Fodor's

PERU

Fodor's Travel Publicati[...]ney, Auckland

www.fodors.com

D0680749

FODOR'S PERU

Writers: David Dudenhoefer, Nicholas Gill, Michael Goodwin, Maureen Santucci

Editor: Salwa Jabado
Editorial Contributors: Bethany Beckerlegge, Andrew Collins, Mark Sullivan, Sue MacCallum-Whitcomb

Production Editor: Carrie Parker
Maps & Illustrations: Mark Stroud, Moon Street Cartography, and David Lindroth *cartographers;* Rebecca Baer, *map editor;* William Wu, *information graphics*
Design: Fabrizio La Rocca, *creative director;* Tina Malaney, Chie Ushio, Jessica Ramirez, *designers;* Melanie Marin, *associate director of photography;* Jennifer Romains, *photo research*
Cover Photo: Front cover: Gonzalo Azumendi/age fotostock [Description: Machu Picchu] Back cover (from left to right): Gail Johnson/Shutterstock; Neale Cousland/Shutterstock; Chris Howey/Shutterstock. Spine: Bartosz Hadyniak/iStockphoto.
Production Manager: Angela McLean

5th Edition

ISBN 978-0-89141-945-7

ISSN 1542-3433

SPECIAL SALES

This book is available at special discounts for bulk purchases for sales promotions or premiums. Special editions, including personalized covers, excerpts of existing books, and corporate imprints, can be created in large quantities for special needs. For more information, write to Special Markets/Premium Sales, 1745 Broadway, MD 3-1, New York, NY 10019, or e-mail specialmarkets@randomhouse.com.

AN IMPORTANT TIP & AN INVITATION

Although all prices, opening times, and other details in this book are based on information supplied to us at press time, changes occur all the time in the travel world, and Fodor's cannot accept responsibility for facts that become outdated or for inadvertent errors or omissions. So **always confirm information when it matters,** especially if you're making a detour to visit a specific place. Your experiences—positive and negative— matter to us. If we have missed or misstated something, **please write to us.** Share your opinion instantly through our online feedback center at fodors.com/contact-us.

PRINTED IN COLOMBIA

10 9 8 7 6 5 4 3 2 1

CONTENTS

ABOUT
THIS GUIDE

Fodor's Ratings

Everything in this guide is worth doing—we don't cover what isn't—but exceptional sights, hotels, and restaurants are recognized with additional accolades. Fodor's Choice★ indicates our top recommendations; ★ highlights places we deem highly recommended. Care to nominate a new place? Visit Fodors.com/contact-us.

Trip Costs

We list prices wherever possible to help you budget well. Hotel and restaurant price categories from $ to $$$$ are noted alongside each recommendation. For hotels, we include the lowest cost of a standard double room in high season. For restaurants, we cite the average price of a main course at dinner or, if dinner isn't served, at lunch. For attractions, we always list adult admission fees; discounts are usually available for children, students, and senior citizens.

Hotels

Our local writers vet every hotel to recommend the best overnights in each price category, from budget to expensive. Unless otherwise specified, you can expect private bath, phone, and TV in your room. For expanded hotel reviews, facilities, and deals visit Fodors.com.

Restaurants

Unless we state otherwise, restaurants are open for lunch and dinner daily. We mention dress code only when there's a specific requirement and reservations only when they're essential or not accepted. To make restaurant reservations, visit Fodors.com.

Credit Cards

The hotels and restaurants in this guide typically accept credit cards. If not, we'll say so.

Ratings
★ Fodor's Choice
★ Highly recommended
☺ Family-friendly

Listings
⊠ Address
⊠ Branch address
☎ Telephone
🖷 Fax
⊕ Website
✉ E-mail
🎫 Admission fee
🕙 Open/closed times
Ⓜ Subway
⊹ Directions or Map coordinates

Hotels & Restaurants
🏨 Hotel
🛏 Number of rooms
🍽 Meal plans
✗ Restaurant
🍴 Reservations
🎩 Dress code
▭ No credit cards
$ Price

Other
⇨ See also
☞ Take note
🏌 Golf facilities

Experience Peru

WHAT'S WHERE

The following numbers refer to chapters in the book.

2 Lima. In Peru's cultural and political center, experience some of the best dining in the Americas, vibrant nightlife, and great museums and churches. See the Catedral and the catacombs at the Iglesia de San Francisco, and stroll about Miraflores for shops and eats.

Fishing boats.

3 The Southern Coast. Head south for wines and piscos around Ica, dune-boarding in Huacachina, the mysterious Nazca Lines, and the marine life of the Paracas National Preserve. The inland area, particularly Pisco, was devastated by an earthquake in 2007, but is rebuilding.

4 The Southern Andes and Lake Titicaca. Colca and Cotahuasi canyons are the world's two deepest canyons. Peru's "second city" Arequipa may also be its most attractive. Lake Titicaca is the

Pisac.

world's highest navigable lake and home to the floating Uros Islands.

5 Cusco and the Sacred Valley. Cusco (11,500 feet above sea level) is a necessary stop on your journey to Machu Picchu. The former Inca capital is gorgeous, and packed with fine restaurants, hotels, churches, and museums. Visit the nearby Inca ruins of Sacsayhuamán, take a day trip to the Pisac market and Ollantaytambo, and spend a night in the Sacred Valley.

6 Machu Picchu. The great Machu Picchu, crowded or not crowded, misty rains or clear skies, never ceases to enthrall, and the Inca Trail is still the great hiking pilgrimage. Stay in Aguas Calientes for the best access.

7 Amazon Basin. Peru's vast tract of the Amazon may contain the world's greatest biodiversity. Fly into

Iquitos or Puerto Maldonado for the wildlife preserves, jungle lodges, rain-forest hikes, and boat excursions.

8 The Central Highlands. Festivals and market towns dominate Huancayo and the Mantaro Valley, while the passionate Semana Santa celebrations are the rage in Ayacucho. From Lima to Huancayo, the world's highest railroad tops out at 15,685 feet.

9 The North Coast and the Northern Highlands. Go up the coast for beach life and inland to the Cordillera Blanca for some of the world's highest mountains. Many of Peru's greatest archaeological discoveries were made in the north. Sites are still being uncovered near Chiclayo, Trujillo, and Chachapoyas.

Camp near Laguna Satuna, Cordillera Blanca.

PERU PLANNER

Time

Peru shares the Eastern Standard Time zone with New York and Miami when the U.S. East Coast is not on daylight saving time. So when it's noon in Lima it will be 11 am in Dallas and 9 am in Los Angeles.

Connectivity

Cell phone coverage and wireless Internet access are increasingly common in Peru, which means you can take your smart phone and laptop with you if you want to. Check with your carrier to see if your cell phone will work in Peru, and what the rates are. It is probably expensive, so keep in mind that there are *locutorios* (phone centers) all over Lima and other cities, and calling cards for sale at most convenience stores and pharmacies, which means you can call home for pennies a minute. You can also buy a prepay cell phone for around $40. All but the cheapest hotels—even some of the jungle lodges—have Wi-Fi, which is free at all but the most expensive hotels. If you don't want to carry a laptop, most hotels also have computers for guest use, and there are Internet cafés all over the country that charge S/1 or S/2 an hour.

Health and Safety

Peru is safer than it has been in years, but standard travel precautions apply. Remember: you represent enormous wealth to the typical person here; the budget for your trip might exceed what many Peruvians earn in a year. Conceal your valuables, watch your things, avoid deserted streets, walk purposefully, take taxis at night, and be vigilant if somebody invades your personal space, or if there is a scene of commotion, either of which may be done to distract you. Bag slashers and pickpockets tend to work in markets and on buses; keep track of your valuables in any crowded place.

In terms of health and sanitation, few visitors experience anything worse than a bout of traveler's diarrhea. If you stick to upscale eateries in well-trodden destinations, you may minimize even those problems. Be wary of raw foods (peel your fruit!), and don't drink tap water. If you visit the Amazon Basin, you should get vaccinated against yellow fever. Check with your physician about any other pretravel immunizations or medications at least a month before you leave, since some vaccines require multiple injections.

High Altitude

Peru's lofty heights present you with both majesty and menace. The Andes, the country's signature geographic feature, provide a glorious backdrop. The 6,768-meter (22,204-feet) Huascarán tops Peru's peaks, and much of the center north–south band of the country sits at 3,000–4,000 meters (9,800–13,000 feet) altitude.

Treat that altitude with respect. Its consequences, locally known as *soroche*, affect many visitors. For most, it's little more than a shortness of breath, which can be minimized by taking it easy the first couple of days and a good intake of nonalcoholic liquids. It occasionally requires immediate descent to lower altitudes. Peruvians swear by tea brewed from coca leaves, a completely legal way (in Peru, at least) to prevent symptoms. We recommend a pretrip check with your doctor to see if any underlying conditions (hypertension, heart problems, pregnancy) might preclude travel here.

First-Timer?

While Cusco and Machu Picchu are obligatory destinations for a first trip to Peru, the country has much more to offer, as the pages of this guide attest. There is too much to see and do in one trip, so plan your itinerary according to your interests and the season.

Wherever you go, build some downtime into your itinerary, especially your first day in the Andes, when you may feel weak or ill. Don't let all those churches, ruins, convents, and museums blur together. Give yourself enough time to stop and smell the pisco sours.

For years travelers avoided Lima, which would be a mistake. The country's capital is a sprawling metropolis with horrible traffic and more than its share of slums, but the plazas and colonial churches of the historic Centro are impressive, Barranco is charming, and the metropolitan area has the country's best museums and restaurants.

Postpone that diet. "Amazing" is the only way to describe what we think is the hemisphere's best food. A mix of European, indigenous, Asian, and African influences makes Peruvian cuisine remarkably varied and delicious. The seafood is excellent, and the best is found in Lima and other coastal cities, but Cusco and Arequipa have ample selections of restaurants that serve up some tasty regional dishes.

Shopping is another popular distraction from exploring, and the handicraft selection is impressive, especially in Cusco. In the market and all but the fanciest shops in the Andean cities you are expected to bargain, so don't be shy.

Try to learn a few words of Spanish. Outside the tourist industry few people speak much English. Learning some common words and phrases can simplify life, and make your trip more pleasant. (Spanish is a second language for many Peruvians, too.)

Pack reserves of patience. Peru offers a polished tourism product, but schedules occasionally go awry, traffic in the cities is chaotic, and street hawkers or beggars can get on your nerves.

Tipping

A 10% tip suffices in most restaurants unless the service is exceptional. Porters in hotels and airports expect S/2 per bag. There's no need to tip taxi drivers, although many people round up the fare. At bars, tip about S/1 a drink. Bathroom attendants get 50 céntimos; gas-station attendants get 50 céntimos for extra services such as adding air to your tires. Tour guides should get S/20 and bus drivers S/10 each per day.

Electricity

Electrical outlets in Peru are like the ones in the United States and Canada, but the electrical grid runs 220 volts, which will destroy an electronic device made for the 110-volt system of North America unless it has a power adapter. Laptop computers and many other electronic goods have power adapters built into their cords, but if you have any doubts, check before you plug in. Many hotels have a 110-volt outlet in the bathroom for electric shavers and other devices. Unless it is marked otherwise, you can assume that every outlet in Peru is 220.

PERU MADE EASY

How Much Can I See in One Week, or Two Weeks?

The minimum amount of time to experience Peru is one week, but you really should consider setting aside two weeks, because that would allow you to move more slowly and catch a few more of the country's amazing sights. One week is enough time to get a taste of Lima and complete the Cusco—Valle Sagrado—Machu Picchu circuit, either with an Inca Trail trek, or a more leisurely train itinerary. If you don't mind a quick pace, you could do that circuit in four days, then fly to Puerto Maldonado for a couple of nights in the Amazon rain forest at one of the nearby nature lodges.

A two-week trip allows you to visit more of the sites along the Cusco—Machu Picchu route and head deeper into the Amazon rain forest, either in Madre de Dios, or on the Amazon River itself. Or you could do the Lake Titicaca—Arequipa—Colca Canyon circuit. The Nazca—Paracas trip, south of Lima, can also easily be added to the above in a two-week trip. An alternative to the chilly Titicaca—Arequipa circuit is to return to Lima after Machu Picchu and fly to the coastal cities of Trujillo and Chiclayo, both of which lie near important pre-Incan sites. If outdoor adventure is your passion, you could extend your stay in the highlands for a white-water rafting trip or trekking in either the Cusco region or the Cordillera Blanca.

How Difficult Is Peru to Get Around?

A growing selection of domestic flights means it is much easier to move about within Peru these days. Almost every worthwhile destination is within a two-hour flight from Lima. Train travel is limited, but fun and easy. Traveling by car is trickier—roads are improving, but signage is spotty. Buses go everywhere, and the most expensive seats are quite comfortable; only travel with big companies such as Cruz del Sur and Junin. In cities, cabs are abundant and cheap, but check for an official license. Many destinations in the Amazon Basin can only be reached by river, in anything from a motorized dugout to a river cruise boat with comfortable cabins.

Is Machu Picchu Hard to Get To?

Travel to Machu Picchu is almost too easy. Many people do the trip in a day out of Cusco, but it is worth two or three days, with overnights in Aguas Calientes and the Sacred Valley. The most common method is to hop on a train from Ollantaytambo to Aguas Calientes, which is a 20-minute bus trip from the ruins. Or you can do as the Incas did and walk the trail, which is a two- to four-day hike and a highlight for those who do it. Keep in mind that you need to book an Inca Trail trek months ahead of time, though there are alternative routes.

What Languages Do People Speak?

The official language is Spanish and nearly everyone speaks it. But in the highlands the language the Incas spoke, Quechua, is still widely used. Older people in indigenous communities often don't know Spanish, but younger generations do. Aymará, a pre-Inca language, is spoken in the towns around Lake Titicaca, and dozens of native tongues are spoken in the Amazon Basin. And a growing number of Peruvians speak English.

Will I Have Trouble if I Don't Speak Spanish?

No problem. Although it's helpful to know some Spanish, it's not a necessity, especially on an organized tour or in

tourist areas. There's a strong push for tourism professionals to learn English, but cab drivers or store clerks aren't likely to know a lick. We suggest learning a few simple phrases. *Cuánto cuesta?* (How much?) is a good one to start with.

Is the Water Safe to Drink?

Nope. But bottled water is cheap and sold nearly everywhere. Drink as much as you can, it'll help you beat altitude sickness.

Will I Get Sick?

Stomach bugs are a frequent problem for visitors, but if you avoid salads and only eat fruits that you peel, you'll reduce your likelihood of suffering from one. Cebiche and other "raw" seafood dishes popular in Lima also carry a risk, but are so tasty that it would be a shame to avoid them. Bring anti-diarrhea medicines and play it by ear, or tummy.

What Are the Safety Concerns?

Petty crime is the primary concern. You'll probably have a camera, iPod, watch, jewelry, credit cards, cash—everything a thief wants. Pickpocketing and bag slashing are the most common methods. Thieves are fast and sneaky, so be alert, especially in crowded markets and bus stations. Distraction is a common technique, so if a stranger touches you—a wobbly drunk, or somebody who wants to clean off a cream that has inexplicably gotten on your coat—be aware that their accomplice may try to rob you. Never walk on a deserted street at night. There have been cases of several robbers mugging travelers on side streets, but if you stick to the busy streets in Lima's Centro and Barranco, you should be fine. Taxi kidnappings, in which people are forced to withdraw money from ATMs at gunpoint, are also a problem, albeit rare. Use official taxis.

Should I Worry about Altitude Sickness?

Yes and no. If you have health issues, you should check with your doctor before heading to high altitudes. Otherwise, don't worry too much because nearly everyone experiences a little altitude sickness. The lucky ones may have a headache for the first 24 hours, while others may endure several days of fatigue, nausea, and headaches. When up high, lay off the booze, limit physical activity, hydrate, drink lots of coca tea, suck coca hard candy, or chew coca leaves. If the headache persists, take an ibuprofen, hydrate some more, and sleep it off. Some hotels have oxygen, so don't hesitate to ask for it.

Do I Have to Pay Any Fees to Get into the Country?

No. But you pay to get out. The departure tax system (which nearly every South American country embraces) is alive and well in Peru, but the $31 USD fee for international departures from Lima will be included in the cost of your ticket.

Are There Cultural Sensitivities I Should Be Aware Of?

Peruvians are very polite, and it's customary to be the same. You'll notice that men and women kiss each other on the cheek when saying hello, and the same goes for women to women. It's nonsexual and a sign of friendliness. There's no 6 inches of personal space in Peru, it's more like 2: people talk, walk, and sit close in general. Peruvians, like many South American countries, are also on "Latin time," meaning they often arrive late for social engagements, though tours and transportation tend to run on time.

WHAT'S NEW IN PERU

National Trademark

As part of its efforts to promote the country's exports and tourism industry, the government of Peru introduced a national trademark in 2012. You're bound to notice the trademark, which is the word Perú written in cursive with a spiral in the P, on everything from brochures to T-shirts. The curlicue in the P was inspired by the tail of the monkey in the Nazca line figures, so Peru's 21st-century marketing campaign celebrates the country's pre-Columbian heritage.

Treasures Returned

Following his discovery of Machu Picchu in 1911, the American adventurer Hiram Bingham returned to the Incan citadel in 1912 and 1915 on expeditions supported by Yale and the National Geographic Society, and oversaw extensive archaeological excavation. His team uncovered thousands of artifacts including human skeletons and ceramics that were shipped to Yale, where they were studied and displayed for nearly a century. As the centennial of Machu Picchu's discovery approached, Peru launched a diplomatic campaign to pressure Yale to repatriate those artifacts, and in 2011 the university complied, transferring them to the Universidad Nacional de San Antonio Abad. Approximately 500 of those artifacts are new displayed at Casa Choncha, in Cusco.

Amazon Wonder

In November 2011 the Amazon was declared one of the New Seven Wonders of Nature based on an international vote organized by the New7Wonders organization. Though most of the Amazon Rain Forest is in Brazil, Peruvians celebrated the designation, since the river's source is in Peru. Travelers can experience that natural wonder by flying to Iquitos, where boats ply the river to nearby nature lodges and several companies offer three- to seven-night Amazon cruises in small ships.

Museum Makover

Lima's best museum has gotten better. The Museo Arqueológico Rafael Larco Herrera (aka Museo Larco), which was founded in 1926 in a former a colonial hacienda, underwent extensive renovation in 2011. Among the innovations, the museum now stays open till 10 pm, and its garden holds one of the city's best restaurants, making a visit to its exhibits and dinner a convenient option for a night in Lima.

Planes, Trains, and Buses

A combination of public infrastructure and private investment has made Peru an easier country to explore than ever before.

In Lima a new express bus called the Metropolitano provides quick and inexpensive transportation between the neighborhoods of Barranco, Miraflores, and the historic Centro.

The addition of Peruvian Airlines and LCPeru to the list of domestic carriers and an expansion of routes flown by Star Peru, TACA, and LAN means there are more options for flying between Lima and other Peruvian cities than ever before. This is especially good news if you're on a tight budget, since LCPeru, Peruvian Airlines, and Star Peru charge foreigners considerably less than TACA and LAN. Chile's LAN Airlines and Brazil's TAM airlines merged in 2012 to form LATAM, increasing flight options to 150 destinations in 22 countries.

A comparable development in Cusco, where two new companies—Inka Rail and the Machu Picchu Train—now offer service to Machu Picchu, means there are also more options for getting to Peru's top attraction. For years one company, PeruRail, departed from Cusco for Machu Picchu early in the morning and returned in the evening. Trains now run between the Sacred Valley towns of Ollantaytambo and Urubamba and Machu Picchu every hour or two, though PeruRail still offers early-morning departures from the Poroy station, near Cusco.

Machu Picchu Centennial
July 7, 2011, marked the 100th anniversary of American adventurer Hiram Bingham's rediscovery of Machu Picchu. The Peruvian government celebrated Machu Picchu's centennial with a concert and light show, with the participation of international celebrities, which helped push the Incan citadel to the top of many a traveler's list.

Peru's Nobel Laureate
Peruvian writer Mario Vargas Llosa, one of Latin America's most popular authors, won the Nobel Prize for Literature in 2010. The award's announcement sparked widespread celebration in Peru and renewed interest in his work throughout the world. The author of more than a dozen novels and numerous plays, Vargas Llosa is also a respected journalist and essayist; his weekly opinion column appears on Sunday in the principal Spanish-language newspapers.

Mother Nature's Fury
Peru suffers more natural disasters than any other country except Bangladesh. This includes periodic tremors and quakes, such as the 8-magnitude earthquake that shattered the southern coastal cities of Pisco, Ica, and Chincha Alta on August 15, 2007. More frequent disasters are the mudslides and flash floods, known as *huaicos* (pronounced "whycos") that destroy homes, roads, bridges, and lives in the eastern Andes during each December–May rainy season. The most newsworthy huaico in recent years roared down the Vilcabamba River Valley in January 2010, tearing out several kilometers of the railway between Ollantaytambo and Machu Picchu and leaving thousands of tourists stranded in the town of Aguas Calientes until they could be rescued by helicopter. According to scientists, such extreme weather events will happen more frequently due to climate change.

PERU TODAY

Traditional and Chic

With its ancient ruins, snow-capped Andes, and vast Amazon wilderness, Peru has long captured the imagination of people in distant lands. But for much of the 1980s and '90s few dared to visit the country, which was wracked by a violent conflict between the Shining Path guerrilla movement and Peru's armed forces. Even after the violence subsided in the '90s, the country's tourism infrastructure was quite limited, catering primarily to backpackers and other budget travelers.

Thanks to two decades of economic growth and its growing popularity as a tourist destination, Peru now has more options for experiencing its cultural and natural heritage than ever before. A growing number of the country's tourism businesses are becoming environmentally and socially responsible, and the industry is helping countless Peruvian's to work their way out of poverty, which remains the country's biggest problem.

Government

Peru's President Ollanta Humala, who was elected in May of 2011, is a leftist who has implemented market-friendly policies comparable to those of neighbors Brazil and Chile, in order to fund programs to improve life for the approximately 10 million Peruvians who live in poverty. He has built upon the reforms and economic growth of the two democratic administrations that preceded his, which marks a bit of continuity after decades on a political roller coaster (⇨ see Visible History).

Economy

For much of the past decade Peru has experienced some of the highest economic growth in Latin America, averaging nearly 7% annually. Driven by high mineral prices and steady demand from China, the boom has also included growth in exports of agricultural products such as asparagus, coffee, seafood, and textiles, as well as tourism. Per capita income has doubled since 2003, and though much of that increase has gone to the upper echelons, the percentage of Peruvians living in poverty has dropped from 50% to 35%. Tax revenues have likewise grown, which is reflected in the refurbished government buildings, new infrastructure, and a bigger police force. For travelers this means more hotels and restaurants to choose from and safer, cleaner neighborhoods, but also higher prices, and a less favorable exchange rate than in years past.

Social Unrest

Marches and road barricades are part of Peruvian political life as communities, unions, and other groups periodically take to the streets to protest projects or policies they don't like, or to demand government help. The protests usually end peacefully, but over the years there have been occasions where police fire has resulted in deaths. Protests against the proposed Conga gold mine near Cajamarca shut down tourism in that city for much of 2012, and Cusco residents stage frequent protests and strikes, sometimes stranding travelers for a day or two. Unfortunately, many of that region's residents perceive little benefit from tourism and don't hesitate to disrupt transportation to pressure the government to respond to their demands. The likelihood of having a protest interfere with your travels is small, but keep an eye on the local news nevertheless.

Religion

As a result of centuries of Spanish rule, Peru remains predominantly Roman Catholic, with more than 80% of the population identifying themselves as such. Catholicism influences the daily lives of most Peruvians, as well as state affairs. The newly elected president's inauguration ceremony begins with a mass in Lima's Cathedral, for example, and the country's archbishop is frequently in the news. Despite this overwhelming presence, many Peruvians have moved toward Protestantism and Evangelicalism, which currently represent about 12% of the population. Indigenous Peruvians fused Catholicism with their preconquest religion, with Pachamama (Mother Earth) representing the Virgin Mary, so in the highlands people observe both Catholic and pre-Columbian holy dates, with rituals that meld traditions from both cultures. If you're lucky, you'll witness a religious procession, celebration, or other display of faith during your travels in the country.

Sports

As with most of South America, *fútbol* (soccer) is Peru's second religion. The country's best teams are Universitario de Deportes and Alianza Lima, and a game between Universitario and Alianza is considered a "clasico." Peru's national team hasn't managed to qualify for the World Cup in more than two decades, which causes much frustration and debate. The country's female athletes are its greatest source of pride; boxer Kina Malpartida and surfer Sofía Mulanovich have both been world champions in recent years.

Literature

Peru's most famous writer is the Nobel Laureate Mario Vargas Llosa, who has written several books set in Peru, which makes him a good author to read before or during a trip there. *The Story Teller* and *The Green House* are two of his most Peruvian novels, though the comic *Aunt Julia and the Script Writer* and *Captain Pandora and the Special Services* are also set in the country.

Other important 20th-century writers are José María Arguedas, Ciro Alegría, and Manuel Scorza, all of who wrote about the country's indigenous culture. Daniel Alarcón, who was born in Peru but raised in the United States, sets his fiction in the country. Peru's most famous poet is Cesar Vallejo, who only produced three books of poetry, but is considered one of the most innovative poets of the 20th century.

Music

Peruvian music can be split by regions: the sounds of the Andes and the sounds of the coast. "Huayno," the music of the Andes, is traditionally played on acoustic guitars, a small stringed instrument called the charango, and a panpipe called the zampoña, but its more popular form now relies on synthesizers and electric guitars. Coastal "música criolla" has Spanish, Gypsy, and African roots and is played on acoustic guitars and a percussion instrument called the *cajón*—a large wooden box. The late Chabuca Granda popularized this genre, and singers such as Susana Baca, Tania Libertad, and Eva Allyón continue the tradition. Peru's most popular music is probably Cumbia, a Colombian genre popular throughout Latin America, played here with a distinctive Peruvian touch.

QUINTESSENTIAL PERU

Exploring the Past

Machu Picchu is amazing, but there's plenty more to see of Peru's fascinating past. Stand at Cajamarca where Inca Atahualpa was captured by Spanish leader Francisco Pizzaro. Explore the ancient Moche culture by walking about its adobe pyramids. Puzzle over the mysterious Nazca Lines from the sky. Then enjoy city life in Spanish-influenced Lima, Trujillo, and Arequipa, with their colonial-era mansions, churches, monasteries, and museums.

Peruvian history is best understood by visiting its people and experiencing its cultures. The islands of Lake Titicaca reveal a slice of raw ancient Andean culture. It's as if time has frozen while Quechua and Aymará families live and work off the land, eating and dressing as they did in the 16th century. It's not much different in the highlands around Cusco, where Quechua-speaking folks farm terraces thousands of years old.

Savoring the Flavors

Peru's culinary cornucopia is as varied and dazzling as its ancient sites and natural wonders. The traditional cuisines of its three geographic regions—the coast, highlands, and jungle—contain dozens of distinctive dishes, which have in turn inspired countless variations and inventions by the country's chefs. The classic dishes of the coast include some spicy seafood concoctions, as well as stewed or sautéed meats. They are complemented by the hearty soups, potato- and quinoa-based dishes of the highlands, and the tropical flavors of the Amazon Basin, which include river fish and jungle fruits.

Regional cuisines have been melded and reinvented in the kitchens of Peru's hotels and restaurants, making every trip a culinary adventure. The greatest selection of traditional and nouveau Peruvian cuisine can be found in Lima, which has become a destination for gastronomical tours and cooking classes.

Peru's distinctive culture may make it seem like a whole other world. But experiencing it isn't difficult. Sample a few local pleasures and you'll fit right in.

High Living

Life in the Andes, or the *sierra*, has changed little through the centuries. In many villages Quechua is still the only language spoken. There are few cars and computers, no ATMs, and no restaurants, though you will see locals carrying cell phones. Families live in stone and adobe huts and plumbing is a hole in the ground.

Nearly every family raises animals for food and transport. Parents harvest crops from the ancient terraces while children attend school. Cold temperatures call for hearty foods like soup, potatoes, bread, quinoa, and meats.

When it comes to fiestas, these villagers know how to let loose. No major floats needed. Parades consist of local instruments, traditional folk dances that reenact Peruvian history, hand-sewn clothing embroidered with bright colors, a crowd, and lots of alcohol.

Great Outdoors

It may be best known for its cultural treasures, but Peru is also prodigious playground for outdoor enthusiasts of all stripes. The mountains around Cusco, and the Cordillera Blanca, are traversed by an array of trekking routes, whereas their peaks provide challenges for seasoned mountaineers. Several highland rivers offer formidable white-water rafting routes, whereas the lowland rivers are routes for exploring the jungle. The Pacific coast has a dozen world-class surf breaks, as well as smaller swells appropriate for learning that sport.

If you include activities such as mountain biking, paragliding, and zip-line tours through the forest canopy, you'll have enough outdoor adventure options to keep your adrenal glands pumping for much of your vacation.

PERU
TOP ATTRACTIONS

Machu Picchu and the Inca Trail

(A) This "Lost City of the Incas" is the main reason why people come to Peru. The citadel of Machu Picchu was built around the 1450s, only to be abandoned a hundred years later. Spanish conquistadors never found it, and for centuries it stayed hidden. But in 1911 it was rediscovered by an American historian. If you're adventurous, and in good shape, the four-day Inca Trail is the classic route to Machu Picchu.

Colca Canyon

(B) Twice as deep as Arizona's Grand Canyon, Colca Canyon is typically a side trip from Arequipa, which is a three-hour drive away. Adventure enthusiasts head for the Canyon's Colca River for whitewater rafting, while those less inclined toward danger hike along the canyon for gorgeous vistas. The highlight is the Cruz del Condor, a mirador where lucky visitors might spot the Andean condor in flight.

Chan Chan

(C) A UNESCO World Heritage Site since 1986, this archaeological site was home to the second largest pre-Columbian society in South America: the Chimú. The estimated 30,000 Chimú residents built the mud city between 850 and 1470. You can roam the ruins—which contain 10 walled citadels that house burial chambers, ceremonial rooms, and temples—on a day trip from the charming northern city of Trujillo.

Lake Titicaca

(D) At 3,812 meters (12,500 feet), Puno's Lake Titicaca is the highest navigable lake in the world. More than 25 rivers empty into it, and according to Inca legend it was the birthplace of the Sun god who founded the Inca dynasty. On Isla Taquile and other islands here Quechua-speaking people preserve the traditions of their ancestors.

Tambopata National Reserve

(E) This vast protected area near Puerto Maldonado, a short flight east of Cusco, is an excellent place to experience the myriad flora and fauna of the Amazon Basin. A dozen nature lodges scattered along the Tambopata and Madre de Dios rivers provide comfortable bases for hikes, or boat trips into the surrounding wilderness to see several types of monkeys, dinosaurian caimans, giant rodents called capybaras, and some of the reserve's hundreds of bird species.

The Nazca Lines

(F) Between 900 BC and AD 600 the Nazca and Paracas cultures constructed the Nazca Lines: geometric figures drawn into the Pampa Colorado (Red Plain) near Nazca, a city south of Lima. Three hundred geoglyphs and 800 straight lines make up these mysterious figures. No one knows why these massive drawings—which include representations of a lizard, monkey, condor, and spider—were created. The only way to get a good view is to take a flight.

Sacsayhuamán

(G) Machu Picchu isn't the only must-see Inca ruin to visit from Cusco. Used as a fortress during Pizarro's conquest, the military site of Sacsayhuamán is made of huge stone blocks; the largest is 8.5 meters (28 feet) high and weighs more than 300 tons (600,000 pounds). It's believed that some 20,000 men built it.

Cordillera Blanca

(H) The highest part of the Peruvian Andes, the Cordillera Blanca (White Range) has more than 50 peaks that reach 5,500 meters (18,000 feet) or higher, and stretches 20 km (12.5 miles) wide and 180 km (112 miles) long. Mountain climbers and hikers of all skill levels can enjoy this majestic range.

TOP EXPERIENCES

Join a Celebration

Clanging bells, chanting, and wafting incense rouse you before dawn. You peer out your window: scores of people draped in bright colorful costumes walk down the street carrying a saint's figure. Catholic observances, indigenous traditions, and history pack the calendar with *fiestas* (festivals)—from Lima's birthday in January to the nationwide Semana Santa in spring, to the Inca ritual Inti Raymi, held near Cusco on June 24.

Puno is best known for its traditional Carnaval, but each November citizens reenact the birth of the first Inca emperor, Manco Capac, who, legend has it, rose out of Lake Titicaca. Among the crosses, saints, and colorful costumes, townspeople try their luck at bingo, beauty queens compete for the crown, Huayno music blasts from speakers, and the beer flows freely.

Explore a Market

Wandering through a market provides a wonderful window into the lives of local people. All of Peru's cities have central markets, some of the more interesting of which include Cusco's Mercado Central, the Mercado San Camillo in Arequipa, and the market in the neighborhood of Belén, in Iquitos. Certain highland towns are known for their market days, when vendors set up shop on central streets, one of the most popular of which is Pisac, in the Sacred Valley. Vendors pack their stalls with everything from dried potato chunks to medicinal herbs to love potions. They'll likely invite you to step inside for a look, and if you see something you need, don't forget to bargain.

Visit the Wild Things

Squirrel monkeys leap between branches, fish break the muddy water's surface, mealy parrots squawk in the treetops. The colors and sounds of the Amazon Basin's wildlife are unforgettable, and each of those creatures has a story, because they all play specific roles in the complex web of jungle life. Peru is one of the easiest countries in which to experience the beauty and diversity of the Amazon, whether on the river that region was named for or one of its many tributaries. There are dozens of nature lodges and cruise boats that can take you deep into that wilderness to admire its exuberant scenery and see some of the thousands of species that live there, most of which are found nowhere else on Earth.

Enjoy the Dances

Peruvian folkloric dances vary dramatically between the coast and mountains. The coastal *marinera* is performed to the music of a brass band by a courting couple who execute elegant, complex movements, but never touch. Afro-Peruvian dance, which is also coastal, is more sensual, performed to the music of guitars and the rhythm of a cajón, a sonorous wooden box on which the percussionist sits. Andean dances are more varied and spectacular, with many more dancers in colorful costumes. The most impressive one is the *danza de tijeras* (scissors dance), which involves gymnastic leaps with scissors in hand. Folk dancing plays a central role in the country's festivals, but any of the above can be enjoyed at the varied peñas and dinner shows in Lima and other cities.

WHEN TO GO

Most people visit Peru between June and September, which is the dry season in the Sierra (mountains) and the Selva (Amazon Basin), but that is by no means the only time to visit. The best time to go depends on your primary interest, or what regions you want to explore. If you prefer to avoid the crowds or the cold, consider doing your Cusco–Machu Picchu trip in late April, May, October, or November.

The seasons are flipped in the southern hemisphere, but because northern Peru is practically on the equator, "summer" and "winter" mean less in the northern half of the country than in its southern half. The dry season, from May to September, is winter in the southern Andes, where it often freezes at night, but the days are sunny. Lima is enveloped in a chilly fog called the *garúa* for the better part of those months. You may get some rain in the Andes in April and May, but the highland landscapes are a beautiful shade of green then, and there are fewer tourists.

The dry months are the best time to visit the Madre de Dios portion of the Amazon Basin, but you are better off visiting Iquitos and the Amazon River during the "rainy" season, because the water is high then, facilitating access to streams and lakes for wildlife-watching, and it doesn't rain that much more than during the "dry" months.

You'll want to make your reservations far in advance for travel anywhere in Peru during the second half of July or first week of August, when local school vacations add Peruvian tourists to foreign masses.

If you're a surfer and want to spend more time in Lima and the coast, or simply want a break from winter, the December-to-May southern summer is a great time to visit Peru. It may be raining in the Andes and Amazon, but the weather is lovely in Lima and such coastal sites as the Nazca Lines, Paracas, and the pre-Incan ruins near Trujillo and Chiclayo.

Festivals and Celebrations

Fireworks and colorful processions honor the **Virgen de la Candelaria** during the first half of February in Puno, on Lake Titicaca. The faithful follow images of the Virgin Mary through the streets as colorful dancers depict the struggle between good and evil. (The demons always lose.)

Carnaval (February or March) is celebrated with parades and folk dancing in most highland towns, though especially in Cajamarca, Ayacucho, and Huarás.

Semana Santa (March or April) is marked by Holy Week processions countrywide, though Ayacucho's celebrations are the most elaborate.

Thousands flock to the Ausangate Glacier for **Qoyllur Rit'i** (June 9), a religious festival that mixes Incan and Christian rites in Sinakara, Cusco department.

Cusco's spectacular **Inti Raymi** (June 24) marks the winter solstice with a reenactment of an Inca ritual that beseeches the sun to return. The fortress ruins of Sacsayhuamán form the stage for that proverbial cast of thousands.

Firecrackers may rouse you out of bed during Peru's two-day **Fiestas Patrias** (July 28–29), which celebrate the country's independence from Spain in 1821.

Lima and the Central Highlands revere the **Señor de los Milagros** (October 18–28), a colonial-era, dark-skinned Christ statue that survived a 1655 earthquake that destroyed much of the capital.

IF YOU LIKE

Sun, Surf, and Seafood

During the summer months (December–April), beach lovers around Peru head west to enjoy a day of surfing the Pacific Ocean waves, sunbathing, and devouring the country's freshest seafood.

Máncora. This fishing town on Peru's northern coast is the country's worst-kept secret. Ask any Peruvian which is the best beach in Peru and they will all mention this stretch of pale-gray sand lined with coconut palms and hotels. Máncora is sunny year-round and visited by beach lovers from Lima and abroad.

Huanchaco. This beach town west of Trujillo has a long left-hand point break that is complemented by an ample dining and lodging selection. Surfers of all skill levels can find suitable waves year-round, and take lessons, if needed, but the biggest swells roll in between March and August.

Lima. While the ocean views from Miraflores and Barranco are impressive, the capital's greatest marine asset is the food. Lima has restaurants that specialize in everything, but *cebicherías* (restaurants dedicated to seafood) are the place to head for lunch. Check out Punta Sal, Segundo Muelle, and Chef Gaston Acurio's upscale "Cebichería La Mar."

South of Lima. Urbanites from Lima flock southward from December to April to beach resorts such as San Vicente de Cañete, a couple of hours from the capital. Cerro Azul, a small beach town in Cañete, is a tranquil alternative to the beaches closer to Lima. In contrast, Asia, also in Cañete, is where the wealthiest Limeños summer.

Ancient Archaeological Sites

The main reason most travelers visit Peru is to see the ancient ruins left by the Inca and older civilizations. Machu Picchu is the biggie, but don't stop there. Here are a few archaeological sites that are worth the trip.

Caral. Four hours north of Lima, the archaeological ruins of Caral in the Supe Valley shocked the world when their origins were discovered to date back to 2627 BC—1,500 years earlier than what was believed to be the age of South America's oldest civilization. Growing numbers of visitors make the day trip to Peru's most recently discovered ancient wonder.

Chan Chan. This capital of the pre-Inca Chimú empire was the largest pre-Columbian city in the Americas and the largest adobe city in the world. A 5-km (3-mile) trip from the northern city of Trujillo, Chan Chan is a UNESCO World Heritage Site. It's threatened by erosion because of its close proximity to the coast, which experiences heavy seasonal rains.

Choquequirau. The Inca ruins of Choquequirau, in Cusco province, is the ideal destination for hikers who want to stray from the beaten trail. Five-day trekking tours are available to this remote site, which has been called "Machu Picchu's sacred sister" because of the similarities in architecture.

Ollantaytambo. Sixty kilometers (37 miles) northwest of Cusco, the extensive Inca fortress of Ollantaytambo is one of the few locations where the Incas managed to defeat Spanish conquistadors. The fort held a temple, with a ceremonial center greeting those who manage to get to the top.

Natural Beauty

With more than 50 natural areas or conservation units—in the form of national parks, reserves, sanctuaries, and protected rain forests—Peru is a great place to experience tropical nature.

Colca Canyon and Cotahuasi Canyon. The two deepest canyons in the world are in Peru's dry, southern Andes. Dipping down 10,600 feet and 11,000 feet respectively, they are skirted by hiking trails, whereas the rivers that flow through them offer intense kayaking and rafting. Near this exceptional geology are villages offering glimpses into the indigenous culture.

Huascarán National Park. Towering over the town of Huaraz, this park was established to protect the flora and fauna and landscapes of the Cordillera Blanca, or "White Mountain Chain." A UNESCO World Heritage Site, it is home to such rare species as the spectacled bear and the Andean condor.

Manu Biosphere Reserve. This remote protected area extends from the cloud forest to the rain forest, and is home to an array of rare species that includes the cock of the rock, giant river otter, and jaguar. Its mountains, rivers, ox-bow lakes, and forests are also stunningly beautiful.

Tambopata National Park. This vast rainforest reserve covers an area where relatively few people live, so it suffers less hunting than other areas of the Amazon Basin, and is consequently one of the best places to see wildlife. This, together with its proximity to the Puerto Maldonado airport, make Tambopata one of the country's most popular natural destinations.

Museums

It could be argued that Peru is one big open-air museum. However, a little background information before you head to the ruins is always helpful. Museums in Peru do an excellent job of documenting the history and culture of a country overflowing with both.

Museo de Oro. Lima's Gold Museum has an extensive collection of pre-Columbian jewelry, pottery, textiles and other artifacts; not just gold. You should, however, visit it with a guide or pay for the recorded tour, in order to better understand what you're admiring.

Museo Nacional Sicán. Twenty kilometers (12.5 miles) north of Chiclayo, this modern museum focuses on the ancient Sicán civilization, which originated in AD 750. Learn about the life and death of one of their leaders, the Lord of Sicán, who represented the "natural world" in their culture.

Museo Rafael Larco Herrera. Recently refurbished, Lima's finest museum was constructed on the site of a pre-Columbian pyramid. It's most famous for its titillating collection of erotic ceramics, but it has more than 40,000 other ceramic pieces, textiles, and gold work on display.

Museo Santury. Home to the famed "Juanita, the Inca princess" mummy, the Museo de la Universidad Católica de Santa María, as it's formally known, is an obligatory stop for anyone visiting the city of Arequipa. Juanita was discovered in southern Peru and is now kept in a cold glass box to preserve her body so that future visitors can learn about her sacrificial death.

TOUR OPERATORS

Why Go with an Operator?

There are plenty of good reasons to entrust the details of your Peru travels to a tour company, and convenience and security are high among them. Do you prefer to have your itinerary planned to the minutest details? If so, you can save time that you might otherwise spend researching and booking your trip by letting travel professionals take care of it. And once your trip has begun, you can see more in less time on a tour. You'll also get more out of your trip if you have a Peruvian guide who can point out and explain things that you might otherwise miss. You can rest assured that if something goes wrong someone will straighten things out for you, and in the unlikely event that you have an accident, they'll take care of you.

On the other hand, if you prefer flexibility and spontaneity, you'll probably want to do things on your own, or hire a guide for day trips. There are areas, or activities, for which you can't avoid joining a tour. For many outdoor adventures, such as trekking or a trip into the Amazon rain forest, you simply have to travel with an outfitter. In the case of the Amazon, this might simply be the eco-lodge you visit. There will also be moments when you'll want things explained, or want to do a specific excursion or event if you're traveling independently. You can always book a day tour, or a short itinerary, from a local operator. You also have the option of simply showing up and hiring a guide in places such as Machu Picchu, or other archaeological sites, where authorized freelance guides are available for hire at the entrance.

Whether you take a packaged tour for your entire Peru trip or prefer to book shorter itineraries with several outfitters, the decision of which tour operator or operators to use will likely be the most important one you make for your vacation. We've consequently compiled a list of the some of the best tour companies operating in Peru, from the big international outfitters to the best local companies, to provide a good range of specializations and budget options.

Who's Who

There is no shortage of companies selling tours to Peru, but not all of them have the same level of experience and reputation. Most U.S., Canadian, and British tour companies offering trips to Peru merely sell tours that are designed and run by Peruvian operators. However, there are also international companies that run their own shows in Peru. Others send a trip leader to accompany each group, who will often team up with a Peruvian guide, while the tour is operated by one or more Peruvian companies.

If you've traveled with a company to other destinations and had good experiences, you have good reason to use them in Peru. Though you may be reluctant to buy a package directly from a Peruvian company, keep in mind that you may get the same tour you would buy from a U.S. company for considerably less money. If you want to stray from the beaten path, you may have no choice but to book directly with a Peruvian company. Rest assured that the local operators included in this section have decades of experience and good reputations.

Where to Go

While every company offers trips to Machu Picchu—Peru's must-see attraction—the country has much more to offer, including the Amazon wilderness, vibrant indigenous cultures, colonial cities, and jaw-dropping mountain landscapes. The great thing is

that many of those attractions are easy to combine with Machu Picchu.

Nearly all first-time visitors do some sort of a Cusco/Sacred Valley/Machu Picchu combination, a tour that every company offers. Whether you hike there on a four-day Inca Trail trek or roll in luxuriously on Orient Express's classic *Hiram Bingham* train, Machu Picchu is all that it is cracked up to be. There is enough to see between that ancient citadel, the Sacred Valley, and Cusco to fill a week, though many people cover the area in a few days. Many tours combine Machu Picchu and Cusco with the rain forest of nearby Madre de Dios, whereas others combine it with southern attractions such as Lake Titicaca, Arequipa, and the Colca Canyon or a cruise on the Amazon River. A longer extension or second trip is needed to include the ancient sites and impressive landscapes of northern Peru.

What to Do

Peru's combination of culture, history, scenery, and biodiversity make it a great place to visit, and you get exposure to all of the above on the classic Cusco–Machu Picchu trip. It is also a world-class destination for people who want to concentrate their vacations on one thing, be it bird-watching (Peru is the number-two country for avian diversity), surfing (the swells are sometimes as big as Hawaii's), or trekking (there are countless highland trails). Travelers with that kind of focus will want to book their tour with an outfitter that specializes in their passion, and we've included experts in each of those activities here.

The following outfitters are some of the best international and local tour outfitters offering trips in Peru, ranging from companies that accommodate thousands of tourists per month to smaller operations

that specialize in custom tours. While nearly all of them offer Cusco–Machu Picchu tours, some have expertise, or hotels in certain regions, while others focus on specific activities.

TOUR OPERATORS

Abercrombie & Kent. Established in 1962, this respected company offers a good selection of Peru itineraries that includes such emblematic attractions as Machu Picchu and the Amazon River as well as less-visited sites such as the Colca Canyon. The company also runs tours that combine Peru with Ecuador's Galápagos Islands or other South American destinations, and trips specifically for families. Itineraries last anywhere from 8 to 18 days.

Destinations serviced: Lima, Cusco, Machu Picchu, Sacred Valley, Amazon River, Colca Canyon, and Paracas.

Most popular package: Wonders of Peru & the Galápagos, 13 days, from $10,745 per person. Combines time in Cusco, the Sacred Valley, and Machu Picchu with a five-night cruise though the Galapagos Islands.

Customized trips: Yes.

What they do best: Provide quality guides, luxury accomodations, and unforgettable experiences.

Corporate responsibility: Support an organization in the Sacred Valley that provides meals, medical care, and education for children from poor families. ☎ 888/611–4711 *in U.S.* ⊕ *www. abercrombiekent.com.*

Adventure Life. The South and Central America specialist Adventure Life has plenty of options for active travelers, including treks on the Inca Trail and less-hiked routes such as Ausangate Glacier

and the Cordillera Blanca, white-water rafting, and trips into the rain forest of Manu and Tambopata. They also offer less strenuous options, ranging from the classic Cusco-Machu Picchu tour to trips to pre-Incan sites in northern Peru. For travelers who want more contact with local people, they offer homestays and extensions volunteering at one of the various projects the company supports.

Destinations serviced: Lima, Cusco, Sacred Valley, Machu Picchu, Inca Trail, Ausengate, Lake Titicaca, Manu, Tambopata, Amazon River, Paracas, Trujillo, Chiclayo, Huaraz.

Most popular packages: Machu Picchu by Train, seven days, $1,775 per person; Cusco, Sacred Valley, and Machu Picchu. Andean Multisport with Machu Picchu, 10 days, $2,395, combines mountain biking, hiking, rafting, and two days in Machu Picchu, with a mix of nights camping or in hotels.

Customized trips: Yes.

What they do best: Take travelers off the beaten track to experience Peru's amazing scenery, nature, and culture up close.

Corporate responsibility: Treat porters and other local staff well; work with rural communities to improve their conditions; support a shelter for single mothers; work with the Rainforest Alliance to make tours sustainable. ☎ *800/344–6118 in U.S.* ⊕ *www.adventure-life.com.*

Andean Treks. A pioneer in outfitting Inca Trail treks, Andean Treks was one of the first companies to organize treks to less-visited areas such as Choquequirao and Ausangate. From its humble beginnings outfitting hikes in 1980, Andean Treks grew to include an array of nonhiking trips in the highlands and the Amazon Basin,

and eventually expanded to cover Argentina, Bolivia, Chile, and Ecuador as well. Their trips range from strenuous treks with overnights in tents or rustic lodges to Amazon cruises or tours of Lake Titicaca.

Destinations serviced: Cusco, Sacred Valley, Inca Trail, Machu Picchu, Choquequirao, Ausengate, Salcantay, Cordillera Blanca, Lake Titicaca, Arequipa, Colca Canyon, Tambopata, Amazon River, Nazca, Trujillo, Chiclayo.

Most popular packages: Inca Trail to Machu Picchu, five days, from $935 per person, the classic trek, should be booked five months in advance. Moonstone to Sun Temple trek, five days, from $870 per person, an alternative route to Machu Picchu.

Customized trips: Yes

What they do best: Outfit quality treks through several cordilleras with experienced guides and arrange custom trips for an array of travelers.

Corporate responsibility: Provide employment, school supplies, and other support for rural communities while working to reinforce traditional values. ☎ *800/683–8148 in U.S.,* *617/924–1974* ⊕ *www.andeantreks.com.*

Manu Expeditions. One of the country's oldest outdoor operators, this Anglo-Peruvian company offers an excellent selection of trips into the Manu Biosphere, trekking on the Inca Trail and alternative routes, horseback excursions, white-water rafting, and top-notch bird-watching tours.

Destinations serviced: Cusco, Manu Biosphere Reserve, Sacred Valley, Inca Trail, Machu Picchu, Choququirao.

Most popular package: Complete Manu Biosphere Reserve Experience, nine days, from $2,445 per person, from the cloud forest down into the rain forest of the

Manu Biosphere with nights at the Cock of the Rock Lodge, Romero Rainforest Lodge, and the Manu Wildlife Center.

Customized trips: Yes.

What they do best: Take clients deep into wilderness, help them see wildlife, and explain the ecology of the rain forest.

Corporate responsibility: The company hires local people and purchases products from rural communities, practices sustainable tourism, and works with conservation organizations. ☎ *84/225–990 Peru* ⊕ *www.manuexpeditions.com.*

Condor Travel. Quite possibly Peru's largest tour company, Condor Travel operates many packaged tours sold by U.S. and European companies. They also sell their own packages and tours operated by smaller Peruvian companies. Condor Travel offers one of the most complete selections of tours and destinations in Peru, including golf, trekking, bird-watching, and adventure packages, for considerably less than U.S. companies.

Destinations serviced: All tourist destinations in Peru and other South American nations.

Most popular package: Enigmas of Peru, 12 days, from $1,600, combines Lima, the Nazca Lines, Paracas, Cusco, the Sacred Valley, Machu Picchu, and Lake Titicaca, with stays in midrange hotels.

Customized trips: Yes.

What they do best: They operate trips to both classic and off-the-beaten-track destinations.

Corporate responsibility: Condor Travel works with the Rainforest Alliance to make its tours sustainable and runs a community development project near the Inca Trail. ☎ *877/236–7199 in U.S., 1/615–3000 Peru* ⊕ *www.condortravel.com.*

Earthwatch. A nonprofit organization that provides volunteers and uses trip revenues to support scientific research, Earthwatch allows travelers to work on studies, enriching their understanding of the natural world while contributing to conservation. In Peru, Earthwatch runs expeditions up the Amazon Basin that let travelers participate in wildlife surveys in Pacaya-Samiria National Reserve. Some of those expeditions cater to teenagers. Fees for participating in Earthwatch expeditions are tax deductible.

Destinations serviced: Amazon River.

Most popular package: Amazon Riverboat Exploration, 8 days, from $2,775 per person; participants contribute to long-term survey of wildlife populations.

Customized trips: No.

What they do best: Allow travelers to contribute to the understanding and conservation of nature.

Corporate responsibility: All Earthwatch profits support scientific research and conservation. ☎ *800/776–0188 in U.S., 44/1865–318–838 in U.K.* ⊕ *www.earthwatch.org.*

Field Guides. The international bird-watching specialist Field Guides runs half a dozen tours to different regions of Peru led by expert birding guides, who help their clients spot as many of the country's more than 1,800 bird species as possible.

Destinations serviced: Cusco, Sacred Valley, Machu Picchu, Manu, Tambopata, Amazon River, northwest Peru.

Most popular package: Machu Picchu & Abra Malaga, 10 days, starting at $4,170 per person, travels from the highlands to the cloud forest to the Amazon Basin.

Customized trips: No.

What they do best: Getting bird-watchers to areas where they can see the greatest variety of species possible.

Corporate responsibility: Field guides makes regular contributions to various conservation organizations. ☎ 800/728–4953 in U.S. ⊕ fieldguides.com.

InkaNatura Travel. One of the country's oldest ecotourism companies, InkaNatura Travel offers trips to lodges deep in the wilderness of the Manu Biosphere Reserve and Tambopata National Reserve, in the Amazon Basin. They also arrange tours to Cusco and Machu Picchu, and the archaeological sites and beaches of northern Peru. They cater to bird-watchers, nature lovers, archaeology buffs, and travelers who want to experience a bit of everything.

Destinations serviced: Manu, Tambopata, Cusco, Sacred Valley, Inca Trail, Machu Picchu, Trujillo, Chiclayo, Chachapoyas, Kuelap, Cajamarca, Mancora, Punta Sal.

Most popular packages: Bio Trip Manu, six days, from $1,639 per person, from the cloud forest to the rain forest of the Manu Biosphere Reserve, with overnights at the Cock of the Rock Lodge, Pantiacolla Lodge, and Manu Wildlife Center.

Customized trips: Yes.

What they do best: Help travelers experience the flora and fauna of the Amazon Basin.

Corporate responsibility: A portion of profits is donated to Peru Verde, a nonprofit groups that promotes conservation, wildlife monitoring and sustainable development. ☎ 1/203–5000 Peru ⊕ www.inkanatura.com.

Inkaterra. This small Peruvian company runs luxury trips that combine access to the rain forest of Madre de Dios with the classic Cusco–Machu Picchu route.

They also operate bird-watching tours and longer trips that visit other sites in southern Peru.

Destinations serviced: Cusco, Sacred Valley, Machu Picchu, Madre de Dios, Arequipa, Colca Canyon, Lake Titicaca.

Most popular package: Inkaterra's Flagship Tour, seven days, starting at $2,950, combines the Amazon Rain Forest, Cusco, and Machu Picchu, with nights in some of the country's best hotels.

Customized trips: Yes.

What they do best: Provide high-quality service and accommodations and exposure to some of the country's greatest attractions.

Corporate responsibility: The company conserves 42,000 acres of rain forest in Madre de Dios, supports scientific research, and has adopted sustainable tourism. Its tours are carbon neutral. ☎ 800/442–5042 in U.S. and Canada, 0/808/101–2224 in U.K., 1/610–0400 in Peru ⊕ www.inkaterra.com.

Orient Express. This venerable company offers a small selection of luxury itineraries in Peru using its own trains and hotels, which are some of the best in the country: the Miraflores Park Hotel, the Palacio Nazarenas, and Hotel Monasterio in Cusco, the Hotel Rio Sagrado, and the Machu Picchu Sanctuary Lodge. Their journeys are all variations on the classic Cusco–Machu Picchu circuit.

Destinations serviced: Most popular package: Lima, Cusco, Sacred Valley, Machu Picchu.

Most popular package: Unmissable Peru, eight days, starting at $5,178 per person, combines Lima, the Sacred Valley, Cusco, Machu Picchu, and a trip on the luxurious Hiram Bingham train.

Customized trips: Yes

What they do best: Luxury tours to Peru's top sites, with first class train and accommodations.

Corporate responsibility: The company has provided support for various schools, an orphanage, and an organic gardening center. ☎ 800/524–2420 in U.S., 44/207–921–4010 in U.K., 1/612–6700 in Peru ⊕ www.orient-express.com.

Overseas Adventure Travel. This U.S. company offers midrange tours with small groups (usually 10–16 travelers) led by knowledgeable guides that give travelers opportunities to meet local people. Their most popular Peru tour combines Cusco and Machu Picchu with the Galápagos, with possible extensions on the Amazon River or Lake Titicaca and La Paz, Bolivia.

Destinations serviced: Lima, Cusco, Sacred Valley, Machu Picchu, Amazon, Lake Titicaca.

Most popular package: Machu Picchu & the Galápagos, 16 days, from $5,295, combines Cusco, the Sacred Valley, and Machu Picchu with the Galápagos and Quito, Ecuador.

Customized trips: No.

What they do best: Provide quality guided tours to top sights at competitive prices.

Corporate responsibility: The company funds the Grand Circle Foundation, which provides school supplies and other support to six schools in poor Peruvian communities in the Sacred Valley and Amazon Basin. ☎ 800/955–1925 in U.S. ⊕ www.oattravel.com.

Green Tracks. Founded by an American biologist, this small company specializes in helping nature lovers experience the fauna and flora of the Amazon rain forest, and they often arrange trips for groups with very specific interests. They also offer trips to Cuzco, Machu Picchu, and other popular areas.

Destinations serviced: Amazon River, Manu, Tambopata, Inca Trail, Machu Picchu, Like Titicaca, Nazca, Trujillo, Chiclayo, Cajamarca, Chachapoyas, Kuelap.

Most popular package: Amazon Wildlife Cruise, seven days, from $2,500, departing Iquitos in a restored, historic river boat, this one-week cruise heads up the Amazon River into the Pacaya Samiria National Reserve.

Customized trips: Yes.

What they do best: Help nature lovers and specialists get deep into the Amazon wilderness with quality guides and information.

Corporate responsibility: Company facilitates scientific research and environmental education, and provides income for remote communities. ☎ 800/892–1035 in U.S., 970/884–6107 ⊕ www.greentracks.com.

International Expeditions. An ecotourism pioneer, International Expeditions specializes in taking travelers deep into tropical nature and helping them experience local wildlife and culture while mitigating tourism's negative impacts. The company has been running Peru trips for more than three decades and it offers longer itineraries to its most popular and off-the-beaten-path attractions. Its tours feature small groups led by knowledgeable local guides and competitive prices.

Destinations serviced: Lima, Cuzco, Sacred Valley, Inca Trail. Machu Picchu, Amazon River, Puno, Lake Titicaca, Colca Valley, Arequipa, Trujillo, Chiclayo, Chaparri Nature Reserve, Gochta Waterfall, Kuelap. Madre de Dios.

Most popular package: Amazon Voyage, eight days, from $3,898 per person, after sightseeing in Lima, travelers fly to Iquitos to start a six-day cruise up the Amazon and Ucayali Rivers to the Pacaya-Samira Reserve.

Customized trips: Yes.

What they do best: Allow travelers to experience Peru's varied natural and cultural attractions safely and in comfort.

Corporate responsibility: The company promotes conservation on the Amazon River while improving life in local communities by donating water treatment plants, improving education 120 rural schools, and sponsoring an urban garden project in Iquitos. ☎ *800/234–9620 or 205/253–1114 ⊕ www.ietravel.com.*

Kuoda Travel. Cusco-based Kuoda Travel specializes in personalized, custom itineraries, primarily for families and couples. The owner, Mery Calderon, manages the business, which has a series of suggested itineraries, but works with clients to customize them to their needs.

Destinations serviced: Lima, Cusco, Sacred Valley, Machu Picchu, Tambopata, Arequipa, Colca Canyon, Puno, Lake Titicaca, Amazon River, Nazca.

Most popular package: the Jungle, Machu Picchu, and Lake Titicaca, 12 days, starting at $3,200, starts with three nights at the Reserva Amazonica, in Madre de Dios, followed by Cusco, the Sacred Valley, and Machu Picchu and ending with a couple days at Lake Titicaca.

Customized trips: Yes.

What they do best: Plan and run trips that cater to the interests and needs of each client.

Corporate responsibility: The company has a small foundation that runs education programs in two Sacred Valley communities. ☎ *800/986–4150 in U.S. and Canada, 84/221–773 in Peru ⊕ www. kuodatravel.com.*

PACKING AND PREPARATIONS

What you pack depends on where and when you travel. If you're heading to several regions, you'll need a good variety of clothing. If you visit the Amazon Basin or Andes between November and May, pack rain gear and a few plastic bags to protect cameras and other items. Good walking shoes or boots are essential everywhere, as are sunblock and insect repellent.

Clothing

Peru's varied geography means a diversity of climates, with the major climate regions being the Costa (coast), the Sierra (mountains), and the Selva (Amazon rain forest). Add to this the fact that southern Peru experiences distinct summer and winter, which are the opposite of the northern hemisphere's seasons, whereas northern Peru has less seasonal variation. When it's torrid in Manhattan, Lima is chilly and gray, but when New Yorkers are bundling up, Lima is hot and sunny. It can get quite cool in the mountains at night, with frequent freezes between June and September, but it is warm and sunny during the day then. The coast is a desert, but it rains most afternoons in the mountains from October to May and pretty much year-round in the Amazon Basin, though more between October and May. If you visit then, you'll need rain gear. However, the mountains don't get as cold at night during the rainy months, so you won't need that down jacket.

The best policy is to bring a good mix of clothes that go well together so that you can layer, since a mountain day begins brisk, but quickly warms. Once the clouds roll in, or the sun gets low, you'll need a raincoat or a jacket. Rather than packing a sweater, hat, and gloves, you may want to buy them in Lima or Cusco, where the shops and markets hold a kaleidoscopic selection of sheep and alpaca wool clothing.

You'll want light clothing, a hat, and rain gear for the Amazon Basin, where it is usually scorching. Long pants and sleeves will help you avoid mosquito bites and sunburn. Keep in mind that the Madre de Dios region gets little rain from May to September, when it gets hit by occasional cold fronts that can make you break out your mountain clothes.

Toiletries

Sunblock is essential everywhere, and can be purchased at any Peruvian pharmacy. Insect repellent, preferably with DEET, is essential in the Amazon Basin and eastern Andes (Machu Picchu), but the local brands aren't as good as what you can buy at home. Pack an antidiarrhea medicine, such as Imodium, just in case, and always carry a small packet of tissues, since bathrooms don't always have toilet paper. You'll want a skin moisturizer if you spend much time in the mountains between May and October. If your camera, travel alarm, or other electronic goods use unusual-size disposable batteries, pack extras.

Vaccines

The Centers for Disease Control and Prevention recommend that travelers to Peru be up to date on routine shots and consult their doctor about getting vaccinated against hepatitis A and B and typhoid. Travelers heading to the Amazon Basin should get a yellow fever vaccine and consider taking an antimalarial drug other than chloroquine. However, diligent use of insect repellent, long pants, and long-sleeve shirts is the best policy in the jungle, because it can protect you against various mosquito-borne diseases.

GREAT ITINERARIES

If this will be your first trip to Peru, Cusco and Machu Picchu are practically obligatory. The question is "what else?" And the answer depends on how much time you have and what your interests are. You can combine Machu Picchu with a number of other Andean attractions, the Amazon rain forest, or pre-Inca archaeological sites on the coast. If this is not your first trip to Peru, the last itineraries in this section offer you something a little different.

ESSENTIAL PERU

The former Inca capital of Cusco and citadel of Machu Picchu are two of the most impressive places in South America and the reasons that most people visit Peru. If you only have a week, this is where you head, but it is easy and highly recommended to combine a Machu Picchu pilgrimage with a visit to the rain forest, either in the nearby Madre de Dios province or on the Amazon River proper.

Day 1: Lima

Lima has more to see than you could possibly pack into a day. You should definitely take a three-hour tour of Lima's historic Centro, or give yourself that much time to explore it on your own. In the afternoon, head to Pueblo Libre to visit the Museo Nacional de Antropología y Arqueología and the Museo Rafael Larco Herrera, or take a taxi out to the suburb of Monterrico to visit the Museo de Oro (Gold Museum). In the evening, stroll around historic Barranco and have a drink, and perhaps dinner, there or at the Huaca Pucllana, where you have the option of exploring a pre-Inca site before you eat. ⇨ *Lima, Chapter 2.*

Day 2: Cusco

From Lima, take an early-morning flight to the ancient Inca capital of Cusco. Try to get seats on the left side of the plane for an amazing view of snow-draped peaks toward the end of the flight. You'll want to take it easy upon arriving in Cusco, which is perched at almost 11,000 feet above sea level. Take a half-day tour, or visit such sights as the Cathedral, Qorikancha, the Museo de Arte Precolombino, and the Museo Hilario Mendivil on your own. Be sure to visit the Plaza de Armas at night, before dining at one of the city's many excellent restaurants. ⇨ *Cusco and the Sacred Valley, Chapter 5.*

Day 3: Sacred Valley

Dedicate this day to the sights of the surrounding highlands, starting with Sacsayhuamán, the Inca ruins outside of town. You could do a day trip to the Sacred Valley, or spend this night at one of the many hotels located there. The valley holds an array of interesting sites, such as the market town of Pisac, Chinchero, and the massive Inca fortress at Ollantaytambo. It is also lower, and thus warmer, than Cusco, and lies on the route to Machu Picchu, which means you can catch a later train there. ⇨ *Cusco and the Sacred Valley, Chapter 5.*

Days 4 and 5: Machu Picchu

Start this day with the train trip to Machu Picchu, which winds its way past indigenous villages, snowcapped mountains, Inca ruins, and luxuriant forest to the town of Aguas Calientes. Check into your hotel, then spend the afternoon exploring Machu Picchu, the majestic citadel of the Incas. Head up the steep trail on the left shortly after entering the park and climb to the upper part of the ruins for a panoramic view before you start exploring.

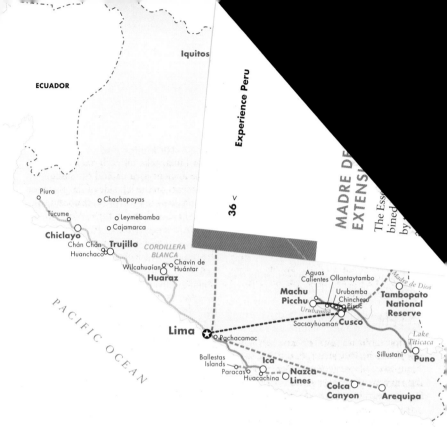

Before it gets dark, stroll up to the hot springs in the valley above Aguas Calientes, which is a lovely spot even if you don't get in the water.

On Day 5, get up early to explore a bit of Machu Picchu before it gets crowded. If you're up for a tough hike up a steep, slightly treacherous trail, climb Huayna Picchu, the backdrop mountain, for vertiginous views of the ruins and surrounding jungle. Or take the longer hike through the forest to the Temple of the Moon (be sure to slather on the insect repellent first). After all the hiking, you should be ready for a leisurely three-course lunch at the Fodor's Choice Indio Feliz, in Aguas Calientes. In the afternoon or evening, take the train back to Cusco. ⇨ *Machu Picchu and the Inca Trail, Chapter 6.*

Day 6: Cusco to Lima

Take advantage of the morning to visit a site you missed on your first day in Cusco, or to visit a few of the city's countless shops and markets. Fly to Lima (one hour) early enough to have lunch at one of the city's cebicherías. Use the afternoon to visit a museum or another attraction you missed on your first day there. You may want to catch a folklore show with dinner, or sample the nightlife in Miraflores or Barranco.

DIOS
ON

ntial Peru tour can easily be com-
with a visit to the Amazon Basin
aking a short flight from Cusco to the
djacent Madre de Dios region on Day 6.

Days 6–9: Manu or Tambopata

Take an early-morning flight from Cusco
to Puerto Maldonado, where someone
from your lodge will meet you and take
you to your lodging by boat. Your next
three days will be filled with constant
exposure to tropical nature on rain-forest hikes, boat trips on oxbow lakes, and
wildlife observation at *collpas* (clay licks),
from towers that let you ascend into the
rain-forest canopy, or from the porch of
your bungalow. Some lodges also offer
contact with local indigenous peoples.
⇨ *The Amazon Basin, Chapter 7.*

Day 10: Lima

Travel by boat and air back to Cusco and/
or Lima. Follow Day 6 of the Essential
Peru itinerary.

AMAZON RIVER EXTENSION

An alternative to the nature lodges of
Madre de Dios is to visit the Amazon River
proper, with a three-night river cruise and
some time in the port city of Iquitos.

Day 6: Cusco

Take advantage of an additional day in
Cusco to visit some of the sites you missed
on your first day there and spend more
time in the city's shops and markets.
⇨ *Cusco and the Sacred Valley, Chapter 5.*

Days 7–10: Iquitos and Amazon Cruise

Fly to Lima early and catch a flight to
Iquitos, a historic Amazon port city in the
northeast corner of the country. Board a
riverboat for a three-day cruise up the
Amazon River to the Pacaya Samiria
Reserve, where you'll explore Amazon
tributaries and oxbow lakes in smaller
boats to experience the area's exceptional biodiversity. ⇨ *The Amazon Basin,
Chapter 7.*

Day 11: Iquitos to Lima

Disembark in Iquitos and either spend a
night there, to visit some of the nearby
sites, or fly directly back to Lima. Follow
Day 6 of the Essential Peru itinerary.

CLASSIC ANDEAN JOURNEY

Day 1: Lima

Follow Day 1 of the Essential Peru itinerary.

Day 2: Arequipa

From Lima, take an early-morning flight
to Arequipa, a lovely colonial city with
a backdrop of snowcapped volcanoes.
Explore the city's historic center with its
rambling Monasterio de Santa Catalina
and the Museo Santuarios Andinos, home
of a pre-Columbian mummy known as
"Juanita." Be sure to enjoy some traditional arequipeña cooking, such as *rocoto
relleno* (a hot pepper stuffed with beef), or
chupe de camarones (river prawn chowder). ⇨ *The Southern Andes and Lake
Titicaca, Chapter 4.*

Days 3: Colca Canyon

Rise early for the drive to Colca Canyon, the deepest canyon in the world and
one of the best places in Peru to spot an
Andean condor. After lunch, take a hike
along the canyon's edge or go horseback

riding. ⇨ *The Southern Andes and Lake Titicaca, Chapter 4.*

Days 4 and 5: Puno and Lake Titicaca

Rise early and head to Cruz del Condor, the best place to spot those massive birds. Spend the rest of the day traveling overland through a series of Andean landscapes to Puno, on Lake Titicaca, the highest navigable lake in the world. Puno's 3,830-meter (12,500-feet) altitude can take your breath away, so have a light dinner and rest for the day ahead.

Rise early on Day 5 and take a boat tour of Lake Titicaca, stopping at one of the Uros Islands, man-made, floating islands that hold small communities, and Isla Taquile, a naturally occurring island whose indigenous inhabitants are famous for their weaving skills. In the afternoon, visit the pre-Inca burial ground and stone *chullpas* at Sillustani. ⇨ *The Southern Andes and Lake Titicaca, Chapter 4.*

Days 6 and 7: Cusco

Catch the early morning train from Puno for a full-day trip across more Andean landscapes to the ancient Inca capital of Cusco, a 330-meter (1,083-foot) drop in altitude. Follow Days 2 and 3 of the Essential Peru itinerary.

Days 8 and 9: Machu Picchu

Follow Days 4 and 5 of the Essential Peru itinerary.

Day 10: Cusco to Lima

Follow Day 6 of the Essential Peru itinerary.

APURIMAC RIVER AND INCA TRAIL

Adventurous travelers in good physical condition can combine two of Peru's top outdoor tours—white-water rafting on the Apurimac River and the hike on the Inca Trail to Machu Picchu—for two weeks of adrenaline, exercise, and phenomenal scenery.

Day 1: Lima

Follow Day 1 of the Essential Peru itinerary.

Day 2: Cusco

Follow Day 2 of the Essential Peru itinerary.

Days 3–6: Apurimac River

Spend the next four days paddling down the legendary Apurimac River (Class III–IV), one of the Amazon's main tributaries and Peru's premier white-water route. The trip begins with a four-hour drive from Cusco to Naihua, where the river trip begins. You'll spend the next three days navigating rapids, admiring the surrounding rain forest, and camping near the riverbank. The last day on the river ends around noon, after which you'll have lunch and be driven to Cusco (five hours).

Day 7: Cusco

You'll probably want to relax this day, but Cusco has plenty of sights to tempt you. Or follow Day 3 of the Essential Peru itinerary.

Days 8–12: Inca Trail and Machu Picchu

Rise early this morning and catch the train to Machu Picchu, but get off at Km 82, where the four-day trek on the Inca Trail begins. You'll start by following the Urubamba River to the ruins of Llactapata, from which you climb slowly to the first campsite, at 9,691 feet. The next day is the toughest; you'll hike over Warmiwanusca pass (13,776 feet) and camp at 11,833 feet. On Day 3 of the trek, you hike over two passes and visit several small Inca ruins. The last day is short, mostly downhill. You may have the option of rising early to reach Machu Picchu's Inti Punku (Sun Gate) by sunrise. Spend the morning or day exploring

Machu Picchu, then bus down to Aguas Calientes for a hot shower and a sumptuous meal at El Indio Feliz.

Rise early on the morning of Day 12 to explore Machu Picchu before it gets crowded. Be sure to climb Huayna Picchu, if you didn't the day before. Catch an afternoon train to Cusco, where great restaurants and nightlife await. ⇨ *Machu Picchu and the Inca Trail, Chapter 6.*

Day 13: Cusco to Lima
Follow Day 6 of the Essential Peru itinerary.

NORTH COAST AND MACHU PICCHU

This trip lets you trace the development of Lima's indigenous cultures by combining the pre-Inca archaeological sites of northern Peru with the classic Inca sites of southern Peru. It also lets you explore several colonial cities and sample Peru's geographic diversity, starting in the coastal desert, moving into the Andes, and then descending to the edge of the Amazon Basin.

Day 1: Lima
Follow Day 1 of the Essential Peru itinerary.

Days 2 and 3: Chiclayo
Catch an early flight to the northern city of Chiclayo, which lies near some of the country's most important pre-Inca sites. A small, pleasant city near several excellent museums and a dilapidated beach town called Pimentel, Chiclayo is noticeably warmer and sunnier than Lima. Spend two days visiting the nearby pyramids at Túcume, the Museo Nacional Sicán, the Museo Brüning, and Museo Tumbas de Sipán. ⇨ *The North Coast and Northern highlands, Chapter 9.*

Days 4 and 5: Trujillo
Catch an early flight (40 minutes) or travel by land (3–4 hours) south to Trujillo, an attractive colonial city near the ancient structures of two other pre-Inca cultures. After checking into your hotel, explore the old city, which holds some well-preserved colonial and 19th-century architecture. In the afternoon, head to the rambling ruins of Chan Chan, with its lovely bas-relief adobe walls. On Day 5, visit the archaeological sites of Huaca de La Luna and Huaca del Sol, and the beach/fishing port of Huanchaco, where fishermen still use the tiny, pre-Columbian reed boats called *caballitos de totora.* ⇨ *The North Coast and Northern Highlands, Chapter 9.*

Day 6: Lima
Take a quick flight back to Lima and visit some of the sights you didn't have time for on Day 1. Be sure to hit Barranco, a lovely area for an evening stroll, cocktail, or dinner. ⇨ *Lima, Chapter 2.*

Day 7: Cusco
Follow Day 2 of the Essential Peru itinerary.

Day 8: Sacred Valley
Follow Day 3 of the Essential Peru itinerary.

Days 9 and 10: Machu Picchu
Follow Days 4 and 5 of the Essential Peru itinerary.

Day 11: Cusco to Lima
Follow Day 6 of the Essential Peru itinerary.

SOUTHERN COAST AND CORDILLERA BLANCA

This tour combines cultural and natural wonders and takes you through an array of landscapes—from the desert to offshore islands to snowcapped mountains.

Day 1: Lima
Follow Day 1 of the Essential Peru itinerary.

Days 2 and 3: Ica
Head south on the Pan-American Highway for four hours to Ica. Try to visit the archaeological site of Tambo Colorado en route. After checking into your hotel, head for the Huacachina oasis for a dune buggy ride or sand-boarding, or arrange a tour of one of the nearby wineries. ⇨ *The Southern Coast, Chapter 3.*

Day 4: Nazca and Paracas
In the morning, board a small plane for a flight over the enigmatic Nazca Lines. Then transfer to Paracas, on the coast. In the afternoon, take a boat tour to the Ballestas Islands, where you'll see thousands of sea lions, birds, and tiny Humboldt penguins, as well as the massive candelabra etched on a hillside. ⇨ *The Southern Coast, Chapter 3.*

Day 5: Lima
The next day, return to Lima, stopping at the pre-Inca site of Pachacamac on the way. Sightsee and shop in the afternoon, then enjoy a memorable meal at one of the city's great restaurants. ⇨ *Lima, Chapter 2.*

Days 6–10: Huaraz
Travel overland to Huaraz, in the country's central Andes, where you'll want to take it easy while you acclimatize. Visit the nearby Wari ruins of Wilcahuaían. If you're up for it, spend the next four days trekking on the Santa Cruz circuit, a gorgeous route into the heart of the Cordillera Blanca. If you aren't up for the trek, spend a couple of days doing less strenuous hikes to one of the Cordilleras turquoise lakes and the ruins of Chavín de Huantar. ⇨ *The North Coast and Northern Highlands, Chapter 9.*

Day 11: Huaraz to Lima
Travel overland back to Lima. Follow Day 6 of the Essential Peru itinerary once you arrive.

NORTHERN ANDES AND CULTURES

The Northern Andes have some of Peru's most spectacular landscapes, the second most impressive Inca site after Machu Picchu (Kuelap), and the ancient city of Cajamarca. However, the precipitous terrain and bad roads dissuade some travelers from going there, and the big tour companies tend to ignore the region. Peruvian tour operators, on the other hand, can help you explore this remote but fascinating region.

Day 1: Lima
Follow Day 1 of the Essential Peru itinerary.

Day 2: Chiclayo
Catch an early flight to the northern city of Chiclayo, which lies near some of the country's most important pre-Inca sites. Spend the day visiting the nearby Museo Nacional Sicán, the Museo Tumbas de Sipán, and the pyramids at Túcume. ⇨ *The North Coast and Northern Highlands, Chapter 9.*

Days 3 and 4: Chachapoyas
Rise early for a long but impressive overland journey deep into the Andes. You'll wind your way up out of the coastal desert into the mountains and through various semi-arid valleys until you reach the lush Uctubamba Valley. You'll arrive in the picturesque mountain town of Chachapoyas around dusk, as the air grows chilly. Check into your hotel and enjoy a hearty dinner.

After breakfast on Day 4, travel up the beautiful Uctubamba Valley to Karajia and "Pueblo de los Muertos" to see the funerary statues of the Chacapoya culture. Look for birds and other wildlife and enjoy the lush scenery en route. Return to Chachapoyas in the late afternoon and explore its small historic center. ⇨ *The North Coast and Northern Highlands, Chapter 9.*

Day 5: Kuelap and Leymebamba

After breakfast, drive for approximately four hours up the Uctubamba Valley to the massive Inca fortress of Kuelap. Spend several hours exploring that vast site, which contains more than 400 structures and is hemmed by lush vegetation. From Kuelap, continue up the valley to the timeless town of Leymebamba, known for its handicrafts. ⇨ *The North Coast and Northern Highlands, Chapter 9.*

Days 6–8: Cajamarca

Travel to Cajamarca via Balzas, where you can stop at a museum with a large collection of mummies and an orchid garden. From there you'll head over two cordilleras and through the Marañon Canyon, passing some phenomenal scenery. Early in the evening you'll arrive in the historic city of Cajamarca, where the Spanish conquistadores captured and killed Atahualpa, the last Inca. Cajamarca is perched at 2,650 meters (8,612 feet), so it is quite cool.

Start Day 7 by climbing to the top of Cerro Santa Apolonia for a panoramic view of the city. Then explore the old part of town with its colonial churches and other structures. Be sure to visit the rambling Complejo de Belén and the Baños del Inca, where you can soak in the same mineral waters that the Inca enjoyed. On Day 8, visit the pre-Inca site of Cumbe Mayo, and hike a section of the Inca Road, such as the stretch to Combayo. ⇨ *The North Coast and Northern Highlands, Chapter 9.*

Day 9: Lima

Fly back to Lima in the morning. Once there, follow Day 6 of the Essential Peru itinerary.

VISIBLE HISTORY

by Paul Steele

About 15,000 years ago, the first people to inhabit what is now Peru filtered down from North and Central America. They were confronted by diverse and extreme environments at varying altitudes. An ocean rich in fish contrasts with sterile coastal valleys that are only habitable where rivers cut through the desert. To the east the valleys and high plateau of the Andes mountains slope down to the Amazon rainforest, home to exotic foods, animals, and medicinal plants.

Modern Peru incorporates all of these environmental zones. Long before the centralized state of the Inca empire, people recognized the need to secure access to varied resources and products. Images of animals and plants from coast and jungle are found on pottery and stone monuments in highland Chavin culture, c. 400 BC.

Around AD 500 the Nazca Lines etched out in the desert also featured exotic jungle animals.

In the 15th century the Incas achieved unprecedented control over people, food crops, plants, and domesticated animals that incorporated coast, highlands, and the semitropical valleys. Attempts to control coca leaf production in the warmer valleys may explain Machu Picchu, which guards an important trading route.

When the Spaniards arrived in the 16th century, the search for El Dorado, the fabled city of gold, extended the Viceroyalty of Peru into the Amazon lowlands. Since independence in 1821, disputes, wars, and treaties over Amazon territory have been fueled increasingly by the knowledge of mineral oil and natural gas under the forest floor.

(far left) Moche ceramic, portrait of a priest; (above) Cerro Sechin ca. 1000 BC on Peru coast; (left) Mummified corpse skull.

2600–1000 BC
BIG OLD BUILDINGS

Peru's first monumental structures were also the earliest throughout the Americas. Coastal sites like Aspero and Caral have platform mounds, circular sunken courtyards, and large plazas that allowed public civic-ceremonial participation. At Garagay and Cerro Sechin mud and adobe relief sculptures show images connected to death, human disfigurement, and human to animal transformation. A developing art style characterized by pronounced facial features like fanged teeth and pendant-iris eyes reached its height later in Chavin culture.

■ Visit:
Kotosh (⇨ Ch. 8),
Sechín (⇨ Ch. 9).

900–200 BC
CHAVIN CULTURE

Chavin de Huantar, a site not far from Huaraz, was famous for its shamans or religious leaders who predicted the future. A distinctive and complex imagery on carved stone monuments like the Lanzón and Tello Obelisk featured animals and plants from the coast, highlands, and especially the jungle. The decline of Chavin de Huantar coincided with the emergence of other oracle temples such as Pachacamac, south of modern Lima. The distinctive Chavin art style, however, continued to influence later cultures throughout Peru, including Paracas on the south coast.

■ Visit:
Chavin de Huantar (⇨ Ch. 9).

600–50 BC
ALL WRAPPED UP IN PARACAS

On the Paracas Peninsula the remains of an ancient burial practice are strewn across the desert. Corpses were wrapped in layers of textiles, placed in baskets, and buried in the sand. Many elaborately woven and embroidered garments that could be tens of meters long were only used to bury the dead and never worn in life. The mummy bundles of high status individuals were often accompanied by offerings of gold objects, exotic shells, and animal skins and feathers.

■ Visit:
Pachacamac (⇨ Ch. 3).

(above) Chavin de Huantar; (top right) Huaca de la Luna deity; (bottom right) Nazca ground picture of whale.

THE NASCANS

50 BC–AD 700

On Peru's south coast followed the Nasca, who are famous for the geoglyph desert markings known as the Nazca Lines. Thousands of long straight lines were constructed over many centuries, while around fifty animal outlines date to a more concise period of AD 400–600. An extensive system of underground aqueducts channeled water from distant mountains. In such a barren environment the Nazca Lines were probably linked closely to a cult primarily devoted to the mountain water source.

■ Visit:
Cahuachi (⇨ Ch. 3),
Nazca Lines (⇨ Ch. 3).

MOCHE KINGDOM

AD 100–800

On Peru's north coast the Moche or Mochica controlled a number of coastal river valleys. Large scale irrigation projects extended cultivable land. The Temples of the Sun and Moon close to the modern city of Trujillo were constructed from millions of adobe or mud bricks and were some of the largest buildings anywhere in the ancient Americas. The high quality of Moche burial goods for individuals like the Lord of Sipan indicated a wide social gulf not previously seen in Peru. Full-time artisans produced metalwork and ceramics for Moche lords. The pottery in particular is famous for the realistic portrayal of individuals and for the naturalistic scenes of combat, capture, and sacrifice that could have been narrative stories from Moche mythology and history. Some themes like the sacrificing of war captives in the presence of the Lord of Sipan and the Owl Priest were probably reenacted in real life. A number of severe droughts and devastating el niños rains precipitated the decline of the Moche.

■ Visit:
Pañamarca(⇨ Ch. 9),
Huaca de la Luna (⇨ Ch. 9),
Huaca del Sol (⇨ Ch. 9).

	Wari Empire begins	Chachapoyas kingdom begins
	EXTENSIVE ROAD NETWORK CREATED	
550	750	950

(above) Wari face neck jar; (top right) Chan Chan, (bottom right) Kuelap.

WELCOME TO THE WARI EMPIRE
550–950

A new dominant highland group, the Wari, or Huari, originated close to the modern city of Ayacucho. Wari administrative centers, storage facilities, and an extensive road network were forerunners to the organizational systems of the Inca empire. The Wari were influenced by the iconographic tradition of a rival site, Tiahuanaco, in what is now Bolivia, which exerted control over the extreme south of Peru. After Wari control collapsed, regional kingdoms and localized warfare continued until the expansion of the Inca empire.

■ Visit:
Pikillacta (⇨ Ch. 5), Santuario Histórico Pampas de Ayacucho (⇨ Ch. 8).

CHIMU KINGDOM
900–1470

On the north coast the Chimu or Chimor succeeded the Moche controlling the coastal river valleys as far south as Lima. The capital Chan Chan was a bustling urban sprawl that surrounded at least 13 high-walled citadels of the Chimu lords. The city was built close to the ocean shore and continual coastal uplift meant that access to fresh water from deep wells was a constant problem. An extensive canal network to channel water from rivers never worked properly.

■ Visit:
Chan Chan (⇨ Ch. 9), Huaca Esmeralda (⇨ Ch. 9).

THE FIGHTIN' CHACHAPOYAS
800–1480

In the cloud forests of the eastern Andean slopes the Chachapoyas kingdom put up fierce resistance against the Incas. The Chachapoyas are famous for their mummified dead placed in cliff-top niches and for high quality circular stone buildings at sites like Kuelap, one of the largest citadels in the world. Kuelap may have been designed as a fortification against the Wari. Later the Incas imposed harsh penalties on the Chachapoyas who subsequently sided with the Spaniards.

■ Visit:
Kuelap (Cuelap) (⇨ Ch. 9).

(left) Mama Occlo, wife and sister of Manco Capac, founder of the Inca dynasty, carrying the Moon; (above) Machu Picchu.

INCA ORIGINS

C. 1400

The Inca empire spanned a relatively short period in Peruvian history. The mythical origins of the first Inca Manco Capac, who emerged from a cave, is typical of Peruvian ancestor tradition. Spanish chroniclers recorded at least 10 subsequent Inca rulers although in reality the earlier kings were probably not real people. The famous Inca, Pachacuti, is credited with expansion from the capital Cusco. Inca iconographic tradition that followed geometric and abstract designs left no representational images of its rulers.

■ Visit:
Isla del Sol (⇨ Ch. 4).

INCA EMPIRE

1450–1527

Within three generations the Incas had expanded far beyond the boundaries of modern Peru to central Chile in the south and past the equator to the north. The Amazon basin was an environment they did not successfully penetrate. Although the Incas fought battles, it was a two-way process of negotiation with *curacas,* the local chiefs that brought many ethnic groups under control. The empire was divided into four *suyu* or parts, centered on Cusco. At a lower level communities were organized into decimal units ranging from 10 households up to a province of 40,000 households. Individual work for the state was known as *mit'a.* Communities forcibly resettled to foreign lands were called *mitimaes.* The Incas kept a regular population census and record of all the sacred idols and shrines. The Incas spread the language Quechua that is still spoken throughout most of Peru and in neighboring countries.

■ Visit:
Ollantaytambo(⇨ Ch. 5),
Machu Picchu (⇨ Ch. 6),
Ruins at Pisac (⇨ Ch. 5).

(above) The execution of Tupa Amaru; (left) Francisco Pizarro, Diego de Almagro, and Fernando de Luque planning the conquest of Peru.

ARRIVAL OF THE CONQUISTADORS

1527–1542

The Spanish conquistadors arrived on the coast of Ecuador and northern Peru bringing European diseases like smallpox that ravaged the indigenous population and killed the Inca king. They also introduced the name Peru. In 1532 a small band of conquistadors led by Francisco Pizarro first encountered the Inca ruler Atahualpa in Cajamarca. This famous confrontation of Old and New World cultures culminated with the capture of Atahualpa, who was later strangled. The Spaniards arrived in Cusco in 1533 and immediately took the city residences and country estates of the Inca elite for themselves. The resistance of Manco Inca could not drive the Spaniards out of Cusco, and by the end of the 1530s the Inca loyal supporters had retreated to Ollantaytambo, and then to the forested region of Vilcabamba that became the focus of Inca resistance for the next 30 years. In 1542 the Viceroyalty of Peru was created and a new capital city, Lima, became the political and economic center of Spain's possessions in South America.

■ Visit:
Cajamarca (⇨ Ch. 9),
Sacsayhuemán (⇨ Ch. 5).

END OF THE INCAS

1542–1572

A relatively small number of Spaniards overthrew the Incas because of support from many groups disaffected under Inca rule. Native Peruvians quickly realized, however, that these new lighter-skinned people were intent on dismantling their whole way of life. The 1560s nativist movement Taqui Onqoy, meaning dancing sickness, called on native gods to expel the Spaniards and their religion. In 1572 the Inca Tupa Amaru, mistakenly called Tupac Amaru, was captured and executed in public in Cusco.

■ Visit:
Cusco (⇨ Ch. 5).

(above) Battle of Ayacucho, Bolivar's forces establish Peruvian independence from Spain 1824; (left) Simon Bolivar, aka "The Liberator."

IN FOCUS VISIBLE HISTORY

1

SPANISH COLONIAL RULE

1572–1770

The Spanish crown increasingly sought more direct control over its American empire. A new viceroy, Toledo, stepped up the policy of *reducciones* in which formerly dispersed native communities were resettled into more easily controlled towns. This made it easier to baptize the native population into the Catholic church. The indigenous population was forced to work in mines such as Potosí, which became the biggest urban center in the Americas. Huge quantities of gold and silver were shipped to the Caribbean and then to Europe, and helped fund Spain's wars in Europe. Spanish hacienda estates introduced new food crops such as wheat, and new livestock like pigs and cows. The scale of native depopulation—more acute on the coast—is today reflected by the number of abandoned hillside terraces. The Inca elite and local chiefs started to adopt European dress; some found ways to prosper under new colonial regulations (like avoiding Spanish taxes if demonstrating Inca ancestry).

■ Visit:
Colonial architecture of Arequipa (⇨ Ch. 4),
Ayacucho (⇨ Ch. 8),
Cusco (⇨ Ch. 5),
Lima (⇨ Ch. 2),
Trujillo (⇨ Ch. 9).

END OF COLONIAL RULE

1770–1824

The execution of the last Inca ruler in 1572 did not stop continued rebellions against Spanish colonial rule. In the eighteenth century an uprising led by the local chief José Gabriel Condorcanqui, who called himself Tupa Amaru II, foreshadowed the wars of independence that ended colonial rule in Peru and elsewhere in the Americas. Peru declared its independence in 1821 and again in 1824, when Símon Bólivar arrived from Colombia to defeat the remaining royalist forces at the battle of Ayacucho.

■ Visit:
Pampas de Quinua
(⇨ Ch. 8).

(above) Ollanta Humala; (right) Lima, Peru.

REPUBLICAN ERA

1824–1900

Despite an initial 20 years of chaos, when every year seemed to bring a new regime, the young republic was attractive to foreign business interests. Particularly lucrative for Peru were the export of cotton and guano—nitrate-rich bird droppings used for fertilizer. Peru benefited from foreign investment such as railroad building, but an increasing national foreign debt was unsustainable without significant industrial development. Disputes with neighboring countries, especially the War of the Pacific against Chile in which Lima was sacked, land to the south ceded, and the country bankrupted, deeply affected the nation.

20TH-CENTURY PERU

1900–2000

For much of the nineteenth century Peru was led by presidents with military backgrounds, and military coups were interspersed with periods of civilian governments. The largest popular political movement, Alianza Popular Revolucionaria Americana, was founded by Victor Raul Haya de la Torre in the 1920s. Democratically elected presidents were rare. Old institutions like the haciendas declined and many are now abandoned ruins. In contrast, Lima's population increased rapidly with the growth of shanty towns called pueblos jóvenes.

RECENTLY . . .

1980–PRESENT

In the 1980s, the Shining Path guerrilla movement raged a ruthless war against the government that claimed tens of thousands of lives. The capture of its leader, Abimael Guzman, in 1992 marked the beginning of tourism's rebirth. President Alberto Fujimori, who served from 1990 to 2000, defeated the Shining Path through draconian measures, such as shuttering congress. He is now in prison for corruption and human rights abuses. Fujimori was succeeded by Peru's first president of indigenous descent, Alejandro Toledo (2001–06). The current president, Ollanta Humala, was elected in 2011 on promises to help Peru's poorest citizens.

Lima

WORD OF MOUTH

"Lima is spectacular. You will want to stay as we did in the nice Miraflores area, which is right along the ocean. This area is beautiful, upscale and safe: it looks like central Paris. Excellent shops and, of course, restaurants."

—tecolote

WELCOME TO LIMA

TOP REASONS TO GO

★ **Neptune's Bounty:** You'll quickly encounter *cebiche*—slices of raw fish or shellfish marinated in lemon juice with onions and hot peppers. Also try the *corvina* (sea bass) and *lenguado* (sole).

★ **Lima Baroque:** In El Centro, Iglesia de San Francisco's facade is considered the height of the "Lima Baroque" style of architecture. The crypt below stores the bones of dearly departed monks.

★ **Cool Digs:** More than 30 archaeological digs are around Lima, such as the pre-Inca temple Huaca Pucllana in Miraflores and the Huaca Huallamarca temple in San Isidro.

★ **Handicrafts:** Calle Alcanflores, which runs through Miraflores, has stores selling everything from hand-carved wooden masks to silver-filigree jewelry.

★ **Park Life:** On weekends families and couples fill Lima's parks, especially the ones that line Miraflores's ocean-view *malecónes,* such as the incomparable Parque del Amor.

1 El Centro. The Plaza Mayor (the city's main square) and nearby Plaza San Martin are two of the most spectacular public spaces in South America. Nearly every block has something to catch your eye, whether it's the elaborate facade of a church or the enclosed wooden balconies on centuries-old houses, but unfortunately, much of the neighborhood is dilapidated.

2 San Isidro. The city's nicest residential neighborhood surrounds Parque El Olivar, a grove of olive trees, where half-timbered homes are set among the gnarled trunks. Nearby are the city's oldest golf course and an array of banks and businesses, but the main attraction for travelers is its selection of restaurants and hotels.

3 Miraflores. A mix of modern and early 20th-century, Miraflores has the city's best selection of hotels, restaurants, bars, and boutiques, which are a draw for locals, so the neighborhood is always full of people. Visit Parque del Amor and the string of other parks along the malecón, which runs along the coastal cliffs—the view is unforgettable.

4 Barranco. The city's most bohemian, but also most charming, neighborhood,

Barranco combines historic architecture with ocean views. Bars and seafood eateries line the Bajada Los Baños, a cobblestone path leading down to the beach. In the evening it fills with young people in search of a good time.

5 Pueblo Libre. This neighborhood feels like a village, which is exactly what Pueblo Libre was until the city's borders pushed outward. The city's best museum, the Museo Arqueológico Rafael Larco Herrera, is here.

2

GETTING ORIENTED

Most of Lima's colonial-era churches and mansions are in **El Centro,** along the streets surrounding the Plaza de Armas. From there a speedy express-way called Paseo de la República (aka Via Espress) or a traffic-clogged thor-oughfare called Avenida Arequipa takes you south to **San Isidro** and **Miraflores,** two fairly upscale neighbor-hoods where you'll find the bulk of the city's dining and lodging options. East of Miraflores is **Barranco,** where colonial architec-ture is complemented by a bohemian ambience.

Banco de Credito, Lima.

Updated
by David
Dudenhoefer

When people discuss great South American cities, Lima is often overlooked. But Peru's capital can hold its own against its neighbors. It has an oceanfront setting, colonial-era splendor, sophisticated dining, and nonstop nightlife.

It's true that the city—clogged with traffic and choked with fumes—doesn't make a good first impression, especially since the airport is in an industrial neighborhood. But wander around the regal edifices surrounding the Plaza de Armas, among the gnarled olive trees of San Isidro's Parque El Olivar, or along the winding lanes in the coastal community of Barranco, and you'll find yourself charmed.

In 1535 Francisco Pizarro found the perfect place for the capital of Spain's colonial empire. On a natural port, the so-called Ciudad de los Reyes (City of Kings) allowed Spain to ship home all the gold the conquistador plundered from the Inca. Lima served as the capital of Spain's South American empire for 300 years, and it's safe to say that no other colonial city enjoyed such power and prestige during this period.

When Peru declared its independence from Spain in 1821, the declaration was read in the square that Pizarro had so carefully designed. Many of the colonial-era buildings around the Plaza de Armas are standing today. Walk a few blocks in any direction for churches and elegant houses that reveal just how wealthy this city once was. But the poor state of most buildings attests to the fact that the country's wealthy families have moved to neighborhoods to the south over the past century.

The walls that surrounded the city were demolished in 1870, making way for unprecedented growth. A former hacienda became the graceful residential neighborhood of San Isidro. In the early 1920s the construction of tree-lined Avenida Arequipa, heralded the development of neighborhoods like bustling Miraflores and bohemian Barranco.

Almost a third of the country's population of 29 million lives in the metropolitan area, many of them in relatively poor *conos:* newer neighborhoods on the outskirts of the city. Most residents of those neighborhoods moved there from mountain villages during the political violence and poverty that marked the 1980s and '90s, when crime increased dramatically. During the past decade the country has enjoyed peace, steady economic growth, and decreasing crime, which have been accompanied by many improvements and refurbishment in the city. Residents who used to steer clear of the historic center now stroll along its streets. And many travelers who once would have avoided the city altogether now plan to spend a day here and end up staying two or three.

PLANNING

WHEN TO GO

The weather in Lima is a relative opposite of North America's. Summer, from December to April, is largely sunny with temperatures regularly rising above 80°F, whereas the nights and mornings are cool. From May to November it is mostly cloudy and cool, sometimes dipping below 60°F, though there are occasional sunny days. The coastal region gets little precipitation, so you'll rarely find your plans ruined by rain, but there are winter days that start with a miserable foggy drizzle.

GETTING HERE AND AROUND

AIR TRAVEL

If you're flying to Peru, you'll touch down at Aeropuerto Internacional Jorge Chávez, in the northern neighborhood of El Callao. Once you're in the main terminal, hundreds of people will be waiting. Do yourself a favor and arrange through your hotel for a transfer. Otherwise, hire a cab from one of the companies that have desks in the corridor outside of customs.

Contacts CMV Taxi ☎ *01/517–1891.* **Taxi Green** ☎ *01/484–4001.*

Various airlines handle domestic flights, so getting to and from the major tourist destinations is no problem. LAN is the carrier with the most national flights, with a dozen flights per day to Cusco and several daily departures to Arequipa, Cajamarca, Chiclayo, Iquitos, Juliaca (Puno), Piura, Puerto Maldonado, Trujillo, and Tumbes. Taca is a close second, with daily flights to Arequipa, Cusco, Piura, Puerto Maldonado, and Trujillo. These are the most convenient airlines, but also the most expensive, charging foreigners at least twice as much as locals. Peruvian Airlines offers the best deals for travelers, with daily flights to Arequipa, Cusco, Iquitos, Piura, and Tacna, on the border with Chile. Star Peru is relatively inexpensive and flies to Ayacucho, Cusco, Huanuco, Iquitos, Juliaca, Puerto Maldonado, and Trujillo. The smaller LCPeru also has competitive rates, and flies to Ayacucho, Cajamarca, Cusco, Huanuco, and Huaraz.

Airport Information Aeropuerto Internacional Jorge Chávez ⊠ *Av. Faucett, El Callao* ☎ *1/517–3100* ⊕ *www.lap.com.pe.*

Carriers LAN ⊠ *Av. José Pardo 513, Miraflores* ☎ *01/213-8200* ⊕ *www.lan.com.* **LC Peru** ⊠ *Av. Pablo Carriquirry 857, San Isidro* ☎ *1/204–1313* ⊕ *www.lcperu.pe.* **Peruvian Airlines** ⊠ *Av. José Pardo 495, Miraflores* ☎ *1/716-6000* ⊕ *www.peruvianairlines.pe.* **Star Peru** ⊠ *Av. José Pardo 485, Miraflores* ☎ *1/705-9000* ⊕ *www.starperu.com.* **Taca** ⊠ *Av. José Pardo 811, Miraflores* ☎ *1/511-8222* ⊕ *www.taca.com.*

BUS TRAVEL

Two types of buses—regular-size *micros* and the van-size *combis*—patrol the streets of Lima. Fares are cheap, usually S/1–S/2 for a ride, but don't expect a lot of comfort. Watch your belongings, as pickpockets and bag-slashers are sometimes a problem. A quicker and safer way to travel between Barranco, Miraflores, and El Centro is El Metropolitano, a modern bus that runs down the middle of the Paseo de la Republica to the underground Estación Central, in front of the Sheraton Lima Hotel. El Metropolitano runs from 6 am to 10 pm and each trip costs S/1.50, but it gets quite crowded during rush hour. The system uses rechargeable electronic cards that you can buy from a vending machine for S/5. Stations on Avenida Bolgnesia in Barranco and Avenida Benavides in Miraflores are walking distance from hotels, but the route is rather far from most San Isidro lodgings.

Contacts Metropolitano ☎ 1/203–9000 ⊕ www.metropolitano.com.pe.

CAR TRAVEL

Lima is a difficult and confusing city to drive in, but most rental agencies also offer the services of a driver. In addition to offices downtown, Avis, Budget, and Hertz have branches at Jorge Chávez International Airport that are open 24 hours.

Contacts Avis ✉ Av. 28 de Julio 587, Miraflores ☎ 1/444–0450. **Budget** ✉ Av. Larco 998, Miraflores ☎ 01/444–4546. **Hertz** ✉ Av. Diez Canseco 218, Miraflores ☎ 1/445–5716. **National** ✉ Av. Costanera No. 1380, San Miguel ☎ 1/578–7878.

TAXI TRAVEL

Taxis are the best way to get around Lima. Use only taxis painted with a company's logo and that have the driver's license prominently displayed. You need to negotiate the fare before you get in. A journey between two adjacent neighborhoods should cost between S/5 and S/8; longer trips run between S/10 to S/25. If you hire one of the taxis parked in front of the tourist hotels, the price will be roughly double. If you're going to spend the day sightseeing, consider hiring a taxi for the day, which should cost about S/15–S/20 per hour.

Contacts Taxi Lima ☎ 9951/85800 ⊕ www.taxilimaperu.com. **Taxi Móvil** ☎ 1/422–6890. **Taxi Seguro** ☎ 1/241–9292. **Yellow Taxi** ☎ 1/561–1111.

HEALTH AND SAFETY

Drink only bottled water. Avoid lettuce and other raw vegetables. As for cebiche and *tiradito* (thinly sliced, marinated fish), both made with raw seafood, the citric acid in the lime-juice marinade is as efficient at killing bacteria as cooking, but because they are often prepared to order, let yours stew in the lime juice for a bit before eating to ensure that you don't suffer after enjoying those delicacies.

El Centro is safe during the day, but the neighborhood grows dicey at night, when you should stick to the two main plazas and Jirón de la Union (the pedestrian mall that connects them). Residential neighborhoods like Miraflores, San Isidro, and Barranco have far less street crime, but you should be on your guard away from the main streets. Always be alert for pickpockets in crowded markets and on public transportation.

In case of trouble, contact the Tourist Police. The department is divided into the **northern zone** (☎ *01/423–3500*), which includes El Centro, and the **southern zone** (☎ *01/243–2190*), which includes Barranco, Miraflores, and San Isidro. English-speaking officers will help you negotiate the system. For emergencies, call the **police** (☎ *105*) and **fire** (☎ *116*) emergency numbers.

EMERGENCIES

Several clinics have English-speaking staff, including the Clinica Anglo-Americana and Clinica El Golf. Both are in San Isidro. There is a pharmacy on every other (or every third) block on Lima main streets.

Hospitals Clinica Anglo-Americana ✉ *Av. Alfredo Salazar 350, San Isidro* ☎ *1/616–8900*. **Clinica El Golf** ✉ *Av. Aurelio Miro Quesada 1030, San Isidro* ☎ *1/631–0000*.

Pharmacies Farmacia Fasa ✉ *Los Eucaliptos 578, San Isidro* ☎ *1/619–0000* ✉ *Av. Larco 129, Miraflores* ☎ *01/619–0000*.

TOURS

Lima has many tour operators with experienced English-speaking guides for local and countrywide sightseeing. The most frequently recommended operator is Lima Vision, which offers various city tours as well as longer tours that combine the city with the pre-Inca site of Pachacámac. Condor Travel offers various city tours, including a gastronomic tour, and can arrange trips to Caral, the oldest city in the Americas. Solmartour has an array of Lima tours and day trips to the archaeological sites of Caral and Pachacámac. Ecocruceros offers half-day boat tours to the Islas Palomino—home to 4,000 sea lions—but it's a chilly excursion from May to December. Turibus and Mirabus offer some of Lima's most affordable city tours in roofless, double-decker buses. Turibus departs from the Larco Mar and Mirabus departs from Parque Kennedy, both in Miraflores. Energetic travelers can pedal their way past Lima's sights on a guided tour with Bike Tours of Lima.

Operators Bike Tours of Lima ✉ *Calle Bolivar 150, Miraflores* ☎ *1/445–3172* ⊕ *www.biketoursoflima.com*. **Condor Travel** ☎ *1/615–3000* ⊕ *www.condortravel.com*. **Ecocruceros** ☎ *1/226–8530* ⊕ *www.islaspalomino. com*. **Lima Vision** ☎ *1/447–7710* ⊕ *www.limavision.com*. **Mirabus** ☎ *1/242–6699* ⊕ *www.mirabusperu.com*. **Solmartour** ☎ *1/444–1313* ⊕ *www.solmar.com. pe*. **TuriBus** ☎ *1/446–7575* ⊕ *www.turibusperu.com*.

VISITOR INFORMATION

Travelers can find information about the city and beyond at iPerú, which has English- and Spanish-language materials. The city runs the Oficina de Información Touristica, or Tourist Information Office, in the rear of the Municipalidad de Lima.

Information iPerú ✉ *Jorge Basadre 610, San Isidro* ☎ *01/421–1627* ⊕ *www.peru.info* ✉ *Larcomar, Malecón de la Reserva and Av. José Larco, Miraflores* ☎ *1/445–9400*. **Oficina de Información Touristica** ✉ *Pasaje de los Escribianos 145, El Centro* ☎ *01/315–1542*.

EXPLORING LIMA

Once a compact city surrounded by small towns, Lima is now a vast metropolitan area that is home to nearly 9 million people. Most of it has little to offer travelers, so you'll want to limit your exploration to the *distritos*, or neighborhoods, listed in this chapter. Most of the city's best hotels and restaurants are located in three adjacent neighborhoods—Barranco, Miraflores, and San Isidro—to the south of the historic center, El Centro, but the bulk of its attractions are clustered in El Centro and nearby Pueblo Libre. You'll consequently need to take taxis between neighborhoods, though an express bus called the Metropolitano provides a quick connection between El Centro and the neighborhoods of Miraflores and Barranco. The airport is in a separate city called El Callao, about half an hour to the west of El Centro and an hour from most hotels. Trips between Barranco and Miraflores or San Isidro should take 10 to 20 minutes, whereas the travel times between any of them and El Centro are 20 to 30 minutes. During the rush hours (7:30 to 9 am and 5:30 to 7:30 pm), however, travel times double.

EL CENTRO

In the colonial era Lima was the seat of power for the viceroyalty of Peru. It held sway over a swath of land that extended from Panama to Chile. With power came money, as is evident by the grand scale on which everything was built. The finely carved doorways of some mansions stand two stories high. At least half a dozen churches would be called cathedrals in any other city. And the Plaza de Armas, the sprawling main square, is spectacular.

But history has not always been kind to the neighborhood known as El Centro. Earthquakes struck in 1687 and 1746, leveling many of the buildings surrounding the Plaza de Armas. Landmarks, such as the Iglesia de San Augustín, were nearly destroyed by artillery fire in skirmishes that have plagued the capital. But more buildings are simply the victims of neglect. It's heartbreaking to see the wall on a colonial-era building buckling, or an intricately carved balcony beyond repair. But the city government has made an effort to restore its historic center. After years of decline, things are steadily improving.

An unhurried visit to the historic district's main attractions takes a full day, with at least an hour devoted to the Museo de Arte Nacional, though you can see a good bit of it all in half a day if you're rushed. ■ **TIP→** Even if you're short on time, don't bypass the guided tour of the underground catacombs of the Iglesia de San Francisco, and don't miss Plaza San Martin.

GETTING AROUND

Chances are you're staying in Miraflores or San Isidro, which are a quick taxi ride from El Centro. Since taxis usually take the expressway, you're downtown in 20 minutes. A slower but more interesting route is to have your driver take Avenida Arequipa and do a loop on Paseo Colón for a look at some lovely architecture. The journey takes a half

HISTORICAL WALK

Almost all of Lima's most interesting historical sites are within walking distance of the Plaza de Armas. The fountain in the center can be used as a slightly off-center compass. The bronze angel's trumpet points due north, where you'll see the Palacio de Gobierno. To the west is the neocolonial Municipalidad de Lima, and to the east are the Catedral and the adjoining Palacio Episcopal. The cathedral, one of the most striking in South America, should be given a look inside. Head north on Jirón Carabaya, the street running beside the Palacio de Gobierno, until you reach the butter-yellow Estación de Desamparados, the former train station. Follow the street as it curves to the east. In a block you'll reach the Iglesia de San Francisco, the most spectacu-lar of the city's colonial-era churches. Explore the eerie catacombs.

hour, longer during rush hour. Once you're in El Centro, the best way to get around is on foot, since the historic area is rather compact.

TOP ATTRACTIONS

Casa Riva-Agüero. A pair of balconies with *celosías*—intricate wood screens through which ladies could watch passersby unobserved—grace the facade of this rambling mansion from 1760. Step inside and the downtown traffic fades away as you stroll across the stone countryard and admire the ancient balconies and woodwork. The Catholic Univer-sity, which administers the landmark, uses it for changing exhibitions, but the real reason to come is for a glimpse into a colonial-era home. ⊠ *Jr. Camaná 459, El Centro* ☎ *1/626–6600* ⬚*S/2* ⊙ *Weekdays 10–7.*

Catedral. The first church on the site was completed in 1625. The lay-out for this immense structure was dictated by Francisco Pizarro, and his basic vision has survived complete rebuilding after earthquakes in 1746 and 1940. Inside are impressive baroque appointments, especially the intricately carved choir stalls. Because of changing tastes, the main altar was replaced around 1800 with one in a neoclassical style. At about the same time the towers that flank the entrance were added. Admission includes a 40-minute tour. Visit the chapel where Pizarro is entombed and the small museum of religious art and artifacts. ⊠ *East side of Plaza de Armas, El Centro* ☎ *1/427–9647* ⬚*S/10* ⊙ *Weekdays 9–5, Sat. 10–1.*

Correo Central. Inaugurated in 1924, this regal structure looks more like a palace than a post office. You can buy a postcard or send a package, but most people come to admire the exuberance of an era when no one thought twice about placing bronze angels atop a civic building. At one time locals deposited letters in the mouth of the bronze lion by the front doors. About half of the building is given over to two museums: the Casa de la Gastronomía Peruana, dedicated to the country's culi-nary traditions, and the Museo Postal y Filatélico, which displays its stamps. The museum entrance is on Jirón Conde Superunda, whereas the post office entrance is on Jirón Camana. ⊠ *Jr. Camana 157, El Centro* ☎ *1/427–9370* ⬚*Free* ⊙ *Mon.–Sat. 8–5, Sun. 9–1. Museums Tues.–Sun. 9–5.*

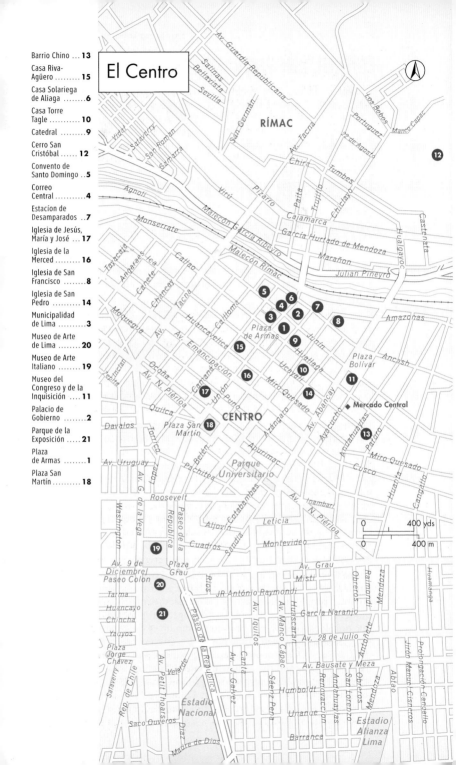

El Centro

Iglesia de la Merced. Nothing about this colonial-era church could be called restrained. Take the unusual baroque facade. Instead of stately columns, the powers-that-be decided they should be wrapped with carefully carved grapevines. Inside are a series of retablos that gradually change from baroque to neoclassical styles. The intricately carved choir stalls, dating from the 18th century,

STREET SMARTS

Although El Centro is safe for daytime strolls, at night you'll want to take a taxi to your destination. If you find yourself on the street with few other people around after dark, it's probably time to hail a cab.

have images of cherubic singers. The first house of worship to be built in Lima, Our Lady of Mercy was commissioned by Hernando Pizarro, brother of the city's founder. He chose the site because it was here that services were first held in the city. ⊠ *Jr. de la Unión at Jr. Miro Quesada, El Centro* ☎ *01/427–8199* ⌦ *Free* ☽ *Tues.–Fri. 10:30–1 and 4–8, Sat. 8–1 and 4–8, Sun. 8–1 and 4–8.*

Iglesia de San Francisco. Bones—including thousands and thousands of human skulls—are piled in eerie geometric patterns in the crypt of this church. This was the city's first cemetery, and the underground tunnels contain the earthly remains of some 75,000 people, which you visit on a tour (available in English). The Church of Saint Francis is the most visited in Lima, mostly because of these catacombs. But it's also the best example of what is known as "Lima Baroque" style of architecture. The handsome carved portal would later influence those on other churches, including the Iglesia de la Merced. The central nave is known for its beautiful ceilings painted in a style called *mudejar* (a blend of Moorish and Spanish designs). On the tour you'll see the adjoining monastery's immense collection of antique texts, some dating back to the 17th century. ⊠ *Jr. Ancash 471, El Centro* ☎ *1/719–7188* ⌦ *S/7* ☽ *Daily 9:30–5:30.*

Fodor's Choice ★

Iglesia de San Pedro. The Jesuits built three churches in rapid succession on this corner, the current one dating from 1638. It remains one of the finest examples of early-colonial religious architecture in Peru. The facade is remarkably restrained, but the interior shows all the extravagance of the era, including a series of baroque retablos thought to be the best in the city. Many have works by Italians like Bernardo Bitti, who arrived on these shores in 1575. His style influenced an entire generation of painters. In the sacristy is *The Coronation of the Virgin*, one of his most famous works. ■ **TIP→** Don't miss the side aisle, where gilded arches lead to chapels decorated with beautiful hand-painted tiles. ⊠ *Jr. Azángaro 451 at Jr. Ucayali, El Centro* ☎ *1/428–3010* ⊕ *www.sanpedrodelima. org* ⌦ *Free* ☽ *Mon.–Sat. 7–12:30 and 5–8, Sun. 7–2 and 5–8.*

Museo de Arte de Lima. Built in 1871 as the Palacio de la Expedición, this mammoth neoclassical structure was designed by the Italian architect Antonio Leonardo, with metal columns from the workshop of Gustav Eiffel (who later built the famous Parisian tower). The ground floor holds temporary exhibitions, usually by international artists, whereas the second floor houses a permanent exhibition that contains a bit of everything, from pre-Columbian artifacts to colonial-era furniture. One

of the highlights is the collection of 2,000-year-old weavings from Para-cas. ■TIP➡ Leave time to sip an espresso in the café near the entrance. ✉ *Paseo Colón 125, El Centro* ☎ *1/423–6332* ⊕ *www.mali.pe* 💲*S/12* 🕐 *Tues.–Sun. 10–8.*

Museo del Congreso y de la Inquisición. Visit the torture chambers of the Spanish Inquisition, where life-size exhibits illustrate methods of extract-ing "confessions" from prisoners accused of crimes against the Catholic Church. You can only visit the museum on hourly tours, and they offer just a few tours in English per day, so you'll want to reserve ahead of time. In contrast to the grisly displays, the 18th-century building is quite lovely, especially the coffered ceilings. ✉ *Jr. Junín 548, El Centro* ☎ *1/311–7777* ⊕ *www.congreso.gob.pe/museo.htm* 💲 *Free* 🕐 *Daily 9–5.*

Palacio de Gobierno. The neobaroque palace north of the Plaza de Armas is the official residence of the president. It was built on the site where Francisco Pizarro was murdered in 1541, and has undergone several reconstructions, the most recent of which was completed in 1938. The best time to visit is at noon, when you can watch soldiers in red-and-blue uniforms conduct an elaborate changing of the guard. It's not Buckingham Palace, but it's impressive. Tours are offered on Saturday at 10 and 11, but you should reserve at least a few days ahead of time. ✉ *Conde de Superunda 1501, El Centro* ☎ *1/311–3908.*

Fodor's Choice **Plaza de Armas.** This massive square has been the center of the city since
★ 1535. Over the years it has served many functions, from an open-air theater for melodramas to an impromptu ring for bullfights. Huge fires once burned in the center for people sentenced to death by the Spanish Inquisition. Much has changed over the years, but one thing remaining is the bronze fountain unveiled in 1651. It was here that José de San Martín declared the country's independence from Spain in 1821. ✉ *Jr. Junín and Jr. Carabaya, El Centro.*

Plaza San Martín. This spectacular plaza is unlike any other in the city. It is surrounded on three sides by neocolonial buildings dating from the 1920s. Presiding over the western edge is the Gran Hotel Bolívar, a pleasant spot for a pisco sour. Even if you aren't thirsty, you should step inside for a look at its elegant lobby. At the plaza's center is a mas-sive statue of José de San Martín, the Argentine general who led the independence of Argentina, Chile, and Peru from Spain. ✉ *Between Jr. de la Unión and Jr. Carabaya, El Centro.*

WORTH NOTING

Barrio Chino. A ceremonial arch at the corner of Ucayali and Andahuay-las marks the entrance to Lima's tiny Chinatown. It consists of little more than a block-long pedestrian mall where the benches and kiosks are topped with traditional Chinese roofs and the street is decorated with tile representations of the Chinese zodiac. The best restaurants are around the corner on Paruro. ✉ *Jr. Ucayali between Andahuaylas and Paruro, El Centro.*

Casa Solariega de Aliaga. Lima's oldest house, commonly known as Casa Aliaga, is a beautiful example of Spanish Colonial architecture a block from the Plaza de Armas. It was built by Jeronimo de Aliaga, one of Pizarro's officers, in 1536. His descendents lived in it for centuries,

RETABLOS EXPLAINED

You can tell a lot about colonial-era churches by their *retablos* (retables), the altarpieces that are almost always massive in scale and over-the-top in ornamentation. Most are made of elaborately carved wood and coated with layer after layer of gold leaf. Indigenous peoples often did the carving, so look for some atypical elements such as symbols of the sun and moon that figure prominently in the local religion. You may be surprised that Jesus is a minor player on many retablos, and on others doesn't appear at all. That's because these retablos often depict the life of the saint for which the church is named. Many churches retain their original baroque retablos, but others saw theirs replaced by the much simpler neoclassical ones with simple columns and spare design. If you wander around the church, you're likely to find the original relegated to one of the side chapels.

restoring it following an earthquake in 1746. Its rooms are furnished with antiques, and its walls decorated with historic paintings and colonial religious art. You must make a reservation to visit the house, so most travelers see it as part of a city tour. ⊠ *Jr. de la Unión 224, El Centro* ☎ *1/427–7736* ⊕ *www.casadealiaga.com* ✉ *S/30* ☼ *Daily 9:30–1 and 2:30–5:45.*

Casa Torre Tagle. This mansion sums up the graceful style of the early 18th century. Flanked by a pair of elegant balconies, the stone entrance is as expertly carved as that of any of the city's churches. It currently holds offices of the Foreign Ministry and is not open to the public, but you can often get a peek inside through an open door, and if you're lucky, the guards may let you step into the courtyard. If so, you might see the tiled ceilings, carved columns, and a 16th-century carriage. Across the street is **Casa Goyeneche**, which was built some 40 years later in 1771, and was clearly influenced by the rococo movement. ⊠ *Jr. Ucayali 363, El Centro* ☎ *1/204–2400.*

Cerro San Cristóbal. Rising over the northeastern edge of the city is this massive hill, recognizable from the cross at its peak—a replica of the one once placed there by Pizarro. On a clear day—more common during the southern summer—you can see most of the city below. The neighborhood at the base of the hill is sketchy, so hire a taxi to take you to the summit and back. At this writing, a new aerial tram is being built. ⊠ *Calle San Cristóbal, El Centro.*

Convento de Santo Domingo. The 16th-century Convent of Saint Dominic offers a glimpse of life in a cloister. This sprawling structure shows the different styles popular during the colonial era in Lima. The bell tower, for instance, has a baroque base built in 1632, but the upper parts rebuilt after an earthquake in 1746 are more rococo in style. The convent's two cloisters are decorated with hand-painted tiles imported from Spain in the early 17th century. The stately library holds 25,000 antiquarian books. If you visit between 1 and 3, you can ascend the bell tower for a view of the old city. The church is quite popular, as it holds the tombs of the first two Peruvian saints, Santa Rosa de Lima and San

San Isidro

Martín de Porres. Independent guides who wait by the entrance offer short tours for a negotiable fee. ⊠ *Conde de Superunda and Camaná, El Centro* ☎ *01/734–1190* ⊕ *www.conventosantodomingolima.org* ⊠ *S/5* ⊙ *Daily 9:30–6:30.*

Estación de Desamparados. Inaugurated in 1912, Desamparados Station was the centerpiece for the continent's first railway, which stretches from the port of Callao to the Andean city of Huancayo. The station was named for a Jesuit church and monastery that stood next door at the time of its construction, but has since been demolished. It now holds the Casa de la Literature Peruana (House of Peruvian Literature), which hosts literary exhibitions. It's well worth stepping inside to admire the building's elegant art nouveau interior, especially the stained-glass skylight. ⊠ *Jr. Ancash 207, El Centro* ☎ *1/426–2573* ⊕ *www.casadelaliteratura.gob.pe* ⊠ *Free* ⊙ *Tues.–Sun. 10:30–7.*

Iglesia de Jesús, María y José. The 1659 Church of Jesus, Mary, and Joseph may be smaller than some of El Centro's other churches, but inside is a feast for the eyes. Baroque retablos representing various saints rise from the main altar and line both walls. ⊠ *Jr. Camaná and Jr. Moquegua, El Centro* ☎ *1/427–6809* ⊠ *Free* ⊙ *Weekdays 7–noon and 3–7, Sat. 7–noon.*

Municipalidad de Lima. Although it resembles the colonial-era buildings that abound in the area, City Hall was constructed in 1944. Step inside to see the stained-glass windows above the marble staircase. To the south of the building is a popular pedestrian walkway called the Paseo Los Escribanos, or Passage of the Scribes, lined with inexpensive restaurants. Here you'll find the entrance to a small gallery run by City Hall that hosts exhibitions by Peruvian artists. In the back of the building is a tourist information office. ✉ *Jr. de la Union 300, El Centro* ☎ *1/315–1542* ☉ *Gallery Tues.–Fri. 10–8, weekends 3–8.*

Museo de Arte Italiano. Italian art in Peru? This small museum is one of the city's most delightful. Most of the art is about a century old, so it captures the exact moment when impressionism was melting into modernism, and the building itself is a work of art. Don't overlook the magnificent iron door, by Alessandro Mazzucotelli. ✉ *Paseo de la República 250, El Centro* ☎ *1/423–9932* 🎟 *S/5* ☉ *Tues.–Sun. 10–5.*

Parque de la Exposición. Eager to prove that it was a world-class capital, Lima hosted an international exposition in 1872. Several of the buildings constructed for the event still stand, including the neoclassical Palacio de la Exposición, which now serves as the Museo de Arte. Stroll through the grounds and you'll find the eye-popping Pabellón Morisco, or Moorish Pavillion. Painstakingly restored, this Gothic-style structure has spiral staircases leading to a stained-glass salon on the second floor. The nearby Pabellón Bizantino, or Byzantine Pavilion, is being slowly refurbished. Despite its name, it most closely resembles a turret from a Victorian-era mansion. ✉ *Av. de la Vega and Av. Grau, El Centro* ☎ *1/423–6332* ☉ *Daily 10–8.*

SAN ISIDRO

While strolling through the ancient olive trees of Parque El Olívar, you might be surprised by the light traffic and pastoral ambiance. But just a few blocks away you'll find the busy boulevards of Camino Real, or Avenida Arequipa, which serve as reminders that San Isidro also holds the offices of the country's largest companies and banks, as well as most foreign embassies. It also has some of the city's best hotels and restaurants, so you are bound to spend some time. However, San Isidro's only real tourist attraction is the Huaca Huallamarca, where you can clamor atop the ruins of a pre-Columbian temple.

Like nearby Miraflores, San Isidro is big on shopping, though more of its boutiques sell designer goods. Its bars serve up the latest cocktails, and its restaurants dish out cuisine from around the world, but it has a more subdued atmosphere than you'll find in the other neighborhoods.

GETTING AROUND
The best way to travel between San Isidro's widely dispersed attractions is by taxi. Walking through the neighborhood takes no more than a few hours. This is probably Lima's safest neighborhood.

Even the statues find love in the Parque del Amor, Miraflores.

TOP ATTRACTIONS

Huaca Huallamarca. The sight of this mud-brick pyramid catches many people off guard. The structure, painstakingly restored on the front side, seems out of place among the neighborhood's towering hotels and apartment buildings. The upper platform affords some nice views of the San Isidro. There's a small museum with displays of objects found at the site, including several mummies. This temple, thought to be a place of worship, predates the Incas. ⊠ *Av. Nicolás de Rivera and Av. El Rosario* ☎ *1/222–4124* 🖃 *S/5* ⊙ *Tues.–Sun 9–5.*

WORTH NOTING

Country Club Lima Hotel. Two royal palms stand guard and a red carpet leads up the stairs to the entrance of this 1926 hotel, widely regarded as the city's most elegant. Even if you stay elsewhere, it's worth dropping by for a a cocktail on the terrace. If you feel like a light meal in the early evening, consider the English-style high tea. ⊠ *Los Eucaliptos 590* ☎ *1/611–9000* ⊕ *www.hotelcountry.com.*

Parque El Olívar. For years this rambling olive grove was slowly disappearing as homes for wealthy citizens were being built on its perimeter. The process was halted in the 1960s, in time to save more than 1,500 gnarled olive trees. Some of the trees are more than a century old and still bear fruit. A network of sidewalks, flowerbeds, fountains, and playgrounds make this 50-acre park a popular spot on weekend afternoons. ⊠ *Av. Los Incas between Choquehuanca and Arce.*

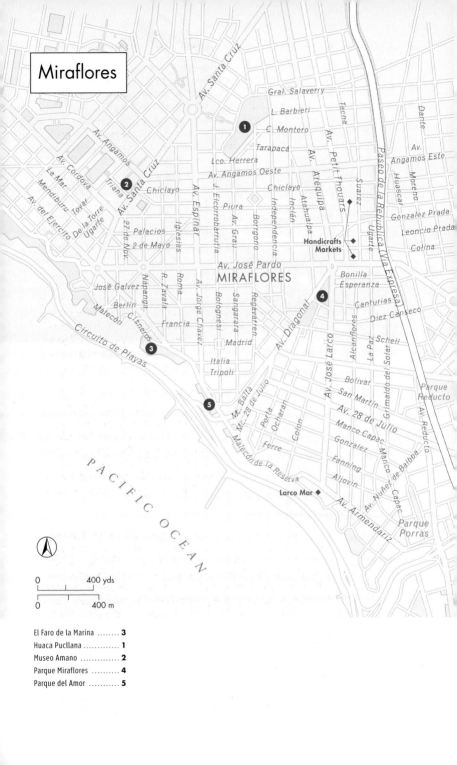

Miraflores

MIRAFLORES

With flower-filled parks and wide swaths of green overlooking the ocean, it's no wonder travelers flock to this seaside suburb. Miraflores has Lima's best selection of hotels and restaurants, which is why most people stay here, but it is also the city's cultural hub. There are plenty of boutiques and galleries, as well as bars, cafés, and dance clubs. Some people who find themselves in Lima for a short time never leave this little haven.

At its center is Parque Miraflores, sitting like a slice of pie between Avenida José Larco and Avenida Diagonal. On the eastern side is the Iglesia de la Virgen Milagrosa, the neighborhood's largest church. The colonial-style building next door is the Palacio Municipal de Miraflores, where most governmental business takes place.

Where you go next depends on your areas of interest. If you're interested in ancient cultures, head to the massive temple of Pucllana. From the top you have a great view of the neighborhood. A tiny Museo Amano, six blocks to the west contains a small but impressive collection of ancient artifacts. If you want to shop, head for Avenida Petit Thouars just a few blocks north of the park, where a series of markets hold dozens of shops that offer some of the best deals in town. For some fresh air and an ocean view, head to Parque del Amor, a wonderful park with a splendid view of the coast and sea below. It attracts young lovers, joggers, paragliding enthusiasts, and just about everyone else on a sunny afternoon.

GETTING AROUND

A popular walk is the 20-minute stroll south from Parque Miraflores down busy Avenida José Larco to Larcomar, an open-air mall built into the side of a cliff, so that it has gorgeous views and ocean breezes to complement the shops, bars, and restaurants. From there you can walk either east or west, since the top of the coast cliff is lined with a series of parks with ocean-view promenades called malecónes. Miraflores is about 10 minutes from San Isidro or Barranco, and 20 minutes from El Centro by taxi or the Metropolitano bus.

TOP ATTRACTIONS

★ **Huaca Pucllana.** Rising out of a nondescript residential neighborhood is this mud-brick pyramid. You'll be amazed at the scale—this pre-Inca *huaca*, or temple, covers several city blocks. The site, which dates back to at least the fourth century, has ongoing excavations, and new discoveries are often announced. A tiny museum highlights some of the finds. Knowledgeable guides, some of whom speak English, will lead you around and over the pyramid to the area that is being excavated. ∎TIP➔ This site is most beautiful at night, when partial tours can be arranged through the adjacent Huaca Pucllana restaurant if you dine there. ⊠ *Calle General Borgoño at Ayacucho* ☎ *1/617–7167* ⊕ *www.mirafloresperu.com/huacapucllana/huaca_pucllana.htm* ⊠ *S/10* ⊙ *Wed.–Mon. 9–4:30.*

Parque del Amor. You could imagine you're in Barcelona when you stroll through this lovely park designed by Peruvian artist Victor Delfin. Like

Antonio Gaudí's Parque Güell, the park that provided the inspiration for this one, the benches are decorated with broken pieces of tile. In keeping with the romantic theme—the name translates as "Park of Love"—the mosaic includes such romantic sayings as *Amor es como luz* ("Love is like light"). The centerpiece is a massive statue of two lovers locked in a rather lewd embrace. ⊠ *Malecón Balta.*

Parque Miraflores. What locals call Parque Miraflores is actually two parks. The smaller section, near the roundabout, is Parque 7 de Junio, whereas the rest of it is Parque Kennedy. To the east of Parque Kennedy stands Miraflores's stately Iglesia de la Virgen Milagrosa (Church of the Miraculous Virgin), built in the 1930s on the site of a colonial church. The equally young colonial-style building behind it is the Palacio Municipal de Miraflores (Town Hall). A tourist-information kiosk sits near the entrance to the church. Several open-air cafés along Parque Kennedy's eastern edge serve decent food. At night a round cement structure in front of those cafés called La Rotonda fills up with handicraft vendors, and the park becomes especially lively. Street vendors sell popcorn and traditional Peruvian desserts such as *mazamora* (a pudding made with blue corn and prunes) and *arroz con leche* (rice pudding). ⊠ *Between Av. José Larco and Av. Diagonal.*

WORTH NOTING

El Faro de la Marina. Constructed in 1900, this little lighthouse a short walk north from the Parque del Amor has guided ships for more than a century. The classically designed tower is still in use today. On sunny afternoons the large park that surrounds it is one of the most popular spots in Miraflores, with paragliders floating overhead and bicyclists and skate boarders rolling along the ocean-view Malecón (promenade). Children of all ages play on the lawns. ⊠ *Malecón Cisneros and Madrid.*

Museo Amano. Although only two rooms, this museum packs a lot into a small space. The private collection of pre-Columbian artifacts includes some of the city's best ceramics. Imaginative displays reveal how cultures in the northern part of the region focused on sculptural images, while those in the south used vivid colors. In between, around present-day Lima, the styles merged. A second room holds an impressive number of weavings, including examples from the Chancay people, who lived in the north between 1000 and 1500. Call ahead to reserve one of the two daily Spanish-language tours, which last an hour and start at 3 and 4. ⊠ *Calle Retiro 160* ☏ *1/441–2909* ⊕ *www.fundacionmuseoamano. org.pe* 🖃 *Free* ☉ *Weekdays 3–5, by appointment only.*

BARRANCO

Barranco is a mix of bohemian, historic, and run down, but the area along the coast is the most charming of Lima's neighborhoods. On weekend nights it's a magnet for young people who come to carouse in its bars and dance clubs. Sleepy during the day, the neighborhood comes to life around sunset, when artisans start hawking their wares on its central square and the bars begin filling up.

Founded toward the end of the 19th century, Barranco was where wealthy Limeños built their summer residences. The streetcar line that

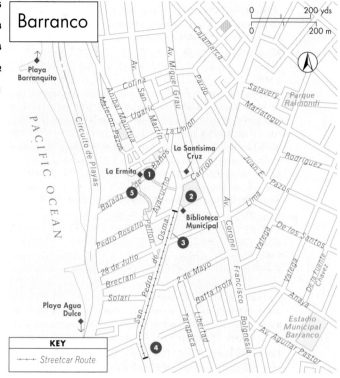

once connected it to El Centro brought crowds of beachgoers on week-ends and holidays. The view proved so irresistible that some built huge mansions on the cliffs above the sea. Many of these have fallen into disrepair, but little by little they are being renovated.

GETTING AROUND

To get your bearings, head to Parque Municipal, one of the nicest of the city's plazas. To the south, the brick-red building with the tower is the Biblioteca Municipal, or Municipal Library. To the north is the parish church called La Santisima Cruz. To the west, steps lead down to Lima's own Bridge of Sighs, the Puente de los Suspiros. Directly below in the shade of ancient trees is the Bajada de Baños, lined with wonder-ful old houses and colorful bougainvillea. Head down this cobblestone street to the waves of Playa Barranquito by day, or to various bars and restaurants by night.

TOP ATTRACTIONS

Bajada de Baños. The cobbled road that leads down to the "Baths"—the beaches—is shaded by massive trees and lined with historic architecture. Once the route that local fishermen used to reach their boats, it is now a popular promenade at night, since many of the former homes that line it hold restaurants and bars. At the bottom of the hill a covered wooden bridge spans a busy road, called Cirquito de Playas, to a coastal sidewalk that leads to several beaches and restaurants. A short walk to the north is Playa Barranquito, and Playa Agua Dulce is half a mile south. ⊠ *1 block west of Parque Municipal, Barranco.*

Fodor'sChoice **Museo Pedro de Osma.** Even if there were no art inside this museum,
★ it would still be worth the trip to see the century-old mansion that houses it. The mansard-roofed structure—with inlaid wood floors, delicately painted ceilings, and breathtaking stained-glass windows in every room—was the home of a wealthy collector of religious art. The best of his collection is permanently on display. The finest of the paintings, the 18th-century *Virgen de Pomato,* represents the Earth, with her mountain-shape cloak covered with garlands of corn. A more modern wing contains some fine pieces of silver, including a lamb-shape incense holder with shining ruby eyes. Make sure to explore the manicured grounds. ⊠ *Av. Pedro de Osma 423* ☎ *1/467–0141* ⊕ *www. museopedrodeosma.org* ⊠ *S/20* ☽ *Tues.–Sun. 10–6.*

★ **Parque Municipal.** Elegant royal palms, swirls of colorful bougainvillea, and the surrounding colonial architecture make this park stand out from others in Lima. The southern end is lined with historic buildings, the most prominent of which is the library, with its yellow clock tower. ▮▮TIP➜ Every evening, artisans who live in the area sell their works here. To the north of the park stands Barranco's bright red Iglesia de la Santísima Cruz (Church of the Holy Cross), which opens for mass every evening, as well as Sunday morning. To the west of the park is a staircase that leads down to the Puente de los Suspiros and the Bajada a los Baños. ⊠ *Between Av. Pedro de Osma and Av. Grau.*

Puente de los Suspiros. The romantically named Bridge of Sighs is a wooden walkway over the tree-shaded Bajada de los Baños. Though the bridge itself is nothing special, the view of the surrounding historic buildings is priceless. the bridge is the most direct route from the Parque Municipal to La Ermita, a lovely little chapel dating from 1882 that is painted a dazzling shade of red. To the left of the church is a path that leads to a scenic overlook. ⊠ *Bajada de los Baños.*

WORTH NOTING

☾ **Museo de la Electricidad.** In front of this tiny museum is a cherry-red *urbanito,* or streetcar, named Breda. From Tuesday to Sunday, for about 80 cents, you can climb aboard and take a three-block trip down tree-lined Avenida Pedro de Osma. The museum's small collection of exhibits on electricity is geared toward school children. ⊠ *Av. Pedro de Osma 105* ☎ *1/477–6577* ⊠ *Free* ☽ *Daily 9–5.*

**NEED A
BREAK?** **La Flor de Canela.** Along a walkway leading past La Ermita is the gingerbread-covered La Flor de Canela, a sweet little café with a porch overlooking much of Barranco. It's a great place for a cup of coffee or a pisco sour. ⊠ *Ermita 102.*

PUEBLO LIBRE

2

Instead of hurrying past, residents of Pueblo Libre often pause to chat with friends. There's a sense of calm here not found elsewhere in the capital. Plaza Bolívar, the park at the heart of Pueblo Libre, is surrounded by colonial-era buildings, many of which are home to shops and restaurants. On the south side, in the Municipalidad de Pueblo Libre, are governmental offices. A small gallery on the ground floor sometimes hosts painting and photography exhibitions.

Despite the pleasant surroundings, there would be little reason to venture this far if it weren't for the presence of two fine museums, the Museo Nacional de Antropología, Arqueología, e Historia del Perú, and the Museo Arqueológico Rafael Larco Herrera.

GETTING AROUND

The most convenient way to reach Pueblo Libre is a taxi ride, which should take 20–30 minutes.

TOP ATTRACTIONS

Fodor's Choice
★

Museo Larco. Fuchsia bougainvillea tumbles over the white walls surrounding the home of the world's largest private collection of pre-Columbian art. The oldest pieces are crude vessels dating back several thousand years. Most intriguing are the thousands of ceramic "portrait heads" crafted more than a millennium ago. Some owners commissioned more than one, allowing you to see how they changed over the course of their lives. The *sala erótica* reveals that these ancient artists were surprisingly uninhibited, creating everyday objects adorned with sexual images. This gallery is across the garden from the rest of the museum. Guides are a good idea, and are just S/25 per group. The café overlooking the museum's garden is an excellent option for lunch or dinner. ⊠ *Av. Bolívar 1515* ☏ *1/461–1312* ⊕ *www.museolarco.org* ⛁ *S/30* ⊙ *Daily 9 am–10 pm.*

WORTH NOTING

Museo Nacional de Antropología, Arqueología e Historia del Perú. The country's most extensive collection of pre-Columbian artifacts can be found at this sprawling museum. Beginning with 8,000-year-old stone tools, Peru's history is revealed through the sleek granite obelisks of the Chavín culture, the intricate weavings of Paraca peoples, and the colorful ceramics of the Moche, Chimú, and Inca civilizations. A fascinating pair of mummies from the Nazca region is thought to be more than 2,500 years old. They are so well preserved that you can still see the grim expressions on their faces. ■ **TIP→** Not all the exhibits are labeled in English, but you can hire a guide for S/15. ⊠ *Plaza Bolívar* ☏ *1/463–5070* ⛁ *S/10* ⊙ *Tues.–Sat. 9–5, Sun. 9–4.*

NEED A DRINK?

Antigua Taberna Queirolo. Be sure to stop by the Antigua Taberna Queirolo, a charming little bar on the west side of Pueblo Libre's central plaza, where locals lean against the marble-top tables and historic photos hang on the walls. The place serves good ham sandwiches smothered in pickled onions and pisco bottled in the factory next door. ⊠ *Jr. San Martín 1090* ☏ *1/461-0441* ⊕ *www.antiguatabernaqueirolo.com.*

ELSEWHERE AROUND LIMA

A few of Lima's most interesting museums are in outlying neighborhoods such as Monterrico and San Borja. The most convenient way to reach them is a quick taxi ride.

TOP ATTRACTIONS

Museo de Oro. When you see examples of how Peru's pre-Columbian societies manipulated gold—from a mantle made of postage-stamp-size pieces worn by a Lambayeque priest to an intricately designed sheet that once decorated an entire wall of the Chimú capital of Chán Chán—you begin to imagine the opulence of the cities that the Spanish conquistadors plundered. The Gold Museum has other interesting items, including a child's poncho of yellow feathers, a skull with a full set of pink quartz teeth, and several mummies. The main floor holds a dull museum of military uniforms and weapons, so most visitors head straight downstairs. None of the displays are particularly well marked, so you may want to rent a recorded tour or visit the museum as part of a city tour. ⊠ *Alonso de Molina 1100, Monterrico, Lima* ☎ *1/345–1271* ⊕ *www.museoroperu.com.pe* 🎫 *S/33* ⊗ *Daily 10:30–6.*

WORTH NOTING

Museo de la Nación. If you know little about the history of Peru, a visit to this museum may leave you overwhelmed. The number of cultures tracked over the centuries makes it easy to confuse the Chimú, the Chincha, and the Chachapoyas. The museum is more manageable if you have a specific interest—for example, if you're planning a trip north to Chiclayo and want to learn more about the Moche people. The museum occupies several floors of the massive Ministry of Culture. At this writing the museum is under renovation, so some exhibits may be closed. ⊠ *Av. Javier Prado Este 2465, San Borja, Lima* ☎ *1/476–9873* ⊕ *www.mcultura.gob.pe* 🎫 *S/10* ⊗ *Tues.–Sun. 9–5.*

Pachacámac. Dating back to the first century, this city of plazas, palaces, and pyramids, many of them painstakingly restored, was for centuries a stronghold of the Huari people. Here they worshipped Pachacámac, creator of the world. It was a pilgrimage site, and people from all over the region came to worship. In the 15th century the city was captured by the Inca, who added structures such as the *Acllahuasi,* the Palace of the Chosen Women. When the Spanish heard of the city, they dispatched troops to plunder its riches. In 1533, two years before the founding of Lima, they marched triumphantly into the city, only to find a few remaining objects in gold. The extensive ruins are spread across a desert ridge with views of the verdant Lurin River valley, the Pacific Ocean, and Pachacámac Island. The site has both pre-Incan temples and several that were built by the Incas, such as the Templo del Inti (Temple of the Sun), with its grand staircase leading up to colonnaded walkways. There is a small but excellent museum and some resident llamas. The easiest way to visit Pachacámac, located 31 km (19 miles) south of Lima, is on a half-day guided tour offered by several Lima agencies. There are also knowledgeable guides available at the entrance (S/20). ⊠ *Carretera Panamericana Sur, Lima* ☎ *1/430–0168* ⊕ *pachacamac.perucultural. org.pe* 🎫 *S/8* ⊗ *Tues.–Sun. 9–4:30.*

OFF THE BEATEN PATH

Caral. Few people realize it, but the oldest urban site in the western hemisphere is just 220 km (120 miles) north of Lima. Caral was first settled around 5,000 BC, long before the rise of ancient Egypt, though Caral's squat Pirámide Mayor is slightly younger than Egypt's Great Pyramid of Giza. It may not be as spectacular as other Peruvian sites, but Caral has some interesting structures that evoke a well-developed people, who archaeologists have dubbed the Caral-Supe Culture. It takes nearly four hours to drive to Caral and it is not easy to find, so the best way to visit it is on an organized tour. ✉ *Carretera Panamericana Norte, Caral, Lima* ☎ *1/205–2500* ⊕ *www.caralperu.gob.pe* 🖅 *S/11* ⊗ *Tues.–Sun. 9–5.*

WHERE TO EAT

Seafood, especially cebiche, is a Peruvian specialty, and the variety of the ingredients and recipes is impressive. Cebiche is traditionally only eaten at lunch, so most cebicherías (seafood restaurants) close in the late afternoon. *Prices in the reviews are the average cost of a main course at dinner or, if dinner is not served, at lunch.*

EL CENTRO

El Centro has both quality cuisine and cheap, filling food. A highlight is the Barrio Chino, packed with dozens of Chinese-Peruvian restaurants called *chifas*, but the run-down neighborhood that surrounds it makes it inadvisable to head there for dinner. Restaurants on the main plazas are better dinner options.

$ ✕ **L'eau Vive.** Calling to mind *The Sound of Music,* the nuns that run
FRENCH this restaurant sing "Ave Maria" every night around 9. The sisters cook French food that, while not extraordinary, is satisfying. Trout baked in cognac and duck in orange sauce are two dishes that bring the locals back. Inexpensive three-course lunch specials pack the dining rooms with workers from nearby offices at 2 pm. In a restored mansion directly across from Palacio Torre Tagle, the restaurant is worth a visit just for a peek inside. Unfortunately, the floors and furnishings don't do justice to the glorious architecture. Ⓢ *Average main: S/23* ✉ *Ucayali 370, El Centro* ☎ *1/427–5612* ⊗ *Closed 3:30–7:30 and Sun.*

$ ✕ **Los Vitrales de Gemma.** Tucked into the courtyard of a colonial-
EUROPEAN style building, this may be the prettiest restaurant in the historic district. Tables covered with peach-color linens are set along a colonnade, under stained-glass windows or beneath a soaring dome. The food is a notch below the ambiance, but decent. In addition to the inexpensive lunch specials, the kitchen offers such options as *lomo saltado* (beef strips sautéed with onions, peppers, and tomato), and *pescado en salsa langostinos* (fish in shrimp sauce). Ⓢ *Average main: S/22* ✉ *Jr. Ucayali 332, El Centro* ☎ *1/426–7796* ⊗ *Closed Sun. No dinner.*

Restaurants ▼

L'eau Vive 3

Los Vitrales de Gemma 2

Tanta 1

Wa Lok 4

Hotels ▼

Gran Hotel Bolívar 1

Sheraton Lima Hotel 2

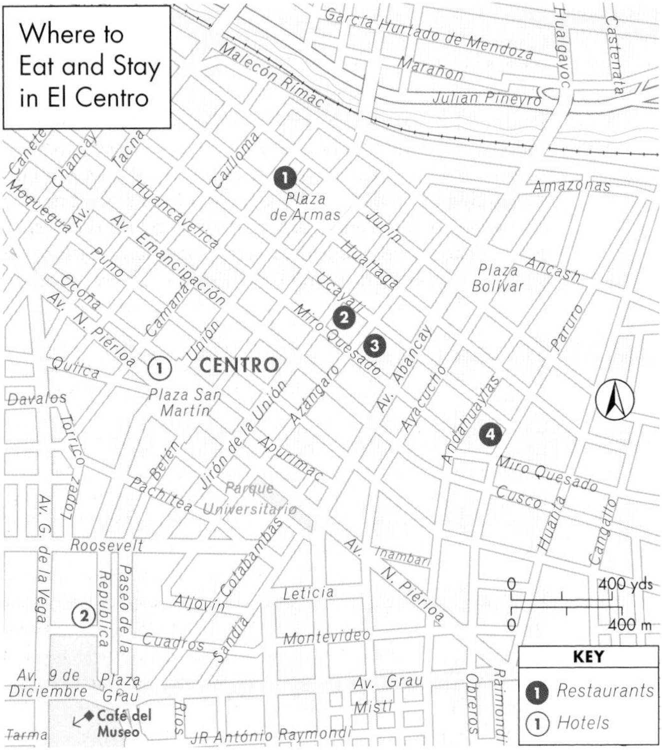

$ PERUVIAN Fodor's Choice ★

🍴 **Tanta.** Nestled behind a hedge of potted plants, this Peruvian fusion restaurant offers an excellent mix of light fare and irresistible desserts. There is an extensive salad selection, and the empanadas, with fillings such as *ají de gallina* (chicken in a creamy pepper sauce) and *lomo saltado* (beef sautéed with tomato and onion), are great. Share an order of *causushis* (cold mashed potato with various fillings), then sample the ravioli *bachiche* (in a spicy cream sauce), or *arroz Tanta*, similar to paella. Save room for a *chocolúcuma* (cream of the native lúcuma fruit encased in dark chocolate), or one of the other pastries. [$] *Average main: S/34* ✉ *Pasaje Escribanos 142, El Centro* ☎ *1/426–7796* 🕓 *Closed Sun. dinner.*

$$ CHINESE

🍴 **Wa Lok.** Of the dozens of chifas in Chinatown, none comes close to Wa Lok. The extensive menu includes such memorable dishes as *langostinos picantes al horno* (spicy broiled shrimp), *kum pou kay tien* (chicken stir-fried with asparagus and yellow peppers), and *lomo de chancho al ajo* (pork loin in a garlic sauce). Vegetarians can choose from more than 30 dishes. The servings are large, so it's best to go with a group and share a few dishes. Though it's open for dinner, the surrounding neighborhood is sketchy at night, so settle for lunch. [$] *Average main: S/40* ✉ *Jr. Paruro 878, El Centro* ☎ *1/427–2750* 🌐 *www.walok.com.pe* 🕓 *No dinner Sun.*

SAN ISIDRO

Most of San Isidro's restaurants are on or near Avenida Conquistadores, the neighborhood's main drag.

$$ FRENCH 🍴 **Chez Philippe.** Though French often connotes fancy, this laid-back restaurant is all about enjoying hearty food at comfortable prices. You enter through a small shop that sells fresh breads and homemade paté to a dining room that evokes a country home, or a popular covered terrace edged with greenery and stacked wood for the oven. The owner is from Alsace, so in addition to French standards such as duck in orange sauce and chicken cordon bleu, he offers *choucroute* (homemade sauerkraut with sausages and pork). Another house specialty is *trucha al horno* (baked trout). ■ **TIP➔ The place also serves excellent pizza, and has a large selection of European beers.** [$] *Average main: S/36* ✉ *Av. Dos de Mayo 748, San Isidro* ☎ *1/222–4953* 🌐 *www.chez-philippe.net* 🕒 *Closed Sun.*

$$ PERUVIAN 🍴 **Lima 27.** There's no sign on this dark grey mansion, and at night the somber edifice with a bright red foyer looks like Dracula's love shack. Step inside and veer right, and you enter a hip little lounge. To the left is a large dining room decorated with original art, though the nicest seating is on the terrace, backed by a brick wall draped with greenery. The food is Peruvian fusion: creative variations on Lima standards and local interpretations of continental cuisine. The results include *risotto de camarones* (river prawn risotto), *cabrito lechón* (roast goat), *atún sellado* (seared tuna steak in a sesame and pepper crust), and *gnocchis crocantes* (crispy gnocchi smothered in a mushroom and artichoke heart ragout). [$] *Average main: S/47* ✉ *Calle Santa Luisa 295, San Isidro* ☎ *1/421–9084* ✍ *Reservations essential* 🕒 *No dinner Sun.*

$$ JAPANESE 🍴 **Matsuei.** The sushi chefs shout out a greeting as you enter the teak-floored dining room of this San Isidro standout. One of the best Japanese restaurants in town, Matsuei specializes in sushi and sashimi. If raw is not your thing, they also offer plenty of hot food such as tempuras, teriyakis, and *kushiyak*, a broiled fillet with a ginger sauce. There's plenty for vegetarians, including *goma nasu,* grilled Japanese eggplant with a sweet sesame glaze. Sushi fans often sit at the bar, but there are tables spread around both floors of this former home. [$] *Average main: S/46* ✉ *Manuel Bañón 260, San Isidro* ☎ *1/422–4323* 🕒 *Closed Sun.*

$$ ECLECTIC ★ 🍴 **Osaka.** Although it has a small sushi bar, Osaka is much more than a Japanese restaurant. It also serves Peruvian standards such as cebiches and tiraditos, as well as Chinese dishes like wontons stuffed with grilled shrimp, and broiled scallops braised in a spicy sauce. Settle into one of the low tables and sink your teeth into seared tuna with a coconut crust and tamarind sauce, or grilled sirloin and sautéed mushrooms atop miso mashed potatoes. It also has a selection of sushi rolls that are perfect for a light meal. [$] *Average main: S/48* ✉ *Av. Conquistadores 999, San Isidro* ☎ *1/222–0405* 🌐 *www.osaka.com.pe* ✍ *Reservations essential* 🕒 *Closed Sun.*

$$$ PERUVIAN 🍴 **Perroquet.** There's not a more elegant dining room than Perroquet, tucked away in the Country Club Lima Hotel. You feel pampered in the main room, with its upholstered chairs and tables almost overloaded with polished crystal and china. If it's a warm enough evening, you

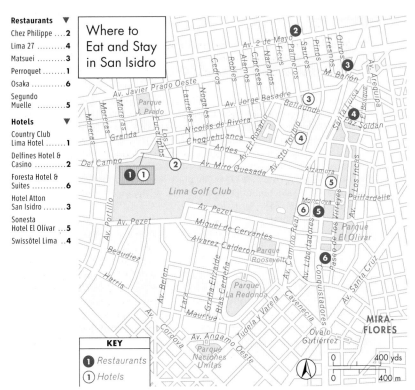

Restaurants ▼
Chez Philippe 2
Lima 27 4
Matsuei 3
Perroquet 1
Osaka 6
Segundo Muelle 5

Hotels ▼
Country Club Lima Hotel 1
Delfines Hotel & Casino 2
Foresta Hotel & Suites 6
Hotel Atton San Isidro 3
Sonesta Hotel El Olívar ... 5
Swissôtel Lima .. 4

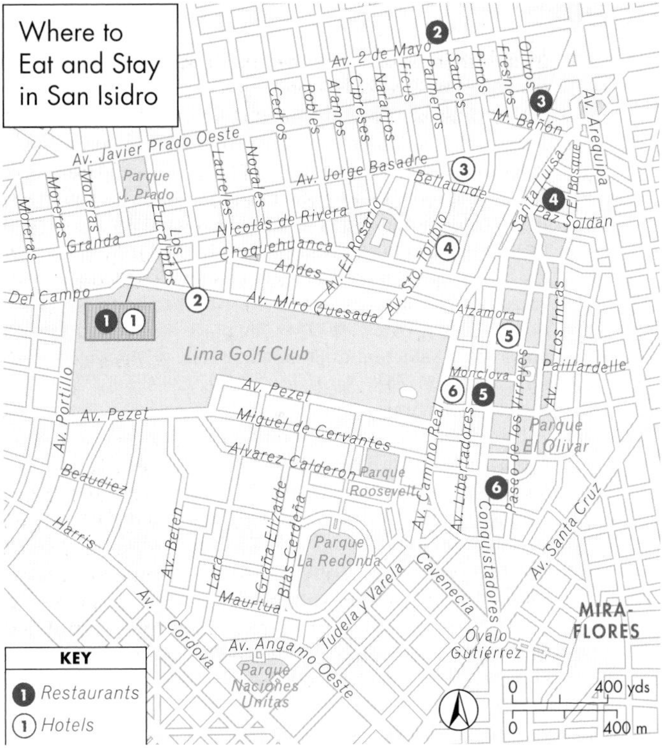

might prefer the terrace and its brass chandeliers. The atmosphere never feels stuffy, and neither does the menu. There are traditional dishes, but they have a modern flair. Try the lamb shank roasted for three hours in red wine and cilantro seeds, the artichoke ravioli, or the lemony *corvina* (sea bass) with *kichwa* (an Andean grain). Or stop by for Sunday brunch. $ *Average main: S/58* ✉ *Country Club Hotel, Los Eucaliptos 50, San Isidro* ☎ *1/611–9000* ✍ *Reservations essential.*

$$ SEAFOOD 🍴 **Segundo Muelle.** This sleek seafood restaurant is one of San Isidro's most popular lunch spots, serving *cebichería* standards and more. Choose from 10 different types of lip-smacking cebiche, or head straight for the *corvina a lo macho* (sea bass in a seafood sauce) or *chita al plato* (whole grilled fish). It also serves a small selection of sushi and sashimi and some excellent rice and pasta dishes, such as *tortellines rellenos de cangrejo y ricotta* (cheese and crab tortellini). $ *Average main: S/37* ✉ *Av. Conquistadores 490, San Isidro* ☎ *01/421–1206* 🌐 *www.segundomuelle.com* 🕒 *No dinner.*

MIRAFLORES

Miraflores has some of Lima's best restaurants. Although inexpensive eateries are clustered around Parque Miraflores, some of the more elegant ones are scattered farther afield and some can only be reached by taxi.

$$$$ ✕ **Astrid y Gaston.** The flagship of Peru's most celebrated chefs (Gastón
PERUVIAN Acurio and his wife Astrid Gutsche), this popular restaurant serves
Fodor's Choice inventive variations on traditional Peruvian cuisine. Acurio is a master
★ of both flavor and presentation. You can't help but watch the kitchen door—each dish the waiters carry out is a work of art. Even a Peruvian standard such as *lomo saltado* (tenderloin slices sautéed with tomato, onions, and ají peppers) gains a new personality here. The menu changes every six months, but is invariably original and delectable. The place has one of the best wine lists in town. ■ TIP➡ Reserve two weeks ahead of time, or arrive early and eat in the bar. $ *Average main: S/70 ⊠ Calle Cantuarias 175, Miraflores* ☎ *1/242–4422* ⊕ *www.astridygaston.com* ⚄ *Reservations essential* ⊗ *Closed 3:30–7 and Sun.*

$$$$ ✕ **Brujas de Cachiche.** Although the name conjures up a haunted house,
PERUVIAN Witches of Cachiche is a modern space with huge windows, soaring ceilings, and modern art. The magic is the cooking, which draws on Peru's traditional cuisines. The results include such delicacies as *corvina en salsa de camarones* (sea bass in a crayfish sauce), *cabrito a la norteña* (stewed goat), and *pato al ají* (a spicy stewed duck). The desgustación, a four-course meal with six items in each course, lets you sample an array of dishes. The wine list has some top South American vintages. ■ TIP➡ The cozy bar in back is a good spot for appetizers or a light meal in the early evening, when most restaurants are closed. $ *Average main: S/52 ⊠ Calle Bolognesi 472, Miraflores* ☎ *1/444–5310* ⊕ *www. brujasdecachiche.com.pe* ⊗ *Closed Sun. night.*

$$$$ ✕ **Central Restaurante.** Hidden on a residential street a few blocks south
PERUVIAN of the Larcomar shopping center is one of Lima's hottest restaurants.
Fodor's Choice The refurbished childhood home of chef Virgilio Martínez, it is now a
★ chic, airy venue for his culinary talents. After years working in some of the best kitchens of Europe and Asia, Martínez returned to Peru to celebrate his country's biodiversity by creating memorable meals using fresh, often organic ingredients. He changes the menu every six months, but it always includes such local delicacies as *paiche* (an Amazon fish), scallops, suckling pig, and baby goat stewed overnight. This place is packed most nights. $ *Average main: S/69 ⊠ Calle Santa Isabel 376, Miraflores* ☎ *1/242–8515* ⊕ *www.centralrestaurante.com.pe* ⚄ *Reservations essential* ⊗ *Closed Sun. No lunch Sat.*

$$$$ ✕ **El Rincón Gaucho.** The cowhide rugs and steer horns on the walls
STEAKHOUSE won't let you forget that this is a steak house. Even the menus are made of hand-tooled leather. But the abundant wine bottles are a reminder that man can't live on meat alone. The Argentine beef, always sliced to order, is displayed just inside the front door. If you want variety, try the *parrillada*, a mixed grill of steaks, kidneys, liver, pork chops, and blood pudding. The order for two will easily satisfy three people. You can't go wrong with a *bife de chorizo*, a thick cut of sirloin. $ *Aver-*

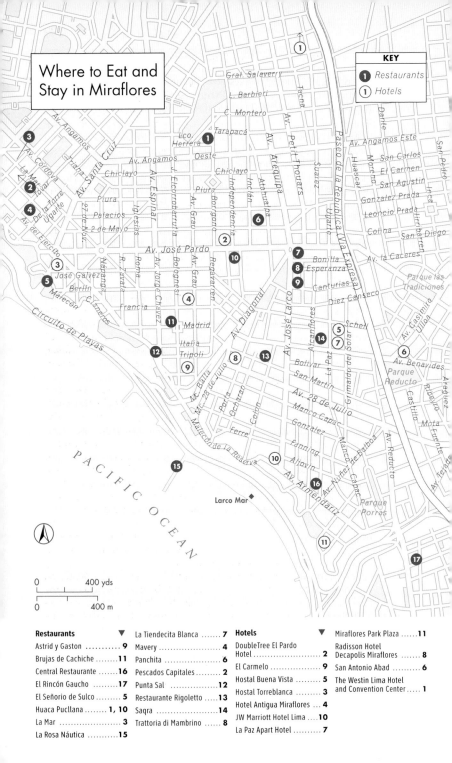

Where to Eat and Stay in Miraflores

KEY
- **1** Restaurants
- **(1)** Hotels

age main: S/65 ✉ *Av. Grau 1540, Barranco* ☎ *1/447–4778* 🌐 *www.rincongauchoperu.com* 🕒 *No dinner Sun.*

$$$ PERUVIAN 🍴 **El Señorío de Sulco.** The owner of this restaurant, Isabel Alvarez, has authored several cookbooks. The antique cooking vessels hanging on the walls reflect her passion for traditional Peruvian cuisine. Start with one of various cebiches or *chupe de camarones* (a creamy river prawn soup) if in season, then move on to *arroz con pato* (rice and duck with a splash of dark beer), *congrio sudado* (a tender whitefish in a spicy broth), or *huatia sulcana* (a traditional beef stew). **TIP→** Weekend lunch buffets offer an excellent opportunity to sample a variety of Peruvian cuisine. [$] *Average main: S/49* ✉ *Malecón Cisneros 1470, Miraflores* ☎ *1/441–0389* 🌐 *www.senoriodesulco.com* 🕒 *No dinner Sun.*

$$$ PERUVIAN Fodor's Choice ★ 🍴 **Huaca Pucllana.** You feel like a part of history at this beautiful restaurant, which faces the ruins of a 1,500-year-old pyramid. Rough-hewn columns hold up the dining room's soaring ceiling, but the best tables are outside, with a view of the huaca, which is spectacularly lit at night. **TIP→** A 20-minute, partial tour of those ruins is available to restaurant customers from 7:30 to 10:30, except on Tuesday. The *novo andino* cuisine served here improves on old recipes, such as *pastel de choclo* (a corn and beef casserole) and *chupe de corvina* (a creamy sea bass soup). It is one of the few places you can try *paiche*, an Amazon fish whose meat resembles swordfish, and the *cabrito al horno* (roasted kid) is simply a work of art. [$] *Average main: S/52* ✉ *Huaca Pucllana, Calle General Borgoño at Ayacucho, Miraflores* ☎ *1/445–4042* 🌐 *www.resthuacapucllana.com* ✍ *Reservations essential.*

$$$ SEAFOOD Fodor's Choice ★ 🍴 **La Mar.** Chef Gastón Acurio's reinvention of the traditional cebichería is not only one of Lima's most popular lunch spots, it is also the model for a franchise now found in six cities, including San Francisco. The decor is minimalist, with plenty of rock, bamboo, and palms along one wall, but the menu is kaleidoscopic. Start by sharing a *desgustación de cebiche* (various types of fish or seafood marinated in lime juice), or a *bandeja de causas* (various mashed-potato appetizers with seafood and mayonnaise fillings), then try the *saltado Pacífico* (sautéed seafood served over squash ravioli), *anticuchos de pulpo* (grilled octopus in an herb sauce atop squashed potatoes), or the catch of the day. The servings tend to be large. **TIP→** The place doesn't take reservations, so arrive before 1 or you'll wait an hour for a table. [$] *Average main: S/46* ✉ *Av. La Mar 770, Miraflores* ☎ *01/421–3365* 🌐 *www.lamarcebicheria.com* ✍ *Reservations not accepted* 🕒 *No dinner.*

$$$$ SEAFOOD 🍴 **La Rosa Náutica.** One of the most recognizable landmarks in Miraflores, La Rosa Náutica is a rambling Victorian-style building perched over the Pacific at the end of a long pier. Its gazebo-like dining rooms have spectacular views of the water, where surfers ride the breakers by day. Stop by in the late afternoon for a drink, as the sunsets can be stunning. Signature appetizers include grilled octopus, scallops sautéed with hot peppers, and a mixed fish, scallops, and octopus *cebiche* (marinated in lime juice). Sea bass is served various ways, such as sautéed in a pernod sauce with scallops and shrimp, or grilled with a leek fondue sauce. The meat dishes include chateaubriand. [$] *Average main: S/65* ✉ *Espigón 4, Circuito de Playas, Miraflores* ☎ *1/445–0149* 🌐 *www.larosanautica.com.*

$$$
SWISS

✕ **La Tiendecita Blanca.** This old-fashioned eatery first flung open its doors in 1937, and little has changed since then. The fancifully painted woodwork on the doors and along the ceiling conjure up the Old Country. *Rösti* (grated potatoes with bacon and cheese) and five kinds of fondue, including a tasty version with ripe tomatoes, are among the traditional Swiss options. The kitchen also offers three-course meals, as well as sandwiches and other light fare. You may want to fast-forward to dessert, as the glass case is filled with eye-popping pastries. On a nice day the front terrace is a great people-watching spot. $ *Average main: S/58* ⊠ *Av. José Larco 111, Miraflores* ☎ *1/445–9797* ⊕ *www. latiendecitablanca.com.pe.*

$
ARGENTINE

✕ **Mavery.** This small restaurant on a busy avenue evokes the country with its rustic log walls and tables made from sliced tree trunks. It specializes in that favorite Argentine snack: the empanada. There are nine types on offer, from the traditional *carne* (ground beef) to *cangrejo y queso* (crabmeat and cheese), as well as dozens of pizzas and pasta dishes. Another option is *pastel de choclo* (corn casserole with beef, raisins, and olives). The food and prices make this a popular nightspot. $ *Average main: S/20* ⊠ *Av. Del Ejercito 182, Miraflores* ☎ *1/441–3134.*

$$$
STEAKHOUSE
Fodor's Choice
★

✕ **Panchita.** The neighborhood's premier steak house is more than that, since in addition to prime cuts of beef the menu features such Peruvian specialties as *cochinillo* (roast suckling pig) with *tacu tacu* (mixed rice and beans) and grilled Chilean salmon. The U.S. beef is pricy, but the Brazilian beef is excellent. Try one of the Argentine malbecs on the wine list. The airy dining room has minimal decoration, but the colorful bar in the corner has a wild collection of statues and handblown glass. The service is first-rate, and the desserts are to die for. It's no wonder the place is usually packed. $ *Average main: S/60* ⊠ *Av. Dos de Mayo 298, Miraflores* ☎ *1/242–5957* ⚄ *Reservations essential* ⊗ *No dinner Sun.*

$$
SEAFOOD
Fodor's Choice
★

✕ **Pescados Capitales.** This vast restaurant with a laid-back ambience is one of the best places in Lima for seafood, and it consequently gets packed at lunch. The name is a play on the Spanish term for the seven deadly sins, but the only one they're promoting is gluttony—and quite effectively at that. Consider such starters as *tequeños capitales* (shrimp eggrolls), tuna cebiche, or grilled octopus. The grilled rockfish in a crispy garlic sauce is a sin worth committing, but so is the shrimp *picante* (in a spicy cream sauce) and *arroz con mariscos* (rice with seafood). So toss morality to the wind, and dig in! ■TIP→ Very close to San Isidro, this place is the only cebichería that opens for dinner. $ *Average main: S/49* ⊠ *Av. La Mar 1337, Miraflores* ☎ *1/421–8808* ⊕ *www. pescadoscapitales.com* ⚄ *Reservations essential.*

$$
SEAFOOD
Fodor's Choice
★

✕ **Punta Sal.** On a sunny afternoon the view of the sea and the paragliders from the upper floors of this restaurant is as good as the food. But the real excitement is on the platters streaming out of the kitchen, such as the *tiradito criollo* (thin slices of marinated fish covered in a yellow pepper sauce), or *conchitas a la parmesana* (scallops in shells smothered in toasted cheese). *Piqueos*, platters with various dishes, are fun to share. You can have your sole or sea bass cooked one of 10 different ways, including *al ajillo* (sautéed with garlic), *a la Chorrillana* (in a tomato, onion, and chile sauce), or *en salsa de mariscos* (in a seafood sauce). **■ TIP→ Arrive before 1 or call ahead to researve a window table on the third floor.** [$] *Average main: S/38* ✉ *Malecón Cisneros at Av. Tripoli, Miraflores* ☎ *1/242–4524* 🌐 *www.puntasal.com* 🕓 *No dinner.*

$ ITALIAN 🍴 **Restaurante Rigoletto.** On a quiet street two blocks from the busy intersection of Larco and Benavides, this small restaurant in a nicely renovated house is known for its authentic southern Italian cuisine. The Peruvian owners worked at a couple of Miami's best Italian eateries before deciding to serve their favorite dishes to the folks back home. The menu includes homemade pasta dishes, including linguini in pesto with *gamberi* (shrimp) and fettuccine *alla boscaiola* (in a mushroom cream sauce), a small selection of risottos, and a traditional osso buco. The consistent food, reasonable prices, and attentive service keep the locals coming back. [$] *Average main: S/32* ✉ *Calle Colón 161, Miraflores* ☎ *1/444–3046* 🌐 *www.restauranterigoletto.com* 🕓 *No dinner Sun.*

$$ PERUVIAN 🍴 **Saqra.** The name of this attractive eatery is a Quechua word for "mischievous child," which explains the decor of antique toys and eclectic art. It also refers to the playful variations on Peruvian cuisine, such as gnocchi served in a *huancaina* (spicy cheese) sauce, or panko-crusted prawns with a passion fruit–ginger-pisco sauce. Start with cream of artichoke soup with smoked trout and fennel, or grilled octopus in a tomato vinagrette atop mashed potatoes. Desserts are equally inventive; try pineapple *picarones* (fried dounuts) with fig syrup and coconut ice cream, or carob raisin cream pastries with an elderberry sauce. [$] *Average main: S/37* ✉ *Pasaje El Suche, Av. La Paz 646, Miraflores* ☎ *1/650–8884* 🌐 *www.saqra.pe* 🕓 *Closed Sun.*

$$ ITALIAN 🍴 **Trattoria di Mambrino.** After a quarter century in business, this trattoria remains one of Lima's best Italian restaurants. You can watch cooks stuff the ravioli and drape the fettuccine on long wooden rods in the kitchen. But the proof is on the plate: delicious dishes like artichoke ravioli and fettuccine magnifico (with a prosciutto, Parmesan, and white truffle sauce) leave you satisfied but not stuffed. **■ TIP→ Be sure to leave room for dessert.** Co-owner Sandra Plevisanni is one of the country's best pastry chefs, so it would be a crime to leave without trying one of her creations. The only caveat is the service, which can be slow. [$] *Average main: S/42* ✉ *Manuel Bonilla 106, Miraflores* ☎ *1/446–7002.*

BARRANCO

In keeping with its reputation as a bohemian neighborhood, Barranco has a slew of bars and cozy cafés, but it also has a few nice restaurants. The most picturesque of those eateries are around the Bajada a los Baños and the Puente de los Suspiros.

$ ITALIAN 🍴 **Antica Pizzeria.** This Italian-style eatery is the place to head on a cool night, because it offers a cozy ambience and good food. Rough-hewn tables are surrounded by old pots and pans hanging from the walls; the rafters hold wooden barrels. The extensive menu includes a wide array of salads, fresh pasta served with your choice of a dozen sauces, and more than 50 different kinds of pizza cooked in the wood-fired oven. You can't go wrong with dishes like risotto with *langostino* (shrimp) or ravioli stuffed with *granchio* (crab). [$] *Average main: S/34* ✉ *Av. San Martín and Jr. Alfonso Ugarte, Barranco* ☎ *1/247–3443* 🌐 *www.anticapizzeria.com.pe.*

Where to Eat and Stay in Barranco

KEY

① *Restaurants*

① *Hotels*

$$ ✕ **Cala.** One of the city's few waterfront dining options, Cala is a
PERUVIAN   chic, modern restaurant set behind a rocky beach. The dining room
★   is upstairs, with a wall of glass on the ocean side. From the balcony
you can hear the cries of seagulls and the waves washing the stones
back and forth. The kitchen offers an inventive selection of Peruvian
nouveau cuisine, with an emphasis on fresh seafood. Signature dishes
include grilled grouper served with olive gazpacho, lamb ravioli with
squash confit, and fried snapper on a bed of mashed corn and portobello
mushrooms. The desserts are also excellent; try the lucuma tiramisu
made with local fruit. There's lighter fare in the ground-floor lounge
or on the adjacent terrace. $ *Average main: S/45* ⊠ *Playa Barranquita,
Circuito de las Playas, Barranco* ☎ *1/252–9187* ⊕ *www.calarestaurante.
com* ⊘ *No dinner Sun.*

$ ✕ **Las Mesitas.** Filled with a dozen or so marble-topped tables, this small,
PERUVIAN   old-fashioned café is half a block north of Parque Municipal. The con-
stant stream of Limeños are drawn by the traditional recipies and rea-
sonable prices. Share a few *humitas,* steamed tamales that you season
with pickled onions and bright yellow ají hot sauce, or try the local
specialty, *pescado a la chorrillana* (fish in a tomato, onion and hot
pepper sauce), or *arroz con pato* (a rice and duck dish seasoned with
beer). If the floor's pinwheel design doesn't put you off balance, then
the spinning dessert display certainly will. Try the *manjar de lucuma,*

Continued on page 88

FOOD IN PERU
by Mark Sullivan

When Peruvians talk about *comida criolla*, or typical food, they aren't talking about just one thing. This is a vast country, and dishes on the table in coastal Trujillo might be nowhere in mountainous Cusco. And all bets are off once you reach places like Iquitos, where the surrounding jungle yields exotic flavors.

REGIONAL CUISINE

THE CAPITAL

Lima cooks up the widest variety of Peruvian and international foods. One of the most influential immigrant communities is the Chinese, who serve traditional dishes in restaurants called *chifas*. One favorite, *lomo saltado*, strips of beef sautéed with onions, tomatoes, and friend potatoes, is now considered a local dish.

THE COAST

When you talk about the cuisine of the country's vast coastal region, you are talking about seafood. Peruvians are very particular about their fish, insisting that it should be pulled from the sea that morning. The most common dish is *cebiche*, raw fish "cooked" in lemon or lime juice. It comes in endless variations—all delicious.

THE ALTIPLANO

Hearty fare awaits in the altiplano. Because it keeps so well over the winter, the potato is the staple of many dishes, including the ubiquitous *cau cau*, or tripe simmered with potatoes and peppers. A special treat is *pachamanca*, a Peruvian-style barbecue where meat and potatoes are cooked in a hole in the ground lined with hot rocks. In Huancayo, the local specialty is *papa a la huancaina*, boiled potato covered in yellow chili-cheese sauce.

THE AMAZON

Fish is a staple in the Amazon, and you'll know why once you taste paiche and other species unknown outside this area. One of the best ways to try local fish is *patarashca*, or fish wrapped in banana leaves and cooked over an open fire. Restaurants here are very simple, often just a few tables around an outdoor grill.

A woman preparing *anticuchos*.

Cebiche dish.

IT'S ALL ABOUT THE FISH

Peru's high-altitude lakes, including Lake Titicaca, and rivers spawn some very tastey *trucha* (trout).

In Peru, restaurants known as *cebicherías* serve more than the marinated fish called ceviche. The menu may intimidate those who can't tell *lenguado* (sole) from *langosta* (lobster). Don't worry—just order a series of dishes to share. Local families pass around huge platters of *pescado* until they are picked clean, then gesture to the server for the next course.

The fragrant *sopa de mariscos* is soup overflowing with *chorros* (mussels) still in their shells. *Tiradito* is similar to cebiche but leaves off the onions and adds a spicy yellow-pepper sauce. A platter of *chicharrones de calamar*, little ringlets of deep-fried squid, should be given a squeeze of lime. For a nice filet or whole fish, many restaurants suggest a dozen or more preparations. It's best grilled, or *a la plancha*.

ON THE SIDE

ELOTE
A pile of large-kernel corn.

Camote
Boiled sweet potatoes. The sweetness is a wonderful contrast to the citrus marinade.

Cancha
A basket full of fried corn that's usually roasted on the premises. Highly addictive.

Chifles
A northern coast specialty of thin slices of fried banana.

Zarandajas
A bean dish served in the northern coast.

A simple boiled potato
A dish you'll recognize.

SPUD COUNTRY

POTATO ON THE PLATE

The potato, or its cousin the yucca, is rarely absent from a Peruvian table. Any restaurant offering *comida criolla,* or traditional cuisine, will doubtless serve *cau cau* (tripe simmered with potatoes and peppers), *papa a la huancaina* (potatoes in a spicy cheese sauce), or *ocopa* (boiled potatoes in peanut sauce). Just about everywhere you can find a version of *lomo saltado,* made from strips of beef sautéed with tomatoes, onions, and fried potatoes. Some 600,000 Peruvian farmers, most with small lots in the highlands, grow more than 3,250,000 tons of potatoes a year.

POTATO HISTORY

The potato comes from the Andes of Peru and Chile (not Idaho or Ireland), where it has been grown on the mountain terraces for thousands of years. There are endless varieties of this durable tuber: more than 7,000 of them, some of which are hardy enough to be cultivated at 15,000 feet. The Spanish introduced potatoes to Europe in the late 1500s.

(above) Preparing *pachamanca;* (left) Discovering the potato.

GET YOUR PURPLE POTATOES HERE!

Peru's potatoes appear in all colors of the spectrum, including purple, red, pink, and blue. They also come in many strange shapes.

SCIENCE POTATO

The International Potato Center (Centro Internacional de la Papa), outside of Lima, conducts spud research to help farmers and open markets, particularly for the great variety of Andean potatoes. They recently sent 35 million potato seeds for safe-keeping to a genetic storage facility to Svaldbard, Norway, a large island of ice that is above the arctic circle—just so the Peruvian potato can outlive us all.

OTHER STAPLES

CORN: Almost as important as potatoes is corn. You might be surprised to find that the kernels are more than twice as large as their North American friends. Most corn dishes are very simple, such as the tamale-like *humitas*, but some are more complex, like the stew called *pepián de choclo*. A favorite in the humid lowlands is *inchi capi*, a chicken dish served with peanuts and toasted corn. A sweet purple corn is the basis for *chicha morada*, a thick beverage, and *mazamorra*, an even thicker jelly used in desserts. Even ancient Peruvians loved popcorn, kernels were found in tombs 1000 years old in eastern Peru. Also discovered were ceramic popcorn poppers from 3000 AD.

PEPPERS: Few Peruvian dishes don't include *ají*, the potent hot peppers grown all over the country. You'll find several everywhere—*amarillo* (yellow pepper), *rocoto* (a reddish variety), and *panca* (a lovely chocolate brown variety), but there are hundreds of regional favorites. Some, like ají *norteño*, are named for the region of origin, others, like the cherry-sized ají *cereza*, are named for what they resemble. Such is the case with the ají *pinguita de mono*, which, roughly translated, means "small monkey penis." It is one of the hottest that you'll find.

Hot pepper tip: Never rub your eyes after handling a hot pepper, and avoid contact with your skin.

FOR ADVENTUROUS EATERS

CUY: What was served at the Last Supper? According to baroque paintings hanging in the Iglesia de San Francisco in Lima and the Cathedral in Cusco, it was guinea pig. Both paintings show a platter in the middle of the table with a whole roasted guinea pig, including the head and feet.

This dish, called *cuy chactado* or simply *cuy*, has long been a staple of the altiplano. Cuy is a bit hard to swallow, mostly because it is served whole. The flavor is like pork, and can be sweet and tender if carefully cooked.

ANTICUCHOS: When a street vendor fires up his grill, the savory scent of *anticuchos* will catch your attention. Beef hearts in the Andes are a delicacy. Marinated in herbs and spices, these strips of meat are incredibly tender. They have become popular in urban areas, and you're likely to run across restaurants called *anticucherías* in Lima and other cities.

ALPACA: Nearly every visitor to Cusco and the surrounding region will be offered a steak made of alpaca. It's not an especially tasty piece of meat, which may be why locals don't eat it very often. But go ahead—you can impress the folks back home.

(Top, right) *humita*; (bottom) Peruvian eating guinea pig.

a pudding made from a native fruit, or *mazamorra morada,* a pudding with prunes and blue corn juice. [$] *Average main: S/18* ✉ *Av. Grau 341, Barranco* ☎ *1/477–4199.*

$$ SEAFOOD 🍴 **La Pescaderia.** This tastefully restored historic building on Barranco's busy Avenida Grau holds one of the city's newest *cebicherías* (restaurants specializing in seafood marinated in lime juice). Its spacious main dining room is the kind of clean, well-lighted place that might please Hemingway, whose photo hangs on the wall, posing next to a massive marlin. The menu combines seafood standards with a small selection of sushi and sashimi. If you prefer a hot meal, try the shrimp and asparagus risotto, salmon and ricotta ravioli, or a fish *sudado* (cooked in a spicy broth). [$] *Average main: S/39* ✉ *Av. Grau 689, Barranco* ☎ *1/586–8423* 🌐 *www.lapescaderia.pe* ⏲ *Closed Mon. No dinner.*

$ PERUVIAN 🍴 **Songoro Cosongo.** Eating here may by the closest you come to dining with a Peruvian family, because this family-run restaurant serves the kind of traditional dishes that Limeños have eaten for generations. Located in a massive, red adobe house at the top of the steps to the Puente de los Suspiros, the restaurant's walls are decorated with a hodge-podge of historic photos and prints. Local musicians often perform traditional *música criolla* at night. The menu includes such standards as *ají de gallina* (shredded chicken in a pepper cream sauce), *lomo saltado* (tenderloin slices sautéed with tomato, onions, and peppers) and *sudado de pescado* (fish filet in spicy broth). For dessert, try *picarones* (sweet-potato donuts served with molasses) or a *bruselina de lúcuma* (a crispy cake layered with cream and a native fruit). [$] *Average main: S/34* ✉ *Ayacucho 281, Barranco* ☎ *1/247–4730* 🌐 *www.songorocosongo.com.*

PUEBLO LIBRE

$ PERUVIAN ★ 🍴 **Café del Museo.** Sequestered inside the walls of the Museo Larco, this is one of Lima's most charming eateries. The dining room occupies an 18th-century building decorated with religious art, whereas tables on the terrace overlook a garden with blazing bougainvillea, ancient statues, and colonial amphorae. The Peruvian fusion menu offers everything from snacks, such as empanadas and sandwiches, to full dinners. Try the ravioli stuffed with squash; spaghettini with a *huancaina* (spicy cheese) shrimp sauce; or the *seco de cordero* (stewed lamb) served with rice, beans, and yuca. [$] *Average main: S/35* ✉ *Av. Bolivar 1515, Pueblo Libre* ☎ *1/462–4757* 🌐 *www.cafedelmuseo.com.*

WHERE TO STAY

THE SCENE

Lima isn't lacking for lodging—you can't go far before you see the flurry of flags above a doorway indicating that international travelers are welcome. If you have some money to spend, the capital has some astonishing accommodations. For something special, pass by the towers of glass and steel and head to such charmers as the Miraflores Park Plaza, the Country Club Lima Hotel, or the Gran Hotel Bolívar.

	Neighborhood Vibe	Pros	Cons
EL CENTRO	Colonial-era splendor	Walking distance to the city's best-known sights	Clogged with traffic by day, deserted at night
SAN ISIDRO	Mostly residential area with a few commercial strips	Peace and quiet, especially around Parque El Olivar	No major sights, a bit far from the action
MIRAFLORES	Bustling neighborhood filled with parks and galleries	Hundreds of dining options, seaside setting, pretty parks	Traffic noise permeates even the side streets
BARRANCO	Bohemian, historic atmosphere, appeals to younger people	Plenty of bars and restaurants, lovely architecture	Area to the east of Metropolitano is sketchy

PLANNING

There are plenty of low-cost lodgings in Lima, many of them on quiet streets in the Miraflores and Barranco districts. These areas are safe, so you don't have to worry about taking a stroll during the day, and they're quick cab rides from El Centro. The only decent hotel near the airport is in its parking lot, and is quite pricy, but it's just a 30-minute drive to the historic center, except during rush hour.

Although the historic center is safer than it once was, it has few decent hotels. If you decide to stay near the heart of the city, remember that you really can't go for a stroll at night. You'll also have far fewer options in terms of bars and restaurants than in other neighborhoods. *Prices in the reviews are the lowest cost of a standard double room in high season.*

AIRPORT

$$$$ **Hotel Costa del Sol Ramada.** Lima's only airport hotel makes up for
HOTEL   the lack of a view with a soothing, minimalist interior and a wide array of services. **Pros:** next to the airport; excellent rooms and facilities. **Cons:** expensive; some street noise. $ *Rooms from: S/950 ⊠ Aeropuerto Internacional Jorge Chávez, Av. Elmer Faucett ☎ 01/711–2000 ⊕ www.costadelsolperu.com ⌑ 120 rooms, 10 suites ⦿ Breakfast.*

EL CENTRO

$ **Gran Hotel Bolívar.** Tastes may have changed since 1924, but this
HOTEL   grande dame retains the grandeur of the days when guests included Ernest Hemingway. **Pros:** historic atmosphere; convenient location; good value. **Cons:** rooms are a bit threadbare; Wi-Fi works only in some rooms. $ *Rooms from: S/195 ⊠ Plaza San Martín, Jr. de la Unión 958, El Centro ☎ 1/619–7171 ⊕ www.granhotelbolivar.com.pe ⌑ 80 rooms, 19 suites ⦿ Breakfast.*

$$$$ **Sheraton Lima Hotel.** This massive hotel is a helpful landmark, as its
HOTEL   concrete facade is visible from far away. **Pros:** plenty of amenities; central location. **Cons:** Wi-Fi is extra; far from most bars and restaurants. $ *Rooms from: S/900 ⊠ Paseo de la República 170, El Centro ☎ 1/315–5000 ⊕ www.sheraton.com ⌑ 410 rooms, 21 suites ⦿ Breakfast.*

SAN ISIDRO

$$$$ **Country Club Lima Hotel.** Priceless paintings from the Museo Pedro de
HOTEL   Osma hang in the lobby and in each room in this luxurious landmark.
Fodor's Choice   **Pros:** architectural gem; doting service; excellent restaurant. **Cons:** a
★   bit removed from the action; new wing less charming. $ *Rooms from:*
S/1440 ⊠ *Los Eucaliptos 590, San Isidro* ☎ *1/611–9000* ⊕ *www.*
hotelcountry.com ⤵ *75 rooms, 7 suites* ❍| *Breakfast.*

$$$ **Delfines Hotel & Casino.** Once one of Lima's best hotels, Delfines's star
HOTEL   has faded slightly, but to compensate it's charging very competitive rates.
Pros: good rates; quiet location; nice views. **Cons:** decor a bit dated.
$ *Rooms from: S/470* ⊠ *Los Eucaliptos 555, San Isidro* ☎ *1/215–7000*
⊕ *www.losdelfineshotel.com* ⤵ *182 rooms, 24 suites* ❍| *Breakfast.*

$$$$ **Foresta Hotel & Suites.** With dozens of bars and restaurants within
HOTEL   walking distance, this hotel puts you in the middle of the action.
Pros: central location; offers discounted rates. **Cons:** chain-hotel feel.
$ *Rooms from: S/625* ⊠ *Av. Libertadores 490, San Isidro* ☎ *1/630–*
0000 ⊕ *www.foresta-hotel.pe* ⤵ *45 rooms, 5 suites* ❍| *Breakfast.*

$$$$ **Hotel Atton San Isidro.** This plain cement building with square windows
HOTEL   doesn't look like much from the street, but step into its sleek lobby
lined with couches and armchairs and you begin to see why it's one of
Lima's most popular hotels. **Pros:** friendly staff; convenient location;
regularly discounted rates. **Cons:** nothing Peruvian about the decor.
$ *Rooms from: S/660* ⊠ *Av. Jorge Bassadre 595, San Isidro* ☎ *1/208–*
1200 ⊕ *www.atton.com* ⤵ *148 rooms, 14 suites* ❍| *Breakfast.*

$$$$ **Sonesta Hotel El Olívar.** Standing at the edge of an old olive grove,
HOTEL   this luminous hotel has one of the most relaxed settings in San Isidro.
Fodor's Choice   **Pros:** lovely location; near shops and restaurants; usually offers dis-
★   counted rates. **Cons:** standards smallish; interior rooms dark. $ *Rooms*
from: S/1180 ⊠ *Pancho Fierro 194, San Isidro* ☎ *1/712–6000* ⊕ *www.*
sonestaperu.com ⤵ *134 rooms, 11 suites* ❍| *Breakfast.*

$$$$ **Swissôtel Lima.** A popular hotel with business travelers, the Swissô-
HOTEL   tel towers over a cul-de-sac in an office complex a few blocks San
★   Isidro's shops and restaurants. **Pros:** plush rooms; friendly service;
quiet; good restaurants. **Cons:** room decor is slightly dated. $ *Rooms*
from: S/1100 ⊠ *Centro Empresarial Real, Via Central 150, San Isidro*
☎ *1/421–4400* ⊕ *www.swissotel.com/hoteles/lima* ⤵ *223 rooms, 21*
suites ❍| *Breakfast.*

MIRAFLORES

$$$$ **DoubleTree El Pardo Hotel.** This is one hotel where you won't want to go
HOTEL   straight to your room. **Pros:** lots of services; near dining options; walk-
ing distance from Miraflores sights. **Cons:** impersonal feel. $ *Rooms*
from: S/1161 ⊠ *Jr. Independencia 141, Miraflores* ☎ *01/617–1000*
⊕ *www.doubletree.com* ⤵ *136 rooms, 15 suites* ❍| *Breakfast.*

$ **El Carmelo.** A stone's throw from Parque del Amor, this little hotel
HOTEL   is also just four blocks from Parque Miraflores. **Pros:** a block from
the oceanfront park; good value. **Cons:** basic rooms on a busy street.
$ *Rooms from: S/145* ⊠ *Bolognesi 749, Miraflores* ☎ *1/446–0575*
⊕ *www.hostalelcarmelo.com.pe* ⤵ *21 rooms.*

Changing of the guard, Peru-style, in front of the Palacio de Gobierno (Government Palace) in El Centro

$
B&B/INN

Hostal Buena Vista. This colonial-style house furnished with antiques and hemmed by an exuberant garden is one of Lima's loveliest B&Bs. **Pros:** charming house; near restaurants and bars; good value. **Cons:** street noise, especially in rooms 13 and 14. *$ Rooms from: S/130 ⊠ Grimaldo del Solar 202, Miraflores ☎ 1/447–3178 ⊕ www. hostalbuenavista.com ⟿ 19 rooms ⟊ Breakfast.*

$
HOTEL

Hostal Torreblanca. The name refers to the little white tower on the top floor of this rust-color, colonial-style building. **Pros:** good value; near oceanfront park. **Cons:** smallish rooms; on a busy traffic circle. *$ Rooms from: S/176 ⊠ Av. José Pardo 1453, Miraflores ☎ 1/242–1876 ⊕ www.torreblancaperu.com ⟿ 30 rooms ⟊ Breakfast.*

$
B&B/INN
Fodor's Choice
★

Hotel Antigua Miraflores. In a salmon-color mansion dating back nearly a century, this elegantly appointed hotel offers spacious, comfortable rooms and friendly service at a reasonable price. **Pros:** nice ambience; pleasant staff; short walk from restaurants. **Cons:** newer rooms have less charm. *$ Rooms from: S/240 ⊠ Av. Grau 350, Miraflores ☎ 1/201– 2060 ⊕ www.peru-hotels-inns.com ⟿ 65 rooms, 9 suites.*

$$
HOTEL

La Paz Apart Hotel. Each of the suites in this five-story hotel has a dining and living room in front and a bedroom in back, making it popular with travelers who are staying for more than a few days. **Pros:** convenient location; big rooms. **Cons:** lacks a Peruvian feel; street noise. *$ Rooms from: S/280 ⊠ Av. La Paz 679, Miraflores ☎ 1/242–9350 ⊕ www.lapazaparthotel.com ⟿ 3 rooms, 22 apartments ⟊ Breakfast.*

$$$$
HOTEL
★

JW Marriott Hotel Lima. In addition to being in the heart of the action, across the street from the Larcomar shopping mall, rooms in this gleaming glass tower have impressive ocean views. **Pros:** nice rooms; impressive ocean views; near shops, bars, and restaurants. **Cons:** on a busy intersection. $ *Rooms from: S/775* ⊠ *Malecón de la Reserva at Av. José Larco, Miraflores* ☎ *1/217–7000* ⊕ *www.marriotthotels.com* ⤴ *288 rooms, 12 suites.*

$$$$
HOTEL
Fodor's Choice
★

⊡ Miraflores Park Plaza. From the moment you step into the elegant lobby with its polished marble floors and high columns, it is clear that this is one of the city's best hotels. **Pros:** luxurious rooms; amazing ocean views; friendly staff. **Cons:** city-view rooms disappointing. $ *Rooms from: S/1880* ⊠ *Malecón de la Reserva 1035, Miraflores* ☎ *1/610–4000* ⊕ *www.miraflorespark.com* ⤴ *64 rooms, 17 suites* ⦿| *Breakfast.*

$$$$
HOTEL

⊡ Radisson Hotel Decapolis Miraflores. Bright, comfortable rooms, a convenient location, and a tendency to charge significantly less than the rack rate make this hotel a good option for travelers who like high-end amenities but don't want to pay a fortune for them. **Pros:** convenient location; competitive rates; some ocean views. **Cons:** everything on a smaller scale than the luxury hotels. $ *Rooms from: S/650* ⊠ *Av. 28 de Julio 151, Miraflores* ☎ *1/625–1200* ⊕ *www.radisson.com/miraflores-hotel-pe-lima18/peflores* ⤴ *105 rooms* ⦿| *Breakfast.*

$
B&B/INN
★

⊡ San Antonio Abad. This mansion in a residential neighborhood offers ambience, tranquillity, and very reasonable rates. **Pros:** colonial-style building; convenient location; good breakfast. **Cons:** some dated furnishings. $ *Rooms from: S/180* ⊠ *Ramón Ribeyro 301, Miraflores* ☎ *1/447–6766* ⊕ *www.hotelsanantonioabad.com* ⤴ *24 rooms* ⦿| *Breakfast.*

$$$$
HOTEL
Fodor's Choice
★

⊡ The Westin Lima Hotel and Convention Center. This 30-story glass tower is impressive from the moment you step into the airy lobby, with its soaring walls of aluminum and glass, geometric patterns, and abundant art.The innovative design extends to the guest rooms, which have walk-in closets, marble baths with tubs and showers, and walls of glass through which you can admire the urban panorama. **Pros:** attractive rooms and public areas; friendly service; indoor pool. **Cons:** far from sights. $ *Rooms from: S/850* ⊠ *Calle Las Begonias 450, at Av. Javier Prado, Miraflores* ☎ *1/201–5000* ⊕ *www.starwoodhotels.com* ⤴ *238 rooms, 63 suites* ⦿| *No meals.*

BARRANCO

$
B&B/INN

⊡ 3B Barranco's Bed & Breakfast. Travelers who are watching their budget appreciate this modern B&B's sleek rooms, convenient location, and reasonable rates. **Pros:** quiet rooms; reasonable rates. **Cons:** lacks personality. $ *Rooms from: S/210* ⊠ *Jr. Centenario 130, Barranco* ☎ *1/247–6915* ⊕ *www.3bhostal.com* ⤴ *16 rooms* ⦿| *Breakfast.*

$$
B&B/INN
Fodor's Choice
★

⊡ Second Home Peru. This 100-year-old Tudor-style house on a cliff overlooking the sea is Lima's loveliest lodging option. **Pros:** gorgeous setting; great view; near restaurants and bars. **Cons:** limited guest services. $ *Rooms from: S/325* ⊠ *Ca. Domeyer 366, Barranco* ☎ *01/247–5522* ⊕ *www.secondhomeperu.com* ⤴ *8 rooms* ⦿| *Breakfast.*

NIGHTLIFE AND THE ARTS

Lima may not be the city that doesn't sleep, but it certainly can't be getting enough rest. Limeños love to go out, as you'll notice on any Friday or Saturday night. Early in the evening they're clustered around movie theaters and concert halls, while late at night they are piling into taxis headed to the bars and clubs of Miraflores and Barranco. Ask at your hotel for a free copy of *Peru Guide,* an English-language monthly full of information on bars and clubs as well as galleries and performances.

THE ARTS

GALLERIES

Miraflores is full of art galleries that show the works of Peruvian and occasionally foreign artists.

Instituto Cultural Peruano Norteamericano. The gallery in the lower floor of the Instituto Cultural Peruano Norteamericano exhibits both contemporary art and traditional handicrafts. ⊠ *Instituto Cultural Peruano Norteamericano, Av. Angamos Oeste at Av. Arequipa, Miraflores* ☎ *1/706–7000.*

Sala Luis Miró Quesada. In the rear of the Municipalidad de Miraflores, around the corner from Parque Miraflores, the Sala Luis Miró Quesada sponsors exhibits of sculpture, painting, and photography. ⊠ *Municipalidad de Miraflores, Av. José Larco and Calle Diez Canseco, Miraflores* ☎ *1/617–7264.*

MUSIC

Auditorio Los Incas. The Orquestra Sinfónica Nacional performs frequently in the Auditorio Los Incas in the Museo de la Nación. ⊠ *Museo de la Nación, Av. Javier Prado Este 2465, San Borja* ☎ *1/225–8882.*

Centro Cultural Juan Parra del Riego. In the heart of Barranco, the Centro Cultural Juan Parra del Riego sponsors exhibitions by local artists, as well as occasional plays. ⊠ *Av. Pedro de Osma 135, Barranco* ☎ *1/247–8643.*

Centro Cultural Ricardo Palma. A few blocks from Parque Miraflores, the theater in the Centro Cultural Ricardo Palma hosts frequent concerts, as well as films, theater, dance and poetry readings. ⊠ *Av. José Larco 770, Miraflores* ☎ *1/446–3959.*

Instituto Cultural Peruano Norteamericano. The Instituto Cultural Peruano Norteamericano offers frequent concerts ranging from jazz to classical to folk, as well as dance and theater. ⊠ *Av. Angamos Oeste and Av. Arequipa, Miraflores* ☎ *01/706–7000* ⊕ *www6.icpna.edu.pe/home.aspx.*

NIGHTLIFE

EL CENTRO

BARS

El Bolivarcito. Legend has it that the pisco sour was invented by a bartender at the Gran Hotel Bolivar, and it remains a popular spot to imbibe that tangy cocktail. You can have one in El Bolivarcito, the popular bar to the right of the hotel's entrance, overlooking Plaza San

The courtyard of the mansion-museum Casa Riva-Agüero in El Centro

Martín, or step inside and veer to the left to the main bar and restaurant, which has also has tables on a side terrace. ✉ *Gran Hotel Bolivar, Jr. de la Unión 958, El Centro* ☎ *1/619–7171.*

SAN ISIDRO

BARS

Chocolate Bar. Above the restaurant Como Agua Para Chocolate, Chocolate Bar has more than 40 types of tequila and serves a damn good margarita. ✉ *Pancho Fierro 108, San Isidro* ☎ *1/222–0174.*

MIRAFLORES

BARS

Art Deco Lounge. This popular bar in an early-20th-century home a few blocks east of Parque Miraflores has a very cool vibe, with smooth house music and groovy lighting. ✉ *Manuel Bonilla 227, Miraflores* ☎ *1/242–3969.*

Ayahuasca. The refurbished 19th-century mansion that houses Ayahuasca would be worth visiting even if it wasn't Barranco's most chic bar. The wild decor—it is named for a hallucinogen used by Amazonian Indians—and tasty tapas only add to the allure. ✉ *Av. Prolongación San Martín 130, Barranco* ☎ *1/9810–44745* ⊕ *www. ayahuascarestobar.com.*

Bar Huaringas. On the second floor of a lovely old house next to the restaurant Brujas de Cachiche, Bar Huaringas is a pleasant place for a drink, though it can get packed on weekends. ✉ *Ovalo Bolognesi, Miraflores* ☎ *1/222–2147.*

Peña Party

Popular weekend destinations are *peñas,* bars that offer *música criolla,* rhythmic ballads performed with guitars and *cajones* (wooden boxes used for percussion). Peñas that cater to tourists, however, offer a more varied show that includes folk music and dancing from the country's coastal and Andean regions.

Junius. In the DoubleTree Hotel, Junius has dinner shows featuring traditional music and dances of the coast and the mountains. It's geared mostly to tourists, with shows nightly from 8 to 10:30. ⊠ *DoubleTree Hotel, Av. Independencia 125, Miraflores* ☎ *1/617–1000* ⊕ *www.junius.com.pe.*

La Candelaria. Vying for both the local and tourist markets, La Candelaria is located in a lovely old building in Barranco. Shows combining the folklore of the coast, mountains, and jungle start at 10:30 on Friday and Saturday night. There's a cover charge for the show, and food and drink are à la carte. ⊠ *Av. Bolognesi 292, Barranco* ☎ *1/247–1314* ⊕ *www.lacandelariaperu.com.*

La Dama Juana. The most tourist-friendly peña, La Dama Juana offers 90-minute shows in an atmospheric Spanish colonial-style building in Barranco. Performances start at 8:30, and the traditional Peruvian buffet is presented at 7:30. ⊠ *Av. República de Panama 230, Barranco* ☎ *1/248–7547* ⊕ *www.ladamajuana.com.pe.*

DANCE CLUBS

Son de Cuba. There are plenty of places to dance in Miraflores, but this Cuban-owned bar is among the most entertaining. On weekends it offers salsa classes from 7 to 9, and a live band plays Cuban beats from 11:30 to 2:30. It also presents short concerts around midnight on Wednesday and Thursday, and the DJ spins Latin dance music the rest of the time. ⊠ *Calle de la Pizza 277, Miraflores* ☎ *445–1444.*

GAY AND LESBIAN CLUBS

Downtown Vale Todo. After midnight, head to the most popular disco, Downtown Todo Vale. A balcony filled with comfy couches overlooks the cavernous dance floor. Psychotic drag queens dressed as hula dancers or space mutants shout epithets from the stage at the appreciative crowd of men and women. ⊠ *Pasaje Los Pinos 160, Miraflores* ☎ *01/446–8222* ⊕ *www.mundovaletodo.com.*

Legendaris. With its big dance floor and convenient location a few blocks west of Parque Miraflores' southern end, Legendaris caters to a young, mostly gay and lesbian crowd. ⊠ *Calle Berlin 363, Miraflores* ☎ *1/446–3435.*

LIVE MUSIC

Cocodrilo Verde. Two blocks west of Parque Kennedy, Cocodrilo Verde features some of Peru's best musicians and visiting acts that play everything from jazz to salsa to bossa nova. Shows start anytime from 9 to 11, depending on the night. ⊠ *Francisco de Paula Camino 226, Miraflores* ☎ *1/242–7583* ⊕ *www.cocodriloverde.com.*

El Tayta. On the second floor of an old building across from Parque Kennedy, El Tayta has live guitar music, mostly Latin, and opens up an adjacent dance club on weekends. It also serves appetizers. ⊠ *Av. José Larco 421, Miraflores* ☎ *1/242–4958* ⊕ *www.eltayta.com.*

Jazz Zone. It's easy to miss the Jazz Zone, hidden in a colonial-style shopping complex called El Suche. Head up a bright red stairway to the dimly lit second-story lounge for performances of everything from Latin jazz to flamenco. It has two shows per night, at 8 and 10:30, and often offers salsa for the second show on Friday. ⊠ *Av. La Paz 656, Miraflores* ☎ *1/241–8139* ⊕ *www.jazzzoneperu.com.*

Marcelino. One of a dozen spots on the famous Calle de las Pizzas in Miraflores, Marcelino has the distinction of being the only one to offer live *musica criollo* (traditional Afro-Peruvian music). The show starts at 11 pm on Friday and Saturday night. ⊠ *Pasaje San Ramón 260, Miraflores* ☎ *1/9460–11795.*

BARRANCO
BARS
La Posada del Mirador. When you're in Barranco, a pleasant place to start off the evening is La Posada del Mirador, at the end of the path behind La Ermita. The bar has a second-story balcony that looks out to sea, making this a great place to watch the sunset or enjoy a nightcap. ⊠ *Ermita 104, Barranco* ☎ *1/256–1796.*

Picas. In a remodeled old building next to the Puente de los Suspiros, Picas is the hippest bar on the Bajada de Baños. It also has an excellent kitchen, making it a good option for a late-night snack. ⊠ *Bajada de Baños 340, Barranco* ☎ *1/252–8095* ⊕ *www.picas.com.pe.*

Santos. Popular with a young crowd, Santos occupies one floor of a historic building up the steps from the Puente de los Suspiros. Its long balcony overlooking the Bajada de los Baños affords one of the best views in Barranco. ⊠ *Jr. Zepita 203, Barranco* ☎ *1/247–4609.*

DANCE CLUBS
Zipango. One of several dance clubs on Barranco's popular Pasaje Sánchez Carrión, Zipango occupies a slightly dilapidated 19-century house. It has a large dance floor where a young crowd shakes its stuff. ⊠ *Pasaje Sánchez Carrión 131, Barranco* ☎ *1/402–7429* ⊕ *www.zipango.com.pe.*

LIVE MUSIC
La Noche. La Noche is in a funky old house at the far end of a pedestrian street. The local rock bands booked here may or may not be your cup of tea, but it's a great place for a drink even if you don't stay for the show. ⊠ *Bolognesi 307, Barranco* ☎ *1/247–1012* ⊕ *www.lanoche.com.pe.*

Posada del Ángel. Posada del Ángel is decorated with a wild collection of antiques and art, including statues of angels. It's one of the few bars in Barranco where you can actually hold a conversation, and the guitarists who perform Latin American classics from 10 pm to 2 am are usually quite good. Besides this branch, there are two others in Barranco at Prolongación San Martín 157 and Avenida Pedro de Osma 222. ⊠ *Av. Pedro de Osma 164, Barranco* ☎ *1/247–0341.*

SHOPPING

Hundreds of stores around Lima offer traditional crafts of the highest quality. The same goes for silver and gold jewelry. Wander down Avenida La Paz in Miraflores and you'll be astounded at the number of shops selling one-of-a-kind pieces of jewelry; the street also yields clothing and antiques at reasonable prices. Miraflores is also full of crafts shops, many of them along Avenida Petit Thouars. For upscale merchandise, many people now turn to the boutiques of San Isidro. For original works of art, the bohemian neighborhood of Barranco has some excellent small galleries.

EL CENTRO

MARKETS

Mercado Central. The official name is Mercado Municipal Gran Mariscal Ramón Castilla, but Limeños simply call this massive market the Mercado Central. Its hundreds of vendors display the ingredients of the city's varied cuisine, including hooks hung with slabs of meat and poultry and trays piled high with seafood. Wheels of cheese are stacked above tubs of olives, open sacks hold everything from dried potato chunks to ají peppers, and bundles of spices lie next to natural remedies. ✉ *Jr. Ucayali 640, at Jr. Ayacucho, El Centro* ☎ *1/427–5182.*

JEWELRY

Camusso. For sterling you can't beat the classic designs at Camusso, a local *platería*, or silver shop, that opened its doors in 1933. Call ahead for a free guided tour of the factory, which is a few blocks west of El Centro. There's also a shop in San Isidro at Avenida Rivera Navarrete 788. ✉ *Av. Oscar Benavides 679, El Centro* ☎ *1/425–0260* ⊕ *www. camusso.com.pe.*

SAN ISIDRO

HANDICRAFTS

Agua y Tierra. Ceramics, hand-painted fabrics, and other handicrafts of the country's Amazonian Indians decorate the windows of this small shop two blocks east of Parque Miraflores. ✉ *Diez Canseco 298, at Alcanfores, San Isidro* ☎ *444–6980.*

Anonima. This shop is known for its lovely jewelry, wooden games, handmade glass bowls, and other objects in wonderfully wacky color combinations. ✉ *Av. Libertadores 256, San Isidro* ☎ *1/222–2382.*

Indigo. On a quiet street in San Isidro, Indigo lets you wander through at least half a dozen different rooms filled with unique items. There's a selection of whimsical ceramics inspired by traditional designs, as well as modern pieces. In the center of it all is an open-air café. ✉ *Av. El Bosque 260, San Isidro* ☎ *1/440–3099* ⊕ *www.galeriaindigo.com.pe.*

Kolke. Walking through the gates of Kolke puts you inside a walled courtyard filled with tropical plants. You'll love the handmade items, including leather picture frames and bowls and boxes made of Peruvian hardwoods. ✉ *Av. Conquistadores 325, San Isidro* ☏ *1/421–0688* ⊕ *www.kolkeperu.com.*

JEWELERY

Ilaria. Chic designs fashioned in silver are the trademark of Ilaria, which also has a shop in San Isidro at Los Eucaliptos 578. Also look for branches in major hotels, malls, and the airport. ✉ *Av. Dos de Mayo 308, San Isidro* ☏ *1/221–8575* ⊕ *www.ilariainternational.com.*

MIRAFLORES

MARKETS

On the northern edge of Miraflores, Avenida Petit Thouars has half a dozen markets crammed with vendors. They all carry pretty much the same merchandise.

Artesanías Miraflores. To get a rough idea of what an alpaca sweater or woven wallet should cost, head to Artesanías Miraflores. It's small but has a little of everything. ✉ *Av. Petit Thouars 5541, Miraflores.*

La Portada del Sol. Excellent quality goods can be found at La Portada del Sol. In this miniature mall the vendors show off their wares in glass cases lighted with halogen lamps. Some even accept credit cards. ✉ *Av. Petit Thouars 5411, Miraflores.*

Mercado Indios. Ask a local about the best place for handicrafts and you'll probably be told to go to Mercado Indios. The selection ranges from mass-produced souvenirs to one-of-a-kind pieces, and since most vendors will bargain, you can often get a very good deal. ✉ *Av. Petit Thouars 5245, Miraflores.*

ANTIQUES

Dozens of shops selling *antigüedades* line Avenida La Paz, making this street in Miraflores a favorite destination for shoppers.

Antigüedades Siglo XVIII. This silver shop specializes in ornate picture frames and *milagros,* or miracles—heart-shape charms that are placed at the feet of a saint's statue as the physical representation of prayers. ✉ *Av. La Paz 397, Miraflores* ☏ *1/445–8915.*

El Detalle. It may be small, but El Detalle holds an incredible variety of antiques, including many smaller items. ✉ *Av. La Paz 668, Miraflores* ☏ *1/242–4698.*

El Frailero. Brooding saints dominate the walls of El Frailero. These small statues and paintings, most of which were made for private homes, date back to the colonial period. ✉ *Av. La Paz 551, Miraflores* ☏ *1/447–2823.*

CLOTHING

All Alpaca. One of several shops specializing in alpaca clothing, All Alpaca sells sweaters and other items in sophisticated styles. There's a second shop in San Isidro at Avenida Emilio Cavenecia 209. ✉ *Av. Schell 375, Miraflores* ☏ *1/446–0565.*

Fodor's Choice   **Kuna.** Lots of stores stock clothing made of alpaca, but Kuna is one of
★   the few to also offer articles made from vicuña. This cousin of the llama produces the world's finest wool. It's fashioned into scarves, sweaters, and even knee-length coats. Other locations are on Avenida Jorge

Bassadre in San Isidro and in the Larcomar shopping center on Malecón de la Reserva in Miraflores. ⊠ *Av. Larco 671, Miraflores* ☎ *1/447–1623* ⊕ *www.kuna.com.pe.*

La Casa de la Alpaca. Bright colors reign at La Casa de la Alpaca. The patterns are updated takes on Andean designs. ⊠ *Av. La Paz 665, Miraflores* ☎ *01/447–6271.*

HANDICRAFTS

La Floristeria. The tiny but charming La Floristeria, in the front the Pasaje El Suche complex, is packed with quality handicrafts: retablos, jewelry, weavings, candles. ⊠ *Av. La Paz 644, Miraflores* ☎ *01/444–2288.*

Raices Peru. Tiny *retablos* (boxes filled with scenes of village life) are among the eye-catching objects at Raices Peru. ⊠ *Av. La Paz 588, Miraflores* ☎ *1/447–7457.*

MALLS

Larcomar. Right in the heart of things is Larcomar, a surprisingly appealing open-air shopping center in Miraflores. It's built into the cliff at the end of Avenida José Larco, so it's almost invisible from the street. The dozens of shops, bars, and restaurants are terraced, and some of them have impressive views of the coast and ocean below. ⊠ *Malecón de la Reserva and Av. José Larco, Miraflores* ☎ *1/620–6000* ⊕ *www.larcomar.com.*

BARRANCO

HANDICRAFTS

Fodor's Choice ★   **Dédalo.** Housed in a restored mansion where Barranco's stately Avenida Sáenz Peña meets the Malecón, Dédalo is worth a visit even if you don't want to shop. It is packed with the colorful works of dozens of independent artists and artisans and the little café in the back garden is a pleasant place to take a break from exploring Barranco. ⊠ *Av. Sáenz Peña 295, Barranco* ☎ *1/652–5400* ⊕ *www.dedalomarket.com.*

PUEBLO LIBRE

Santiago Queirolo. Founded in 1880, Santiago Queirolo has had years to perfect its pisco, and even won the prize for the country's best pisco back in 2002. Besides four types of pisco, it bottles nine types of wine, none of which are especially good. The lunch specials, on the other hand, are usually worth stopping for. ⊠ *Av. San Martín 1062, Pueblo Libre* ☎ *1/461–0441* ⊕ *www.santiagoqueirolo.com.*

SPORTS AND THE OUTDOORS

BEACHES

BARRANCO

Playa Barranquito. A short walk north of the pedestrian bridge at the bottom of Barranco's Bajada de Baños, this narrow beach is one of Lima's most popular. The sand is dark gray, and when the sea is rough it is unsafe for swimming. That doesn't keep Playa Barranquito from getting packed on weekends from December to April, when vendors stroll through the crowd selling snacks. There are several restaurants nearby if you want a proper meal. It's a quiet spot the rest of the year except for the cries of seagulls and the rumble of cars passing on the Circuito de Playas. **Amenities:** food and drink; parking (fee); toilets. **Best for:** sunset; walking. ⊠ *Circuito de Playas, ½ km (¼ mile) north of Bajada de los Baños, Barranco.*

Punta Hermosa. The road here may pass some ugly architecture, but this crescent of beige sand cropped by black rocks is worth the trip. When the waves are big, surfers ride the break on the beach's northern end. Ceramic benches shaped like surfboards decorate a nearby promenade. There is a small selection of restaurants and cafés on the promenade's northern end, which can be quite lively on a summer afternoon. ⚠ The rip currents can be dangerous, especially when the waves are bigger. **Amenities:** food and drink. **Best for:** surfing; swimming; walking. ⊠ *Carretera Panamericana Sur Km 40, Punta Hermosa.*

ELSEWHERE AROUND LIMA

Playa Agua Dulce. The nicest of Lima's public beaches, Playa Agua Dulce is a wide swath of gray sand that slopes into calm water. It gets packed on weekends from December to April, when vendors wander through the crowd and families enjoy picnic lunches. Consequently, the sand has tiny scraps of litter mixed in. The view of a nearby fishing pier and several neighborhoods along the nearby ridge is quite nice. **Amenities:** parking, toilets. **Best for:** sunset; swimming. ⊠ *Circuito de Playas, 1 km (½ mile) south of Bajada los Baños, Chorrillos.*

Playa San Pedro. Stretching for more than a mile along the coast near the archaeological site of Pachacámac, this wide beach offers a cleaner sea and sand than the beaches near Barranco. It overlooks a collection of rocky islands, the largest of which is Isla Pachacámac. It can get quite busy on summer holidays and weekends, as the dozens of seafood restaurants that line it attest. However, it's big enough to never feel crowded. Most of those restaurants have tables on the beach, and vendors rent beach chairs and umbrellas. ⚠ If the waves are big, don't go in past your waist, since rough surf creates rip currents here. **Amenities:** food and drink; parking; toilets. **Best for:** sunset; swimming; walking. ⊠ *Carretera Panamericana Sur Km 32.*

The Southern Coast

WORD OF MOUTH

"We visited Huacachina during our trip to Peru and had a blast! The dune buggy ride was fantastic! We went out for about two hours and got to try out maybe eight or so progressively bigger dunes. At the end, we stopped at the top of a dune to watch a beautiful sunset over the oasis."

—abennis

WELCOME TO THE SOUTHERN COAST

TOP REASONS TO GO

★ **Mysteries in the Desert.** Marvel over the mysterious Nazca Lines, giant shapes and figures etched into the desert floor by an enigmatic ancient civilization, from the sky.

★ **Island Life.** Boats cruise around the Islas Ballestas for viewing sea lions, condors, flamingos, and millions of guano-producing seabirds in the Paracas National Reserve.

★ **Fun with Grapes.** Go wine tasting in the grape-growing valleys of Lunahuaná and Ica and sample Peru's most famous drink, pisco, in the best *bodegas* (traditional wineries).

★ **Staying Seaside.** Sprawling luxury coastal resorts have sprung up in Paracas. Kick back at the spa or infinity pool and enjoy these posh leisure palaces as bases for exploring area attractions.

★ **Sandboarding.** Test your nerve and skill sandboarding down the giant dunes at the oasis town of Huacachina, then nurse your injuries in the lagoon's magical healing waters.

1 **North of Pisco.**
Escape from the noise and chaos in Lima by heading to the gorgeous Lunahuaná river valley, or by exploring the Inca burial site at Tambo Colorado. You'll find white-water rafting on Class IV rapids, and more relaxing opportunities, too—like chilling out with a plate of *langostinos* while sipping pisco from a rustic distillery.

Pucusana

TO LIMA, PUNTA HERMOSA & PUNTA ROCAS

1S

Puerto Viejo — Mala

Asia

Quilmaná
Punta Corriente — Lunahuaná Valley
Cerro Azul — 24 — Lunahuaná
San Vicente de Cañete — Imperial

1

Cinco Cruces

Palca

1S

Chincha

ISLAS DE CHINCHA — *Bahía Paracas* — San Clemente — Tan Col
ISLAS BALLESTAS — Pisco — Humay
Puerto San Martín
ISLAS SAGAYÁI — Pozo Sante
Peninsula de Paracas
Paracas National Reserve — T A B L A S A   D E   I C A

Laguna Grande
Punta Carreta
Bahía Independencia — Carhua
ISLA INDEPENDENCIA
Punta Grande

P A C I F I C

Punta de Asma

Faro del Infiernillo

O C E A N

Sandboarding

Desert lagoon, Huacachina, Ica.

2 Pisco and the Paracas Peninsula.

Rugged beaches and tiny rocky islands swarm with amazing wildlife on this part of the Peruvian coast, where a new wave of modern resorts has reenergized the shoreline. In the town of Pisco the always dusty streets remain even more so as residents continue the long process of rebuilding their lives after the disastrous earthquake in 2007.

3 Ica and Nazca.

Lush wine-producing valleys, peaceful desert oases, and the enigmatic signs of some of the world's most fascinating ancient cultures hide amid the arid coastal desert in this fascinating corner of Peru. Taste famous wines and potent piscos in Ica, test your skills on a sandboard in Huacachina, and tackle the mysteries of the Nazca Lines in Nazca.

GETTING ORIENTED

3

Southern Peru is connected to Lima by the Pan-American Highway, which runs down the coast to Pisco and the Paracas Peninsula before cutting inland to Ica and Nazca. Between Lima and Pisco are a variety of small coastal towns all located just off the Panamericana. Towns are laid out in the usual Spanish colonial fashion around a central Plaza de Armas. This is usually a good place to look for services such as banks, lodgings, and transport.

Man showing off Peruvian grapes.

Updated by
Nicholas Gill

From vineyards to arid coastal desert, surf beaches to rolling sand dunes, the area south of Lima is wild, contradictory, and fascinating. Jump a bus on the Pan-American Highway, which cuts a black ribbon of concrete south all the way to Chile, and you'll see mile after mile of nothing but sand, cactus, and wind-torn brush clinging to the stark, rocky earth.

It seems arid and inhospitable, yet keep traveling and you'll begin to discover the reasons why this region has been home to some of the world's most amazing ancient civilizations. Lush desert oases hide among the sweeping dunes, fertile river valleys tuck swatches of green into the gray folds of the mountains, and amazing wildlife lounges offshore on rocky islands.

This region was home to the Nazca, a pre-Colombian civilization that created the enigmatic Nazca Lines. ■TIP➔ Hundreds of giant diagrams depicting animals, humans, and perfectly drawn geometric shapes are etched into the desert floor over areas so vast that they can only be seen properly from the air. The mystery of how, why, and who they were created for is unexplained, although theories range from irrigation systems to launch pads for alien spacecraft.

This is also where the Paracas culture arrived as early as 1300 BC and over the next thousand years established a line of fishing villages that exist today. The Paracas are long gone, and the Inca Empire conquered the region in the 16th century, yet the Paracas left behind some of Peru's most advanced weavings, ceramics, stone carvings, metal jewelry, and thousands of eerie cemeteries in the desert.

Yet it's not all ancient civilizations, pottery, and mysterious drawings. With a sunny climate, great wines, and charming fishing villages, this region has been a favorite holiday destination for generations of Limeños anxious to escape the big city. It's also been a commercial hub. For years during the mid-19th century the region was the center of Peru's riches, which took the rather odorous form of guano—bird droppings (found in vast quantities on the islands off the coast of Paracas) that are a rich source of natural fertilizer. Shipped to America and Europe from the deep-water port of Pisco, the trade proved so lucrative that there was even a war over it—the Guano War of 1865–66 in which Spain battled Peru for possession of the nearby Chincha Islands.

Today the region capitalizes on its natural beauty, abundant wildlife, and enigmatic archaeological sites to draw tourists from all parts of the world. When the earthquake struck the coast of Pisco on August 15, 2007, it was a double calamity for the region. Settled above the Nazca and South American tectonic plates, southern Peru is no stranger to earthquakes, and Pisco town has been destroyed several times over the course of its history. Tsunamis, some 7 meters (23 feet) high, often accompany the quakes and can splash in as much as 1 km (½ mile) from the coast. The 2007 quake that leveled much of Pisco and left the fishing industry in tatters due to boat damage also severely affected the region's tourism. As people struggled in the aftermath to rebuild houses, churches, hospitals, and roads, reduced tourist numbers have further strained the precarious economy.

With wines and piscos to taste in Ica, dunes to board down in Huacachina, mysterious lines to puzzle over in Nazca, idyllic coastal resorts in Paracas, and tranquil fishing villages along the coast, this part of Peru can seduce and charm you. Forget the whistle-stop tour and hire a car or take a bus along the Panamericana, stopping whenever and wherever you feel the urge. From Lima the road leads to the towns of Pisco and Paracas, where you can choose side trips southwest to Paracas National Reserve, the Islas Ballestas, or east to Ayacucho. Continuing south, you'll pass through the desert towns of Ica and Nazca, the take-off point for flights over the Nazca Lines as well as trips east to Cusco and Machu Picchu. Farther south is the lovely colonial town of Arequipa, the largest settlement in the region, as well as the gateway to some of the world's deepest canyons and Lake Titicaca. From Arequipa, it's a long, parched desert drive to Tacna at the Chilean border. The "gringo trail" it may be, but just because the path is well-beaten doesn't mean there's not always something new to discover.

PLANNING

WHEN TO GO

Although the weather in southern Peru is fairly even and arid throughout the year, the best time to visit is in summer and autumn, November through April, when the rivers are ripe for rafting and kayaking and harvest festivals spice up the small towns. Around Christmas, Carnival, the grape harvest, Easter, the mid-June religious festivals, and Peru's independence day in July, hotels are often booked to capacity.

GETTING HERE AND AROUND

With the Panamericana following the coastline all the way to Chile, southern Peru is prime territory to explore by road. Bus travel is easy and inexpensive. Larger companies such as Cruz del Sur serve all major towns. Minivans, called combis, and share taxis shuttle between smaller towns and usually depart from the Plaza de Armas.

AIR TRAVEL

Although there is talk of building an international airport near Pisco, right now there are only landing strips in Nazca and Paracas that do not accept commercial traffic. The nearest airport to this region is in Lima, where ground transportation can be arranged via bus or tour operator.

BUS TRAVEL

Numerous companies work the route from Lima to Arequipa. Always take the best service you can afford—aside from the comfort issue, cheaper carriers have less stringent safety standards and the section of highway between Pisco and Tacna is notorious for robbery, especially on overnight services. Cruz del Sur and Ormeño provide the most reliable service and have the most departures from Ica, while the quality of vehicles and onboard service is notoriously patchy with other operators.

CAR TRAVEL

The Pan-American Highway runs the length of southern Peru, some of it along the coast, some through desert, and some over plateaus and mountains. It's paved and in good condition, but have fully equipped first-aid and repair kits packed. Besides breakdowns, hazards include potholes, rock slides, sandstorms, and heat. You'll find many service stations along this route, most of which have clean bathrooms and convenience stores. Off the highway conditions are less predictable. Roads may be poor in the eastern highlands and around the Paracas Reserve. Four-wheel-drive vehicles are recommended for all driving except on the main highway and within major cities.

Your only real options to rent a car are in Lima or Arequipa.

HEALTH AND SAFETY

The main health advice for the rest of Peru also applies to this region: Don't drink the water (or use ice), and don't eat raw or undercooked food.

Theft can be a problem in crowded tourist areas, such as beaches or on economy-class transport. Police are helpful to most foreign travelers, but procedures can be slow, so take care with your valuables. If you lose something important, like your passport, report it to the police and to your embassy.

RESTAURANTS

Casual dress is the order of the day. Reservations are seldom necessary. If you're on a budget, look for the excellent-value set menus at lunchtime, where a three-course meal can be as little as S/10. Throughout the south seafood is king, and your chef might blend local farm goods and the catch of the day with international seasonings. In Ica, try *tejas,* candies made of *manjar blanco,* a sweet, puddinglike milk spread. A treat available only during harvest festivals is *cachina,* a partially fermented wine. *Prices in the reviews are the average cost of a main course at dinner or, if dinner is not served, at lunch.*

HOTELS

Accommodations in southern Peru range from luxury resorts to spartan *hostals* that run less than S/30 per night. Hotels rated $$$$ usually have more than standard amenities, which might include such on-site extras as a spa, sports facilities, and business and travel services, and such room amenities as minibars, safes, faxes, or data ports. Hotels rated $$$ and $$ might have only some of the extras. Accommodations rated $ are basic and may have shared baths or be outside the central tourist area. If you're arriving without a reservation, most towns have accommodations around the Plaza de Armas or transport stations. *Prices in the reviews are the lowest cost of a standard double room in high season.*

NORTH OF PISCO

Tired of the noise, smog, and traffic chaos of Lima? A couple of hours' drive south is all that's required to leave behind any trace of the big city. Tranquil fishing villages, opportunities for white-water rafting, and even some significant Inca ruins are highlights of this easily accessible section of the Peruvian coast. This area is the favored weekend getaway for many Limeños, some who have grand summer residences that lie side-by-side with local fishermen's and farmers' houses. Follow their lead and head south to enjoy the sun, smog-free air, and overflowing plates of hearty criollo cooking.

GETTING HERE AND AROUND

Traveling from town to town is easy in this part of Peru—distances are short and no town is more than an hour or so from the last. ■ TIP➔ Car rental is a convenient way to get around, although you'll have to organize this in Lima, as there are no rental services between Lima and Arequipa. If you don't have a rental car, hotels and travel agencies in Ica and Paracas offer four-hour tours of Tambo Colorado for around S/150.

Minibuses (called combis) shuttle between most towns and are the cheapest, although not the most comfortable, way of getting around. Look on the side of the combi for the painted signs displaying its route. If you choose to travel by taxi, agree on a price before setting off.

From Cerro Azul, combis depart to Cañete from the Plaza de Armas for S/2. To get to Lunahuaná, take a combi from Canete to Imperial for S/0.70, then another combi to Lunahuaná for S/3. Perubus and Flores both offer a bus service between Cañete and Pisco for S/3.

LUNAHUANÁ

14 km (8 miles) east of Cerro Azul; 150 km (93 miles) south of Lima; 85 km (54 miles) north of Pisco.

Flanked by arid mountains, the beautiful valley of the Río Cañete cuts a swathe of green inland from Cañete to reach the tiny but charming town of Lunahuaná, nestled against the river. It's the center for some of Peru's best white-water rafting. The season is from December to March, when the water is at its highest, creating rapids that can reach up to

CLOSE UP

Surfing

South of Lima you'll find a string of sandy beaches, most of them backed by massive sand dunes. The water is cold and rough, the waves are big, and lifeguards are nonexistent.

Sound appealing? Then pick up your board and head south to see why Peru is becoming one of South America's hottest surfing destinations.

For a sure bet, head to **Punta Hermosa**, a town near Km 44 on the Pan-American Highway (about an hour's drive south of Lima), which, with its numerous reefs and coves, has the highest concentration of quality surf spots and breaks all year round.

Fancy yourself a pro? The largest waves in South America, some 7 meters (23 feet) high, roll into nearby **Pico Alto**, with nearly 20 good breaks around the Pico Alto Surf Camp. Paddle out from Punta Hermosa via Playa Norte to reach the reef, although be warned—these waves are for the very experienced and crazy only!

Excellent surfing is also much closer to shore at the town of **Cerro Azul**, at Km 132 of the Panamericana. Long tubular waves break right in front of the town, so be prepared for an audience. A pleasant fishing village, Cerro Azul is a popular weekend and holiday destination and the beach gets crowded during peak times. Go midweek if you want the place to yourself.

Peru doesn't have a huge surfing tradition, but to see where a small slice of local history was made, head to **Punta Rocas**, 42 km (26 miles) south of Lima, where in 1965 Peruvian surfer Felipe Pomar converted himself into something of a national

Costa Verde

hero when he won the World Surfing Championships. The reefbreak here provides a classic wave for beginners and advanced surfers alike.

There's even some decent surfing in the middle of Lima. Just off the coast of Miraflores, on the **Costa Verde** beach road, you can find four surfable beaches, all within a 15-minute walk of each other. Right near the Rosa Nautica restaurant, Redondo, Makaha, La Pampilla, and Waikiki are breaks for beginners, but with their proximity to the city the water can be more than a little polluted. Think you've just paddled past a jellyfish? It's more likely a plastic bag.

Surfing in Peru is best from March to December, with May probably being ideal. While the climate is dry year-round, in winter the Pacific Ocean can get very chilly (although it's never particularly warm and wetsuits are advisable year-round), and coastal fog can leave you with little to look at.

—Katy Morrison

Class IV. Most of the year, however, the river is suitable for beginners. Rafting companies offering trips line Calle Grau in town.

If you're more interested in whetting your palate, Lunahuaná is a great spot to enjoy the products of the region—wines and piscos from the surrounding wineries and freshwater prawns straight from the river. **TIP→ In March you can celebrate the opening of the grape pressing season at the Fiesta de la Vendimia.** The rest of the year, join the locals and while away the afternoon trying the variety of cocktails from the pisco stands dotted around the flower-filled main plaza—the *maracuya* (passion fruit) sour is a winner. If the cocktails, sun, and lazy atmosphere don't get the better of you, just down the road from Lunahuaná lie the **Incahuasi** ruins—an Inca site said to have been the military headquarters of Túpac Yupanqui. There's not a great deal to see, although Inca enthusiasts may find it interesting.

GRAPE HARVEST

If you happen to be in the San Vicente de Cañete region in March, drop by Cañete, which holds one of Peru's most exciting Fiestas de la Vendimia (grape-harvest festivals) on the first weekend of that month. The event stems from the town's proximity to the **Valle Cañete**, best known for its fertile vineyards that produce some of Peru's greatest wines. During the rest of the year there's little in Cañete to hold your interest, and most people head straight to the far nicer town of Cerro Azul, 30 minutes to the north.

3

GETTING HERE AND AROUND

To reach Lunahuaná, take a bus to Km 143 on the Pan-American Highway to the turnoff to San Vicente de Cañete and Imperial. There you can catch a combi for the hour-long ride to Lunahuaná for S/7.50.

ESSENTIALS

Tour Operators Hemiriver Adventures ☎ *01/534–7342* 🌐 *www.hemiriver.com.* **Warko Adventures** ☎ *01/99713–0206* 🌐 *www.warkoadventures.com.*

WHERE TO STAY

$$ HOTEL 🏨 **Los Palomas de Lunahuaná.** Set on a curve of the Rio Canete, the mostly white, very contemporary Los Palomas is a laid-back, rambling property surrounded by nature. **Pros:** nice pub; great regional food in the restaurant; beautiful pool area. **Cons:** mediocre service. [$] *Rooms from: S/287* ✉ *Langla, Km 35* ☎ *51/99567–4019* 🌐 *hotellospalomos.com* 🛏 *12 rooms, 5 suites* 🍴 *Breakfast.*

$$$ B&B/INN ALL-INCLUSIVE 🏨 **Refugio Viñak.** Operated by the same company that runs the luxury lodge-to-lodge trek on the Salkantay trail in the Cusco area, Mountain Lodges of Peru, this cozy lodge enjoys a breathtaking setting high in the Andean foothills, many kilometers past Lunahuaná—the property accesses more than 80 km (50 miles) of hiking trails. **Pros:** stunning setting; family-size rooms; all-inclusive. **Cons:** extremely remote. [$] *Rooms from: S/412* ✉ *110 km northeast of Lunahuaná* ☎ *51/421–7777* 🌐 *www.refugiosdelperu.com* 🛏 *10 rooms, 1 bungalow* 🍴 *All-inclusive.*

$ 🏨 **Río Alto Hotel.** Just ½ km from
HOTEL   Lunahuana, this hacienda-style
hotel has a family vibe and is popular with visitors from Lima. **Pros:**
riverside location; pool; flower-
filled terrace to kick back in. **Cons:**
small rooms; out of town location;
no travel services. [$] *Rooms from:
S/177* ✉ *Cañete–Lunahuana Hwy.,
Km 39.5* ☎ *01/284–1125* ⊕ *www.
rioaltohotel.com* ⤳ *23 rooms, 2
bungalows* ⦿ *Breakfast.*

$ 🏨 **Villasol Hotel.** Listen to the sounds
HOTEL   of the Rio Cañete from your room
or enjoy the river views while floating lazily in the swimming pool at
this large hotel that makes the most
of its spectacular riverside location.
Pros: riverside location; spectacular
pool area; river views from some
rooms. **Cons:** some rooms only
have views to the lawn; unimagina-
tive room furnishings; parking on
the front lawns. [$] *Rooms from: S/160* ✉ *Cañete–Lunahuana Hwy.,
Km 37.5* ☎ *51/284–1127* ⊕ *www.hotelvillasolperu.com* ⤳ *55 rooms*
⦿ *Breakfast.*

AFRO-PERUVIAN BEAT

A sprawling town midway
between Cañete and Pisco, Chincha is famous for its riotous Afro-
Peruvian music. If you're nearby
during late February, head here
to celebrate the Fiesta de Verano
Negro, when Chincha's neighborhood of El Carmen shakes its
booty day and night in the peñas
and music clubs. A highlight is
El Alcatraz, a dance in which a
hip-swiveling male dancer tries to
set his partner's cloth tail on fire
with a candle. Outside of festival
time, there are several good pisco
bodegas to tour, a couple of excellent criollo restaurants, and Casa
Andina's pleasant Chincha Sausal
Hotel, but not much else.

TAMBO COLORADO

*132 km (84 miles) southeast of Lunahuaná; 48 km (30 miles) south-
east of Pisco.*

GETTING HERE AND AROUND

There is no public transportation to Tambo Colorado. Most hotels and
travel agencies in Ica and Paracas offer four-hour tours of the archaeological site for around S/75.

EXPLORING

Fodor'sChoice   **Tambo Colorado.** Tambo Colorado is one of Peru's most underrated
★   archaeological sites. This centuries-old burial site, extremely well-preserved in this bone-dry setting, was discovered beneath the sand dunes
by Peruvian archaeologist Julio Tello in 1925. Dating back to the 15th
century, Tambo Colorado or Pucahuasi in Quechua (*Huasi* means "rest-
ing place," and *puca* means "red," after the color of the stone it was
built from), is thought to have been an important Inca administrative
center for passing traffic on the road to Cusco. It was also where Inca
runners waited to relay messages. With runners waiting at similar stations every 7 or so kilometers, messages could be passed from one end
of the country to the other in just 24 hours.

The site comprises several sections laid out around a large central plaza.
▦ **TIP→ Notice that the plaza's distinctive trapezoid shape is reflected
throughout the site—look for trapezoid windows and other openings—and**

thought to have been an earthquake-proofing measure, necessary in this extremely volatile region. The site has withstood the test of time, but that hasn't stopped generations of visitors from etching personalized graffiti into its walls. A small museum is on-site, which has some of Julio Tello's original finds, including funeral *fards* (burial cocoons), dating from 1300 BC to AD 200 and wrapped in bright cotton and wool textiles embroidered with detailed patterns. Some skulls showed evidence of trepanation, a sophisticated medical procedure involving the insertion of metal plates to replace sections of bone broken in battles where rocks were used as weapons. Samples from Tello's original dig are also on display at the Museo Julio Tello near Paracas. ⊠ *Paracas Bay* ☜ *S/7.50* ☉ *Daily 9–5.*

Huaytara. Catch your breath and drive up to this beautiful modern Catholic church built on the foundation of an Inca temple 2,800 meters (9,200 feet) above sea level.

Puente Colgante. If you have time, drive up the road past Tambo Colorado to this suspension bridge. The original wooden bridge built in the early-20th century and a newer one installed in 2004 span the river side by side. If you're brave, cross the older version.

PISCO AND THE PARACAS PENINSULA

With spectacular natural surroundings and diverse wildlife, Pisco and neighboring Paracas have long been featured as stops on Peru's well-beaten tourist trail. At less than half a day's drive from the capital, for many years Pisco was a favorite holiday destination for Limeños anxious to escape the big smoke. Sadly, the earthquake that struck in August 2007 left little of the colonial town standing and both the city and country reeling from the scale of the destruction. Life continues, however, and as Pisco has struggled to rebuild, the town of Paracas is booming, and several major new resorts have opened recently with more on the way. The rugged coastline of the Paracas Peninsula and spectacular rocky Ballestas Islands draw visitors keen to experience the area's wild scenery and to see flamingos, penguins, sea lions, and every imaginable type of guano-producing seabird.

PISCO

30 km (19 miles) south of Chincha.

Lending its name to the clear brandy that is Peru's favorite tipple and a source of fierce national pride, the coastal town of Pisco and its surroundings hold a special place in the national psyche. It's the point where the Argentinean hero General San Martín landed with his troops to fight for Peru's freedom from Spanish rule. It's the city from which *pisco* was first exported, and it's also an important seaport that had its heyday during the 1920s, when guano (bird droppings used as fertilizer) from the nearby Islas Ballestas were worth nearly as much as gold.

Modern-day Pisco shows little evidence of its celebrated past. Instead, what you'll find is a city struggling to get back on its feet after the disaster of August 2007, when a magnitude 8 earthquake shook the town for three minutes. Disregard for planning permission, illegal building extensions, and the use of adobe (mud brick) as the main building material had left a vast number of Pisco's buildings unable to withstand the quake, and hundreds of lives were lost as homes, churches, and hospitals collapsed during the tremor.

Undoubtedly a town that's had more than its fair share of hardship and natural disaster, Pisco had suffered from earthquake damage prior to 2007. The city stands where it does today because an earthquake in 1687—and pirate attacks in its aftermath—destroyed so many structures that viceroy Count de la Monclova decided to give up on the old location and start afresh where the city lies today.

Modern-day Pisco is a shadow of its former self, and most travelers base themselves in Paracas, just a few kilometers down the coast. For travelers wishing to assist Pisco's recovery, there are numerous opportunities to volunteer. While organizations active in the area vary over time, a good place to start looking for current opportunities is ⊕ *www.idealist.org*. Even those without the time to volunteer should know that every nuevo sol spent in local businesses is contributing to rebuilding the region's economy.

GETTING HERE AND AROUND

Transport within Pisco is generally not necessary: the central area is easily covered on foot, although those venturing out at night should take a taxi. If you arrive by bus, you may find yourself dropped off at the Pisco turnoff on the Panamericana rather than in the town itself—ask for a direct service. If you do end up disembarking on the highway, there are taxis waiting, which make the run into town for around S/5. Drivers who work this route have a bad reputation for taking travelers only to hotels from which they receive a commission—always insist on being taken to the destination of your choice and ignore anyone who tells you that the hotel has closed, moved, or changed its name.

ESSENTIALS

Bus Contacts Empresa José de San Martín ⊠ *2 de Mayo y San Martín* ☏ *034/543-167.* **Ormeño** ⊠ *Calle San Francisco 259* ☏ *056/532-764* ⊕ *www.grupo-ormeno.com.pe.* **Paracas Express** ⊠ *Pan-American Hwy., Km 447* ☏ *056/533-623.* **San Martín** ⊠ *San Martín 199* ☏ *056/522-743 or 051/363-631.*

Currency Banco de Crédito ⊠ *Plaza de Armas* ☏ *056/532342.* **Banco de la Nación** ⊠ *Calle San Fransisco, primera cuadra.*

Medical San Juan de Dios (Hospital) ⊠ *Calle San Juan de Dios, tercera cuadra* ☏ *056/532332.*

Police Comisaría Sectorial ⊠ *Calle San Fransisco, primera cuadra* ☏ *056/532-884.*

WHERE TO EAT AND STAY

The 2007 earthquake destroyed many accommodations in Pisco, and most have closed up shop or moved to nearby Paracas, which has become the base for most travelers here. It's recommended to stay in

Pisco

Pedemonte
Comercio
San Juan de Dios
Ayacucho
San Clemente

← **1 2**

Bolognesi
San Francisco

Plazuela ◆

Plaza
de Armas
San Martin
◆ Cathedral
Ruins

← TO
ACOREMA

Callao
Perez Figuerola

KEY

1 *Restaurants*

① *Hotels*

0   200 yrds
0   200 meters

Paracas, but if you must stay in Pisco the Hostal San Isidro is structurally sound and has been repaired since the quake. If you decide to stay elsewhere, stay away from hotels housed in precarious-looking multi-story adobe constructions.

$ ✕ **As de Oros.** Open since 1976, As de Oros has been steadily sprucing
SEAFOOD   up the its sprawling cafeteria-like restaurant, even adding a pool and disco in recent years. Regardless, the reason to come here remains the terrific local cuisine, especially fresh seafood. Try the tangy cebiche or one of the seafood stews; if you like heartier fare, sample roast chicken and grilled meats. If you want to nosh between meals, there are plenty of salads, soups, coffees, and desserts. $ *Average main: S/15 ⊠ Av. San Martín 472 ☎ 056/532–010 ⊕ www.asdeoros. pe ⊗ Closed Mon.*

$ ✕ **La Viña de Huber.** Locals recommend this restaurant on the outskirts
PERUVIAN   of town as the best around, and judging from the lunchtime crowds, they can't be too far wrong. Run by three brothers who take turns in the kitchen, this friendly spot cooks up hip modern Peruvian cuisine with enticing dishes such as sole fillets rolled with bacon and served with passion fruit dipping sauce, or fish stuffed with spinach and sautéed in a pisco and pecan broth. Everything is delicious and the portions are enormous so order a few dishes to share. $ *Average*

Pisco Country

El pisco es Peruano! And don't try to tell the locals any different. This clear brandy that takes its name from the port town of Pisco is Peru's favorite tipple and a source of fierce national pride. It would take a brave and foolish man to raise the suggestion that pisco was invented in Spain, or worse still, in neighboring Chile. Yes, when in Peru, the only thing you need to know is that el pisco es 100% Peruano.

Fiery and potent, pisco is hands-down the most popular liquor in Peru, and is drunk on just about every social occasion. Invited to someone's house for dinner? Chances are you'll be welcomed with a Pisco Sour, a tart cocktail made from pisco, lime juice, egg white, sugar, and bitters. Heading to a party? You're sure to see at least a couple of people drinking Peru Libres—a Peruvian take on the classic cuba libre, using pisco instead of rum and mixed with Coca-Cola. Of course, the real way to drink pisco is *a lo macho*—strong and straight up. It will certainly put hair on your chest.

Pisco is derived from grapes, like wine, but is technically an *aguardiente,* or brandy. Through a special distillation process involving a serpentine copper pipe, the fermented grapes are vaporized and then chilled to produce a clear liquor. In Peru there are multiple variations of pisco: the single-grape *pisco puro*; a blend of grapes, such as quebranta mixed with torontel and muscatel, called *pisco acholado*; straight muscatel grapes make *pisco aromatico;* and *pisco mosto verde,* in which the green musts are distilled during the fermentation process.

Legend has it that pisco got its name from sailors who tired of asking for "aguardiente de Pisco" and shortened the term to pisco. (The name meant "place of many birds" in the language of the indigenous people, and it still refers to the port city as well as a nearby river.)

Today Peru produces more than 7.5 million liters annually, 40% of which is exported to the United States. In 1988w the liquor was designated a national patrimony, and each year Peruvians celebrate an annual Pisco Festival in March as well as the National Day of the Pisco Sour every February 8.

Bottoms up!

—Brian Kluepfel and Katy Morrison

---

main: S/12 ⊠ *Prolg. Cerro Azul, next to Parque Zonal* ☎ *056/536–609* ▬ *No credit cards.*

$ **☷ Hostal San Isidro.** A relaxing oasis away from the dust of the Pisco
B&B/INN streets, this friendly, family-run guesthouse is a top place to drop your bags and rest your weary bones. **Pros:** very welcoming hosts; great pool; free laundry service. **Cons:** near the cemetery; expensive dorm rooms; high walls somewhat fortresslike. $ *Rooms from: S/94* ⊠ *San Clemente 103* ☎☎ *056/536–471* ⊕ *www.sanisidrohostal.com* ↗ *18 rooms.*

PARACAS

15 km (10 miles) south of Pisco.

After the 2007 quake, Paracas quickly leapfrogged Pisco as the most important tourist hub on the south coast. Several major coastal resorts from big-name chains like Doubletree and Libertador (now part of Starwood) have since opened and others are planned. The small-town feel and cluster of petite inns and restaurants around a central fishing pier are still there, though for the passing tourist the exploring options have quadrupled. Apart from being the launching point for trips in the Paracas National Reserve and Islas Ballestas, this is a good base for pisco tasting or dune-buggy riding near Ica and for trips to the Nazca Lines.

GETTING HERE AND AROUND

A taxi from Pisco to Paracas runs about S/15, or you can take a half-hour Chaco–Paracas–Museo *combi* to El Chaco for S/2. From Paracas, you can catch a slow motorboat to the reserve and islands.

To visit the Islas Ballestas, you must be on a registered tour, which usually means an hour or two cruising around the islands among sea lions and birds. Motorboat tours usually leave from the El Chaco jetty at 8 and 10 am. For the calmest seas, take the early tour. ■ **TIP →** You'll be in the open wind, sun, and waves during boat trips, so dress appropriately,

CLOSE UP

Area Tours

In Ica, Pelican Travel Service offers tours of the city and can arrange trips to Paracas National Park and the Nazca Lines. One fellow you can't miss in Ica is Roberto Penny Cabrera, a direct descendent of Ica's founding family, with a home right on the Plaza de Armas. After a long career in mining, Roberto started his company, Ica Desert Trip Peru, and began offering tours of the nearby desert in his fully equipped four-wheel-drive Jeep. He's fascinated with the fossils of gigantic sharks and whales he's come across and has a collection of huge incisors that would make Peter Benchley jump.

Guided tours of Paracas National Park and the Ballestas Islands are offered by Zarcillo Connections in Paracas. Ballestas Travel represents several agencies that sell park packages. Just about every hotel in Pisco and Paracas will assist in booking tours, and most include transport to and from the dock at Paracas. Make sure your boat has life jackets.

Most hotels can arrange tours of the Nazca Lines, but several travel companies also specialize in local explorations. The going rate for a flight over the lines ranges US$90–US$140, depending on the season. Book ahead, because the flights are often sold out. The inexpensive and often recommended Alegría Tours includes stops at several archaeological sites, maps, guides, and options for hiking the area. Nasca Trails arranges flights over the Nazca Lines, trips to the Pampas Galeras vicuña reserve, and tours of the Cementerio Chauchills in Spanish, Italian, French, German, and English.

Make sure the guide or agency is licensed and experienced. Professional guides must be approved by the Ministry of Tourism, so ask for identification before you hire.

ICA

Huacachina Tours. Huacachina Tours ⊠ *Perotti s/n, Balneario de Huacachina, Ica* ☎ *051/113–252* ⊕ *www.huacachina.com.*

Ica Desert Trip Peru (Roberto Penny Cabrera). Ica Desert Trip Peru (Roberto Penny Cabrera) ⊠ *Bolivar 178, Ica* ☎ *956/624–868.*

NAZCA LINES

Alegría Tours. Alegría Tours ⊠ *Calle Lima 168, Nazca* ☎ *056/522–444, 056/506–722* ⊕ *www.hotelalegria.net.*

Nasca Trails. Nasca Trails ⊠ *Jr. Bolognesi 299, Nazca* ☎ *056/522–858.*

PARACAS AND ISLAS BALLESTAS

Ballestas Travel. Ballestas Travel ☎ *01/257–1146* ⊕ *www.ballestastravel.com.*

Pelican Travel Service. Pelican Travel Service ⊠ *Independencia 156, Galerías Siesta, Ica* ☎ *051/456–7802.*

Peru Kite. Peru Kite ⊠ *Paracas L-10, Paracas* ☎ *01/959–524–940* ⊕ *www.perukite.com.*

Tikariy. Tikariy ⊠ *Hotel Libertador* ☎ *056/58–1333* ⊕ *www.tikariy.com.pe.*

Zarcillo Connections ⊠ *Paracas* ☎ *056/536–636* ⊕ *www.zarcilloconnections.com.*

and prepare your camera for the mists in July and August. It takes about an hour to reach the park from the jetty; you're close when you can see the Candelabra etched in the coastal hills. A two-hour tour costs around S/80. Some tours continue on to visit the Paracas Peninsula during the afternoon for around S/30 extra.

ESSENTIALS

Tour Operators Ballestas Expeditions ☎ *056/532-373.*

BEACHES

Most beaches at Paracas are rugged and scenic, top-notch for walking but dangerous for swimming due to rip tides and undertow. Beware in the shallows, too—there are often stingrays and giant jellyfish. Calmer stretches include La Catedral, La Mina, and Mendieta, as well as Atenas, a prime windsurfing section. Dirt roads lead farther to Playa Mendieta and Playa Carhaus. Small, open restaurant shacks line the more popular beaches.

EXPLORING

Fodor's Choice
★
Islas Ballestas. Spectacular rocks pummeled by waves and wind into *ballestas* (arched bows) along the cliffs mark this haven of jagged outcrops and rugged beaches that shelter thousands of marine birds and sea lions. You're not allowed to walk on shore, but you wouldn't want to—the land is calf-deep in *guano* (bird droppings). ■ TIP→ Bring a hat, as tourists are moving targets for multitudes of guano-dropping seabirds. Also, be prepared for the smell—between the sea lions and the birds the odor can drop you to your knees. A boat provides the best views of the abundant wildlife: sea lions laze on the rocks surrounded by Humboldt penguins, pelicans, seals, boobies, cormorants, and even condors, which make celebrity appearances for the appreciative crowds in February and March. On route to the islands is Punta Pejerrey, the northernmost point of the isthmus and the best spot for viewing the enormous, cactus-shape **Candelabra** carved in the cliffs. It's variously said to represent a symbol of the power of the northern Chavín culture, a Masonic symbol placed on the hillside by General Jose San Martín, leader of the liberation movement, or a pre-Inca religious figure.

Fodor's Choice
★
Reserva Nacional de Paracas. If a two-hour jaunt around the Islas Ballestas doesn't satisfy your thirst for guano, sea lions, and sea birds, then a land trip to this 280,000-hectare (700,000-plus-acre) park just might. The stunning coastal reserve, on a peninsula south of Pisco, teems with wildlife. Pelicans, condors, and red-and-white flamingos congregate and breed here; the latter are said to have inspired the red-and-white independence flag General San Martín designed when he liberated Peru. On shore you can't miss the sound (or the smell) of the hundreds of sea lions, while in the water you might spot penguins, sea turtles, dolphins, manta rays, and even hammerhead sharks.

Named for the blustering *paracas* (sandstorms) that buffet the west coast each winter, the Reserva Nacional de Paracas is Peru's first park for marine conservation. Organized tours take you along the thin dirt tracks that crisscross the peninsula, passing by sheltered lagoons, rugged cliffs full of caves, and small fishing villages. This is prime walking territory, where you can stroll from the bay to the **Julio Tello Museum,** and

Seals observe congregation of floating humans at Isla Ballestas.

on to the fishing village of **Lagunilla** 5 km (3 miles) farther across the neck of the peninsula. Adjacent to the museum are colonies of flamingos, best seen June through July (and absent January through March, when they fly to Sierra). Hike another 6 km (4 miles) to reach **Mirador de Lobos** (Sea-Lion Lookout) at Punta El Arquillo. Carved into the highest point in the cliffs above Paracas Bay, 14 km (9 miles) from the museum is the **Candelabra.** Note that you must hire a guide to explore the land trails. Minibus tours of the entire park can be arranged through local hotels and travel agencies for about S/35–S/50 for five hours.

WHERE TO EAT AND STAY

Sleepy Paracas really only comes alive during the Peruvian summer (December to March), when city dwellers arrive to set up residence in their shorefront holiday homes. If visiting out of season, be warned—many hotels close during the low season, or scale back their service and concentrate on repairs.

$

SEAFOOD

✕ **El Chorito.** Spacious, light-filled, and with minimalistic white decor and polished wood, this eatery would not look out of place in a much larger and more cosmopolitan city. The emphasis is on seafood, dished up in delicious creations such as *conchitas à la parmesana* (baked mussels with Parmesan cheese). The dish to try is the cebiche *asesino,* or "killer cebiche," which packs a spicy punch. $ *Average main: S/14* ⊠ *Av. Paracas s/n, in front of Plazuela Abelarolo Quiñorez* 🖀 *056/545–045* 🕑 *No dinner.*

$$$

RESORT

🏨 **Doubletree Hotel Paracas.** The first resort hotel to hit the Paracas coast, this all-suite, family-friendly retreat opened in 2009 and sits just a few steps down the beach from the newer and more luxurious Libertador. **Pros:** Club de Paco kids' club, variety of dining options. **Cons:** pools can become overcrowded during summer weekends, adults without kids might be turned off. $ *Rooms from: S/389* ✉ *Lote 30–34, Urb. Santo Domingo* ☎ *51/617–1000* ⊕ *doubletree3.hilton.com* ↘ *124 suites* ⦿ *No meals.*

$$$
RESORT
Fodor'sChoice
★

⛾ **Hotel Paracas Libertador.** The best of the new resorts to have opened in Paracas in recent years, the ultrachic Libertador, now part of Starwood's swanky Luxury Collection, was created from the rubble of the once famous Hotel Paracas, destroyed in the 2007 earthquake. **Pros:** beach-front location; sea views; one of Peru's most luxurious hotels. **Cons:** wind can pick up at times near the pool. $ *Rooms from: S/444* ✉ *Av. Paracas 173* ☎ *056/581–333* ⊕ *www.libertador.com.pe* ↘ *120 rooms.*

$$$$
RESORT

⛾ **La Haceinda Bahia Paracas.** Opened in 2009, La Hacienda may not be as flashy as the nearby Libertador or Doubletree, but it's nearly as nice. **Pros:** package deals; amazing pool. **Cons:** slow during the week; only one restaurant; expensive. $ *Rooms from: S/574* ✉ *Santo Domingo Lote 25* ☎ *056/213–1000* ⊕ *www.hoteleslahacienda.com* ↘ *68 rooms* ⦿ *Breakfast.*

$
B&B/INN

⛾ **Refugio del Pirata.** Friendly and terrifically located for those heading out to early-morning boat tours, this ramshackle guesthouse is popular with backpackers and tour groups alike. **Pros:** central location in town; terrific terrace with port views; easy to organize tours via the affiliated travel agency on the ground floor. **Cons:** no restaurant; rooms lack style. $ *Rooms from: S/105* ✉ *Av. Paracas Lote 6* ☎ *056/545–054* ⊕ *refugio-delpirata.com* ↘ *14 rooms.*

ICA AND NAZCA

South of Pisco, the thin black highway cuts through desert vast and pale as cracked parchment, and there's nothing but sand and sky as far as the eye can see. As you gaze out the bus window at mile upon endless mile of arid coastal desert, you'd be forgiven for thinking that there's little to hold your attention in this part of Peru.

You couldn't be more wrong. With good wines, year-round sunshine, spectacular desert landscapes, and giant desert drawings left by one of the world's most mysterious and enigmatic ancient cultures, there's definitely more to this region than meets the eye.

Head to Nazca to puzzle over the mystery of the world-famous Nazca Lines—giant drawings of animals, geometric shapes, and perfectly straight lines that stretch for miles across the desert floor. Who created them and why? Theories range from ancient irrigation systems to alien-spaceship landing sites. Hop on a light aircraft for a dizzying overflight and try and cook up your own theory.

Or try tackling the easier problem of discerning which of Ica's numerous bodegas produces the best pisco, and if you're around in March, have a go at stamping the grapes during the pressing season.

Adrenaline seekers will find their mecca in Huacachina, where the dazzling dunes can be explored in a hair-raising dune buggy ride or sliding down on a sandboard. The oasis town just outside Ica also draws the health-conscious, who come to enjoy the lagoon's reputedly magical healing qualities.

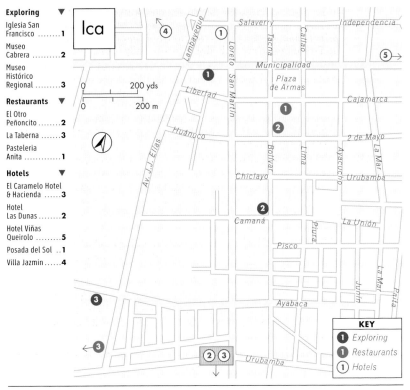

ICA

56 km (35 miles) southeast of Paracas.

A bustling commercial city with chaotic traffic and horn-happy drivers, Ica challenges you to find its attractive side. Step outside the city center, however, and you'll see why this town was the Nazca capital between AD 300 and 800, and why the Nazca people couldn't have picked a better place to center their desert civilization. Set in a patch of verdant fields and abutted by snow-covered mountains, Ica is serene, relaxing, and cheerful, with helpful residents—likely due as much to the nearly never-ending sunshine as to the vast selection of high-quality wines and piscos produced by dozens of local bodegas. This is a town of laughter and festivals, most notably the Fiesta de Vendimia, the wine-harvest celebration that takes place each year in early March. Ica is also famous for its pecans and its high-stepping horses called *caballos de paso*.

The city center's colonial look comes from its European heritage. Ica was founded by the Spanish in 1536, making it one of the oldest towns in southern Peru. The city suffered badly in the 2007 earthquake, however, and sadly many of the colonial-era buildings, including most of the famous churches, were damaged.

Today Peru's richest wine-growing region is a source of national pride, and its fine bodegas are a major attraction. Most are open all year, but the best time to visit is February to April, during the grape harvest. The Tacama and Ocucaje bodegas are generally considered to have the best-quality wines, and the Quebranta and Italia grape varietals are well regarded. ■ TIP➜ The Peruvian autumn is the season for Ica's Fiesta de la Vendimia, where you can enjoy parades, sports competitions, local music, and dancing, and even catch beauty queens stamping grapes. It's also a great time to be introduced to the vast selection of local wines and piscos, as well as an opportunity to try homemade concoctions not yet on the market.

The city's excitement also heightens for such festivals as February's Carnival, Semana Santa in March or April, and the all-night pilgrimages of El Señor de Luren in March and October. Other fun times to visit are during Ica Week, around June 17, which celebrates the city's founding, and the annual Ica Tourist Festival in late September.

GETTING HERE AND AROUND

Surrounded as it is by vineyards, tourism in Ica is all about wineries. Most are close to the city and are easily accessed by road. ■ TIP➜ If you don't have your own car (or you don't want to be designated driver on a winery trip), pick the wineries you'd like to see and ask a taxi driver to give you a price. Or hop on one of the prearranged tours offered by most hotels. The going rate for a four-hour taxi ride taking in three wineries close to the city is around S/50; if you go on a formal tour you'll pay up to S/40 per person.

Taxis in Ica include the noisy but distinctive three-wheeled "mototaxis." A taxi ride between Ica and Huacachina costs S/5–S/8.

The bus company Ormeños has the most departures from Ica, though dozens of other companies also make trips north or south along the Panamericana. Buses usually depart from the park at the western end of Salaverry and go to Lima (5 hours, S/20), Pisco (1 hour, S/5), and Nazca (3 hours, S/10). Taxis *colectivos* to Lima (3½ hours, S/50) and Nazca (2 hours, S/15) leave from the southwest corner of Municipalidad and Lambayeque when full.

ESSENTIALS

Bus Contacts Ormeño ✉ *Lambayeque 180* ☎ *056/215–600* ⊕ *www.grupo-ormeno.com.pe.*

Currency Banco de Crédito ✉ *Av. Grau 105* ☎ *056/235–959* ⊕ *www.viabcp.com.*

Mail Post Office ✉ *Av. San Martin 521* ☎ *056/233–881.* **DHL** ✉ *Av. Conde de Nieva 841* ☎ *056/517–2500.*

Visitor Information Inrena ✉ *Lambayeque 169* ☎ *056/214–223.*

EXPLORING

Iglesia San Francisco. Soaring ceilings, ornate stained-glass windows, and the fact that it's the only one of Ica's colonial era churches left standing after the 2007 earthquake make this the city's grandest religious building. Yet even this colossal monument didn't escape the quake unscathed.

▓**TIP➜** If you look on the floor toward the front of the church you can see the gouges left in the marble blocks by falling pieces of the church altar. It's said that the statues of the saints stood serenely throughout the quake and didn't move an inch. ✉ *At Avs. Municipalidad y San Martín* ✇ *Free* ☉ *Mon.–Sat. 6:30–9:30 and 4:30–7:30.*

Museo Cabrera. Curious to find the *real* meaning of the Nazca Lines? Head to this small, unmarked building on the Plaza de Armas, which contains a collection of more than 10,000 intricately carved stones and boulders depicting varied pre-Colombian themes ranging from ancient surgical techniques to dinosaurs. The charismatic and eccentric owner, Dr. Javier Cabrera, has studied the stones for many years and is more than happy to explain to you how they prove the existence of an advanced pre-Colombian society who created the Nazca Lines as a magnetic landing strip for their spacecraft (he even has the diagram to prove it!). ✉ *Bolívar 170* ☎ *056/231–933 or 056/213–026* ⊕ *www.museodepiedrasgrabadasdeica.com.pe* ✇ *S/10 with guided tour* ☉ *Weekdays 9:30–1 and 4:30–7, weekends by appointment only.*

Fodor's Choice ★ **Museo Histórico Regional.** It may be a little out of the way, but don't let that stop you from visiting this fantastic museum with a vast and well-preserved collection on regional history—particularly from the Inca, Nazca, and Paracas cultures. Note the quipas, mysterious knotted, colored threads thought to have been used to count commodities and quantities of food. ▓**TIP➜** Fans of the macabre will love the mummy display, where you can see everything from human mummies to a mummified bird. The squeamish can head out back to view a scale model of the Nazca Lines from an observation tower. You can also buy maps (S/0.50) and paintings of Nazca motifs (S/4). The museum is about 1½ km (1 miles) from town. It's not advisable to walk, so take the opportunity to jump into one of the distinctive three-wheeled *mototaxis* that will make the trip for around S/2. ✉ *Ayabaca s/n* ☎ *056/234–383* ✇ *S/11, plus S/4 camera fee* ☉ *Weekdays 8–7, Sat. 9–6, Sun. 9–1:30, or by appointment.*

WINERIES

If you can't imagine anything better than sampling different varieties of wine and pisco at nine in the morning, then these winery tours are most definitely for you. Most wineries in the Ica region make their living from tourism and as a way of boosting sales devote a good portion of the winery tour to the tasting room. Tours are free, although the guides do appreciate tips.

▓**TIP➜** Peruvians like their wines sweet and their pisco strong. If you're unused to drinking spirits straight up, follow this tried-and-true Peruvian technique for a smoother drop—after swirling the pisco around the glass, inhale the vapors. Before exhaling, take the pisco into your mouth and taste the flavor for four seconds. As you swallow, exhale!

Bodega El Carmen. Look for this small winery on the right side of the road when you're driving south into Ica; it makes a good stop for sampling fine pisco. Look for the ancient grape press, which was made from an enormous tree trunk. ✉ *3 km (2 miles) north of Ica, Guadalupe* ☎ *056/222–890* ✇ *Free* ☉ *Mon.–Sat. 10–4.*

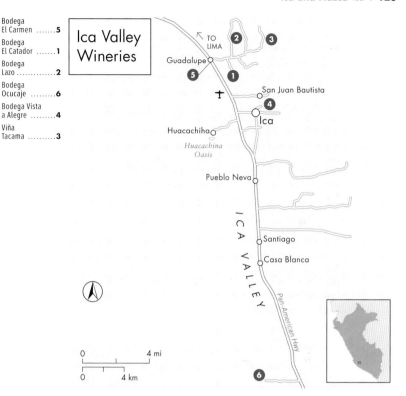

Ica Valley
Wineries

TO
LIMA

Guadalupe

San Juan Bautista

Ica

Huacachiha

*Huacachina
Oasis*

Pueblo Neva

Santiago

Casa Blanca

ICA VALLEY

Pan-American Hwy

0   4 mi

0   4 km

3

Bodega El Catador. A favorite stop on the tour circuit, this family-run winery produces wines and some of the region's finest pisco. If you're here in March, watch out for the annual Fiesta de Uva where the year's festival queen tours the vineyard and gets her feet wet in the opening of the grape-pressing season. If you miss the festival, check out the photos in the small museum near the restaurant. The excellent Taberna restaurant and bar is open for lunch after a hard morning's wine tasting. If you don't want to drive, take a taxi or wait at the second block of Moquegua for Bus 6 (S/1), which passes by about every half hour. ⊠ *Pan-American Hwy. S, Km 294, Fondo Tres Equinas 102* ☎ *056/403–427* ☜ *Free* ⊙ *Daily 8–6.*

Bodega Lazo. One of the more fun alcohol-making operations to visit is owned by Elar Bolivar, who claims to be a direct descendent of the Libertador Simón Bolívar himself (some locals shrug their shoulders at this boast). Regardless, Elar's small artisanal operation includes a creepy collection of shrunken heads (Dutch tourists, he says, who didn't pay their drink tab), ancient cash registers, fencing equipment, and copies of some of the paintings in Ica's regional museum. The question is, who really has the originals—Elar or the museum? As part of your visit, you can taste the bodega's recently made pisco, straight from the clay vessel. Some organized tours include this bodega as part of a tour. It's not a safe walk from town, so take a cab if you come on your own. ✉ *Camino de Reyes s/n, San Juan Bautista* ☎ *056/771–008* 🌐 *www.bodegalazo.com* 🎟 *Free.*

Bodega Vista Alegre. A sunny brick archway welcomes you to this large, pleasant winery, which has been producing fine wines, pisco, and sangria since it was founded by the Picasso brothers in 1857. The largest winery in the valley, this former monastery is a popular tour bus stop so come early to avoid the groups. Tours in English or Spanish take you through the vast pisco and wine-making facilities at this industrial winery before depositing you in the tasting room. Take a taxi or city bus 8 or 13 to get there. *Don't walk from downtown Ica,* as robberies have been reported along this route. ✉ *Camina a la Tinguiña, Km 205* ☎ *056/232–919* 🌐 *www.vistaalegre.com.pe* 🎟 *Free* 🕓 *Weekdays 9–2.*

Viña Tacama. After suffering earthquake damage in 2007, this 16th-century farm hacienda has taken the opportunity to overhaul its now very modern operation. Internationally renowned, it produces some of Peru's best labels, particularly the Blanco de Blancos wine and the Demonio de los Andes line of piscos. Stroll through the rolling vineyards—still watered by the Achirana irrigation canal built by the Inca—before sampling the end result. The estate is about 11 km (7 miles) north from town. ✉ *Camina a la Tinguiña s/n* ☎ *056/228–395* 🌐 *www.tacama.com* 🎟 *Free* 🕓 *Daily 9–4:30.*

WHERE TO EAT AND STAY

$ PERUVIAN 🍴 **El Otro Peñoncito.** Three generations have had a hand in this family business, one of the oldest and most respected restaurants in Ica. Dishing up traditional Peruvian cuisine and the self-proclaimed best pisco sours around, this classic spot is a welcome change from the usual fried chicken and rice joints on every other corner. Local specialties include the *pollo a la Iqueña* (chicken in a rich pecan, pisco, and spinach sauce) and the traditional *papas a la huancaina* (potatoes with cheese sauce). Owner Hary Hernandez says he won't accept credit cards, although precious stones, gold, and silver are fine. Art by Iqueño artists adorns the walls. [$] *Average main: S/25* ✉ *Bolívar 255* ☎ *056/233–921* 💳 *No credit cards.*

$ PERUVIAN 🍴 **La Taberna.** After a hard morning's wine tasting, stop in this cheerful open-air restaurant in Bodega El Catador to take in some carbohydrates and soak up the pisco. Like an outdoor rural dining room, this pleasant spot dishes up local specialties such as *carapulcra con sopa seca*, a stew of dried potatoes and dried meat, washed down with one of El Catador's excellent wines. If you want to keep up the pace, Catador's bar with its extensive range of piscos is within arm's reach. [$] *Average main: S/30* ✉ *José Carrasco González, Km 296* ☎ *056/403–295* 🕓 *No dinner.*

$ CAFÉ 🍴 **Pasteleria Anita.** High ceilings lend an openness to this popular café and bakery on the Plaza de Armas, which makes it perfect for people-watching. Everything from cappuccino to shrimp cocktail is available, and although it's not the cheapest venue in town, the range of delicious pastries and locally famous *tejas* (manjar blanco or chocolate-coated pecans) make it a top pick for sweet tooths. [$] *Average main: S/12* ✉ *Jr. Libertad 133, Plaza de Armas* ☎ *056/218–582.*

$ **El Carmelo Hotel & Hacienda.** Hotel or bodega-related theme park?
HOTEL   **Pros:** wicker-filled open-air sitting room; chance to see the pisco-making
process up close; zoo to entertain the kids. **Cons:** out of town location; rooms are on the small side; beds are in need of upgrade. $ *Rooms from: S/170* ⊠ *Pan-American Hwy., Km 301.2* ☎☎ *056/232–191* ⊕ *www.elcarmelohotelhacienda.com* ⤴ *58 rooms.*

$$ **Hotel Las Dunas.** For a taste of the good life, Peruvian style, head to
RESORT   this top-end resort on the road between Ica and Huacachina. **Pros:** beautiful grounds; activities for children; decent restaurant. **Cons:** out of town; resort aesthetic. $ *Rooms from: S/294* ⊠ *La Angostura 400* ☎ *056/256–224* ⊕ *www.lasdunashotel.com* ⤴ *130 rooms, 3 suites.*

$$ **Hotel Viñas Queirolo.** There's no better property in the country for
HOTEL   experiencing Peru's wine and pisco industry than this charming bodega-
Fodor's Choice   based hacienda surrounded by Santiago Queirolo's verdant vineyards.
★   **Pros:** atmospheric, authentic, unique in the region. **Cons:** a bit out of the way, making local transportation impractical. $ *Rooms from: S/340* ⊠ *Carretera a San José de los Molinos* ☎☎ *056/254–119* ⊕ *www. hotelvinasqueirolo.com* ⤴ *20 rooms* ❍ *Breakfast.*

$ **Posada del Sol.** Surly staff and a noisy street frontage take the shine
B&B/INN   off this small hotel in central Ica, yet given the dearth of decent lodgings it remains one of the best options in town. **Pros:** central location near the Plaza de Armas; secure; comfortable beds. **Cons:** basic; noisy street frontage; standard rooms only have internal windows. $ *Rooms from: S/60* ⊠ *Esquina Loreto y Salvaverry 193* ☎ *056/238–446* ⤴ *50 rooms.*

$ **Villa Jazmin.** This more intimate rival to Las Dunas garnishes rave
HOTEL   reviews. **Pros:** relatively new, clean, and less crowded than other Ica resorts. **Cons:** rooms can be dark; the pool is more for lounging than swimming. $ *Rooms from: S/157* ⊠ *Los Girasoles MZ C-1, La Angostura* ☎ *056/258–179* ⊕ *www.villajazmin.net* ⤴ *20 rooms.*

SHOPPING

Ica is an excellent place to pick up Peruvian handicrafts with regional styles and motifs. Tapestries and textiles woven in naturally colored llama and alpaca wool often have images of the Nazca Lines and historical figures. In particular, look for *alfombras* (rugs), *colchas* (blankets), and *tapices* (hangings).

HUACACHINA

5 km (3 miles) southwest of Ica.

Drive 10 minutes through the pale, mountainous sand dunes southwest of Ica and you'll suddenly see a gathering of attractive, pastel-color buildings surrounding a patch of green. It's not an oasis on the horizon, but rather the lakeside resort of Laguna de Huacachina, a palm-fringed lagoon of jade-color waters whose sulfurous properties are reputed to have healing powers. The view is breathtaking: a collection of attractive, colonial-style hotels in front of a golden beach and with a backdrop of snow-covered peaks against the distant sky. In the 1920s Peru's elite traveled here for the ultimate holiday, and today the spacious resorts still beckon. The lake is also a pilgrimage site for those with health and skin problems, sandboarders who want to tackle the 100-meter

(325-foot) dunes, and budget travelers who pitch tents in the sand or sleep under the stars.

GETTING HERE AND AROUND

Huacachina sits on the opposite side of the highway from the center of Ica. Take any bus to Ica and hire a mototaxi to the oasis for about S/8–S/10.

EN ROUTE **Bodega Ocucaje.** About 40 km (27 miles) southeast of Huacachina is Bodega Ocucaje, a famous winery in an old Spanish mansion, whose vintages—including the famous Vino Fond de Cave—are considered among Peru's best. **TIP→** **Because of the isolation, the bodega gets few visitors, so be sure to call ahead. Also on the property is the Ocucaje Sun & Wine Resort. Heavily damaged in the 2007 earthquake, it's reopened but has yet to live up to its former reputation.** ✉ *Av. Principal s/n* ☎ *056/836–101* 🌐 *www.ocucaje.com* 🎟 *S/15* 🕑 *Weekdays 9–noon and 2–5, Sat. 9–noon.*

WHERE TO EAT AND STAY

$ PERUVIAN 🍴 **Arturo's Restaurant Taberna.** In a town severely lacking dining options, this restaurant holds some promise. With plastic furniture and a concrete floor, it's not winning any style prizes, but the hearty Peruvian cooking hits the spot and with most meals going for around S/10 to S/15 it's by far the best deal on food in town. Owner Arturo has grand plans to turn it into a more upmarket eatery, so expect changes. There's a good selection of wines from the local bodegas, and prices are almost as cheap as buying direct from the winery. [$] *Average main: S/10* ✉ *Av. Perotti, lote 3* 💳 *No credit cards.*

$ B&B/INN 🏨 **Carola del Sur.** This place is party central—just follow the sounds of Bob Marley drifting on the night air and you'll be sure to end up here. **Pros:** good restaurant and bar; pool has views of the dunes; Huacachina's largest and longest running dune buggy service. **Cons:** terrible fluorescent lighting in the rooms; small windows; loud music makes getting an early night impossible. [$] *Rooms from: S/50* ✉ *Av Perotti s/n, Balneario de Huacachina* ☎ *056/215–439* 🌐 *www.casa-de-arena-hotels.com* 🛏 *50 rooms* 💳 *No credit cards.*

$ B&B/INN Fodor's Choice ★ 🏨 **El Hauchachinero.** Hands-down Huacachina's best budget lodging, this is a beautiful bargain in the oasis of Peru. **Pros:** fantastic pool area with hammocks for lounging; dune-buggy service and sandboard rental; attractively furnished rooms and common areas. **Cons:** often full; noisy parrots. [$] *Rooms from: S/160* ✉ *Av. Perotti, Balnearia de Huacachina* ☎ *056/271–435* 🌐 *www.elhuacachinero.com* 🛏 *24 rooms, 3 without bath* 🍽 *Breakfast.*

$ B&B/INN 🏨 **Hosteria Suiza.** It may not be the most jumping joint in town, but this guesthouse is a good spot for enjoying the beauty of the desert landscape and lush oasis without having to deal with the constant party that exists in some other hotels. **Pros:** peaceful atmosphere; lovely garden; friendly staff; great pool. **Cons:** restaurant only serves breakfast; furnishings are a little old-fashioned. [$] *Rooms from: S/204* ✉ *Balneario de Huacachina* ☎ *056/238–762* 🌐 *www.hosteriasuiza.com.pe* 🛏 *17 rooms* 🍽 *Breakfast.*

$ HOTEL 🏨 **Hotel Mossone.** Imagine life as it was in Huacachina's heyday in the oasis's original hotel. **Pros:** fantastic location in front of the lagoon;

great pool; the elegant lounge bar is the best spot in town from which to watch the sun set over the dunes. **Cons:** rooms look a little tired; hotel is often full with tour groups. $ *Rooms from: S/174* ✉ *Balneario de Huacachina s/n* ☎ *056/213–630, 01/261–9605 in Lima* ⤸ *41 rooms.*

SPORTS AND THE OUTDOORS
SANDBOARDING

Ever fancied having a go at snowboarding but chickened out at the thought of all those painful next-day bruises? Welcome to the new adventure sport of sandboarding, a softer and warmer way to hit the slopes. Surrounded by dunes, Huacachina is the sandboarding capital of the world: every year European sports fans arrive here in droves to practice for the international sand-surfing competitions on Cerro Blanco, the massive dune 14 km (8 miles) north of Nazca.

With no rope tows or chairlifts to get you up the dunes, the easiest way to have a go at sandboarding is to go on a dune buggy tour, offered by just about every hotel in town. In these converted vehicles you'll be driven (quickly) to the top of the dunes, upon which you can board, slide, or slither down to be picked up again at the bottom. Drivers push their vehicles hard, so be prepared for some heart-stopping moments. Carola del Sur guesthouse has the biggest fleet of dune buggies and runs two tours daily at 10 am and 4 pm. The tours last around two hours and cost S/45. It's best to go in the morning or late afternoon, when the sand is not as hot and doesn't melt the wax off your board.

NAZCA

120 km (75 miles) southeast of Ica.

What do a giant hummingbird, a monkey, and an astronaut have in common? Well, apart from the fact that they're all etched into the floor of the desert near Nazca, no one really seems to know. Welcome to one of the world's greatest mysteries—the enigmatic Nazca Lines. A mirage of green in the desert, lined with cotton fields and orchards and bordered by crisp mountain peaks, Nazca was a quiet colonial town unnoticed by the rest of the world until 1901, when Peruvian archaeologist Max Uhle excavated sites around Nazca and discovered the remains of a unique pre-Colombian culture. Set 598 meters (1,961 feet) above sea level, the town has a dry climate—scorching by day, nippy by night—that was instrumental in preserving centuries-old relics from Inca and pre-Columbian tribes. ■ TIP➔ The area has more than 100 cemeteries, where the humidity-free climate has helped preserve priceless jewelry, textiles, pottery, and mummies. Overlooking the parched scene is the 2,078-meter (6,815-foot) Cerro Blanco, the highest sand dune in the world.

GETTING HERE AND AROUND

Be prepared: Nazca is all about tours and it may seem like everyone in town is trying to sell you one at once. The minute you poke your nose outside the bus door you'll be swamped with offers for flights over the lines, hotels, and trips to the Chauchilla cemetery. Be wise about any offers made to you by touts at the bus station—if it's cheap, there's probably a good reason why. That said, a tour with a reputable agency is a great way to catch all of Nazca's major sites. Recommended agencies include Alegria Tours and Nasca Trails.

All buses arrive and depart from the *óvalo* (roundabout). To see the lines from ground level, taxis will make the 30-minute run out to the mirador for around S/50, or do it the local way and catch any northbound bus along the Panamericana for just S/3. ■ TIP→ Flights over the Lines are best in early morning, before the sun gets too high and winds make flying uncomfortable. Standard flights last around 30 minutes and cost between $120 USD and $160 USD, depending on the season. You'll also have to pay an airport tax of S/10 (watch out for cheeky operators who will try and tell you that the tax is $10 USD; it's not!). You can buy flight tickets from travel agencies and many hotels in town, or directly from the airline offices near the airport. Buying tickets in advance will save you time. Tickets are available on the spot at the airport, but as planes won't take off until all seats are filled you may spend most of your morning hanging around the dusty Panamerica Sur watching while others take off and land.

FLIGHTS FOR THE LINES   Nazca Lines flights depart from the small Aeropuerto Nazca, cost S/315 for a 40-minute flight plus lunch, a tour of Nazca's archaeological museum, and a trip to the *mirador*. Note that these flights are often overbooked year-round; arrive early to check in for your flight, as many are full and there's a chance you'll get bumped if you're late. Nazca Airlines and upstarts Aero Palpa, Aero Paracas, and Taxi Aereo all offer services. As these latter lines are small operations with varying office hours, check at the airport for schedules. Most sightseeing flights depart from Nazca, although Aero Paracas also originates in Lima and Pisco.

Safety records for many of the airlines are spotty at best. In 2010 seven tourists were killed when their Nazca Airlines flight crashed into the desert. Airlines change owners and names frequently, so it's hard to know exactly who you are flying with. Check with PromPeru in Lima before booking a flight.

ESSENTIALS

Air Carriers Aero Paracas ☎ 01/265–8073 or 01/265–8173 ⊕ www.aeroparacas.com. **Nazca Airlines.** ☎ 056/224–6373 ⊕ www.nazcagroup.com.

Bus Contacts Cruz del Sur ☎ 034/522–484 ⊕ www.cruzdelsur.com.pe. **Expreso Wari** ☎ 056/229134 ⊕ www.expresowari.com.pe.

Currency Banco de Crédito ✉ Lima 495 ⊕ www.viabcp.com.

Internet Speed Service ✉ Bolognesi 299 ☎ 056/522–176.

Medical Es Salud ✉ Juan Matta 613 ☎ 056/522–446. **Hospital de Apoyo** ✉ Calle Callao s/n ☎ 056/522–486.

Police Comisaría Sectorial ✉ Av. Los Incas ☎ 056/522–2084.

Continued on page 134

by Ruth Anne Phillips

NAZCA LINES

On the surface of the southern Peruvian coastal desert or "Pampa" between the Nazca and Ingenio River valleys are the Nazca Lines. The Nazca Lines are enormous figures, geometric designs and straight lines etched into the desert's surface called geoglyphs. There are more than 1,000 enormous figures, geometric shapes and straight lines, some arranged as ray centers. While the most famous of the lines appear on the Pampa de San José near Nazca as well as on the hillsides of the valleys of the Río Grande de Nazca, the geoglyphs are throughout a larger area that comprises 400 square miles.

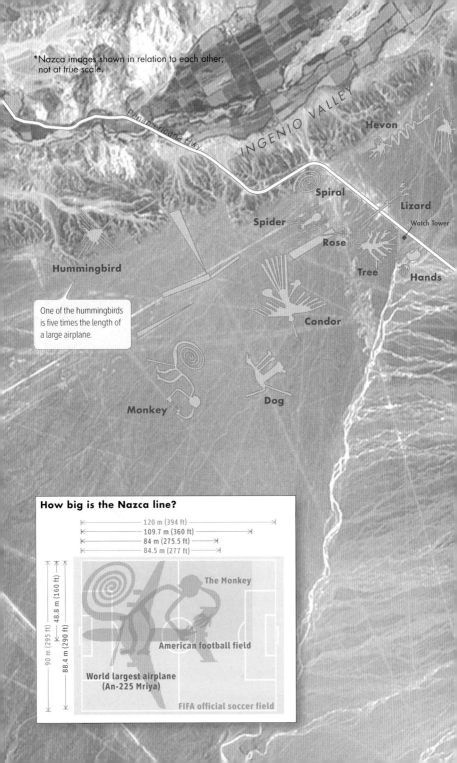

*Nazca images shown in relation to each other; not at true scale.

Panamericana Hwy.

INGENIO VALLEY

Hevon

Spiral

Lizard

Watch Tower

Spider

Rose

Hummingbird

Tree

Hands

One of the hummingbirds is five times the length of a large airplane.

Condor

Monkey

Dog

How big is the Nazca line?

120 m (394 ft)
109.7 m (360 ft)
84 m (275.5 ft)
84.5 m (277 ft)

90 m (295 ft)
48.8 m (160 ft)
88.4 m (290 ft)

The Monkey

American football field

World largest airplane
(An-225 Mriya)

FIFA official soccer field

Shell

Parrot

THINGS TO LOOK FOR

The biomorphic designs include monkeys, birds, a spider, plants, and a number of fantastical combinations and somewhat abstracted humanoid creatures. One of the monkeys is 180 feet long while a hummingbird is five times the length of a large airplane. At least 227 spirals, zigzags, triangles, quadrangles, and trapezoids make up the geometric designs, with one trapezoid measuring over 2,700 feet by 300

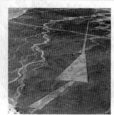

A trapezoid.

feet. The straight lines represent the greatest proportion of the geoglyphs: 800 single or parallel lines stretch on for miles, ranging in width from less than two feet to hundreds of feet.

Many of the lines haphazardly overlap each other, which indicates that as a group they were not pre-planned.

CONSTRUCTION

Modern archaeologists have recreated surprisingly simple construction methods for the geoglyphs using basic surveying techniques. Sight poles guided the construction of straight lines and strings tied to posts helped create circular designs. Wooden posts that may have been used as guides or end markers and an abundance of fancy potsherds, possibly used in rituals, have been found along many of the lines.

AGE

The extremely dry climatic conditions of the Pampa have helped preserve the lines; most date from c. 500 AD, during the florescence of the Nazca culture (c. 1–700 AD). A small number, however, may date to after the Nazca period to as late as 1000 AD.

Panamericana Hwy. (18 miles from Nazca to Ingenio Valley)

TO NAZCA

Astronaut

HISTORY AND MYSTERY

An archaeologist examines the lines.

Though the Nazca Lines are difficult to see from the ground due to their enormous size, some can be seen from nearby hillsides. It's widely believed that the lines were first properly seen from an airplane, but they were "discovered" by archaeologists working near Cahuachi in the mid-1920s. American archaeologist, Alfred L. Kroeber was the first to describe them in 1926, but it was Peruvian archaeologist Toribio Mejía Xesspe who conducted the first extensive studies of the Nazca Lines around the same time.

By the late 1920s, commercial planes began flying over the Pampa and many reported seeing the Nazca Lines from the air. It was not until American geographer and historian, Paul Kosok and his second wife Rose, flew over the Nazca drainage area in 1941, however,

that the Nazca Lines became a widely known phenomenon in the United States and Europe.

THE CREATIVE PROCESS

The dry desert plain acts as a giant scratchpad as the darker oxidized surface can be swept away to reveal the lighter, pale pink subsurface. Many of the shapes are made with one continuous line that has piles of dark rocks lining the edges creating a dark border.

Stylistic comparisons between the figural Nazca Lines and images that appear on Nazca ceramics have helped establish their age.

THEORIES ABOUND

The Nazca Lines have incited various scholarly and popular theories for their construction and significance. Kroeber and Xesspe, observing the lines from the ground, believed that they served as sacred pathways. Kosok, seeing the lines from the air, observed the sun setting over the end of one line on the day of the winter solstice and thought they must have marked important astronomical events. German mathematician Maria Reiche, who studied the lines and lived near them for decades, expanded upon Kosok's astronomical theories. Modern scholars, however, have demonstrated that the lines' alignment to celestial events occurred at a frequency no greater than chance. Other theories posit that they were made for earth, mountain, or sky deities. After Cahuachi was determined in the 1980s to have been a large pilgrimage center, the idea that the lines acted as a sacred pathway has gained new momentum. Another plausible theory suggests that the Nazca Lines marked underground water sources.

IT'S THE ALIENS, OF COURSE

Popular theories have promoted the "mystery" of the Nazca Lines. One influential author, Erich von Däniken, suggested in his 1968 best-selling book *Chariots of the Gods* (reprinted several times and made into a film) that these giant geoglyphs were created as landing

Spaceman figure, San Jose Pampa

markers for extraterrestrials. Archaeologists and other scientists have dismissed these theories. The aliens deny them as well.

VISITING THE NAZCA LINES

The "Candelabra of the Andes" or the "Paracas Candelabra" on the Peninsula de Paracas.

The best way to view the Nazca Lines is by air in small, low-flying aircraft. Local companies offer flights usually in the early morning, when viewing conditions are best. You can fly over several birds, a few fish, a monkey, a spider, a flower, a condor, and/or several unidentified figures. While seeing the amazing Nazca Lines is a great experience, the sometimes questionable-looking airplanes with their strong fumes and pilots who seem to enjoy making nausea-inducing turns and twists can be worrisome. Because of poor safety records, planes are often grounded. Check with your tour operator before booking a trip with any local airline.

Nazca

KEY

1 Exploring
1 Restaurants
1 Hotels

Exploring	▼	Restaurants	▼	Hotels	▼
Museo Antonini **2**		Chifa Nam Kug **3**		Casa Andina **3**	
Tallera de Artesania		Restaurant Don Carlos **2**		Hotel Alegría **1**	
de Andres Calle Flores **1**		Via la Encantada **1**		Hotel Cantayo	
				Spa & Resort **6**	
				Hotel Maison Suisse **4**	
				Hotel Majoro **5**	
				Hotel Nazca Lines **2**	

EXPLORING

Cahuachi Pyramids. Within a walled, 4,050-square-yard courtyard west of the Nazca Lines is an ancient ceremonial and pilgrimage site. Six adobe pyramids, the highest of which is about 21 meters (70 feet), stand above a network of rooms and connecting corridors. Grain and water silos are also inside, and several large cemeteries lie outside the walls. Used by the early Nazca culture, the site is estimated to have existed for about two centuries before being abandoned about AD 200. Cahuachi takes its name from the word *qahuachi* (meddlesome). El Estaquería, with its mummification pillars, is nearby. Tours from Nazca visit both sites for around S/120 and take four hours. ⊠ *34 km (21 miles) west of Nazca* ⊆ *Free* ⊙ *Daily 8–5.*

Casa-Museo Maria Reiche. To see where a lifelong obsession with the Nazca Lines can lead you, head to the former home of the German anthropologist who devoted her life to studying the mystery of the lines. There's little explanatory material among the pottery, textiles, mummies, and skeletons from the Paracas, Nazca, Wari, Chincha, and Inca cultures, so don't expect any of the area's mysteries to be solved here, but the museum does a great job of showing the environment in which Maria Reiche lived and worked, and her vast collection of tools, notes, and sketches is impressive. Reiche, who died in 1998, is buried here in a small tomb. A scale model of the lines is behind the house. Take a bus from the Ormeño terminal to the Km 416 marker to reach the museum, which is 1 km (½ mile) from town. ⊠ *Pan-American Hwy., Km 416, San Pablo* ☎ *034/255734* ⊆ *S/5* ⊙ *Daily 9–4.*

Cementerio de Chauchilla. In the midst of the pale, scorched desert, the ancient cemetery is scattered with sun-bleached skulls and shards of pottery. *Huaqueros* (grave robbers) have ransacked the site over the years, and while up until a couple of years ago the mummies unearthed by their looting erupted from the earth in a jumble of bones and threadbare weavings, they are now housed neatly inside a dozen or so covered tombs. It's nevertheless an eerie sight, as the mummies still have hair attached, as well as mottled, brown-rose skin stretched around empty eye sockets and gaping mouths with missing teeth. Some are wrapped in tattered burial sacks, though the jewelry and ceramics with which they were laid to rest are long gone. Tours from town take about three hours and cost around S/40. Visits to the cemetery are also packaged with Nazca Lines flights. ⊠ *30 km (19 miles) from Nazca, the last 12 km (7 miles) of which is unpaved* ⊆ *S/5* ⊙ *Daily 8–6.*

El Estaquería. The wooden pillars here, carved of *huarango* wood and placed on mud-brick platforms, were once thought to have been an astronomical observatory. More recent theories, however, lean toward their use in mummification rituals, perhaps to dry bodies of deceased tribal members. You can take a private tour of the site for about S/25 with a three-person minimum. ⊠ *34 km (21 miles) west of Nazca* ⊆ *Free* ⊙ *Daily 8–4.*

Museo Antonini. For an overview of the Nazca culture and the various archaeological sites in the region, this Italian-run museum is the best in town. The displays, made up of materials excavated from the surrounding archaeological digs, are heavy on scientific information and light on entertainment, although the display of Nazcan trophy skulls will appeal to the morbid among us and textiles fans will appreciate the display of painted fabrics from the ancient adobe city of Cahuachi. All the signage is in Spanish, so ask for the translation book at the front desk. Don't miss the still-working Nascan aqueduct in the back garden. ✉ *Av. de la Cultura 600* ☎ *056/265–421* 🎟 *S/15, S/20 with a camera* 🕒 *Daily 9–7.*

Fodor's Choice ★ **Nazca Lines.** Even with the knowledge of the Nazca culture obtained from the archaeological discoveries, it was not until 1929 that the Nazca Lines were discovered, when American scientist Paul Kosok looked out of his plane window as he flew over them. Almost invisible from ground level, the Lines were made by removing the surface stones and piling them beside the lighter soil underneath. More than 300 geometrical and biomorphic figures, some measuring up to 300 meters (1,000 feet) across, are etched into the desert floor, including a hummingbird, a monkey, a spider, a pelican, a condor, a whale, and an "astronaut," so named because of his goldfish-bowl-shape head. Theories abound as to their purpose, and some have devoted their lives to the study of the Lines. Probably the most famous person to investigate the origin of the Nazca Lines was Kosok's translator, German scientist Dr. Maria Reiche, who studied the Lines from 1940 until her death in 1998. ✉ *Pampas de San José, 20 km (12 miles) north of Nazca town.*

Tallera de Artesania de Andres Calle Flores. Everyone comes to Nazca for the Lines, but it's worth visiting Mr. Flores, a 91-year-old wonder who years ago discovered old pottery remnants and started making new pottery based on old designs and forms. Andres's son, Tobi, hosts a funny and informative talk in the kiln and workshop, and afterward you can purchase some beautiful pottery for S/30 to S/60. It's a quick walk across the bridge from downtown Nazca; at night, take a cab. ✉ *Pje. Torrico 240, off Av. San Carlos* ☎ *056/522–319* 🎟 *Free* 🕒 *By appointment only.*

WHERE TO EAT

$ CHINESE 🍴 **Chifa Nam Kug.** Enduringly popular, this landmark chifa near the Plaza de Armas continues to satisfy the crowds with cheap Chinese fare. There's not much that sets this chifa apart from any other in Peru, but the food is delicious and a two-course lunch is just S/5. Fried rice dominates the menu, but the garlic beef and fried prawns entrées are excellent. [$] *Average main: S/8* ✉ *Bolognesi 448* ☎ *056/522–151* 💳 *No credit cards.*

$ PERUVIAN 🍴 **Restaurant Don Carlos.** For a truly local experience, follow the crowds to this tiny restaurant, which dishes up tasty Peruvian meals in huge portions. The restaurant won't dazzle you with its design, but what it lacks in style it more than makes up for with home-style Peruvian cuisine just like your grandmother used to make (or your grandmother's Peruvian cousin). The set-lunch—a soup, a main course, and a drink—is a steal at only S/4.50 and you may need to fight to get a table. The menu changes daily but specialties include *aji de gallina,* chicken in creamy hollandaise sauce served with boiled rice and a sliced egg.

There's no street sign; look for "Restaurant" painted over the door. $ *Average main: S/20* ✉ *Calle Fermín del Castillo 375* ☎ *056/524–087* ▭ *No credit cards.*

$

PERUVIAN

Fodor's Choice

★

✕ **Via La Encantada.** This stylish eatery on restaurant row adds some class to the Nazca dining scene, which is otherwise dominated by mediocre hotel restaurants. ▮**TIP**➔ With food that is as modern as the decor, this is the best spot in town to try Peruvian-fusion cuisine. The *pollo a lo Oporto*, chicken in a port wine sauce, is a standout, as is the cocktail list, including the tri-color Macchu Pichu pisco cocktail. Head upstairs for a spot on the balcony overlooking the street, and while there, sneak a peek through the back window and you can see the parrilla chef working over the restaurant's giant barbecue. $ *Average main: S/25* ✉ *Calle Bolognesi 282* ☎ *056/524–316* ⊕ *hotellaencantada.com.pe.*

WHERE TO STAY

$

HOTEL

Fodor's Choice

★

🛏 **Casa Andina.** A relative newcomer, this hotel, part of a national chain, offers the best value for the money of any of Nazca's top-end lodgings. **Pros:** Wi-Fi; welcoming service. **Cons:** small pool. $ *Rooms from: S/208* ✉ *Bolognesi 367* ☎ *056/523–563* ⊕ *www.casa-andina.com* 🛏 *60 rooms* ❏*Breakfast.*

$

HOTEL

🛏 **Hotel Alegría.** Long a favorite with travelers, this classic Nazca hotel has recently had a facelift and is now better than ever. **Pros:** friendly staff; good pool; book exchange. **Cons:** smallish rooms; no Internet access; often full. $ *Rooms from: S/156* ✉ *Calle Lima 166* ☎☎ *056/522–702* ⊕ *www.hotelalegria.net* 🛏 *42 rooms, 3 bungalows* ❏*Breakfast.*

$$$$

RESORT

🛏 **Hotel Cantayo Spa & Resort.** At this sprawling hacienda-style resort a 10 minutes' drive from the center of Nasca, the Italian owners have created an eclectic look that adds elements of the Far East to a peaceful farmhouse setting. $ *Rooms from: S/587* ✉ *Pan-American Hwy. S, desvío Puquio Km 3–Km 4* ☎ *056/522–264* ⊕ *www.casahotelperu.com* 🛏 *38 rooms, 2 suites* ❏*Breakfast.*

$

HOTEL

🛏 **Hotel Maison Suisse.** Although a bit worn-looking these days, this long-running hotel across from the airport provides a peaceful green refuge from the Nazca dust. **Pros:** peaceful; convenient for the airport; lovely garden. **Cons:** out of town; small pool; tired decor. $ *Rooms from: S/194* ✉ *Km 445, Pan-American Hwy. S* ☎☎ *056/522–434* ⊕ *www.nazcagroup.com* 🛏 *39 rooms, 6 suites* ❏*Breakfast.*

$$

HOTEL

🛏 **Hotel Majoro.** In fragrant gardens surrounded by cotton fields, this quiet, 80-year-old hacienda and former Augustine convent 1½ km (1 miles) from the airport offers a taste of life on a coastal farm. **Pros:** peaceful atmosphere; charming gardens; good travel services. **Cons:** out of town; popular with tour groups; some airplane noise. $ *Rooms from: S/260* ✉ *Pan-American Hwy. S, Km 452* ☎ *056/522–481, 01/451–3897 in Lima* ⊕ *www.hotelmajoro.com* 🛏 *62 rooms* ❏*Breakfast.*

$$

HOTEL

Fodor's Choice

★

🛏 **Hotel Nazca Lines.** Mixing colonial elegance with all the mod-cons, this once top-end hotel is a Nazca landmark. **Pros:** magnificent pool; nightly lectures; colonial charm. **Cons:** busy staff; tour groups; dated. $ *Rooms from: S/221* ✉ *Jr. Bolognesi 147* ☎ *056/522–293, 01/261–9605 in Lima* 🛏 *78 rooms* ❏*Breakfast.*

The Southern Andes and Lake Titicaca

WORD OF MOUTH

"After a wonderful soak in Chivay's hot springs, we boarded the bus for our trip back to Arequipa. The highway took us over the pass at 14,000 feet or so, where we got to see flocks of both alpacas and vicuñas."

—Yokena

WELCOME TO THE SOUTHERN ANDES AND LAKE TITICACA

TOP REASONS TO GO

★ **Wild Rivers:** Fantastic rapids and gorges make Colca Canyon and Cotahuasi Canyon the region's best-known kayaking and rafting spots.

★ **Folk Fiestas:** Whether it's the Virgen del Candelaria festival in Puno, Arequipa's annual anniversary, or Semana Santa in Chivay, Peru's culture is celebrated with more than 300 festive folkloric dances featuring brightly colored costumes.

★ **Wildlife:** Llamas, vicuñas, and alpacas roam the Reserva Nacional Salinas y Aguada Blanca, giant Andean condors soar above Colca Canyon, and rare bird species nest at Lake Titicaca and in other high mountain lakes.

★ **Shopping:** Along with Arequipa's alpaca stores, this region is also a mine of yarn, leather products, guitars, and antiques.

★ **Floating Islands:** On Lake Titicaca, made from the lake's totora reeds, the series of Uros islands float, providing residence to more than 3,000 Aymará and Quechua inhabitants.

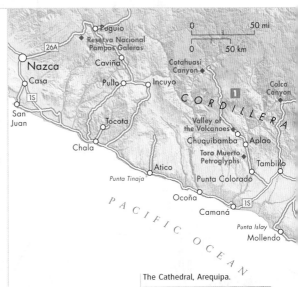

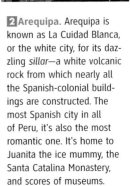

The Cathedral, Arequipa.

1 Canyon Country. Dusty and dry, this is a place of striking geology, wildlife, and history. It's also a playground for adventure sports lovers. Four hours northeast of Arequipa is Colca Canyon, the second deepest gorge in the world. It's home to the intense Río Colca, 14 tiny villages, the giant Andean condor, and great hiking. Ten hours away is Colca's sister gorge, the world's deepest canyon, Cotahuasi Canyon.

2 Arequipa. Arequipa is known as La Cuidad Blanca, or the white city, for its dazzling *sillar*—a white volcanic rock from which nearly all the Spanish-colonial buildings are constructed. The most Spanish city in all of Peru, it's also the most romantic one. It's home to Juanita the ice mummy, the Santa Catalina Monastery, and scores of museums.

GETTING ORIENTED

A good jumping-off point is Arequipa. Acclimatize while taking in the sights, then head to the Colca Canyon. The four-hour drive travels over Patapampa Pass, for views of the Valley of the Volcanoes, and through the Reserva Nacional Salinas y Aguada Blanca, where herds of wild vicuñas, llamas, and alpacas graze. At the canyon you can go on a multiday hike or relax at a resort, but nearly everyone comes to spy condors at Cruz del Condor. Afterward, head back to Arequipa and on to Puno and Lake Titicaca, where you can book an overnight island homestay, visit the floating islands, or see the Sillustani ruins. From Puno some head to Bolivia (⇨ see Chapter 10), while others go to Cusco by train, bus, or plane. Similarly, you can travel to Puno from Cusco and begin your exploration in the opposite direction.

3 **Puno and Lake Titicaca.** Known as the folkloric capital of Peru, Puno's annual festivals shine with elaborate costumes, music, and dancing in the streets. Puno has quality hotels and good restaurants, and it's the jumping-off point to Lake Titicaca, the world's highest navigable lake and the reason travelers come here. Outdoor adventures and unique island cultures are found throughout the lake's 62 islands.

Children in traditional costume

Updated by
Nicholas Gill

Though often overshadowed by Cusco and the Sacred Valley, the south of Peru has some of the most dynamic, jaw-dropping geography and exciting cultural attractions anywhere in the country.

Arequipa, Peru's second-largest city, is a Spanish-colonial maze, with volcanic white sillar buildings, well-groomed plazas, and wonderful food, museums, and designer alpaca products. Arequipa is close to Colca Canyon, where many head to see the famed gorge for its stunning beauty, depth, and Andean condors. Several hours farther out is the very remote Cotahuasi Canyon, the world's deepest gorge.

Second in tourism to Machu Picchu, Lake Titicaca is home to the floating islands. The Uros islands are nearly 40 man-made islands—constructed from the lake's tortora reeds—and are literally floating. The natives are the Quechua and Aymará peoples, who still speak their respective languages.

Puno, an agricultural city on the shores of Titicaca, is the jumping-off point for exploring the lake, and is Peru's folkloric capital. A dusty-brown city most of the time, Puno is a colorful whirlwind during festivals. The region's many fiestas feature elaborate costumes, story-telling dances, music, and lots of merrymaking. Each November and February Puno puts on two spectacular shows for local holidays.

PLANNING

WHEN TO GO

In the mountains and high plains the blistering sun keeps you warm from May through early November, but nights get cold. Rainy season is from mid-November until April, when it's cooler and cloudy, but rain isn't a guarantee. Use sunscreen, even if it's cloudy.

GETTING HERE AND AROUND

AIR TRAVEL

Flights take between 30 minutes and an hour to fly anywhere in southern Peru, and a one-way ticket costs $50 to $150 USD. LAN (⊕ *www.lan.com*) has daily flights between Lima and Rodríguez Ballón

Airport, 7 km (4½ miles) from Arequipa. Peruvian Airlines (⊕ *www. peruvianairlines.com.pe*), Taca (⊕ *www.taca.com*), and Star Peru (⊕ *www.starperu.com*) also have daily flights. Only LAN offers daily flights to Aeropuerto Manco Cápac in Juliaca, the closest airport to Puno and Lake Titicaca. It takes 45 minutes to drive from Juliaca to downtown Puno. Chilean Sky Airlines (⊕ *www.skyairlines.cl*) also flies between Arequipa and several destinations in northern Chile.

BUS TRAVEL

The road between Arequipa and Puno has been paved, so instead of 20 hours the trip now takes only about six. Service is also good between Puno and Cusco, and so is the road between Puno and Copacabana in Bolivia. Cruz del Sur (⊕ *www.cruzdelsur.com.pe*), CIVA, Tour Peru, Inka Express, Flores, and Ormeño (⊕ *www.grupo-ormeno.com.pe*) have offices in Puno and Arequipa, and each runs multiple daily buses between the two cities. For your comfort and safety, take the best service you can afford. There has been crime on night buses from Arequipa to Nazca and from Puno to Cusco. Several bus companies sell tickets that go direct, so buy one of those or be prepared for a long slog during which drivers stop for every passerby. Bus stations in Peru are known for crime, mostly theft of your belongings, so always hold on to your bags.

CAR TRAVEL

Car-rental services are in Arequipa center and at the airport. Keep your car travel to daylight hours: night driving poses a number of risks—blockades, crime on tourists, and steep roads. A 4x4 is needed for the canyons. While the road from Arequipa to Chivay has improved, the last hour of the journey is rough and has steep cliffs. Use even more caution if traveling into Cotahuasi Canyon: only a quarter of the 10-hour ride is paved.

TAXI TRAVEL

Ask any Arequipeño and they'll tell you Arequipa has three major concerns: earthquakes, the looming threat of volcanoes, and taxis.

Arequipa has the most taxis per capita of any city in Peru. Pint-size yellow cars, namely miniature Daewoo Ticos, clog the streets. Pollution is high, accidents aplenty, and rush-hour traffic rivals that of Los Angeles.

About 40 years ago driving taxis became the hot job to have, especially for young people looking to make a quick sole. As the industry grew, immigrants from Bolivia, Chile, and elsewhere came swarming in, creating stiff competition. Soon paying off government agents for valid taxi licenses became commonplace. Officially, this practice no longer occurs, but there remains an overload of little yellow hotwheels. A 2006 United Nations study on air pollution in Arequipa said that on average 50 cars per minute cross the Plaza de Armas. The study also said that since 1992 the number of taxis in Arequipa has increased by more than 250%.

TRAIN TRAVEL

Train travel on PeruRail (⊕ *www.perurail.com*) is slow but scenic, and more relaxing than a bus blasting reggaeton. A Pullman train ticket means more comfort, not to mention a meal and increased security. The train only goes from Cusco to Puno. It's a popular way to take in the dramatic change of scenery as you ride over La Raya Pass at 4,315 meters (14,156 feet). The trip takes about nine hours and includes a stop at the highest point. For a full listing of PeruRail trips, check out ⊕ *www.perurail.com*. It's now possible to book online.

HEALTH AND SAFETY

Visiting mountain towns and Lake Titicaca can bring on *soroche* (altitude sickness). Temporary cures include *mate de coca* (coca tea) and *chancaca* (crystallized pure cane sugar). Drink lots of bottled water and forgo alcohol, coffee, and heavy meals.

Colca Canyon is generally safe, as are Arequipa and Puno. However, don't walk alone at night, know where your money is, and educate yourself on the good and bad parts of town. Police presence has increased in Arequipa. Use only recommended taxi companies or have someone call you one. But walking around the plaza, even at night, is safe in Arequipa. Hiking El Misti alone is not recommended. Puno is generally safe in the tourist areas, but at night the port and the hills should be avoided.

RESTAURANTS

You can find everything from *cuy* (guinea pig) to wood-fired pizza at the many excellent restaurants in Arequipa and Puno, where cuisine ranges from sophisticated Novo Andino cuisine to traditional fare and international grub. Food in Arequipa is known for strong, fresh flavors, from herbs and spices to vegetables served with native Andean foods like alpaca steaks. In the mountains the cool, thin Andean air calls for hearty, savory soups and heaps and heaps of carbs in the form of the potato. Whether they're fried, boiled, baked, with cheese, in soup, or alone, potatoes you will be eating. In Puno fresh fish from the lake is served in almost every restaurant. Puno also has a special affection for adobe-oven, wood-fired pizza. *Prices in the reviews are the average cost of a main course at dinner or, if dinner is not served, at lunch.*

HOTELS

Arequipa and Puno are overloaded with hotels. This is good for you, the traveler, considering that you reap the benefit of great service for a low price. Puno lives and breathes for tourists. While a growing number of resorts and chain hotels are set along the lakeside, most of the properties within the city are small boutique hotels with local owners pining to get in on the tourist boom in this otherwise agricultural town. As a commercial business center, Arequipa has more high-end hotels that cater to business travelers, and given its fame for being the romance city, it also has lots of small inns. *Prices in the reviews are the lowest cost of a standard double room in high season.*

CLOSE UP

On The Menu

With its altitude and cool weather, southern Peru is famous for its hearty and savory soups. Quinoa and potatoes typically provide the base, and with the emergence of Novo Andino cuisine, the addition of meats, vegetables, and spices makes these soups meals unto themselves. Cheese, potatoes, cuy, and quinoa make up the diets in traditional villages around Lake Titicaca and the canyons.

SEAFOOD
In coastal towns you'll dine in *cebicherías* and more upscale *marisquerías* (seafood restaurants). The best are along the coast and in Puno.

cebiche: Fish or shellfish (marinated in lime juice, cilantro, onions, tomatoes, and chilies), served raw as a salad or cocktail and usually accompanied by *canchas,* toasted corn kernels sprinkled with salt. *Cebiche mixto* is a mix of shellfish and fish and is best along the coast.

escabeche: Raw fish and prawns with chilies, cheese chunks, sliced eggs, olives, and onions, found in Arequipa.

MEATS
Cuy chactado: Roasted guinea pig.

Filet de cuy: A Novo Andino style of cuy cut in fillets instead of whole; found in Arequipa.

Lomo a la huancaina: Beef strips with egg and cheese sauce.

Rocoto relleno: Baked spicy red peppers stuffed with ground beef, olives, and queso fresco.

SOUPS AND STEWS
Chupe de camarones: Spicy shrimp stew; found on the coast.

Chupe verde: Potatoes, cheese, eggs, and herbs; found in Arequipa and the canyon country.

Créma de quinoa: Creamed soup made of quinoa. Found in mountainous areas like Lake Titicaca and the canyon country.

Hualpa chupe: Chicken, chilies, and spices; found in Arequipa.

Mollejitas: Chicken innards are a specialty in Arequipa.

Sopa a la criolla: Onions, peppers, and potatoes; found in Arequipa.

DESSERTS
Alfajores: Shortbread.

Churros: Fried dough sprinkled with sugar.

Cocadas al horno: Macaroons.

Ganja blanco: Boiled evaporated milk and sugar mixed with pineapple or peanuts.

Mazamorra morada: Purple maize, cinnamon, milk, and sugar—a specialty from small street stands in Arequipa.

Queso helado: The signature ice cream of Arequipa. Creamy coconut ice cream with cinnamon.

REFRESHMENTS
The fizzy red soda Cola Esococia is the local soda brand. Regional beers include Cusqueña and Arequipeña. *Chicha* (a fermented corn drink) is the national beverage for fiestas and celebrations, not to be confused with *chicha morada* (a nonalcoholic drink from purple corn). *Vino Calliente* is hot-mulled red wine served across the country but especially in the highlands and in Puno.

4

CROSSING INTO CHILE

The border with Chile, about 40 km (25 miles) from Tacna or 440 km (272 miles) from Arequipa, is open daily and very easy to cross. All you need is your passport. From Tacna there are scores of colectivos that will give you a ride to the other side for S/20, or you can take a bus headed to Arica from Tacna, departing hourly. You can also take the train, which leaves several times a day.

Typically, drivers will help with border formalities, even the colectivos. The road journey takes about an hour. Any train aficionado will enjoy the slow, somewhat bumpy, but beautiful train ride from Tacna to Arica, which takes more than an hour and costs S/6.

CANYON COUNTRY

Colca and Cotahuasi canyons, the two deepest canyons on earth, are two of Peru's greatest natural wonders. Colca is the far more visited, more accessible of the two, and recently has a seen a boom in five-star resorts and laid-back family inns. Cotahuasi, a little more than 150 meters (500 feet) deeper than Colca, is much more remote and only reached by the most rugged adventurers, though if you can withstand long, bumpy hours in a car or bus, you'll find an unspoiled terrain rarely visited by outsiders.

COTAHUASI VILLAGE AND VICINITY

379 km (236 miles) north of Arequipa.

Cotahuasi is the largest town in canyon country and the first you'll stumble upon. In the hills at 2,680 meters (8,620 feet), whitewashed colonial-style homes line slim, straight lanes before a backdrop of Cerro Hiunao. Most visitors kick off their stay in this Quechua-speaking community of 3,500 residents, where there are a few basic hostels, restaurants, a small *tienda* (grocery store), a bell tower, and the Plaza de Armas. It's also where most hiking trails begin or end. Many families rent *burros* (mules) to tourists to help carry their load, especially kayakers who walk eight hours down to the gorge with their boats.

Three hours farther south along a thin track against the canyon wall—which climbs to 400 meters (1,312 feet) above the river—you'll reach Chaupo, a settlement surrounded by groves of fruit trees. You can camp here and hike through Velinga to ruins at Huña before reaching Quechualla, where you can see the ancient farming terraces of Maucullachta, an old Wari city across the gorge.

In Cotahuasi Village the route forks, leading northeast along the Río Cotahuasi or due north. Either way is possible by 4x4, colectivo, or on foot. Heading northeast, about 10 km out of town, you'll discover the village of Tomepampa. After that is the small town of Alca, near the hot springs of Luicho. Even farther east is Puica, at 3,700 meters (8,440 feet). Traveling northwest from Cotahuasi Village will lead you to Pampamarca, a town known for weaving exquisite rugs. Two hours by car, Pampamarca is three hours from the hot springs of Josla and Uskuni.

GETTING HERE AND AROUND

Cotahuasi Canyon is a travel destination in the making, but outside of expert extreme sports enthusiasts, few people venture here. If you're not taking a bus or coming with a tour operator, driving anything but

> **ADVANCE PREP**
>
> Cotahuasi is not traveler savvy yet, so it's not possible to show up in a town, buy a map, hire a guide, and get on your way. You'll want to buy a map of the canyon at the Instituto Geográfico Militar in Lima or at the South American Explorers clubhouse in Lima or Cusco.

a 4x4 is asking for trouble. The jagged, rocky dirt roads are full of cliffs and narrow corners. Dry for most of the year, the roads get muddy from December to April (rainy season), a time when you're also likely to encounter random streams flowing across the road.

Hire a guide, regardless of season and not just for safety: Since this region is so remote, you're likely to see a lot more with a guide. All buses travel through the night. Three bus companies go from Arequipa to Cotahuasi daily; each leaves around 5 pm, arriving in Cotahuasi Village in time for sunrise: Transportes Cromotex (☎ 054/421–555), Transportes Reyna (☎ 054/430–612), and Alex Bus (☎ 054/424–605).

TIP→ If you're driving, know that gas stations are few on the long stretch between Corire (near Toro Muerto) and the village of Cotahuasi.

EXPLORING

Cataratas de Sipia. Below the village of Cotahuasi is the valley of Piro, the gateway to the canyon, which is close to this 150-meter (462-foot), 10-meter-wide waterfall. **TIP→** Sipia Falls is the most-visited attraction in the entire canyon.

Cotahuasi Canyon. Colca Canyon may be the region's most famous natural attraction, but at 3,354 meters (11,001 feet), Cotahuasi is the world's deepest gorge, beating Colca Canyon by 163 meters (534 feet). It's nearly twice as deep as the Grand Canyon. The canyon has been carved by the Río Cotahuasi, which changes into the Río Ocuña before connecting to the Pacific. Its deepest point is at Ninochaco, below the quaint administrative capital of Quechualla and accessible only by kayak. Kayak explorations first documented the area in the mid-1990s and measured its depth. Since then, paddling the Cotahuasi River's Class V rapids is to kayakers what scaling Mount Everest is to mountaineers.

The ride from Arequipa to the Cotahuasi Canyon ranks with the great scenic roads of the world. As you pass Corire and Toro Muerto, the road rides the western side of snow-capped Nevado Coropuno (6,424 meters, 21,079 feet), Peru's third-highest volcano, for spectacular views as you descend into the valley of Cotahuasi. **TIP→** Logistically speaking, it's a bumpy 11- to 13-hour bus ride or 10 hours by four-wheel drive from Arequipa. The pavement ends in Chuquibamba. Some of the road from Chuquibamba to Cotahuasi, the longest stretch of the ride, is in the process of being graded. There's no fee to enter the canyon.

4

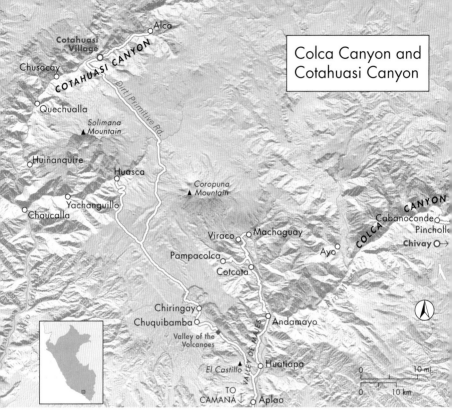

Colca Canyon and Cotahuasi Canyon

Alca

Cotahuasi Village

Chusacay

COTAHUASI CANYON

Quechualla

Dirt Primitive Rd

Solimana ▲ Mountain

Huiñanquire

Huasca

Coropuna ▲ Mountain

Yachanguillo

Chaucalla

COLCA CANYON

Cabanoconde

Pincholle

Chivay O →

Viraco

Machaguay

Ayo

Pampacolca

Cotcota

Río Molles

Chiringayo

Chuquibamba

Andamayo

Valley of the Volcanoes

VALLE DE MAJES

El Castillo

Huatiapa

TO CAMANÁ

Aplao

0   10 mi
0   10 km

SPORTS AND THE OUTDOORS

Many operators in Arequipa and Cusco offer multiday excursions. Most tours are at least four days, five nights, and some last up to 17 nights. A few local hikers provide custom tours for visitors as well.

HIKING

Cotahuasi Canyon is an awesome place to explore by foot. The backdrop of snowcapped Volcano Coropuna and Solimana is fantastic, the high desert plains offer a rest from the steep upward rocky canyon terrain, and the untouched villages provide a cultural aspect. Hikes can go between 1,830 meters (6,000 feet) and 6,400 meters (21,000 feet) in height, so prepare for the altitude. Temperatures remain about 65–70°F during the day, dipping below 45°F on any given night. Ancient Inca paths wind throughout the canyon and its terraces. ■TIP→ Beware: Many of these ancient trails are narrow, rocky, and hang over the side of the canyon. Newer trails parallel some of the ancient ones, and are generally safer.

Sipia Falls is a solid three- to four-hour trek from Cotahuasi Village, and it's a hard-on-your-knees hike down that includes two bridge crossings, but the first taste of being in the canyon is a surreal experience. It's also possible to reach the falls by hailing a colectivo or driving your own 4x4 from the Cotahuasi road to the Sipia Bridge, where the road ends. From here it's a 45-minute hike to the falls.

If you're going on a multiday excursion, continue on the trail from Cotahuasi to Sipia to the Chaupo Valley and the citrus-tree village of Velinga, a good place to camp. From Velinga it's on to Quechualla, where you'll pass through

the 1,000-year-old Wari ruins, rock forests, and cactus forests. One of the last major points along this route is Huachuy, where you can again camp. Beyond this point things get trickier, as you'll have to cross the Rió Cotahuasi. Many guides use a cable system to reach Yachau Oasis, Chaucalla Valley, and eventually Iquipi Valley.

4

WHITE-WATER RAFTING

Kayakers and white-water rafters can challenge the rapids anywhere from the upper Cotahuasi, near the village, almost to the Pacific. The river is divided into four sections: the Headwaters, beginning upstream from Cotahuasi Village, Aimaña Gorge, Flatwater Canyon, and the Lower Canyon.

The Lower Canyon is a mix of Class III and V rapids, without much portage. Most rafting tour operators put in at the village of Velinga and use this part of the river for tours. These tours are done fairly frequently by operators from Arequipa. Depending upon skill level, adventure-craving kayakers tend to put in upriver and have to portage on several occasions.

Kayakers put in at Headwaters in the village of Chuela. Here the rapids ring in at a Class III, but by the time the Aimaña Gorge starts the waters tug at Class V. White-water season is June through November, when the rapids are Class III to V. But the best time to go is mid-May to mid-June. The water is snowmelt, so wet suits are necessary.

CHIVAY

136 km (85 miles) north of Arequipa.

The largest town in the Colca Canyon region is Chivay, a small, battered-looking village with a population of 3,000. Most tourist facilities are here, which are not many, but include restaurants, hotels, a medical clinic, and a tourist information center. As you approach Chivay, you'll pass through a stone archway signifying the town entrance, where AUTOCOLCA, the government authority over Colca Canyon, stops cars to ask if they are headed to see the condors. If you're headed to Cruz del Condor or any of the churches in the 14 villages you must purchase a S/35 entry ticket, which will be asked for again at the entrance of the Mirador. Nearly all agency tours do not include this entry fee in their all price.

Chivay marks the eastern end of the canyon's rim; the other end is Cabanaconde, a developing village where most multiday hikes into the canyon begin and end. As you come into Chivay the road splits off into two: one, less traveled because of its rocky rutted surface, goes along the canyon's northern edge to the villages of Coporaque, Ichupampa, and Lari; the other follows the southern rim, and although it's a bumpy dirt road, it's better for travel and leads to Cruz del Condor and the small towns of Yanque, Maca, and Cabanaconde.

GETTING HERE AND AROUND

You can explore the area by hiring a private guide, renting a four-wheel-drive vehicle, joining a tour from Arequipa, or going by bus. A standard two-wheel-drive car won't do. Arequipa is the jumping-off point for nearly everyone headed to Colca Canyon, and most will either come on a tour or take a bus that stops at either Chivay, the first town you come to, which takes about five hours to reach from Arequipa, or Cabanaconde, about another hour farther. Sporadic combi service links each town in the middle.

> ### VALLEY OF THE VOLCANOES
>
> This spectacular, 65-km (40-mile) crevasse north of Colca Canyon includes a line of 80 extinct craters and cinder cones. Looming over the scene is active Volcán Coropuna, the third-highest peak in Peru. Andagua, at the head of the valley, has the best tourist facilities in the area. The valley is about five hours by a rocky, half-paved, half-dirt road from Colca Canyon. There are several multi-day hikes from Colca Canyon that must be arranged in Arequipa. If you're going to Cotahuasi or Colca Canyon, you're bound to pass through this high-altitude valley.

Chivay is a four-hour drive from Arequipa. The road takes you through the Reserva Nacional Aguada Blanca y Salinas and over the Patapampa Pass, where at 4,825 meters (15,830 feet) you can view nearly the entire Valley of Volcanoes. The road is paved only about half of the way; going toward Patapampa Pass is dirt, but has been graded and smoothed out. The last quarter of the ride is rocky. Most who visit Colca Canyon experience altitude problems along the way, so bring plenty of water. Some of the nicer hotels will have oxygen tanks.

Taxis are a good way to go from town to town if long hikes or mountain biking aren't your thing. Taxis line up around the Plaza de Armas in Chivay. Most rides will cost S/30–S/55.

EXPLORING

Colca Canyon. Flying overhead, you can't miss the green, fertile trough as it cuts through the barren terrain, but it's all an illusion; only scrub brush and cactus cling to the canyon's sheer basalt sides and miles of ancient terraces. ■ TIP➜ The canyon is named for the stone warehouses (colcas) used to store grain by an ancient society living along the walls of the gorge.

Carved into the foothills of the snow-covered Andes and sliced by the silvery Río Colca, Colca Canyon drops 3,182 meters (10,607 feet) down. The more adventurous can embark on a multiday hike into the canyon—typically a two-, three-, or five-day excursion. Bird lovers (and anyone with an eye for amazement) can visit the Cruz del Condor. Culture seekers can spend a night with a native family. Light

Llamas take the high road in Colca Canyon.

hikers and archaeology aficionados can observe points along the rim, or those seeking pure relaxation can hit one of the all-inclusive lodges with horseback riding and thermal baths.

Cruz del Condor is a haunt for the giant birds, particularly at dawn, when they soar on the winds rising from the deep valley. At 1,200 meters (4,000 feet), the "condor cross" precipice, between the villages Pinchollo and Cabanaconde, is the best place to spot them. ■ TIP➔ From June to August you're likely to spot close to 20 or more condors during a morning visit. By October and November many of the female birds are nesting, so your chances of eyeing flocks are slim, but you'll likely spot a few birds.

SPORTS AND THE OUTDOORS

Most organized adventure sport activities should be arranged from Arequipa, especially kayaking, rafting, and multiday treks into the canyon. Many upper-tier hotels and resorts offer packages, have their own tour guides, and have activities like horseback riding and mountain-bike rentals. So check with your hotel before booking anything else. There's only one official tour operator in Chivay, and it specializes in mountain-bike rentals. However, local guides for hiking can be hired by asking around; the most experienced guides are in Cabanaconde and Chivay. The average price is S/80 or $30 USD a day for a local guide.

HIKING

Bring lots of water (the valley has water, but it's grossly expensive, as it's "imported" from Arequipa), sunscreen, a hat, good hiking shoes, high-energy snacks, and sugar or coca leaves to alleviate the altitude sickness. And layer your clothes—one minute the wind may be fierce and the next you may be sweltering in the strong sun.

Along the canyon: Along the south side of the canyon it's possible to do an easy hike from the observation points between Cruz del Condor and Pinchollo. Paths are along the canyon rim most of the way; however, in some places you have to walk along the road. The closer to Cruz del Condor you are, the better the paths and lookouts get.

> ### SCARY BRIDGES
>
> A hallmark of Cotahausi Canyon is its bridges, which are all hanging (and swinging) across the Río Cotahuasi. They're cool to look at, nerve-racking to consider, but there's only one way over.

Another short hike, but more uphill, is on the north rim starting in Coporaque. At the Plaza de Armas, in the corner to the left of the church, you'll see an archway. Go through the archway and take a right uphill and you'll be on the trail, which goes from wide to narrow, but is defined. ■ **TIP→** Following it up about an hour, you'll come to ancient burial tombs (look down) with actual skeletons. The trail climbs up a cliff, which overlooks the valley. It's about a two-hour hike to the top, and in some spots is very steep and rocks are crumbly. After the tombs the path becomes confusing and splits in many directions.

Into the canyon: Trails into the canyon are many as well as rough and unmarked, so venture down with a guide. Several adventure-tour operators provide government-certified hiking guides; local guides are also easily found. Packages range from two- to eight-day treks. The Cabanaconde area is the entry point for most of these.

The most popular multiday hike is the three-day/two-night trek. Starting about 20 minutes (on foot) east of Cabanaconde at Pampa San Miguel, the trail to San Juan Chuccho (one of the larger villages along the river) begins. The steep slope has loose gravel and takes about four hours. In San Juan Chuccho sleeping options are family-run hostels or a campsite. Day two consists of hiking on fairly even terrain through the small villages of Tapay, Cosnirhua, and Malata before crossing the river and into the lush green village of Sangalle, or as locals call it, Oasis, a mini-paradise along the Río Colca, with hot springs and waterfalls. On day three, you'll hike four to five hours uphill to the rim and arrive in Cabanaconde by lunch.

We do not recommend hiking alone here. So many paths are in this area that it can be overwhelming to even the most experienced trekkers.

TOUR OPERATORS IN AREQUIPA For the standard one- or two-day tours of Colca Canyon most agencies pool their customers, so quality varies little.

Carlos Zárate Aventuras. For about S/140 per day you can hire Carlos Zárate Aventuras and his hiking and mountain guides, who conduct tours in Spanish, English, and French. ⊠ *Santa Catalina 204* ☎ *054/263–107* ⊕ *www.zarateadventures.com.*

Colca Trek. Colca Trek is a specialist in longer trekking tours and comes highly recommended. ⊠ *Jerusalén 401-B* ☎ *054/206–217.*

Canyon Life

Quechua farmers once irrigated narrow, stacked terraces of volcanic earth along the canyon rim to make this a productive farming area. These ancient fields are still used for quinoa and kiwicha grains, and barley grown here is used to brew Arequipeña beer.

Most of those who live along the rim today are Collagua Indians, whose settlements date back more than 2,000 years. Their traditions persevered through the centuries. In these unspoiled Andean villages you'll still see Collaguas and Cabana people wearing traditional clothing and embroidered hats. Spanish influence is evident in Achoma, Maca, Pinchollo, and Yanque, with their gleaming white sillar (volcanic-stone) churches.

Steeped in colorful folklore tradition, locals like a good fiesta. Some of the larger festivals include La Virgen del Candelaria, a two-day fiesta in Chivay on February 2 and 3; later in the month Carnivál is celebrated throughout the valley. Semana Santa (holy week) in April is heavily observed, but for a more colorful party don't miss Chivay's annual anniversary fiesta on June 21. From July 14 to 17 the Virgen del Carmen, one of the larger celebrations kicks off with parades on both ends of the canyon: Cabanaconde and Chivay. All Saints Day is well honored on November 1 and 2 as is La Virgen Imaculada on December 8.

Condor Travel. Upscale travelers go with Condor Travel. ☒ *Santa Catalina 210, in La Casona de Santa Catalina shopping center* ☎ *054/237–821* ⊕ *www.condortravel.com* ☒ *Santa Catalina 117.*

Giardino. Slightly less expensive, but still good, is Giardino ☒ *Jerusalén 604-A* ☎ *054/221–345* ⊕ *www.giardinotours.com.*

Land Adventures. Other travelers interested in multiday trekking trips of Colca Canyon, Misti, and Chachani use Land Adventures ☒ *Santa Catalina 118-B* ☎ *054/204–872* ⊕ *www.landadventures.net.*

WHITE-WATER RAFTING

The Río Colca is a finicky river. Highly skilled paddlers long to run this Class IV–V river. Depending upon the season, the water level and the seismic activity of the local volcanoes, the rapids change frequently. In some areas it's more than a Class V and in other areas it's slow enough that it could be considered a Class II–III. Below Colca Canyon conditions on the Río Majes (the large downstream section of the Río Colca) are reliable with superb white-water rafting. Skilled rafters start in Huambo by renting mules for S/20 and for the next eight hours descend to the river. The waters at this point rank in at Class III, but when the Río Mamacocha dumps in, it's Class IV and V rapids.

Paddlers who have tried to run the entire river through the canyon have failed more often than succeeded. There are a few well-known operators to consider, which is important given the river's intensity.

TOUR OPERATORS

Bio Bio Expeditions. The king of all kayaking and rafting operators around the world, Bio Bio Expeditions puts on multiday runs down the Colca and Cotahuasi rivers. All guides are trained in first aid and swiftwater rescue. ⊠ *Jerusalén 408-A, Arequipa* ☎ *800/246–7238* ⊕ *www.bbxrafting.com.*

Apumayo Expediciones. Class IV, V, and VI rafting adventures through the Colca Canyon are operated May through September by Apumayo Expediciones. ⊠ *Garcilaso 316-A, Cusco* ☎🖨 *084/246–018* ⊕ *www. apumayo.com.*

WHERE TO EAT AND STAY

Chivay is tiny, but has plenty of small budget hotels and a few restaurants. You'll come into town on 22 de Agosto, which leads to the Plaza de Armas, where you'll find **Inka's Restaurant and Coffee Bar, McElroy's Pub** (a gringo magnet owned by a true Irishman), and **El Balcón de Don Zacarias**, which serves very good traditional food.

If you're planning on staying one night in Colca Canyon it makes sense to stay in Chivay. If you'll be in the area for longer, we recommend one of the lodges in the valley, which are more inclusive and offer activities like hiking, biking, horseback riding, and have a restaurant on-site.

$
B&B/INN

Casa Andina. This hotel from the national chain of the same name seems like a Swiss ski lodge, with stand-alone bungalow-style cabins made of locally quarried rock. **Pros:** planetarium and observatory; good breakfast; cozy lounge and fireplace. **Cons:** no easy access to the outdoors; small bathrooms. $ *Rooms from: S/222* ⊠ *Calle Huayna Capac s/n, Chivay* ☎ *051/213–9739* ⊕ *www.casa-andina.com* 🛏 *52 rooms* ⦿*Breakfast.*

$$$
RESORT

Colca Lodge. The hotel's understated look, with adobe and clay walls and thatched roof, compliment the terrain. **Pros:** lots of activities; full-service spa; hot springs; solar heating. **Cons:** hot springs are closed in February and March; rooms are plain. $ *Rooms from: S/454* ⊠ *Fundo Puye s/n, Caylloma, Yanque* ☎ *054/202–587* ⊕ *www.colca-lodge.com* 🛏 *45 rooms* ⦿*Breakfast.*

$
B&B/INN

La Casa de Mama Yacchi. Perhaps the best food around, and the best pillows, too. **Pros:** delicious food; good water pressure and pillows. **Cons:** gets cold; far from Cruz del Condor. $ *Rooms from: S/182* ⊠ *Calle Jerusalén 606, Coporaque* ☎ *054/241–206* ⊕ *www. lacasademamayacchi.com* 🛏 *28 rooms* ▭ *No credit cards* ⦿*Breakfast.*

$$$$
RESORT
Fodor's Choice
★

Las Casitas del Colca. It doesn't get better than this, at least not in Colca. **Pros:** beautiful rooms; heated floors; private hot springs; top-notch service. **Cons:** pricey. $ *Rooms from: S/524* ⊠ *Parque Curiña, Yanque* ☎ *051/959–672688* ⊕ *www.lascasitasdelcolca.com* 🛏 *19 rooms, 1 suite* ⦿*Breakfast.*

CLOSE UP

Llamas, Vicunas and Alpacas

Alpaca

Llamas, vicuñas, guanacos, and alpacas roam the highlands of Peru, but unfortunately not in the great herds of pre-Inca times. However, there are always a few around, especially the domesticated llama and alpaca. The sly vicuña, like the guanaco, refuses domestication. Here's a primer on how to tell them apart.

The alpaca is the cute and cuddly one, especially while still a baby. It grows a luxurious, long wool coat that comes in as many as 20 colors, and its wool is used in knitting sweaters and weaving rugs and wall hangings. Its finest wool is from the first shearing, and is called "baby alpaca." When full-grown it's close to 1½ meters (5 feet) tall and weighs about 48 kg (106 pounds). Its size and the shortness of its neck distinguish it from the llama. There are two types of alpaca: the common huancayo with short thick legs; and the less-predominant suri, which is a bit taller, and also nicknamed the Bob Marley for its shaggy curly

dreadlocks that grow around its face and chest.

The guanaco, a cousin of the delicate vicuña, is a thin-legged, wild endangered camelid, with a coarse reddish-brown coat and a soft white underbelly. Its hair is challenging to weave on its own, so often it's mixed with other fibers, like alpaca. The guanaco weighs about 200 pounds and can be up to 5 feet long and 3–4 feet high. Eighty percent of guanacos live in Patagonia, but the other 20% are scattered across the altiplano of southern Peru, Chile, and Bolivia. It's the only camelid that can live both at sea level and in the high-altitude Andes.

The llama is the pack animal with a coarse coat in as many as 50 colors, though one that's unsuitable for weavings or fine wearing apparel. It can reach almost 2 meters (6 feet) from its hoofs to the top of its elongated neck and long, curved ears. It can carry 40–60 kilograms (88–132 pounds), depending on the length of the trip. It can also have some nasty habits, like spitting in your eye or kicking you if you get too close to its hind legs.

The vicuña has a more delicate appearance. It will hold still (with help) for shearing, and its wool is the most desirable. It's protected by the Peruvian government, as it was almost killed off by unrestricted hunting. It's the smallest of the Andean camelids, at 1.3 meters (4 feet), and weighs about 40 kg (88 pounds) at maturity. It's found mostly at altitudes over 3,600 meters (12,000 feet).

—By Joan Gonzalez

4

$ B&B/INN 🏨 **Pozo del Cielo.** Across the river on top of a hill on the outskirts of Chivay sits one of the most quaint lodges in the valley. **Pros:** hot-water bottles at bedtime for extra warmth; on the outskirts of Chivay; good views. **Cons:** must walk outside to get to breakfast; no closets. [$] *Rooms from: S/248* ✉ *Calle Huáscar B-3 Sacsayhuaman, Chivay* ☎ *054/346–547* 🌐 *www.pozodelcielo.com.pe* 🛏 *20 rooms* 🍴 *Breakfast.*

BRING CASH!

There are ATMs in Chivay but nowhere else in the Colca Canyon or valley area. Soles and U.S. dollars (no bills larger than $10 USD) are accepted.

HOMESTAYS In the small settlements of Cabanaconde, Coporaque, Ichupampa, Madrigal, and Yanque you can experience local life by staying with families. In addition to exploring ruins and historic sites with family guides, you'll help out with daily chores and participate in seasonal festivities. This option is difficult to arrange in advance and from afar, but possible. Colonial Tours in Arequipa can make advance arrangements, but details will be limited. These types of trips cost only about $35–$40 USD, including private transportation to the canyon from Arequipa.

If you don't mind uncertainty, it's quite simple to come to Chivay or Cabanaconde and ask around about staying with a family. Locals are friendly and know families in the canyon who want visitors. Arriving as early as possible is essential. It takes a few hours to network, find a family, and travel to their village.

AREQUIPA

150 km (93 miles) south of Colca Canyon; 200 km (124 miles) south of Cotahuasi Canyon.

Cradled by three steep, gargantuan, snow-covered volcanoes, the jaw-dropping white-stoned Arequipa (population 58,000), one of the most visually stunning cities in Peru, shines under the striking sun at 2,350 meters (7,709 feet). This settlement of 1 million residents grew from a collection of Spanish-colonial churches and homes constructed from white sillar (volcanic stone) gathered from the surrounding terrain. The result is nothing less than a work of art—short, gleaming white buildings contrast with the charcoal-color mountain backdrop of El Misti, a perfectly shaped cone volcano.

The town was a gathering of Aymará Indians and Inca when Garci Manuel de Carbajal and nearly 100 more Spaniards founded the city on August 15, 1540. After the Spanish arrived, the town grew into the region's most profitable center for farming and cattle-raising—businesses still important to Arequipa's economy. The settlement was also on the silver route linking the coast to the Bolivian mines. By the 1800s Arequipa had more Spanish settlers than any town in the south.

Arequipeños call their home Cuidad Blanca, "White City," and the "Independent Republic of Arequipa"—they have made several attempts to secede from Peru and even designed the city's own passport and flag. Today the town is abuzz with adventure outfitters leading tours in the surrounding canyons, bars and cafés in 500-year-old sillar buildings, and the finest alpaca threads anywhere in the country. ■ **TIP→** On August 15, parades, fireworks, bullfights, and dancing celebrate the city's founding.

Arequipa enjoys fresh, crisp air, and warm days averaging 23°C (73°F) and comfortable nights at 14°C

(57°F). To make up for the lack of rain, the Río Chili waters the surrounding foothills, which were once farmed by the Inca and now stretch into rows of alfalfa and onions.

GETTING HERE AND AROUND

Arequipa's airport is large, and it's easy to hail a taxi to your hotel. Many hotels also offer pickup and drop-off. The cost is about S/15.

Walking is the best option around the city center. Most sights, shops, and restaurants are near the Plaza de Armas. For a quick, cheap tour, spend S/5 and catch a Vallecito bus for a 1½-hour circuit around Calles Jerusalén and San Juan de Díos. Taxis are everywhere, and cost about S/3–S/6 to get around the center or to Vallecito.

Arequipa has two bus terminals side by side on Avenida Ibañez and Avenida Andrés Avelino Cáceres. Most people leave out of the older Terminal Terreste, where most bus companies have offices, while the newer terminal Terrapuerto sees less traffic.

TIMING

Most sites are open morning and afternoon, but close for a couple of hours at midday. Churches usually open 7 to 9 am and 6 to 8 pm, before and after services.

SAFETY AND PRECAUTIONS

Wear comfortable walking shoes and bring a hat, sunscreen, a Spanish dictionary, some small change, and a good map of town. Be street-smart in the Arequipa market area—access your cash discreetly and keep your valuables close. At 2,300 meters (7,500 feet), Arequipa is quite high. If you're coming directly from Lima or from the coast, carve out a day or two for acclimatization.

ESSENTIALS

Currency Banco Continental BBVA ⊠ *San Francisco 108* ☎ *054/215–060.* **Banco de Crédito BCP** ⊠ *San Juan de Dios 123* ☎ *054/283–741.* **Banco de Trabajo** ⊠ *Calle Moral 201.* **Caja Municipal Arequipa** ⊠ *La Merced 106.* **Scotiabank** ⊠ *Mercaderes 410.*

Internet C@tedral Internet ⊠ *Pasaje Catedral 101* ☎🖨 *054/282–074.* **Cybermarket** ⊠ *Santa Catalina 115* ☎🖨 *054/284–306.*

Mail DHL ⊠ *Santa Catalina 115* ☎ *054/234–288.***SERPOST Arequipa** ⊠ *Calle Moral 118* ☎ *054/215–247* ⊕ *www.serpost.com.pe* ☾ *Mon.–Sat. 8–8, Sun. 9–2.*

Medical Clínica Arequipa SA ⊠ *Puente Grau y Av. Bolognesi* ☎ *054/599–000.* **Honorio Delgado Espinoza Regional Hospital** ⊠ *Av. A. Carrión s/n*

☎ *054/231–818 or 054/219–702.* **Hospital Goyeneche** ✉ *Av. Goyeneche s/n, Cerado* ☎ *054/231–313.*

Police Police ✉ *Av. Emmel 106, Yanahuara* ☎ *054/254–020.* **Policía de Tourismo** ✉ *Jerusalén 315* ☎ *054/201–258.*

Rental Car Akal Rent A Car ✉ *Francisco Mostajo 204, Yanahuara* ☎ *054/272–663* ⊕ *www.akalrentacar.com.* **Exodo** ✉ *Manuél Belgrado F-1, Urb. Alvarez Thomas* ☎ *054/423–756.* **Hertz** ✉ *Palacio Viejo 214* ☎ *054/282–519* ⊕ *www.hertz.com* ✉ *Rodriguez Ballón Airport* ☎ *054/445–576* ⊕ *www.hertz.com.*

Taxi 454545 ☎ *054/454–545.***Taxi Turismo Arequipa** ☎ *054/458–888 or 054/459–090* ⊕ *www.taxiturismo.com.pe.*

Visitor Information Iperu Oficina de Información Turística ✉ *Portal de la Municipalidad 110, Plaza de Armas* ☎ *054/223–265* ✉ *Santa Catalina 210, Casona Santa Catalina* ☎ *054/221–227* ✉ *Rodríguez Ballón Airport, 1st fl., Main Hall* ☎ *054/444–564.* **Touring and Automobile Club of Peru** ✉ *Goyeneche 313* ☎ *054/603–131 or 054/603–333.*

EXPLORING

TOP ATTRACTIONS

Casa del Moral. One of the oldest architectural landmarks from the Arequipa Baroque period was named for the ancient *mora* tree (mulberry tree) growing in the center of the main patio. One of the town's most unusual buildings, it now houses the Banco Sur, but it's open to the public. Over the front door, carved into a white sillar portal, is the Spanish coat of arms as well as a baroque-mestizo design that combines puma heads with darting snakes from their mouths—motifs found on Nazca textiles and pottery. The interior of the house is like a small museum with alpaca rugs and soaring ceilings, polished period furniture, and a gallery of colonial period Cusco School paintings. Originally a lovely old colonial home, it was bought in the 1940s by the British consul and renovated to its former elegance in the early 1990s. ✉ *Moral 318 and Bolívar* ☎ *054/285–371* 🎟 *S/6* ⊙ *Mon.–Sat. 9–5, holidays 9–1.*

Fodor's Choice **Catedral.** You can't miss the imposing twin bell towers of this 1612 ★ cathedral, whose facade guards the entire eastern flank of the Plaza de Armas. ■**TIP→** As the sun sets the imperial reflection gives the Cathedral an amber hue. The inside has high-vaulted ceilings above a beautiful Belgian organ. The ornate wooden pulpit, carved by French artist Rigot in 1879, was transported here in the early 1900s. In the back, look for the Virgin of the Sighs statue in her white wedding dress, and the figure of Beata Ana de Los Angeles, a nun from the Santa Catalina monastery who was beatified by Pope John Paul II when he stayed in Arequipa in 1990. A fire in 1844 destroyed much of the cathedral, as did an 1868 earthquake, so parts have a neoclassical look. In 2001 another earthquake damaged one of the bell towers, which was repaired to match its sister tower. ✉ *Plaza de Armas, between Santa Catalina and San Francisco* ☎ *054/23–2635* 🎟 *S/7* ⊙ *Daily 7–11 and 4–7.*

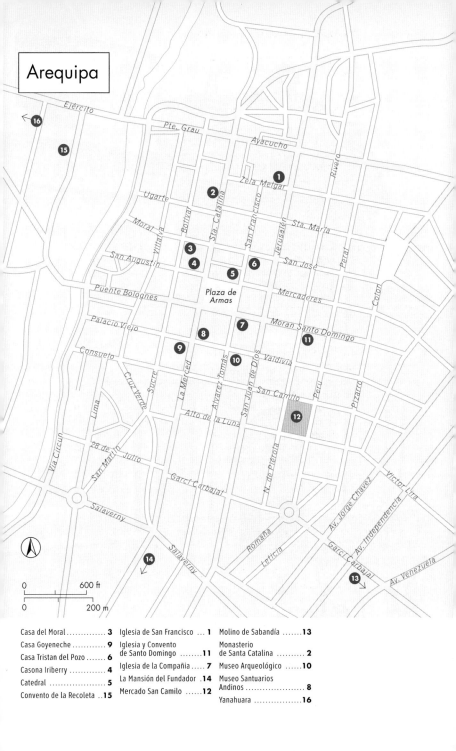

Arequipa

Iglesia de la Compañía. Representative of 17th-century religious architecture, the complex was built by the Jesuits in 1573. ■TIP➡ A series of bone-white buildings incorporate many decorative styles and touches. The detail carved into the sillar arcades is spectacular. The side portal, built in 1654, and main facade, built in 1698, show examples of Andean mestizo style with carved flowers, spirals, birds—and angels with Indian faces—along gently curving archways and spiral pillars. Inside, **Capilla St. Ignatius** (St. Ignatius Chapel) has a polychrome cupola and 66 canvases from the Cusco School, including original 17th-century oil paintings by Bernardo Bitti. Hike up to the steeple at sunset for sweeping views of Arequipa. The former monastery houses some of the most upscale stores in the city and contains two cloisters, which can be entered from General Morán or Palacio Viejo. The main building is on the southeast corner of the Plaza de Armas. ⊠ *General Morán at Álvarez Tomás* ☎ *054/21–2141* ⌖ *Chapel S/6* ☉ *Church weekdays 9–12:30 and 3–6:30, Sat. 3–4:30, Sun. 5–6 pm.*

♻ **Monasterio de Santa Catalina.** A city unto itself, this 5-acre complex of
Fodor'sChoice mud-brick, Iberian-style buildings surrounded by vibrant fortress-like
★ walls and separated by neat, open plazas and colorful gardens, is a working convent and one of Peru's most famed cultural treasures. ■TIP➡ Founded in 1579 and closed to the public for the first 400 years, Santa Catalina was an exclusive retreat for the daughters of Arequipa's wealthiest colonial patrons. Visitors can catch a peek at life in this historic monastery. Narrow streets run past the Courtyard of Silence, where teenage nuns lived during their first year, and the Cloister of Oranges, where nuns decorated their rooms with lace sheets, silk curtains, and antique furnishings. Though about 400 nuns once lived here, fewer than 30 do today. Admission includes a one-hour guided tour (tip S/10–S/20) in English. Afterward, head to the cafeteria for the nuns' famous *torta de naranja* (orange cake), pastries, and tea. There are night tours on Tuesday and Thursday, but check the times before you go, as they sometimes change. ⊠ *Santa Catalina 301* ☎ *054/221–213* ⊕ *www. santacatalina.org.pe* ⌖ *S/35* ☉ *Mon., Fri.–Sun. 8–5; Tues.–Thurs. 8–8. Last entry 1 hr before closing.*

Fodor'sChoice **Museo Santuarios Andinos.** Referred to as the Juanita Museum, this fas-
★ cinating little museum at the Universidad Católica Santa Maria holds the frozen bodies of four young girls who were apparently sacrificed more than 500 years ago by the Inca to appease the gods. The "Juanita" mummy, said to be frozen around the age of 13, was the first mummy found in 1995 near the summit of Mt. Ampato by local climber Miguel Zarate and anthropologist Johan Reinhard. ■TIP➡ When neighboring Volcán Sabancaya erupted, the ice that held Juanita in her sacrificial tomb melted and she rolled partway down the mountain and into a crater. English-speaking guides will show you around the museum, and you can watch a video detailing the expedition. ⊠ *La Merced 110* ☎☎ *054/215–013* ⌖ *S/15* ☉ *Mon.–Sat. 9–6, Sun. 9–3.*

WORTH NOTING

Casa Goyeneche. This attractive Spanish-colonial home was built in 1888. Ask the guard for a tour, and you'll enter through a pretty courtyard and an ornate set of wooden doors to view rooms decorated in

Courtyard in Monasterio de Santa Catalina, Arequipa

period-style antiques and Cusco School paintings. ✉ *La Merced 201 y Palacio Viejo* ☎ *054/352–674* 🖹 *Free, but if you get a tour a small donation is expected* ⊗ *Weekdays 9:15–3.*

Casa Tristan del Pozo. This small museum and art gallery was built in 1738 and is now the Banco Continental. Look for the elaborate puma heads spouting water. Inside you'll find colonial paintings, ornate Peruvian costumes, and furniture. ✉ *San Francisco 108* ☎ *054/21–1101* 🖹 *Free* ⊗ *Weekdays 9:15–6:30, Sat. 9:30–12:30.*

Casona Iriberry. Unlike the other mansions, Casona Iriberry has religious overtones. Small scriptures are etched into its structure, exemplifying Arequipa's catholic roots. The back of the house is now the Centro Cultural Cháves la Rosa, which houses some of the city's most important contemporary arts venues, including photography exhibits, concerts, and films. The front of the compound is filled with colonial-period furniture, paintings, and decor. ✉ *Plaza de Armas, San Augustin y Santa Catalina* ☎ *054/20–4482* 🖹 *Free to look around, admission price for certain events* ⊗ *Mon.–Sat. 9–1 and 4–8.*

Convento de la Recoleta. One of Peru's most extensive and valuable libraries is in this 1648 Franciscan monastery. With several cloisters and museums on-site, it's a wonderful place to research regional history and culture. Start in the massive, wood-paneled, wood-floored library, where monks in brown robes quietly browse 20,000 ancient books and maps, the most valuable of which were printed before 1500 and are kept in glass cases. Pre-Columbian artifacts and objects collected by missionaries to the Amazon are on display, as is a selection of elegant colonial and religious artwork. Guides are available, just remember to tip. To reach the monastery, cross the Río Chili by Puente Grau. It's a 10- to 15-minute walk from the Plaza de Armas. ⊠ *Recoleta 117* ☎ *054/27–0966* 🖅 *S/5* ◷ *Mon.–Sat. 9–noon and 3–5.*

Iglesia de San Francisco. This 16th-century church has survived numerous natural disasters, including several earthquakes that cracked its cupola. Inside, near the polished silver altar, is the little chapel of the Sorrowful Virgin, where the all-important Virgin Mary statue is stored. ▉ **TIP→** On December 8, during Arequipa's Feast of the Immaculate Conception, the Virgin is paraded around the city all night atop an ornate carriage and surrounded by images of saints and angels. A throng of pilgrims carry flowers and candles. Visit the adjoining convent (S/5) to see Arequipa's largest painting and a museum of 17th-century religious furniture and paintings. ⊠ *Zela 103* ☎ *054/223–048* 🖅 *Free* ◷ *Church: Weekdays 7–10 am and 4–8, Sat 4–8, Sun. 7–12:45 and 6–8. Convent: Mon.–Sat. 9–noon and 3–5.*

Iglesia y Convento de Santo Domingo. With hints of Islam in its elegant brick arches and stone domes, this cathedral carries an aura of elegance. Step inside to view simple furnishings and sunlight streaming through stained-glass windows as small silver candles flicker along the back wall near the altar. A working Dominican monastery is in back. ⊠ *Santo Domingo y Piérola* ☎ *054/213–511* 🖅 *Free* ◷ *Weekdays 7–noon and 3:30–7:45, Sat. 6:45–9 and 3–7:45, Sun. 5:30–1.*

La Mansión del Fundador. First owned by the founder of Arequipa Don Garcí Manuel de Carbajal, La Mansión del Fundador is a restored colonial home and church. Alongside the Río Sabandía, the sillar-made home perches over a cliff and is about 20 minutes from the center of town. Said to have been built for Carbajal's son, it became a Jesuit retreat in the 16th century and in the 1800s was remodeled by Juan Crisostomo de Goyeneche y Aguerreverre. While intimate, the chapel is small and simple, but the home is noted for its vaulted arch ceilings and spacious patio. There's also a cafeteria with a bar on-site. To reach the home, go past Tingo along Avenida Huasacanche. ⊠ *Av. Paisajesta s/n, about 6.5 km outside of Arequipa, Socobaya* ☎ *054/442–460* ⊕ *www. lamansiondelfundador.com* 🖅 *S/12* ◷ *Daily 9–5.*

Mercado San Camilo. This jam-packed collection of shops sells everything from snacks and local produce to clothing and household goods. It's an excellent place to spot rare types of potatoes, sample queso helado, or eat *chicharrones* (deep-fried pork). It's on Calle San Camilo, between Avenidas Peru and Piérola. ⊠ *San Camilo 352* 🖅 *Free* ◷ *Daily 7–5.*

Molino de Sabandía. There's a colorful story behind the area's first stone *molina* (mill), 7 km (4 miles) southeast of Arequipa. Built in 1621 in the gorgeous Paucarpata countryside, the mill fell into ruin over the next century. Famous architect Luis Felipe Calle was restoring the Arequipa mansion that now houses the Central Reserve Bank in 1966 when he was asked to work on the mill project. By 1973 the restoration of the volcanic-stone structure was complete—and Calle liked the new version so much that he bought it, got it working again, and opened it for visitors to tour. Bring your swimsuit and walking shoes in good weather;

Short Trips from Arequipa

Reserva Nacional Salinas y Aguada Blanca. Herds of beige-and-white vicuñas, llamas, and alpacas graze together on the sparse plant life in the midst of the open fields that encompass this vast nature reserve of desert, grass, and flamingo-filled lakes. Wear good walking shoes for the uneven terrain and bring binoculars. Also bring a hat, sunscreen, and a warm jacket, as the park sits at a crisp 3,900 meters (12,800 feet). The reserve is 35 km (22 miles) north of Arequipa, just beyond El Misti. If you're headed to Colca Canyon or Puno from Arequipa, you have to pass through the reserve to get there.

Yura. About a half-hour drive from Arequipa, this serene little town is settled in the western foothills of the Volcán Chachani. Take the road 27 km (17 miles) farther to reach these rustic thermal baths where you can take a dip in naturally heated water that ranges from 70 to 82°F. You can soak in any weather and enjoy a picnic along the river in summertime. Admission to the hot springs is S/10, and they're open daily from sunrise until 3 pm. From San Juan de Dios, you can catch buses to Yura for S/3.

there's a pool and trails around the lovely countryside. Adjoining the site is Yumina, which has numerous Inca agricultural terraces. If you're not driving, flag a taxi for S/20 or take a colectivo from Socabaya in Arequipa to about 2 km (1 miles) past Paucarpata. ⊠ *8 km (5 miles) south of Arequipa, Sabandia* ⌨ *S/7* ☉ *Daily 9–5.*

Museo Arqueológico. With a solid collection of native pottery and textiles, human-sacrificed bones, along with gold and silver offerings from Inca times, this archaeology museum at the Universidad de San Augustín provides a background on local archaeology and ruins. Apply to the director for an appointment to visit; once you're approved, you'll have an expert guide to tell all the stories behind the displays. ⊠ *Av. Independencia, between La Salle y Santa Rosa* ☎ *054/288–881* ⌨ *S/3* ☉ *Weekdays 9–4.*

Yanahuara. The eclectic little suburb of Yanahuara, northwest of the city, is perfect for lunch or a late afternoon stroll. The neighborhood is above Arequipa and has amazing views over the city at the lookout constructed of sillar stone arches. On a clear day views of volcanos El Misti, Chachani, and Picchu can be had. Stop in at the 1783, mestizo-style Iglesia Yanahuara. The interior has wrought-iron chandeliers and gilt sanctuaries surrounding the nave. Ask to see the glass coffin that holds a statue of Christ used in parades on holy days. To reach Yanahuara, head across the Avenida Grau bridge, then continue on Avenida Ejército to Avenida Lima, and from here, it's five blocks to the Plaza. It's a 15-minute walk or an eight-minute cab ride from the city center.

WHERE TO EAT

Comida Arequipa (Arequipan cuisine) is a special version of *comida criolla*. Perhaps the most famous dish is *rocoto relleno*, a large, spicy red pepper stuffed with meat, onions, and cheese. Other specialties to try are *cuy chactado* (roasted guinea pig), and *adobo* (pork stew), a local cure for hangovers. *Picanterías* are where locals head for good, basic Peruvian meals and cold Arequipeña beer served with *cancha* (fried, salted corn kernals).

The west side of the Plaza de Armas has dozens of restaurants along the balcony above the Portal San Augustín. The first blocks of Calle San Francisco and Calle Santa Catalina north of the Plaza de Armas are lined with cafés, restaurants, and bars.

$ ✕ **Café Peña Anuschka.** European expats and travelers craving the sour
GERMAN flavorings of German cuisine frequent this busy, dinner-only restaurant. You can also drop in after supper for a fruity cocktail or coffee and a freshly baked German pastry. The café, open 7–9 pm, transforms into a peña with live music Friday and Saturday nights. $ *Average main: S/15* ⊠ *Santa Catalina 204* ☎ *054/213–221* ▭ *No credit cards* ⊘ *Closed Sun. No lunch.*

$ ✕ **Chi Cha.** Celebu-chef Gastón Acurio's stylish Peruvian bistro serves
PERUVIAN up a wide range of contemporary Peruvian fare ranging from regional
Fodor'sChoice specialties to national plates in what feels like a trendy extension of the
★ Santa Catalina monastery, right across the street. Start your meal with a pisco-based cocktail that uses Peruvian fruits like tumbo or camu camu, and then make your way around the menu sampling traditional Arequipeñan dishes such as adobo or rocoto relleno, or more creative, Novo Andino plates like the chupe de camarones pizza and alpaca ossobuco. $ *Average main: S/30* ⊠ *Santa Catalina 210* ☎ *054/28–7360* ⊕ *www.chicha.com.pe.*

$ ✕ **Crepisimo.** This artistic, Euro-styled restaurant offers more than 100
FRENCH crepes, filled with a variety of sauces, as entrées and desserts. Little sister to the Zig Zag restaurant on Calle Zela, look for such crêpe specialties as the *Cubana*, filled with banana slices, sugar, and rum. Exotic fruit juices like the *boa–boa* (tropical fruit punch) can be had, as can a glass of *vino* (wine) or high-grade espresso drinks. Check out the terrace for great views of the Monastery de Santa Catalina and volcanoes. Look for the restaurant in the Alianza Francesa compound. Open until 11:30. $ *Average main: S/22* ⊠ *Santa Catalina 208* ☎ *054/206–020* ⊕ *www. crepisimo.com.*

$ ✕ **Cusco Coffee Company.** If you're missing home, this Starbucks-esque
CAFÉ coffee shop, owned by a Peruvian and American couple, will fix any caffeine craving. You can order-up fresh ground coffee drinks, or if tea is your thing, go for a maté (try the eucalyptus), and there's a small selection of desserts. Comfortable leather couches make this a great place to plan your day or read the *International Herald Tribune*. $ *Average main: S/8* ⊠ *La Merced 135* ☎ *054/281–152.*

$ ✕ **El Mesón del Virrey.** This spacious upscale restaurant is donned in
PERUVIAN antiqued Spanish-colonial motif. The meat-heavy menu is infused with Italian and coastal influences. ■**TIP➔** Quinoa con camarones (quinoa

with shrimp) is one of the best dishes in Arequipa. Much like a risotto, the quinoa is cooked in a creamy tomato sauce with vegetables and a large fresh jumbo-size shrimp that looks more like a lobster. Lamb, beef, alpaca, and ostrich can also be enjoyed. The pisco sour is one of the best around. Hear live music nightly from 8 to 10. [$] *Average main: S/20* ✉ *San Francisco 305* ☎ *054/202–080.*

$ FAST FOOD 🍴 **El Turko.** If you thought Arequipa, like most other Peruvian cities, lacked variety in terms of its restaurants, guess again. This local fast-food chain serving doner kebabs—sometimes including Peruvian sauces like *ocopa* or local sausages—is in a beautiful colonial building with rescued murals, and it's one of the town's best places for an inexpensive, quick bite at any time of the day. There are additional locations in surrounding districts. [$] *Average main: S/10* ✉ *San Francisco 225* ☎ *054/227–779* 🌐 *www.elturko.com.pe.*

$ SEAFOOD Fodor's Choice ★ 🍴 **Fory Fay Cevicheria.** Ask any Arequipeño to name their favorite fish joint and Fory Fay tops the list. For more than two decades they've served some of the freshest cebiche around. Personable owner Alex Aller grew up in the coastal port of Mollendo and travels there often to check on the catch. Fishing bric-a-brac and photos of New York, where Aller once lived, line the walls. [$] *Average main: S/15* ✉ *Alvarez Thomas 221* ☎ *054/242–400* ⏲ *No dinner.*

$ CAFÉ 🍴 **Helados Artika.** The small, retro-style *helados* (ice-cream) café next to La Compañía is the perfect stop after shopping around town. We recommend the famous Arequipeño *queso helado*, or cheese ice cream—it's sweet milk with cinnamon and a dash of coconut. If you're in for a fruitier treat go for a scoop of the guanabana. Open from 8 am until 10 pm. [$] *Average main: S/8* ✉ *Morán 120* ☎ *054/284–915* 💳 *No credit cards.*

$ PERUVIAN Fodor's Choice ★ 🍴 **La Nueva Palomino.** Chef Monica Huertas, who uses many of the same classic recipes her mother and her grandmother used that date back more than a century, is one of the great promoters of Arequipeñan cuisine. Her preparations of regional standards such as rocoto relleno, adobo, *lechón al horno* (oven roasted pork), chupe de camarones, and queso helado have become the definitive recipes. This sprawling *picanteria* (simple, traditional restaurant) with a maze of pleasant patios and dining rooms is a great place to come to on the weekend and spend the entire day eating, drinking, and listening to live music. [$] *Average main: S/25* ✉ *Psje Leoncio Prado 122, Yanahuara* ☎ *054/252–393* ⏲ *No dinner.*

$$ ITALIAN 🍴 **La Trattoria del Monasterio.** This intimate restaurant serves some of the best Italian food in southern Peru. Its location in the Monasterio de Santa Catalina (the entrance is outside the compound) is enough to make this place special. Homemade pastas, ravioli, gnocchi, risottos, paired with seafood, meats and creative, savory sauces are offered. There's an extensive wine list. [$] *Average main: S/40* ✉ *Santa Catalina 309* ☎ *054/204–062.*

$ VEGETARIAN 🍴 **Lakshmivan.** A herbivore's paradise, this tasty vegetarian restaurant will delight any traveler in search of leafy greens. Inexpensive and mostly organic, it's been an Arequipa staple for nearly three decades. Specializing in soups and salads (16 different kinds), all meals fuse

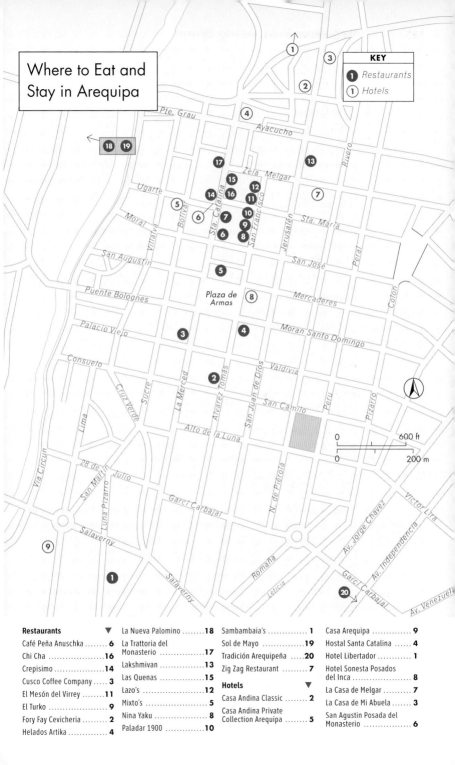

Where to Eat and Stay in Arequipa

KEY

🛈 Restaurants
① Hotels

healthy ingredients with Peruvian flavors. You can sit outside in the courtyard among the colorful blossoms and birds, or inside, amid dazzling watercolor portraits by local artists. [$] *Average main: S/12* ✉ *Jerusalén 408* ☎ *054/228–768* 💳 *No credit cards.*

$ PERUVIAN 🍴 **Las Quenas.** This rustic restaurant, filled with antiques and musical instruments, offers complete immersion into Arequipeñan life and traditions. Lunch and tea are served daily, but set dinners are the specialty, served nightly except Sunday to the accompaniment of a live folkloric performance. Dinners start at 8, and there's an extra S/5 charge if you stay for the music, which lasts until after midnight. [$] *Average main: S/16* ✉ *Santa Catalina 302* ☎ *054/281–115* 🕒 *Closed Sun.*

$ STEAKHOUSE 🍴 **Lazos.** With the same owner as Zingaro next door and Crepisimo nearby, this is Arequipa's finest *parrilla*. Meat is what you come here for—and they have lots of it, from thick regional cuts like Peruvian *picana* and Argentine *asado de tira* to alpaca served with a passion fruit sauce. The beautiful, narrow, arched dining room with white sillar walls makes you question whether you should be paying more for the expertly cooked meat. **TIP→ The wine list is quite global, though you'll find better values if you stick with Argentina and Chile.** [$] *Average main: S/24* ✉ *San Francisco 313* ☎ *054/215–729.*

$ SEAFOOD 🍴 **Mixto's.** Above the Catedral, this ultraromantic spot serves up some great seafood dishes. Cebiche is the focus, but you'll also find shellfish empanadas and mixed stews. They also serve pastas, salads, and grilled meats. It's not the culinary gem it once was, but the food remains good and it's a beautiful spot. On the terrace above the Catedral entrance, the views of the city and El Misti are stunning. [$] *Average main: S/25* ✉ *Pasaje Catedral 115* ☎ *054/205–343.*

$ PERUVIAN 🍴 **Nina Yaku.** This exclusive Novo Andino restaurant creates innovative Peruvian-style pastas, meats, and vegetarian dishes, all presented artfully. Drizzled in flavorful sauces, from sweet and tangy to savory and rich, the alpaca and beef are especially appetizing. It's a relaxing spot for after-dinner cocktails; ask for the *vino caliente,* mulled hot red wine. [$] *Average main: S/18* ✉ *San Francisco 211* ☎ *054/281–432* 🕒 *Closed Sun.*

$ PERUVIAN Fodor's Choice ★ 🍴 **Paladar 1900.** The latest eatery from the restaurateur known as El Turko is by far his best yet and easily one of Arequipa's top restaurants. The contemporary digs, which have moved from Calle Villaba to a more pedestrian-friendly location on Calle San Francisco, are the place where Arequipa's sophisticated elite come to wine and dine. The lengthy menu is adventurous and travels to the Mediterranean, Middle East, Southeast Asia, Switzerland, and of course, Peru. Start with the Escribano fusion, a typical Arequipeñan salad that adds octopus, and then move on to one of the heartier entrées like the Bardo Immortal (corn cake stuffed with shrimp tails) or a 350-gram cut of Argentinian Bife Ancho. Finish your evening with a lucuma version of the classic Peruvian sweet, *suspiro a la limeña*, or a shot of pisco. Note: Paladar's pisco and wine selections are tops in the city. [$] *Average main: S/30* ✉ *San Francisco 227* ☎ *054/226–295* 🌐 *www.paladar.com.pe.*

$
PERUVIAN
✗ **Sambambaia's.** Specializing in classic Andean meat and fish dishes, try the chef's favorite, a tender, juicy lomo al vino tinto, but if you're craving more familiar fare, order a wood-oven pizza or the grilled chicken. Live Latin jazz plays on Friday nights; if you're not eating dinner, you can pay S/5 for the performance, which begins at 8. In the quiet residential neighborhood of Vallecito, it's a 10-minute walk from the Plaza de Armas. $ *Average main: S/16* ⊠ *Luna Pizarro 304, Vallecito* ☎ *054/223–657.*

$
PERUVIAN
✗ **Sol de Mayo.** This charming garden restaurant in the colonial Yanahuara neighborhood is worth the expense to taste true Arequipan cooking. Specialties include *ocopa arequipeña* (boiled potato slices in spicy sauce and melted cheese), and *rocoto relleno* (spicy peppers stuffed with cheese, meat, and raisins). $ *Average main: S/25* ⊠ *Jerusalén 207, Yanahuara* ☎ *054/254–148* ⊘ *No dinner.*

$
PERUVIAN
✗ **Tradición Arequipeña.** It may be a S/10 taxi ride to this restaurant in the Paucarpata district, but locals come in droves for the fantastic Arequipan food. The decor is Peruvian country, but the flavors lean toward Creole. Get ready for *cuy chactado* (deep-fried guina pig) and *ocopa arequipeña* (potato-based dish with garlic, olives, onion, and fresh cheese). If you crave seafood, try the *chupe de camarones* (a creamy shrimp chowder). Open from noon to 7, it's primarily a lunch-only venue Sunday through Thursday, but on Friday and Saturday it doesn't close until 10 (sometimes later) when live music can be heard, including an orchestra on Saturday nights. Reservations recommended. $ *Average main: S/25* ⊠ *Dolores 111, Paucarpata* ☎ *054/426–467.*

$$
FRENCH
✗ **Zig Zag Restaurant.** Everything at Zig Zag—from its grand iron spiral staircase to its Novo Andino cuisine, extensive wine list, and decadent desserts—is done with exquisite detail and attention. ■**TIP**➔ See that spiral staircase? It was built by Gustave Eiffel. Using a fusion of gourmet techniques from the Alps and Andes, the menu is a harmonious mix of fresh local foods. Try the quinoa potato gnocchi, the meat fondue, or the notable Trios, a prime cut of three meats: alpaca, ostrich, and beef, slow-cooked and served on a hot stone with three dipping sauces. Call ahead and reserve one of the romantic balcony nooks. Top it all off with a chocolate mousse. $ *Average main: S/36* ⊠ *Zela 210* ☎ *054/206–020* ⊕ *www.zigzagrestaurant.com.*

WHERE TO STAY

Arequipa has one of the highest-quality collections of inns and hotels anywhere in Peru. While the larger resorts and chain hotels tend to cater to tour groups and business travelers, there are dozens of charming, small, independently run bed-and-breakfasts within a few blocks of the Plaza de Armas.

$
B&B/INN
🏨 **Casa Andina Classic.** The Peruvian equivalent to a Holiday Inn, the cookie-cutter rooms, nicely decorated with Andean textiles, are comfortable but basic. **Pros:** good location; good breakfast; clean. **Cons:** tour-group heavy; flat pillows; bad ventilation. $ *Rooms from: S/232* ⊠ *Calle Jerusalén 603* ☎ *054/202–070* ⊕ *www.casa-andina.com* ⤵ *103 rooms, 1 suite* ◎ *Breakfast.*

$$$
HOTEL
Fodor's Choice
★

🏨 **Casa Andina Private Collection Arequipa.** As upscale as it gets, this is the place to go for top-of-the-line amenities. **Pros:** historic building; comfortable bedding; large bathrooms. **Cons:** modern rooms do not match the colonial ones. $ *Rooms from: S/385 ⊠ Ugarte 403 ☎ 054/226–907 ⊕ www.casa-andina.com ⤳ 41 rooms, 7 suites �‖ Breakfast.*

$
B&B/INN
Fodor's Choice
★

🏨 **Casa Arequipa.** With 11 individually designed rooms, all decked out in luxuriously high-quality motifs and bedding, every last detail has been thought of—and applied. **Pros:** impeccable service; new and comfortable bedding; quiet neighborhood. **Cons:** not near any stores; need a taxi at night. $ *Rooms from: S/194 ⊠ Av. Lima 409, Vallecito ☎ 054/231–933 ⊕ www.arequipacasa.com ⤳ 11 rooms �‖ Breakfast.*

$
B&B/INN

🏨 **Hostal Santa Catalina.** This bright-yellow hostel (and it's very much like a youth hostel, minus the youth part) offers shared and private quarters. **Pros:** great place to meet other travelers; central location; friendly staff. **Cons:** old furniture and bedding; a bit noisy; some communal bathrooms. $ *Rooms from: S/60 ⊠ Santa Catalina 500 ☎ 054/221–766 ⊕ www.hostalsantacatalinaperu.com ⤳ 8 rooms, 3 dorms ═ No credit cards �‖ No meals.*

$$$
RESORT
★

🏨 **Hotel Libertador.** Amid sprawling gardens, this 1940 Spanish-colonial villa is an oasis in Old Arequipa. **Pros:** well kept; helpful staff; Jacuzzi and sauna. **Cons:** older building; far from town. $ *Rooms from: S/465 ⊠ Plaza Bolívar, Selva Alegre ☎ 511/518–6500 or 877/778–2281 ⊕ www.libertador.com.pe ⤳ 80 rooms, 8 suites �‖ Breakfast.*

$$
HOTEL

🏨 **Hotel Sonesta Posadas del Inca.** You don't get any more central than this upscale hotel with top-rate modern facilities and services and a superb location on Plaza de Armas. **Pros:** superb views of plaza; great value; bilingual staff; late check-out. **Cons:** older; little colonial feel. $ *Rooms from: S/260 ⊠ Portal de Flores 116 ☎ 054/215–530 ⊕ www.sonesta. com ⤳ 57 rooms, 1 suite �‖ Breakfast.*

$
B&B/INN

🏨 **La Casa de Melgar.** In a beautiful tiled courtyard surrounded by fragrant blossoms and dotted with trees is this 18th-century home, believed to have been the one-time temporary residence of Mariano Melgar, Peru's most romantic 19th-century poet. **Pros:** high on the charm scale; garden is great for relaxing; quiet; close to shops and restaurants. **Cons:** rooms can get cold in rainy season; some have thin walls; front desk staff can be curt. $ *Rooms from: S/198 ⊠ Melgar 108 ☎☎ 054/222–459 ⊕ www.lacasademelgar.com ⤳ 30 rooms, 1 suite �‖ Breakfast.*

$
HOTEL
☺

🏨 **La Casa de Mi Abuela.** An old stone wall circles this famous budget-traveler haunt. **Pros:** best breakfast buffet in town; free airport pickup; large grounds; security gate. **Cons:** standard room bathrooms are old and small; lots of tour groups. $ *Rooms from: S/154 ⊠ Calle Jerusalén 606 ☎ 054/241–206 ⊕ www.lacasademiabuela.com ⤳ 57 rooms �‖ Breakfast.*

$$
HOTEL

🏨 **San Agustin Posada del Monasterio.** Designed from an 18th-century sillar building directly across from the Santa Catalina Monastery, this new property helps fill the much desired higher-end demand in Arequipa's historic center. **Pros:** excellent location; historic atmosphere. **Cons:** generic decor. $ *Rooms from: S/284 ⊠ Calle Santa Catalina 300 ☎ 511/203–2840 ⊕ www.hotelessanagustin.com.pe ⤳ 47 rooms; 2 suites �‖ Breakfast.*

NIGHTLIFE

Peñas start the party early, around 8 or 9 pm, and many of the traditional restaurants sponsor a show on Friday and Saturday nights. A quiet restaurant can quickly turn into a Broadway-like show and you could very well become the star.

Most of the after-dark entertainment revolves around a number of cafés and bars near the city center along Calle San Francisco. Close by on Calle Zela, near the Catedral de San Francisco, bars seem to change daily, and on Calle Santa Catalina you'll find small cafés that suit the more artsy, avant-garde folk. In a seedier section across town, teenagers and twentysomething Arequipeños head to discos and salsatecas on Avenida Dolores.

BARS

Ad Libitum. Head to this relaxed artistic heaven popular with thirsty locals for cheap cocktails and fun music. ⊠ *San Francisco 233* ☎ *054/993–1034.*

Café Bar Istanbul. This tiny eclectic bar is great for martinis and small bites. ⊠ *San Francisco 231-A* ☎ *54/203–862.*

Café y Vino. For something a bit more relaxed, climb up to the second floor of the beautiful Claustros de la Compinia complex to this small wine bar and café serving light snacks. Try some of the French owner's own pisco. ⊠ *Morán 118* ☎ *054/283–371.*

Casona Forum. Enter a large sillar building called Casona Forum and chill in one of five bars: Retro, Forum, Terrasse, Club Zero, and Chill Out Sofa Bar. At Retro you can enjoy live concerts and dance to hits from the 1970s and 1980s. Over at Zero, belly up to the pub-styled bar, grab a beer, and shoot some pool. While you can dine at Forum among tropical furnishings or dance the night away, at Terrasse you can eat among great views and sharpen your karaoke skills. ⊠ *San Francisco 317* ☎ *054/204–294* ⊕ *www.casonaforum.com.*

Déja Vu. Open 9 am to 4 am, Déja Vu is a popular place to have a light meal. The two-floor venue has live Latin pop music and/or a DJ spinning every night with a dance club downstairs. ⊠ *San Francisco 319B* ☎ *054/221–904.*

GAY AND LESBIAN

Although not as gay-friendly as Lima, there's a small progressive gay and lesbian scene.

SKP. This gay and lesbian disco opens at 8 pm; there's no cover charge before 11 pm. Closed Monday and Tuesday. ⊠ *Calle Villalba 205* ☎ *054/934–7169.*

Two One Two. Another of the city's popular gay clubs, Two One Two has covers up to S/40 but sometimes admission is free. ⊠ *Av. Ejercito 311.*

LIVE MUSIC

Instituto Cultural Peruano Norteamericano. This is a regular venue for evening concerts of traditional and classical music. ⊠ *Melgar 109* ☎ *054/243–201* ⊕ *www.cultural.edu.pe.*

Kibosh. This lively and much-frequented dance bar has good pizza and beer. ⊠ *Zela 205* ☎ *054/203–837.*

La Troica. Open Monday through Saturday from 7 pm, La Troica specializes in Afro-Peruvian music, but also has groups from all over South America and sometimes a folkloric show on Saturday. For other good peña shows, consider Las Quenas and Tradicion Arequipeña (see restaurants). ✉ *Calle Jerusalén 522-A* ☎ *054/225–690.*

SHOPPING

Arequipa has the widest selection of Peruvian crafts in the south. Alpaca and llama wool is woven into brightly patterned sweaters, ponchos, hats, scarves, and gloves, as well as wall hangings, blankets, and carpets. Look for *chullos* (woolen knitted caps with ear flaps and ties), transported from the Lake Titicaca region. Ceramic *toros* (bulls) are a local favorite to hold flowers or money, and you can even see them sitting in the rafters of homes to bring good luck.

At the Plaza San Francisco, the cathedral steps are the site of a daily flea market that has delicate handmade jewelry. Across the street at the Fundo el Fierro, crafts vendors tout bargains on clothing, ceramics, jewelry, and knickknacks in a cobblestone courtyard; deals can be had until about 8 pm. Arequipa is also an excellent place to purchase inexpensive but well-constructed handmade guitars. Avenida Bolognesi has lines of such workshops. Behind the cathedral on the narrow Pasaje Catedral, boutiques sell jewelry and knickknacks made of Arequipa agate and along Santa Catalina there are many clothing stores.

In recent years several upscale shopping centers have popped up.

MALLS

Casona de Santa Catalina. A number of upscale shops like Kuna and Tienda del Ekeko are housed at this complex ✉ *Santa Catalina 210* ☎ *054/281–334.*

Patio del Ekeko. This is a good shopping complex to scout quality souvenirs, with a branch of alpaca store Kuna and an artisanal foodstuff shop. ✉ *Mercaderes 141* ☎ *054/215–861.*

SPECIALTY SHOPS
ANTIQUES

Arequipa is a great place to pick up colonial-era antiques, high-quality copies of Pre-Colombian ceramics, and even authentic Inca archeological pieces. Most shops are found on Santa Catalina facing the monastery.

Curiosidades. This five-and-dime type of curiosity shop sells everything from furniture and weapons to postcards and silver. ✉ *Zela 207* ☎ *054/232–703.*

Antiquedades y Objectos de Arte. This colorful shop carries large furniture pieces and vintage tapestries. Cash only. ✉ *Santa Catalina 406* ☎ *054/229–103.*

El Anticuario. This mom-and-pop shop resells treasures from tables to teapots. All credit cards accepted. Will assist in shipping. ✉ *Santa Catalina 300* ☎ *054/234–474.*

DESIGNER ALPACA CLOTHING

Arequipa is churning out scores of fashionistas who are responsible for creating some of the country's most sophisticated alpaca knits. Since many couturiers make their home in Arequipa, a few have alpaca clothing outlets. **Incalpaca** is the maker of the Kuna, Alpaca 111, TUMI, and CONDOR labels and has two factory outlets in Arequipa, a small one in the Claustros de la Compañia, and a larger one 15 minutes outside of town at Avenida Juan Bustamante s/n, in the Tahuaycani district. The Michell Group, the umbrella company of Sol Alpaca, has an ecotourist center called **Mundo Alpaca** in Alameda San Lázaro, an upscale boutique with a camelid zoo, an art gallery, and textile museum.

Jenny Duarte. For fine dresses with a French-trained local designer there's Jenny Duarte, who doesn't shy away from using alpaca and other regional fibers. ⊠ *Claustros de la Compañia, General Morán 118* ☎ *054/283–693* ⊕ *www.jennyduarteperu.com.*

Kuna. Formerly called Alpaca 111, Kuna is the go-to destination for alpaca scarves, gloves, socks, sweaters, and jackets. ⊠ *Santa Catalina 210* ☎ *054/282–485* ⊕ *www.kuna.com.pe.*

Ranticuy Baby Alpaca. Here you'll find intricately designed sweaters and accessories made with lots of bright colors. ⊠ *Claustros de la Compañia, General Morán 118* ☎ *054/232–801.*

Sol Alpaca. The Michell Group's Sol Alpaca has gone haute couture, constructing fine-quality knits, helping hoist Peru onto the international fashion scene. ⊠ *Santa Catalina 210* ☎ *054/221–454.*

JEWELRY

L. Paulet. Stop here for high-quality, reasonably priced jewelry. ⊠ *Claustros de la Compañia, General Morán 118* ☎ *054/287–786.*

SPORTING GOODS

Camping Equipment. This is a great source of everything for a last-minute outdoor adventure. ⊠ *Jerusalén 307* ☎ *054/331–248.*

WOOL

Alpa Wool. If you're looking for baby alpaca yarn Alpa Wool carries a small selection of high-quality and cheap baby alpaca yarn. ⊠ *Santa Catalina 120-B* ☎ *054/220–992.*

PUNO AND LAKE TITICACA

Lake Titicaca is one of the most breathtaking parts of Peru, though that may have something to do with the altitude. The azure-blue waters of the lake paired with an even bluer sky are a sight to behold indeed. The region is one of the most culturally significant places in Peru. There are not only more festivals here than anywhere else, but Quechua and Aymará people who inhabit isolated islands like Taquile and Amantani have preserved their customs over centuries with little change. The Islas de Uros, made of floating tortora islands, are a magical display of color and originality. This is where the Incas were born, and ancient ruins, such as those at Sullustani, are scattered all over the area. For many travelers a visit to Lake Titicaca is the highlight of their trip.

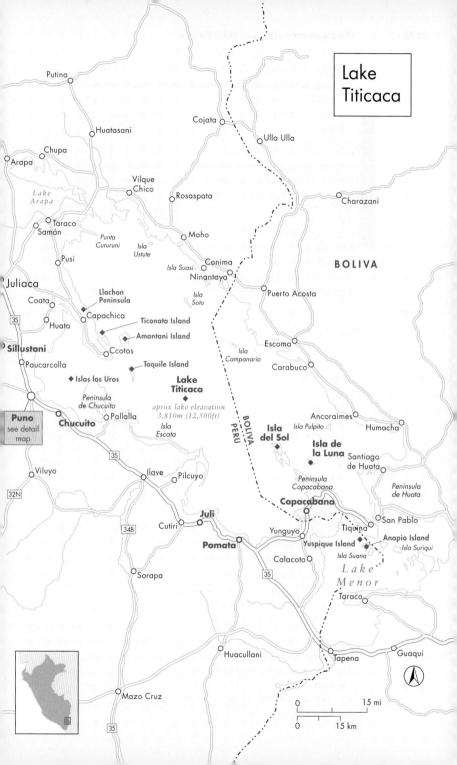

Lake Titicaca

Putina

Huatasani

Chupa

Arapa

Lake Arapa

Taraco
Samán

Pusi

Juliaca

Coata

Huata

Sillustani

Paucarcolla

Puno
see detail
map

Chucuito

Viluyo

32N

34B

Cutiri

Pomata

Sorapa

Vilque
Chico

Rosaspata

Punta
Cururuni

*Isla
Ustute*

Llachon
Peninsula

Capachica

Ticonata Island

Amantani Island

Ccotos

Taquile Island

Islas los Uros

Peninsula
de Chucuito

Pallalla

*Isla
Escata*

3S

Ilave

Pilcuyo

Juli

Huacullani

Mazo Cruz

35

Cojata

Ulla Ulla

Moho

Isla Suasi Conima

Ninantaya

*Isla
Soto*

Puerto Acosta

Charazani

BOLIVA

Escoma

*Isla
Campanario*

Carabuco

**Lake
Titicaca**

*aprox lake eleavation
3,810m (12,500ft)*

**BOLIVA
PERU**

Ancoraimes

Isla Pulpito

Humacha

**Isla
del Sol**

**Isla de
la Luna**

Santiago
de Huata

*Peninsula
de Huata*

Peninsula
Copacabana

Copacabana

Yunguyo

Tiquina

San Pablo

Anapia Island

Isla Suriqui

Yuspique Island

Isla Suana

*Lake
Menor*

Calacoto

Taraco

Huacullani

Tapena

Guaqui

0   15 mi

0   15 km

Festival Time!

Although any time of year is suitable for traveling to Puno and Lake Titicaca, visiting during a festival of dance, song, and parades is ideal. The streets are flooded with people; the folklore experience is passionate and very fun. Preserving the choreography of more than 140 typical dances, Puno's most memorable celebration is the Festival of the Virgin de la Candelaria (candle), held on February 2 and during carnival. A cast of several hundred elaborately costumed Andean singers, dancers, and bands from neighboring communities parades through the streets carrying the rosy-white-complexioned statue of the Virgin. During the rest of the year, the statue rests on the altar of the San Juan Bautista Church. Puno week, as it's informally known, occurs the first week of November and is equally fun. When Puno isn't having a celebration, it reverts to its true character, that of a small, poor Andean agricultural town. On the lake, Isla Taquile celebrates a vivid festival the last week of July.

PUNO

975 km (609 miles) southeast of Lima.

Puno doesn't win any beauty pageants—brown unfinished cement homes, old paved roads, and a dusty desert have dominated the landscape for years. It's a sharp contrast to Puno's immediate neighbor, Lake Titicaca. Some people arrive in town and scram to find a trip on the lake. Don't let the dreary look of Puno stop you from exploring its shores; it's considered Peru's folklore capital.

Puno retains traits of the Aymará, Quechua, and Spanish cultures that settled on the northwestern shores of the lake. Their influence is in the art, music, dance, and dress of today's inhabitants, who call themselves "Children of the Sacred Lake." Much of the city's character comes from the continuation of ancient traditions—at least once a month a parade or a festival celebrates some recent or historic event.

GETTING HERE AND AROUND

Although Puno does not have an airport, you can fly into Juliaca's Aeropuerto Manco Capac, about one hour away. The airport is only served by LAN airlines (⊕ *www.lan.com*) for flights between Juliaca and Lima, sometimes stopping in Arequipa, once per day. Most hotels in Puno will pick you up on arrival; otherwise you can take one of the waiting tourist buses (S/15).

The Terrestre bus terminal is at 1 de Mayo 703, and Bolívar and many companies also have offices here. Puno is a connection point for trips between Arequipa, Cusco, and La Paz, Bolivia, so there are frequent buses throughout the day for each destination.

The train station for PeruRail for the daily trip to/from Cusco, Estación Huanchaq (☎ 084/238–722), is at the end of Avenida Sol on Avenida La Torre just outside of the center of town.

Restaurants, shops, Internet services, banks, and drugstores line the four-block pedestrian-only street Jirón Lima, between Pino Park (sometimes called Parque San Juan after the San Juan Bautista Church nearby) and the Plaza de Armas.

Puno has tricycle taxis, which resemble Asian tuk-tuks and are driven by bicycle peddlers with a carriage and cost only S/1 to go nearly anywhere in the city. However, if you're heading to a mirador high up on the hill and you don't want the peddler to keel over, take an auto taxi, which costs S/5.

SAFETY AND PRECAUTIONS

At 3,827 meters (12,553 feet) above sea level, Puno challenges your system, so eat lightly, skip the alcohol (trust us!), forgo your morning jog, and take it easy your first two or three days.

■TIP➜ Walking around the port after dark is not smart. When the sun goes down, the port gets desolate, and unsuspecting tourists become targets for crime. So if you're at the handicraft market or are getting back from an outing on the lake and suddenly it's dusk, catch a cab.

ESSENTIALS

Bus CIVA ✉ Terminal Terrestre C-35 ☎ 051/365–882 ⊕ www.civa.com.pe. **Cruz del Sur** ✉ Terminal Terrestre C-10 ☎ 051/368–524 ⊕ www.cruzdelsur. pe. **Flores** ✉ Terminal Terrestre C-5, 6, 7, 8 ☎ 051/366–734 ⊕ www.floreshnos. net. **Inka Express** ✉ Jr. Melgar N 226 ☎ 051/365–654. **Julsa** ✉ Terminal Terrestre C-10 ☎ 051/364–080. **Ormeño** ✉ Terminal Terrestre C-11 ☎ 051/368–176 ⊕ www.grupo-ormeno.com.pe. **Tour Peru** ✉ Terminal Terrestre C-10 ☎ 051/365–517 ⊕ www.tourperu.com.pe. **Turismo Mer** ✉ Terminal Terrestre C-10 ☎ 051/245–171 ⊕ www.turismomer.com.

Currency Banco Continental BBVA ✉ 400 Jr. Lima. **Banco de Crédito BCP** ✉ Jr. Lima 510 ☎ 051/352–119. **Scotiabank** ✉ Plaza de Armas, corner of Duestra and Jr. Lima.

Internet Choz@Net ✉ Jr. Lima 339, 2nd fl. ☎ 051/367–195. **La Casa del Corregidor** ✉ Deustua 576 ☎ 051/351–921 ☾ Tues.–Sat. 10–10.

Mail SERPOST Puno ✉ Av. Moquegua 269 ☎ 051/351–141 ☾ Mon.–Sat. 8–8.

Medical Carlos Monge Medrano Hospital ✉ Huancane Hwy., Km 2, sector San Ramon, Juliaca ☎ 051/321–901 or 051/321–750 ☾ Daily 24 hrs. **Manuel Nuñez Butron National Hospital** ✉ Av. El Sol 1022 ☎ 051/351–021 or 051/369–286 ☾ Daily 24 hours.

Police Police ✉ Jr. Deustua 530 ☎ 051/366–271 or 051/353–988. **Policía de Tourismo** ✉ Jr. Deustua 538 ☎ 051/354–764, 051/354–774, or 051/353–3988.

Taxis Radio Taxi Milenium ☎ 051/353–134. **Servitaxi Turistico** ☎ 051/369–000.

Trains PeruRail ✉ Estacion Puno, La Torre 224 ☎ 084/238–722 ⊕ www.perurail.com ☾ Weekdays 7–5, weekends 7–noon.

Visitor Information Iperu Oficina Información Turística ✉ Corner of Jr. Deustua and Jr. Lima, Plaza de Armas ☎ 051/365–088.

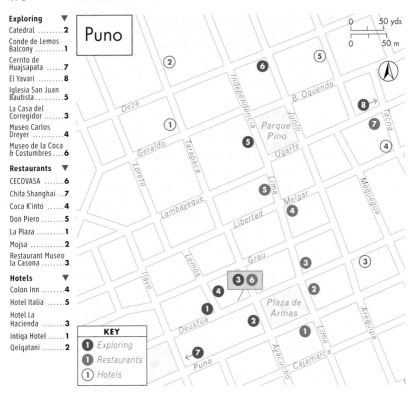

EXPLORING

TOP ATTRACTIONS

Conde de Lemos Balcony. An intricately carved wooden balcony marks the home where viceroy Conde de Lemos stayed when he arrived in Puno to counter rebellion around 1668. Behind the Catedral, it is today home of the National Culture Institute of Puno. ⊠ *Corner of Calles Deustua and Conde de Lemos* ⊒ *Free* ☉ *Weekdays 8:30–4.*

Fodor'sChoice
★
La Casa del Corregidor. Reconstructed more than five times, this 17th-century colonial, once a chaplaincy, is now a brightly colored cultural center. It was originally home to Silvestre de Valdés, a Catholic priest who served as a *corregidor* (a Spanish official who acts as governor, judge, and tax collector) and oversaw construction of the nearby Catedral. The house had a long history of changing owners until its present owner, Sra. Ana Maria Piño Jordán, bought it at public auction. Now a vibrant cultural locale, with an arts cooperative, it houses a fair-trade café and a few upscale handicraft stores. The exhibition hall displays works by local artists and hosts music events. ⊠ *Deustua 576* ☎ *051/351–921* ⊕ *www.casadelcorregidor.pe* ☉ *Wed.–Fri. 10–10, Sat. 10–2:30 and 5–10.*

WORTH NOTING

Catedral. Etchings of flowers, fruits, and mermaids playing an Andean guitar called the *charango* grace the entrance of the Spanish baroque-style church. Sculpted by Peruvian architect Simon de Asto, the 17th-century stone cathedral has one of the more eclectically carved facades of any church in the area. Plain on the inside, its main decorations are a silver-plated altar and paintings from the Cusco School. ⊠ *Plaza de Armas* ✉ *Free* ☼ *Weekdays 7–noon and 3–6, Sat. 7–noon and 3–7.*

Cerrito de Huajsapata. A statue honoring Manco Cápac, the first Inca and founder of the Inca empire, sits on this hill overlooking Puno. Legend has it that there are caves and subterranean paths in the monument, which connect Puno with the Koricancha Temple in Cusco. It's technically a 10-minute walk from town, but it's all uphill and a bit off the beaten path where a few robberies have been reported, so stick with a group or take a taxi. ⊠ *4 blocks southwest of Plaza de Armas.*

El Yavari. The restored Victorian iron ship was built in Birmingham, England, in 1861. It was subcontracted by the Peruvian Navy to patrol the waters of Titicaca, so it was dismantled and its 2,766 pieces and two crankshafts were loaded onto a freighter and shipped to the Peruvian Port of Arica on the Pacific coast, which today belongs to Chile. Mules and porters carried the pieces 290 miles through the Andes Mountains to Puno. The journey took six years and it was Christmas Day 1870 before it was reassembled and launched on Lake Titicaca. Now a museum and sometimes bed-and-breakfast, it's docked at the end of a pier by the Sonesta Posada del Inca Hotel. After remaining idle for 40 years, the vessel took a trial run in 1999 after volunteers rebuilt its engine. ⊠ *Av. Sesquicentenario 610, Sector Huaje, pier behind Sonesta Posada del Inca Hotel* ☎ *051/369–329* ⊕ *www.yavari. org* ✉ *Donation* ☼ *Daily 8:30–6.*

Iglesia San Juan Bautista. This 18th-century church has been entrusted with the care of the Virgin of the Candlemas, the focus of Puno's most important yearly celebration in February, the Festival de la Virgen de la Candelaria. The statue rests on the main altar. ⊠ *Jr. Lima and Parque Pino.*

Museo Carlos Dreyer. An exhibit of 501 gold pieces called the "Great Treasure of Sillustani" has classified the intimate museum as one of the most important regional archaeological museums in southern Peru. The museum is named for famed Puno painter and antiques collector Carlos Dreyer Spohr. You can view the oil canvasses by Dreyer and explore exhibits of pre-Hispanic and colonial art, weavings, silver, copper works, delicate Aymará pottery, pre-Inca stone sculptures, and historical Spanish documents on the founding of Puno. ⊠ *Conde de Lemos 289* ✉ *S/15* ☼ *Mon.–Sat. 9:30–7:30, Sun. 2–7:30.*

Museo de la Coca y Costumbres. A hidden gem, this museum pays tribute to the infamous coca leaf and Peruvian folklore. The quaint museum, tucked away on a second-floor building, is sliced into rooms, one that houses the folklore exhibit and the other displays everything you'd ever want to know about the coca leaf. Presented in English and Spanish, displays are well constructed with educational videos and photographs.

The mission is not to promote coca, but merely to share the plant's history and culture. You can enlist the help of a bilingual guide if you wish or mosey on your own. The folklore exhibit displays elaborately constructed costumes worn during festivals and shares the history behind the dances. ✉ *Jr. Deza 301* ☎ *051/977–0360* 🌐 *www.museodelacoca.com* 🎫 *S/5* ⏲ *Daily 9–1 and 3–8.*

WHERE TO EAT

Many small restaurants line Jirón Lima, and include a mix of Novo Andino and classic regional foods. On the menu you'll find fresh fish from the lake, an abundance of quinoa dishes, along with typical Peruvian fare like *lechón al horno o cancacho* (highly spiced baked suckling pig); *pesque o queso de quinua* (resembling ground-up barley), prepared with cheese and served with fish fillet in tomato sauce; *chairo* (lamb and tripe broth cooked with vegetables, and frozen-dried potato known as *chuño*). Particularly good are *trucha* (trout) and *pejerrey* (Kingfish mackerel) from the lake.

$ CAFÉ 🍴 **CECOVASA.** In La Casa del Corregidor, this charming and poetic café is run by a union of eight cooperatives and coffee producers who grow and sell organic fair-trade coffee from Puno's eastern regions that was recently named among the world's best. Eight java varieties are available to taste, along with a collection of teas, cocktails, smoothies, and healthy café foods including salads, soups, sandwiches, along with more sweet treats like cakes and pies. A book exchange and sun-filled patio make this a great relaxation station. [$] *Average main: S/6* ✉ *Deustua 576, La Casa del Corregidor* ☎ *051/351–921* 💳 *No credit cards.*

$ CHINESE 🍴 **Chifa Shanghai.** Among the half dozen *chifas*—the Peruvian name for Chinese restaurants—around the central market, Chifa Shanghai is the best. This is where the locals go and at night the place gets crowded. Though you wouldn't know it by the grungy interior, Shanghai is among a chain of chifas scattered around Peru. The menu is varied and includes chifa classics, and set menus for less than S/.10 pair wonton soup with dishes such as Aeropuerto (fried rice and noodles) or Chi Jau Kay (breaded pork). [$] *Average main: S/10* ✉ *Arbulu 169* ☎ *051/167–171.*

$ PERUVIAN Fodor's Choice ★ 🍴 **Coco K'intu.** While Novo Andino cuisine is all the rage around Peru, it had yet to really hit Puno until this restaurant opened. It's not nearly as creative as restaurants in Cusco or Arequipa, but several traditional dishes make creative, sophisticated, downright delicious entrées. The food bursts with flavor, especially the *sopa incasica,* a thick, creamy quinoa soup with peppers and onions, and a kick of spice. Slow-cooked alpaca entrées include the alpaca *con salsa de maracuya,* a tender alpaca steak cooked in a passion-fruit sauce. Open for breakfast, lunch, and dinner. [$] *Average main: S/18* ✉ *Jr. Lima 401* ☎ *051/365–566.*

$ PERUVIAN 🍴 **Don Piero.** Colorful paintings of Quecha people partaking in various rituals hang above you as you enjoy such typical dishes as barbecued chicken, fresh lake fish (pejerrey and trucha) fried in oil and garnished with potatoes and toasted chili peppers. Local musicians entertain on most nights. [$] *Average main: S/20* ✉ *Lima 364* ☎ *051/365–943* 💳 *No credit cards.*

$ PERUVIAN 🍴 **La Plaza.** A grand colonial dining room with hand-carved fixtures gives this restaurant a sense of old-world Europe. Prices are inversely proportional to the large portions, so try a hearty regional dish like *chairo puneño* (soup with dehydrated potatoes and beef), cuy, or trucha. A separate location named La Hosteria, two blocks away on Avenida Lima, has a similar menu. $ *Average main: S/25* ⊠ *Jr. Puno 425, Plaza de Armas* 🕾🕾 *051/366–871.*

$ ✕ **Mojsa.** The window seats overlooking the Plaza de Armas are for
PERUVIAN a romantic dinner or a cup of fresh local coffee. Mojsa, which mean "delicious" in Aymara language, serves reasonably priced Novo Andino cuisine, fused with fresh traditional and criollo flavors. Tender, juicy cuts of grilled beef and alpaca for less than S/20 are favorties, but creative pastas and crispy brick-oven pizza are also good. $ *Average main: S/18* ⊠ *Lima 635, Plaza de Armas* 🕾 *051/363–182.*

$ ✕ **Restaurant Museo La Casona.** Museum-like, this quaint two-decades-old
PERUVIAN institution is filled with wrought-iron antiques and artwork including a display of antique irons and sewing machines. Divided into four intimate rooms, the polished hardwood floors, lace tablecloths, and burning candles make it feel like having dinner at great-grandma's. Luckily there are no old home odors here, only savory aromas of hearty soups and grilled meats and fish. Try local fare, such as *lomo de* alpaca (alpaca steak) or one of their thick soups (the cream of quinoa is amazing) made with vegetables and meat or fish. Ask for the Menu Turistico and have a great set meal for S/25, and a pisco sour for less than S/6. $ *Average main: S/25* ⊠ *Av. Lima 423* 🕾 *051/351–108 or 051/967–9207* ⊕ *www.lacasona-restaurant.com.*

WHERE TO STAY

Puno can be cold, so bring warm clothes. Not even the fanciest hotels have internal heating systems, but most have portable electric heaters. Air-conditioning is unheard of here; you won't miss it. Always ask about heat when you book, and ask for extra blankets. As Puno has few notable attractions, there is less of a need to stay in town as in other Peruvian cities. A surge of new hotel development has occurred on the lakeshore outside of town, particularly at the higher end, which aims to give a more authentic Titicaca experience.

$$$ 🖵 **Casa Andina Private Collection.** Out of the two Casa Andina properties
HOTEL in Puno (the other is a less expensive Casa Andina Classic property), this lakeside hotel is the best. **Pros:** good atmosphere; oxygen tank; great terrace. **Cons:** gets cold; rooms are small. $ *Rooms from: S/455* ⊠ *Av. Sesquicentenario 1970-1972, Sector Huaje* 🕾 *051/363–992* ⊕ *www.casa-andina.com* ⬎ *45 rooms, 1 suite* ⦿| *Breakfast.*

$$$$ 🖵 **Casa Andina Private Collection Suasi.** An ecological paradise for those
RESORT who can afford it, at this exclusive hotel on Isla Suasi, on a remote
ⓒ end of Lake Titicaca, you can hike among wild llamas, canoe, study
Fodor'sChoice astronomy, learn Andean spirituality, marvel at flower-filled terraces,
★ discuss ecosystems, or just relax with a massage. **Pros:** cultural activities; child-friendly. **Cons:** charges extra for transportation. $ *Rooms from: S/600* ⊠ *Isla Suasi Lago Titicaca* 🕾 *511/213–9739* ⊕ *www.casa-andina. com* ⬎ *24 rooms, 2 suites* ⦿| *Multiple meal plans.*

$ 🖵 **Colon Inn.** With an air of old Europe, this Belgian-owned 19th-century
B&B/INN republican-era inn is draped in dark mahogany wood and colonial furnishings. **Pros:** a hospitable staff speaks English; free coca tea is always

on hand; great water pressure. **Cons:** dark decor; small bathrooms. $ *Rooms from: S/168* ✉ *Calle Tacna 290* ☎ *051/351–432* ⊕ *www.coloninn.com* ⤵ *22 rooms, 1 suite* ✺ *Breakfast.*

$
B&B/INN

✺ **Hotel Italia.** A lovely, flower-filled courtyard, rooftop terrace, and scrumptious restaurant are all pluses at this hotel a block from Parque Pino. **Pros:** friendly Peruvian–Italian owner is always around to help; excellent soups; active communal lounge. **Cons:** furniture is old and bathrooms are small. $ *Rooms from: S/130* ✉ *Theodoro Valcarcel 122* ☎ *051/367–706* ⊕ *www.hotelitaliaperu.com* ⤵ *32 rooms* ✺ *Breakfast.*

$
HOTEL

✺ **Hotel La Hacienda.** Panoramic views of Lake Titicaca and its surroundings can be viewed from the endless window-filled restaurant atop of this Spanish-colonial hotel, two blocks from Plaza de Armas. **Pros:** free Internet; large bathrooms; complimentary pisco sour upon arrival. **Cons:** can be noisy along Avenida Deustua. $ *Rooms from: S/234* ✉ *Deustua 297* ☎ *051/365–134* ⊕ *www.lahaciendapuno.com* ⤵ *58 rooms* ✺ *Breakfast.*

$
B&B/INN

✺ **Intiqa Hotel.** Looking as if it were lifted out of Miraflores, all the rooms are spacious, sleek, and modern, and have lots of natural light, flat-screen TVs with DIRECTV, plush brown bedding, and polished hardwood floors. **Pros:** big bathrooms; spacious rooms; new. **Cons:** breakfast café doesn't have enough seating. $ *Rooms from: S/203* ✉ *Tarapacá 272* ☎ *051/366–900* ⊕ *www.intiqahotel.com* ⤵ *17 rooms* ✺ *Breakfast.*

$$$$
RESORT

✺ **Libertador Hotel Isla Esteves.** The Libertador, a gleaming white, futuristic-looking, low-rise hotel, which functions more like a resort, is 5 km (3 miles) from Puno. **Pros:** knowledgeable staff; on the lake; heating; Jacuzzi and sauna. **Cons:** 10 minutes from town; rooms lack charm. $ *Rooms from: S/549* ✉ *Isla Esteves* ☎ *511/518–6500 or 877/778–2281* ⊕ *www.libertador.com.pe* ⤵ *111 rooms, 12 suites* ✺ *Breakfast.*

$
B&B/INN

✺ **Qelqatani.** This small hotel owned by tour operator Arcobaleno on a quiet street about a five-minute walk from Jirón Lima is an affordable and cozy place to lay your head after a day on the lake. **Pros:** excellent staff; quiet; good place to meet other travelers; helpful travel agency. **Cons:** dark interior; older building. $ *Rooms from: S/80* ✉ *Tarapacá 355* ☎ *051/351–470* ⊕ *www.qelqatani.com* ⤵ *40 rooms, 2 suites* ✺ *Breakfast.*

$$
HOTEL

✺ **Sonesta Posadas del Inca.** Weavings, polished wood, and native art give character to this thoroughly modern Sonesta hotel on the shores of Lake Titicaca. **Pros:** on the lake; good heating; comfortable beds; near El Yavari. **Cons:** five minutes from town. $ *Rooms from: S/312* ✉ *Sesquicentenario 610, Sector Huaje* ☎ *051/364–111* ⊕ *www.sonesta.com* ⤵ *62 rooms* ✺ *Breakfast.*

$$$$
RESORT
ALL-INCLUSIVE
Fodor's Choice
★

✺ **Titilaka.** The best hotel on the lake, period, this stylish ecotourism resort with contemporary flair offers an off-the-beaten-path location, overlooking the lake next to the Chucuito Peninsula, on Peninsula Titilaka, about a 30-minute boat ride from Puno. **Pros:** all inclusive; heated floors. **Cons:** secluded; far from Puno; slow Internet connection. $ *Rooms from: S/1880* ✉ *Huenccalla, Centro Poblado Menor de Titilaka, District of Plateria, Peninsula Titilaka* ☎ *511/700–5100 or 866/628–1777* ⊕ *www.titilaka.com* ⤵ *18 suites* ✺ *All-inclusive.*

$ B&B/INN **Yavari B&B.** The old iron ship that has long been docked in front of the Hotel Sonesta has been turned into one of Puno's most unique bed-and-breakfasts. **Pros:** unique experience. **Cons:** you'll live like a sailor. [$] *Rooms from: S/200* ✉ *Muelle de Hotel Sonesta Posadas el Inca* ☎ *051/369–329* 🛏 *2 rooms* 💳 *No credit cards.*

NIGHTLIFE

There are dozens of small bars and lounges packed inside of Jirón Lima, often one flight up from the street.

Clan Destino. This popular spot lures in young travelers off the street with two-for-one happy hour specials that seem to go on all night. ✉ *Lima 355* ☎ *051/368–252.*

Colors Lounge. For a more posh experience, the Colors Lounge is the most Manhattan-styled bar in Puno and attracts an older crowd. The food, however, is hit or miss. ✉ *Lima 342* ☎ *051/369–254.*

IncaBar. After dinner the restaurant IncaBar turns into a low-key lounge where you'll find a thirties-and-over crowd. ✉ *Jr. Lima 348* ☎ *051/368–031.*

Kamizaraky Rock Pub. For live rock and pizza check out Kamizaraky Rock Pub. ✉ *Pasaje Grau 148.*

Positive. One of the best pubs in town, Positive is a cozy watering hole that plays reggae and rock while serving up an eclectic cocktail menu, which includes drinks like the Amanti Island for S/12. ✉ *Jr. Lima 378, 1st fl.*

Pub Ekeko's. This lively pub is a town staple for soccer. When there are no games on, there's music and dancing. The quiet downstairs venue serves wood-fired pizza. ✉ *Lima 365* ☎ *051/365–986.*

SHOPPING

Casa del Artesano. This is a good source for locally made alpaca items, including sweaters, scarves, and ponchos. Also look for Puno's signature pottery, the Torito de Pucara (Little Bull from Pucará). The pot is a receptacle used to hold a mixture of the bull's blood with chicha in a cattle-branding ceremony. If you don't find what you want here, just walk on down Calle Lima, as there are more artisans' shops along the way. ✉ *Lima 549.*

La Casona Parodi. This is a collection of small high-end shops selling alpaca sweaters, jewelry, and handicrafts. ✉ *Jr. Lima 316.*

Kuna. For fine alpaca clothing head to branch of the Peruvian retail chain. ✉ *Jr. Lima 401* ☎ *051/366–050.*

Mercado Artesanal. Model reed boats, small stone carvings, and alpaca-wool articles are among the local crafts sold near the Port at Puno's Mercado Artesanal. If you find you aren't dressed for Puno's chilly evenings, it's the place to buy a good woolen poncho for less than $10 USD. Open 8–6. Make sure you know where your wallet or purse is while you're snapping a photo of the colorful market. **TIP→** Never walk to the docks after the sun has set; robberies are frequent at night. ✉ *Av. Simon Bolivar and Jr. El Puerto.*

Q'ori Ch'aska. At this small store you'll find ceramics and jewelry. ✉ *Jr. Lima 435* ☎ *051/364–148.*

4

LAKE TITICACA

Forms Puno's eastern shoreline.

Stunning, unpredictable, and enormous, Lake Titicaca is a world of unique flora, fauna, cultures, and geology. Lago Titicaca, which means lake of the gray (*titi*) puma (*caca*) in Quechua, borders Peru and Bolivia, with Peru's largest portion to the northwest. While Peru boasts the largest port in Puno (57% of the lake is in Peru), Bolivia's side has Isla del Sol and Isla de la Luna, two beautiful islands with great views and Inca ruins. The lake itself is larger than Puerto Rico, with an average depth of 7.5 meters (25 feet) and a minimum temperature of 38°F. Lake Titicaca gains 5 feet of water in summer (rainy season) and loses 5 feet in winter (dry season).

The Bahía de Puno, separated from the lake proper by the two jutting peninsulas of Capaschica and Chucuito, is home to the descendents of the Uro people, who are now mixed with the Aymará and Quechua. The lakeshores are lush with totora reeds—valuable as building material, cattle fodder, and, in times of famine, food for humans.

Although it's generally cold, the beaming sun keeps you warm and, if you don't watch it, burned.

GETTING HERE AND AROUND

A boat is necessary for traveling the lake. Most people go to the islands with a tour, but colectivo boats in Puno Bay will transport you for S/25–S/40. Most boats are super slow, super old, and they won't leave port unless at least 10 people are smooshed aboard. A four-hour trip will take only an hour in one of the newer speedboats that the higher-end tour companies now use.

ESSENTIALS

TOURS OF LAKE TITICACA Excursions to the floating islands of the Uros as well as to any of the islands on Lake Titicaca can be arranged through tour agencies in Puno. Most tours depart between 7:30 and 9 am, as the lake can become choppy in the afternoon. For Amantani and Taquile, you also can take the local boat at the Puno dock for about the same price as a tour, although boats don't usually depart without at least 10 passengers.

All Ways Travel ✉ *Jr. Tacna 285* ☎ *051/353–979* ⊕ *www.titicacaperu.com.*

The Andean Experience. The Andean Experience ✉ *Saenz Pena 129, Lima 4* ☎ *051/1700–5170* ⊕ *www.andean-experience.com.*

Condor Travel ✉ *Tarapacá* ☎ *051/364–763* ⊕ *www.condortravel.com.*

Edgar Adventures ✉ *Jr. Lima 328* ☎ *051/353–444* ⊕ *www.edgaradventures.com.*

Explorandes ✉ *Jr. Bolognesi 334* ☎ *051/367–747* ⊕ *www.explorandes.com.*

Kontiki Tours ✉ *Jr. Melgar 188* ☎ *051/353–473* ⊕ *www.kontikiperu.com.*

Solmartour ✉ *Jr. Libertad 229–231* ☎ *051/352–901* ⊕ *www.solmar.com.pe.*

Traficoperu ✉ *Av. Pardo 620 oficina 506, Lima 18* ☎ *051/447–1676* ⊕ *www.traficoperu.com.*

Continued on page 191

THE ISLANDS
of Lake Titicaca

According to legend, under orders from their father, the Sun God, the first Inca—Manco Cápac—and his sister—Mama Ocllo rose from the deep blue waters of Lake Titicaca and founded the Inca empire. Watching the mysterious play of light on the water and the shadows on the mountains, you may become a believer of the Inca myth.

Reed Boat Head, Uros

This is the altiplano—the high plains of Peru, where the earth has been raised so close to the sky that the area takes on a luminous quality. Lake Titicaca's sharp, sparkling blue waters may make you think of some place far from the altiplano, perhaps someplace warm. Then its chill will slap you back to reality and you realize that you're at the world's highest navigable lake, 12,500 feet above sea level. The lake's surface covers 8,562 sq km (3340 sq miles) and drops down 282 meters (925 ft) at its deepest.

Most of Lake Titicaca is a National Reserve dedicated to conserving the region's plant and animal life while promoting sustainable use of its resources. The reserve extends from the Bay of Puno to the peninsula of Capachica. It's divided into two sectors: one surrounds the Bay of Puno and protects the resources of the Uros-Chuluni communities; the other, in the Huancané area, preserves the totora-reed water fields and protects the nesting area of more than 60 bird species, including the Titicaca grebe.

THE FLOATING ISLANDS

Uru indian woman and totora reeds boat.

ISLAS LOS UROS

Islas Los Uros, known as the Floating Islands, are man-made islands woven together with tótora reeds that grow in the lake shallows. Replenished often with layers because the underbelly reeds rot, these tiny islands resemble floating bails of hay. Walking on them feels like walking on a big waterlogged sponge, but they are sturdy.

VISITING

Trips to the Los Uros typically take 30 minutes and can be arranged from the port in the Puno Bay or with a guide through one of the many agencies in town. While some travelers marvel at these 62-plus islands, some call them floating souvenir stands. Yes, locals sell trinkets, but visiting the floating islands is a glimpse into one of the region's oldest cultures, the Uros. Now mixed with Aymara culture it's a form of human habitation that evolved over centuries. The closest group of "floating museums" is 7 km (4.35 miles) from Puno.

ISLAND LIFE

The islanders make their living by fishing, trapping birds, and selling visitors well-made miniature reed boats, weavings, and collages depicting island life. You can hire an islander to take you for a ride in a reed boat. Although there's no running water, progress has come to some of the islands in the form of solar-powered energy and telephone stations. Seventh Day Adventists converted the inhabitants of one island and built a church and school.

HOMESTAY TIP

It's tradition for most families not to have visitors help in the kitchen, and on several islands families will not eat with visitors. It's also customary to bring a gift—usually essentials like fruit, dried grains, matches, and candles.

TAQUILE & AMANTANI ISLANDS

Folk dances on Taquile island.

TAQUILE ISLAND

35 km (22 miles) east of Puno in the high altitude sunshine, Taquile's brown dusty landscape contrasts with green terraces, bright flowers, and the surrounding blue waters. Snow-capped Bolivian mountains loom in the distance.

Taquile folk are known for weaving some of Peru's loveliest textiles, and men create textiles as much as the women. Islanders still wear traditional dress and have successfully maintained the cooperative lifestyle of their ancestors. The annual Taquile festival the third week of July is a great time to visit.

Taquile is on a steep hill with curvy long trails, which lead to the main square. There are many ways to reach the top of Taquile where there are Inca and Tiahuanaco ruins—you can climb up the 533 stone steps, or take a longer path.

AMANTANI ISLAND

The island of Amantani is 45 km (28 miles) from Puno and almost three hours away by boat from Taquile. Amantani has pre-Inca ruins, and a larger, mainly agrarian society, whose traditional way of life has been less exposed to the outside world until recently. Not as pretty as Taquile, Amantani is dusty and brown.

Locals were losing population to the mainland before a community-based project helped them dive into the tourist industry and organize homestays. Although the project has been a success, make sure you will be your host's only guests for a more intimate experience.

Most of the younger generations speak Spanish and even a smidgen of English, but the older generation speaks only Quechua. Amantani has a population of 3,500 Quechua. Sacred rituals are held in its two pre-Inca temples, dedicated to the earth's fertility.

Amantani woman spinning yarn from wool.

ISLA DEL SOL, BOLIVIA

Adventurous travelers, with a couple days to spare, will want to journey on to Bolivia. After crossing the border, and getting to the pleasant lakeside town of Copacabana (visit the striking Moorish-style cathedral), go on by boat to the Isla del Sol, Lake Titicaca's largest island, where there are tremendous views, Inca ruins, and hotels.

Isla del Sol is the best place to visit and to stay on the lake and is the mythological birthplace of the pre-Inca and Inca. The views of the Cordillera Real mountains are amazing, especially at dawn and dusk, and the island has beautiful white sandy beaches and an extraordinary terraced landscape. Ruins include the Inca palace of Pilkokaina and a strange rock formation said to be the birthplace of the sun and moon, and an excellent Inca trail across the island. Alternatively, you can just laze around and soak up the cosmic energy.

En route to Isla del Sol, boats sometimes stop at **Isla de la Luna**, where the ruins of Iñacuy date back to the Inca conquest. You'll find an ancient con-

vent called Ajlla Wasi (House of the Chosen Women). Stone steps lead up to the unrestored ruins of the convent.

The legends that rise out of Lake Titicaca are no more mysterious than discoveries made in its depths. In 2000 an international diving expedition bumped into what is believed to be a 1,000-year-old pre-Inca temple. The stone structure is 660 feet long and 160 feet wide, with a wall 2,699 feet long. The discovery was made between Copacabana and the Sun and Moon islands.

(pictured top and bottom) Isla del Sol, the Island of the Sun, on Lake Titicaca, Bolivia.

EXPLORING

Anapia and Yuspique Island. In the Winaymarka section of Lake Titicaca, near the Bolivian border are the Aymara-speaking islands of Anapia and Yuspique. This off-the-beaten-path two-day trip can be done with a tour operator or on your own. With 280 families living on the islands, very few people speak English or even Spanish, but rather traditional Aymara.

The trip usually begins in Puno, where you board a bus for two hours to the village of Yunguyo near Punta Hermosa, where you catch a 1.5-hour sailboat ride to the flat but fertile Anapia. On arrival hosts will meet visitors and guide them back to their family's home for an overnight stay. The day is then spent farming, tending to the animals, or playing with the children, and also includes a hiking trip to nearby Yuspique Island, where lunch is cooked by the women on the beach. Typically, *huatia*, potatoes cooked in a natural clay oven and buried in hot soil with lots of herbs, is served along with fresh fish. Yuspique is not very populated, but is home to more than 100 wild vincuñas.

After returning to Anapia you'll follow an evening's activities of traditional family life, such as music or dance. All Ways Travel and Edgar Adventures run tours. Proceeds go to the families. You can do this trip on your own for about $60 USD by following the itinerary and taking a water colectivo from Punta Hermosa to Anapia. Public transportation to the islands only runs on Thursday and Sunday.

Llachon Peninsula. One of the peninsulas that form the bay of Puno, Llachon juts out on the lake near Amantani and Taquile. ■**TIP**➜ The land is dry and barren with rows of pre-Inca terraces, and original ancient paths and trails, which are great for exploring. Locals are more than willing to guide visitors on a light trek to Cerro Auki Carus. Here a circular temple remains the sacred place for villagers to honor the Pachamama (Mother Earth). As the highest point on the peninsula, Cerro Auki Carus serves as an excellent viewpoint to admire the splendor of Lake Titicaca. You can venture out yourself from the port in Puno via water colectivo and then arrange a homestay once in Llachon, or for slightly more money, you can have a tour operator arrange the accommodations for you. By land back from Puno it's about 2–3 hours. Llachon is also a great place to kayak. Tour operator Explorandes has lots of kayak trips around here.

Ticonata Island. A hidden island in a corner of Lake Titicaca, Ticonata is one of the greener islands on the lake. It has a warm microclimate that allows lush green grass to grow, crops to bloom, and many birds to be spied. In 2004 the Quechua-speaking natives of this island were nearly gone—only two families remained on the island. But a community-based project began to teach locals how to use their resources for travel tourism. Today more than a dozen families have returned and ancient island practices are being taught to younger generations. Only a small number of visitors are allowed at a time and the focus of a trip is to help families farm and fish while learning the ancient traditions of the Ticonatas.

It's typically a two-day trip that starts by visiting the floating islands, then the Capachica Peninsula and Llachon, where you can hike through an original pre-Inca path or kayak in the lake. Following a picnic lunch, you head to Ticonata eco-village where you overnight in thatched-roof homes. ■ TIP➔ After helping families farm or fish, you help prepare dinner, followed by a bonfire and native dances. In the morning you'll head two hours to Amantani Island by rustic sailboats and then back to Puno by late afternoon. Most visits need to be arranged by Edgar Adventures. A group tour is easier to book, but a private tour is an option as is volunteering on the island for several days.

SILLUSTANI

30 km (19 miles) northwest of Puno.

Sillustani. High on a hauntingly beautiful peninsula in Lake Umayo is the necropolis of Sillustani. Twenty-eight stone burial towers represent a city of the dead that both predated and coincided with the Inca empire. ■ TIP➔ The proper name for a tower is ayawasi (home of the dead), but they're generally referred to as chullpas, which are actually the shrouds used to cover the mummies inside. This was the land of the Aymará-speaking Colla people, and the precision of their masonry rivals that of the Inca. Sillustani's mystique is heightened by the view it provides over Lake Umayo and its mesa-shape island, El Sombrero, as well as by the utter silence that prevails, broken only by the wind over the water and the cries of lake birds.

Most of the chullpas date from the 14th and 15th centuries, but some were erected as early as AD 900. The tallest, known as the Lizard because of a carving on one of its massive stones, has a circumference of 28 feet. An unusual architectural aspect of the chullpas is that the circumference is smaller at the bottom than the top. To fully appreciate Sillustani, it's necessary to make the long climb to the top; fortunately, the steps are wide and it's an easy climb. Some schoolchildren will put on dances; if you take photos of mothers and children, and pet alpacas, a donation of a few soles will be appreciated.

CHUCUITO

20 km (12 miles) southeast of Puno.

Chucuito (in Aymará: Choque-Huito, Mountain of Gold) is the first of several small towns that dot the lake as you travel from Puno into Bolivia. If you aren't interested in architecture, colonial churches, or don't care to see another undeveloped Peruvian town, then chances are you won't enjoy these little towns. Having said that, Chucuito, surrounded by hillsides crisscrossed with agricultural terraces, has one novelty you won't find elsewhere—its Temple of Fertility, or Templo de Inca Uyu.

The temple is the most interesting thing to see in Chucuito. Almost a ghost town, the main plaza has a large stone Inca sundial as its centerpiece. There are two Renaissance-style 16th-century churches, **La Ascunción** alongside the plaza and the **Santo Domingo** on the east side of town. Neither one has been maintained, but both are open for services.

Templo de Inca Uyu. This "temple" doesn't quite meet the dictionary's description of a temple as a stately edifice, but that's what it's called. ■ TIP→ It's an outdoor area surrounded by a pre-Inca and Inca-made stone walls that block the view of a "garden" of anatomically correct phallic stone sculptures. Each 3-foot-tall penis statue points toward the sky at the Inca sun god, or toward the ground to the Pachamana, the mother earth. It's better known as the Temple of the Phallus. In ancient times it was—and is still today—visited by females who sit for hours on the little statues believing it will increase their fertility. 🎟 *S/5.*

TOTORA REEDS

The totora reeds of Islas los Uros are 70% chloride and 30% iodine and calcium. Once the reed is pulled from its root, the white base known as *chullo* is often eaten for its iodine or wrapped around wounds to relieve pain or cure hangovers. It can also serve as a natural "cooling pack" by splitting it open and placing it on the forehead. Uros commonly use it to brew reed flower tea, and in desperate times it can be eaten as food.

WHERE TO STAY

$ HOTEL 🏨 **Taypikala Hotel & Spa.** Owned by an Aymara shaman and healer, the design of this building, a stone's throw from the Templo de Fertilidad, is as unusual as you will find in Peru. **Pros:** creative. **Cons:** far from Puno. [$] *Rooms from: S/175* ✉ *Chucuito, Calle Sandia* ☎ *051/792–252* 🌐 *www.taypikala.com* 🛏 *39 rooms, 2 suites.*

JULI

On Lake Titicaca, 84 km (52 miles) southeast of Puno.

At one time this village may have been an important Aymará religious center, and it has served as a Jesuit training center for missionaries from Paraguay and Bolivia. Juli has been called "Little Roma" because of its disproportionate number of churches. Four interesting churches in various stages of restoration are **San Pedro Mártir, Santa Cruz de Jerusalén, Asunción,** and **San Juan de Letrán.** The latter has 80 paintings from the Cusco School and huge windows worked in stone. Juli has a Saturday morning bartering market in the main square. It's not a handicraft market, but a produce and animal market where the barter system is in full effect and the trade of animals is interesting to watch. It starts at 9 am and is done by noon. The drive from Puno to Juli takes about 1½ hours.

POMATA

108 km (67 miles) southeast of Puno.

Santiago Apóstol de Nuestra Señora del Rosario. The main attraction in the small lakeside town of Pomata is the church of Santiago Apóstol de Nuestra Señora del Rosario. It was built of pink granite in the 18th century and has paintings from the Cusco School and the Flemish School. Its mestizo baroque carvings and translucent alabaster windows are spectacular. Its altars are covered in gold leaf. Pomata is also famous for its fine pottery, especially for its Toritos de Pucará (bull figures).

A boat sails across Lake Titicaca, on the border between Bolivia and Peru.

BOLIVIAN SIDE OF LAKE TITICACA

You'll hear lots of talk about crossing Lake Titicaca from Peru to Bolivia via hydrofoil or catamaran. At this time you cannot go completely across without stopping at the border and walking from Peru into Bolivia or vice versa. ■ TIP➔ You can still use hydrofoils (only through Crillón Tours) and catamarans in your journey to Bolivia's side of the lake from Copacabana on the Bolivian side, then on to the Sun and Moon islands for an overnight or two on Sun Island.

CROSSING THE BORDER

Bolivia now requires U.S. citizens to obtain a visa to travel in the country. For a price tag of $150 USD, the visa is good for up to 90 days in a calendar year. The application can be done by mail or in person at any Bolivian Consulate or border crossing, not by the Internet. Additionally, a yellow fever vaccination certificate (approximately $150 USD, valid for 10 years) is necessary for Americans to show upon entry. The vaccine must be taken at least 10 days before exposure.

If you're taking a bus from Puno, three hours into the ride the bus will stop just after Yunguyo for border-crossing procedures. Most higher-end bus services hand you immigration forms on the bus. As you leave Peru you'll get off to get an exit stamp from the Peruvian immigration, and then walk through to the small Bolivian immigration building, where you get an entrance stamp and will have to show your visa. From there you catch up with your bus, which will be waiting for you. Keep all immigration documents, your passport, and visa safe; you may need these when leaving Bolivia. The border closes at 6 pm daily.

Those entering from Peru generally overnight in Copacabana, a pleasant, if touristy, town that provides easy access to the lake and the surrounding countryside. Buses from Puno to Copacabana are available through Tour Peru. They cost S/20 and depart from the Puno Bus Terminal at 7:30 am daily. Many buses continue on to La Paz.

GETTING AROUND

The border-crossing tours have packages from $150 USD to $400 USD. Reputable agencies include Crillón Tours and Transturin Ltd; based in Bolivia, tours go from Puno to La Paz and vice versa. Both include pickup from your hotel in Puno and transfer by first-class bus to the border in Yunguyo (a three-hour drive). After crossing the border you take a bus to Copacabana, a funky beach town (30 minutes). The most expensive—and comfortable way—to get to Isla del Sol and Isla de la Luna is by Crillón Tours hydrofoil from the **Inca Utama Hotel,** but cheaper boats leave from Copacabana at 8:30 and 1:30 daily. The journey takes about two hours and costs (Bs)20. Once you are on the island it's walking all the way, unless a mule has been organized through your hotel ahead of time. The tourist office, on the northern side of Isla del Sol, offers private guides for (Bs)100, or (Bs)10 per person when booking groups of 10 or more.

4

ESSENTIALS

Boat Transportation Andes Amazonia. Andes Amazonia ☎ *591/2244–0242 in Bolivia* 🌐 *www.andes-amazonia.com.*

Bus Transportation Tour Peru. Tour Peru ☎ *51/676–600.*

Tour Operators Crillón Tours ☎ *591/233–7533 in Bolivia, 305/358–5853 in U.S.* 🌐 *www.titicaca.com.* **Edgar Adventures** ☎ *051/353–444* 🌐 *www.edgaradventures.com.* **Transturin** ☎ *591/2242–2222 in Bolvia* 🌐 *www.transturin.com.*

WHERE TO STAY

$$$ RESORT 🏨 **Inca Utama Hotel & Spa.** The best lodging on Lake Titicaca's Bolivian side is the Inca Utama Hotel & Spa at Huatajata, home harbor for Crillón Tours' hydrofoils on Lake Titicaca. **Pros:** educational programs replace television; fireplace bar; hydrofoil transportation. **Cons:** difficult location; nothing else in the area. [$] *Rooms from: (Bs)1150* ✉ *86 Carretera Asfaltada, off highway from La Paz to Copacabana (Km 80), Huatajata, Bolivia* ☎ *02/233–7533* 🌐 *www.incautama.com* 🛏 *65 rooms, 4 suites* 🍴 *Breakfast.*

COPACABANA, BOLIVIA

79 km (49 miles) from Huatajata.

Copacabana, a pleasant, if touristy town, provides easy access to the lake, the islands, and the surrounding countryside. It is also a major pilgrimage destination for devout Bolivians at Easter, and lost South American hippies all year. A highlight is watching the sunset over the water from the Stations of the Cross, the highest point of Copacabana.

GETTING HERE AND AROUND

Tour Peru has buses departing from the main terminal in Puno at around 7:30 am and 2:30 pm for S/20; the ride takes around 3½ to 4 hours. Buses returning back to Puno leave Copacabana around 7:30 am and 1:30 pm. It's theoretically possible to drive a rental car from Puno to Copacabana, but passing through Bolivian customs, even if you have all of your paperwork in order, can be a time-consuming hassle. It's easier just to go with public transportation, as a car isn't really needed once you reach Copacabana. In the center of Copacabana's main plaza, the tourist booth is the place to find information about the area.

ESSENTIALS

Bank Prodem ⊠ *Av. 6 de Agosto s/n entre Calles Oruro y Pando, Copacabana, Bolivia* ☎ *591/2862–2183* ⊙ *Closed Mon.*

Bus Transportation Tour Peru ⊠ *Jr Tacna 285, Ofc 103, Copacabana, Bolivia* ☎ *951–676–600.*

Internet Internet Café ⊠ *Av. 6 de Agosto, Copacabana, Bolivia.*

Pharmacy Farmacia ⊠ *Northwest corner of Plaza 2 de Febrero, Copacabana, Bolivia* ☎ *591/795–42606* ⊙ *8 am–10 pm.*

Police Police ⊠ *Plaza 2 de Febrero, north end, Copacabana, Bolivia* ☎ *02/222–5016 or 800–108–687.*

Post Office Copacabana Post Office ⊠ *Plaza de Febrero, Copacabana, Bolivia.*

Visitor Information Centro de Informacion Turistica ⊠ *Av. 16 de Julio, esq Av. 6 de Agosto, Copacabana, Bolivia* ⊙ *Wed.–Sun. 8–noon and 2–6.*

EXPLORING

Cerro Calvario. Marking the highest point of Copacabana are the Stations of the Cross, built in the 1950s for the thousands of pilgrims who summit the hill for prayer and penance on Good Friday. For many tourists, these stone monuments serve as the ideal spot to admire the city and watch the sunset. ⊠ *Trail begins near red chapel at end of Calle Destacamento 211, Copacabana, Bolivia.*

Copacabana Cathedral. The town's breathtaking Moorish-style cathedral, built between 1610 and 1619, is where you'll find the striking sculpture of the Virgin of Copacabana. There was no choice but to build the church, because the statue, carved by Francisco Yupanqui in 1592, was already drawing pilgrims in search of miracles. If you see decorated cars lined up in front of the cathedral, the owners are waiting to have them blessed for safe travel. Walk around to a side door on the left and light a candle for those you wish to remember, then admire the gaudy glitter and wealth of the church interior itself. Throngs of young Paceños do the three-day walk to Copacabana from La Paz to pay homage to the statue with a candlelight procession on Good Friday. They also make the trip here when they buy a new car, lining up in front of the church for a *ch'alla*, or ritual blessing. You can combine your visit with the semi-scramble up past Cerro Calvario (Calvary Hill) on the point above the town. If the climb doesn't knock you out, the view will. ⊠ *Copacabana, Bolivia.*

Horca del Inca. Dating back to 14th century BC, this structure was originally built by the pre-Inca Chiripa culture as an astronomical observatory. Four of the seven horizontal rock slabs were later destroyed by the Spanish who believed gold was hidden inside. The remains of the ruins show signs of vandalism, yet still warrant a visit for those wanting to blend culture and exercise. The slope is steep and rather challenging, but the view of Lake Titicaca will help alleviate the pain. ✉ *Southeast part of city, Copacabana, Bolivia* 🎟 *(Bs)15* ⏲ *7–6.*

WHERE TO EAT

Copacabana has a wide array of hotels, hostels, international cafés, and bars and pizza joints, which reflects its popularity as a weekend destination from La Paz and as the crossing point for travelers from Peru. There's a lot of competition, so most are good value—the best thing to do for lunch or dinner is wander along the two main streets and window-shop first. You can find the famous trout dishes everywhere.

$ CAFÉ 🍴 **Condor and The Eagle Café.** If you are dying for a decent cup of organic coffee, this is the place to get your caffeine fix. This cozy spot operates as a bookstore, Internet café, and breakfast house. Power up with a bowl of muesli mixed with natural yogurt, fresh fruit, and honey, or grab a cappuccino and brownie to go. They have a wide variety of American classics for sale as well as handmade arts and crafts. [$] *Average main: (Bs)15* ✉ *Av. 6 de Agosto and Calle Bolivar, across from Plaza Sucre, Copacabana, Bolivia* 🌐 *www.facebook.com/elcondoryelaguilacafe* 💳 *No credit cards* ⏲ *Closed Wed.*

$$ VEGETARIAN 🍴 **Kala Uta.** Good things come to those who wait at this slow-food, mostly vegetarian restaurant. Homemade pizza, pasta, and salad are all on the menu, as is trout prepared 20 different ways. Main courses come with quinoa, corn, or sweet potatoes. For dessert, take your pick from flan, crepes, or flambé. [$] *Average main: (Bs)45* ✉ *Av. 6 de Agosto, across from Plaza Sucre, Copacabana, Bolivia* ☎ *749–01288* 💳 *No credit cards.*

$$ SEAFOOD 🍴 **Snack 6 de Agosto.** Although it serves various entrées, this place is best known for its trout, fresh from Lake Titicaca. There's also a selection of vegetarian dishes, including a flavorful quinoa soup. [$] *Average main: (Bs)60* ✉ *Av. 6 de Agosto, Copacabana, Bolivia* ☎ *02/0862–2114.*

$$ VEGETARIAN 🍴 **Sujna Wasi.** This Spanish-owned restaurant is tiny, with seating for fewer than two-dozen people. It's the place to come in Copacabana for vegetarian food. They also serve trout with quinoa and great breakfasts from 7–11 daily. The restaurant has a small library with books, maps, and travel information. [$] *Average main: (Bs)55* ✉ *Calle General Gonzalo Jaúregui 127, Copacabana, Bolivia* ☎ *02/7486–1624* 💳 *No credit cards.*

WHERE TO STAY

$$ B&B/INN 🏨 **Ambassador Hotel.** This hotel near the lake is aligned with a youth hostel, which means it offers special rates for students. **Pros:** right on the beach. **Cons:** rubbish from the lake close by; no Internet; somewhat tacky decor in the lobby. [$] *Rooms from: (Bs)120* ✉ *Calle General Gonzalo Jaúregui, Plaza Sucre, Copacabana, Bolivia* ☎ *02/862–2216* 🛏 *42 rooms* 💳 *No credit cards* 🍽 *Breakfast.*

DID YOU KNOW?

According to legend, Isla del Sol is where the Inca Empire was founded when Manco Kapac and Mama Ojllo, son and daughter of the Sun god Inti, came down to Earth to improve the life of the altiplano people.

$ **Hotel La Cupula.** It's worth staying on in Copacabana just to enjoy
B&B/INN   this alternative-style hotel tucked below the hills at one corner of the
Fodor'sChoice   bay. **Pros:** alternative vibe; great vegetarian breakfasts; the penthouse
★   room—if you can get it. **Cons:** breakfast not included; no Internet; staff
can be hard to locate; some rooms lack private bathrooms. $ *Rooms*
from: (Bs)220 ⊠ *Calle Michel Pérez 1–3, Copacabana, Bolivia*
🕾 *02/862–2029* ⊕ *www.hotelcupula.com* ⤴ *17 rooms, 3 with shared*
bath; 6 suites ⊠ *No meals.*

$$$ **Hotel Rosario Del Lago Titicaca.** One of the nicest accommodations in
HOTEL   Copacabana, this colonial-style hotel is a few blocks from the main
Fodor'sChoice   plaza. **Pros:** friendly staff; good buffet breakfast; the view of the sun-
★   set from any of the rooms; heaters in the rooms. **Cons:** no closets;
no Wi-Fi in the rooms. $ *Rooms from: (Bs)693* ⊠ *Calle Rigoberto*
Paredes and Av. Costanera, Copacabana, Bolivia 🕾 *02/862–2141,*
02/245–1341 in La Paz ⊕ *www.hotelrosario.com/lago* ⤴ *24 rooms,*
1 suite ⊠ *Breakfast.*

ISLA DEL SOL AND ISLA DE LA LUNA, BOLIVIA

12 km (7½ miles) north of Copacabana.

GETTING HERE AND AROUND

The most expensive—and comfortable—way to get here is by hydrofoil
from the **Inca Utama Hotel** in Huatajata, but cheaper boats leave from
Copacabana at 8:30 am and 1:30 pm and return from Isla del Sol south
port at 8:30 am, 10:30 am, and 3:30 pm. The journey from Copacabana
takes about two hours and costs (Bs)20. Once you are on the island,
it's walking all the way, unless a mule has been organized through your
hotel ahead of time. The tourist office, located on the northern side of
Isla del Sol, offers private guides for (Bs)100, or (Bs)10 per person when
booking groups of 10 or more.

ESSENTIALS

Boat Transportation Andes Amazonia ⊠ *Av. 6 de Agosto, Esq Plaza Sucre,*
Copacabana, Bolivia 🕾 *02/862-2616* ⊕ *www.andesamazoniabolivia.com*
⌔ *(Bs)20* ⏱ *9:30–noon and 3-6.*

Visitor Information Asociacion Turismo Comunitario ⊠ *North port, Isla del*
Sol, Bolivia 🕾 *719-15544 or 772-99088.*

Fodor'sChoice   **Isla del Sol.** The largest of Lake Titicaca's islands, Isla del Sol is the best
★   place to visit and stay on the lake. The views of the Cordillera Real
mountains are amazing, especially at dawn and dusk, and the island
has beautiful white sandy beaches and an extraordinary terraced land-
scape. There are ruins, including the Inca palace of Pilkokaina and a
strange rock formation said to be the birthplace of the sun and moon,
and an excellent Inca trail across the island. Some travelers take a boat
to the northern community of Challa Pampa and then hike 3–4 hours
to the southern community of Yumani where most accommodations
(and the main "village") can be found. Although rewarding, the island
trail is void of shade with only three spots to buy water along the way.
If your goal is to just laze around and soak up the cosmic energy, then
be sure to disembark at the southern boat port of Yumani, unless you

are staying at one of the few hotels on the north side. One of the best beaches on Isla del Sol is located on the north end, directly behind the museum. Regardless of your destination, plan on hiking at least 30 minutes uphill from the boat port. Nearly every property is staggered high on the slope, which means that both altitude and fitness should be taken into consideration. ✉ *Bolivia.*

Isla de la Luna. En route to Isla del Sol, boats sometimes stop at Isla de la Luna, where the ruins of Iñacuy date back to the Inca conquest. You'll find an ancient convent called Ajlla Wasi (House of the Chosen Women). Stone steps lead up to the unrestored ruins of the convent. ✉ *Bolivia.*

4

WHERE TO STAY

You will be amply rewarded for your climb up the steps from the port—the higher you go, the cheaper the hostels or *posadas*. They are almost all good, if basic. The north side of the island is more barren but also has attractive options, including a place on the beach itself.

$ B&B/INN 🏨 **Hostal Pacha-Mama.** Located at the north end of the island, this low-budget hostel is a bit unkempt, but it's right on Challapampa beach and has hot showers. **Pros:** cheap as they come; the hot water is a novelty. **Cons:** be prepared to rough it in the rooms; on a very busy road; endless partying. [$] *Rooms from: (Bs)140* ✉ *Isla del Sol North, Playa, Bolivia* ☎ *02/735–30261* 🛏 *20 rooms* 💳 *No credit cards* 🍴 *No meals.*

$$$$ B&B/INN 🏨 **La Estancia Ecolodge.** Staggered on a hillside, each bungalow (named for flora) has an unobstructed view of Lake Titicaca, making it the perfect place to watch the sunrise. **Pros:** excellent views; great showers; dinners integrate local flavors. **Cons:** unlit paths at night; overpriced; arrangements must be made through La Paz office. [$] *Rooms from: (Bs)1100* ✉ *South end of Isla del Sol, Bolivia* ☎ *02/244–2727* 🌐 *www.ecolodge-laketiticaca.com* 🛏 *15 rooms* 🍴 *Some meals.*

$$$ B&B/INN Fodor's Choice ★ 🏨 **La Posada del Inca.** Your stay at this lovely posada begins with a 30-minute mule ride (a llama carries your luggage) from the boat dock to the garden-lobby where fruit trees shade handmade reed couches. **Pros:** high standard of service; good food; pleasant garden setting. **Cons:** the pricing; slightly out of place on the island. [$] *Rooms from: (Bs)1000* ✉ *Isla del Sol, Bolivia* ☎ *02/233–7533* 🌐 *www.titicaca.com* 🛏 *21 rooms* 🍴 *Some meals.*

Cusco and the Sacred Valley

WORD OF MOUTH

"I would have to say I loved Cusco/Sacred Valley the best. It has such an interesting history, and beautiful topography. The countryside is beautiful and rich with color...The food was amazing, organic and healthy, the pisco sours were sublime (no pun intended) and the people were fantastic!."

—clelbong

WELCOME TO CUSCO AND THE SACRED VALLEY

Santo Domingo Church in Cuzco

TOP REASONS TO GO

★ **Alpaca Clothing:** Nothing says "Cusco" quite like a sweater, shawl, poncho, or scarf woven from the hair of the alpaca.

★ **Andean Cuisine:** Where else in the world will you find roasted *cuy* (guinea pig) and alpaca steaks rubbing shoulders on fine-dining menus?

★ **Inca Architecture:** How did the Inca construct stone walls so precisely using 15th-century technology? How could they position a temple so it would be illuminated best at the exact moment of the solstice?

★ **Layered Religion:** Take a closer look at the walls— every Catholic church was built on the site, and often the foundation, of an Inca *huaca,* or sacred place.

★ **Hotels with History:** Cusco's hostelries brim with history. Many are former convents, monasteries, dwellings of sacred women, or palaces of Spanish conquerors.

★ **Sacred Playground:** The Sacred Valley is an adventurer's playground for hiking, biking, and rafting.

CORDILLERA URUBAMBA

Ollantaytambo
Salineras
Maras
Moray
Huayllabamba
Urubamba
Yucay
Huayllabamba
Racchi
Chinchero
Huarocondo
Lake Huaypo
Lake Piuray
Ch'uso
Zurite
Izcuchaca
Anta
Poroy
Tambomachay
2
Cusco
1

1 Cusco. You'll be missing out if you skip Cusco on your way to Machu Picchu or the Sacred Valley. This city is a mix of new and old: ancient Inca walls holding up baroque colonial buildings, inside of which lie some of the city's most contemporary restaurants and shops. Colonial churches and cultural museums dot the plaza, while funky modern cafés sit side by side with traditional galleries of Cusqueñan art in San Blas. Inca gems are everywhere, even along the traffic-heavy business district of Avenida El Sol, home of Cusco's star attraction, the Qorikancha Sun Temple.

2 Side Trips—The Southeastern Urubamba Valley. What really made the Inca civilization so successful? Their appreciation of a good view! Gorgeous Andean landscapes characterize almost every important Inca site in the area surrounding Cusco. For a bird's-eye perspective on the city, head uphill to the second most famous Inca site of them all—Sacsayhuamán.

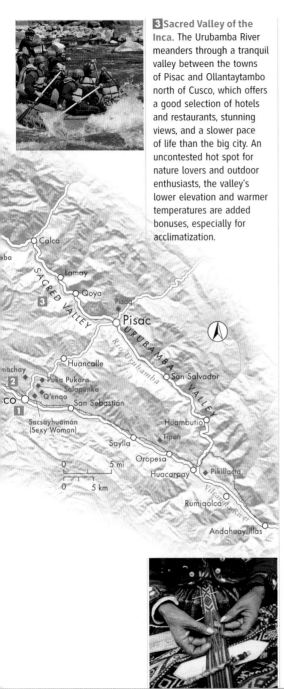

3 Sacred Valley of the Inca. The Urubamba River meanders through a tranquil valley between the towns of Pisac and Ollantaytambo north of Cusco, which offers a good selection of hotels and restaurants, stunning views, and a slower pace of life than the big city. An uncontested hot spot for nature lovers and outdoor enthusiasts, the valley's lower elevation and warmer temperatures are added bonuses, especially for acclimatization.

GETTING ORIENTED

At the center of Cusco is the colonial Plaza de Armas, slightly sloped, with streets heading downhill, most prominently the Avenida El Sol, leading to the more modern sections of the city. Heading uphill takes you to the city's older neighborhoods, notably the artisan quarter of San Blas and its web of pedestrian-only walkways. If you look up and to the left, you'll see that towering over the lot is the archaeological site of Sacsayhuamán, which sits just to the left of the Christo Blanco. This white Christ statue is most clearly seen at night when it's lighted by floodlights. The Urubamba mountain range on the north side and Cusco and environs on the south side watch over the river basin known as the Sacred Valley. Transportation to the Sacred Valley is straightforward, with roads fanning out from Urubamba, the valley's small hub city, and back to Cusco.

Updated by Maureen Santucci

"Bienvenidos a la ciudad imperial del Cusco" announces the flight attendant when your plane touches down at a lofty 3,300 meters above sea level. "Welcome to the imperial city of Cusco." This greeting hints at what you're in for in Cusco, one of the world's great travel destinations.

The city has stood for nine centuries, a wellspring of culture and tradition soaring above the fertile Andean Valley. The area's rich history springs forth from the Inca tale that describes how Manco Capac and his sister-consort Mama Ocllo were sent by the Sun and Moon to enlighten the people of Peru. Setting off from Lake Titicaca with the directive to settle only where their golden staff could be plunged fully into the soil, they traveled far across the altiplano until reaching the fertile soils surrounding present-day Cusco. They envisioned Qosqo (Cusco) in the shape of a puma, the animal representation of the Earth in the indigenous cosmos, which you can still see today on city maps. But not all was Inca in southern Peru. Not far from Cusco sits Pikillacta, a pre-Inca city constructed by the Wari culture that thrived between AD 600 and 1000. It's an indication that this territory, like most of Peru, was the site of sophisticated civilizations long before the Inca appeared.

By the time Francisco Pizarro and the Spanish conquistadors arrived in 1532, the Inca Empire had spread from modern-day Ecuador in the north down through Peru and Bolivia to Chile. Sadly, the city's grandeur could do little to save an Empire weakened by internal strife and civil war. Stocked with guns and horses, which the Inca had never seen, and carrying new diseases, against which they had no immunity, the Spanish arrived with the upper hand, despite smaller numbers. In 1532, the Spanish seized Atahualpa, the recently instated Inca ruler, while he was in Cajamarca to subdue rebellious forces. The Inca's crumbling house of cards came tumbling down, though pockets of resistance remained for years in places like Ollantaytambo.

After sacking the Inca Empire, Spanish colonists instated new political and religious systems, superimposing their beliefs onto the old society and its structures. They looted gold, silver, and stone and built their own churches, monasteries, convents, and palaces directly onto the foundations of the Inca sites. This is one of the most striking aspects of the city today. The Santo Domingo church was built on top of the Qorikancha, the Temple of the Sun. And it's downright ironic to think of the cloistered convent of Santa Catalina occupying the same site as the equally cloistered Acllawasi, the home of the Inca chosen women, who were selected to serve the sun in the Qorikancha temple. The cultural combination appears in countless other ways: witness the pumas carved into the cathedral doors. The city also gave its name to the Cusqueña school of art, in which New World artists combined Andean motifs with European-style painting, usually on religious themes. You'll chance on paintings that could be by Van Dyck but for the Inca robes on New Testament figures, and Last Supper diners digging into an Andean feast of guinea pig and fermented corn.

Throughout the Cusco region you'll witness this odd juxtaposition of imperial and colonial, indigenous and Spanish. Traditionally clad Quechua-speaking women sell their wares in front of a part-Inca, part-colonial structure as a business executive of European heritage walks by carrying on a cell-phone conversation. The two cultures coexist, but have not entirely embraced each other even five centuries after the conquest.

The Río Urubamba flows, at its closest, about 30 km (18 miles) north of Cusco and passes through a valley about 300 meters (980 feet) lower in elevation than Cusco. The northwestern part of this river basin, romantically labeled the Sacred Valley of the Inca, contains some of the region's most appealing towns and fascinating pre-Columbian ruins. A growing number of visitors are heading here directly upon arrival in Cusco to acclimatize. The valley's altitude is slightly lower and its temperatures slightly higher, and make for a physically easier introduction to this part of Peru.

PLANNING

WHEN TO GO
Cusco's high season is June through early September (winter in the southern hemisphere) and the days around the Christmas and Easter holidays. Winter means drier weather and easier traveling, but higher lodging prices and larger crowds. Prices and visitor numbers drop dramatically during the November through March summer rainy season, except around the holidays.

PLANNING YOUR TIME
The typical tour of the Cusco region combines the city with the Sacred Valley and Machu Picchu in three whirlwind days, including the full Boleto Turístico. We recommend devoting five days to get the most out of your visit—including one day to get acclimated to the high altitude.

GETTING HERE AND AROUND
AIR TRAVEL
LAN Peru (⊕ *www.lan.com*) connects Cusco with Lima, Arequipa, Juilaca, and Puerto Maldonado. Peruvian Airlines (⊕ *www.peruvianairlines. pe*) offers connecting service from Lima to Cusco, Arequipa, Tacna, and Iquitos. Star Perú (⊕ *www.starperu.com*) and TACA Peru (⊕ *www.taca.*

com) fly from Cusco to Lima. You can find offices for LAN, Taca, and StarPeru along the Avenida del Sol; Peruvian Airlines is located on Calle Medio just off the Plaza de Armas in Cusco.

BUS TRAVEL

Cusco's main bus terminal is at the Terminal Terrestre in Santiago, not

HEY TOURIST!

The ubiquitous "tourist informa-tion" signs are storefront travel agencies anxious to sell you tours rather than provide unbiased, offi-cial sources of information.

far from the airport. The best company running from Cusco is Cruz del Sur (⊕ *www.cruzdelsur.com.pe*), which has its own terminal on Avenida Industrial in Bancopata. Bus travel between Cusco and the Sacred Val-ley is cheap, frequent . . . and sometimes accident-prone; taxis (shared or private) are by far the better option.

CAR TRAVEL

For exploring the Sacred Valley, a car is the best option. The vehicular tourist route ends at Ollantaytambo. Cusco is the only place to rent a vehicle. However, you won't need or want to drive inside the city; heavy traffic, lack of parking, and narrow streets, many of them pedestrian only, make a car a burden. Driving anywhere in Peru seems to have its own unwritten rules, so hiring a car and driver or going by taxi is the usually the safest option.

TAXI TRAVEL

Cusco's licensed taxis have a small official taxi sticker on the windshield, but these are difficult to see. Choose ones that have the name and num-ber of a company on the top. Fares are S/3 within the central city and S/4 after 10 pm. Have your hotel or restaurant call a taxi for you at night.

Mototaxis—three-wheeled motorized vehicles with room for two pas-sengers—ply the streets of Sacred Valley towns. Touring the Sacred Val-ley from Cusco with one of the city's taxis costs about $60–$70 USD, but depends largely on your negotiating skills.

TRAIN TRAVEL

PeruRail is the most established operator in Peru; its *Andean Explorer* train departs from Cusco (at Wanchaq Station on Pachacutec) Mon-day, Wednesday, and Saturday at 8 am for Puno. There is an additional train on Friday April to October.) The scenic journey takes 10 hours. Three classes of daily service to Machu Picchu depart from Cusco's Poroy station. Trains depart early in the morning—with the luxury *Hiram Bingham* service departing from Poroy at 9 am. Trains depart throughout the day from the Ollantaytambo station. Purchase tickets in advance from the PeruRail sales office in the Plaza de Armas, online (⊕ *www.perurail.com*), or from a travel agency. ⇨ *For more informa-tion see Train Travel in Chapter 6, Machu Picchu and the Inca Trail.*

HEALTH AND SAFETY

ALTITUDE SICKNESS

Known as *soroche,* you'll likely encounter altitude sickness at Cusco's 3,500-meter (11,500-foot) elevation. Drink lots of fluids but eliminate or minimize alcohol and caffeine consumption. Many hotels have an oxygen supply for their guests' use. The prescription drug acetazolamide can help. Check with your physician about this (allergies to the drug are not uncommon), and about traveling here if you have a heart condition or high blood pressure, or are pregnant.

⚠ Warning: Sorojchi pills are a Bolivian-made altitude-sickness remedy whose advertising pictures a tourist vomiting at Machu Picchu. Its safety has not been documented, and it only contains pain relievers and caffeine, so we don't recommend it.

SAFETY
Security has improved dramatically in Cusco. A huge police presence is on the streets, especially around tourist centers such as the Plaza de Armas. Nonetheless, petty crime, such as pickpocketing, is not uncommon: use extra vigilance in crowded markets or when getting on and off buses and trains. Robbers have also targeted late-night and early-morning revelers stumbling back to their hotels. Women should not leave drinks unattended at dance clubs; there have been cases in which drinks have been tampered with.

WATER
Tap water is not safe to drink here. Stick with the bottled variety, *con gas* (carbonated) or *sin gas* (plain).

DISCOUNTS AND DEALS
Offering access to 16 of Cusco's best-known tourist attractions, the Boleto Turístico (tourist ticket) is the all-in-one answer to your tourism needs. There are four different passes you can purchase. For S/130 you can get a 10-day pass that lets you visit all 16 sites in the city and around the Sacred Valley. Alternatively, you can opt for one of three amended circuits outlined in the Boleto Parcial, each S/70. Although always subject to change, the participating sites have remained the same for some time. Certain big-name attractions (such as the Catedral) have withdrawn from the Boleto Turístico in order to levy their own fees. Regardless, if you want to see sites like Sacsayhuamán and Pisac, you have to buy the ticket, which can be purchased at the **Comite de Servicios Integrados Turisticos Culturales del Cusco** *(COSITUC) (⊠ Av. El Sol 103 ☎ 084/261–465 Ext. 203 ⊕ www.cosituc.gob.pe)*, open daily 8–6.

South American Explorers. This is a membership organization. Its $60 USD annual dues get you a wealth of information as well as discounts at local establishments. It has clubhouses in Cusco, Lima, and other South American cities. ⊠ *Atoqsaycuchi 670 ☎ 084/245–484 ⊕ www. saexplorers.org ⊗ Weekdays 9:30–5, Sat. 9:30–1.*

TOURS
One of the most important decisions you'll make when planning your trip is whether or not you want to engage the services of a travel agency. If you speak Spanish and are only doing a quick Lima-Cusco-Machu Picchu trip, it may not be so necessary. If not, there are reasons you might consider doing so.

When you hire an agency, you'll be met at each arrival by a driver with a sign bearing your name. If there are problems—your hotel loses the reservation, there is a strike keeping you from your next destination, inclement weather grounds your flight—you will have someone on the ground to help you find solutions. Traveling between destinations is also made easier by the fact that the agency will know when the buses, flights, or trains are available. They can plan an itinerary for you taking these things into account, so that you make the most of the time you have available to travel.

The biggest two concerns most people have when considering using an agency are price and being restricted to a specific itinerary. If you choose a moderately priced Peruvian agency (these are typically ones that will charge about $600 USD for a Classic Inca Trail), the percentage that they will mark-up a personalized itinerary usually isn't that much beyond what you would pay doing it yourself. As for restrictions, be sure to make it clear to them what your priorities are, and if you want some down time in places, let them know.

Another question when booking tours is whether to go for a group tour or book a private one. Prices can vary from place to place, but if you are working with an agency, be sure to ask what the difference in price is. For example, a tour to the Sacred Valley with a group is about $20 USD, not including lunch or admissions. Group size can be up to 30 people and, when it is not high season, you may end up in a bilingual group where more explanation is often given in whichever language the bulk of the group speaks.

You can get the same tour in private service for around $185 USD for up to six people. Whether it is worth it to you or not will depend on your interests. You'll be able to hear your guide better, explanations can be geared toward your particular obsessions (history, culture, architecture, plants, etc.), you can decide what sites you want to see, and stay as long as you like rather than being herded back onto the bus before you're done. Making your own decisions is key. If you get tired of seeing "rocks," however impressively they have been assembled, you can get your guide to take you to a site that's off the beaten path, on a walk through the country, or to the best chicheria.

■ **TIP➡** If you need to pay in dollars, as agencies sometimes request, they cannot be even the slightest bit torn. When it comes to soles, many shops do not have change, so it's best to use the larger bills at higher-end shops and restaurants so that you will have small change for the smaller ones.

If you want to spend time in Lima, plan to do so at the end of your trip. That way if you run into transportation problems, you will be less likely to miss your flight home.

SELECTING A TOUR OPERATOR

"Holaaaa—trip to Machu Picchu?" With so many touts in Cusco's streets hawking tours to Peru's most famous sight, it's tempting to just buy one in order to make them stop asking. Anyone who offers an Inca Trail trek departing tomorrow should be taken with more than a grain of salt—Inca Trail walks need to be booked months in advance. Don't make arrangements or give money to someone claiming to be a travel agent if they approach you on the street or at the airport in Cusco or Lima. Instead, choose an agency that has a physical address. Better yet, select one that is listed here or on ⊕ *www.peru.info.* ⇨ *Below are several reputable travel agencies.*

TOUR OPERATORS

Amazonas Explorer. This guide has more than 20 years of experience organizing top-quality alternative adventure and cultural tours. All guides are safety certified and equipment is top-shelf. One percent of profits are donated to sustainable tourism and native tree planting. ✉ *Av. Collasuyo 910* ☎ *084/252–846* ⊕ *www.amazonasexplorer.com.*

Andina Travel. Specializing in trekking and alternatives to the Inca Trail, Andina Travel also offers standard Sacred Valley and Machu Picchu tours as well as biking and rafting. ☎ *084/251–892* ⊕ *www. andinatravel.com.*

Another Planet. For custom-built hiking, biking, rafting and city tours, as well as healing retreats, check out Another Planet. The foreign-owned and family operated company has more than 15 years of guiding experience, and also runs the popular Casa de la Gringa Hostal and Andean Wings Boutique Hotel. ☎ *084/243–166* ⊕ *www.andeanwingshotel.com.*

Apumayo Expediciones. This operator offers a full gamut of adventure tours and nonconventional treks, including trips geared toward the disabled. ☎ *084/246–018* ⊕ *www.apumayo.com.*

Aspiring Adventures. Started by two long-time professionals in adventure travel, this agency specializes in tours that go off the beaten path. In addition to visiting the must-see sights, you will have the opportunity to engage with the Peruvian culture in a much more intimate way than with the typical canned tours. This boutique company excels in personal service, ensuring that the trip you get exceeds even the highest of expectations. ☎ *877/438–1354* in *U.S. and Canada, 643/489–7474 worldwide* ⊕ *www.aspiringadventures.com.*

Cusco Top Travel & Treks. Run by the wildly talented and witty David Choque, this guide specializes in a range of packaged and comfort-class custom-built tours. ☎ *084/251–864* ⊕ *www.cuscotoptravelperu.com.*

El Chalan. This operator organizes single and multiday horseback riding treks for all levels (beginner to professional) throughout the Sacred Valley. Riders and horses alike are carefully tended to and looked after. ☎ *984/737–897or 084/201–541* ⊕ *www.ranchoelchalan.com.*

Enigma. Specializing in small, customized adventure trips, you can enjoy trekking, rafting, mountain climbing, mountain biking, or horseback riding led by professional guides. ☎ *084/222–155* ⊕ *www. enigmaperu.com.*

Explorandes. This is a large and long-running company that organizes customized guided trips and expeditions through the Andes in Peru and Ecuador, including rafting and trekking trips around Cusco. ☎ *084/238–380* ⊕ *www.explorandes.com.*

Inkaterra. A top-end agency specializing in nature-and-culture oriented trips and a 30-year veteran of sustainable tourism, the company customizes tours around Cusco and the Sacred Valley with however much guide accompaniment you desire. ☎ *800/442–5042* ⊕ *www.inkaterra.com.*

Intrepid Travel. This Australian company offers a variety of itineraries using Peruvian tour leaders as well local guides when appropriate. Group size averages around 10 people and tours are geared toward a balanced mix of planned activities and free time. ☎ *613/9473–2673 Australia* ⊕ *www.intrepidtravel.com.*

Kuoda Travel. For top-tier personalized tours, including an eight-day journey from the Amazon to Cusco and the Sacred Valley and outstanding service, try Kuoda Travel. ☎ *084/221–773, 800/986–4150 in U.S. and Canada* ⊕ *www.kuodatravel.com.*

River Explorers. Contact River Explorers for one- to six-day rafting and kayaking excursions on the Urubamba and Apurimac rivers and standard trekking tours. ☎ *084/260–926* ⊕ *www.riverexplorers.com.*

SAS Travel. Cusco-based SAS Travel has made a name for itself in trekking circles, but can also customize tours and accommodations. ☎ *084/291–194* ⊕ *www.sastravelperu.com.*

TopTurPeru. An internationally recognized, local company run by Raul Castelo and family. An archaeoastronomy expert, Raul has been sought out by National Geographic and other documentary-filmmaking entities worldwide. ☎ *084/243–234* ⊕ *www.topturperu.com.*

Wayki Trek. A unique, indigenously managed operator specializing in Inca Trail and alternative trekking. They are known for great guides and excellent customer service. ☎ *084/224–092* ⊕ *www.waykitrek.net.*

Wilderness Travel. The company offers a variety of itineraries for touring around the Cusco region and visiting Machu Picchu, depending on how active you want to be. A luxury trek features stays at mountain lodges rather than tents. ☎ *800/368–2794 in U.S.* ⊕ *www. wildernesstravel.com.*

X-treme Tourbulencia. This agency leads mountain climbing, biking, trekking, and multisport trips. ☎ *084/222–405, 702/560–7220 in U.S. and Canada* ⊕ *www.x-tremetourbulencia.com.*

CUSCO

If you arrive in Cusco with the intention of hopping on the train to Machu Picchu the next morning, you'll probably only have time to take a stroll through the Plaza de Armas and visit Qorikancha (Temple of the Sun) and the Catedral. However, the city merits exploration, either at the start or end of your trip. We recommend spending at least two days in Cusco, giving you time to acclimate to the altitude and get to know this city of terra-cotta roofs and cobblestone streets. The churches and some restaurants close for a few hours in the middle of the day. Some of the city's museums close on Sunday, but most are open, sometimes with shorter hours.

Cusco takes its newest role as tourist favorite in stride, and absorbs thousands of travelers with an ample supply of lodgings, restaurants, and services. That a polished infrastructure exists in such a remote, high-elevation locale is a pleasant surprise.

GETTING AROUND

Cusco's Aeropuerto Internacional Teniente Alejandro Velasco Astete (CUZ) is about 15 minutes from the center of town. An army of taxis waits at the exit from baggage claim, and they charge wildly varying

ACCLIMATIZING WITH COCA TEA

Take it easy! Cusco is a breathless 3,300 meters (10,825 feet) above sea level—a fact you'll very soon appreciate as you huff and puff your way up its steep cobbled streets. With 30% less oxygen in the atmosphere, the best way to avoid altitude sickness is to take it easy on your first few days. There's no point in dashing off on that Inca hike if you're not acclimatized—altitude sickness is uncomfortable at best and can be very dangerous.

Locals swear by *mate de coca,* an herbal tea brewed from coca leaves that helps with altitude acclimatization. Indigenous peoples have chewed the leaves of the coca plant for centuries to cope with Andean elevations. But the brewing of the leaves in an herbal tea is considered a more refined and completely legal way to ingest the substance, in Andean nations at least. Most restaurants and virtually all hotels have leaves and hot water available constantly.

rates to take you to the city center. Compare some rates, have your hotel pick you up, or carry your bags out to the street, where the standard price to the center is S/6.

Cusco's center city is most enjoyably explored on foot. Many of the streets open to vehicular traffic are so narrow that it's simply faster to walk. ■TIP➔ Cusco streets have a habit of changing names every few blocks, or even every block. Many streets bear a common Spanish name that everyone uses, but have newly designated street signs with an old Quechua name in order to highlight the city's Inca heritage: the Plaza de Armas is Haukaypata, the Plaza Regocijo is Kusipata, Triunfo is Sunturwasi, Loreto is Intikijlli, Arequipa is Q'aphchijk'ijllu, and intermittent blocks of Avenida El Sol are labeled Mut'uchaka. And so on.

Report any problems with tour companies, hotels, restaurants, and so on to INDECOPI, a tourist-focused government agency.

ESSENTIALS

Airport Aeropuerto Internacional Teniente Alejandro Velasco Astete ✉ *Av. Velasco Astete s/n* ☎ *084/222-611.*

Bus Cruz del Sur ✉ *Av. Industrial 121, Bancopata* ☎ *084/720-444* ⊕ *www.cruzdelsur.com.pe.* **Ormeño** ✉ *Terminal Terrestre de Cuzco* ☎ *084/261-704 or 084/241-426, 014/721-710 Lima* ⊕ *www.grupo-ormeno.com.pe.*

Currency Banco de Crédito. This bank also has ATMS in the Plaza de Armas and the Plaza San Blas. ✉ *Av. El Sol 189* ☎ *01/311-9898* ⊕ *www.viabcp.com.* **Western Union** ✉ *Maruri 310* ☎ *084/248-028.*

Mail DHL ✉ *Av. El Sol 608.* **Scharff International/FedEx** ✉ *Tacna 208-Wanchaq* ☎ *084/264-141.* **SERPOST** ✉ *Av. El Sol 800* ☎ *084/224-212.*

Medical Clínica Pardo ✉ *Av. de la Cultura 710, Plaza Tupac Amaru* ☎ *084/240-387.* **Dr. Eduardo Luna.** Dr. Luna specializes in travel medicine, will make visits to hotels, and speaks English. ✉ *Cusco* ☎ *984/761-277.* **Hospital Regional** ✉ *Av. de la Cultura s/n-Wanchaq* ☎ *084/223-691.*

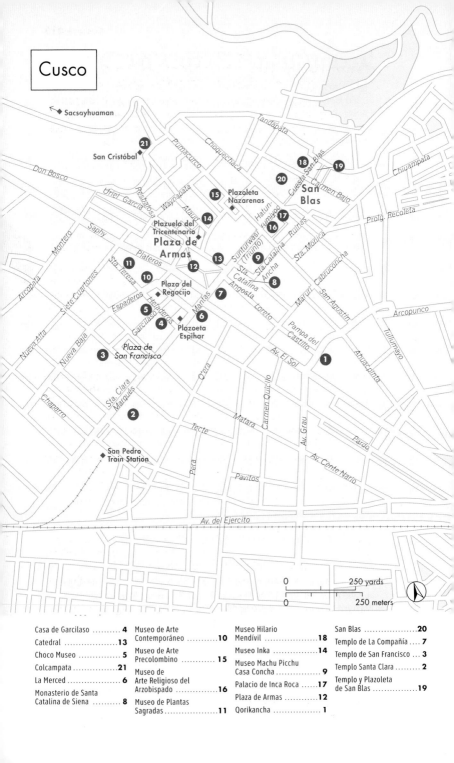

Cusco

Sacsayhuaman

Police INDECOPI ⊠ *Urb. Constancia Mz A-11-12, Wanchaq* ☎ *084/252–987*
⊕ *www.indecopi.gob.pe.* **Policia Nacional** ⊠ *Plaza Tupac Amaru* ☎ *084/249–654.* **Tourism Police (POLTUR).** ⊠ *Plaza Tupac Amaru* ☎ *084/235–123.*

Rental Car Atix Rent A Car ⊠ *Garcilaso 210, Office 125, Cusco* ☎ *084/241–824.* **Hertz** ⊠ *Av. El Sol 803* ☎ *084/248–800* ⊕ *www.gygrentacar.com.* **Manu Rent A Car** ⊠ *Av. El Sol 520, Cusco* ☎ *084/233–382* ⊕ *www.manurentacar.com.* **OSDI Rent-a-Car** ⊠ *Urb. Mateo Pumacahua B-10* ☎ *084/251–616.*

Taxi Alo Cusco ☎ *084/222–222.* **Llama Taxi** ☎ *084/222–000.*
Taxi Turismo Cusco ☎ *084/245–000.*

Train PeruRail. There is a second ticket office in Plaza Regocijo. ⊠ *Portal de Carnes 214, Plaza de Armas* ☎ *084/581–414* ⊕ *www.perurail.com* ⊙ *Daily 7 am–9:30 pm.* **Inca Rail** ⊠ *Portal de Panes 105, Plaza de Armas* ☎ *084/233–030* ⊕ *www.incarail.com* ⊙ *Weekdays 8–6, weekends 9–6.* **Machu Picchu Train** ⊠ *Av. El Sol 576* ☎ *084/221–199* ⊕ *www.machupicchutrain.com* ⊙ *Mon.–Sat. 8–8, Sun. 8–noon.*

Visitor Information DIRCETUR (*Dirección Regional de Comercio Exterior y Turismo).* ⊠ *Mantas 114* ☎ *084/222–032* ⊕ *www.dirceturcusco.gob.pe* ⊙ *Mon.–Sat. 8–8, Sun. 9–2.* **iPerú** ⊠ *Portal de Harinas 177* ☎ *084/252–974* ⊙ *Daily 8–8.*

EXPLORING

PLAZA DE ARMAS

For thousands of years the heart of Cusco, formerly called Haukaypata and now known as the **Plaza de Armas,** has served as the pulse of the city. Yet where you once would have found Inca ceremonies and parades in front of the many palaces that stood here, today you'll find a more modern procession of postcard sellers, shoe-shiners, and photographers angling for your attention. It's no surprise that they congregate here—with the stupendous **Catedral** dominating the northeastern side of the Plaza, the ornate **Templo de La Compañía** sitting to the southeast, and gorgeous Spanish-colonial arcades forming the other two sides, the Plaza is one of the most spectacular areas of Cusco.

TOP ATTRACTIONS

Fodor's Choice ★ **Catedral.** Dominating the Plaza de Armas, the monumental cathedral is one of Cusco's grandest buildings. Built in 1550 on the site of the palace of the Inca Wiracocha and using stones looted from the nearby Inca fortress of Sacsayhuamán, the cathedral is a perfect example of the imposition of the Catholic faith on the indigenous population. The grander the building, went the theory, the more impressive (and seductive) the faith. With soaring ceilings, baroque carvings, enormous oil paintings, and glittering gold-and-silver altars, the cathedral certainly seemed to achieve its aim.

Today Cusco's Catedral is one of the town's star attractions, noted mainly for its amazing collection of colonial art that mixes Christian and non-Christian imagery. Entering the Catedral from the Sagrada Familia chapel, head to your right to the first nave where you'll find the famous oil painting (reputed to be the oldest in Cusco) depicting the earthquake that rocked the town in 1650. Among the depictions

of burning houses and people flee-
ing, you'll see a procession in the
Plaza. Legend has it that during the
earthquake, the citizens took out
from the Catedral a statue of Jesus
on the cross and paraded it around
the Plaza—halting the quake in its
tracks. This statue, now known
as the Señor de los Temblores, or
Lord of the Earthquakes, is Cusco's
patron, and you'll find him depicted
in many Cusqueñan paintings.

To see the famous statue, head
across the Catedral to the other
side, where in the nave and to the
right of the passage connecting the
Catedral to the adjoining Iglesia del
Triumfo, you'll find el Señor himself. The dark color of his skin is often
claimed to be a representation of the indigenous people of Cusco; actually, it's the effect of years of candle smoke on the native materials used
in its fabrication.

> **UNA FOTO AMIGO?**
>
> Cusco is one of the most colorful
> cities in the world, and you can't
> be here for more than five minutes
> without noticing all the women
> and young children walking the
> streets in full traditional costume,
> most towing a llama or endear-
> ingly cuddling a lamb or puppy.
> They are more than happy to pose
> for photos. In fact, that's how they
> make their money, so make sure
> you pay up when asked. The going
> rate for a photo is S/1.

Those interested in the crossover between indigenous and Catholic iconography will find lots to look at. Figures of pumas, the Inca representation of the earth, are carved on the enormous main doors, and in
the adjoining Iglesia del Triumfo you'll see an Andean Christ in one of
the altars flanking the exit. ■ TIP➡ No one should miss the spectacular
Last Supper, painted by the indigenous artist Marcos Zapata, where you'll
see the diners tucking into a delicious feast of cuy (guinea pig) and chicha
(corn beverage)!

The cathedral's centerpieces are its massive, solid-silver altar, and the
enormous 1659 María Angola bell, the largest in South America, which
hangs in one of the towers and can be heard from miles away. Behind
the main altar is the original wooden *altar primitivo* dedicated to St.
Paul. The 64-seat cedar choir has rows of carved saints, popes, and
bishops, all in stunning detail down to their delicately articulated hands.
■ TIP➡ If you're interested in a more in-depth look, enlist the services of a
guide—you'll find them right outside the Catedral. Agree on a price before
you start, it will cost a minimum of S/30 per group. Alternatively, there
is now a free audio guide. ⊠ *Plaza de Armas* ☎ *084/254–285* 🖅 *S/25;
combined admission with Templo de San Blas and Museo de Arte Religioso S/40* ⊙ *Daily 10–6.*

Plaza de Armas. With park benches, green lawns, and splendid views of
the Catedral, Cusco's gorgeous colonial Plaza de Armas invites you to
stay awhile. Pull up one of those park benches and the world will come
to you—without moving an inch you'll be able to purchase postcards,
paintings, and snacks, organize a trip to Machu Picchu, get your pho-
tograph taken, and get those dirty boots polished. ■ TIP➡ What you
see today is a direct descendant of imperial Cusco's central square, which
the Inca called the Haukaypata (the only name indicated on today's street

signs) and which extended as far as the Plaza del Regocijo. According to belief, this was the exact center of the Inca empire, Tawantinsuyo, the Four Corners of the Earth. Today, continuing the tradition, it's the tourism epicenter. From the plaza you'll see the Catedral and Iglesia de la Compañía on two sides, and the graceful archways of the colo-

> **RAINBOW FLAGS**
>
> All the rainbow flags on the Plaza de Armas and elsewhere may make Cusco seem really gay-friendly. But those flags are actu-ally the flag of Cusco, based on the banner of the Inca empire.

nial *portales,* or covered arcades, lining the other sides. Soft lighting bathes the plaza each evening and creates one of Cusco's iconic views. Many of the city's frequent parades (and some protests) pass through the Plaza, especially on Sundays. Enjoy the views of colonial Cusco, but remember that any attempt to sit on one of those inviting green lawns will prompt furious whistle-blowing from the guards. ⊠ *Plaza de Armas.*

WORTH NOTING

Templo de La Compañía. With its ornately carved facade, this Jesuit church on the Plaza gives the Catedral a run for its money in the beauty stakes. The Compañía, constructed by the Jesuits in the 17th century, was intended to be the most splendid church in Cusco, which didn't sit too well with the archbishop. The beauty contest between the churches grew so heated that the pope was forced to intervene. He ruled in favor of the Catedral, but by that time the Iglesia was nearly finished, complete with baroque facade to rival the Catedral's grandeur. The interior is not nearly so splendid, however, although it's worth seeing the paint-ings on either side of the entrance depicting the intercultural marriage between a Spanish conquistador and an Inca princess. If you don't have a Boleto Turístico, the church is open several times a day for mass and tourists are admitted under the condition that they participate in the mass—start wandering around and taking photos and you'll be shown the door. ⊠ *Plaza de Armas* ☜ *S/10* ⊙ *Mon.–Sat. 9–11:30 and 1–5:30, Sun. 9–11 and 1–5:30; Masses: Mon.–Sat. noon and 6 pm, Sun. 11:30 am, and 6 and 7 pm.*

NORTH OF THE PLAZA DE ARMAS

Directly north of the Plaza de Armas, behind La Catedral and to the east and west for about three blocks is a section of the city that boasts scores of upscale shops, fine restaurants, and some of the city's newest cultural museums, Museo Inka and Museo de Arte Precolombino. Walk 15 minutes to the northwest to Colcampata, said to be the palace of the first Inca ruler, Manco Cápac. The charming Plazoleta Nazarenas is the perfect place to stroll around, and is far quieter than the bustling Plaza de Armas. Many travelers often mistake this section for the art-ists' neighborhood of San Blas, but San Blas requires a bit more of a hike, about two steep blocks farther, uphill.

TOP ATTRACTIONS

Museo Inka. Everyone comes to "ooh" and "eeww" over this archaeo-logical museum's collection of eight Inca mummies, but the entire facil-ity serves as a comprehensive introduction to pre-Columbian Andean

INTI RAYMI

Inti is the Quechua name for the sun, which the Inca worshipped. Inca rulers were considered to be descended from Inti, thus legitimizing their authority over the people. The most important festival was Inti Raymi, held on June 24, marking the winter solstice and the beginning of the new year. Each June Cusco is once again home to the Inti Raymi celebration, which begins at Qoricancha with dances and processions, making its way to Sacsayhuamán, where a variety of ceremonies are performed. There is a cost to the festivities at Sacsayhuamán, but those held in the center of Cusco are free. ■TIP➜ If you plan to travel to Peru at this time, reservations should be made well ahead of time due to the influx of visitors.

culture. Jam-packed with textiles, ceramics, and dioramas, there's a lot to see here, and displays bear labels in Spanish and English. One room is dedicated to the story of Mamakuka ("Mother Coca"), and documents indigenous people's use of the coca leaf for religious and medicinal purposes. ■TIP➜ Visit the Museo de Plantas Sagradas for more information about coca leaves. The building was once the palace of Admiral Francisco Aldrete Maldonado, the reason for its common designation as the Palacio del Almirante (Admiral's Palace). ✉ *Ataúd at Córdoba del Tucumán* ☎ *084/237–380* 💲*S/10* 🕓 *Weekdays 8–6, Sat. 9–4.*

WORTH NOTING

OFF THE BEATEN PATH

Colcampata. To behold colonial Cusco in all its beauty, take the 15-minute walk up to Colcampata. Following Procuradores from the Plaza de Armas to Waynapata and then Resbalosa, you'll come to a steep cobblestone staircase with a wonderful view of La Compañía. Continuing to climb, you'll find the church of San Cristóbal, which is of little intrinsic interest but affords another magnificent panorama of the city. The church stands atop Colcampata, believed to have been the palace of the first Inca ruler, Manco Cápac. The Inca wall to the right of the church has 11 niches in which soldiers may once have stood guard. Farther up the road, the lane on the left leads to a post-conquest Inca gateway beside a magnificent Spanish mansion.

Fodor'sChoice ★ **Museo de Arte Precolombino.** For a different perspective on pre-Colombian ceramics head to this spectacular museum, known as MAP, where art and pre-Colombian culture merge seamlessly. Twelve rooms in the 1580 Casa Cabrera, which was used as the convent of Santa Clara until the 17th century, showcase an astounding collection of pre-Columbian art from the 13th to 16th centuries, mostly in the form of carvings, ceramics, and jewelry. The art and artifacts were made by the Huari and Nasca, as well as the Inca, cultures. The stylish displays have excellent labels in Spanish and English that place the artifacts in their artistic and historical context. On the walls is commentary from European artists on South American art. Swiss artist Paul Klee wrote: "I wish I was newly born, and totally ignorant of Europe, innocent of facts and fashions, to be almost primitive." Most Cusco museums close at dark but MAP remains open every evening. For a break after a walk around, find your way to the on-site cafe, one of Cusco's best restaurants (reservations are required for dinner). ✉ *Plazoleta Nazarenas 231* ☎ *084/233–210* ⊕ *map. museolarco.org* 🖫 *S/20* ⊗ *Daily 8 am–10 pm.*

EAST OF THE PLAZA DE ARMAS

TOP ATTRACTIONS

Museo Machu Picchu Casa Concha. Artifacts that Hiram Bingham unearthed during his 1911 "discovery" of Machu Picchu and brought back to Yale University resided with the university for a century. After a hotly contested custody battle, an agreement was reached between Peru and Yale and the artifacts began to be returned to Peru in 2011. Some of them can now be seen on display at this small but fascinating museum housed in a colonial mansion built atop the palace of Tupac Yupanqui. While the artifacts are interesting, the real reason to go is for the video, which presents research findings on these pieces. If you have the time, visit the museum before your trip to Machu Picchu for a deeper understanding of what is currently known, and still unknown, about this wonder of the world. ✉ *Calle Santa Catalina Ancha 320* ☎ *084/255–535* 🖫 *S/20* ⊗ *Weekdays 9–5, Sat. 9–1.*

WORTH NOTING

Monasterio de Santa Catalina de Siena. An extensive collection of Cusqueñan religious art is the draw at this still-working Dominican convent, which incorporates a 1610 church with high and low choirs and baroque friezes. Although there's not much to show of it these days, the convent represents another example of the pasting of Catholic religion over indigenous faiths—it was built on the site of the Acllawasi, the house of some 3,000 Inca chosen women dedicated to teaching, weaving Inca ceremonial robes, and worship of Inti, the Inca sun god. The entire complex was given a face-lift in 2010. ✉ *Santa Catalina Angosta 401* 🖫 *S/8; S/15 combined ticket includes Qorikancha* ⊗ *Mon.–Sat. 8:30–5:30, Sun. 2–5.*

Museo de Arte Religioso del Arzobispado. The building may be on the dark and musty side, but this San Blas museum has a remarkable collection of religious art. Originally the site of the Inca Roca's Hatun Rumiyoq palace, then the juxtaposed Moorish-style palace of the Marqués de Buenavista, the building reverted to the archdiocese of Cusco and served as the archbishop's residence. In this primary repository of religious art in the city many of the paintings in the collection are anonymous, but you'll notice some by the renowned indigenous artist Marcos Zapata. A highlight is a series of 17th-century paintings that depict the city's Corpus Christi procession. Free audio guides are available. ✉ *Hatun Rumiyoq and Herejes, San Blas* ☎ *084/225–211* 🖫 *S/15; S/40 combined admission with Catedral and the Templo de San Blas* ⊗ *Daily 8–6.*

CORPUS CHRISTI FESTIVAL

Cusco's Corpus Christi festival in late May or June is a deeply religious affair with mass in the Plaza de Armas surrounded by 15 statues of virgins and saints. The statues are brought from churches in nearby districts, which come to Cusco to be blessed. In the early afternoon, the beaded, brocaded, 15-foot statues are hoisted onto the shoulders of teams of men and promenaded around the plaza, genuflecting at various altars and ending at the Cathedral. It's a day-long party where the whole city crams into the Plaza de Armas to watch the parade, eat, drink, and make merry. ■TIP➔ Cusco's Plaza de Armas has many restaurants and bars, like the Crown Cafe and Bar, with a view of the action if you want to stay above the fray. Go early for the best views.

Palacio de Inca Roca. Inca Roca lived in the 13th or 14th century. Halfway along his palace's side wall, nestled amid other stones, is a famous 12-angled stone, an example of masterly Inca masonry. There's nothing sacred about the 12 angles: Inca masons were famous for incorporating stones with many more sides than 12 into their buildings. If you can't spot the famous stone from the crowds taking photos, ask one of the shopkeepers or the elaborately dressed Inca figure hanging out along the street to point it out. Around the corner is a series of stones on the wall that form the shapes of a puma and a serpent. Kids often hang out there and trace the forms for a small tip. ⊠ *Hatun Rumiyoc and Palacio.*

SOUTH OF THE PLAZA DE ARMAS

After the colonial charm of central Cusco and San Blas, head south of the plaza for a timely reminder that you're still in Peru. Traffic, smog, and horn-happy drivers welcome you to the noisy and unattractive Avenida El Sol, where the colonial charm of the city is hidden but for one glaring exception: Cusco's if-you-have-time-for-only-one-thing tourist attraction, the Qorikancha, or temple of the sun. Don't miss it. ■TIP➔ Plaza Regocijo, while still southwest of the plaza, has re-created itself in the last five years from a once low-level tourist area to a clean, upscale plaza (catering to Cusqueños and travelers alike) with gourmet restaurants and high-end shopping.

TOP ATTRACTIONS

Fodor's Choice
★

Qorikancha. If the Spanish came to the new world looking for El Dorado, the lost city of gold, they must have thought they'd found it when they laid eyes on Qorikancha. Built during the reign of the Inca Pachacutec to honor the Sun, Tawantinsuyos' most important divinity, Qorikancha translates as "Court of Gold." Conquistadors' jaws must have dropped when they saw the gold-plated walls of the temple glinting in the sunlight. Then their fingers must have started working because all that remains today is the masterful stonework.

If Cusco was constructed to represent a puma, then Qorikancha was positioned as the animal's loins, the center from which all creation emanated; 4,000 priests and attendants are thought to have lived within its confines. Walls and altars were plated with gold, and in the center of the complex sat a giant gold disc, positioned to reflect the sun and bathe the temple in light. At the summer solstice, sunlight reflected into a niche in the wall where only the Inca were permitted to sit. Terraces that face it were once filled with life-size gold-and-silver statues of plants and animals. ■TIP→ Much of the wealth was removed to pay ransom for the captive Inca ruler Atahualpa during the Spanish conquest, blood money paid in vain since Atahualpa was later murdered. Eventually, Francisco Pizarro awarded the site to his brother Juan. Upon Juan's death, the structure passed to the Dominicans, who began to construct the church of Santo Domingo, using stones from the temple and creating perhaps Cusco's most jarring imperial–colonial architectural juxtaposition.

An ingenious restoration to recover both buildings after the 1953 earthquake lets you see how the church was built on and around the walls and chambers of the temple. In the Inca parts of the structure left exposed, estimated to be about 40% of the original temple, you can admire the mortarless masonry, earthquake-proof trapezoidal doorways, curved retaining wall, and exquisite carvings that exemplify the artistic and engineering skills of the Inca. Bilingual guides are available for a separate fee. A small museum down the hill with an entrance on Avenida El Sol contains a few artifacts from the site but doesn't warrant a huge amount of your time. ■TIP→ Only entrance to the museum is covered in the Boleto Turístico. A separate fee is applied to enter the ruins and the church. For S/15 you can buy a ticket that grants you entrance to the Convento Santa Catalina, and Qorikancha's ruins and church. ⊠ *Pampa del Castillo at Plazoleta Santo Domingo* ☎ *Ruins and church, S/10; museum, Boleto Turístico* ⊙ *Ruins and church: Mon.–Sat. 8:30–6:30, Sun. 2–5; museum: Mon.–Sat. 9–6, Sun. 8–1.*

WORTH NOTING

La Merced. The church may be overshadowed by the more famous Catedral and Iglesia de la Compañía, but La Merced contains one of the city's most priceless treasures—the Custodia, a solid gold container for communion wafers more than a meter high and encrusted with thousands of precious stones. Rebuilt in the 17th century, this monastery, with two stories of portals and a colonial fountain, gardens, and benches, has a spectacular series of murals that depict the life of the founder of the Mercedarian order, St. Peter of Nolasco. A small museum is found to the side of the church. ⊠ *Mantas 121* ☎ *Free for church, S/6 museum* ⊙ *Church: Mon.–Sat. 7–8 am and 5–8 pm; museum: Mon.–Sat. 8–12:30 and 2–5:30.*

Templo Santa Clara. Austere from the outside, this incredible 1588 church takes the prize for most eccentric interior decoration. Thousands of mirrors cover the interior, competing with the gold-laminated altar for glittery prominence. Legend has it that the mirrors were placed inside in order to tempt locals into church. Built in old Inca style, using stone looted from Inca ruins, this is a great example of the lengths that the Spanish went to in order to attract indigenous converts to the Catholic faith. ⊠ *Santa Clara s/n* ☎ *Free* ⊙ *Daily 9–noon and 3–5.*

WEST OF THE PLAZA DE ARMAS

Casa de Garcilaso (*Museum of Regional History*). You'll find a bit of everything in this spot, which may leave you feeling like you've seen it all before. Colonial building? Check. Cusqueña-school paintings? Check. Ancient pottery? Check. Inca mummy? Check. This is the colonial childhood home of Inca Garcilaso de la Vega, the famous chronicler of the Spanish conquest and illegitimate son of one of Pizarro's captains and an Inca princess. Inside the mansion, with its cobblestone courtyard, is the Museo de Historia Regional, with Cusqueña-school paintings and pre-Inca mummies—one from Nazca has a 1½-meter (5-foot) braid—and ceramics, metal objects, and other artifacts. ⊠ *Heladeros at Garcilaso* ☎ *084/223–245* ⌧ *Boleto Turístico* ⊗ *Daily 8–5.*

🐦 **ChocoMuseo.** This museum provides a delicious introduction to the history and process of chocolate-making, from cacao bean to bar. Workshops allow you to make your own sweets; they are offered three times a day for a minimum of three people at an additional cost of S/70, and advance reservations are required. ⊠ *Plaza Regocijo, Calle Garcilaso 210, 2nd fl., Plaza Regocijo* ☎ *084/244–765* ⊕ *www.chocomuseo.com.*

Museo de Arte Contemporáneo. Take a refreshing turn back toward the present in this city of history. As is typically the case in Cusco, the museum is housed in a colonial mansion. However, the art exhibits, which rotate constantly, display some of the best work that contemporary Peruvian artists have to offer. ⊠ *Kusipata s/n, Plaza Regocijo* ☎ *084/240–006* ⌧ *Boleto Turístico* ⊗ *Mon.–Sat. 8–6.*

Museo de Plantas Sagradas. Many people are familiar with the coca plant only as the source of cocaine until they land in Cusco, where it is offered at every stop for helping with the effects of altitude. If this dichotomy has made you curious, stop by the museum of sacred plants to learn about the science and history of coca as well as its traditional uses, both medicinal and religious. Also covered are tobacco, ayahuasca, san pedro, and a host of other plants used for millennia by the Andean and Amazonian people. It's a great opportunity to get a more thorough understanding about plants that were, and still are, a vital part of the indigenous cultures of Peru. ⊠ *Santa Teresa 351* ☎ *084/222–214* ⊕ *www.museoplantascusco.org.*

Templo de San Francisco. Close to the Plaza de Armas, the Plaza de San Francisco is a local hangout. There's not a lot to see in the plaza itself, but if you've wandered this way, the Templo de San Francisco church is interesting for its macabre sepulchers with arrangements of bones and skulls, some pinned to the wall to spell out morbid sayings. A small museum of religious art with paintings by Cusqueña-school artists Marcos Zapata and Diego Quispe Tito is in the church sacristy. ⊠ *3 blocks south of Plaza de Armas, Plaza de San Francisco* ☎ *084/221–361* ⌧ *S/5* ⊗ *Weekdays 9–noon and 3–5.*

SAN BLAS

Huff and puff your way up the narrow cobbled streets north of the Plaza de Armas about four steep blocks to the trendy artisan district of San Blas. This is *the* spot in Cusco to pick up treasures such as ornate Escuela Cusqueña–style paintings and carved traditional masks. The streets are steep, but you'll have plenty of opportunity to catch your breath admiring the spectacular views along the way.

TOP ATTRACTIONS

Museo Hilario Mendívil. As San Blas's most famous son, the former home of 20th-century Peruvian religious artist Hilario Mendívil (1929–77) makes a good stop if you have an interest in Cusqeñan art and iconography. Legend has it that Mendívil saw llamas parading in the Corpus Christi procession as a child and later infused this image into his religious art, depicting all his figures with long, llama-like necks. ▉TIP➡ In the small gallery are the maguey-wood and rice-plaster sculptures of the Virgin with the elongated necks that were the artist's trademark. There's also a shop selling Mendívil-style work. ⊠ *Plazoleta San Blas 634, San Blas* ☎ *084/240–527* ☁ *Free* ☉ *Mon.–Sat. 9–1 and 2–6.*

San Blas. For spectacular views over Cusco's terra-cotta rooftops, head to San Blas. This is where the Incas brought the choicest artists and artisans, culled from recent conquests, to bolster their own knowledge base. The district has maintained its Bohemian roots for centuries and remains one of the city's most picturesque districts with whitewashed adobe homes and bright-blue doors. ▉TIP➡ The area and the surrounds is one of the trendier parts of Cusco, with several of the city's choicest restaurants and bars opening their doors here. The Cuesta de San Blas (San Blas Hill), one of the main entrances into the area, is sprinkled with galleries that sell paintings in the Cusqueña-school style of the 16th through 18th centuries. Many of the stone streets are built as stairs or slopes (not for cars) and have religious motifs carved into them. ⊠ *San Blas.*

WORTH NOTING

Templo y Plazoleta de San Blas. The little square in San Blas has a simple adobe church with one of the jewels of colonial art in the Americas— the pulpit of San Blas, an intricately carved 17th-century cedar pulpit, arguably Latin America's most ornate. Tradition holds that the work was hewn from a single tree trunk, but experts now believe it was assembled from 1,200 individually carved pieces. Figures of Martin Luther, John Calvin, and Henry VIII—all opponents of Catholicism— as well as those representing the seven deadly sins are condemned for eternity to hold up the pulpit's base. The work is dominated by the triumphant figure of Christ. At his feet rests a human skull, not carved, but the real thing. It's thought to belong to Juan Tomás Tuyrutupac, the creator of the pulpit. ⊠ *Plazoleta de San Blas, San Blas* ☎ *084/254–057* ☁ *S/15; S/40 combined entrance with Catedral and Museo de Arte Relgioso* ☉ *Church: Mon.–Sun. 8–6.*

WHERE TO EAT

Cusco's dining scene is surprisingly vast. Gone are the days when visitors only had touristy restaurants with ubiquitous Andean pan flute players to choose from. You'll encounter everything from Andean grills to Middle Eastern kebab shops. Restaurant employees on Cusco's Plaza de Armas and Plateros and Procuradores streets—any of these could be renamed "Restaurant Row"—stand in their doorways, touting their establishments, menus in hand, to entice you. Browsing many menus,

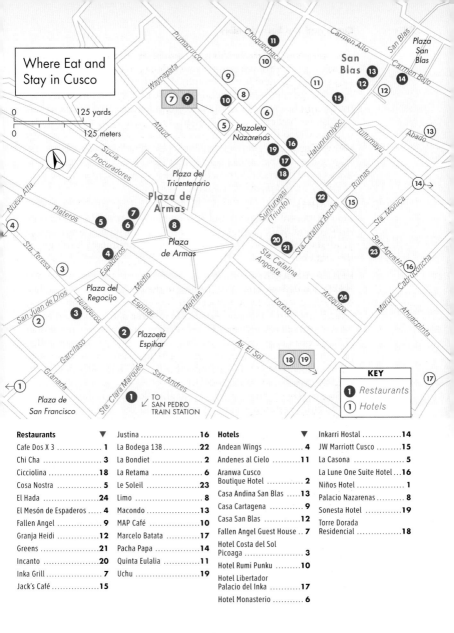

Where Eat and Stay in Cusco

0 ———— 125 yards
0 ———— 125 meters

KEY

🛑 Restaurants
🔵 Hotels

you will come across the Andean specialties of cuy and alpaca. The former is guinea pig and is usually served roasted (sometimes with peppers stuffed charmingly in its mouth). The latter is the cute furry llama-like creature you'll see wandering the Cusco streets with its indigenous owner for photo ops. In addition to the wider variety of cuisines, there are also far higher-quality restaurants than there once were. You may not find Cusco to be as cheap a place to eat as before, however, what you will pay for a gourmet meal at a place like MAP Café is far less than you would pay at its equivalent in New York or Los Angeles and just as good. *Prices in the reviews are the average cost of a main course at dinner or, if dinner is not served, at lunch.*

MEAL TIMES

Lunch is served between 1 and 3. Dinner begins around 7, with prime rush around 8:30, and most restaurants start winding down service at about 9:30. Most places do stay open continually throughout the afternoon.

PLAZA DE ARMAS

$ PERUVIAN 🍴 **El Mesón de Espaderos.** You'll drink in the city's history as you dine on a rustic second-floor terrace with stucco walls and high-beamed ceilings above the Plaza de Armas. **TIP→ The parrilladas (barbecued meats) are the best in Cusco.** The platter for one person is more than enough for two, and the *Parrilla Inca,* with its mix of Andean meats, provides a good opportunity to try cuy. Vegetarians may want to pass, or resign themselves to dining from the salad bar. [$] *Average main: S/30* ✉ *Espaderos 105* ☎ *084/235–307.*

$$ PERUVIAN Fodor's Choice ★ 🍴 **Greens.** The reputation for top-quality, locally produced organic food at this restaurant extends well beyond the cobblestone streets of Cusco—travelers as far away as the Sacred Valley rave about the homemade wheat pasta dishes and overstuffed sandwiches. The only problem you'll have here is figuring out which of the Peruvian fusion creations to try. Start with a fresh fruit juice or tea infusion and be sure to save room for one of the great dessert options. Their organic offerings also extend to beer and wine. Future plans include opening for breakfast. [$] *Average main: S/43* ✉ *Santa Catalina Angosta 135, 2nd fl., Plaza de Armas* ☎ *084/243–379* 🌐 *www.cuscorestaurants.com* ✍ *Reservations essential.*

$$ MEDITERRANEAN 🍴 **Incanto.** Stylish contemporary design in an Andean setting has made this large upmarket restaurant near the Plaza a hit with those looking for a classy night out. Dishing up Mediterranean-Andean fusion cuisine as well as more traditional dishes such as delicious thin-crust pizza, this has got to be one of the only places in the world where you'll find ravioli *aji de gallina,* a traditional creamy chicken sauce usually served with rice, on the menu. Wander down the back to the open kitchen, and don't forget to have a look at the original Inca wall on the way. [$] *Average main: S/43* ✉ *Catalina Angosta 135, Plaza de Armas* ☎ *084/254–753* 🌐 *www.cuscorestaurants.com.*

$$ PERUVIAN 👶 🍴 **Inka Grill.** Centrally located in the Plaza de Armas, this popular restaurant offers a wide variety of Peruvian and international fare. From fresh quinoa-battered shrimp salad to homemade ravioli in Andean herb sauce, the extensive menu, including a number of vegetarian options,

is sure to please even the pickiest of palettes. Cozy and chic, order up a glass of red and listen to the live nightly music. $ *Average main: S/36* ⊠ *Portal de Panes 115, Plaza de Armas* ☎ *084/262–992* ⊕ *www. cuscorestaurants.com* ⚓ *Reservations essential.*

$$ ✕ **La Retama.** One of the better offerings on the Plaza, this tourist-ori-
PERUVIAN ented second-floor eatery wins points for its view over the Catedral and Iglesia de la Compañía. Pull up a stool on the balcony to drink in the vista while you tuck into an Andean river trout in garlic sauce or alpaca steak accompanied by elderberries. A cozy fireplace, Andean tapestries, and a nightly folk-music show complete the experience. Make reservations for the dinner buffet (S/50); you can also order à la carte. $ *Average main: S/37* ⊠ *Portal de Panes 123, Plaza de Armas* ☎ *084/242–620* ⊕ *www.laretama.info.*

$$ ✕ **Limo.** For an excellent view of the Plaza de Armas with food and
PERUVIAN drinks to match, this is the perfect place to enjoy a drink before dinner as the sun sets behind the surrounding mountains. Limo is known for its cebiche and fish dishes, but there is plenty more to choose from. In addition to traditional Peruvian food, there are fusion dishes using local ingredients such as grilled alpaca with rosemary or quinoa risotto. Limo is also known for its pisco drinks, and for good reason. $ *Average main: S/43* ⊠ *Portal de Carnes 236, Plaza de Armas* ☎ *084/240–668* ⊕ *www. cuscorestaurants.com* ⚓ *Reservations essential.*

NORTH OF PLAZA DE ARMAS

$$ ✕ **Fallen Angel.** Come for the kitschy, fun, over-the-top decor—take your
EUROPEAN pick of seating from a brass daybed, a heart-shape couch, or leopard-
★ and cheetah-print stools, and dine off bathtubs that double as fish tanks covered with glass tops, watched over all the while by baroque angels, flying pigs, and disco balls in all sizes. A massive angel sculpture presides over the courtyard, whose walls are painted to look like a sky full of clouds. This was one of Francisco Pizarro's houses, and it's doubtful that he envisioned anything so avant-garde. The steak-driven menu, just like the decoration, is absolutely fabulous, darling. The decor encourages you to indulge, and you won't want to pass up a sinful dessert. There are plenty of tables, but if your heart is set on dinner here, make a reservation. ■ TIP→ Fallen Angel rents out similarly decorated, uniquely luxurious rooms upstairs starting at $280 USD per night. $ *Average main: S/47* ⊠ *Plazoleta Nazarenas 221* ☎ *084/258–184* ⊕ *www.fallenangelincusco.com.*

$$$ ✕ **MAP Café.** Museum eateries don't routinely warrant separate guide
PERUVIAN listings, but this small, glass-enclosed, elegant café inside the courtyard
Fodor'sChoice of the Museo de Arte Precolombino is actually one of the city's top
★ restaurants—it has top prices to boot, but it's still a bargain compared to what this quality meal would cost in New York or Los Angeles. Of its novel and exciting twists on traditional Peruvian cuisine, try the chicken estofado with goat cheese and raisins or the pork adobo with ravioli. The dessert presentation is so amazing that your first instinct will be that you don't want to eat it—but you'll be glad you did. ■ TIP→ The menu is prix-fixe after 6 pm (S/165), and you can choose one each from any of the appetizers, main dishes, and desserts; between 3 and 6 pm only dessert and coffee are served. $ *Average main: S/61* ⊠ *Plazoleta Nazarenas 231* ☎ *084/242–476* ⊕ *www.cuscorestaurants.com* ⚓ *Reservations essential.*

EAST OF THE PLAZA DE ARMAS

$$ ✕ **Cicciolina.** Everyone seems to know everyone and greet each other
MEDITERRANEAN with a peck on the cheek at this second-floor eatery, part lively tapas
Fodor's Choice bar, part sit-down, candlelit restaurant. On the tapas side, the bar
★ wraps around the kitchen area where a small army of cooks prepare
your food. You'll strain to see as they set out each new tapas plate—
perhaps some duck prosciutto or prawns and sweet potato in wasabi
sauce—and be tempted to say, "I want one of those." The restaurant
half of Cicciolina is much more subdued, with homemade pastas and
delicious selections of fish, meat, and poultry dishes, not to mention
a nice wine list. You can order off the restaurant menu in the tapas
bar, but not the other way around. Note that, while not required,
reservations are very strongly encouraged and available only through
the website. $ *Average main: S/43 ⊠ Sunturwasi 393, 2nd fl., Triunfo
☎ 084/239–510 ⊕ www.cicciolinacuzco.com.*

$ ✕ **El Hada.** If you're looking for dessert or something sweet to tide you
CAFÉ over until your next meal, you can't do better than the artisanal ice
cream you'll find here. Unique flavors such as orange cardamom and
Madagascar cinnamon along with the use of only the best ingredients
combine to provide you with a treat that is truly something special.
There is great coffee too. $ *Average main: S/7 ⊠ Calle Arequipa 167
☎ 084/253–744 ⊕ www.elhada.com ⊟ No credit cards.*

$ ✕ **Justina.** With so many places around Cusco offering pizza, you may
PIZZA start to crave it. If so, this is one of the best places to go. Pizza is the
only thing that's served here, along with reasonably priced Chilean
wine. The atmosphere is relaxed and cozy, with just a few tables, so get
here early. $ *Average main: S/28 ⊠ Calle Palacio 110 ☎ 084/255–475
⊟ No credit cards ⊘ Closed Sun. No lunch.*

$ ✕ **La Bodega 138.** The wide selection of pizzas, pastas, soups, and salads
PIZZA here, as well as a few great desserts, ensure that you will leave feeling
satisfied. The unique blue cheese, bacon, and sauco pizza in particular
can't be beat. Be sure to accompany it with one of their reasonably
priced wines. $ *Average main: S/25 ⊠ Herrajes 138 ☎ 084/260–272
⊟ No credit cards ⊘ Closed Sun.*

$$$ ✕ **Le Soleil.** If you're in Peru and missing Paris, you're in luck. Unlike many
FRENCH of the higher-end restaurants in Cusco, this is not Peruvian fusion—it is
French cuisine through and through, right down to the imported wine
and the fabulous crème brûlée. In addition to à la carte, there are also tasting menus of either five or eight courses, allowing you to sample a variety
of dishes like foie gras, escargots, and duck confit for S/116 and S/159
respectively. $ *Average main: S/51 ⊠ Calle San Agustin 275 ☎ 084/240–
543 ⊕ www.restaurantelesoleilcusco.com ⌂ Reservations essential.*

$$ ✕ **Marcelo Batata.** The ambience here is a nice blend of friendly, upscale,
PERUVIAN and romantic, with a rooftop terrace and a cozy interior dining room
with red-painted walls. Start with a drink made from one of the many
pisco macerations made in-house. Peruvian fusion is the restaurant's
specialty, and the alpaca steaks are some of the best in town; other
options include melt-in-your mouth chicken in aguaymanto sauce.
$ *Average main: S/37 ⊠ Calle Palacio 121, 2nd fl. ☎ 084/222–424
⊕ www.cuzcodining.com/marcelo-batata.htm ⌂ Reservations essential.*

$$
PERUVIAN
✕ **Uchu.** Although you could make a meal out of the many tasty appetizers at this upscale and minimalist-design spot, the real highlight is cooking an entrée at your table on a heated volcanic stone. Whether you choose beef, alpaca, fish, or shrimp (or any combination), your selection will be the choicest and freshest cut, guaranteed to melt in your mouth. It comes to your table seared on the outside, allowing you to complete the cooking to your personal preference. Cooking on the hot stone is unlike other techniques for cooking at the table; there is no smoke or strong odor to follow you home. $ *Average main: S/43* ✉ *Calle Palacio 135* ☎ *084/246–598* ⊕ *www.cuzcodining.com/uchu.htm* ✍ *Reservations essential.*

> **CORN 1000 WAYS**
>
> Corn is a staple of the Peruvian diet—wander the streets of Cusco long enough and you'll soon see it being popped, steamed, and roasted into a healthy carbo-snack. *Chicha*, a corn beer drunk at room temperature and sold from rural homes that display a red flag (and in many restaurants) is a surprisingly tasty take on the old corncob, but can have adverse effects on the foreign tummy. You may want to stick to the nonalcoholic chicha morada made from purple corn.

SOUTH OF PLAZA DE ARMAS

$
CAFÉ
✕ **Cafe Dos X 3.** Pouring some of the best coffee in the city from a special house blend, this café is a Cusco icon. Martin Chambi photos help locate the cafe in Peru, but the jazz playing and bohemian atmosphere make this café feel more cosmopolitan. It's a great place for a quick bite, as well as to pick up flyers on current cultural offerings. Try the passionfruit cheesecake or tiramisu with your cappuccino and then head next door to the Cusco School of Fine Arts to see what they have on display. $ *Average main: S/5* ✉ *Calle Marqués 271* ☎ *084/232–661* ⊘ *No dinner.*

$
CAFÉ
✕ **La Bondiet.** Although we all know that you come to Peru to experience Peru, sometimes you need a break. This is a great spot to regroup and recaffeinate after a hard morning's sightseeing. The coffee is quality, there's a huge range of mouthwatering cakes and slices to dig into, and you can also grab breakfast and sandwiches. $ *Average main: S/13* ✉ *Heladeros 118* ☎ *084/246–823* ⊘ *No dinner.* ✉ *Plateros 363* ☎ *084/222–671* ⊕ *www.labondietcusco.com* ⊘ *No dinner.*

WEST OF THE PLAZA DE ARMAS

$$
PERUVIAN
✕ **Chi Cha.** Inspired by Gastón Acurio—renowned chef and godfather of the Nuevo-Andino culinary craze—this hip and hopping restaurant dishes up regional Cusqueña cuisine with a modern twist. If you haven't tried cuy yet, this trendy, open-kitchen restaurant may inspire you to pull the trigger with its *chaufa* (a type of Peruvian-Chinese fried rice) with guinea pig. Those who are intrigued but not ready for the guinea pig plunge can still experience the thrill of trying traditional recipes peppered with innovative additions: consider *kapchi de habas* (fava bean casserole) or *anticuchos* (Peruvian kebabs). Standbys like pizza and pasta are top-notch if that's more your speed, and the cocktails aren't too shabby either. $ *Average main: S/46* ✉ *Plaza Regocijo 261, 2nd fl., Plaza Regocijo* ☎ *084/240–520.*

$
ITALIAN

✕**Cosa Nostra.** Lots of restaurants in Cusco say they serve Italian food but this is undoubtedly the best and most authentic of the bunch. Owned by a transplant from Italy, you'll want to try a bit of everything here from the homemade bread with olive oil and balsamic vinegar to the tiramisu and perfect cappuccino for dessert. In between, you have a wide variety of choices including several types of lasagnas and other pastas, some dishes featuring ingredients brought over from Europe, and a lovely Italian syrah to go with it. $ *Average main: S/34* ✉ *Calle Plateros 358-A, 2nd fl.* ☎ *084/232–992* ⊕ *www.cosanostraristorante.com* ◷ *Closed Sun.*

SAN BLAS

$
INTERNATIONAL

✕**Granja Heidi.** Don't be mistaken: Heidi is not the owner, but rather the mule who resides on the nearby farm where the owners get much of the produce for this San Blas restaurant. Yep, it's all about the farm here, especially the farm-fresh yogurt—something definitely worth trying. Lunch and dinner are quite satisfying, with plenty of choices of soups, salads, crepes, meat, and vegetarian plates. Save room for one of the yummy desserts and coffee. $ *Average main: S/33* ✉ *Cuesta San Blas 525* ☎ *084/238–383* ▭ *No credit cards* ◷ *Closed Sun.*

$
CAFÉ
★

✕**Jack's Cafe.** Scrumptious breakfasts can be had all day at this bright and busy Aussie- and Irish-owned café in San Blas. Order up granola and yogurt, large fluffy pancakes, or a grand "brekkie" (breakfast) with bacon and eggs. Also on the menu are gourmet sandwiches, fresh salads, and a variety of other satisfying dishes. Jack's is a standout hit. Come during peak season and you may have to line up to get a table. Everything is prepared in-house, including the delicious breads, and the coffee and hot chocolate are excellent. This jumping spot stays open well into the night. $ *Average main: S/17* ✉ *Choquechaca 509* ☎ *084/254–606* ⊕ *jackscafecusco.com* ▭ *No credit cards.*

$
LATIN AMERICAN

✕**Macondo.** Walking through this shop off the busy Cuesta San Blas, part art gallery, part café, and more hip than ever, you may think you took a wrong turn and ended up in New York City. The menu features some healthy dishes and some splurges, and this is a great spot for coffee and breakfast in the morning. The house wine is a South African shiraz. There are just seven small tables, so make reservations, especially for dinner. Come for the food, but be sure to check out the contemporary artwork for sale, rare for this history-focused city. $ *Average main: S/33* ✉ *Cuesta San Blas 571* ☎ *084/227–887* ⊕ *www.macondoincusco.com* ✍ *Reservations essential.*

$$
PERUVIAN
☾
Fodor's Choice
★

✕**Pacha Papa.** If you've been putting off trying the famous Andean dishes of guinea pig or alpaca, then wait no longer. This fabulous restaurant is hands-down the best place in town for Peruvian food. Modeled after a typical Peruvian open-air *quinta*, wooden tables are scattered around a large patio. The menu takes influences from all over Peru, and the waiters are happy to explain what makes each dish special. Try the delicious *anticuchas de* alpaca, skewers of tender alpaca meat with local spices, and don't miss the sensational *adobo de chancho*, a tangy pork stew with meat that melts in your mouth. For a special treat, go for the underground-oven baked *pachamanca*, a stew where different types of meats are slow roasted together with potatoes and aromatic herbs (*pacha* is Quechua for ground, *manca* means pot): This dish, as well as the cuy, has to be ordered 24 hours in advance, so plan ahead. This is a great place to go for breakfast as well, with fabulous fruit juices. [$] *Average main: S/37* ✉ *Plazoleta San Blas 120* ☎ *084/241–318* 🌐 *www.cuscorestaurants.com.*

$ PERUVIAN 🍴 **Quinta Eulalia.** A *quinta* is a típico semi-open-air Peruvian restaurant, and Eulalia's is the oldest such place in the city, cooking up hearty, filling portions of down-home food since 1941. Only open for lunch, its specialties include *chicharrones* (fried pork and cabbage), *trucha al horno* (oven-baked trout), *lechon* (suckling pig), and *cuy chactado* (deep-fried guinea pig). Eat your fill, and enjoy one of the Peruvian beers along with the traditional criolla music. [$] *Average main: S/26* ✉ *Choquechaca 384, San Blas* ☎ *084/234–495* 💳 *No credit cards* 🕓 *No dinner.*

WHERE TO STAY

No matter what your travel budget, you won't be priced out of the market staying in Cusco: luxury hotels, backpackers' digs, and everything in between await. Most lodgings discount rates during the unofficial off-season of September through May. With a few exceptions, absent are the international hotel chains. In their place are smaller, top-end, independently run lodgings offering impeccable service, even if some lack swimming pools and concierges. Lodgings in all price ranges, whether in a former 17th-century convent or newly built, mimic the old Spanish-colonial style of construction arranged around a central courtyard or patio.

You may have to adjust your internal thermostat in moderate or budget lodgings at this altitude, but all provide extra blankets and may have electric heaters available at an extra charge. High-end establishments have heating. Most places provide hot water around the clock, but if you're wondering, just ask if there's *agua caliente.* Many accommodations keep an oxygen supply on hand for those having trouble adjusting to the thin air.

PLANNING

Lodgings in Cusco keep shockingly early checkout times. (Flights to Cusco arrive early in the morning.) **TIP→ Expect to have to vacate your room by 9 or 10 am, though this is less strictly enforced in the off-season.** All lodgings will hold your luggage if you're not leaving town until later in the day, as well as while you are off on a trek. Breakfast, at least a continental one (and sometimes something more ample), is included in all lodging rates. *Prices in the reviews are the lowest cost of a standard double room in high season.*

NORTH OF PLAZA DE ARMAS

$$$$ HOTEL Fodor's Choice ★ 🏨 **Casa Cartagena.** Just a few blocks north of the Plaza de Armas on a quiet cobblestone street lies this elegant boutique hotel of spacious rooms decorated with trendy lamps and contemporary Italian furniture. **Pros:** in the historic center of Cusco; excellent breakfast and service; L'Occitane bath products; free Wi-Fi. **Cons:** thin walls; pricey. [$] *Rooms from: S/1350* ✉ *Pumacurco 336* ☎ *084/224–356* 🌐 *www.casacartagena.com* 🛏 *16 suites* 🍴 *Breakfast.*

$$$$ **Fallen Angel Guest House.** This luxury boutique hotel features four
HOTEL   of the most unusually designed suites you will find anywhere—picture
a lofted bedroom with blue and brown floral wallpaper, a claw-foot
tub with a red canopy curtain, chandeliers, and modern art everywhere. **Pros:** a unique experience; excellent service; fantastic breakfast
included. **Cons:** may be noisy, as it is above the Fallen Angel restaurant,
which stays open until 11. $ *Rooms from: S/780* ⊠ *Plazoleta Nazare-
nas 221, San Blas* ☎ *084/258–184* ⊕ *www.fallenangelincusco.com* ⤴ *4
suites* ⦿ *Breakfast.*

$$$$ **Hotel Monasterio.** One of Cusco's top hotels, this beautifully restored
HOTEL   1592 monastery of San Antonio Abad is a national historic monument.
Fodor'sChoice   **Pros:** stylish rooms with all the conveniences; stunning public spaces;
★   attentive service. **Cons:** rooms are small for the price tag; *everything*
(including Internet access) is charged. $ *Rooms from: S/1995* ⊠ *Palacio
140, Plazoleta Nazarenas* ☎ *084/604–000 or 01/610–8300* ⊕ *www.
monasteriohotel.com* ⤴ *120 rooms, 6 suites* ⦿ *Breakfast.*

$$$$ **La Casona.** Colonial with a touch of class, this 11-suite boutique *casa*
HOTEL   comes complete with a manicured interior courtyard, stately sitting
Fodor'sChoice   and dining areas, and rooms with heated floors, antique-looking but
★   modern bathtubs, and marbled showers. **Pros:** serenely situated and
spoil-yourself stylish. **Cons:** books up fast in high season. $ *Rooms
from: S/1087* ⊠ *Plaza Nazarenas 113* ☎ *084/245–314 or 084/234–010*
⊕ *www.inkaterra.com* ⤴ *11 suites* ⦿ *Breakfast.*

$$$$ **Palacio Nazarenas.** Following years of careful renovation and rebuild-
HOTEL   ing, Palazio Nazarenas opened in June 2012 as one of Cuzco's most
Fodor'sChoice   glamorous hotels. **Pros:** excellent and friendly staff; historic setting;
★   central location; top-notch spa. **Cons:** not all rooms have balconies.
$ *Rooms from: S/1547* ⊠ *Plaza Nazarenas 144* ☎ *84/582–222* ⊕ *www.
palacionazarenas.com* ⤴ *55 suites* ⦿ *No meals.*

EAST OF THE PLAZA DE ARMAS

$ **Inkarri Hostal.** If all you want is a clean and comfortable place to lay
HOTEL   your head, you'll be pleasantly surprised at how much more you get
here. **Pros:** great service; comfy beds; heaters available for an extra
fee. **Cons:** basic amenities. $ *Rooms from: S/130* ⊠ *Collacalle 204*
☎ *084/242–692* ⊕ *www.inkarrihostal.com* ⤴ *36 rooms* ⦿ *Breakfast.*

$$$$ **JW Marriott Cusco.** Step through the enormous original 16th-century
HOTEL   doorway and into the plush lobby for a feel of this property, a beautiful and comfortable blend of old and new. **Pros:** large comfortable
rooms; close to the historic center; steeped in history. **Cons:** not everyone will appreciate the blending of past and present. $ *Rooms from:
S/1027* ⊠ *Calle Ruinas 432 and San Agustín* ☎ *084/582–200* ⊕ *www.
jwmarriottcusco.com* ⤴ *146 rooms, 7 suites* ⦿ *Breakfast.*

$$$$ **La Lune One Suite Hotel.** If you're looking for a place to stay where
HOTEL   your every need will be taken care of, it's tough to get more personalized
service than can be had in a hotel with just one suite. **Pros:** unparalleled
luxury and service. **Cons:** doesn't offer a historical ambience; books up
fast. $ *Rooms from: S/650* ⊠ *Calle San Agustin 275* ☎ *084/240–543*
⊕ *www.onesuitehotelcusco.com* ⤴ *1 suite* ⦿ *Multiple meal plans.*

$$$$ **Hotel Libertador Palacio del Inka.** Close enough, but still removed from
HOTEL   the hubbub of the Plaza de Armas, the glass-covered lobby of this hotel

may look like an airport, but it gives you a good idea of the sleek contemporary design that is the signature of this hotel chain. **Pros:** contemporary rooms with all the conveniences; some rooms have views to the Sun Temple; close to the action but not in the thick of it. **Cons:** modern rooms lack the character of some other lodgings; customer service is reportedly uneven. [$] *Rooms from: S/1560* ✉ *Plazoleta Santo Domingo 259* ☎ *084/231–961, 01/518–6500 reservations* 🌐 *www.libertador.com.pe* 🛏 *250 rooms, 4 suites* 🍴 *Breakfast.*

SOUTH OF PLAZA DE ARMAS

$$$ HOTEL 🏨 **Sonesta Hotel.** The sleek yet comfortable lobby introduces you to this hotel's conservative yet friendly style; this hotel is popular with business travelers and tourists alike. **Pros:** newly renovated and clean; comfortable lobby; friendly staff; in-room safes hold laptops; heat. **Cons:** a 10-minute stroll to get into town; not a historic landmark. [$] *Rooms from: S/416* ✉ *Av. El Sol 954* ☎ *084/581–200* 🌐 *www.sonesta.com/cusco* 🛏 *98 rooms* 🍴 *Breakfast.*

$$ HOTEL 🏨 **Torre Dorada Residencial.** What this hotel lacks in location, it more than makes up for with its cheerful staff and clean, comfortable rooms. **Pros:** quiet and comfortable, with a noteworthy staff and variety of other travelers; some rooms have views. **Cons:** a bit far from the center of town, but there is a free shuttle service to the Plaza de Armas. [$] *Rooms from: S/286* ✉ *Calle los Cipreses N-5, Huancaro* ☎ *084/241–698* 🌐 *www.torredorada.com.pe* 🛏 *18 rooms* 🍴 *Breakfast.*

WEST OF THE PLAZA DE ARMAS

$$$$ HOTEL 🏨 **Andean Wings.** Housed in a 16th-century colonial mansion, this boutique does an outstanding job of blending the historical backdrop with a modern and artistic design—each room is unique and decorated with original artwork, sometimes with chandeliers, canopy beds, or Jacuzzi tubs. **Pros:** luxurious rooms; attentive service; design a visual feast. **Cons:** some rooms are smaller with less light; not all designs may be to your taste. [$] *Rooms from: S/546* ✉ *Siete Cuartones 225* ☎ *084/243–166* 🌐 *www.andeanwings.com* 🛏 *11 rooms, 5 suites.*

$$$$ HOTEL 🏨 **Aranwa Cusco Boutique Hotel.** Everywhere you look, there are original pieces of art juxtaposed with modern furnishings at this luxurious boutique hotel housed in a 16th-century colonial mansion. **Pros:** luxury service; historic setting; intimate feel. **Cons:** some rooms have better views than others. [$] *Rooms from: S/980* ✉ *San Juan de Dios 255* ☎ *084/604–444* 🌐 *www.aranwahotels.com* 🛏 *39 rooms, 4 suites* 🍴 *Breakfast.*

$$$$ HOTEL 🏨 **Hotel Costa del Sol Picoaga.** An upscale option at a fraction of the price of some Cusco lodgings, this hotel, now a Costa del Sol by Ramada, mixes the best of the new and old Cusco. **Pros:** excellent value for top-end lodging; mix of modern and colonial room options. **Cons:** rooms on the modern side of the hotel are a bit lacking in charm. [$] *Rooms from: S/535* ✉ *Calle Santa Teresa 344* ☎ *084/252–330* 🌐 *www.costadelsolperu.com* 🛏 *76 rooms, 2 suites* 🍴 *Breakfast.*

$ HOTEL 🏨 **Niños Hotel.** If you prefer lodging with a social conscience—and even if you don't—this is a great budget find; proceeds from your stay at the "Children's Hotel" provide medical and dental care, food, and recreation for disadvantaged Cusqueño children who attend day care on the premises and cheerfully greet you as you pass through the court-yard. **Pros:** wonderfully welcoming staff; charming colonial building; you can sleep soundly with the knowledge that your money is going to a good cause. **Cons:** slightly out of the way; some rooms are small and very basic; books up fast. $ *Rooms from: S/130* ⊠ *Meloq 442* 🏨 *084/231–424* ⊕ *www.ninoshotel.com* ↝ *20 rooms, 13 with bath* ▭ *No credit cards* ⦿ *No meals.*

SAN BLAS

$ ⊡ **Andenes al Cielo.** This boutique hotel housed in a colonial mansion

HOTEL   is located just a few blocks from the Plaza de Armas but offers a quiet respite from the crowds there. **Pros:** low cost for a central location; comfortable rooms; lovely setting. **Cons:** not as luxurious as some of the other Cusco choices; not all rooms have heat yet. $ *Rooms from: S/182* ⊠ *176 Calle Choquechaca, San Blas* ☎ *084/222–237* ⊕ *www. andenesalcielo.com* ↝ *13 rooms, 2 suites* ⦿ *Breakfast.*

$$$ ⊡ **Casa Andina San Blas.** Part of a national chain, all of the Casa Andina

HOTEL   hotels exude professionalism and are great value for money, but each

Fodor's Choice   hotel differs in style—the San Blas branch, in a colonial house perched

★   up on the hillside, offers great views over the city's terra-cotta rooftops. **Pros:** good value for top-end lodgings; excellent location with spectacu-lar views over Cusco; professional atmosphere and pleasant service. **Cons:** can be a hard walk uphill to get here; some rooms have subpar views over the neighboring houses. $ *Rooms from: S/445* ⊠ *Chihuam-pata 278* ☎ *084/263–694, 1/213–9720 Lima reservations* ⊕ *www.casa-andina.com* ↝ *36 rooms, 1 suite* ⦿ *Breakfast.*

$$ ⊡ **Casa San Blas.** This small hotel with a large staff—there's a 2-to-1

HOTEL   staff-to-guest ratio—prides itself on exceptional service and the rooms

☾   are quite comfortable, with colonial-style furniture and hardwood floors, but with more modern amenities than this restored 250-year-old house would imply. **Pros:** fabulous views; warm welcome from staff; fantastic location. **Cons:** it's a steep uphill walk to get here. $ *Rooms from: S/360* ⊠ *Tocuyeros 566, San Blas* ☎ *084/237–900, 888/569–1769 in North America* ⊕ *www.casasanblas.com* ↝ *12 rooms, 5 suites, 1 apartment* ⦿ *Breakfast.*

$$ ⊡ **Hotel Rumi Punku.** A massive stone door—that's what Rumi Punku

HOTEL   means in Quechua—opens onto a rambling complex of balconies, patios, gardens, courtyards, terraces, fireplace, and bits of Inca wall scattered here and there linking a series of pleasantly furnished rooms with hardwood floors and comfy beds covered with plush blankets. **Pros:** great views from the upstairs sauna ($15 USD extra); charming rambling layout; great value for the money. **Cons:** located a bit uphill. $ *Rooms from: S/260* ⊠ *Choquechaca 339* ☎ *084/221–102* ⊕ *www. rumipunku.com* ↝ *40 rooms, 1 suite* ⦿ *Breakfast.*

THE ARTS

FOLKLORE

If you don't fancy the show at the Qosqo Centro de Arte Nativo, many of the restaurants around the Plaza de Armas (like Inka Grill) offer you a similar package. Starting at around 8 pm you'll be treated to an Andean folkloric show while you're dining, the cost of which is usually included in the meal price.

La Retama. At La Retama you'll enjoy Andean music during dinner each evening. ⊠ *Portal de Panes 123, Plaza de Armas* ☎ *084/242–620* ⊕ *www.laretama.info.*

Paititi. There is a folklore show during dinner here most nights. ⊠ *Portal de Carrizos 270, Plaza de Armas* ☎ *084/252–686.*

Qosqo Centro de Arte Nativo. A fun addition to the Boleto Turístico scheme is the Qosqo Centro de Arte Nativo. The cultural center holds hour-long folkloric dance performances in its auditorium each night at 6:30 and 8, with introductions in Spanish and English. You may be one of the lucky audience members called up to participate in the final number. ⊠ *Av. El Sol 872* ☎ *084/227–901.*

Tunupa. There is a nightly folklore show here along with fine dining. ⊠ *Portal de Confiturías 233, Plaza de Armas* ☎ *084/252–936.*

LECTURES

South American Explorers. If you're up for an intellectual, but fun, evening, South American Explorers holds talks on themes of tourist or cultural interest almost every week. The subject might be a mini-Quechua lesson, Peruvian food and drink, a shamanic ceremony, or the screening of a Latin American film. The cost and schedule varies; check the website for information. The gatherings are a great way to meet other travelers. ⊠ *Atoqsaycuchi 670, San Blas* ☎ *084/245–484* ⊕ *www.saexplorers.org.*

THEATER

ICPNAC Cusco. Created to promote understanding between Peru and the U.S. through educational and cultural programs, this center also puts on some of the most varied cultural offerings in the city. It also has a small art gallery with new shows every month. ⊠ *Av. Tulumayo 125, Cusco* ☎ *084/224–112* ⊕ *www.icpnacusco.org.*

NIGHTLIFE

Cusco is full of bars and discos with live music and DJs playing everything from U.S. rock to Andean folk. Though dance clubs sometimes levy a cover charge, there's usually someone out front handing out free passes to tourists. Many clubs cater to an under-thirty crowd. Bars, especially around the Plaza de Armas, frequently position someone in front to entice you in with a coupon for a free drink, but that drink is usually made with the cheapest, gut-rottingest alcohol the bar has available. The drinks may not be great, and the music may not have changed much in the last five (or 10) years, but they're good fun if you want to get your dance on. On the brighter side, in recent years as Cusco's culinary scene has moved in, so have more upscale, less clubby lounges.

PLAZA DE ARMAS
BARS AND PUBS

The Cross Keys. For a cold beer and English soccer broadcast via satellite, try this classy pub that will make London expats homesick. Challenge the regulars to a game of darts at your own risk. ⊠ *Triunfo 350 2nd fl., Plaza de Armas* ☏ *084/229–227* ⊕ *www.cross-keys-pub-cusco-peru.com.*

Limo. For upscale drinks, check out the bar at Limo. While also functioning as a high-end restaurant, the bar here mixes some of the tastiest pisco drinks—in any variation or flavor—around. Not cheap, but if you like pisco sours, don't miss it. ⊠ *Portal de Carnes 236, 2nd fl., Plaza de Armas* ☏ *084/240–668* ⊕ *www.cuscorestaurants.com.*

Norton Rat's Tavern. The second-floor tavern has a great outdoor balcony overlooking the Plaza de Armas, perfect for enjoying a beer (especially if you want an import) and watching the people go by. ⊠ *Santa Catalina Angosta N. 116, Plaza de Armas.*

Paddy Flaherty's. The second-floor, dark-wood Paddy Flaherty's mixes pints of Guinness and old-fashioned Irish pub grub with Philly steaks, pita sandwiches, and chicken baguettes. ⊠ *Triunfo 124, Plaza de Armas* ☏ *084/247–719* ⊕ *www.paddysirishbarcusco.com.*

DANCE CLUBS

The Muse. Although also a restaurant serving up great international comfort food, this locale is becoming more and more known for the great music that can be found here nightly. Of particular note is the live salsa every Friday and Saturday night. ⊠ *Triunfo 338, Plaza de Armas* ☏ *084/242–030.*

Mythology. Always full, with a mixed crowd of generally young Peruvians and foreigners, the club offers free salsa lessons from about 9 to 11 nightly. After that, you can literally dance the night away to a mix of music from the 1980s to today. ⊠ *Portal de Carnes 298.*

Ukukus. Dance the night away at Ukukus, a hugely popular pub and disco that hops with a young crowd most mornings until 5 am. ⊠ *Plateros 316, 2nd fl.* ☏ *084/254–911* ⊕ *www.ukukusbar.com.*

NORTH OF PLAZA DE ARMAS
DANCE CLUBS

Groove. Hands down one of the best dance clubs in Cusco, they play a more modern music set than you will find in most of the other clubs, which tend to play the same songs over and over again. Also check out their lounge on Tecsacocha. ⊠ *Waynapata 194.*

GAY AND LESBIAN

Rainbow flags fly everywhere in Cusco and you might think the city is just really gay-friendly. But you're actually seeing the flag of Cusco, based on the banner of Tawantinsuyo, the Inca empire. The gay scene is actually pretty limited.

Fallen Angel. This bar and restaurant sponsors occasional gay and lesbian events, such as cabaret nights, holiday celebrations, and parties. Check out the website for dates and more information. ⊠ *Plazoleta Nazarenas 221* ☏ *084/258–184* ⊕ *www.fallenangelincusco.com.*

EAST OF PLAZA DE ARMAS
BARS AND PUBS

The Frogs. One of the best bars in Cusco, this is always a fun place to hang out, with plenty of comfy seating and frequently featuring live bands. ✉ *Calle Warankalqui 185* ☎ *084/221–762.*

Museo del Pisco. If you only have time for one bar while you're in Cusco, this should be it. Not only do they serve up great pisco drinks, you can also get a pisco tasting on the fly. If learning about Peru's national liquor is on your must-do list, check their schedule, as they often host special pisco tastings with guest experts. There's great ambience as well as tapas if you want to nosh as you drink. ✉ *Santa Catalina Ancha 398* ☎ *084/262–709* ⊕ *www.museodelpisco.org.*

SAN BLAS
BARS AND PUBS

7 Angelitos Cafe. In San Blas, the intimate 7 Angelitos Cafe often highlights live local bands of many genres including rock and salsa. ✉ *Siete Angelitos 638, San Blas.*

Muse Too. While you're in San Blas you should check out this small, sleek euro-styled café that serves drinks and has live music nightly. ✉ *Tandapata 917, San Blas* ☎ *998/170–084.*

SHOPPING

Cusco is full of traditional crafts, artwork, and clothing made of alpaca, llama, or sheep wool. Beware of acrylic fakes. For the best quality products, shop in the higher-end stores. The export of artifacts would require a government permit, so banish any thoughts of waltzing off with the Inca ruler Pachacutec's cape for a song.

Vendors, often children, will approach you relentlessly on the Plaza de Armas. They sell postcards, finger puppets, drawings, and CDs of Andean music. A simple "no, gracias" is usually enough to indicate you're not interested; if that doesn't work, just keep walking and say it again. Going to art school is a popular thing for students, so you may find some nice paintings in the mix. Several enclosed crafts markets are good bets for bargains. Even the upscale shops are sometimes amenable to offering a discount if these three conditions are met: 1) it's the September–May off-season; 2) you came into the store on your own, without a guide who will expect a commission from the shop; and 3) you pay in cash. General rule of thumb: the more you buy, the more of a discount you'll get.

PLAZA DE ARMAS
ART AND REPLICAS

Ilaria. This is Cusco's finest jewelry store, with an ample selection of replicas of colonial-era pieces. The internationally recognized shop is based in Lima, though there are multiple locations in Cusco, including ones in the Monasterio, Libertador, Casa Andina Private Collection, and Marriott hotels. ⊠ *Portal de Carrizos 258, Plaza de Armas* ☎ *084/246–253* ⊕ *www.ilariainternational.com.*

CRAFTS AND GIFTS

Arte y Canela. If you're looking for modern twists on folkloric crafts, check out Arte y Canela, which sells a variety of high-end silver jewelry and household goods, all with a regional artistic flair. ⊠ *Portal de Panes 143, Plaza de Armas* ☎ *084/221–519* ⊕ *www.arteycanela.com.*

TEXTILES

Alpaca's Best. With several stores in Cusco, Alpaca's Best sells quality knits, but also has a good selection of jewelry. ⊠ *Portal Confiturias 221, Plaza de Armas* ☎ *084/249–406.*

Ethnic Peru. For fine alpaca coats, sweaters, scarves, and shawls, check out this shop; there are two other central locations at Santa Catalina Ancha and Limacpampa Chico. ⊠ *Portal Mantas 114, Plaza de Armas* ☎ *084/232–775* ⊕ *www.ethnicperu.com.*

Kuna. Long-established and übermodern Kuna has alpaca garments, and is one of the only authorized distributors of high-quality vicuña scarves and sweaters. Run by Peruvian design company Alpaca 111, they have shops at the Plaza Regocijo, the Libertador and Monasterio hotels as well as at the airport. ⊠ *Portal de Panes 127, Plaza de Armas* ☎ *084/243–191.*

SPORTING GOODS

The North Face. There are now two locations for this well-known supplier of outdoor wear, one right on the Plaza de Armas and the other at Plazoleta Espinar 188. It's best to buy directly from the company, as there have been problems with inferior knock-off products being sold with the North Face label. ⊠ *Portal de Comercio 195, Plaza de Armas, Cusco* ☎ *084/232–130.*

RKF. Forget to pack your winter jacket for the Inca Trail? No problem: Check out RKF, where you'll find a variety of quality (mostly imported) outdoor goods like North Face jackets and Merrill boots. ⊠ *Portal Carrizos 252, Plaza de Armas* ☎ *084/254–895.*

NORTH OF THE PLAZA DE ARMAS

CERAMICS

Seminario. Seminario is the Cusco shop of famed ceramics maker Pablo Seminario, now housed in the MAP museum building. Prices are lower at the source, in the Sacred Valley town of Urubamba. ⊠ *Plaza Nazarenas 231* ☎ *084/246–097* ⊕ *www.ceramicaseminario.com.*

TEXTILES

La Casa de la Llama. Alpaca gets the camelid's share of attention for use in making fine garments, but La Casa de la Llama sells a fine selection of expensive clothing made from the softer hairs sheared from its namesake animal's chest and neck. It's difficult to tell the difference in texture between llama and adult alpaca, at least in this shop. There are some nice gifts for little ones here as well. ⊠ *Palacio 121* ☎ *084/240–813.*

CLOSE UP

Alpaca Or Acrylic?

Vendors and hole-in-the-wall shop-keepers will beckon you in to look at their wares: "One of a kind," they proudly proclaim. "Baby alpaca, hand woven by my grandmother on her deathbed. It's yours for S/70."

Price should be the first giveaway. A real baby-alpaca sweater would sell for more than S/200. So maintain your skepticism even if the label boldly states "100% baby alpaca." False labels are common on acrylic-blend clothing throughout the Cusco area. Which brings us to our next clue: A good-quality label should show the maker's or seller's name and address. You're more likely to find quality goods at an upscale shop, of which there are several around town. Such a business is just not going to gamble its reputation on inferior products.

Texture is the classic piece of evidence. Baby-alpaca products use hairs, 16–18 microns in diameter, taken from the animal's first clipping. Subsequent shearings from a more mature alpaca yield hairs with a 20-micron diameter, still quite soft, but never matching the legendary tenderness of baby alpaca. (For that reason, women tend toward baby-alpaca products; men navigate toward regular alpaca.) A blend with llama or sheep's wool is slightly rougher to the touch and, for some people, itchier to the skin. And if the garment is too silky, it's likely a synthetic blend. (The occasional 100% polyester product is passed off as alpaca to unsuspecting buyers.)

While "one of a kind" denotes uniqueness—and, again, be aware that much of what is claimed to be handmade here really comes from a factory—the experts say there is nothing wrong with factory-made alpaca products. A garment really woven by someone's grandmother lacks a certain degree of quality control, and you may find later that the dyes run or the seams come undone.

—by Jeffrey Van Fleet

SOUTH OF PLAZA DE ARMAS

ART AND REPLICAS

Fractal Dragon Art Gallery. Even if you aren't looking to bring home artwork, this gallery is worth browsing through. The director is a Cusqueña artist herself and each month she chooses a contemporary up-and-coming artist to display in the gallery. These works of art will give you an opportunity to learn more about the current culture of Cusco and Peru, rather than the traditional painting and crafts. The cultural center upstairs showcases a variety of special events including music, theater, storytelling, and more. ⊠ *Calle Arequipa/Q'hapchik'jllu 159 and 175* ☎ *084/255–860* ⊕ *www.fractaldragon.com* ☉ *Closed Sun.*

CRAFTS

Galería Latina. This reasonably priced crafts shop has many original pieces including tapestries, ceramics, and alpaca clothing. ⊠ *Calle Mantas 118* ☎ *084/228–931.*

SPAS

Healing House. After a day of touring, climbing up and down hundreds of steps, you may be ready for a massage. Healing House is the place to go for a professional treatment with European- and American-trained therapists. This nonprofit also offers yoga classes, a variety of other therapies, as well as seminars, and provides low-cost or free treatments and workshops to locals with limited resources. Limited rooms are available to rent in shared housing for those wanting a more spiritual place to stay. ✉ *555 Qanchipata, San Blas* ☎ *974/962–350* ⊕ *www. healinghousecusco.com.*

SPORTING GOODS

Tatoo. If you are looking for technical trekking gear you'll likely find it at Tatoo. ✉ *Medio 130, Plaza de Armas* ☎ *084/254–211.*

TEXTILES

Center for Traditional Textiles of Cusco. Sweaters, ponchos, scarves, and wall hangings are sold at fair-trade prices at this nonprofit organization dedicated to the survival of traditional weaving. Weavers from local villages work in the shop, and the on-site museum has informative exhibits about weaving techniques and the customs behind traditional costume. ✉ *Av. El Sol 603* ☎ *084/228–117.*

Centro Artesanal Cusco. The municipal government operates the Centro Artesanal Cusco, containing 340 stands of artisan vendors. This is often your best bet for buying those souvenirs that you've seen everywhere but not gotten around to purchasing. Prices are typically negotiable (and often cheaper than you will find in Pisac), and the more you buy at one stall, the better discount you are likely to get. ✉ *Tullumayo and El Sol.*

El Palacio de Las Lanas. If you'd rather knit your own sweater than buy one, there are many places where you can buy yarn. Take a walk over toward the San Pedro market, where you will find a number of yarn stores, such as this one, where you can buy packets of the famous baby alpaca yarn. ✉ *Tupac Amaru 155* ☎ *084/228–741 or 974/286–272.*

WEST OF THE PLAZA DE ARMAS

TEXTILES

Sol Alpaca's. Offering fine garments made from alpaca and vicuña fibers, this store is part of the Michell Group, which has more than 75 years of know-how in processing alpaca and is the leading alpaca producer and exporter in the world. There are also stores on Calle Espaderos and in the Plaza Nazarenas. ✉ *Santa Teresa 317, Plaza Regocijo* ☎ *084/232–687.*

SAN BLAS

CERAMICS

Galería Mérida. In San Blas, the Galería Mérida sells the much-imitated ceramics of Edilberto Mérida. His characters are so expressive you can practically hear them as you browse through the gallery, which doubles as a museum where you can learn more about this award-winning Peruvian artist and his work. ✉ *Carmen Alto 133, San Blas* ☎ *084/221–714* ⊘ *Closed Sun.*

CRAFTS AND GIFTS

Galería Mendívil. Religious art, including elaborately costumed statues of the Virgin Mary, is sold at the shop at the Galería Mendívil. The popular Museo Hilario Mendívil is located across the plaza. ⊠ *Plazoleta San Blas 615-619* ☎ *084/240–527 or 084/274–6622.*

SIDE TRIPS FROM CUSCO

Cusco may be enchantingly beautiful, but with the constant hassle to *buy buy buy*, it's not the most relaxing place on earth. Yet just outside the city lies one of Peru's most spectacular and serene regions, filled with Andean mountains, tiny hamlets, and ancient Inca ruins. In a half-day trip you can visit some of Peru's greatest historical areas and monuments, just beyond Cusco's city limits, such as Sacsayhuamán, perched high on a hill overlooking the city, or the spectacular sights of Qenko, Puka Pukara, and Tambomachay.

The Urubamba Valley, located northwest of Cusco and functioning as the gateway to the Sacred Valley of the Inca, which extends farther northwest, attracts the puma's share of visitors going to Machu Picchu, especially those looking to catch their breath—and some R&R—in the region's idyllic setting. Additionally, the Valle del Sur, a stretch of highway running southeast of Cusco to Sicuani, boasts lesser-known, but equally impressive, Inca and pre-Inca sites.

GETTING HERE AND AROUND

The sites immediately north of Cusco (Sacsayhuamán, Qenko, Puka Pukara, and Tambomachay) are best and most easily taken in via an organized tour. Although both the Urubamba Valley and Valle del Sur are readily accessible by public transportation, most travelers prefer the convenience of a tour to bouncing between buses—the entire sightseeing circuit is about 170 km (105 miles).

Tours are easily organized from one of the many kiosks in Cusco ($15–$30 USD), or if you prefer a more intimate, less tourist-driven trip you can hire a taxi ($60–$70 USD) and a guide ($60 USD).

SACSAYHUAMÁN

2 km (1 miles) north of Cusco.

GETTING HERE AND AROUND

Sacsayhuamán sits a stone's throw from Cusco and is easily visited in a half-day organized tour (the typical tour also includes Puka Pukara, Qenko, and Tambomachay. A so-called "mystical tour" typically takes in the Templo de la Luna and other surrounding sites. If your lungs and legs are up to it, the self-guided 40-minute ascent to Sacsayhuamán offers an eye-catching introduction to colonial Cusco. The walk starts from the Plaza de Armas and winds uphill along the pedestrian-only Resbalosa Street. Make your way past San Cristóbal Church, hang a left at the outstretched arms of the white statue of Christ, and you're almost there. ⊠ *Km 2, Hwy. to Pisac* ☎ *No phone* 💳 *Boleto Turístico* ☉ *Daily 7–6.*

EXPLORING

Fodor's Choice ★ **Sacsayhuamán.** Towering high above Cusco, the ruins of Sacsayhuamán are a constant reminder of the city's Inca roots. You may have to stretch your imagination to visualize how it was during Inca times—much of the site was used as a convenient source of building material by the conquering Spanish, but plenty remains to be marveled at. Huge stone blocks beg the question of how they were carved and maneuvered into position, and the masterful masonry is awe-inspiring. If you're not moved by stonework, the spectacular views over the city are just as eye-catching.

If the Incas designed Cusco in the shape of a puma, then Sacsayhuamán represents its ferocious head.

ACCLIMATIZING IN THE SACRED VALLEY

An increasingly popular option for acclimatizing is to touch down in Cusco and head directly to the Sacred Valley. The patchwork of pastures rolls loosely alongside rocky red cliffs, and life sways lazily to the sibilant croon of the Urubamba river; a balmy and breath-catching 2,000 meters (6,562 feet) below the clamoring cobblestone streets of Cusco. Most Sacred Valley hotels will provide transportation to and from the airport in Cusco on request, but be sure to ask about price. It may be cheaper to arrange your own taxi.

■TIP→ Perhaps the most important Inca monument after Machu Picchu, Sacsayhuamán is thought to have been a religious complex during Inca times. That being said, from its strategic position high above Cusco, it was also excellently placed to defend the city, and its zigzag walls and cross-fire parapets allowed defenders to rain destruction on attackers from two sides.

Construction of the site began in the 1440s, during the reign of the Inca Pachacutec. It's thought that 20,000 workers were needed for Sacsayhuamán's construction, cutting the astonishingly massive limestone, diorite, and andesite blocks—the largest gets varying estimates of anywhere between 125 and 350 tons—rolling them to the site, and assembling them in traditional Inca style to achieve a perfect fit without mortar. The probable translation of Sacsayhuamán, "city of stone," seems apt. The Inca Manco Cápac II, installed as puppet ruler after the conquest, retook the fortress and led a mutiny against Juan Pizarro and the Spanish in 1536. Fighting raged for 10 months in a valiant but unsuccessful bid by the Inca to reclaim their empire. History records that thousands of corpses from both sides littered the grounds and were devoured by condors at the end of the battle.

Today only the outer walls remain of the original fortress city, which the Spanish tore down after the rebellion and then ransacked for years as a source of construction materials for their new city down the hill, a practice that continued until the mid-20th century. One-fifth of the original complex is left; nonetheless, the site is impressive. Sacsayhuamán's three original towers, used for provisions, no longer stand, though the foundations of two are still visible. The so-called Inca's Throne, the Suchuna, remains, presumed used by the emperor for reviewing troops. Today those parade grounds, the Explanada, are the ending point for

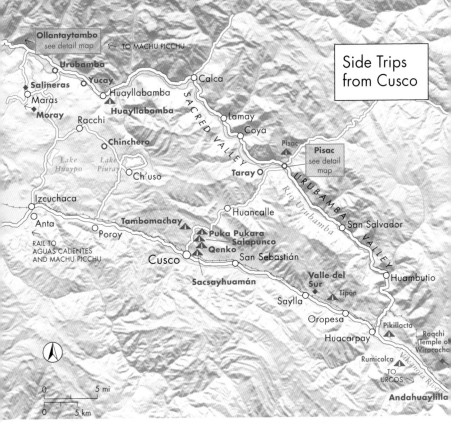

TO MACHU PICCHU

Side Trips
from Cusco

Ollantaytambo
see detail map
Urubamba
Salineras
Maras   Yucay
Moray   Huayllabamba
Racchi   Huayllabamba
Chinchero
Lake   Lake
Huaypo   Piuray   Ch'uso
Izcuchaca
Anta   Poroy   Tambomachay
RAIL TO
AGUAS CALIENTES
AND MACHU PICCHU
Cusco   Puka Pukara
Salapunco
Qenko
San Sebastián
Sacsayhuamán
Saylla
Calca
Lamay
Coya
Pisac
Pisac
see detail
map
Taray
Huancalle
San Salvador
Valle del
Sur   Tipón
Huambutio
Oropesa
Huacarpay   Pikillacta
Raqchi
(Temple of
Wiracocha
Rumicolca
TO
URCOS
Andahuaylilla

SACRED VALLEY
URUBAMBA VALLEY
Río Urubamba
Vilcanota River

0   5 mi
0   5 km

the June 24 Inti Raymi festival of the sun, commemorating the winter solstice and Cusco's most famous celebration.

These closest Inca ruins to Cusco make a straightforward half-day trip from the city, and provide a great view over Cusco's orange rooftops. If you don't have a car, take a taxi, or if you want to test yourself, the ruins are a steep 25-minute walk up from the Plaza de Armas. ■TIP→ A large map at both entrances shows the layout of Sacsayhuamán, but once you enter, signage and explanations are minimal. Self-appointed guides populate the entrances and can give you a two-hour tour (for about S/40 or S/50; negotiate ahead of time). Most are competent and knowledgeable, but depending on their perspective you'll get a strictly historic, strictly mystical, strictly architectural, or all-of-the-above type tour. (But all work the standard joke into their spiel that the name of the site is pronounced "sexy woman.")

It's theoretically possible to sneak into Sacsayhuamán after hours, but lighting is poor, surfaces are uneven, and robberies have occurred at night. ⊠ 2 km (1 mile) north of Cusco ⊠ Boleto Turistico ⊘ 7 am–5 pm.

QENKO

4 km (2½ miles) north of Cusco.

Qenko. It may be a fairly serene location these days, but Qenko, which means "zigzag," was once the site of one of the Incas' most intriguing and potentially macabre rituals. Named after the zigzagging channels carved into the surface, Qenko is a large rock thought to have been the site of an annual preplanting ritual in which priests standing on the top poured *chicha*, or llama blood, into a ceremonial pipe, allowing it to make its way down the channel. If the blood flowed left, it boded poor fertility for the coming season. If the liquid continued the full length of the pipe, it spelled a bountiful harvest. ■TIP➔ **Today you won't see any blood, but the carved channels still exist and you can climb to the top to see how they zigzag their way down.** Other symbolic carvings mix it up on the rock face, too—the eagle-eyed might spot a puma, condor, and a llama. ⊠ *Km 4, Hwy. to Pisac* 🖾 *Boleto Turístico* ☉ *Daily 7–6.*

PUKA PUKARA

10 km (6 miles) north of Cusco.

Puka Pukara. Little is known of the archaeological ruins of Puka Pukara, a pink-stone site guarding the road to the Sacred Valley. Some archaeologists believe the complex was a fort—its name means "red fort"—but others claim it served as a hunting lodge and storage place used by the Inca nobility. Current theory holds that this center, likely built during the reign of the Inca Pachacutec, served all those functions. Whatever it was, it was put in the right place. Near Tambomachay, this enigmatic spot provides spectacular views over the Sacred Valley. Pull up a rock and ponder the mystery yourself. ⊠ *Km 10, Hwy. to Pisac* 🖾 *Boleto Turístico* ☉ *Daily 7–6.*

TAMBOMACHAY

11 km (6½ miles) north of Cusco.

Tambomachay. Ancient fountains preside over this tranquil and secluded spot, which is commonly known as "El Baño del Inca," or, Inca's Bath. The name actually means "cavern lodge" and the site is a three-tiered *huaca* built of elaborate stonework over a natural spring, which is thought to have been used for ritual showers. Interpretations differ, but the site was likely a place where water, considered a source of life, was worshipped (or perhaps just a nice place to take a bath). The huaca is almost certain to have been the scene of sacred ablutions and purifying ceremonies for Inca rulers and royal women. ⊠ *Km 11, Hwy. to Pisac* 🖾 *Boleto Turístico* ☉ *Daily 7–6.*

VALLE DEL SUR

The Río Urubamba runs northwest and southeast from Cusco. The northwest sector of the river basin is the romantically named "Sacred Valley of the Inca," but along the highway that runs southeast of Cusco to Sicuani the region locals call the Valle del Sur is just as interesting.

Peruvian women lead camelids by the Inca site of Sacsayhuamán.

The area abounds with opportunities for off-the-beaten-path exploration. Detour to the tiny town of Oropesa and get to know this self-proclaimed capital of brick-oven bread making; a tradition that's sustained local families for more than 90 years. Or you can side-trip to more pre-Inca and Inca sites. Apart from Andahuayillas and Raqchi, you'll have the ruins to yourself. Only admission to Tipón and Pikillacta is included in the Boleto Turístico. ⇨ *See Buying a Boleto Turístico, above.*

TIPÓN
26 km (15½ miles) southeast of Cusco.

Tipón. Everyone has heard that the Incas were good engineers, but for a real look at just how good they were at land and water management, head to Tipón. Twenty kilometers (12 miles) or so south of Cusco, Tipón is a series of terraces, hidden from the valley below, crisscrossed by stone aqueducts and carved irrigation channels that edge up a narrow pass in the mountains. A spring fed the site and continually replenished a 900-cubic-meter reservoir that supplied water to crops growing on the terraces. ■TIP→ So superb was the technology that several of the terraces are still in use today, and still supplied by the same watering system developed centuries ago. The ruins of a stone temple of undetermined function guard the system, and higher up the mountain are terraces yet to be completely excavated. The rough dirt track that leads to the complex is not in the best of shape and requires some effort to navigate. If you visit without your own car, either walk up (about two hours each way) or take one of the taxis waiting at the turnoff from the main road. ⊠ *4 km (2½ miles) north of Km 23, Hwy. to Urcos* ☷ *Boleto Turístico* ☉ *Daily 7–6.*

PIKILLACTA

6 km (3½ miles) east of Tipón; 7 km (4 miles) south of Oropesa.

Pikillacta. For a reminder that civilizations existed in this region before the Incas, head to Pikillacta, a vast city of 700 buildings from the pre-Inca Wari culture, which flourished between AD 600 and 1000. Over a 2-km site you'll see what remains of what was once a vast walled city with enclosing walls reaching up to 7 meters (23 feet) in height and many two-story buildings, which were entered via ladders to doorways on the second floor. Little is known about the Wari culture, whose empire once stretched from near Cajamarca to the border of the Tiahuanaco near Lake Titicaca. It's clear, however, that they had a genius for farming in a harsh environment and like the Incas built sophisticated urban centers such as Pikillacta (which means the "place of the flea"). At the thatch-roofed excavation sites, uncovered walls show the city's stones were once covered with plaster and whitewashed. A small museum at the entrance houses a scattering of artifacts collected during site excavation, along with a complete dinosaur skeleton. Across the road lies a beautiful lagoon, Lago de Lucre. ⊠ *Km 32, Hwy. to Urcos* 🎫 *Boleto Turístico* ⊗ *Daily 7–6.*

> **DID YOU KNOW?**
>
> Quechua is not a written language. Therefore, there is no written history of the Inca before the time of the Spanish conquest. For this reason, much of what is believed about the local history is speculation. Don't be surprised if you hear different guides offering different versions of the past. Take it all with a grain of salt and feel free to make up your own theories!

RUMICOLCA

3 km (2 miles) east of San Pedro de Cacha.

Rumicolca. An enormous 12-meter- (39-foot-) high gate dating from the Wari period stands at Rumicolca, sitting a healthy walk uphill from the highway. The Inca enhanced the original construction of their predecessors, fortifying it with andesite stone and using the gate as a border checkpoint and customs post. ⊠ *Km 32, Hwy. to Urcos* 🎫 *Free* ⊗ *Daily 24 hrs.*

ANDAHUAYLILLAS

40 km (32 miles) southeast of Cusco.

Andahuaylillas. The main attraction of the small town of Andahuaylillas, 8 km (5 miles) southeast of Pikillacta, is a small 17th-century adobe-towered church built by the Jesuits on the central plaza over the remains of an Inca temple. The contrast between the simple exterior and the rich, expressive, colonial baroque art inside is notable: fine examples of the Cusqueña school of art decorate the upper interior walls. ■ **TIP➔** It's the ceiling that is its special claim to fame, for which it is known as the Sistine Chapel of America. ⊠ *Km 40, Hwy. to Urcos* 🎫 *S/10* ⊗ *Daily 7:30–5:30. Masses: Tues. and Thurs. 8 am, Sat. 6:30 pm, Sun. 10:30 am.*

RAQCHI (TEMPLE OF WIRACOCHA)

4 km (2½ miles) east of San Pedro de Cacha.

Raqchi. (Temple of Wiracocha). The ruins of this large temple in the ancient town of Raqchi give little indication of their original purpose, but if size counts, then they are truly impressive. ■TIP→ Huge external walls up to 12 meters (39 feet) high still tower overhead. You'll be forgiven for thinking that the place was once an Inca version of the Colossium, or a football stadium. Legend has it that the Temple of Raqchi was built in homage to the god Viracocha, to ask his intercession in keeping the nearby Quimsa Chata volcano in check. The ploy worked only some of the time. The site, with its huge adobe walls atop a limestone foundation, performed multiple duties as temple, fortress, barracks, and storage facility. ⊠ *Km 80, Urcos–Puno Hwy.* ⬚*S/10* ☉ *Daily 9–5:30.*

SACRED VALLEY OF THE INCA

A pleasant climate, fertile soil, and proximity to Cusco made the Urubamba River valley a favorite with Inca nobles, many of whom are believed to have had private country homes here. Inca remains, ruins, and agricultural terraces lie throughout the length of this so-called Sacred Valley of the Inca. Cusco is hardly the proverbial urban jungle, but in comparison the Sacred Valley is positively captivating with its lower elevation, fresher air, warmer temperatures, and rural charm. You may find yourself joining the growing ranks of visitors who base themselves out here and make Cusco their day trip, rather than the other way around.

WHEN TO GO

The valley has increasingly taken on a dual personality, depending on the time of day, day of the week, and month of the year. Blame it on Pisac and its famous market. Every Cusco travel agency offers a day tour of the Sacred Valley, with emphasis on Tuesday, Thursday, and Sunday to coincide with the town's larger market days, and they all seem to follow the same schedule: morning shopping in Pisac, buffet lunch in Urubamba, afternoon browsing in Ollantaytambo. You can almost always sign up for one of these tours at the last minute—even early on the morning of the tour—especially if you're here in the September-to-May off-season. On nonmarket days and during the off-season, however, Pisac and the rest of the Sacred Valley is quieter. In any case, the valley deserves more than a rushed day tour if you have the time.

GETTING AROUND

Highways are good and traffic is relatively light in the Sacred Valley, but any trip entails a series of twisting, turning roads as you head out of the mountains near Cusco and descend into the valley. Most people get here by way of an organized tour. However, you can hire a taxi to take you around the valley. Alternatively, you can take a collectivo taxi or van from Cusco ($2–$3.50 USD). They depart daily from Pavitos, close to the intersection with Avenida Grau. ■TIP→ Watch for the rooftop bulls as you pass through the valley. The road to Machu Picchu ends in Ollantaytambo; beyond that point it's rail only.

TARAY

23 km (14 miles) north of Cusco.

The road from Cusco leads directly to the town of Taray. The Pisac market beckons a few kilometers down the road, but Taray makes a worthwhile pre-Pisac shopping stop. Devastating flooding in March 2010 destroyed nearly 80% of the town's homes. However, a herculean effort has been made to get the town's main infrastructure up and running at full steam again.

DID YOU KNOW?

Those ceramic bulls often seen on rooftops, especially in the Sacred Valley, are for good luck. The custom began in Pucara (between Cusco and Puno) and the beasts are believed to protect the home and family, bringing good luck, health and wealth. There is usually a cross in between the pair and there may be other elements as well, such as a condor, sacred in the Andes.

Awana Kancha. Loosely translated as "palace of weaving," Awana Kancha provides an opportunity to see products made from South America's four camelids (alpaca, llama, vicuña, and guanaco) from start to finish: the animal, the shearing, the textile weaving and dyeing, and the finished products, which you can purchase in the showroom. It makes a great stop for the whole family, as kids can feed the camelids on-site. ✉ *Km 23, Carretera a Pisac* 🌐 *www.awanakancha.com* 🎟 *Free* 🕒 *Daily 8–5.*

PISAC

9 km (5 miles) north of Taray.

The colorful colonial town of Pisac, replete with Quechua-language masses in a simple stone church, a well-known market, and fortress ruins, comes into view as you wind your way down the highway from Cusco. (You're dropping about 600 meters [1,970 feet] in elevation when you come out here from the big city.) Pisac, home to about 4,000 people, anchors the eastern end of the Sacred Valley and, like much of the region, has experienced a surge of growth in recent years, with new hotels and restaurants popping up in and around town. An orderly grid of streets forms the center of town, most hemmed in by a hodgepodge of colonial and modern stucco or adobe buildings, and just wide enough for one car at a time. (Walking is easier and far more enjoyable.) The level of congestion (and fun) increases dramatically each Tuesday, Thursday, and especially Sunday, when one of Peru's most celebrated markets comes into its own, but much more spectacular are the ruins above. Admission to the ruins is included in both the Boleto Turístico and Boleto Parcial.

WHERE TO EAT AND STAY

$ PERUVIAN 🍴 **Horno Pumachayoq.** The empanadas are fantastic, but that's not the only reason to stop by at this classic empanada place. The real hook is a "cuy castle," a sort of Barbie mansion for guinea pigs. But rest assured, there are no cuy empanadas on the menu. [$] *Average main: S/3* ✉ *Carretera a Pisac Ruinas s/n, Pisac* 🕒 *No dinner.*

$ ✕ **Mullu Café.** Rustic but stylish,
PERUVIAN Mullu Café has a cosmopolitan flair
and specializes in Andean fusion
fare. The food and drinks, along
with the upbeat atmosphere, can't
be topped. Grab a table for dinner
overlooking the Plaza de Armas
and you might think you were in
Cusco for the night. If you're looking for a lunch spot, come early as
the place tends to fill up. $ *Average
main: S/29* ✉ *Plaza de Armas 352*
☎ *084/203–073* ⊕ *www.mullu.pe.*

$ ✕ **Panadería.** The unnamed bak-
BAKERY ery just off the Plaza Constitución
★ is a Pisac institution. Empanadas
(some vegetarian) and homemade
breads are delivered from the clay
oven and into your hands. The lines are long on Tuesday, Thursday,
and Sunday market days but it's worth the wait. $ *Average main: S/3*
✉ *Mariscal Castilla 372* ⊟ No credit cards ☾ No dinner.

$ ✕ **Trattoria Escondida.** A welcome addition to the culinary offerings in
ITALIAN Pisac, this restaurant offers Italian food with some Peruvian twists con-
cocted by an American chef. The ingredients are sourced locally and
purchased daily, ensuring that everything is fresh. Continuing on the
theme of freshness, pastas are made in-house. The restaurant is literally
built into the mountain, as you will notice by the huge rock forming part
of one wall. The locale doubles as a community space, with frequent
live music, art openings, and the like. Located across the street from
Melissa Wasi, the restaurant closes early, so be sure to call ahead. $ *Av-
erage main: S/22* ✉ *Rinconada, Sector Matará, Pisac* ☎ *084/791–938*
☾ *Closed Tues. and Wed.*

$ ✕ **Ulrike's Café.** German transplant Ulrike Simic and company dish up
CAFÉ food all day long, making this the perfect refueling stop during a day of
market shopping and sightseeing. Breakfast gets underway, before the
market does, at 8 am. ■**TIP→** Stop by for the S/20 prix-fixe lunch, with
a lot of vegetarian options on the menu, a real rarity in this part of Peru.
They've got good à la carte soups and pizzas, too, and yummy brownies,
muffins, cheesecake, and chocolate-chip cookies for dessert. $ *Aver-
age main: S/18* ✉ *Calle Pardo 613* ☎ *084/203–195* ⊟ No credit cards.

$ ⌂ **The Green House.** With just four rooms, this small hotel offers a quiet
HOTEL getaway in a gorgeous country setting—it's perfect for getting in some
nature without having to rough it. **Pros:** quiet and friendly; beautiful grounds. **Cons:** remote location. $ *Rooms from: S/210* ✉ *Carret-
era Pisac-Ollantaytambo Km 60.2, Huaran* ☎ *984/115–375* ⊕ *www.
thegreenhouseperu.com* ⤺ *4 rooms* ⦿*Breakfast.*

$ ⌂ **Hotel Royal Inka Pisac.** Just outside of town is a branch of Peru's Royal
HOTEL Inka hotel chain, and the closest lodging to the Pisac ruins. **Pros:** lots of
activities; clean and comfortable. **Cons:** outside of town. $ *Rooms from:*

BOLETO TURÍSTICO

Four Sacred Valley sites (Pisac,
Chinchero, Moray, and Ollantaytambo) fall under Cusco's Boleto
Turístico scheme ⇨ see *Discounts
and Deals* at the start of this
chapter. The ticket's 10-day valid-
ity lets you take in these four
attractions as well, and is the only
way to gain admission. An abbreviated S/70 ticket, valid for two
days, also gains you admission to
the four sites in the valley. Moray
is not included in the standard
Sacred Valley tour.

Restaurants ▼

Horno Pumachayoq **4**
Mullu Café **3**
Panaderia **1**
Trattoria Escondida **5**
Ulrike's Cafe **2**

Hotels ▼

The Green House **4**
Hotel Royal Inka Pisac **2**
Paz y Luz **3**
Pisac Inn **1**

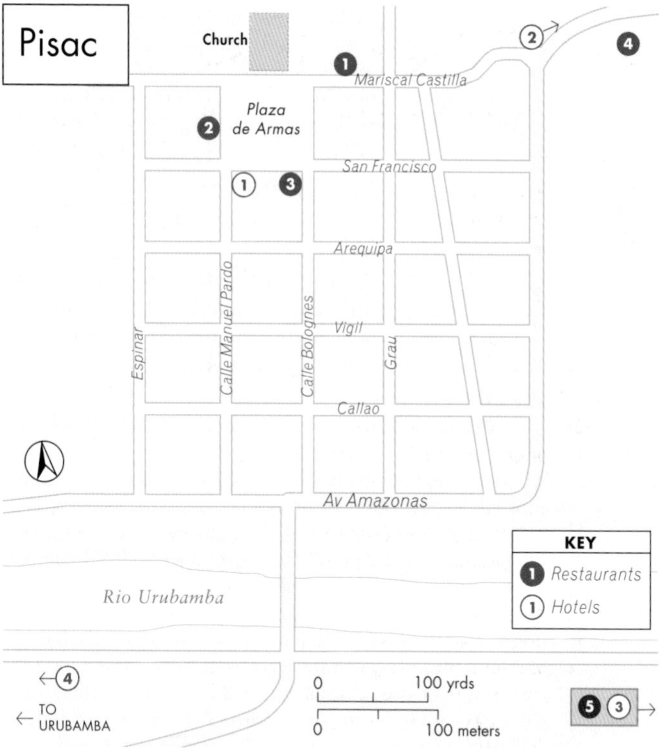

S/208 ✉ *Km 1½, Carretera a Pisac Ruinas* ☎ *084/203–064, 866/554–6028 in North America* 🌐 *www.royalinkahotel.com* 🛏 *80 rooms* 🍴 *Breakfast.*

$ HOTEL 👶 🏨 **Paz y Luz.** Bright airy rooms, sky-lighted bathrooms, and mountain views characterize this growing hotel just outside of town. **Pros:** excellent for families and big groups, especially conference cadres. **Cons:** not the most centrally located. [$] *Rooms from: S/170* ✉ *1 km (½ mile) past the bridge, on the right* ☎ *084/203–204* 🌐 *www.pazyluzperu.com* 🛏 *22 rooms, 2 suites, 3 bungalows* 💳 *No credit cards* 🍴 *Breakfast.*

$ HOTEL 👶 🏨 **Pisac Inn.** Renovated in 2010, this already homey place now boasts an even brighter face, and it's on the main square. **Pros:** convenient location; serene space. **Cons:** basic room amenities. [$] *Rooms from: S/143* ✉ *Plaza de Armas* ☎ *084/203–062* 🌐 *www.pisacinn.com* 🛏 *12 rooms* 🍴 *Breakfast.*

HUAYLLABAMBA

On your way from Pisac to Yucay/Urubamba, you will pass through this small town. There's not much reason to stop unless you happen to be staying at the Aranwa, but that alone might be reason enough.

$$$$ HOTEL 🏨 **Aranwa Sacred Valley Hotel and Wellness.** Set in the beautiful Sacred Valley, the hotel's riverside location is enough to make your stress melt away, add to that an extensive wellness center with treatments

featuring local ingredients and therapies, hydrotherapy pools, yoga, a fitness center, and more, and your trip to Peru may turn into a wellness retreat. **Pros:** excellent service; beautiful property; extensive wellness treatments. **Cons:** located in a remote area. $ *Rooms from: S/728* ⊠ *Antigua Hacienda Yaravilca, Huayllabamba* ☎ *084/205–080* ⊕ *www. aranwahotels.com* ↪ *101 rooms, 14 suites* ◯ *Breakfast.*

YUCAY

46 km (28 miles) northwest of Pisac.

Just a bit outside the much larger Urubamba, Yucay proper is only a few streets wide, with a collection of attractive colonial-era adobe and stucco buildings and a pair of good-choice lodgings on opposite sides of a grassy plaza in the center of town.

WHERE TO STAY

$$
HOTEL

La Casona de Yucay. The 1810 home of Manuel de Orihuela hosted South American liberator Simón Bolívar, and you can stay in Room 136, where he slept during his 1825 visit. **Pros:** historic setting amidst beautiful landscapes. **Cons:** not much else in Yucay itself. $ *Rooms from: S/299* ⊠ *Av. San Martín 104, Plaza Manco II* ☎ *084/201–116* ⊕ *www. hotelcasonayucay.com* ↪ *50 rooms, 3 suites* ◯ *Breakfast.*

$$$
HOTEL
★

Sonesta Posada del Inca Valle Sagrado. In the heart of the Sacred Valley is this 300-year-old former convent (monastery) whose rooms, with tile floors, wood ceilings, and hand-carved headboards, have balconies that overlook the gardens or the terraced hillsides. **Pros:** good restaurant; historic setting. **Cons:** although a good base for the valley, there's not much else in Yucay $ *Rooms from: S/468* ⊠ *Plaza Manco II 123* ☎ *084/201–107, 01/712–6060 in Lima, 800/766–3782 in North America* ⊕ *www. sonesta.com/SacredValley* ↪ *83 rooms, 4 suites* ◯ *Some meals.*

URUBAMBA

2 km (1 mile) west of Yucay; 29 km (17 miles) northwest of Chinchero.

Spanish naturalist Antonio de León Pinedo rhapsodized that Urubamba must have been the biblical Garden of Eden, but you'll be forgiven if your first glance at the place causes you to doubt that lofty claim: the highway leading into and bypassing the city, the Sacred Valley's administrative, economic, and geographic center, shows you miles of gas stations and convenience stores. But get off the highway and get lost in the countryside, awash in flowers and pisonay trees, and enjoy the spectacular views of the nearby mountains and you might agree with León Pinedo after all. Urubamba holds little of historic interest, but the gorgeous scenery, a growing selection of top-notch hotels, and easy access to Machu Picchu rail service make the town an appealing place in which to base yourself.

ESSENTIALS

Currency Banco de la Nación ⊠ *Av. Señor de Torrechayoc y Jr. Sagrario* ☎ *084/201–291.*

Mail SERPOST ⊠ *Jr. Comercio 407.*

CLOSE UP

Trails Other Than The Inca Trail

Trekking to this Inca site of Choquequirao is a serious trek of at least four days.

The popularity of the Inca Trail and the scarcity of available spots have led to the opening of several alternative hikes of varying length and difficulty.

The four- to seven-day **Salcantay** trek (typically five) is named for the 6,270-meter (20,500-foot) peak of the same name. It begins at Mollepata, four hours by road from Cusco, and is a strenuous hike that goes through a 4,800-meter (15,700-foot) pass. The seven-day version of the Salcantay excursion joins the Inca Trail at Huayllabamba, and for this one you need an Inca trail permit.

The **Ausangate** trek takes its name from the Nevado Ausangate, 6,372 meters (20,900 feet) in elevation, and requires a day of travel each way from Cusco in addition to the standard five to six days on the trail. Nearly the entire excursion takes you on terrain over 4,000 meters (13,100 feet) high.

Multiday hikes through the **Lares Valley**, north of Urubamba and Ollantaytambo, offer a little bit of everything for anyone who enjoys the outdoors; a series of ancient trails once used by the Inca wind their way through native forests and past lakes fed by runoff from the snowcapped mountains nearby. Excursions also offer a cultural dimension, with stops at several traditional Quechua villages along the way. The Lares trek compares in difficulty to the Inca Trail.

The lesser-known but remarkably rewarding trek to **Choquequirao** (Cradle of Gold) takes in stunning Andean scenery as you make your way to ruins that have been heralded as Machu Picchu's "Sacred Sister." The site, another long-lost Inca city still under excavation and not yet engulfed by mass tourism, sits at 3,100 meters (10,180 feet). The four-day trek entails a series of steep ascents and descents. If you have more time, you can continue trekking on to Machu Picchu from here.

The **Chinchero–Huayllabamba** trek has two selling points: it can be accomplished in one day—about six hours—and is downhill much of the way, although portions get steep. The hike begins in Chinchero, north of Cusco, and follows an Inca trail that offers splendid views as you descend into the Sacred Valley toward the small village of Huayllabamba.

5

WHERE TO EAT AND STAY

$
PERUVIAN

✕ **El Huacatay.** The best restaurant in Urubamba, possibly in the Valley, El Huacatay was serving Peruvian fusion cuisine before it became trendy in an intimate ambience and with a lovely garden. All that experience has certainly stood them in good stead and you're likely to need some time to decide between all the enticing possibilities on the menu. Still, you can never go wrong with an alpaca tenderloin or pumpkin tortellini. There are plenty of vegetarian choices as well. Be sure to save room for the frozen passionfruit cheesecake. $ *Average main: S/34* ✉ *Jr. Arica 620, Urubamba* ☎ *084/201–790* ⊕ *www.elhuacatay.com* ✑ *Reservations essential* ☾ *Closed Sun.*

$
HOTEL

🛏 **Hospedaje Los Jardines.** Some remodeling coupled with the carefully tended and colorful grounds continues to sustain this longtime favorite in the center of town. **Pros:** cozy setting; good value. **Cons:** service is very hands-off, so not for people seeking instant attention when needed; breakfast available for a fee. $ *Rooms from: S/80* ✉ *Jr. Convencion 459* ☎ *084/201–331* ⊕ *www.los-jardines-urubamba.com* ⤺ *11 rooms* ⦿ *No meals.*

$$$$
HOTEL

🛏 **Hotel Libertador Tambo del Inka.** The sprawling complex sits on the edge of Urubamba's curving river—all state-of-the-art, environmentally friendly rooms have hardwood floors, two beds, and great mountain views. **Pros:** secluded with riverfront views; green hotel. **Cons:** huge modern resort; not for those seeking intimate atmosphere. $ *Rooms from: S/793* ✉ *Av. Ferrocarril s/n* ☎ *511/518–6500 or 084/581–777* ⊕ *www.libertador.com.pe* ⤺ *116 room, 12 suites* ⦿ *Breakfast.*

$$
HOTEL

🛏 **Hotel San Agustín (Monasterio de la Recoleta).** Part of a Peruvian hotel chain, this is the quintessential two-in-one lodging—on the main road is a modern hacienda-style hotel with gleaming rooms, modern services, and all the comforts you could desire, and up the hill is the scaled-up Recoleta, a 16th-century Franciscan monastery with a cavernous dining room, guest rooms with hardwood floors, white walls, and Cusqueña paintings, and a bell tower with great views of the valley. **Pros:** historic setting. **Cons:** slightly outside of town. $ *Rooms from: S/325* ✉ *Km 69, Carretera Pisac–Ollantaytambo* ☎ *084/201–443 or 084/201–666* ⊕ *www.hotelessanagustin.com.pe* ⤺ *92 rooms, 10 suites* ⦿ *Breakfast.*

$
HOTEL

🛏 **Posada Las Casitas del Arco Iris.** An incredibly tranquil and cozy retreat in the gorgeous Urubamba countryside, you'll have even more peace of mind knowing that your soles are helping fund health care and education for underprivileged children and adults. **Pros:** gorgeous landscape; private comfortable rooms; bargain prices; charitable organization. **Cons:** remote location. $ *Rooms from: S/208* ✉ *Querocancha, Urubamba* ☎ *084/201–484* ⊕ *www.lascasitasdelarcoiris.com* ⤺ *8 bungalows, 3 rooms* ⦿ *Breakfast.*

$$$$
HOTEL
☾

🛏 **Rio Sagrado.** Sprawled across 2.5 hectares of greenery, and situated alongside the Urubamba River, this retreat offers tranquillity and comfort. **Pros:** self-sufficient, serene, and personalized service. **Cons:** a bit outside of town. $ *Rooms from: S/845* ✉ *Km 75.8 Carratera Cusco-Urubamba* ☎ *084/201–631 or 511/610–8300* ⊕ *www.riosagrado.com* ⤺ *21 rooms, 2 villas* ⦿ *Breakfast.*

Continued on page 263

Valley in the vicinity of Ollantaytambo near Cusco, Peru.

TOURING THE SACRED VALLEY

by Jeffery Van Fleet

You've come to Cusco to see Machu Picchu, but you'll spend at least one day touring the Sacred Valley. Not only is it chock-full of major archaeological sights, but its small towns and easy-living pace invite you to slow down. If the Inca emperors favored the warm, fertile valley as a place for cultivation and recreation, why not you?

The Sacred Valley follows the Urubamba River from the town of Pisac, about 30 km (18 miles) northeast of Cusco, and ends 60 km (36 miles) northwest of Cusco at Ollantaytambo. Beyond that point, the cliffs flanking the river grow closer together, and the agriculturally rich floodplain thins to a gorge as the Urubamba begins its abrupt descent toward the Amazon basin.

What makes the valley "sacred"? The Inca named rivers by sector and called this stretch of the Urubamba Wilcamayu, "the sacred river" because it reflects the Milky Way at that point. Spanish explorers applied the concept to the entire valley, calling it the Valle Sagrado. The tourist industry likes the appealing, evocative name, too.

The entire area, though very rural, is served by good roads and public transportation except to the Moray and Salineras sites. The best options are to hire a car and driver or take a tour.

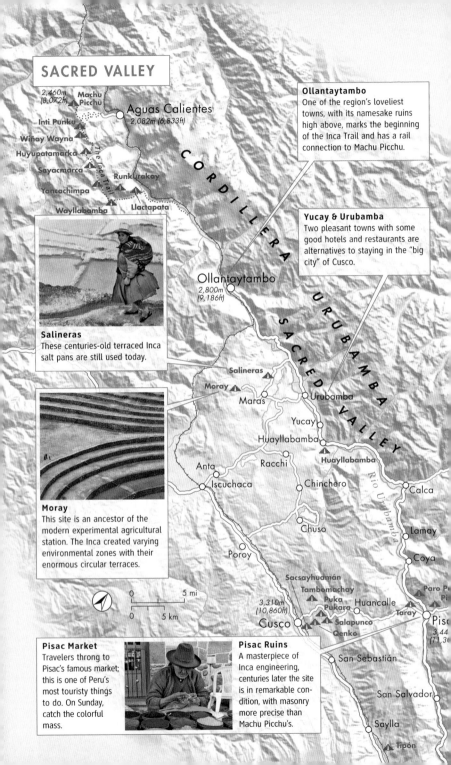

SACRED VALLEY

2,460m (8,072ft) Machu Picchu

Aguas Calientes
2,082m (6,833ft)

Inti Punku

Wiñay Wayna

Huyupatamarka

Sayacmarca

Yancachimpa

Runkurakay

Wayllabamba

Llactapata

The Inca Trail

C O R D I L L E R A

U R U B A M B A

Ollantaytambo
One of the region's loveliest towns, with its namesake ruins high above, marks the beginning of the Inca Trail and has a rail connection to Machu Picchu.

Yucay & Urubamba
Two pleasant towns with some good hotels and restaurants are alternatives to staying in the "big city" of Cusco.

Ollantaytambo
2,800m (9,186ft)

S A C R E D   V A L L E Y

Salineras
These centuries-old terraced Inca salt pans are still used today.

Salineras

Moray

Maras

Urubamba

Yucay

Huayllabamba

Huayllabamba

Racchi

Moray
This site is an ancestor of the modern experimental agricultural station. The Inca created varying environmental zones with their enormous circular terraces.

Anta

Iscuchaca

Chinchero

Calca

Chuso

Lamay

Poroy

Coya

Río Urubamba

0   5 mi
0   5 km

Sacsayhuamán

Tambomachay

Puka Pukara

Huancalle

Paro Po
Pi

3,310m (10,860ft)

Salapunco

Taray

Qenko

Cusco

Pisa

San Sebastián

3,44
(1,3)

Pisac Market
Travelers throng to Pisac's famous market; this is one of Peru's most touristy things to do. On Sunday, catch the colorful mass.

Pisac Ruins
A masterpiece of Inca engineering, centuries later the site is in remarkable condition, with masonry more precise than Machu Picchu's.

San Salvador

Saylla

Tipón

PISAC

Pisac market vendor

PISAC MARKET

Pisac's famous market is held every day but is even larger on Tuesday, Thursday, and Sunday when the ever-present ceramics, jewelry and textiles share the stage with fruits, vegetables, and grains, spilling over and onto the side streets. Sellers set up shop about 9 am on market days and start packing up at about 5 pm. The market is not so different from many others you'll see around Peru, only larger. Go on Sunday if your schedule permits; you'll have a chance to take in the 11 am Quechua Mass at the Iglesia San Pedro Apóstolo and watch the elaborate costumed procession led by the mayor, who carries his *varayoc*, a ceremonial staff, out of the church afterward. ☉ *Daily 9–5.*

PISAC RUINS

From the market area, drive or take a taxi S/15–S/20 one-way up the winding road to the Inca ruins of Pisac. Visiting on market day is your best bet for finding easy transportation up; the alternative is a steep two-hour walk from town. It's most crowded on Sunday; the rest of the week there will be fewer people.

Archaeologists originally thought the ruins were a fortress to defend against fierce Antis (jungle peoples), though there's little evidence that battles were fought here. Now it seems that Pisac was a bit of everything: citadel, religious site, observatory, and residence, and may have served as a refuge in times of siege. The complex also has a temple to the sun and an astronomical observatory, from which priests calculated the growing season each year. Narrow trails wind tortuously between and through solid rock. You may find yourself practically alone on the series of paths in the mountains that lead you among the ruins, through caves, and past the largest known Inca cemetery (the Inca buried their dead in tombs high on the cliffs). Just as spectacular *as* the site are the views *from* it.

Farther above are more ruins and burial grounds, still in the process of being excavated. ✉ *Boleto Turístico* ☉ *Daily 7–6.*

Inca Pisac ruins on a high bluff.

OLLANTAYTAMBO

Women in Ollantaytambo, Peru.

The town is pronounced "oy-yahn-tie-tahm-bo" but everyone calls it "Ollanta"—or "Olly"—for short. It was named for Ollantay, the Inca general who expanded the frontiers of Tawantinsuyo as far north as Colombia and as far south as Argentina during the reign of the Inca Pachacutec. The general asked for the hand of the emperor's daughter, a request Pachacutec refused. Accomplished though Ollantay was, he was still a commoner. The general rebelled against the ruler and ensconced himself in his fortress. Legend has it that the princess was imprisoned until her more tolerant brother took the throne. Whatever the story, you too will fall in love when you glimpse the stone streets and houses,

Inca ruins, Ollantaytambo.

mountain scenery, some of the most lush territory in the valley, and great ruins.

FORTRESS OF OLLANTAYTAMBO

Walk above the town to a formidable stone structure where massive terraces climb to the peak. It was the valley's main defense against the Antis tribes from the neighboring rain forests. Construction began during the reign of Pachacutec but was never completed. The rose-color granite used was not mined in this part of the valley. The elaborate walled complex contained a temple to the sun, used for astronomical observation, as well as the Baños de la Ñusta (ceremonial princess baths), leading archaeologists to believe that Ollantaytambo existed for more than defensive purposes, as was typical with Inca constructions.

The fortress was the site of the greatest Inca victory over the Spanish during the wars of conquest. The Manco Inca fled here in 1537 with a contingent of troops after the disastrous loss at Sacsayhuamán and routed Spanish forces under Hernando Pizarro. The victory was short-lived: Pizarro regrouped and took the fortress. ⊠ *Plaza Mañay Raquy* 🎫 *Boleto Turístico* 🕙 *Daily 7–6.*

OLLANTAYTAMBO HERITAGE TRAIL

Attribute the town's distinctive appearance to Inca organization. They based their communities on the unit of the cancha, a walled city block, each with one entrance leading to an interior courtyard, surrounded by a collection of houses. The system is most obvious in the center of town around the main plaza. You'll find the most welcoming of these self-contained communities at Calle del Medio. A tourist information office in the Plaza de Armas can help direct you.

$$$$
HOTEL
Fodor'sChoice
★

Sol y Luna Lodge & Spa. You can't help but relax the minute you set foot on this property featuring bungalows surrounded by gorgeous flower gardens. **Pros:** tranquil setting; many activities. **Cons:** a few miles outside of town but easy to get to. $ *Rooms from: S/572* ✉ *Fundo Huincho, 2 km west of Urubamba* ☎ *084/201–620* ⊕ *www.hotelsolyluna.com* �ъ *24 bungalows* ⦿ *Breakfast.*

SHOPPING

Cerámica Seminario. Cusco transplants and husband-and-wife team Pablo Seminario and Marilú Bejar and their German shepherds run the Cerámica Seminario in the center of town. They take the valley's distinctive red clay and turn it into ceramic works using modern adaptations of ancient indigenous techniques and designs. More than a shop or art gallery, here you have the ability to view the workshop where the magic happens. ✉ *Berriozabal 111* ☎ *084/201–002* ⊕ *www.ceramicaseminario.com* ⊗ *Daily 8–7.*

5

CHINCHERO

28 km (17 miles) northwest of Cusco.

Indigenous lore says that Chinchero, one of the valley's major Inca cities, was the birthplace of the rainbow. Frequent sightings during the rainy season might convince you of the legend's truth. Chinchero is one of the few sites in the Sacred Valley that's higher (3,800 meters or 12,500 feet) than Cusco.

Today tourists and locals frequent the colorful Sunday artisan market on the central plaza, an affair that gets rave reviews as being more authentic and less touristed than the larger market in neighboring Pisac. A corresponding Chinchero produce market for locals takes place at the entrance to town. The market is there on other days, but on Sunday there are artisans who travel from the high mountain villages to sell their wares.

Amble about the collection of winding streets and adobe houses, but be sure to eventually make your way toward one of the weaving cooperatives, where a gaggle of local women will entertain you into understanding the art of making those lovely alpaca sweaters you eyed in the market.

EXPLORING

Church. A 1607 colonial church in the central plaza above the market was built on top of the limestone remains of an Inca palace, thought to be the country estate of the Inca Tupac Yupanqui, the son of Pachacutec. ▤ *Boleto Turístico* ⊗ *Daily 9–3.*

WHERE TO STAY

$
HOTEL

La Casa de Barro. This "house of adobe," with its ochre walls and eucalyptus-wood roof, is the main lodging option here, and it's just fine if you're looking for a cute hotel and don't mind being a little way from town. **Pros:** cozy setting; good value. **Cons:** isolated location. $ *Rooms from: S/130* ✉ *Miraflores 147* ☎ *084/306–031* ⊕ *www.lacasadebarro.com* ➪ *11 rooms* ▭ *No credit cards* ⦿ *Breakfast.*

MORAY AND SALINERAS

48 km (29 miles) northwest of Cusco.

Moray and Salineras. Scientists still marvel at the agricultural technology the Inca used at **Moray**. Taking advantage of four natural depressions in the ground and angles of sunlight, indigenous engineers fashioned concentric circular irrigation terraces, 150 meters (500 feet) from top to bottom, and could create a difference of 15°C (60°F) from top to bottom. The result was a series of engineered mini-climates perfect for adapting, experimenting, mixing, matching, and cultivating foods, especially varieties of maize, the staple of the Inca empire, normally impossible to grow at this altitude. Though the technology is attributed to the Inca, the lower portions of the complex are thought to date from the pre–Inca Wari culture. Entrance to Moray is included in the Boleto Turístico.

The famed terraced Inca salt pans of **Salineras** are still in use and also take advantage of a natural phenomenon: the Inca dug shallow pools into a sloped hillside. The pools filled with water, and upon evaporation salt crystallized and could be harvested. It costs S/5 per person, but is well worth it. They're difficult to reach via a tour, and almost impossible during the rainy season. No public transportation serves Moray or Salineras. A taxi can be hired from Maras, the closest village, or from Cusco. Alternatively, it's a two-hour hike from Maras to either site. ✉ *Maras* ✉ *Moray: Boleto Turístico, Salineras: S/5.*

OLLANTAYTAMBO

19 km (11 miles) west of Urubamba.

Poll visitors for their favorite Sacred Valley community, and the answer will likely be Ollantaytambo—endearingly nicknamed Olly or Ollanta—which lies at the valley's northwestern entrance. Ollantaytambo's traditional air has not been stifled by the invasion of tourists. Ask around for the local *mercado*, situated just off the Plaza de Armas, close to the pickup point for collectivos and taxis. This busy marketplace quietly evades tourism's grasp and offers a behind-the-scenes peak at life beyond the ruins. The juice stations on the second floor, toward the back, might just be the town's best-kept secret.

■ **TIP➔** Ollantaytambo makes a superb base for exploring the Sacred Valley and has convenient rail connections to Machu Picchu.

Ollantaytambo is also the kickoff point for the Inca Trail. You'll start here at nearby Km 82 if you wish to hike to the Lost City, and lodging here will give you a bit more time to sleep before hiking. Walk up to discover the **fortress of Ollantaytambo**, one of the most fantastic ruins in the Sacred Valley.

ESSENTIALS

BCP ATM, on Ventidero 248 inside the entrance to Hostal Sauce, is the most reliable ATM in town. There is also one in the Plaza de Armas if the other one isn't working.

ATMs BCP ATM ✉ *Ventiderio 248, inside entrance to Hostal Sauce.*

EXPLORING

Awamaki. If you've made it to the Sacred Valley, you've likely seen your share of woven garments. But it's worth swinging by this fair-trade shop just down the road from the Plaza de Armas on the way to the ruins. All goods are produced as part of the Awamaki weaving project, which supports a cooperative of Quechua women from the Patacancha Valley. The organization also offers a variety of cultural tours, including homestays and weaving courses, all of which you can find out about at the shop. ⊠ *Pilcohausi s/n* ☎ *084/204–149* ⊕ *www.awamaki.org* ☾ *Daily 10–6.*

WHERE TO EAT

$ ✕ **Blue Puppy.** With a varied menu of light-bites like soups, salads, and
PERUVIAN   quesadillas, a selection of pastas and pizzas, and a number of vegetarian options, this is an especially good choice for groups. The location on the second floor in a corner of the Plaza de Armas affords some views of the mountains that surround the town. Padded chairs and couches provide more comfortable seating than many places in town. $ *Average main: S/28* ⊠ *Plaza de Armas, Calle del Horno s/n* ⊕ *www.cuzcodining.com.*

$ ✕ **Café Mayu.** We recommend hunkering down for at least a day or
CAFÉ   two in Ollantaytambo, but if you've only got time for a pit stop, Café Mayu is conveniently located right at the train station. This tiny spot serves up big-city-style coffee and some quick bites like empanadas. The chocolate-chip cookies are as good as they smell, but you can't go wrong with the other baked goods here, either. $ *Average main: S/6* ⊠ *Train Station* ☎ *084/204–014* ▬ *No credit cards.*

$ ✕ **Hearts Café.** w✕ **La Esquina.** For a quick bite, healthy or indulgent, this
CAFÉ   café on the Plaza de Armas is a good bet. Breakfast, sandwiches, soups, and salads will all keep you going as you walk around the ruins, and the baked goods, coffees, and English teas make for great pick-me-ups in the afternoon. $ *Average main: S/13* ⊠ *Plaza de Armas* ☎ *084/204–078* ▬ *No credit cards.*

$ ✕ **Mayupata.** Spacious and airy, furnished with large wooden tables and
PERUVIAN   chairs, this restaurant has the unmistakable air of a tourist-friendly Andean establishment. The menu ranges from traditional Peruvian grilled meats and fish to slightly edgier dishes like Andean ravioli (filled with alpaca). For an all-around good meal, try their specialty— mayupata trucha—with a miracuya-sour cocktail. You'll also find foreigner-friendly staples like wood-oven pizza and Asian fusion plates. $ *Average main: S/28* ⊠ *Jr. Concepcíon s/n* ☎ *084/204–009.*

$ ✕ **Pachamama.** Linen tablecloths, carefully folded napkins, and cruets
PIZZA   of olive oil and balsamic vinegar give this pizzeria-restaurant the mark of a sophisticated European eatery. Tables already set with wine glasses invite you to relax and order a bottle. Formerly closer to the ruins, the restaurant is now situated on the Plaza de Armas. Known for pizza, the restaurant also features Peruvian dishes, pasta and more. $ *Average main: S/23* ⊠ *Plaza de Armas* ☎ *084/204–168.*

$ ✕ **Puka Rumi.** Where it lacks the polish and charm of other places in
MEXICAN   town, Puka Rumi gains ground with its colossal burritos and chicken fajitas—served with a tabletop's worth of sides, including a heaping bowl of homemade guacamole. The menu isn't strictly Mexican, despite what they claim; like the patrons, you'll find an international mix. The

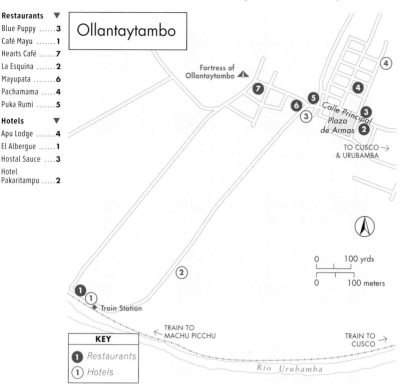

Ollantaytambo

Fortress of
Ollantaytambo

Calle Principal
Plaza
de Armas

TO CUSCO →
& URUBAMBA

0   100 yrds

0   100 meters

5

Train Station

TRAIN TO
← MACHU PICCHU

TRAIN TO →
CUSCO

Rio Urubamba

KEY

① *Restaurants*

① *Hotels*

restaurant is managed by the same folks who run the popular KB Tambo Hotel and Tours, so grab a brochure and organize a tour if the mood strikes. $ *Average main: S/18* ✉ *Calle Ventiderio s/n* ☎ *084/204–151.*

WHERE TO STAY

$ 🏨 **Apu Lodge.** Surrounded by flowers and maturing gardens, Apu Lodge
HOTEL commands a delightful view of the Ollantaytambo ruins from its private
♻ grassy perch and is well worth the five-minute meander up cobbled Inca streets from the center of town. **Pros:** gorgeous location and lovely rooms. **Cons:** a few blocks from the center of town. $ *Rooms from: S/160* ✉ *Lari Calle* ☎ *084/797–162* ⊕ *www.apulodge.com* ⤳ *10 rooms, 1 suite* ▭ *No credit cards* 🍴 *Breakfast.*

$ 🏨 **El Albergue.** Right at the train station, the town's first hotel, El
HOTEL Albergue, features spacious rooms with dark-wood accents and his-
♻ toric black-and-white photos of the region. **Pros:** convenient to rail station; relaxing sauna. **Cons:** books up fast. $ *Rooms from: S/204* ✉ *Estación de Ferrocarril* ☎☎ *084/204–014* ⊕ *www.elalbergue.com* ⤳ *16 rooms* 🍴 *Breakfast.*

$ 🏨 **Apu Lodge.** Surrounded by flowers and maturing gardens, Apu Lodge
HOTEL commands a delightful view of the Ollantaytambo ruins from its private
♻ grassy perch and is well worth the five-minute meander up cobbled Inca streets from the center of town. **Pros:** gorgeous location and lovely

rooms. **Cons:** a few blocks from the center of town. $ *Rooms from: S/160* ✉ *Lari Calle* ☎ *084/797–162* ⊕ *www.apulodge.com* ⤳ *10 rooms, 1 suite* ⊟ *No credit cards* ⦿ *Breakfast.*

$$ ⛻ **Hostal Sauce.** Thanks to its hillside location, this hotel features some vaulted-ceiling rooms with a superb view of the Ollantaytambo ruins. **Pros:** clean and modern

HOTEL

WIFI IN OLLY

Wi-Fi is nearly everywhere in town. Many hotels offer computer terminals and a place to check your email or to look up tour information. There are also some cafés along and near the Plaza de Armas.

furnishings; new bedding; good value; great views; ATM on premises. **Cons:** no elevator; lots of stairs. $ *Rooms from: S/280* ✉ *Ventiderio 248* ☎ *084/204–044* ⊕ *www.hostalsauce.com.pe* ⤳ *8 rooms* ⦿ *Breakfast.*

$$$ ⛻ **Hotel Pakaritampu.** Ollantaytambo's best lodging, with a Quechua name that translates as "house of dawn," has reading rooms with fireplaces and Cusqueño art that invite you to settle in with a good book and a hot cup of coffee on a chilly evening. **Pros:** tranquil setting; good restaurant. **Cons:** not for partiers. $ *Rooms from: S/437* ✉ *Av. Ferrocarril s/n* ☎ *084/204–020, 01/242–6278 in Lima* ⊕ *www.pakaritampu.com* ⤳ *37 rooms, 1 suite* ⦿ *Breakfast.*

HOTEL
Fodor's Choice
★

Machu Picchu and the Inca Trail

WORD OF MOUTH

"Our first glimpse of Machu Picchu was just spectacular! At each and every turn, the view was breath-taking. I kept imagining the almost impossible feat of building this "Incan city" all those centuries ago, using only ingenuity and man power. It is impossible to describe; one must go to see it for oneself!"

—wkwb42a

WELCOME TO MACHU PICCHU AND THE INCA TRAIL

TOP REASONS TO GO

★ **Discover Ancient Kingdoms:** Hiram Bingham "discovered" Machu Picchu in 1911. Your first glimpse of the fabled city will be your own discovery, and every bit as exciting.

★ **The Trail:** The four-day hike of the Inca Trail from near Ollantaytambo to Machu Picchu is Peru's best-known outdoor expedition. Spaces fill up quickly, but never fear: tour operators have opened up some alternative treks.

★ **Ye Olde Technology:** It was the 15th century, yet the Inca made the stones fit perfectly without mortar. The sun illuminates the windows at the solstice, and the crops grow in an inhospitable climate. And they did it all without bulldozers, tractors, or Google Earth.

★ **Mystery:** Mystics, shamans, spiritualists, astrologers, and UFO spotters, professionals and wannabes, flock to this serene region to contemplate history's secrets.

★ **Majestic Scenery:** The area's stunning mountain landscapes surround you.

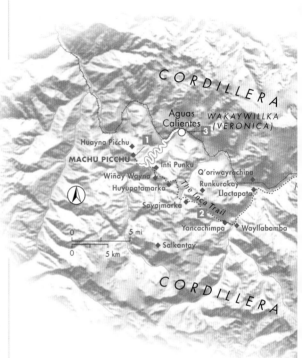

1 Machu Picchu.
The two words that are synonymous with Peru evoke images of centuries-old Inca emperors and rituals. Yet no one knows for certain what purpose this mountaintop citadel served or why it was abandoned. Machu Picchu is an easy day trip from Cusco, but an overnight in Aguas Calientes or Ollantaytambo gives you more time to explore and devise your own theories.

2 The Inca Trail.
A 43-km (26-mile) sector of the original Inca supply route between Cusco and Machu Picchu has become one of the world's signature treks. No question: You need to be in good shape, and the four-day excursion can be rough going at times, but it's guaranteed to generate bragging rights and immense satisfaction upon completion.

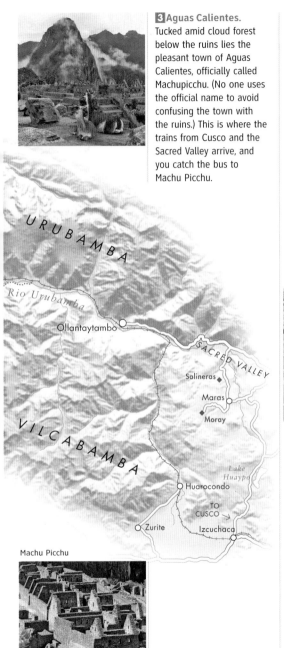

3 **Aguas Calientes.**
Tucked amid cloud forest below the ruins lies the pleasant town of Aguas Calientes, officially called Machupicchu. (No one uses the official name to avoid confusing the town with the ruins.) This is where the trains from Cusco and the Sacred Valley arrive, and you catch the bus to Machu Picchu.

Machu Picchu

GETTING ORIENTED

The famed ruins of Machu Picchu, accessible only via rail or foot, lie farther down the Río Urubamba, in the cloud forest on the Andean slopes above the jungle. Cusco, the region's largest city, is about 112 km (70 miles) southeast.

6

Inca Drawbridge, Machu Picchu.

Updated by
Maureen
Santucci

More and more people are putting Machu Picchu on their bucket lists each year, and it lives up to its fame as one of the New 7 Wonders of the World. It is indeed a wondrous site to see, so don't let the need to check off a box on your to-do list get in the way of taking the time to really appreciate it. If you can, go there by trekking the Inca Trail—sleeping in the Andes, walking on paths that the Incas themselves took to get to this sacred site, and entering at dawn through the Sun Gate is absolutely breathtaking. Take some time as well to relax in Aguas Calientes before rushing back to Cusco. It may not have the same charm as that colonial city, but being nestled among green mountains, not to mention getting a hot shower and massage in after hiking around Machu Picchu, is definitely the icing on the cake.

PLANNING

WHEN TO GO

All the high-season/low-season trade-offs are here. Winter (June through August) means drier weather and easier traveling, but it's prime vacation time for those in the northern hemisphere. Don't forget that three major observances—Inti Raymi (June 24), Peru's Independence Day (July 28), and Santa Rosa de Lima (August 30)—fall during this time, and translate into exceptionally heavy concentrations of Peruvian travelers. (Also consider that Sundays are free for Cusqueños.) The result is higher lodging prices and larger crowds at these times. Prices and visitor numbers drop dramatically during the summer rainy season (October through April). Note that January is the height of rainy season, and the

Inca Trail is closed in February. For near-ideal weather and manageable crowds, consider a spring or fall trip.

Entrance to Machu Picchu is now limited to 2,500 visitors a day. In low season this won't present a problem, but if you are traveling during the winter months, be sure to purchase your entrance tickets well ahead of time. If your heart is set on hiking Huayna Picchu, you should purchase tickets in advance regardless of the season. If you are not using an agency, you can purchase tickets yourself online at ⊕ *www. machupicchu.gob.pe.*

Although many travelers day-trip to Machu Picchu, an overnight in Aguas Calientes (the town below the site) lets you experience the ruins long after the day-trippers have left, and before the first train and tour groups arrive in the morning. ■TIP➔ When booking your return train, it's best not to do that for the same day you are flying out of Cusco, just to be safe.

GETTING HERE AND AROUND

Unless you're hiking in to Machu Picchu, you must first catch a train to Aguas Calientes. From here there is an official Consettur tourist bus that takes you to the famed ruins. The 20-minute ride offers hair-raising turns and stunning views of the Vilcanota Valley below. You cannot drive yourself here.

BUS TRAVEL

If you don't plan on walking up to Machu Picchu (about an hour up the road from Aguas Calientes), you will have to catch a bus, easily identifiable by the Consettur name on the front. Consettur buses depart from the intersection of Imperio de los Incas Avenue and the Aguas Calientes River. Tickets cost $9 USD one way or $17 USD round-trip, and can be purchased in advance from the small kiosk across the street from the departure point. Buses leave every 10 minutes starting at 5:30 am. During peak season, lines for the first bus can get long, so it's recommended that you arrive by 5 am or earlier.

TRAIN TRAVEL

It's an easy train ride from Ollantaytambo to Machu Picchu. Most visitors board the train in Ollantaytambo. as there are more options available. Although it is technically possible to take the train from Cusco to Ollantaytambo, taxis are a much cheaper and more readily available method of getting to the Sacred Valley. And, considering that the "Cusco" station is actually at Poroy, far more convenient.

PeruRail is the longest-standing operator, and offers services from Cusco, Urubamba, Ollantaytambo, and Aguas Calientes. The luxury *Hiram Bingham* train leaves from Cusco's Poroy station, a 15-minute taxi ride from the Plaza de Armas, and makes a stop in Ollantaytambo. The *Vistadome* and the *Expedition* (formerly known as the *Backpacker*) trains depart from both Poroy as well as Ollantaytambo. There is also one *Vistadome* per day traveling to and from Urubamba, which also stops in Ollantaytambo.

PeruRail held a near monopoly over train travel from Cusco and Ollantaytambo to Machu Picchu for more than 10 years, but now two additional companies have entered the picture: Inca Rail and the

6

Machu Picchu Train. The new trains allow for more frequent and easier travel from the Sacred Valley, specifically from Ollantaytambo to Aguas Calientes.

Most tour packages include rail tickets as well as bus transport to and from Aguas Calientes and Machu Picchu and admission to the ruins and lodging if you plan to stay overnight. Tourists are not permitted to ride the Tren Local, the less expensive cars intended for local residents only.

PERURAIL At least two *Vistadome* trains depart from Cusco's Poroy station daily for Aguas Calientes, near Machu Picchu. One leaves at 6:40 am and arrives in Aguas Calientes at 9:52, and the other departs at 8:25 am. Return trains from Aguas Calientes are at 3:20 pm, arriving in Cusco at 7:05, and at 5:27 pm. Snacks and beverages are included in the price, and the cars have sky domes for great views. The return trip includes a fashion show and folklore dancing.

PeruRail also offers a more economical coach, the *Expedition*, to replace their old budget trains. The new cars have comfortable seats and tables, with sky windows for a full peek of the Sacred Valley. As PeruRail's cheapest option, the *Expedition* departs from Poroy Station at 7:42 am and arrives in Aguas Calientes at 10:51 am. The return train departs from Aguas Calientes at 4:43 pm, arriving in Cusco at 8:23 pm. Conditions are comparable to second-class trains in Western Europe and are plenty comfortable. PeruRail's luxury *Hiram Bingham* train provides a class of service unto itself (with prices to match). The train departs at 9:05 am, arriving in Aguas Calientes at 12:24 pm. It leaves Aguas Calientes at 5:50 pm and arrives back in Cusco at 9:16 pm. Trains consist of two dining cars, a bar car, and a kitchen car, and evoke the glamour of the old Orient Express rail service, which comes as no surprise, since Orient Express is the parent company of PeruRail. The round-trip price tag includes brunch on the trip to Machu Picchu, bus transport from Aguas Calientes up to the ruins and back in vehicles exclusively reserved for *Hiram Bingham* clients, admission to the ruins, guide services while there, and an afternoon buffet tea at the Machu Picchu Sanctuary Lodge. The trip back entails cocktails, live entertainment, and a four-course dinner. Trains stop at Ollantaytambo, Km 88 (optional start of the Inca Trail), and Km 104 (the launch point of an abbreviated two-day Inca Trail); the latter two stops are only with prior notice by the trekking company. Arrival is in Aguas Calientes, where you catch the Consettur buses up to the ruins.

If you're using the Sacred Valley as your base, PeruRail operates a daily *Vistadome* train departing from Ollantaytambo at 7:05, 8, and 8:53 am and 1:27 and 3:37 pm. A daily *Expedition* train departs from Ollantaytambo at 5:10, 6:10, and 7:45 am. Travel between Ollantaytambo and Urubamba takes slight less than an hour and a half. There is one daily *Vistadome* from the Urubamba station at Tambo del Inca, which departs at 6:50 am daily, arriving in Aguas Calientes at 9:24 am. The train departs from Aguas Calientes at 3:48 pm, arriving back in Urubamba at 6:43 pm. This train also stops at Rio Sagrado.

New for 2013 is a two-tiered pricing schedule, depending on the date of travel. In low season (January 1–March 31; November 15–December

20), a round-trip ticket on the *Hiram Bingham* is $650 USD, while in high season it is $691 USD. Pricing on the *Vistadome* and *Expedition* varies in the same way, however, different prices also apply with this train depending on the time of day you are traveling as well, so that a low-season train from Ollantaytambo can vary from $102 to $130 USD round-trip on *Vistadome* and between $87 and $106 USD round-trip on *Expedition* One-way-only rates are higher as well.

A full train schedule is available on PeruRail's website, and timetable fliers can be picked up from the office in the Plaza de Armas.

PeruRail's service is generally punctual. Schedules and rates are always subject to change, and there may be fewer trains per day to choose from during the December to March low season.

In theory, same-day tickets can be purchased, but waiting that late is risky. Procure tickets in advance from PeruRail's sales office in the Plaza de Armas in Cusco (⊠ *Portal de Carnes 214, Plaza de Armas*) every day, including weekends and holidays, from 8 am to 10 pm. You can also purchase tickets online at ⊕ *www.perurail.com*, or by phone at ☎ *084/581–414.*

INCA RAIL Inca Rail runs trains from Ollantaytambo to Aguas Calientes and vice versa three times daily. Trains leaves Ollantaytambo at 6:40 and 11:15 am and 4:36 pm. Trains depart from Aguas Calientes for Ollantaytambo at 8:30 am and 2:30 and 7 pm.

There are three types of tickets offered on Inca Rail: Tourist Class, which costs $106 USD round-trip, Executive Class, which will cost you $120 USD round-trip, and First Class, which costs $180 USD round-trip. These are 2012 rates; as of this writing, the 2013 rates had not been released. To purchase tickets you can go to the kiosk at the train station in Aguas Calientes or to the office just outside the rail stop in Ollantaytambo. In Cusco you can also buy tickets at the office in the Plaza de Armas (⊠ *Portal de Panes, 105*) or by phone at ☎ *084/233–030.* It is also possible to purchase at ⊕ *www.inkarail.com,* but that could get cumbersome because it requires a bank and wire transfer.

MACHU PICCHU TRAIN The Machu Picchu Train runs between Ollantaytambo and Aguas Calientes with trains departing from each station three times per day. From the Sacred Valley, the trains depart at 7:20 and 11:30 am and 12:36 pm. The return trains from Aguas Calientes are at 10:32 am and 4:12 and 7:15 pm. The 2012 rate is $126 USD round-trip. Check their website for more information (⊕ *www.machupicchutrain.com*). Tickets can be purchased at their Cusco office (⊠ *Av. El Sol 576*) or on their website using PayPal.

Train Contacts Inca Rail ⊠ *Ticket Office, Portal de Panes, 105, Plaza de Armas, Cusco* ☎ *084/581–860 office, 084/233–030 reservations* ⊕ *www.incarail.com.* **Machu Picchu Train** ⊠ *Av. El Sol 576, Cusco* ☎ *084/221–199* ⊕ *www.machupicchutrain.com.* **PeruRail** ⊠ *Ticket Office, Portal de Carnes 214, Plaza de Armas, Cusco* ☎ *084/581–414* ⊕ *www.perurail.com.*

HEALTH AND SAFETY
Machu Picchu is a breath-catching 1,000 meters (3,300 feet) *lower* than Cusco. The Inca Trail, however, at its highest point reaches 4,200 meters (13,776 feet). To be on the safe side about altitude effects, locally

known as *soroche*, get an ample intake of fluids and eliminate or minimize alcohol and caffeine consumption. (Both can cause dehydration, already a problem at high altitudes.) Smoking aggravates the problem. Some hotels have an oxygen supply for their guests' use. The prescription drug acetazolamide can help offset the alkalosis caused by low oxygen at high elevations, but bear in mind that you need to start taking it before you get to altitude and that, as a sulfa-based drug, it causes allergic reactions in some.

Tap water is generally not safe to drink. Stick with the bottled variety, *con gas* (carbonated) or *sin gas* (plain). The San Luis and Cielo brands are for sale everywhere.

Aguas Calientes is quite small, with an active police force and is very safe. Mudslides are an occasional problem from October to April, and severe rains in those months can occasionally (though rarely) interfere with train service.

RESTAURANTS

The town of Aguas Calientes near Machu Picchu has numerous restaurants, each offering its own take on traveler-tested and approved plates like pizza, Mexican, Chinese, and typical Andean food. Recently Andean fusion, a gourmet play on traditional Peruvian high-mountain fare, has also found its way to this once gastronomically boring town. Restaurants are busiest between 1 and 3, and then again when dinner begins around 7 and tour groups tend to be gathering. However, most places are open all afternoon if you wish to eat in between those times. Things typically start winding down around 9. *Prices in the reviews are the average cost of a main course at dinner or, if dinner is not served, at lunch.*

HOTELS

There is only one hotel at Machu Picchu itself and that is the Machu Picchu Sanctuary Lodge. It will cost you to stay there no doubt, as it's an exclusive property owned by Orient-Express, the same company that operates PeruRail, but it's also the only place you can sit in a Jacuzzi and look at the Inca city long after the crowds have left. In Aguas Calientes you'll find many hostels and cheaper hotels lining the railroad tracks—that's not as down-at-the-heels as it first sounds: many rooms have great waterfront views. Aguas Calientes' budget lodgings are utilitarian places to lay your head, with a bed, a table, a bathroom, and little else. A handful of hotels offer surprising luxury for such an isolated location. Their rates can be shockingly luxurious, too.

Not even the top luxury hotels can meet their guests inside the train station anymore. They and all other hotels will meet you just outside the front gate and help you to and from the station with your bags. Lodgings keep surprisingly early checkout times. (Hotels free up the rooms for mid-morning Cusco–Ollantaytambo–Machu Picchu trains.) Expect to vacate by 9 am, unless you are in one of the more expensive lodging choices, though this is less strictly enforced in the off season. All hotels will hold your luggage if you're not leaving town until later in the day.

Many hotels keep the same official rates year-round, but unofficially discount rates during the off season of mid-September through May. It also pays to check the hotel website, if they have one, for current promotions. *Prices in the reviews are the lowest cost of a standard double room in high season.*

TOURS

The following Cusco-based operators run either four-day or two-day treks to Machu Picchu, along the famed Inca Trail. Most companies also provide alternative multiday Inca Trail treks including the Lares Valley, Salkantay, and Choquequirao. These treks often are cheaper in cost and just as magnificent, if not more challenging. The average cost of a four-day Inca Trail excursion runs about $600 USD per person, but this can depend on the number of people in the group. Bear in mind that it does not pay to bargain hunt for this excursion. Cheap cost will generally mean lesser quality service as well as poorer treatment for porters. Most companies listed can also organize one-day tours to Machu Picchu from Cusco as well. ⇨ *For more information about seeing the region with a tour operator, also see Chapter 5, Planning section.*

PERU-BASED GUIDES

Amazonas Explorer. For more than 20 years, this company has specialized in adventure tours, with or without the entire family. They are known for using top-quality equipment and the best guides around. ⊠ *Av. Collasuyo 910, Cusco* ☎ *084/252–846* ⊕ *www.amazonasexplorer.com.*

CuscoTopTravel&Treks. Run by the wildly talented and witty David Choque, who specializes in a range of packaged and comfort-class custom-built multiday treks along the Inca Trail and the Sacred Valley. They also offer one-day tours to Machu Picchu. ☎ *084/251–864* ⊕ *www.cuscotoptravelperu.com.*

Pachamama Explorers. This company has more than 12 years experience with a specialty in trekking the Inca Trail and alternatives as well as in creating customized itineraries. They promoted porter welfare before regulations were set in place. ⊠ *Calle Umanchata 140, Cusco* ☎ *084/226–570* ⊕ *www.pmexplorers.com.*

SAS. One of the longest-running operators in the region, they offer just about any hiking tour from the four-day Inca Trail trek to a variety of alternative treks. ☎ *084/249–194* ⊕ *www.sastravelperu.com.*

Sun Gate Tours. Specialists in trekking tours including the Classic and Short Inca Trail options, Sun Gate Tours also provides a variety of non-trekking tours to Machu Picchu. ☎ *084/232–046* ⊕ *www.sungatetours.com.*

United Mice. One of the more popular Inca Trail operators, United Mice have been guiding adventurers on multiday hikes since 1990. They offer a variety of alternative Inca trail treks from across the Sacred Valley. ☎ *084/221–139* ⊕ *www.unitedmice.com.*

U.S. AND CANADA-BASED GUIDES

Backroads. This active travel company provides luxury all-inclusive trips in Peru for families and individuals. Packages include Inca Trail trekking trips, lodge-to-lodge hiking to Machu Picchu, and culturally oriented excursions. ☎ *800/462–2848* ⊕ *www.backroads.com.*

G Adventures. Although recently changed from GAP Adventures to G Adventures, this is still the same ecoconscious, Canadian-run tour company that provides multiple levels of trips based on comfort and activity styles. They offer traditional Inca Trail treks and alternative Inca Trail multiday hikes. Many can be combined with other G Adventure tours of Peru. Check out last-minute deals on the website. ☎ 416/260–0999 ⊕ www.gadventures.com.

Wilderness Travel. This company specializes in small group, family, and private journeys, with an emphasis on education. Along with the classic Inca Trail and the upscale lodge-to-lodge trek to Machu Picchu, they also offer some more unusual options. ☎ 800/368–2794 ⊕ www.wildernesstravel.com.

> **INDIGENOUS TERMINOLOGY**
>
> Stick to the term "indigenous" (*indígena*) to describe Peru's Inca-descended peoples. Avoid "Indian" (*indio*), which is considered pejorative here, that is, unless you're describing an Indian restaurant. Likewise, among people in Peru, "native" (*nativo*) and "tribe" (*tribú*) conjure up images best left to old Tarzan movies.

AGUAS CALIENTES

But for the grace of Machu Picchu discoverer Hiram Bingham, Aguas Calientes would be just another remote, forgotten crossroads. But Bingham's discovery in 1911, and the tourist boom decades later, forever changed the community. At just 2,050 meters (6,724 feet) above sea level, Aguas Calientes will seem downright balmy if you've just arrived from Cusco. There are but two major streets—Avenida Pachacutec leads uphill from the Plaza de Armas, and Avenida Imperio de los Incas isn't a street at all, but the railroad tracks; there's no vehicular traffic on the former except the buses that ferry tourists to the ruins. You'll have little sense of Aguas Calientes if you do the standard day trip from Cusco. But the cloud-forest town pulses to a very lively tourist beat with hotels, restaurants, hot springs, and a surprising amount of activity, even after the last afternoon train has returned to Cusco. It also provides a great opportunity to wander around the high jungle, particularly welcome if you aren't going to make it to the Amazon. Although you won't see wildlife other than several species of hummingbirds, the flora (especially the many varieties of orchids) are worth taking a wander to see. You can find information about the easy and relatively flat walk to Mandor Waterfalls or the more intense hike up Putucusi Mountain at the local iPeru office. ■ **TIP** ➜ Stay two nights in town if you can so you can take as long as you like visiting Machu Picchu and then relax and enjoy a hot shower after tramping around.

GETTING HERE AND AROUND

Trains to Aguas Calientes depart daily from Cusco's Poroy Station, as well as from Ollantaytambo and Urubamba. In spite of its steep side streets, the city is small and easily explored by ambling about on foot.

ESSENTIALS

Currency Banco de Crédito ✉ Av. Imperio de los Incas s/n ☎ 084/211–342. **Banco de la Nación** ✉ Av. Imperio de los Incas 540 ☎ 084/211–323.

Mail SERPOST ✉ Collaraymy L-13.

Visitor Information iPeru. You'll find all the local tourist information available here and a representative happy to help. ✉ *Av. Pachacutec Cuadro 1 s/n* ☎ *084/211–104* 🕒 *Mon.–Sat. 9–1, 2–6, Sun. 9–1.*

EXPLORING

Aguas Termales. Aguas Calientes (literally "hot waters") takes its name from these thermal springs that sit above town. Don't expect Baden-Baden, but if you aren't too fussy, this can be a refreshing dip at the end of a hot day, where you can sip a pisco sour while you lounge. Towels and even bathing suits are available for rental just outside the baths. ✉ *Top of Av. Pachacutec* 🎟 *S/10* 🕒 *Daily 5 am–8 pm.*

Mercado Artesanal (*Craft Market*). A warren of vendors' stalls lines the couple of blocks between the train station and the bus stop for shuttle transport up to the ruins. You can find some souvenirs here that you may not see in Cusco. The prices for crafts such as textiles, bags, and magnets may or may not be cheaper (this largely depends on your negotiating skill and patience), but it's a great way to spend time before your train leaves. ✉ *Near train station* 🕒 *Daily 10–8, some stalls open as early as 7.*

6

Museo de Sitio Manuel Chávez Ballón. The museum, dedicated to the history, culture, and rediscovery of Machu Picchu, sits on the way up to the ruins about 2 km (1 mile) from the edge of town at the entrance to the national park. Hoofing it is the best way to get here. Plan on about a 30-minute walk. You'll get a bit more insight at the Casa Concha museum in Cusco, where the artifacts returned from Yale are being exhibited, but there are some interesting pieces on display here, some recovered as recently as 2004. Admission also includes entrance to a small but interesting botanical garden at the same site. ✉ *Puente de Ruinas, 2 km (1 mile) from Aguas Calientes* 🎟 *S/22* 🕒 *Daily 9–4.*

WHERE TO EAT

Pizza once took Aguas Calientes by storm, and while you can still order up a cheesy pie cooked in the traditional Peruvian wood-burning clay ovens, luxury hotel chefs have raised the bar, creating noteworthy Andean fusion, or as sometimes it's referred to, Novo Andino fare, a twist on traditionally bland Peruvian food of the high Andes. The result is creative, gourmet dishes—sometimes influenced by Asian flavors and other times marked by typical California cuisine or European delicacies.

$$
FRENCH
Fodor's Choice ★

🍴 **Indio Feliz.** An engaging French-Peruvian couple manage the best restaurant in Aguas Calientes. Quiche Lorraine, ginger chicken, and spicy *trucha macho* (trout in hot pepper and wine sauce) are favorites on the Peruvian-French fusion menu, and are usually part of the reasonably priced (S/54.50) prix-fixe menu, all accompanied by homemade bread. Top it off with a fine coffee and apple pie or *flan* (creme caramel) for dessert. The decor is worth a visit all on its own, and this is the perfect place for dining with a group of friends or for an intimate dinner for two. [$] *Average main: S/39* ✉ *Lloque Yupanqui 103* ☎ *084/211–090* 🌐 *www.indiofeliz.com.*

Continued on page 297

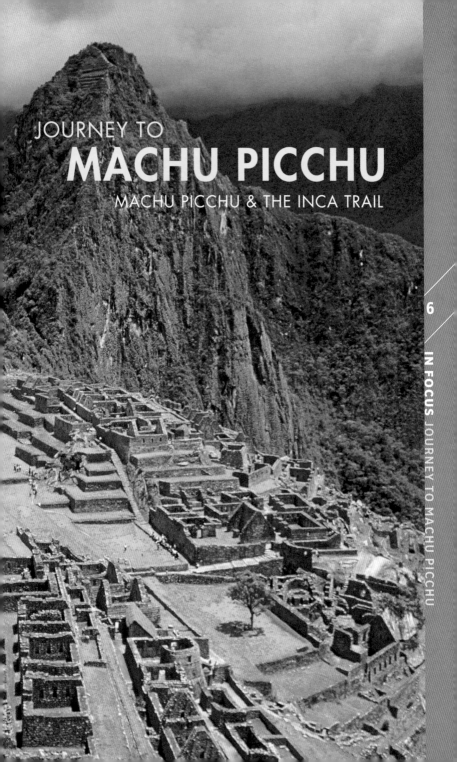

JOURNEY TO
MACHU PICCHU
MACHU PICCHU & THE INCA TRAIL

MACHU PICCHU & THE INCA TRAIL

Guardhouse

The exquisite architecture of the massive Inca stone structures, the formidable backdrop of steep sugarloaf hills, and the Urubamba River winding far below have made Machu Picchu the iconic symbol of Peru. It's a mystical city, the most famous archaeological site in South America, and one of the world's must-see destinations.

The world did not become aware of Machu Picchu's existence until 1911 when Yale University historian Hiram Bingham (1875–1956) announced that he had "discovered" the site. "Rediscovery" is a more accurate term; area residents knew of Machu Picchu's existence all along. This "Lost City of the Inca" was missed by the ravaging conquistadors and survived untouched until the beginning of the 20th century.

You'll be acutely aware that the world has since discovered Machu Picchu if you visit during the June–mid-September high season. Machu Picchu absorbs the huge numbers of visitors, though, and even in the highest of the high season, its beauty is so spectacular that it rarely disappoints.

DISCOVERY

American explorer and historian Hiram Bingham, with the aid of local guides, came across the Lost City in 1911. Though the name appeared on maps as early as 1860, previous attempts to find the site failed. Bingham erred in recognizing what he had uncovered. The historian assumed he had stumbled upon Vilcabamba, the last real stronghold of the Inca. (The actual ruins of Vilcabamba lie deep in the rain forest, and were uncovered in the 1960s.)

Bingham, who later served as governor of and senator from Connecticut, transported—some say stole—many of Machu Picchu's artifacts to Yale in 1912. Although they were intended to be on a short term loan, the artifacts did not begin to make their way back to Peru until 2011. They are now housed in the Museo Machu Picchu Casa Concha in Cusco.

In 1915, Bingham announced his discovery of the Inca Trail. As with Machu Picchu, his "discovery" was a little disingenuous. Locals knew about the trail, and that it had served as a supply route between Cusco and Machu Picchu during Inca times. Parts of it were used during the colonial and early republican eras as well.

Though archaeological adventuring is viewed differently now, Bingham's slog to find Machu Picchu and the Inca Trail was no easy feat. Look up from Aguas Calientes, and you still won't know it's there.

HISTORY

Ever since Bingham came across Machu Picchu, its history has been debated. It was likely a small city of some 200 homes and 1,000 residents, with agricultural terraces to supply the population's needs and a strategic position that overlooked—but could not be seen from—the valley floor.

New theories suggest that the city was a transit station for products, such as coca and hearts of palm that were grown in the lowlands and sent to Cusco. Exactly when Machu Picchu was built is not known, but one theory suggests that it was a country estate of an Inca ruler named Pachacutec, which

means its golden age was in the mid-15th century.

Historians have discredited the romantic theory of Machu Picchu as a refuge of the chosen Inca women after the Spanish conquest; analysis shows a 50/50 split of male and female remains.

The site's belated discovery may indicate that the Inca deserted Machu Picchu before the Spanish conquest. The reason for the city's presumed abandonment is as mysterious as its original function. Some archaeologists suggest that the water supply simply ran out. Some guess that disease ravaged the city. Others surmise it was the death of Pachacutec, after which his estate was no longer needed.

"INDIANA" BINGHAM

Hiram Bingham at Machu Picchu, 1912.

A globe-trotting archaeological explorer, which was an especially romantic figure in early 20th century America, Hiram Bingham was a model for the Indiana Jones character in the film *Raiders of the Lost Ark*.

1 Storage Houses

2 Guardhouse

EXPLORING THE RUINS

Everyone must go through the main entrance to have their ticket stamped. Those arriving from the Inca Trail enter the park via a path leading past the Guardhouse, away from the main entrance but they must exit the park, then enter again through the ticket booth. From there you work your way up through the agricultural areas and to the urban sectors.

There are almost no signs inside to explain what you're seeing; booklets and maps are for sale at the entrance. Restrooms are outside the front gate, but not inside the ruins. You can exit and re-enter as many times as you'd like as long as you show your ticket.

The English-language names to the structures within the city were assigned by Bingham. Call it inertia, but those labels have stuck, even though the late Yale historian's nomenclature was mostly offbase.

The Storage Houses are the first structures you encounter after coming through the main entrance. The Inca carved terraces into the hillsides to grow produce and minimize erosion. Corn was the likely crop cultivated. The semitropical climate meant ample rain for most of the year.

The Guardhouse and Funeral Rock are a 20-minute walk up to the left of the entrance, and provide the quintessential Machu Picchu vista. You've seen the photos, yet nothing beats the view in person, especially with a misty sunrise. Bodies of nobles likely lay in state here, where they would have been eviscerated, dried, and prepared for mummification.

The Temple of the Sun is a marvel of perfect Inca stone assembly. On June 21 (winter solstice in the southern hemisphere sometimes June 20 or June 22), sunlight shines through a small, trapezoid-shape window and onto the middle of a large, flat granite stone presumed to be an Inca calendar. Looking out the window, astronomers saw the constellation Pleiades, revered as a symbol of crop fertility. Bingham dubbed the small cave below the Royal Tomb, though no human remains were found at the time of his discovery.

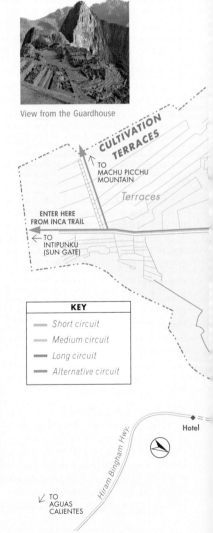

View from the Guardhouse

CULTIVATION TERRACES

TO MACHU PICCHU MOUNTAIN

Terraces

ENTER HERE FROM INCA TRAIL

← TO INTIPUNKU (SUN GATE)

KEY	
—	*Short circuit*
—	*Medium circuit*
—	*Long circuit*
—	*Alternative circuit*

Hotel

Hiram Bingham Hwy.

↙ TO AGUAS CALIENTES

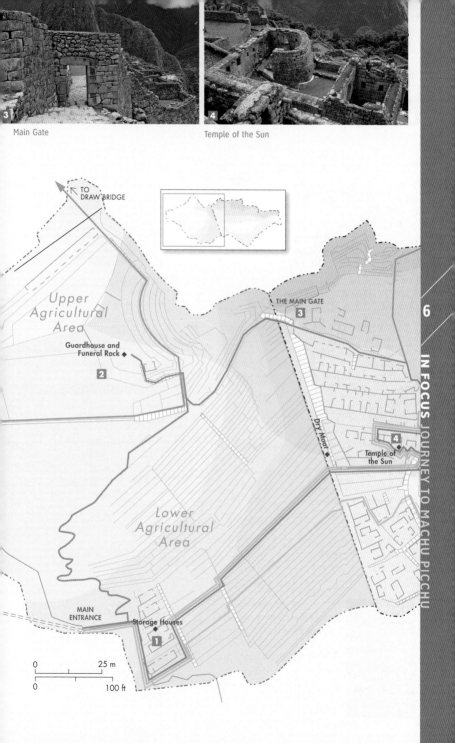

Main Gate

Temple of the Sun

TO
DRAW BRIDGE

Upper
Agricultural
Area

Guardhouse and
Funeral Rock ◆

2

THE MAIN GATE

3

Dry Moat

Temple of
the Sun

◆

4

Lower
Agricultural
Area

MAIN
ENTRANCE

Storage Houses ◆

1

0   25 m

0   100 ft

Principal Temple

Three Windows

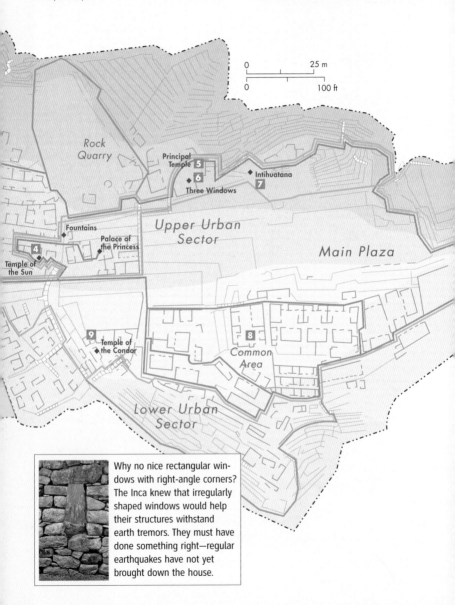

Rock Quarry

Principal Temple **5**

6 Three Windows

◆ Intihuatana **7**

Fountains

Palace of the Princess

4

Temple of the Sun

Upper Urban Sector

Main Plaza

9 Temple of the Condor

8

Common Area

Lower Urban Sector

Why no nice rectangular windows with right-angle corners? The Inca knew that irregularly shaped windows would help their structures withstand earth tremors. They must have done something right—regular earthquakes have not yet brought down the house.

Intihuatana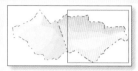

Common Area

Sacred Rock

URBAN SECTOR

TO HUAYNA PICCHU →

KEY

— *Short circuit*

— *Medium circuit*

▬ *Long circuit*

— *Alternative circuit*

Temple of the Condor.

Fountains. A series of 16 small fountains are linked to the Inca worship of water.

Palace of the Princess, a likely misnomer, is a two-story building that adjoins the temple.

The Principal Temple is so dubbed because its masonry is among Machu Picchu's best. The three-walled structure is a masterpiece of mortarless stone construction.

Three Windows. A stone staircase leads to the three-walled structure. The entire east wall is hewn from a single rock with trapezoidal windows cut into it.

Intihuatana. A hillock leads to the "Hitching Post of the Sun." Every important Inca center had one of these vertical stone columns (called gnomons), but their function is unknown. The Spanish destroyed most of them, seeing the posts as objects of pagan worship. Machu Picchu's is one of the few to survive—partially at least. Its top was accidentally knocked off in 2001 during the filming of a Cusqueña beer commercial.

The Sacred Rock takes the shape in miniature of the mountain range visible behind it.

The Common Area covers a large grassy plaza with less elaborately constructed buildings and huts.

Temple of the Condor is so named because the positioning of the stones resembles a giant condor, the symbol of heaven in the Inca cosmos. The structure's many small chambers led Bingham to dub it a "prison," a concept that did not likely exist in Inca society.

DID YOU KNOW?

The step terraces you see here were used to grow crops but their main purpose was to minimize erosion.

THE SKINNY ON MACHU PICCHU

DAY TRIPPING VS. OVERNIGHT

You can visit Machu Picchu on a day trip, but we recommend staying overnight at a hotel in Aguas Calientes. A day trip allows you about four hours at Machu Picchu. If you stay overnight you can wander the ruins after most tourists have gone or in the morning before they arrive.

BUYING A TICKET

It is wise to purchase tickets to Machu Picchu online at least one month in advance (⊕ www. machupicchu.gob.pe/), but if you arrive without an admission ticket, you must purchase one in Aguas Calientes at the **Centro Cultural Machu Picchu** (⊠ *Avenida Pachacutec 103,* ☎ *084/211-196* 🖼 *S/128* ⊘ *Daily 5:10 am– 8:45 pm* 🖿 *No credit cards*). There is no ticket booth at the ruins' entrance. If you are with a tour, the tickets are most likely taken care of for you. Buy your ticket the night before if you want to get in the park right away; bus service begins at 5:30 am. The ticket is valid only for the date it is purchased for. So if you arrive in the afternoon and visit the ruins, then stay the night and want to return the next morning, you'll have to buy two tickets. The park is open from 6 am to 5:30 pm.

CATCHING THE BUS

If you're a day-tripper, follow the crowd out of the rail station about two blocks to the **Consettur Machupicchu** shuttle buses, which ferry you up a series of switchbacks to the ruins, a journey of 20 minutes. Buy your $17 round-trip ($9 one way) ticket at a booth across from the line of buses before boarding. Bus tickets can

be purchased in US dollars or soles. If you're staying overnight, check in to your lodging first, and then come back to buy a bus ticket.

Buses leave Aguas Calientes for the ruins beginning at 5:30 am and continue more or less every 10 minutes, with a big push in mid-morning as the trains arrive, until the historic site closes around 5:30 pm. If you're heading back to Cusco, take the bus back down at least an hour before your train departs. It's also possible to walk to and from the ruins to Aguas Calientes but this hike will take you a good hour and a half either way.

BEING PREPARED

Being high above the valley floor makes you forget that Machu Picchu sits 2,490 meters (8,170 ft) above sea level, a much lower altitude than Cusco. It gets warm, and the ruins have little shade. Sunscreen, a hat, and water are musts. Officially, no food or drinks are permitted, but you can get away with a bottle of water and snacks. Large packs must be left at the entrance. ■**TIP**➔ You have to show your passport to enter—if you want it stamped, stop by the office inside the gate to the left as you enter.

PRACTICALITIES

A snack bar is a few feet from where the buses deposit you at the gate to the ruins, and the **Machu Picchu Sanctuary Lodge** has a S/100 lunch buffet open to the public. Bathrooms cost S/1, and toilet paper is provided. There are no bathrooms inside the ruins but you may exit and re-enter to use them.

THE INCA TRAIL, ABRIDGED

Most Cusco tour operators market a two-day, one-night Inca Trail excursion. An Inca Trail permit is required and you must go with a licensed operator; book well in advance. The excursion begins at **Km 104,** a stop on the Cusco/Sacred Valley–Machu Picchu trains. All of the hiking happens on the first day, and you get to enter Machu Picchu through the Sun Gate and spend the night at a hotel in Aguas Calientes. The second day is not a trail hike, but a visit to the ruins.

Who needs gardeners? Llamas roam Machu Picchu and keep the grass nice and short.

EXPLORING BEYOND THE LOST CITY

Huiñay Huayna

Several trails lead from the site to surrounding ruins.

INTIPUNKO (SUN GATE)
You can take a 45-minute walk on a gentle arc leading uphill to the southeast of the main complex. **Intipunku**, the Sun Gate, is a small ruin in a nearby pass. This small ancient checkpoint is where you'll find that classic view that Inca Trail hikers emerge upon. Some minor ancient outbuildings along the path occasionally host grazing llamas. A two- or three-hour hike beyond the Intipunku along the Inca Trail brings you to the ruins of **Huiñay Huayna**, a terrace complex that climbs a steep mountain slope and includes a set of ritual baths.

INCA BRIDGE
Built rock by rock up a hair-raising stone escarpment, The **Inca Bridge** is yet another example of Inca engineering ingenuity. From the cemetery at Machu Picchu, it's a 30-minute walk along a narrow path.

HUAYNA PICCHU
The **Huayna Picchu** trail, which follows an ancient Inca path, leads up the sugarloaf hill in front of Machu Picchu for an exhilarating trek. Limited to 400 visitors daily at two entrance times (7–8 am and 10–11 am), tickets to the trail must be purchased at the same time as your entrance to Machu Picchu (combined price S/152). The arduous, vertiginous hike up a steep, narrow set of Inca-carved stairs to the summit and back takes between 2 and 3 hours round trip. Bring insect repellent; the gnats can be ferocious.

MACCHU PICCHU MOUNTAIN
Hiking up Machu Picchu mountain is another possibility. Tickets must be purchased at the same time as the entrance to the site itself (combined price S/142). Entrance is allowed between 7 am and 11 am.

Looking down onto Inca ruins at base of Huayna Picchu.

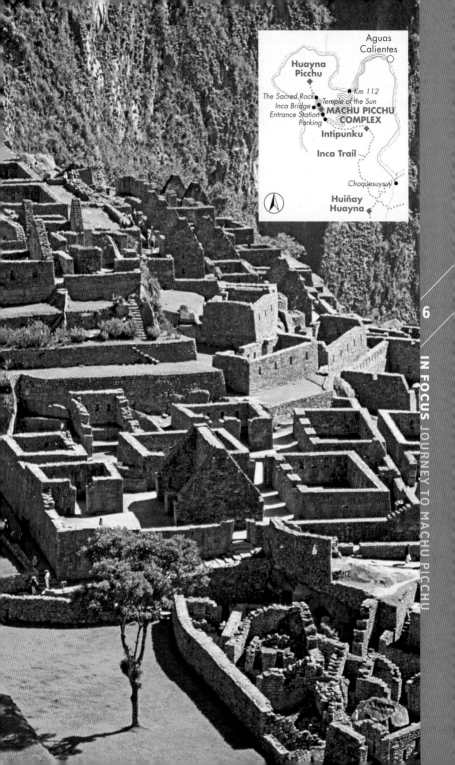

Aguas
Calientes

Huayna
Picchu

The Sacred Rock
Inca Bridge
Entrance Station
Parking

● Km 112
Temple of the Sun
MACHU PICCHU
COMPLEX

Intipunku

Inca Trail

Choquesuysuy ●

Huiñay
Huayna ◆

Walking the Inca trail through the Sacred Valley.

Inca Trail

Patallaqta

Train to Machu Picchu

INCA TRAIL

The Inca Trail (*Camino Inca* in Spanish), a 43-km (26-mile) sector of the stone path that once extended from Cusco to Machu Picchu, is one of the world's signature outdoor excursions. Nothing matches the sensation of walking over the ridge that leads to the Lost City of the Inca just as the sun casts its first yellow glow over the ancient stone buildings.

Though the journey by train is the easiest way to get to Machu Picchu, most travelers who arrive via the Inca Trail wouldn't have done it any other way. There are limits on the number of trail users, but you'll still see a lot of fellow trekkers along the way. The four-day trek takes you past ruins and through stunning scenery, starting in the thin air of the highlands and ending in cloud forests. The orchids, hummingbirds, and spectacular mountains aren't bad either.

The impressive Puyupatamarca ruins.

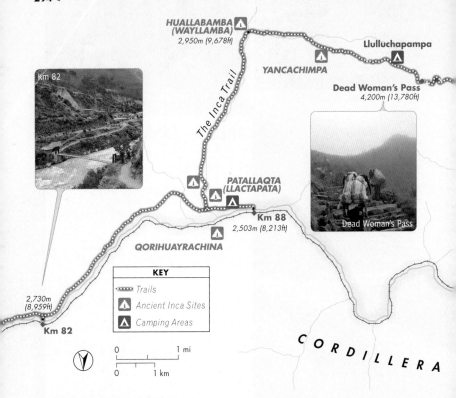

KEY

🏛 Trails

🏛 Ancient Inca Sites

◣ Camping Areas

0   1 mi

0   1 km

HUALLABAMBA (WAYLLAMBA) 2,950m (9,678ft)

YANCACHIMPA

Llulluchapampa

Dead Woman's Pass 4,200m (13,780ft)

The Inca Trail

Km 82

Dead Woman's Pass

PATALLAQTA (LLACTAPATA)

Km 88 2,503m (8,213ft)

QORIHUAYRACHINA

2,730m (8,959ft)

Km 82

CORDILLERA

INCA TRAIL DAY BY DAY

The majority of agencies begin the traditional Inca Trail trek at **Km 82** after a two-to three-hour bus ride from Cusco.

DAY 1

Compared to what lies ahead, the first day's hike is a reasonably easy 11 km (6.8 miles). You'll encounter fantastic ruins almost immediately. An easy ascent takes you to the first of those, **Patallaqta** (also called Llactapata). The name means "town on a hillside" in Quechua, and the ruins are thought to have been a village in Inca times. Bingham and company camped here on their first excursion to Machu Picchu. As at most Inca

sites, you'll see three levels of architecture representing the three spiritual worlds of the Inca—the world above (a guard tower), the world we live in (the main complex), and the world below (the river and hidden aqueducts).

At the end of the day, you arrive at Huayllabamba (also called Wayllamba), the only inhabited village on the trail and your first overnight

DAY 2

It's another 10-km (6.2 mile) hike, but with a gain of 1,200 m (3,940 ft) in elevation. The day is most memorable for the spectacular views and muscular

aches after ascending **Dead Woman's Pass** (also known as Warmiwañuscca) at 4,200 m (13,780 ft). The pass is named for the silhouette created by its mountain ridges—they resemble a woman's head, nose, chin, and chest.

A tricky descent takes you to **Pacaymayu**, the second night's campsite, and you can pat yourself on the back for completing the hardest section of the Inca Trail.

DAY 3

Downhill! You'll cover the most ground today (16 km, 9.9 miles) descending down 1,500 meters

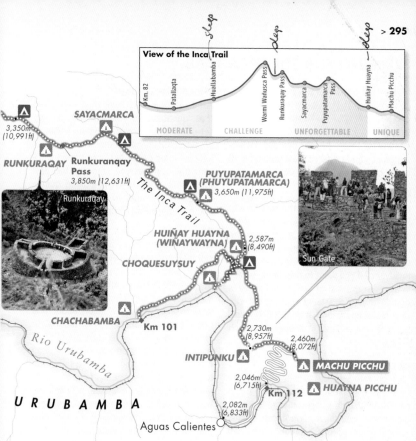

View of the Inca Trail

Km. 82 — Patallaqta — Huallabamba — Warmi Wañusca Pass — Runkuraqay Pass — Sayacmarca — Puyupatamarca Pass — Huiñay Huayna — Machu Picchu

MODERATE · CHALLENGE · UNFORGETTABLE · UNIQUE

SAYACMARCA

3,350m (10,991ft)

RUNKURAQAY · Runkuranqay Pass 3,850m (12,631ft)

Runkuraqay

The Inca Trail

PUYUPATAMARCA (PHUYUPATAMARCA) 3,650m (11,975ft)

HUIÑAY HUAYNA (WIÑAYWAYNA) 2,587m (8,490ft)

Sun Gate

CHOQUESUYSUY

CHACHABAMBA · Km 101

Rio Urubamba

2,730m (8,957ft) · 2,460m (8,072ft)

INTIPUNKU 2,046m (6,715ft)

MACHU PICCHU

Km 112 · **HUATNA PICCHU**

U R U B A M B A

2,082m (6,833ft)

Aguas Calientes

to the subtropical cloud forest where the Amazon basin begins. There's some of the most stunning mountain scenery you'll see during the four days. The ruins of **Runkuraqay** were a circular Inca storage depot for products transported between Machu Picchu and Cusco.

You also pass by **Sayacmarca**, possibly a way station for priests traversing the trail.

Most excursions arrive by mid-afternoon at **Huiñay Huayna** (also known as Wiñaywayna), the third-night's stopping point, at what may now seem a low and balmy

2,712 m (8,900 ft). The first possibility of a hot shower and a cold beer are here.

There is time to see the ruins of **Puyupatamarca** (also known as Phuyupatamarca) a beautifully restored site with ceremonial baths, and perhaps the best ruins on the hike. At this point you catch your first glimpse of Machu Picchu peak, but from the back side.

DAY 4

This is it. Day 4 means the grand finale, arrival at **Machu Picchu**, the reason for the trail in the first place. You'll

be roused from your sleeping bag well before dawn to hike your last 6 km (3.7 miles) to arrive at the ruins in time to catch the sunrise. You'll be amazed at the number of fellow travelers who forget about their aching muscles and sprint this last stretch.

The trail takes you past the **Intipunku**, the Sun Gate. Bask in your first sight of the ruins and your accomplishment, but you'll need to circle around and enter Machu Picchu officially through the entrance gate.

PREPPING FOR THE INCA TRAIL

YOU MUST GO WITH A GUIDE

You must use a licensed tour operator, one accredited by SERNANP, the organization that oversees the trail and limits the number of hikers to 500 per day, including guides and porters. There are some 50 such licensed operators in Cusco.

WHEN TO GO

May through September is the best time to make the four-day trek; rain is more likely in April and October and a certainty the rest of the year. The trail fills up during the dry high season. Make reservations months in advance if you want to hike then—weeks in advance the rest of the year. The trek is doable during the rainy season, but can become slippery and muddy by November. The trail closes for maintenance each February.

GETTING READY

Tour operators in Cusco will tell you the Inca Trail is of "moderate" difficulty, but it can be rough going, especially the first couple of days. You must be in decent shape, even if your agency supplies porters to carry your pack—current regulations limit the porter's load to 20 kg (44 lb) including his own gear. Agencies will typically offer a "half-porter" person with a limit of 7 kg (15 lb) for your personal gear. The trail is often narrow and hair-raising.

As the mountains sometimes rise to over 13,775 feet, be wary of altitude sickness. (Give yourself two or three days in Cusco or the Sacred Valley to acclimatize.)

Your gear should include sturdy hiking boots, a sleeping bag (some outfitters rent them); layered clothing for cold, rainy, and hot weather, a hat, and a towel. Also bring plenty of sunblock and mosquito repellent. Toilet paper is essential; walking sticks can be helpful.

There are seven well-spaced, designated campsites along the trail.

WHILE YOU'RE HIKING

Food: All operators have their own chefs that run ahead of you with the porters, set-up camp, and create culinary feasts for breakfast, lunch, and dinner. This will probably be some of the best camp food you'll ever have and maybe some of the best food while in Peru. We're talking quinoa porridge with blueberries, chicken soup, and gourmet pasta dishes.

Coca Leaves: Although after Day 2 it is a gradual descent into Machu Picchu, you're still high enough to feel the thin air. You'll notice porters chewing coca throughout the trek. Coca leaves are a mild stimulant as well as an appetite, pain, and hunger suppressant. You'll only need about one bag of your own (about S/1) for the trail. To properly enjoy the leaves, take about 15 of them and pick the stems off. Stack them on top of each other and roll into a tight little bundle. Place the bundle between your gum and cheek on one side, allowing the leaves to soften up for about two minutes. Eventually start chewing to let the juice out. It's quite a bitter taste, but you'll feel better. All tour operators will also serve tea during coca breaks.

Bathrooms: Toilets could be a lot worse. You won't be able to sit down, but most porcelain-lined holes in the ground do flush. Bathrooms usually have working sinks. You must bring your own toilet paper wherever you go. Camp sites all have toilets, but the trail itself does not.

Luggage: Check with your tour operator before you go, and pack as lightly as possible. If you hire porters, they're probably going to be carrying a lot more than just your things on their backs. An American-style backwoods backpack may not be the right piece of luggage—it weighs a lot on its own and is an awkward shape for the porters to incorporate into their massive bundles. A simple duffle bag is often best.

$ **La Boulangerie de Paris.** Paris' loss is Aguas Calientes' gain with the
CAFÉ authentic French pastries served up here, as well as coffee, sandwiches
on house artisanal bread, quiche, and more. Eat in or take some of the
delicious choices to go—the excellent boxed lunch options are perfect
for enjoying in Machu Picchu. $ *Average main: S/5 ⌂ Jr. Sinchi Roca*
☎ *084/797–798 ⊕ www.laboulangeriedeparis.net* ▭ *No credit cards*
⊘ *No dinner.*

$$ **Pueblo Viejo.** Hearty food comes easy for this established restaurant.
PERUVIAN Everyone gathers around an open-fire grill in the middle of the res-
taurant, where cuts of beef, alpaca, lamb, and trout are prepared and
served with the typical side dish of fries, rice, or potato. Future plans
include a lunch buffet featuring typical dishes from the coast, the moun-
tains, and the jungle. Live Andean music and a good wine menu keep
this place hopping long after the last tour bus has left town. $ *Average
main: S/41 ⌂ Pachacutec s/n ☎ 084/211–193.*

$$$$ **Qunuq Restaurant.** A must experience for foodies, the culinary offerings
PERUVIAN by Sumaq Hotel's restaurant can easily hold their own against anything
Fodor's Choice the finest restaurants in Lima dish out. As with many of the top gas-
★ tronomic choices in Peru, the menu features a fusion of flavors giving
European dishes like ravioli an Andean slant by stuffing them with *aji
de gallina* as well as infusing traditional Peruvian fare with interna-
tional flair. The cebiche has to be among the best in the country. Other

standout choices include alpaca carpaccio and a melt-in-your-mouth lamb. You'll want to make sure to save room for one of the dessert choices as well. Bear in mind that the room rates at the hotel include lunch or dinner so the restaurant can get a bit packed with groups and it's worth making reservations. $ *Average main: S/67* ⊠ *Av. Hermanos Ayar Mz. 1, L-3* ☎ *084/211–059.*

$$ ✕ **Toto's House.** The sister restaurant to Pueblo Viejo has long tables set

PERUVIAN   up in the center of its cavernous dining room to accommodate tour groups who come for the huge buffet lunch (S/65). Grab one of the smaller tables with a river view by the window or out on the shaded front patio for some good people-watching. Evenings are more sedate—as is the case with the dining scene in most of the restaurants here—with grilled dishes like *trucha andina* (Andean trout), beef, or alpaca set to the entertainment of a folklore music show. $ *Average main: S/50* ⊠ *Av. Imperio de los Incas 600* ☎ *084/211–020.*

$$ ✕ **Tree House Restaurant.** Perched high above the streets of Aguas Calien-

PERUVIAN   tes, this small, wood-panel restaurant serves up some of the best Novo Andino cuisine in town, adding a twist of Italian, Thai, and coastal flavors to typical dishes. Fresh, local ingredients are the backbone for dishes like *quinotto* (similar to risotto but made with quinoa), home-made fettuccine, and fine cuts of beef, fish, and alpaca. The intimate candle-light dining room is small so you may want to make dinner reservations. $ *Average main: S/47* ⊠ *Calle Huanacaure 180* ☎ *084/791–929* ⊕ *www.thetreehouse-peru.com.*

WHERE TO STAY

$$$$ ⚏ **Casa del Sol Boutique Hotel.** The decor and the setting by the river

HOTEL   are what make this hotel special—wood floors, beams, and window frames give rooms an elegant yet warm ambience, textile art adorns the walls, and stone and marble bathrooms blend perfectly with the natural environment outside. **Pros:** beautiful design and lush comfort; less expensive than other luxury options; suites have balconies with Jacuzzis. **Cons:** train noise from tracks just outside the hotel. $ *Rooms from: S/780* ⊠ *Av. Imperio de los Incas 608* ☎ *084/237–333* ⊕ *www. hotelescasadelsol.com* ⮤ *25 rooms, 3 suites* ⍩ *Some meals.*

$$$$ ⚏ **El MaPi.** Designed to save travelers some dollars and cents without

HOTEL   skimping on comfort and class, El MaPi delivers what it promises: simple but stylish rooms, top-tier service, and the same amenities you might expect from one of the more luxurious joints in town. **Pros:** great service; good value. **Cons:** not for those seeking a boutique hotel. $ *Rooms from: S/600* ⊠ *Av. Pachachutec 109* ☎ *084/211–011* ⊕ *www. elmapihotel.com* ⮤ *71 rooms* ⍩ *Breakfast.*

$$ ⚏ **Gringo Bill's Hostal.** Bill has hosted Machu Picchu travelers since 1979,

HOTEL   his was one of the first lodgings in town. **Pros:** cozy setting; good place to meet other travelers; friendly staff. **Cons:** basic; outdoor hot tub doesn't always work; lots of stairs; complaints of roof leaks. $ *Rooms from: S/195* ⊠ *Colla Raymi 104* ☎ *084/211–046* ⊕ *www.gringobills. com* ⮤ *13 rooms, 10 suites* ⍩ *Breakfast.*

$$$$ ⚏ **Hatuchay Tower.** One of the larger, more standard hotels in town,

HOTEL   Hatuchay Tower stands above the river at the edge of town on the

The pros of spending a night at the Sanctuary Lodge, where you can see the Machu Picchu ruins from the property

road heading to the ruins. **Pros:** good location; quiet and comfortable; breakfast and dinner included. **Cons:** not exceptional. Ⓢ *Rooms from: S/943* ✉ *Av. Hermanos Ayar 401* ☎ *084/211–201* ☎ *01/447–8170 in Lima* ⊕ *www.hatuchaytower.com* ⤶ *37 rooms, 5 suites* ⍩ *Some meals.*

$$$$ 🏨 **Hatun Inti.** Polished wood floors, white walls, and tasteful furnishings
HOTEL give this hotel an elegantly rustic and homey feel. **Pros:** prime location; clean; modern. **Cons:** not the cheapest beds in town. Ⓢ *Rooms from: S/625* ✉ *Av. Imperio de los Incas L-23* ☎ *084/211–365* ⊕ *www. grupointi.com* ⤶ *14 rooms* ⍩ *Breakfast.*

$$ 🏨 **Hostal Continental.** This old budget standby is among the better of
HOTEL the lower-cost lodgings in Aguas Calientes, and a definite cut above the standard backpacker digs. **Pros:** hot water; good budget choice. **Cons:** basic. Ⓢ *Rooms from: S/145* ✉ *Av. Imperio de los Incas 400* ☎ *084/211–078* ✉ *sierraandina@gmail.com* ⤶ *16 rooms* ⊟ *No credit cards* ⍩ *Breakfast.*

$ 🏨 **Hotel Presidente.** The Presidente is one of the more moderately priced
HOTEL hotels in Aguas Calientes—about half of the carpeted rooms here have big windows and balconies that overlook the Río Vilcanota (be sure to request this if possible), but none of the rooms have phones, safes, or public Wi-Fi. **Pros:** good value; prime location; nice views. **Cons:** nothing fancy; bathrooms and rooms a bit outdated. Ⓢ *Rooms from: S/197* ✉ *Av. Imperio de los Incas s/n* ☎ *084/211–034* ⤶ *28 rooms* ⍩ *Breakfast.*

$$$$ 🏨 **Inkaterra Machu Picchu.** A five-minute walk from the center of town
HOTEL takes you to this stunning ecolodge made up of rustic, elegant stone
☾ bungalows with exposed beams and cathedral ceilings, set in a minitrop-
Fodor'sChoice ical cloud forest. **Pros:** natural setting; many activities, some included
★ in the price; excellent restaurant with breakfast and dinner included.

Cons: expensive. $ *Rooms from: S/1425* ✉ *Av. Imperio de los Incas s/n* ☎ *084/211–032, 01/610–0400 in Lima, 800/442–5042 in North America* ⊕ *www.inkaterra.com* ⤵ *85 casitas and villas* ⫟⧀ *Some meals.*

$
HOTEL
⬚ **Machupicchu Hostal.** At what is probably one of the best budget deals in town the motel-style rooms all have modern furnishings and renovated bathrooms. **Pros:** good value; river-facing rooms; good location. **Cons:** pretty basic. $ *Rooms from: S/120* ✉ *Av. Imperio de los Incas 135* ☎ *084/211–095* ⤵ *12 rooms* ⫟⧀ *Breakfast.*

$$$$
HOTEL
⬚ **Machu Picchu Sanctuary Lodge.** This upscale hotel at the entrance to Machu Picchu puts you closest to the ruins, a position for which you do pay dearly, but nowhere else can you sit in a hot tub, sip pisco sours or tea, and watch the sunset over the ruins after the last of the tourists depart each afternoon. **Pros:** prime location at ruins' entrance; great astronomy; personalized service; all-inclusive. **Cons:** double the price of other luxury options in Aguas Calientes. $ *Rooms from: S/3600* ✉ *Machu Picchu* ☎ *084/211–094 Hotel, 01/610–8300 in Lima, 800/237–1236 in North America* ⊕ *www.machupicchu.orient-express.com* ⤵ *29 rooms, 2 suites* ⫟⧀ *All meals.*

$
HOTEL
⬚ **Pachamama Inn.** From the comfort of the beds and pillows in this small, budget hotel, you might think you were in a much more expensive place. **Pros:** really comfortable beds, especially for the price; great showers. **Cons:** inner rooms can be noisy as guests leave early in the morning. $ *Rooms from: S/208* ✉ *Calle Chaska Tika 109* ☎ *084/211–352* ⤵ *10 rooms* ⫟⧀ *Breakfast.*

$$$$
HOTEL
Fodor's Choice
★
⬚ **Sumaq Hotel.** The only five-star offering in Aguas Calientes, this large hotel sits at the edge of town alongside the Vilcanota River and offers all the amenities and high level of service you would expect. **Pros:** many amenities; great restaurant with breakfast and lunch or dinner included; cooking class and tea time included; fantastic service. **Cons:** luxury costs. $ *Rooms from: S/1869* ✉ *Av. Hermanos Ayar Mz.1 L-3* ☎ *084/211–059, 01/628–1082 in Lima* ⊕ *www.machupicchuhotels-sumaq.com* ⤵ *46 rooms, 14 suites* ⫟⧀ *Some meals.*

SHOPPING

Otto's Spa. In a place where many of the massage therapists have little or no training, Otto is a real gem—professional and talented. A massage is the perfect way to end a day of hiking around Machu Picchu, especially if you plan to climb Huayna Picchu or hike the Inca Trail. At about S/60 for an hour massage, this is truly a bargain. Call for an appointment if the office is not open; walk-ins are welcome. ✉ *Av. Imperio de los Incas 602* ☎ *984/382–567.*

The Amazon Basin

WORD OF MOUTH

"We saw squirrel monkeys in trees along the shore and watched a small spectacled caiman suffer the continued annoyance of bees landing on its eyelids, which barely protruded from the water. Then we fished for piranha."

—atravelynn

WELCOME TO THE AMAZON BASIN

TOP REASONS TO GO

★ **The River:** The Amazon is a natural choice for adventures, but it is best explored on an organized tour.

★ **Wild Things:** Peru's Amazon Basin has more than 50,000 plant, 1,700 bird, 400 mammal, and 300 reptile species. Bring binoculars.

★ **Sport Fishing:** Anglers can test their skills on dozens of river fish, including the feisty peacock bass.

★ **Nature Lodges:** Staying at a jungle lodge is almost obligatory when visiting the Amazon Basin if you really want to experience the jungle life surrounding you.

★ **Cruising:** An Amazon River cruise to Pacaya Samiria National Reserve is the most comfortable, though expensive, way to explore this vast wilderness.

1 Madre de Dios. The national parks, reserves, and other undeveloped areas of the southern department of Madre de Dios are among the most biologically diverse in the world. Puerto Maldonado is an ugly frontier town that is mostly used by travelers as a place to fly into, board a boat, and head for a jungle lodge.

2 Iquitos and Environs. The jungle-locked city of Iquitos has historic architecture, jungle flavors, and a city-on-the-edge attitude with more than 400,000 cooped-up residents. Nature lodges accessible only by boat offer wildlife observation and rain forest exploration. The region's three top eco-destinations are the Allpahuayo Mishana Nacional Reserve, Tamshiyacu Tahuayo Reserve, and Pacaya Samiria National Reserve.

Iquitos.

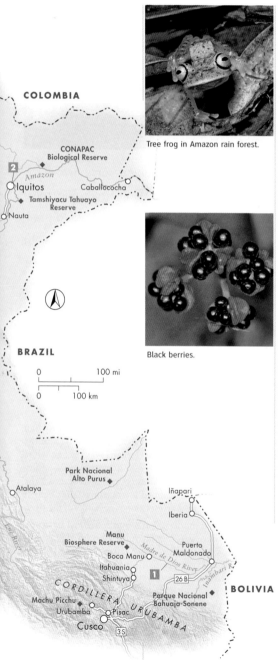

Tree frog in Amazon rain forest.

Black berries.

GETTING ORIENTED

The logistics of travel and isolation make it difficult to visit both the northern and southern Amazon regions—separated by 600 km (370 miles) at their nearest point—during one trip to Peru. The city of Iquitos is the jumping-off point for the northern Amazon; Puerto Maldonado for the southern Amazon tributaries the Madre de Dios and Tambopata rivers. Some 1,200 km (740 miles) and connecting flights back in Lima separate the two cities. The Manu Biosphere Reserve, on the upper Madre de Dios River, is primarily reached by land and river from Cusco. Both the northern and southern regions are dotted with excellent jungle lodges, whereas the Peruvian Amazon can also be experienced on a cruise.

Updated
by David
Dudenhoefer

Peru's least-developed region occupies some two-thirds of the country, an area the size of California. The *selva* (jungle) of the Amazon Basin is drained by the world's second-longest river and its countless tributaries. What eastern Peru lacks in human population it makes up for in sheer plant and animal numbers. There are lodges, cruise boats, and guides for the growing number of people who arrive to see a bit of the region's spectacular wildlife.

The northern Amazon is anchored by the port city of Iquitos—the Amazon Basin's second-biggest city after Manaus, Brazil, and the gateway to the rain forest. From Iquitos you can head out on an Amazon cruise or take a smaller boat to any of a dozen jungle lodges to experience the region's diverse flora and fauna.

Though this area has been inhabited by indigenous groups for more than 5,000 years, it wasn't "civilized" until Jesuit missionaries arrived in the 1500s. The Spanish conquistador Francisco de Orellana was the first white man to see the Amazon. He came upon the great river, which the indigenous people called Tunguragua (King of Waters), on his trip down the Río Napo in search of El Dorado. He dubbed it Amazonas after he met with extreme opposition from female warriors along the banks of the river.

The area was slow to convert to modern ways, and remained basically wild until the 1880s, when there was a great rubber boom. The boom changed the town of Iquitos overnight; rubber barons installed themselves in lavish homes, and the city's population exploded. Indigenous people were put to work, often under slavelike conditions as rubber tappers who headed into the jungle each day to collect the sap from rubber trees scattered through the forest. The boom went bust in the first part of the 20th century, when a British entrepreneur transported some seeds out of Brazil and established plantations on the Malay Peninsula. The invention of synthetic rubber in the mid–20th century only made things worse. You can still see remnants of the boom in the somewhat dilapidated mansions of Iquitos.

Most of the indigenous tribes—many small tribes are found in the region, the Boras, Yaguas, and Orejones being the most numerous—have given up their traditional hunter-gatherer existence and now live in small communities along the backwaters of the great river. You will not see the remote tribes unless you travel far from Iquitos and deep into the jungle, a harrowing and dangerous undertaking. What you will see are people who have adopted western dress and other amenities, but who still live in relative harmony with nature and preserve traditions that date back thousands of years. A common sight might be a fisherman paddling calmly on an Amazon tributary in his dugout canoe, angling to reel in one of its many edible fish.

The lesser-known southern Amazon region is traversed by one of the big river's tributaries—the Río Madre de Dios. Few travelers spend much time in Puerto Maldonado, the capital of Madre de Dios department, using the city instead as a jumping-off point to the Tambopata National Reserve. The Manu Biosphere Reserve is less accessible but more pristine, located on the Upper Madre de Dios River between Cusco and Puerto Malonado. Nonetheless, Tambopata will not disappoint, and much of the jungle outside those protected areas still holds remarkable flora and fauna.

Both Madre de Dios and the Peruvian Amazon are impressive, and while they share much of the same flora and fauna, each region has its own attractions. The Amazon River is notable for its sheer size, and has species that you won't find in Madre de Dios, such as two types of freshwater dolphin and the giant water lily. This region also offers more comfortable access to the jungle, primarily on cruises. Because it has fewer inhabitants, Madre de Dios has more wildlife, including rare creatures like the giant river otter, and large flocks of macaws that gather at its *collpas* (clay licks).

Whichever region you visit, it will be a true adventure. Be prepared to spend some extra soles to get here. Roads, where they exist, are rough-and-tumble, so the preferred mode of transport is by boat. A dry-season visit is recommended—but, of course, "dry" is a euphemism in the rain forest. You'll most likely jet into Iquitos or Puerto Maldonado, respectively the northern and southern gateways to the Amazon, and climb into a boat to reach one of the region's famed nature lodges.

PLANNING

WHEN TO GO

As you might expect, it rains plenty in the Amazon Basin, though that precipitation is somewhat seasonal. Although there's no true dry season in the Iquitos area, it rains less from June to October in Madre de Dios. For Amazon cruises out of Iquitos, high-water season is best (December–June); tributaries become shallow during the dry months, making it hard to get to oxbow lakes.

The southern Amazon Basin has a pronounced dry season between May and October; and while most lodges are open year-round, some Manu lodges close between December and April. Tambopata sees a well-defined wet season/dry season; Manu's rainfall is more evenly dispersed throughout the year. Plan well in advance for trips in July and August, the peak tourist season, when some jungle lodges often take in large groups and cruise boats can be full. During the dry season, especially July and August, sudden *friajes* (cold fronts) bring rain and cold weather to Madre de Dios, so be prepared for the worst. Temperatures can drop from 32°C (90°F) to 10°C (50°F) overnight. No matter when you travel, bring a rain jacket or poncho.

GETTING HERE AND AROUND

AIR TRAVEL

LAN flies to Iquitos five times daily from Lima. Peruvian Airlines and Star Peru each fly to Iquitos twice a day, but charge considerably less than LAN. Iquitos's Aeropuerto Internacional Francisco Secada Vignetta is 8 km (5 miles) from the city center. A taxi to the airport should cost around S/10. LAN has three daily flights from both Lima and Cusco to Aeropuerto Padre Aldámiz, 5 km (3 miles) from the center of Puerto Maldonado. TACA and Star Peru each have one Lima–Puerto Maldonado flight daily, which stop in Cusco. Star Peru usually has the best deals.

BOAT TRAVEL

Boats are the most common form of transportation in the Amazon Basin and the only way to get to most of the nature lodges, with the exception of those in the cloud forests of Manu. If you stay at any of this region's nature lodges, you will be met at the airport in Puerto Maldonado or Iquitos and transported to a riverbank spot where you board a boat that takes you to your lodge. Once there, most excursions will also be by boat. If you opt for an Amazon cruise, you'll spend most of your time on the water.

BUS TRAVEL

The only areas that can be reached by road are Puerto Maldonado and the buffer zone of Manu National Park. The windy road to Puerto Maldonado from Cusco is a 10-hour bus ride that only a backpacker on a very tight budget would take. Several tour companies offer slower, but incredible, overland trips from Cusco to Manu, including nine hours over rugged terrain via Paucartambo. The road plunges spectacularly from the *páramo* (highlands) into the cloud forests, eventually reaching the Alto Madre de Dios River in Atalaya, where travelers board boats to Manu lodges.

HEALTH AND SAFETY

MALARIA

There is no vaccine, but prescription drugs help minimize your likelihood of contracting this mosquito-borne illness. Strains of malaria are resistant to the traditional regimen of chloroquine. There are three recommended alternatives: a weekly dose of mefloquine; a daily dose of doxycycline; or a daily dose of Malarone (*atovaquone/proguanil*). Any regimen must start before arrival and continue beyond departure. Ask your physician. Wear long sleeves and pants if you're out in the evening, and use a mosquito repellent containing DEET whenever you enter the jungle.

YELLOW FEVER

The Peruvian Embassy recommends getting a yellow fever vaccine at least 10 days before visiting the Amazon. Though recent cases of yellow fever have occurred only near Iquitos, southern Amazon lodges in

Manu and Tambopata tend to be sticklers about seeing your yellow fever vaccination certificate. Carry it with you.

EMERGENCIES

The **Policia Nacional** (☎ *082/803–504 or 082/573–605*), Peru's national police force, handles emergencies. At jungle lodges minor emergencies are handled by the staff. For serious emergencies, the lodge must contact medical services in Puerto Maldonado, Cusco, or Iquitos.

RESTAURANTS

You can dine out at restaurants only in Iquitos and Puerto Maldonado, the Amazon Basin's two main cities, and even they have limited choices. Your sole dining option is your lodge if you stay in the jungle. Meals are often served buffet-style at fixed times, with everyone seated around a big table, and you can swap stories with your fellow lodgers about what you saw on your day's excursion. The food, usually made of local ingredients, can be quite tasty. *Prices in the reviews are the average cost of a main course at dinner or, if dinner is not served, at lunch.*

HOTELS

Puerto Maldonado and Iquitos have plenty of small hotels. Iquitos also has a few nicer hotels geared to business travelers. Beyond those urban centers lie the region's jungle lodges. They are reachable only by boat and vary in degree of rusticity and remoteness. They range from tented camps, where rooms consist of a bed inside a screened enclosure under a roof, to upscale eco-lodges with swimming pools and Wi-Fi. Most have limited electricity, however, and only one offers air-conditioning. Showers are often refreshingly cool.

All nature lodges offer fully escorted tours, with packages from one to several nights including guided wildlife-viewing excursions. They all provide mosquito nets and three meals. Most lodges quote rates per person, based on double occupancy, that include meals and transportation plus some tours, and many take so long to reach that the minimum stay is two nights. *The price ranges given for lodges in this chapter reflect the cost of one night's stay for two people, meals included.* All lodges accept soles, and U.S. dollars for drinks and souvenirs.

TOURS

MADRE DE DIOS

InkaNatura Travel. InkaNatura Travel runs tours to its own nature lodges in the Manu Biosphere Reserve and the Tambopata National Reserve. ☎ *1/203–5000* ⊕ *www.inkanatura.com.*

Inkaterra. Inkaterra's tours provide a good introduction to the rain forest without sacrificing comfort. They include overnights at the Reserva Amazónica, a private reserve 30 minutes downriver from Puerto Maldonado, or the Hacienda Concepción, 20 minutes south of Puerto Maldonado, near the Tambopata National Reserve. Both lodges offer a selection of excursions that include rain-forest hikes, a morning on Lake Sandoval, a paddle down Gamitana Creekm, and a canopy walk. ☎ *1/610–0400, 800/442–5042 in U.S. and Canada* ⊕ *www.inkaterra.com.*

Manu Expeditions. The specialists in bird-watching, with decades of experience, Manu Expeditions offers trips into the Manu Biosphere Reserve lasting anywhere from five to nine days, with overnights at several different nature lodges. ☎ 84/225–990 ⊕ www.manuexpeditions.com.

Manu Nature Tours. Manu Nature Tours runs trips into Manu with overnights at a cloud forest lodge and the Manu Lodge, inside Manu National Park. ☎ 84/252–721 ⊕ www.manuperu.com.

Pantiacolla. Pantiacolla organizes three- to nine-day ecotours to Manu that include nights in the cloud forest and rainforest. Their lodges are more rustic, but less expensive than the competition. ☎ 84/238–323 ⊕ www.pantiacolla.com.

Rainforest Expeditions. The Tambopata experts, Rainforest Expeditions runs three- to seven-day nature tours with accommodations at any of the company's three lodges: the Posada Amazonas, Refugio Amazonas and Tambopata Research Center. ✉ Av. Larco 1116, 4to Piso, Miraflores, Lima ☎ 1/719–6422 in Miraflores, 9847–05266 in Cusco, 877/231–9251 in U.S. ⊕ www.perunature.com.

IQUITOS AREA

Amazonia Expeditions. Amazonia Expeditions offers trips to the Tamshiyacu-Tahuayo Reserve: an extremely diverse protected area up the Amazon River from Iquitos, where it operates the Tahuayo Lodge and Research Center Lodge. ☎ 800/262–9669 in U.S. ⊕ www.perujungle.com.

Aqua Expeditions. Aqua Expeditions runs high-end nature cruises up the Amazon from Iquitos to the Pacaya Samiria Reserve, where tributaries and lakes are explored in small boats. Cruises last for three, four, or seven nights. ☎ 1/484–5544 or 65/601–053 ⊕ www.aquaexpeditions.com.

Delfin. Delfin offers four- and five-day Amazon eco-cruises on two boats: the luxurious *Delfin I*, which takes eight passengers, and the larger *Delfin II*, which sleeps 28. Passengers board small boats each day for trips into the Pacaya Samiria Reserve. ☎ 1/719–0998 ⊕ www.delfinamazoncruises.com.

Explorama Tours. Explorama Tours offers trips down the Amazon River lasting anywhere from three to seven days, with stays at its rustic Explorama and ExplorNapo nature lodges or the more comfortable Ceiba Tops. ☎ 65/252–530, 800/707–5275 in U.S. ⊕ www.explorama.com.

Green Tracks. Green Tracks is a U.S.-based company that organizes one-week river expeditions up the Amazon to the Pacaya Samiria Reserve, and books stays at nature lodges in both the Iquitos area and Madre de Dios. ☎ 970/884–6107 ⊕ www.greentracks.com.

International Expeditions. International Expeditions offers 10-day nature cruises to the Pacaya Samira Reserve that go deeper into the jungle and are less expensive that most Amazon cruises. ☎ 800/234–9620 ⊕ www.ietravel.com.

MADRE DE DIOS

Do the math: 20,000 plant, 1,200 butterfly, 1,000 bird, 200 mammal, and 100 reptile species (and many more yet to be identified). The southern sector of Peru's Amazon Basin, most readily approached via Cusco, is famous among birders, whose eyes glaze over in amazement at the dawn spectacle of macaws and parrots gathered at one of the region's famed *collpas* (clay licks). Ornithologists speculate that the birds ingest clay periodically to neutralize toxins in the seeds and fruit they eat. Madre de Dios also offers a rare chance to see large mammals, such as capybaras (dog-sized rodents) and anteaters. If the zoological gods smile upon you, you may even encounter a tapir or a jaguar. Animal and plant life abounds, but this is the least popu-lated of Peru's departments: a scant 76,000 people reside in an area slightly smaller than South Caro-lina, and almost two-thirds of them are in Puerto Maldonado.

> ## RIBEREÑOS
>
> Peruvians in the Amazon region are a mix of native and Spanish ancestry. Ribereños (river people) live simple lives close to the land and water, much like their native ancestors. They depend on fish and crops for their survival. Not far from Iquitos are numerous small communities of the Amazon's original peoples. They include the Yagua, Bora, Huitoto, Ticuna, and Cocama, whose people generally speak very little Spanish. If you do visit a native village, be sure to take small bills (soles or dollars) to buy artisanal items.

The southern Amazon saw little incursion at the time of the Spanish conquest. The discovery in the late 19th century of the *shiringa*, known in the English-speaking world as the rubber tree, changed all of that. Madre de Dios saw outside migration for the first time with the arrival of the *caucheros* (rubber men) and their minions staking out claims. The discovery of gold in the 1970s drew new waves of fortune seekers to the region, and you are bound to encounter mining barges on the river.

Tourism and conservation have triggered the newest generation of explorers in the species-rich southern Amazon. Two areas of Madre de Dios are of special interest. One is around the city of Puerto Mal-donado, including the Tambopata National Reserve and the adjoining Bahuaja-Sonene National Park. Easily accessible, they offer lodges amid primary rain forest and excellent birding. Tambopata also serves sus-tainable agriculture purposes: some 1,500 families in the department collect Brazil nuts from the reserve, an economic incentive to keep the forest intact, rather than cut it down. The Manu Biosphere Reserve, directly north of Cusco, though more difficult to reach, provides unpar-alleled opportunity for observing wildlife in one of the largest virgin rain forests in the New World.

PUERTO MALDONADO

500 km (310 miles) east of Cusco.

The inland port city of Puerto Maldonado lies at the confluence of the Madre de Dios and Tambopata rivers. The capital of the department of Madre de Dios, it is a rough-and-tumble town with 60,000 people and nary a four-wheeled vehicle in sight, but with hundreds of motor-ized two- and three-wheeled motorbikes jockeying for position on its few paved streets.

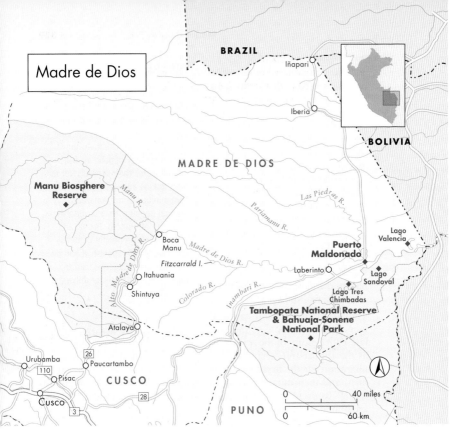

Madre de Dios

The city is named for two explorers who ventured into the region 300 years apart: Spanish conquistador Juan Álvarez de Maldonado passed through in 1566; Peruvian explorer Faustino Maldonado explored the still-wild area in the 1860s, never completing his expedition (he drowned in the Madeira River). Rubber barons founded this youngster of Peruvian cities in 1912, and its history has been a boom-or-bust roller-coaster ride ever since. The collapse of the rubber industry in the 1930s gave way to decades of dormancy that were ended by the discovery of gold in the 1970s and the opening of an airport 10 years later. High prices for gold and steady improvements to the road there—part of a "highway" connecting Peru with Brazil—have brought an influx of settlers in recent years, which has been a scourge for the region's forests and indigenous peoples.

Nevertheless, Puerto Maldonado bills itself as the "Biodiversity Capital of the World," since it is the jumping-off point for visiting the Tambopata National Reserve and surrounding rain forest. ■ TIP➔ Few travelers spend any time in the city, heading from the airport directly to docks, where they board boats to their respective jungle lodges. Still, Puerto Maldonado has a couple of decent hotels that can be used as a base for day trips. And this is the only place to use an ATM machine or cash a traveler's check.

GETTING HERE AND AROUND

It's fun to get around town in Puerto Maldonado's fleet of mototaxis, semi-open three-wheeled motorized vehicles with room for two passengers in the back seat. They patrol the main streets from dawn to well past dusk.

ESSENTIALS

Airport Aeropuerto Internacional Padre José Aldamiz ✉ *Ca. Faucett Km 7* ☎ *82/502-029.*

Currency Banco de Crédito ✉ *Jr. Daniel A. Carrion 201* ☎ *82/571-193.*

Mail SERPOST ✉ *Av. León Velarde 675* ☎ *82/571-088.*

Medical Hospital de Apoyo Santa Rosa ✉ *Jr. Cajamarca 171* ☎ *82/571-019.*

Visitor Information Dirección Regional de Industria y Turismo ✉ *Jr. San Martin Urb. Fonavi F20* ☎ *82/571-164.*

EXPLORING

Plaza Grau. The best view in Puerto Maldonado is from this grassy plaza one block northeast of the Plaza de Armas. The park is dedicated to Miguel Grau, a Peruvian naval officer in the 19th century. But the attraction isn't the bust of him erected there: rather it's the sweeping view of the Rio Madre de Dios, and the rain forest that lines its banks. ✉ *Jr. Bellinghurst at Jr. Arequipa.*

WHERE TO EAT AND STAY

$ PERUVIAN 🍴 **Burgos's Restaurant.** This funky thatch-roofed restaurant has one of Puerto Maldonado's best kitchens, serving up regional dishes and original recipes based on local ingredients. The ambience is appropriately Amazonian, with indigenous art on the walls. **TIP→ Tables in back have great views of the Tambopata River and jungle by day.** Start off with a maracuya sour (a cocktail made with passion fruit and pisco) and some *yucca con salsa hancaina* (fried cassava sticks with a spicy cheese sauce). Then sink your teeth into *pollo con salsa de castaña* (chicken in a Brazil-nut sauce), *pescado con salsa de cocona*, fish fillet in a forest-fruit sauce, or *lomo* (grilled tenderloin) with fried plantain balls and *ensalada de palmito* (heart of palm salad). [$] *Average main: S/22* ✉ *Av. 26 de Diciembre 195* ☎ *82/502-373.*

$ HOTEL 🏨 **Hotel Cabaña Quinta.** The rambling grounds with tropical gardens and Victorian touches could have come right out of a Graham Greene novel. **Pros:** quiet; clean; good restaurant; pleasant staff. **Cons:** basic rooms. [$] *Rooms from: S/170* ✉ *Jr. Moquegua 422* ☎ *82/571-045* 🌐 *www.hotelcabanaquinta.com.pe* 🛏 *62 rooms, 3 suites* 🍽 *Breakfast.*

$ HOTEL 🏨 **Wasaí Maldonado Lodge.** The Wasaí gives you that jungle-lodge feel right in town, a block from the Plaza de Armas. **Pros:** convenient; jungle setting; airport pickup. **Cons:** musty rooms. [$] *Rooms from: S/170* ✉ *Jr. Bellinghurs at Jr. Arequipa* ☎ *82/572-290 or 1/436-8792* 🌐 *www.wasai.com* 🛏 *17 cabins* 🍽 *Breakfast.*

7

TAMBOPATA NATIONAL RESERVE AND
BAHUAJA-SONENE NATIONAL PARK

5 km (3 miles) south of Puerto Maldonado.

GETTING HERE AND AROUND

Tambopata jungle lodges are possibly the easiest places in the world to experience the Amazon rain forest. They are much more accessible—and affordable—than those in the Manu Biosphere Reserve, Madre de Dios's more famous ecotourism area. And Tambopata is no poor man's Manu either—its numbers and diversity of wildlife are very impressive. A half-hour flight from Cusco takes you to Puerto Maldonado, the Tambopata jumping-off point. The closest lodges are less than an hour by boat down the Madre de Dios River, whereas lodges on the Tambopato River take anywhere from two hours to two days to reach. Some of the lodges offer two-night packages, but a three-night stay is really the least you should spend in this area, and if you intend to go deep into Tambopata, you'll need five days.

EXPLORING

Tambopata National Reserve and Bahuaja-Sonene National Park. From Puerto Maldonado, the Madre de Dios River flows east to the Bolivian border. The river defines the northern boundary of the Tambopata National Reserve and passes some nearby, easy-to-reach jungle lodges. The Tambopata River flows out of the reserve and into the Madre de Dios at Puerto Maldonado, and a boat trip up that waterway can take you deep into that protected area: a 3.8-million-acre rain-forest reserve about the size of Connecticut. Officially separate from the reserve, but usually grouped for convenience under the "Tambopata" heading, is the Bahuaja-Sonene National Park, created in 1996 and taking its moniker from the names in the local indigenous Ese'eja language for the Tambopata and Heath rivers, respectively. (The Río Heath forms Peru's southeastern boundary with neighboring Bolivia.) The former Pampas de Río Heath Reserve along the border itself is now incorporated into Bahuaja-Sonene, and encompasses a looks-out-of-place secondary forest more resembling the African savanna than the lush tropical Amazon.

Peru works closely on joint conservation projects with Bolivia, whose adjoining Madidi National Park forms a grand cross-border 7.2-million-acre reserve area. Only environmentally friendly activities are permitted in Tambopata. The area functions partially as a managed tropical-forest reserve, and local communities collect *castañas*, or Brazil nuts, from the forest floor.

Elevations here range from 500 meters (1,640 feet) to a lofty 3,000 meters (9,840 feet), providing fertile homes for an astounding number of animals and plants. The area holds a world record in the number of butterfly species (1,234) recorded by scientists. ■ TIP→ Tambopata contains the largest of Madre de Dios's collpas, the Colpa Chuncho. It's visited by approximately 15 species of parrots and macaws who congregate at dawn to collect a beakful of mineral-rich clay, an important but mysterious part of their diet. ☎ 82/573–278.

Continued on page 317

THE JUNGLE LIFE

by Doug Wechsler

Green-winged Macaw (*Ara chloroptera*) foraging high in rain forest canopy.

An observant naturalist living in the Peruvian Amazon can expect to see something new and exciting every day in his or her life. To the casual traveler much of this life remains hidden at first but reveals itself with careful observation.

Western Amazonia may be the most biologically diverse region on earth. The areas around Puerto Maldonado and Iquitos are two of the best locales to observe this riot of life.

On the Tambopata Reserve, for example, 620 species of birds and more than 1,200 species of butterflies have been sighted within a few miles of Explorer's Inn. To put that into perspective, only about 700 species of birds and 700 species of butterflies breed in all of North America. Within the huge Manu National Park, which includes part of the eastern slope of the Andes, about ¹/₁₀ of the world's bird species can be sighted. A single tree can harbor the same number of ant species as found in the entire British Isles. A single hectare (2.4 acres) of forest might hold nearly 300 species of trees.

This huge diversity owes itself to ideal temperatures and constant moisture for growth of plants and animals and to a mixture of stability and change over the past several million years. The complex structure of the forest leads to many microhabitats for plants and animals. The diversity of plants and animals is overwhelming and the opportunity for new observations is limitless.

STARS OF THE AMAZON

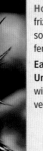

Pink River Dolphin: The long-snouted pink river dolphin enters shallow waters, flooded forest, and even large lakes. Unlike the gray dolphin of river channels, this species rarely jumps out of the water.
Eats: Fish. **Weighs:** 350 lbs. **Myth:** Often blamed for pregnancies when father is unknown.

Red-and-Green Macaw: The loud, raucous shrieks first call attention to red-and-green macaws, the largest members of the parrot family in the Amazon. Clay licks near a number of jungle lodges in Madre de Dios are great places to observe these spectacular birds.
Eats: Seeds of trees and vines. **Weighs:** 3 lbs.
Length: 3 ft. **Odd habit:** Consumes clay from steep banks.

Hoatzin: The clumsy-flying, chicken-sized Hoatzin sports a long frizzled crest and bare blue skin around the eye, suggesting something out of the Jurassic. Its digestive system features a fermentation chamber and is more bovine than avian.
Eats: Leaves, especially arum. **Weighs:** 1.8 lbs.
Unusual feature: Nestlings can climb with claws on their wings. **Favorite Hangout:** Trees and shrubs in swampy vegetation near lakes.

Squirrel Monkey: The small, active squirrel monkeys live in groups of 20 to 100 or more. These common monkeys can be distinguished by a black muzzle and white mask.
Eats: Large insects and fruit. **Weighs:** 2 lbs.
Favorite Hangout: Lower and mid-levels of vine-tangled forest especially near rivers and lakes. **Associates:** Brown capuchin monkeys often hang out with the troop.

Red Howler Monkey: A loud, long, deep, roaring chorus from these large, sedentary, red-haired monkeys announces the coming of dawn, an airplane, or a rainstorm. The swollen throat houses an incredible vocal apparatus.
Eats: Leaves and fruits. **Weighs:** 8 to 23 lbs.
Favorite Hangout: Tree tops and mid-levels of forest.
Unfortunate trait: They will urinate and defecate on you if you walk beneath them.

Three-toed Sloth: This slow-moving, upside down ball of fur is easiest to spot in tree crowns with open growth like cecropias. The dark mask and three large claws on the hands distinguish it from the larger two-toed sloth.

Eats: Leaves. **Weighs:** 5 to 11 lbs. **Favorite Hangout:** Tree tops and mid-levels of forest. **Unusual habit:** Sloths climb to the ground once a week to move their bowels.

Cecropia Tree: The huge, multi-lobed leaves, open growth form, and thin light-colored trunks make cecropias among the most distinctive Amazonian trees. Cecropias are the first trees to shoot up when a forest is cut or a new river island is formed. Their long finger-like fruits are irresistible to birds.

Height: Up to 50 ft. or more. **Bark:** Has bamboo-like rings. **Attracts:** Toucans, tanagers, bats, monkeys, sloths. **Relationships:** The hollow stems house stinging ants that protect the tree—beware.

Horned Screamer: A bare, white quill arches from the crown of this ungainly, dark, turkey-sized bird. Its long toes enable it to walk on floating vegetation. Occasionally it soars among vultures.

Eats: Water plants. **Weighs:** up to 7 lbs. **Favorite Hangout:** Shores of lagoons and lakes. **Relatives:** Screamers are related to ducks and geese—who would have guessed?

Russet-backed Oropendola: What the yellow tailed, crow-sized, oropendola lacks in beauty, it makes up for in its liquid voice. The remarkable three-foot long woven nests dangle in groups from an isolated tree—protection from monkeys.

Eats: Insects and fruit. **Favorite Hangout:** Forest near clearings and rivers. **Look for:** Flocks of hundreds going to and from roosting islands in the river at dusk and dawn.

Giant Amazon Water Lily: This water lily has leaves up to 7 ft. across and 6–12 inch white or pink flowers that bloom at night. The edges of the leaves bend upward. Leaf stems grow with the rising flood.

Length: Stems up to 20 ft. **Eaten by:** Fish eat the seeds. **Favorite Hangout:** River backwaters, oxbow lakes. **Sex changes:** Female parts flower the first night, then the flower turns pink and the male parts open.

7

IN FOCUS THE JUNGLE LIFE

TIPS:

Don't expect all those species to come out and say hello! The Amazon's great biodiversity is made possible by the jungle's sheltering, almost secretive nature. Here are tips to help train your eye to see through nature's camouflage.

1. Listen for movement. Crashing branches are the first clue of monkeys, and rustling leaves betray secretive lizards and snakes.

2. Going upstream on the river means your boat will stay steady close to shore—where all the wildlife is.

3. Look for birds in large mixed-species flocks; stay with the flock while the many birds slowly reveal themselves.

4. Concentrate your observation in the early morning and late afternoon, and take a midday siesta to save energy for night-time exploration.

5. Wear clothes that blend in with the environment. Exception: hummingbird lovers should wear shirts with bright red floral prints.

6. Train your eye to pick out anomalies—what might, at first, seem like an out-of-place ball of debris in the tree could be a sloth.

7. At night, use a bright headlamp or hold a flashlight next to your head to spot eye-shine from mammals, nocturnal birds, frogs, boas, moths, and spiders.

8. Crush leaves and use your nose when getting to know tropical plants.

Reserva Amazonica canopy walkway.

Fodor's Choice ★ **Lago Sandoval.** Changes in the course of Amazon tributaries have created countless oxbow lakes, which are formed when the riverbed shifts and the abandoned bend fills with water. Lago Sandoval, created by the Madre de Dios River, lies just inside the Tambopata National Reserve, a short trip from Puerto Maldonado. It is a lovely sight, hemmed with lush jungle and a wall of *aguaje* palms on one end. It is also an ideal spot for wildlife watching. Herons, egrets, kingfishers, and other waterfowl hunt along its edges; several species of monkeys forage in the lakeside foliage; and chestnut-fronted macaws fly squawking overhead. A family of elusive giant otters lives in Lake Sandoval, making it one of the few places you can hope to see that endangered species. The lake is a 30-minute boat ride east from Puerto Maldonado. Once you disembark, there's a flat-but-muddy 3-km (1.8-mile) hike to the actual lake. ✉ *14 km (9 miles) east of Puerto Maldonado.*

★ **Lago Tres Chimbadas.** This oxbow lake, a short hike from the Tambopata River, is a great place to see wildlife, including the endangered giant river otter. It is also home to side-necked turtles, hoatzins, sun grebes, and dozens of other bird species. Its dark waters hold black caimans (reptiles that resemble small alligators) and a plethora of piranhas, so try to resist any urge you have to go for a swim. Most people visit Tres Chimbadas on an early morning excursion from the nearby Posada Amazonas. ✉ *42 km (26 miles) southeast of Puerto Maldonado.*

Lago Valencia. Two hours northeast of Puerto Maldonado, across the Madre de Dios River from the Tambopata Reserve, is the oxbow lake of Lago Valencia. It is bigger than Lago Sandoval, but because it has a large community that can be reached by road, it has less wildlife. Some lodges offer day trips to the lake, which is good for piranha fishing and bird watching. ✉ *23 km (14 miles) east of Puerto Maldonado.*

7

WHERE TO STAY

Eco-lodges in this area can only be reached by boat and range from the jungle luxury of Inkaterra's Reserva Amazónica to the rustic Tambopata Research Center, deep inside the Tambopata National Reserve. Rates for all lodges include transportation, bilingual nature guides, three meals per day, and varied excursions. The Hacienda Concepción and Reserva Amazónica are the region's most accessible lodges. They lie less than an hour down the Madre de Dios River from Puerto Maldonado, whereas the Sandoval Lake Lodge requires an additional 90-minute hike. The next closest is Posada Amazonas, which is two hours from Puerto Maldonado, up the Tambopata River. The rest require boat trips ranging from three to five hours. Whichever lodge you choose, you will be met at the Puerto Maldonado Airport and transported to and from the lodge by bus and boat.

$$$$ RESORT 🏨 **Explorer's Inn.** Founded in 1975, this lodge on the Tambopata River was one of the country's ecotourism pioneers, and dozens of biological studies have been completed in its forest. It accommodates tourists and visiting scientists alike in thatched-roof bungalows, and the selling point here is exposure to nature rather than comfort. **Pros:** knowledgeable guides; in the Tambopata Reserve; responsible tourism. **Cons:** rustic; basic meals. [$] *Rooms from: S/535* ✉ *Tambopata River, 58 km*

CLOSE UP

Jungle Days

The knock at the door comes early. "*¡Buenos días!* Good morning!" It's 5 am and your guide is rousing you for the dawn excursion to the nearby *collpa de guacamayos*. He doesn't want you to miss the riotous, colorful spectacle of hundreds of parrots and macaws descending to the vertical clay lick to ingest mineral-rich earth. Roll over and go back to sleep? Blasphemy! You're in the Amazon.

A stay at any of the remote Iquitos or Madre de Dios lodges is not for the faint of heart. You'll need to gear up for a different type of vacation experience. Relaxing and luxuriating it will not be, although some facilities are quite comfortable. Your days will be packed with activities: bird- and wildlife-watching, boat trips, rainforest hikes, visits to indigenous communities, kayaking, and so on. You'll be with guides from the minute you're picked up in Iquitos, Puerto Maldonado, or Cusco. Most lodges hire top-notch guides who know their areas well, and you'll be forever amazed at their ability to spot that camouflaged howler monkey from a hundred paces.

The lodge should provide mosquito netting and sheets or blankets, and some type of lantern for your room. (Don't expect electricity.) But check the lodge's website, or with your tour operator, for a list of what to bring and what the lodge provides. Your required inventory will vary proportionally by just how much you have to rough it. Pack sunscreen, sunglasses, insect repellent, a hat, hiking boots, sandals, light shoes, a waterproof bag, and a flashlight. Also, a light, loose-fitting, long-sleeve shirt and equally loose-fitting long trousers and socks are musts for the evening when the mosquitoes come out. Carry your yellow fever vaccination certificate and prescription for malaria prevention, plus an extra supply of any medicine you might be taking. Bring along antidiarrheal medication, too. You'll need a small day-pack for the numerous guided hikes. Also bring binoculars and a camera, as well as plastic bags to protect your belongings from the rain and humidity. Everything is usually included in the package price, though soft drinks, beer, wine, and cocktails carry a hefty markup.

Few things are more enjoyable at a jungle lodge than dinner at the end of the day. You'll dine family-style around a common table, discussing the day's sightings, comparing notes well into the evening, knowing full well there will be another 5 am knock in the morning.

—By Jeffrey Van Fleet

(36 miles) southwest of Puerto Maldonado ☎ *1/447–8888* ⊕ *www.explorersinn.com* ↻ *30 rooms* ⊙ *All meals.*

$$$$ 🏨 **Hacienda Concepción.** Owned by Inkaterra, Hacienda Concepción
RESORT   is a good option for travelers who want to experience the rain forest in comfort or are short on time. **Pros:** easy to reach; comfortable, screened rooms; near Lago Sandoval; competitively priced. **Cons:** less natural experience than at other lodges. ⓢ *Rooms from: S/730* ⊠ *8 km (5 miles) east of Puerto Maldonado* ☎ *800/442–5042 in U.S. and Canada, 808/101–2224 in U.K., 1/422–6574 in Peru* ⊕ *www.byinkaterra.com/hacienda-concepcion/* ↻ *8 rooms, 12 bungalows* ⊙ *All meals.*

$$$$
RESORT
Fodor's Choice
★

☷ **Heath River Wildlife Center.** The spacious screened bungalows at this InkaNatura-owned lodge are among the most comfortable eco-accommodations in Madre de Dios, and they're ideal for full-blown wildlife fans: in fact, guests frequently see such rare animals as tapirs or jaguars. **Pros:** lots of wildlife; macaw clay lick; nice bungalows. **Cons:** remote. $ *Rooms from: S/995* ⊠ *123 km (76 miles), or 5 hrs by boat, east of Puerto Maldonado* ☎ *1/203–5000* ⊕ *www.inkanatura.com* ⤶ *10 bungalows* ⑩ *All meals.*

$$$$
RESORT
Fodor's Choice
★

☷ **Posada Amazonas.** Since this open-air lodge is surrounded by forest, you may spot birds and monkeys right from your room or the restaurant. **Pros:** lots of wildlife; excellent service; great excursions; massage; lodge benefits local people. **Cons:** noise from neighboring guest rooms. $ *Rooms from: S/975* ⊠ *Tambopata River, 40 km (25 miles) southwest of Puerto Maldonado* ☎ *1/719–6422 or 9935–12265, 877/231–9251 in U.S.* ⊕ *www.perunature.com* ⤶ *30 rooms* ⑩ *All meals.*

$$$$
RESORT
☙

☷ **Refugio Amazonas.** Rooms separated by cane walls in long, thatched buildings, an airy bar and restaurant, and a jungle setting make the Refugio comparable to Posada Amazonas. **Pros:** surrounded by rain forest; children's program; sustainable. **Cons:** no screens; noise audible from other rooms. $ *Rooms from: S/975* ⊠ *Tambopata River, 80 km (50 miles) southwest of Puerto Maldonado* ☎ *1/719–6422 or 9935–12265, 877/231–9251 in U.S.* ⊕ *www.perunature.com* ⤶ *32 rooms* ⑩ *All meals.*

$$$$
RESORT

☷ **Reserva Amazónica.** A 30-minute boat ride down the Madre de Dios River from Puerto Maldonado, this is the region's fanciest and most expensive lodge. **Pros:** easy to get to; excursions included in rates; environmentally friendly. **Cons:** bungalows are close enough to hear neighbors; engine noise from the river annoying; expensive. $ *Rooms from: S/1350* ⊠ *Km 15, Madre de Dios River* ☎ *1/610–0400, 855/409–1456 in U.S., 808/101–2224 in U.K.* ⊕ *www.inkaterra.com* ⤶ *33 rooms, 2 suites* ⑩ *All meals.*

$$$$
RESORT
★

☷ **Sandoval Lake Lodge.** Despite its proximity to Puerto Maldonado, this lodge (owned by InkaNatura Travel) puts you in the midst of Amazonian nature. **Pros:** beautiful location; screened rooms and restaurant; lots of wildlife; sustainable. **Cons:** the boat-hike-boat access isn't for everyone. $ *Rooms from: S/845* ⊠ *14 km (9 miles) east of Puerto Maldonado* ☎ *1/203–5000* ⊕ *www.inkanatura.com* ⤶ *25 rooms* ⑩ *All meals.*

$$$$
RESORT

☷ **Tambopata Ecolodge.** This lodge, about four hours south of Puerto Maldonado on the Tambopata River, has some of the region's most comfortable accommodations. **Pros:** nice rooms; good programs; sustainable. **Cons:** less wildlife than other lodges. $ *Rooms from: S/860* ⊠ *Tambopata River, 70 km (44 miles) southwest of Puerto Maldonado* ☎☎ *84/245–695* ☎ *82/571–397* ⊕ *www.tambopatalodge.com* ⤶ *28 rooms, 6 suites* ⑩ *All meals.*

$$$$
RESORT
Fodor's Choice
★

☷ **Tambopata Research Center.** Eight hours upriver by boat from Puerto Maldonado, in the heart of the Tambopata National Reserve, this rustic lodge is one of the best places in Peru to spot wildlife. **Pros:** deep in the wilderness; lots of wildlife; excellent guides; sustainable. **Cons:** no screens; little privacy. $ *Rooms from: S/1100* ⊠ *Tambopata River,*

7

150 km (93 miles) southwest of Puerto Maldonado ☎ *1/719–6422 or 9935–12265, 877/231–9251 in U.S.* 🌐 *www.perunature.com* 🛏 *18 rooms with shared bath* 🍴 *All meals.*

$$$$ RESORT ★ 🏨 **Wasaí Tambopata Lodge.** This pleasant spot, set deep in the wilderness (it's about a three-hour boat ride up the Tambopata River from Puerto Maldonado), offers comfortable lodgings and lots of wildlife. **Pros:** gorgeous forest; comfortable bungalows; great excursions; sustainable; friendly. **Cons:** original rooms time-worn and not very private. [$] *Rooms from: S/875* ✉ *Tambopata River, 100 km (62 miles) southwest of Puerto Maldonado* ☎ *1/436–8792* 🌐 *www.wasai.com* 🛏 *19 cabins* 🍴 *All meals.*

MANU BIOSPHERE RESERVE

90 km (55 miles) north of Cusco.

GETTING HERE AND AROUND

A Manu excursion is no quick trip. Overland travel from Cusco, the usual embarkation point, takes two days with an overnight in the cloud forest. A charter flight in a twin-engine plane to the small airstrip at Boca Manu could shave that time down to 45 minutes and add a few hundred dollars onto your package price; however, they weren't running at this writing. It is also possible to fly to Puerto Maldonado and travel by land and river to the Manu Wildlife Center, but it's a very long day. Most travelers enter by land and river from Cusco—passing amazing Andean cloud-forest and rain-forest scenery along the way—and depart by river and land to Puerto Maldonado, where they catch a flight to Cusco or Lima. The logistics of travel to this remote part of the Amazon mean you need a minimum of five days for your excursion.

★ **Manu Biosphere Reserve.** Readers of the British children's series *A Bear Called Paddington* know that the title character "came from darkest Peru." The stereotype is quite outdated, of course, but the Manu Biosphere Reserve, which has been called "the most biodiverse park on earth," will conjure up the jungliest Tarzan-movie images you can imagine. And the reserve really does count the Andean spectacled bear, South America's only ursid, and the animal on which Paddington was based, among its 200 mammals.

Straddling the boundary of the Madre de Dios and Cusco provinces, this reserve is Peru's second largest protected area. Manu encompasses more than 4½ million acres of pristine primary tropical-forest wilderness, ranging in altitude from 3,450 meters (12,000 feet) down through cloud forests and into seemingly endless lowland tropical rain forests at 300 meters (less than 1,000 feet). This geographical variety shelters a stunning range of wildlife—and a near total absence of humans and hunting means that the animals here are less skittish and more open to observation. **TIP→ The reserve's 13 monkey species scrutinize visitors with the same curiosity they elicit.** White caimans sun themselves lazily on sandy riverbanks, whereas the larger black ones lurk in the oxbow lakes. With luck, you'll see tapirs at the world's largest tapir collpa. Giant river otters and elusive big cats (jaguars and ocelots among them) sometimes make fleeting appearances. But it's the avian life that has made Manu world famous. The area counts more than 1,000 bird species, fully one-ninth of those known. Some 500 species have been spotted at the Pantiacolla Lodge alone. Birds include macaws, toucans, roseate spoonbills, and 1½-meter- (5-foot-) tall wood storks.

Manu, a UNESCO World Heritage Site, is divided into three distinct zones. The smallest is the so-called "cultural zone" (Zone C), with several indigenous groups and the majority of the jungle lodges. Access is permitted to all—even independent travelers, in theory—though vast distances make this unrealistic for all but the most intrepid. About three times the size of the cultural zone, Manu's "reserve zone" (Zone B) is uninhabited but contains the Manu Lodge. Access is by permit only, and you must be accompanied by a guide from one of the 10 agencies authorized to take people into the area. The western 80% of Manu is designated a national park (Zone A). Authorized researchers and indigenous peoples who reside there are permitted in this zone; visitors may not enter.

WHERE TO STAY

$$$$
RESORT
★
Cock of the Rock Lodge. This lodge stands at the edge of the cloud forest and affords an amazing view of the lush Kosñipata River Valley, in Manu's cultural zone. **Pros:** great bird-watching; gorgeous setting; pleasant climate. **Cons:** not cheap; a seven-hour drive from Cusco. $ *Rooms from: S/1650* ✉ *177 km (110 miles) northeast of Cusco* ☎ *1/203–5000* ⊕ *www.inkanatura.com* ⤳ *12 bungalows* ⦿ *All meals.*

$$$$
RESORT
Manu Cloud Forest Lodge. High in the cloud forest of Manu's cultural zone, this lodge overlooks the rushing Río Unión in an exuberant forest busy with hummingbirds. **Pros:** great scenery; birds. **Cons:** very rustic; reaching it requires a seven-hour drive from Cusco. $ *Rooms from: S/1557* ✉ *About 177 km (110 miles) north of Cusco* ☎ *84/252–721* ⊕ *www.manuperu.com* ⤳ *8 rooms, 4 cabins* ⦿ *All meals.*

$$$$
RESORT
★
Manu Wildlife Center. As its name suggests, the Manu Wildlife Center is a great place for wildlife viewing: after all, this lodge is close to macaw and tapir collpas, and it has 48 km (30 miles) of trails that thread through a forest adjacent to Manu National Park. **Pros:** amazing wildlife; knowledgeable guides. **Cons:** rustic; remote, but not cheap. $ *Rooms from: S/1700* ✉ *Two days by land and river from Cusco, 7 hrs to Puerto Maldonado.* ☎ *84/225–990 or 1/203–5000* ⊕ *www.manuwildlifecenter.com, www.inkanatura.com* ⤳ *22 bungalows* ⦿ *All meals.*

$$$$
RESORT
Pantiacolla Lodge. Named for the mountain range that towers over it, the Pantiacolla Lodge sits in a 900-hectare (2,223-acre) nature reserve in Manu's cultural zone that boasts 600-odd bird species plus an array of mammals that ranges from squirrel monkeys to peccaries. **Pros:** less expensive than competition; great bird-watching. **Cons:** quite rustic; a two-day trip from Cusco. $ *Rooms from: S/940* ✉ *290 km (180 miles) northeast of Cusco* ☎ *84/238–323* ⊕ *www.pantiacolla.com* ⤳ *11 rooms, 8 with shared bath* ⦿ *All meals.*

$$$$
RESORT
Posada San Pedro Lodge. Nestled in the cloud forest of the Manu Biosphere Reserve's cultural zone, midway between Cusco and Boca Manu, this small lodge offers earthy accommodations amid extraordinary scenery and birdlife. **Pros:** great bird-watching. **Cons:** rustic; seven

7

hours from Cusco. [$] *Rooms from: S/848* ✉ *78 km (110 miles) north of Cusco* ☎ *84/238–323* 🌐 *www.pantiacolla.com* 🛏 *8 rooms without bath* 🍴 *All meals.*

$$$$ RESORT 🏨 **Romero Rainforest Lodge.** Offering the newest and most comfortable accommodations in Manu, the Romero Rainforest Lodge is located on the Manu River, inside the National Park's reserved zone. **Pros:** nice rooms; stellar wildlife. **Cons:** takes two full days to reach from Cusco. [$] *Rooms from: S/1700* ✉ *One hr north of Boca Manu, 2 days from Cusco* ☎ *84/225–990* 🌐 *www.manuexpeditions.com* 🛏 *8 rooms* 🍴 *All meals.*

$$$$ RESORT 🏨 **Yine Lodge.** This collection of thatched bungalows at the confluence of the Manu and Madre de Dios Rivers is the result of a project that the Pantiacolla tour company has embarked upon with a Yine community. [$] *Rooms from: S/1180* ✉ *Boca Manu, 2-day trip from Cusco, 8 hrs from Puerto Maldonado* ☎ *84/23800323* 🌐 *www.pantiacolla.com* 🛏 *6 bungalows* 🍴 *All meals.*

IQUITOS AND ENVIRONS

Founded by Jesuit priests in the 1500s, Iquitos was once called the "Pearl of the Amazon." It isn't quite that lustrous today, but it's still a pleasant, friendly town that provides access to the Amazon River, rain-forest wildlife, and various indigenous cultures. Although most travelers fly here specifically for an excursion into the surrounding rain forest, Iquitos has sites nearby that can be visited in a few hours or a day, and deserves at least a night. The city itself may grow on you as you become accustomed to the humid climate and relaxed, easy ways of its citizens. Its revamped Malecón (riverwalk) is a popular place for an evening stroll, and you can enjoy a meal of river fish while floating on that waterway.

GETTING HERE AND AROUND

The best way to travel around the Iquitos area is by boat: hundreds of vessels come and go each day, from tiny dugout canoes bound for jungle enclaves to seagoing ships that travel all the way through Brazil to the Atlantic Ocean.

Various companies run cruises out of Iquitos or the nearby town of Nauta, providing comfortable access to the province's protected areas and indigenous villages. Nature lodges transport guests in swift launches with outboard engines and canvas tops to protect you from the sun and rain.

BORDER CROSSINGS Various companies offer speedboat service to the Brazilian and Colombian borders. It's a 9- to 10-hour boat ride to the border town of Santa Rosa, across the river from Leticia (Colombia) and Tabatinga (Brazil). The one-way trip costs only $80 USD. Each company runs twice a week, so boats depart every day; all the ticket offices are on the 300 block of Calle Raymondi, three blocks north of the Plaza de Armas. Just go there and buy a ticket from the company that departs on the day you want to travel.

American citizens don't need a visa to enter Colombia, but they do need one for Brazil.

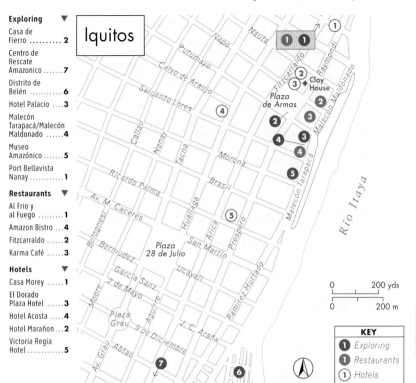

KEY

❶ Exploring

❶ Restaurants

① Hotels

IQUITOS

1,150 km (713 miles) northeast of Lima.

A sultry port town on the Río Amazonas, Iquitos is quite probably the world's largest city that cannot be reached by road. The city has nearly 500,000 inhabitants and is the capital of the vast Loreto department. The area around Iquitos was first inhabited by small, independent Amazonian tribes. In the 1500s Jesuit missionaries began adventuring in the area, trying to Christianize the local population, but the city wasn't officially founded until 1757.

Iquitos saw unprecedented growth and opulence during the rubber boom, but became an Amazonian backwater overnight when the boom went bust. The economy slouched along, barely sustaining itself with logging, exotic-animal exports, and Brazil-nut harvesting. Then in the early 1970s petroleum was discovered. The black gold, along with eco-tourism and logging, have since become the backbone of the region's economy, though drug running also provides significant income.

The city's historic center stretches along a lagoon formed by the Río Itaya, near the confluence of the Río Nanay and the Río Amazonas. Most of its historic buildings, hotels, restaurants, and banks are within blocks of the Plaza de Armas, the main square, and the nearby Malecón Maldonado riverwalk.

GETTING HERE AND AROUND

The most common mode of transportation in Iquitos is the mototaxi, a three-wheeled motorcycle with a canvas top. Service in town costs around S/2, whereas a trip to the outskirts costs around S/10 an hour. Always negotiate the price beforehand. It should cost S/4 to Port Bellavista Nanay, where you can hire a boat to the butterfly farm, serpentarium, and a Yagua or Bora Indian village, although those places are best visited with a guide.

SAFETY AND PRECAUTIONS

While violent crime is not common in Iquitos, pickpocketing and other petty thefts are—especially in and around the neighborhood of Belén. Use common sense when you're out and about. Using mosquito repellent is recommended, too.

ESSENTIALS

Currency BBVA Banco Continental ⊠ *Jr. Putumayo 253* ☎ *65/231–038.* **Banco de Crédito** ⊠ *Av. Putumayo at Jr. Prospero* ☎ *65/234–501.* **Scotiabank** ⊠ *Av. Próspero 278* ☎ *65/232–350.*

Mail Serpost Iquitos ⊠ *Av. Arica 402* ☎ *65/231–915.*

Medical Clínica Adventista Ana Stahl ⊠ *Av. de la Marina 285* ☎ *65/252–528.*

Taxi Taxi Aeropuerto ⊠ *Iquitos* ☎ *65/241–284.* **Taxi Flores** ⊠ *Iquitos* ☎ *65/232–014.*

Tour Operators Dawn on the Amazon ⊠ *Malecón Maldonado 185* ☎ *65/223–730* ⊕ *www.dawnontheamazon.com.* **Grupo Dorado Tours** ⊠ *El Dorado Plaza Hotel, Napo 252* ☎ *65/222–555* ⊕ *www.grupo-dorado.com.*

Visitor Information iPerú ⊠ *Airport* ☎ *65/260–251.* **Tourist Information Office** ⊠ *Napo 161* ☎ *65/236–144.*

EXPLORING

Casa de Fierro. The most interesting structure on the Plaza de Armas is this "Iron House," designed by Gustave Eiffel (of Eiffel Tower fame) and forged in Belgium. A wealthy rubber baron bought the house at the Parisian International Exposition of 1889 and had it shipped to Iquitos, where it was reassembled. The building now houses a pharmacy and a restaurant on the second floor. ⊠ *Putumayo at Jr. Prospero* 🖃 *Free* ☉ *Daily 8 am–midnight.*

Centro de Rescate Amazónico. At this animal rescue center, a short trip south of town, you can get a close look at one of the region's rarest, and most threatened species: the manatee. Despite being protected by Peruvian law, manatees continue to be hunted for their meat. The Centro, a collaboration of the Dallas World Aquarium and Zoo and two Peruvian institutions, raises orphaned manatees and nurses injured ones back to health for eventual release in the wild. It also serves as an environmental education center to raise awareness of the gentle creature's plight. ⊠ *Km 4.6 Carretera Iquitos-Nauta* ☎ *965–834–685* ⊕ *www.acobia-dwazoo.com* 🖃 *By donation* ☉ *Mon.–Sat. 9–3, Sun. noon–3.*

Distrito de Belén (*Belén District*). Iquitos's most fascinating neighborhood lies along the Itaya River. This market sells goods from the area's jungle villages, and you'll find sundry items from love potions to fresh *suri* (palm-tree worms). Although it's not the cleanest or sweetest-smelling spot, it is worth a visit. Near the center of the market is a port where you can head out in a dugout through the floating Belén District. ■ TIP→ This slummy area is often called the Venice of the Amazon (a diplomatic euphemism), but navigating between its floating homes is really a kick. The houses are built on balsa rafts. Most of the year they float placidly on the Amazon; however, during the low-water season (June–November) they sit in the mud and can attract disease-carrying mosquitoes. The area should be avoided then. During high-water season (December–May), you can visit the area on a half-day tour with any Iquitos tour operator. Do not explore Belén on your own—muggings have been reported—and it should be avoided from dusk to dawn. Be wary of pickpockets and bag slashers in and around the market. Stay alert, access your cash discreetly when you need it, and keep your valuables close. ✉ *East end of Jr. 9 de Diciembre.*

Hotel Palacio. Iquitos enjoyed its heyday as a port during the rubber boom a century ago. Some of the wealth of that time can still be detected in the imported *azulejos* (tiles) that cover many of its older buildings. A notable example is the former Hotel Palacio, on the Malecón Tarapacá. The hotel was the city's best when it opened for business in 1908. It has since been converted into an army barracks and is now looking a little worn, but remains a stately building nonetheless. ✉ *Putumayo and Malecón Tarapacá* ☉ *Daily.*

Malecón Tarapacá (aka Malecón Maldonado). During high-water season, this pleasant waterfront walk between Brasil and Pevas is a good place for an evening stroll. You'll find some lovely rubber-boom-era architecture here, and there are a few bars and restaurants on the Malecón's northern end, near the Plaza de Armas. Its southern end gets less traffic, so stick to the three northernmost blocks after 8 pm.

Museo Amazónico. This museum is dedicated to the region's rich indigenous culture, with a few faded paintings and "bronzed" fiberglass statues of local tribespeople made by plastering real people. One room is dedicated to work by local artists. The building itself, a former town hall constructed in 1863, is more attractive than the exhibits thanks to its ornately carved hardwoods and courtyard gardens. ✉ *Malecón Tarapacá 386* ☎ *65/234-031* ✆ *Free* ☉ *Mon.–Sat. 9–1, 2–5.*

NEED A BREAK?

Helados Giornata. The equatorial heat provides ample motivation to pop into Helados Giornata, an ice-cream parlor on the Plaza de Armas that specializes in sherbets made from rain-forest fruits. Try the refreshing *camu camu*, tangy *arazá*, or the sweeter *aguaje* and *ungurahui*. ✉ *Jr. Prospero 139.*

Port Bellavista Nanay. About 3 km (1½ miles) north of downtown Iquitos, at the end of Avenida La Marina, is this muddy beehive of activity with a large open-air market, dilapidated shops selling everything from fruit to moonshine, boats of all shapes and sizes, and seedy bars perched on wooden posts. You can hire a boat to take you to the Bora or Yagua Indian villages, near San Andrés, or the Pilpintuwasi Butterfly Farm. Bringing a donation of school supplies (pencils, crayons, and notebooks) is a kind gesture that will be appreciated by the Boras and Yaguas.

Pilpintuwasi Butterfly Farm. A 20-minute boat ride and a short walk from the port of Bellavista Nany will bring you to Pilpintuwasi Butterfly Farm, which raises some 42 butterfly species and also serves as home for wild animals that have been confiscated from hunters and wildlife traffickers. It thus has macaws, monkeys, a jaguar, a tapir, and other animals. During the dry season you'll need to walk along a forest path for 15 minutes to get there. It's best to go with a guide. A private boat to and from Padre Cocha should cost 30 soles. ⊠ *Near village of Padre Cocha on Nanay River, 20-min. boat trip from Bellavista Nanay* 🕾 *965–932–999* ⊕ *www.amazonanimalorphanage.org* 🖃 *S/20 without transportation* ⊘ *Tues.–Sun. 9:30–4, tours start at 9:30, 11, 12:30, 1:30, and 2:45*

WHERE TO EAT

$$
PERUVIAN
Fodor's Choice
★
×**Al Frío y al Fuego.** Step through the unassuming doorway on Avenida La Marina, descend the long stairway to the dock, and a boat will ferry you to this floating restaurant. At first glance, the thatched structure on a balsa-log raft belies the fine service and excellent Peruvian fusion cuisine that await you. The menu offers innovations on traditional dishes using local ingredients, from *tiradito* (marinated fish strips) in a *cocona* (jungle fruit) sauce to *pescado a la Loretana*, a tender filet of *doncella* (a river fish) in a sweet chili cream sauce served with *chonta* (shredded palm heart) and *tacacho* (fried plantain-and-pork dumplings). If fish isn't your thing, try the steak with cassava gnocchi and onion marmalade. ∎**TIP**➜ The restaurant's floating swimming pool is a great place to spend an afternoon (bring a bathing suit and towel), whereas the view of the city lights makes it equally appealing at night. $ *Average main: S/38* ⊠ *Av. La Marina 134-B, next to "Embarcadero El Huequito"* 🕾 *965–607–474* ⚓ *Reservations essential* ⊘ *Closed Mon. No dinner Sun.*

$
BISTRO
★
×**Amazon Bistro.** This restored rubber-boom-era mansion on the Malecón is well worth a visit—if not for a meal, at least for a drink or much-needed espresso. It has river-view tables on the sidewalk and more inside, either in the main dining room or a wooden mezzanine. The long, French-inspired menu features both simple bistro fare (think escargots or local fish sautéed in butter) as well as more complex favorites such as chicken cordon bleu and tenderloin Chateaubriand. If you're looking for a light meal, the bistro also serves salads, sandwiches, and toasts with toppings, including the classic *croque-monsieur* (ham and cheese). $ *Average main: S/29* ⊠ *Malecón Tarapacá 268* 🕾 *65/600–785.*

$
PERUVIAN
×**Fitzcarraldo.** Conveniently located on the Malecón Maldonado, one block from the Plaza de Armas, this restaurant specializes in Amazonian fish dishes like *dorado* (a white fish) in a *camu camu* (jungle fruit) sauce. Traditional regional specialties, such as the *cecina con tacacho* (a smoked pork steak with fried plantain balls) are also available. Start you meal off with a frothy *caipirinha* (a Brazilian drink made with lime,

sugar, and the sugarcane liquor *cachaça*). You can eat in an air-conditioned room or under ceiling fans in the front dining room. $ *Average main: S/30* ⊠ *Napo and Malecón Maldonado* ☎ 65/236–536.

$ ✕**Karma Café.** This spot serves a mix of international dishes; and free
ECLECTIC Wi-Fi, comfy furnishings (couches supplement the standard wooden chairs), plus a convenient location between the Plaza de Armas and the Malecón make it a popular place for travelers to hang out. The eclectic food selection includes plenty of vegetarian options, along with Thai curries, falafel, river fish, and an array of salads and sandwiches. Great fruit smoothies are an added bonus. At night the eatery continues to serve food but, with the lights dimmed and the music cranked up, transforms itself into more of a lounge. $ *Average main: S/23* ⊠ *Calle Napo 138* ☎ 65/600–576 ▭ *No credit cards* ☾ *Closed Mon.*

WHERE TO STAY

$ 🏨**Casa Morey.** Built by rubber baron Luis Morey in 1913, this restored
B&B/INN mansion is Iquitos's only historic hotel. **Pros:** lovely building; spacious
Fodor'sChoice rooms; friendly staff. **Cons:** restoration could be better. $ *Rooms*
★ *from: S/220* ⊠ *Calle Loreto 200, Plaza Ramón Castilla* ☎ 65/231–913 ⊕ *www.casamorey.com* ↬ *14 rooms* ⏺ *Breakfast.*

$$$$ 🏨**El Dorado Plaza Hotel.** This contemporary hotel is in the heart of Iqui-
HOTEL tos, on the Plaza de Armas, and rooms in front put your fingers on the
★ city's mototaxi pulse. **Pros:** modern; great location; friendly staff; airport shuttle. **Cons:** expensive; some street noise. $ *Rooms from: S/580* ⊠ *Napo 252* ☎ 65/222–555 ⊕ *www.grupo-dorado.com* ↬ *56 rooms, 9 suites* ⏺ *Breakfast.*

$ 🏨**Hotel Acosta.** Nothing fancy here: just a straightforward, decent hotel
HOTEL a couple blocks from the Plaza de Armas. **Pros:** clean rooms; free Wi-Fi and airport transfers. **Cons:** on a busy corner; bland rooms. $ *Rooms from: S/180* ⊠ *Huallaga 254* ☎ 65/321–761 ⊕ *www.hotelacosta.com* ↬ *20 rooms* ⏺ *Breakfast.*

$ 🏨**Hotel Marañon.** Although this hotel is ultraclean and relatively inex-
HOTEL pensive, it has a slightly institutional feel that is due mostly to its tile floors, high ceilings, and unadorned walls. **Pros:** good value; very clean; central location. **Cons:** not the character choice. $ *Rooms from: S/150* ⊠ *Nauta 289, at Fitzcarrald* ☎ 65/242–673 ⊕ *www.hotelmaranon.com* ↬ *38 rooms* ⏺ *Breakfast.*

$$ 🏨**Victoria Regia Hotel.** Named for the giant lily pads found in the region's
HOTEL lakes, this simple hotel has comfortable, carpeted guest rooms, and a fairly central location. **Pros:** good beds; competitive rates; pool; restaurant; Wi-Fi. **Cons:** rooms are on the small side; those in back are a bit dark. $ *Rooms from: S/270* ⊠ *Ricardo Palma 252* ☎☎ 65/231–983 ⊕ *www.victoriaregiahotel.com* ↬ *58 rooms, 6 suites* ⏺ *Breakfast.*

NIGHTLIFE AND THE ARTS

Maybe it's the proximity to the jungle and its innate, inexplicable sensuality. Whatever the reason, Iquitos heats up after dark, and the dancing and bar scene is quite good. You should begin your night with a drink at one of the bars or restaurants along the Malecón Maldonado.

Arandú Bar. Arandú Bar is the most popular bar on the Malecón, with pop and rock music blasting, river views and wild interior murals. ⊠ *Malecón Maldonado 113* ☎ 65/243–434.

CLOSE UP

Cruising the Amazon

The most comfortable way to explore the Amazon and its tributaries is on a river cruise, most of which depart from the port of Nauta, a one-hour drive south from Iquitos. Those cruises head up the Amazon River and its two main tributaries, the Ucayali and Marañón, to take passengers deep into the Reserva Nacional Pacaya Samiria. Because of its distance from Iquitos, Pacaya Samiria is one of the best areas in the region to see wildlife, but it is also one the most difficult to reach. Cruise boats travel to a different area each day, where passengers board smaller vessels to explore narrow rivers, oxbow lakes, and flooded forests. The daily excursions, led by expert guides, may also include forest hikes, dolphin-watching, or a visit to an indigenous village.

River cruises can cost twice as much as a stay in a nature lodge, but they generally offer a higher level of comfort and service, and allow you to visit more areas than you could from a lodge. Delfin operates the most exclusive boat, the *Delfin I*, which has four spacious cabins complete with private balconies. The company's larger *Delfin II* sleeps 28 passengers, but provides the same high level of service. Aqua Expeditions has two comparable boats: the *Aqua*, which sleeps 24 passengers, and the *Aria*, which accommodates 32. Both Delfin and Aqua Expeditions offer three- and four-night cruises, and Aqua Expeditions passengers can combine two tours for a seven-day cruise. International Expeditions runs seven-day cruises on ships with smaller cabins that go farther upriver and cost considerably less than the others. Green Tracks, a smaller company also runs relatively inexpensive seven-day cruises in renovated steamships that forgo luxury but prioritize exposure to nature. No matter which company you choose, an Amazon cruise is sure to be an unforgettable experience.

7

Discotec Noa. Discotec Noa, the biggest and liveliest dance club in town, is open Thursday to Saturday till the wee hours. ⊠ *Fitzcarraldo 298* ☎ *65/222–555.*

La Noche. With tables on the sidewalk and a second-floor balcony, La Noche is a good spot for a quiet drink on the riverwalk. ⊠ *Malecón Maldonado 177* ☎ *65/222–373.*

Texto. This two-level, wood-panel bar, located two blocks north of the Plaza de Armas, lures a young crowd with good music and low prices. It's one of Iquito's most popular watering holes. ⊠ *Raymondi 382* ☎ *65/242–942.*

SHOPPING

Street vendors display their wares on the Malecón Maldonado at night; and around the corner, on the first block of Nauta, by day. Look for pottery, hand-painted cloth from Pucallpa, and jungle items such as preserved piranhas, seed necklaces, fish and animal teeth, blowguns, spears, and balsawood parrots. The **Mercado Belén** is a riot of colors and smells where merchants sell everything from love potions to souvenirs made from snake and caiman skins and toucan beaks, which you should definitely not buy. Beware of pickpockets in that close-quartered market.

Boa Arts. T-shirts emblazoned with images of the region's wildlife and native peoples, painted by local artists, as well as varied handicrafts are on sale around the corner from the Malecón Maldonado at Boa Arts. ⊠ *Putumayo 124* ☎ *65/234–600.*

Casa del Artesano Amazónico. Handicrafts from several of the province's indigenous cultures can be found in the souvenir stands at the Casa del Artesano Amazónico. ⊠ *Malecón Maldonado 167.*

Centro Artesanal Turístico Anaconda. This collection of handicraft stalls on a wooden platform perched over the water is worth wandering through even if you don't want to buy anything. It's down the stairs from the Malecón Maldonado, at the end of Jirón Napo. ⊠ *Malecón Maldonado s/n, down stairway.*

Jirón Nauta. The first block of this street, at the north end of the Malecón Maldonado, is lined with several dozen wooden stalls where vendors (mostly indigenous women) sell their handicrafts. ⊠ *100 block of Jr. Nauta.*

THE PERUVIAN AMAZON

The Amazon Basin is the world's most diverse ecosystem. The numbers of cataloged plant and animal species are astronomical, and scientists are discovering new ones all the time. More than 25,000 classified species of plants are in the Peruvian Amazon (and 80,000 in the entire Amazon Basin), including the 2-meter-wide (6-foot-wide) Victoria Regia water lilies. Scientists have cataloged more than 4,000 species of butterfly and more than 2,000 of fish—a more diverse aquatic life than that of the Atlantic Ocean. Scientists estimate that the world's tropical forests, while comprising only 6% of the Earth's landmass, may hold up to 75% of the planet's plant and animal species. This land is also the largest natural pharmacy in the world: one-fourth of all modern medicines have botanical origins in tropical forests.

Most mammals are nocturnal and difficult to spot, and hunting has made them wary of humans. ▥ TIP➜ You're likely to see an array of birds, butterflies, and monkeys, and if you're lucky you'll spot bufeos (freshwater dolphins) or caimans along the Amazon tributaries.

It's interesting and worthwhile to visit the small villages of indigenous people. When the boat stops at these settlements you'll usually find half the village waiting to sell you handicrafts.

The best way to visit the area is on a prearranged tour with one of the many jungle lodges or cruise boats. All have highly trained naturalist guides. Among the activities offered are nature walks, birding tours, nighttime canoe outings, fishing trips, and forays into indigenous villages. There are also a couple of canopy walkways that will take you into the seldom-explored rain-forest canopy.

GETTING HERE AND AROUND

With the exception of Reserva Nacional Allpahuayo Mishana, which is a 40-minute drive from town, you'll reach the Amazon's sites by water. You basically have two options: travel to a nature lodge in one of that company's boats or take a cruise. The cruises are more expensive, but

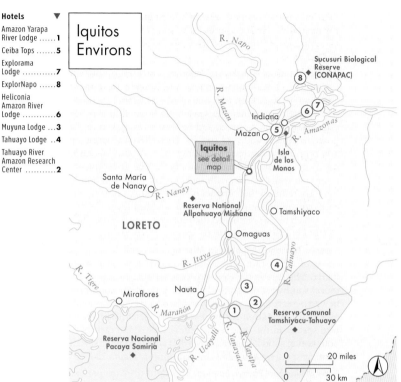

quite comfortable, and they allow you to explore different protected areas on daily excursions in small boats. Otherwise, you can book a stay at a nature lodge, in which case a guide will meet you at the airport, take you to the port, and accompany you to the lodge in a small, fast boat.

ESSENTIALS

Tour Operators Amazonia Expeditions ☎ *800/262–9669* ⊕ *www.perujungle. com.* **Aqua Expeditions** ☎ *866/603–3687 in U.S. and Canada, 1/434–5544* ⊕ *www.aquaexpeditions.com.* **Dawn on the Amazon** ✉ *Malecón Maldonado 185, Iquitos* ☎ *65/223–730* ⊕ *www.dawnontheamazon.com.* **Delfin** ☎ *1/719– 0998* ⊕ *www.delfinamazoncruises.com.* **Explorama Tours** ☎ *65/252–530, 800/707–5275 in U.S. and Canada* ⊕ *www.explorama.com.* **Green Tracks** ☎ *970/884–6107* ⊕ *www.greentracks.com.* **International Expeditions** ☎ *800/234–9620 in U.S.*

EXPLORING

Isla de los Monos. An easy reserve to visit—and a popular spot for explorers of all ages—Isla de los Monos is Peru's "Monkey Island." The 250-hectare (618-acre) island is a private reserve where monkeys that were once held in captivity, or were confiscated from animal traffickers, now live in a natural environment. It's home to eight monkey species, as well as sloths, parrots, macaws and other wildlife. Since most of the animals are former pets, you can get very close to them; maybe closer than you want. It's best to visit the island on a tour from Iquitos of the nearby Ceiba Tops hotel. ⊠ *30 km (18 miles) northeast of Iquitos near Varadero* ☏ *065/233–801* ⊕ *www.monkeyislandperu.com* ✆ *S/20* ⊙ *Daily 6–6.*

Reserva Comunal Tamshiyacu-Tahuayo. Covering approximately 4,144 square km (1,600 square miles), the Reserva Comunal Tamshiyacu-Tahuayo is larger than the state of Rhode Island. It comprises an array of ecosystems that includes seasonally flooded forests, terra firma forests, *aguaje* palm swamps, and oxbow lakes. Taken together, these are home to almost 600 bird species: cocoi herons, wire-tailed manakins, and blue and gold macaws among them. It also has rare primate species, such as saki and uakari monkeys. The government manages the reserve in coordination with local people (they still hunt and fish here, but have reduced their impact on its wildlife). Local eco-lodges provide employment and support education and healthcare in those communities, which has strengthened their interest in protecting the environment. ⊠ *100 km (60 miles) south of Iquitos* ☏ *No phone.*

Reserva Nacional Allpahuayo Mishana. Around Iquitos there are large tracts of virgin rain forest and several reserves worth visiting. Allpahuayo Mishana is the easiest protected area to get to, just 25 km (15 miles) southwest of Iquitos by road. One of the country's smallest and newest reserves, it is not a great place to see large animals, but it is an excellent destination for bird-watchers. Scientists have identified 475 bird species in the reserve, including such avian rarities as the pompadour cotinga and Zimmer's antbird. It is also home to several endangered monkey species. ⊠ *Km 25 Carretera Iquitos-Nauta* ✆ *Free* ⊙ *Daily 6–6.*

Reserva Nacional Pacaya Samiria. This hard-to-reach park sits at the confluence of the Marañón and Ucayali rivers. The reserve is Peru's largest, encompassing more than 20,000 square km (7,722 square miles)—which makes it about the size of El Salvador. The landscape is diverse (picture seasonally flooded forests, oxbow lakes, and vast expanses of lowland rain forest). So are the animals who inhabit it, including pink river dolphins, black caimans, various kinds of monkeys, and more than 500 bird species. As with many South American reserves, there are people living in Pacaya Samiria, around 40,000 according to recent estimates. Park rangers try to balance the needs of these local communities with efforts to protect the environment, and request a minimal S/120 entrance fee to help pay for that work. The park can only be reached by boat, but lies relatively close to the port of Nauta, 100 km (60 miles) south of Iquitos by road. ⊠ *Confluence of Marañón and Ucayali rivers* ⊙ *Daily 6–6.*

Sucusuri Biological Reserve (CONAPAC). This smaller private rain-forest reserve is northeast of Iquitos, near the confluence of the Napo and Amazon rivers. CONAPAC (the Peruvian Amazon Conservation Organization) manages the 1,000-square-km (386-square-miles) multiuse property, known as the Sucusuri Biological Reserve, which can be explored from the ExploNapo lodge. ⊠ *Near confluence of Napo and Amazon rivers, 70 km (43 miles) downriver from Iquitos* ☏ *065/252–530* ⊕ *www.explorama.com* ✆ *Free* ⊙ *Daily.*

WHERE TO STAY

Rates for the rain-forest lodges near Iquitos are high, but they include transportation, meals, and guided excursions. Transportation to the lodges is either by *palmcaris* (large wooden boats with thatched roofs) or speedboats. Three lodges—Ceiba Tops, Explorama Lodge, and ExplorNapo—are owned and operated by Explorama Tours, whereas two—the Tahuayo Lodge and Tahuayo River Amazon Research Center—are owned by Amazonia Expeditions.

$$$$
RESORT
Amazon Yarapa River Lodge. With solar power, a composting program, even a biology lab used by Cornell University, this place is at the forefront of sustainable tourism. **Pros:** in the jungle; good guides; good food. **Cons:** rustic. *Rooms from: S/1440 ⊠ Yarapa River, 150 km (93 miles) southwest of Iquitos ☎ 65/223–320 or 965/931–172, 315/952–6760 in U.S. ⊕ www.yarapa.com ⤥ 16 rooms with shared bath, 8 rooms with private bath ⓘ All meals.*

$$$$
RESORT
★
Ceiba Tops. The most comfortable accommodations of any Amazon eco-lodge are found 45 minutes downriver from Iquitos. **Pros:** amenities in the jungle; great river views; easy to reach. **Cons:** less wildlife than other lodges. *Rooms from: S/1100 ⊠ On Amazon River, 40 km (25 miles) east of Iquitos ☎ 65/252–530, 800/707–5275 in U.S. ⊕ www. explorama.com ⤥ 72 rooms, 3 suites ⓘ All meals.*

$$$$
RESORT
Explorama Lodge. Built in 1964, this is one of Peru's original nature lodges, and it still provides rustic accommodations and access to a private rain-forest reserve. **Pros:** in the jungle; good guides. **Cons:** very rustic; limited wildlife. *Rooms from: S/1000 ⊠ 80 km (50 miles) east of Iquitos ☎ 65/252–530, 800/707–5275 in U.S. ⊕ www.explorama. com ⤥ 55 rooms ⓘ All meals.*

$$$$
RESORT
ExplorNapo Lodge. This remote lodge is at the edge of the CONAPAC Sucusari Biological Reserve, a vast protected forest on the Napo River, 1½ hours by boat from the Explorama Lodge. **Pros:** wildlife; in the jungle. **Cons:** very rustic; pricey. *Rooms from: S/1280 ⊠ On Napo River, 160 km (100 miles) east of Iquitos ☎ 65/252–530, 800/707–5275 in U.S. ⊕ www.explorama.com ⤥ 30 rooms with shared bath ⓘ All meals.*

$$$$
RESORT
Heliconia Amazon River Lodge. An hour and a half down the Amazon River from Iquitos, the Heliconia has some of the nicest facilities on the river. **Pros:** comfortable rooms; pool; Amazon River views. **Cons:** less wildlife than other lodges. *Rooms from: S/850 ⊠ 80 km (50 miles) east of Iquitos ☎ 1/421–9195 or 65/231–983 ⊕ www. amazonriverexpeditions.com ⤥ 21 rooms ⓘ All meals.*

$$$$
RESORT
Fodor's Choice
★
Muyuna Lodge. You must go 140 km (84 miles) up the Amazon and Yanayacu rivers to reach the Muyuna Lodge, poised at the edge of a seasonally-flooded forest; but on arrival you can bed down in some of the nicest accommodations available at any eco-lodge in this region. **Pros:** comfortable bungalows; varied excursions; abundant wildlife; good guides. **Cons:** remote. *Rooms from: S/1080 ⊠ San Juan de Yanayacu, 140 km (87 miles) southwest of Iquitos ☎ 65/242–858 or 965/721–221 ⊕ www.muyuna.com ⤥ 17 cabins ⓘ All meals.*

7

$$$$ RESORT Fodor's Choice ★ 🏨 **Tahuayo Lodge.** This network of thatched buildings perched between the Tahuayo River and a seasonally flooded forest lies just outside the Reserva Comunal Tamshiyacu-Tahuayo. **Pros:** personalized tours; responsible tourism; good food; laundry service; Wi-Fi. **Cons:** you may hear your neighbors. [$] *Rooms from: S/960* ✉ *Río Tahuayo, 145 km (90 miles) south of Iquitos* ☎ *800/262–9669 in U.S., 65/242–792 in Peru* 🌐 *www.perujungle.com* 🛏 *15 rooms, 9 with private bath* 🍴 *All meals.*

$$$$ RESORT ★ 🏨 **Tahuayo River Amazon Research Center.** Staying at this rustic lodge inside the Reserva Comunal Tamshiyacu-Tahuayo means almost constant exposure to tropical nature. **Pros:** deep in the forest; peaceful; lots of wildlife; good food; great guides. **Cons:** not much privacy. [$] *Rooms from: S/960* ✉ *Río Tahuayo, 170 km (106 miles) south of Iquitos* ☎ *800/262–9669 in U.S., 65/242–792 in Peru* 🌐 *www.perujungle.com* 🛏 *8 rooms with shared bath* 🍴 *All meals.*

The Central Highlands

WORD OF MOUTH

"[Huancayo] was quite enjoyable and I managed a visit to the market and had arroz zambito (world's best rice pudding) with a bit of mazzamora morada—2 soles! I did take train both ways, spectacular scenery and fascinating maneuvers."

—mlgb

WELCOME TO
THE CENTRAL HIGHLANDS

TOP REASONS
TO GO

★ **Handicrafts:** Ayacucho has *retablos*—three-dimensional scenes of religious and historical events. Quinua has ceramic workshops. The Mantaro Valley has Mates Burilados, silver filigree, and alpaca textiles.

★ **Highland Cuisine:** Enjoy the sublime delights of freshly caught trout, *pachamanca* (herb-roasted meats, potatoes, and vegetables cooked in an earthen oven), and *papa a la huancaína* (potatoes covered in a spicy cheese sauce).

★ **Market Day:** Villagers trek in with their goods ready to hawk and trade. Head to the Mantaro Valley and there's a market every day.

★ **World's Second-Highest Train:** It's no longer number one, but you can still chug your way from Lima to 4,782 meters (15,685 feet) before dropping down to the valleys surrounding Huancayo.

★ **Jungle Heat:** Drop down to Chanchamayo, near Tarma, to escape the dry highland air and enjoy the soothing warmth of the high jungle.

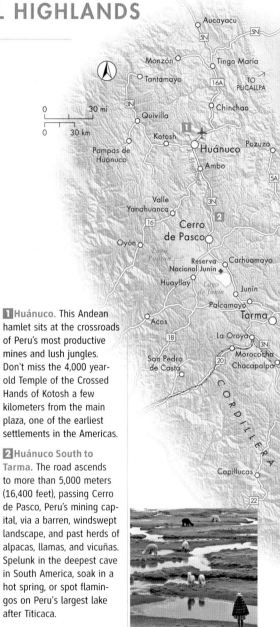

1 Huánuco. This Andean hamlet sits at the crossroads of Peru's most productive mines and lush jungles. Don't miss the 4,000 year-old Temple of the Crossed Hands of Kotosh a few kilometers from the main plaza, one of the earliest settlements in the Americas.

2 Huánuco South to Tarma. The road ascends to more than 5,000 meters (16,400 feet), passing Cerro de Pasco, Peru's mining capital, via a barren, windswept landscape, and past herds of alpacas, llamas, and vicuñas. Spelunk in the deepest cave in South America, soak in a hot spring, or spot flamingos on Peru's largest lake after Titicaca.

3 Tarma South to Huancayo. A quintessential Andean town filled with women in traditional garb, craft capital Huancayo is within a few minutes of vibrant festivals, daily markets, and breathtaking highland scenery. Many come for a weekend on the world's second-highest train, but then stay to study Spanish or explore the small pueblos dotting the surrounding countryside.

4 Huancayo to Ayacucho. Some of the country's worst roads have kept outside influences away, leaving traditional Andean values intact in places such as Huancavelica. These small villages, perched on the side of countless nameless mountains, can induce more than vertigo; *soroche,* or altitude sickness, will strike the uninitiated, so follow the locals by drinking coca tea and taking it easy while enjoying the breathtaking scenery.

5 Ayacucho. Terrorism once cut Ayacucho off from the rest of the country, but with stability, improved roads, and regular flights from Lima, the church-filled town is firmly on the tourist trail. Its centuries-old traditions come to life during the weeklong Semana Santa Easter celebrations, when a passionate and deeply religious fervor blankets the town.

GETTING ORIENTED

A mere hour east of Lima puts you in the foothills of the Andes, a windy, barren landscape where llamas and alpacas graze on vast, puddle-filled fields. Under the blinding highland sun, roads and rails twist around the peaks and pass through ramshackle mountain towns before sliding down through cloud forests and thick jungle en route to Tingo María and Pucallpa. Southeast from Tarma, passing through Huancayo and on to Ayacucho, massive green mountains and the endless *altiplano* (high plains) protect hidden Incan ruins and mesmerizing stone forests.

Huánuco market.

Parque Nacional Yanachaga-Chemillen

Oxapampa

Perené   5S

San Ramón

20A

CORDILLERA

Runatullo

Jauja

Mantaro Valley

Concepción

Huancayo   22

3S

Yauncocha

Izcuchaca

Huancavelica   4

3A

OCCIDENTAL

Santa Inés

Lircay

24A

Rumichaca

ORIENTAL

Huanta   3

Quinua

24B

Ayacucho   5

3

8

Updated
by Michael
Goodwin

The central highlands are where the massive Andes crash into the impenetrable South American rain forests, and winding, cloud-covered mountain roads dip down into stark desert terrain. Defying the land's complexity, its people continue to eke out a hardscrabble life that time has left unchanged.

Most people still depend on the crops they grow and the animals they breed—including guinea pigs and alpaca. Local festivals coincide with the rhythms of the harvest, and traditional recipes and artisanship predate the Inca Empire by hundreds of years. The scenery is stunning, with thundering rivers, blooming potato fields, and hidden waterfalls tucked into the mountainous terrain. Lago de Junín, the country's second-largest lake, sits miles above sea level and crowns the region.

Despite how little daily life seems to have changed, the area has served as the backdrop for some of the most explosive events in Peruvian history: fierce wars between the Inca and the Wanka, the most important battles for independence, and the birth of Peru's devastating terrorist movement. The region gave birth to Sendero Luminoso (the Shining Path) and the Tupac Amarú Revolutionary Movement, revolutionary groups that violently shook Peru's political landscape for over two decades. In the wake of Peru's massive 1969 land reform, the Shining Path's charismatic leader, Abimaél Guzmán Reynoso promised an agrarian paradise to Ayacucho's long disenfranchised *campesinos* (peasants). The central highlands descended into civil war, and more than 60,000 people died at the hands of the Shining Path and government-sponsored paramilitaries before Alberto Fujimori's government captured Guzmán in a Lima suburb in 1992 and Oscar Alberto Ramírez Durand, the leader of the Sendero Rojo offshoot, in 1999. The Shining Path is now a small shadow of its former self, controlling narcotrafficking in the *VRAE* (the Apurímac and Ene river valleys), which abuts the central highlands, and occasionally skirmishing with the Peruvian military. Fujimori now resides in the same prison as his foe Guzmán, having been convicted of human rights abuses committed during the 1992 *auto-golpe* (self-coup) that gave him unlimited power. Now, apart from narcotrafficking and the occasional protest from coca growers and unions, the region is relatively calm.

This beautiful region is gaining prominence and greater integration with the rest of Peru along with improved security and transportation options have opened up this remote region to adventurers and cultural travelers alike.

No one knows when the first cultures settled on the *puna* (highland plains), or how long they stayed. ■TIP➔ Archaeologists found what they believe to be the oldest village in Peru at Lauricocha, near Huánuco, and one of the oldest temples in the Americas, at Kotosh. Other nearby archaeological sites at Tantamayo and Garu also show that indigenous cultures thrived here long before the Inca or Spanish conquistadors ever reached the area.

When the Inca arrived in the late 1400s, they incorporated the already stable northern settlement of Huánuco into their empire. It eventually became an important stop along their route between the capital at Cusco and the northern hub of Cajamarca, and today Inca ruins are scattered along the *pampas*. The Spanish built a colonial city at Huánuco in 1539, and the area quickly gained the attention of Spanish explorers, who turned Cerro de Pasco's buried gold, silver, copper, and coal into the center of the mining industry north of the Amazon basin. They ruled the region—and the country—until 1824, when Simón Bolívar's troops claimed Peru's autonomy by defeating the Spanish on the Pampas de Quinua near Ayacucho.

PLANNING

8

WHEN TO GO

This region's best weather falls in the dry season—May through October—when the skies are clear and daytime temperatures are moderate (nights can be frigid). The rainy season is November through April, when many roads are inaccessible.

GETTING HERE AND AROUND
AIR TRAVEL
The airline LC Perú (⊕ *www.lcperu.com.pe*) flies from Lima to Ayacucho, Jauja, and Huánuco. Star Perú (⊕ *www.starperu.com*) flies from Lima to Ayacucho and Huánuco. Airlines often cancel flights due to unpredictable weather; always confirm your flight, even outside the rainy season.

BUS TRAVEL
Lima is the country's travel hub. Ormeño, Cruz del Sur, and Expresa Molina, among others, run overnight services (10 hours) from Lima to Ayacucho. Likewise, ETUCSA, Ormeño, Cruz del Sur, and Expresa Molina have many daily buses between Huancayo and Lima (7 hours). You can also reach Huancayo from Ayacucho (12 hours) by overnight service on Turismo Central and Expresa Molina—but prepare for a very rough road. Expresa Molina and Empresa Hidalgo have buses to Huancavelica. GM international has overnight service (7 hours) between Huánuco and Lima. *Colectivos* (shared taxis) travel between the central

highland cities, and can be quicker though slightly more expensive than bus travel. The location of these *paraderos* (taxi stops) changes, so ask your hotel receptionist for directions.

CAR TRAVEL

The central highlands have some of the country's most scenic driving routes, and paved roads link Lima and Huánuco to the north and Huancayo to the south. It's five hours from the capital to the crossroads at La Oroya, from which a gorgeous Andean panorama stretches in three directions: north toward Huánuco, east toward Tarma, and south to Huancayo. Most sights around Huancayo in the Valle del Mantaro are accessible by car. You should travel the rugged road from Huancayo to Ayacucho in a four-wheel-drive vehicle, and be sure to bring emergency supplies for the 12-hour trip. Except for the highway, there are mostly dirt roads in this region, so be prepared. There is no place to rent a car in this region.

TRAIN TRAVEL

The train journey from the capital is the most memorable travel option, but service is limited, with bi-monthly trips running only from May to November. On the route from Lima to Huancayo, the 12-hour, 335-km (207-mile) railway cuts through the Andes, across mountain slopes, and above deep crevasses where thin waterfalls plunge down into icy streams far below.

HEALTH AND SAFETY

Altitude sickness, or *soroche,* is a common risk in the Andes. Hydrate with water and coca tea, avoid alcohol, and move slowly until you have acclimated.

Safety and security have improved dramatically since Shining Path's heyday in the 1980s, and the central highlands benefit from a strong military presence. Occasional conflicts do shake the area though, with illegal coca growers and militant unions often blocking roads, particularly in the area from Huánuco to Pucallpa. This has little effect on tourism, although a regional strike can throw off a tight itinerary.

Petty crime is rarer in the highlands than in Lima. By staying alert and taking standard precautions, you shouldn't have any trouble. Carry your passport and other important identification on you at all times. Call 105 for an ambulance, the fire department, or the police.

RESTAURANTS

Dining out in the central highlands is a very casual experience. Restaurants are mostly small, family-run eateries serving regional fare. Breakfast is usually bread with jam or butter and juice, but can include anything from eggs to soups. The midday lunch, the day's largest meal, combines soup, salad, and a rice and meat dish. You'll find snacks everywhere, from nuts and fruit to ice cream and pastries. Dinner is after 7 pm and tends to be light. Don't worry about dressing up or making reservations. Tipping isn't customary, but waiters appreciate the extra change. All parts of the animal and almost every animal are considered. Guinea pig husbandry is a centuries-old tradition, so *cuy* served grilled or fried is a menu staple. Highland potatoes, *choclo* (large grained corn), fresh cheese, and rich stews spiced with *aji* (chili pepper) round out the highland culinary experience.

The cuisine of the central highlands, which focuses on local ingredients and techniques, reflects its isolation. Huancayo's local specialty is *papa a la huancaína* (potatoes covered in spicy cheese sauce), served cold with a sliced egg and an olive. *Pachamanca* (herb-roasted meats, potatoes, and vegetables) is wrapped in local herbs, then slow-cooked on hot stones in an earthen oven. Huánuco's favorites include *picante de cuy* (guinea pig in hot-pepper sauce), pachamanca, fried trout, *humitas* (a local tamale made of ground corn and stuffed with cheese or raisins), and *caldo de cabeza* (sheep's-head soup). Ayacucho is famous for its filling, flavorful *puca picante* (a nutty pork-and-potato stew), served with rice and topped with parsley. During Semana Santa, the city's favorite drink is the warm *ponche* (flavored with milk, cinnamon, cloves, sesame, peanuts, walnuts, and sugar). *Prices in the reviews are the average cost of a main course at dinner or, if dinner is not served, at lunch.*

HOTELS

Accommodations in the central highlands lean toward the very basic. Only the largest properties have hot water, TVs, phones, and private baths, and almost none have (or require) air-conditioning. If you don't need pampering, and you don't expect top-quality service, you'll travel easily—and cheaply. The majority of hotels have clean, modest rooms with simple Andean motifs. Bathrooms usually have showers only, and you should confirm that the hot water does function before paying for a room. Most hotels have a restaurant, or at least a dining room with some type of food service. If you want a homestay experience, ask your hotel or a local travel company, who can often hook you up with hosts in the area.

Rooms are usually available, but if you'll be traveling during the region's popular Semana Santa (Holy Week) or Fiestas Patrias (July 28), book tours and hotels early. Also book early around the anniversary of the Battle of Ayacucho in mid-December. *Prices in the reviews are the lowest cost of a standard double room in high season.*

TOURS

Tarma is the gateway to the Reserva Nacional de Junín and high jungle around Chanchamayo, and outfits like Perú Latino Tarma tours and Max Adventures offer day tours to both.

Around Huancayo you can hike, bike, and explore local villages with the amazing Incas del Perú, which also has a Spanish-language school, book exchange, and folk-art collection. They will also arrange volunteering and hiking throughout the Manataro Valley and high jungle, as well as music, cooking, weaving, and gourd-carving workshops. Dargui Tours offers multiday tours of the region, with a focus on the archaeological ruins around Huancayo.

Ayacucho is surrounded by archaeological ruins and natural wonders, all of which can be viewed on a package tour. A&R Tours has city excursions and routes to Huari, Quinua, Valle Huanta, and Vilcashhuamán.

A&R Tours ✉ *9 de Diciembre 130* ☎ *066/311–300.*

Dargui Tours ✉ *Jr. Ancash 367, Ayacucho* ☎ *064/238–100* ⊕ *www.darguitours.com.*

Incas del Perú ✉ *Giráldez 652, Huancayo* ☎ *064/223–303*
⊕ *www.incasdelperu.com.*

Max Adventures ✉ *2 de Mayo 684, Tarma* ☎ *064/323–908.*

Perú Latino Travel Agency ✉ *Lima 320, Tarma* ☎ *064/321–725.*

HUÁNUCO

365 km (226 miles) northeast of Lima; 105 km (65 miles) north of Cerro de Pasco.

At first glance, Huánuco looks like any other Spanish settlement: a picturesque collection of colonial buildings and churches surrounded by rocky, forested mountains and cut through by the Huallaga River. History, however, runs far deeper here. Evidence of some of Peru's earliest human settlements, and some of the oldest ruins in the country, were found nearby at Lauricocha and Kotosh. Pre-Inca ruins have turned up throughout these mountains, notably at Tantamayo and Garu. Huánuco was an Inca stronghold and a convenient stopover on their route from Cusco north to Cajamarca. Thousands of Inca relics litter the surrounding *pampas*.

Huánuco's cool, 1,894-meter (6,212-foot) elevation makes for pleasant winter days and crisp nights, but in the rainy summer a thick mountain fog blankets the town. The Spanish-style architecture reflects the town's 1539 founding, and later buildings tell the story of Huánuco's importance as a cultural hub. Still, the original Peruvian traditions run deep, particularly during the annual Huánuco anniversary celebrations. Mountain hikes, swims in natural pools, and dips in nearby hot springs add to the area's natural appeal.

GETTING HERE AND AROUND

Most of Huánuco can be seen on foot or via short, cheap cab rides. A guide is recommended for exploring beyond the city. The area is a major coca-growing region, and farmers are leery about strange characters hanging about. Tours from several agencies on the Plaza de Armas will bring you to the major sites within a few hours of the city for under S/50. David Figueroa Fernandini Airport (HUU) is 8 km (5 miles) from Huánuco.

ESSENTIALS

Airport David Figueroa Fernandini Airport ✉ *Carretera al Aeropuerto* ☎ *062/513–066.*

Bus Expreso Huallaga ✉ *Huallayco 695* ☎ *062/519–312.* **León de Huánuco** ✉ *Robles 821* ☎ *062/511–489.* **Transportes Rey** ✉ *28 de Julio 1201* ☎ *062/513–623.* **Turismo Central** ✉ *Tarapacá 598* ☎ *062/511–806* ⊕ *www.turismocentral.com.pe.*

Currency Banco de Crédito ✉ *2 de Mayo 1005* ☎ *062/512–213* ✉ *Huánuco 699* ☎ *062/512–213* ⊕ *www.viabcp.com.*

Mail SERPOST ✉ *2 de Mayo 1157* ☎ *062/512–503.*

Visitor Information Incas del Perú ✉ *Av. Giraldez 652, Huancayo* ☎ *064/223–303* ⊕ *www.incasdelperu.org.* **Oficina de Turismo** ✉ *On main plaza, Prado 714* ☎ *064/512–980.*

KEY

1 Exploring
1 Restaurants
① Hotels

0 100 yds
0 100 m

EXPLORING

Iglesia La Merced. The Romanesque Iglesia La Merced was built in 1566 by Royal Ensign Don Pedro Rodriguez. Colonial treasures include a silver tabernacle, paintings of the Cusco School, and the images of the Virgen Purisima and the Corazon de Jesus that were gifts from King Phillip II. ⊠ *Huánuco and Valdizán* ⊠ *Free* ⊘ *Daily 6–10 and 5–8.*

Iglesia San Cristóbal. Fronting a landscape of steep, grassy mountain slopes, the Iglesia San Cristóbal, with its three-tiered bell tower, was the first local church built by the Spanish settlers in 1542. Inside is a valuable collection of colonial-era paintings and baroque wood sculptures of San Agustín, the Virgen de la Asunción, and the Virgen Dolorosa. ⊠ *San Cristóbal y Beraún* ⊠ *Free* ⊘ *Mass time.*

Iglesia San Francisco. The 16th-century Iglesia San Francisco has Cusco School paintings and a few colonial-era antiques. Peek inside to see the spectacular gilt wall and arches behind the altar. ⊠ *2 de Mayo and Beraún* ⊠ *Free* ⊘ *Daily 6–10 am and 5–8 pm.*

Kotosh. Considered to be South America's oldest temple, Kotosh, a 4,000-year-old archaeological site, is famous for the Templo de las Manos Cruzadas (Temple of the Crossed Hands). Some of the oldest Peruvian pottery relics were discovered below one of the niches surrounding the main room of the temple, and the partially restored ruins are thought to have been constructed by the Kotosh, one of the country's earliest cultures. Inside the temple you'll see re-created images of the crossed hands. The original mud set is dated 2000 BC and is on display in Lima's Museo Nacional de Antropología, Arqueología, e Historia del Perú. **TIP→** **The site was named Kotosh, Quechua for "pile," in reference to the piles of rocks found strewn across the fields.** Taxi fare is S/15 for the round-trip journey from Huánuco, including a half hour to sightsee. ✉ *5 km (3 miles) west of Huánuco* 🎟 *S/3.50* 🕑 *Daily dawn–dusk.*

Pampa de Huánuco. Also known as Huánuco Viejo, this was formerly the ancient capital city of Chinchaysuyu, northern portion of the Inca Kingdom. These highland *pampas* contain Incan ruins and are near the town of La Unión, a S/30 ($12 USD) taxi ride from Huánuco. **TIP→** **During the last week of July the Fiesta del Sol (Sun Festival) takes place at the ruins.** ✉ *137 km (85 miles) northwest of Huánuco near the town of La Unión* 🎟 *Free* 🕑 *Daily 24 hrs.*

OFF THE BEATEN PATH

Tomayquichua. This small village was the birthplace of Micaela Villegas, a famous mestiza entertainer in the 18th century and the mistress of Viceroy Manuel de Amat y Juniet, a Spanish military hero and prominent colonial official. Also known as La Perricholi, her story was the basis of Prosper Mérimée's comic novella *Le Carrosse du Saint-Sacrement* and she was an important character along with the Viceroy in Thornton Wilder's *The Bridge of San Luis Rey.* A festival in July with parades, music, and dancing celebrates her vitality. Beautiful mountain views are the main attraction of the 2,000-meter- (6,500-foot-) high area. Sixteenth-century San Miguel Arcángel, one of the first churches built in the Huánuco area, is nearby in the village of Huacar. ✉ *15 km (9 miles) south of Huánuco.*

WHERE TO EAT AND STAY

Restaurants in Huánuco are simple and small, mostly offering local cuisine with a smattering of Chinese and continental selections. Little eateries cluster around the plaza and markets. **TIP→** **Most hotels have a small restaurant, but if yours does not, your host will usually fix a meal on request.** Hotels are basic, with shared cold-water baths at most budget places. Spend a little more and you'll get lots more comfort, including a private bath, hot water, and a better mattress. But don't expect the Ritz.

$ PERUVIAN ★ 🍴 **Recreo El Falcon.** Perched on the banks of the Huallaga River, this family-style restaurant offers the best of Huánuco cooking, including specialties like *gallina con locro* (chicken soup), *pachamanca* (herb-roasted pork with potatoes), and fresh river trout. Come at lunch and lounge on the open-air terrace while you enjoy the view and live music. **TIP→** **Dishes are huge, so be prepared to share.** [$] *Average main: S/18* ✉ *2 de Mayo 190, Huánuco* ☎ *062/513–272* ✍ *Reservations not accepted* 🕑 *No dinner.*

$ B&B/INN Fodor's Choice ★ 🏨 **Casa Hacienda Shismay.** For lovers of beautiful landscapes and peaceful scenery, Casa Hacienda Shismay, founded in 1851, is a slice of paradise in the highlands of Peru. **Pros:** incredible value; romantic; spectacular scenery. **Cons:** 45 minutes from Huánuco; no public transportation; might be too rustic for some. $ *Rooms from: S/90* ✉ *Shismay* ☎ *062/96236–7734 in Shismay, 01/348–6216 in Lima* ⊕ *www. shismay.com* � *4 rooms* ⦿ *Breakfast.*

$ 🛏 **Gran Hotel Cusco.** Its age shows in chipped paint, squeaky pipes, and
HOTEL ceiling cracks, but overall this local favorite has held up okay over the decades and is undergoing renovations that will double its size by 2013. **Pros:** decent price; undergoing renovations. **Cons:** showing its age; lacks frills. $ *Rooms from: S/50* ✉ *Huánuco 616* ☎ *062/515–070* ⊕ *www. hotelcuzcohuanuco.com* ➤ *60 rooms* ▭ *No credit cards* ⦿ *Breakfast.*

$ 🛏 **Grand Hotel Huánuco.** The colonial-style building, built in 1943, is chic,
HOTEL swanky, and completely out of place in simple Huánuco, which explains
★ the business travelers wandering its wide halls. **Pros:** on the plaza; first-class service; good restaurant. **Cons:** rooms overlooking the plaza are noisy. $ *Rooms from: S/210* ✉ *Jr. Dámaso Beraún 775* ☎ *062/512–410* ⊕ *www.grandhotelhuanuco.com* ➤ *32 rooms, 3 suites* ⦿ *Breakfast.*

HUÁNUCO SOUTH TO TARMA

Heading east, the road from modern, sprawling Lima climbs through the Andes, then splits north–south through the highlands. Working its way through the narrow crevasses and up the rugged hillsides of the Valle Mantaro, the northern road speeds endlessly forward at an elevation of 4,250 meters (13,940 feet) atop the earth's largest high-altitude plains. This route north connects the mountain towns of La Oroya, Junín, Cerro de Pasco, and Huánuco, where despite battles for independence and intrusions of modern technology, traditional customs remain the way of life. At an elevation of 3,755 meters (12,316 feet), by the confluence of the Río Mantaro and Río Yauli, La Oroya is a town of 33,000 and a main smelting center for the region's mining industry. From here you can head due east to Tarma or continue north by road or rail to the village of Junín. Still farther northwest along the eastern shores of Lago de Junín are Tambo del Sol and Cerro de Pasco.

At an elevation of 4,333 meters (14,212 feet), with more than 70,000 residents, Cerro de Pasco is the world's highest town of its size. It's also the main center for copper, gold, lead, silver, and zinc mining north of the Amazon basin, as the pit mine-turned-lake at the center of town can attest. Coal is excavated from the Goyllarisquisga canyon 42 km (26 miles) north of town, the highest coal mine in the world.

About 80 km (50 miles) east of town, the Valle de Huachón provides gorgeous mountains for hiking and camping, while the trail north toward Huánuco runs along a spectacular road that plunges nearly 2,500 meters (8,200 feet) in the first 30 km (19 miles). Overlooking the land from an elevation of 1,849 meters (6,065 feet), Huánuco is a pleasant stopover between Lima and thick jungles around Pucullpa, or before heading south toward Huancayo and into the highlands.

8

TANTAMAYO

158 km (98 miles) northwest of Huánuco.

The fields around Tantamayo are rich with pre-Inca ruins, some from the oldest cultures to settle in Peru. Most notable are the thick, seven-story stone skyscrapers of the Yarowilca, who flourished from AD 1200 to 1450. ■ TIP➔ Finds at Susupio, Hapayán, Piruro, and Selmín Granero are the best preserved. The ruins are within easy walking distance of Tantamayo village, which has a hostel and basic restaurants; or catch a bus to Tantamayo and visit the ruins without a guide.

VALLE YANAHUANCA

35 km (22 miles) south of Tingo María; 73 km (45 miles) north of Huancayo; 65 km (40 miles) northwest of Cerro de Pasco.

One of the longest surviving stretches of Inca road, the Qhapaq Nan, passes through the massive rocky outcrops and deep meadows of the Valle Yanahuanca. Forested hills threaded by shallow, pebbled rivers lead 4 km (2½ miles) from the village of Yanahuanca to the village of Huarautambo, where pre-Inca ruins dot the rugged terrain. Continue along the 150-km (93-mile) Inca track and you'll pass La Union, San Marcos, Huari, Llamellin, and San Luis.

RESERVA NACIONAL DE JUNÍN

238 km (148 miles) south of Yanahuanca; 165 km (102 miles) north of Huancayo.

GETTING HERE AND AROUND

Most travelers visit the Reserva Nacional de Junín on a day trip from Tarma.

Reserva Nacional de Junín. This reserve is at the center of the Peruvian puna, the high-altitude cross section of the Andes, which, at 3,900 to 4,500 meters (12,792 to 14,760 feet), is one of the highest regions in which humans live. Its boundaries begin about 10 km (6 miles) north of town along the shores of Lago de Junín, which, at 14 km (9 miles) wide and 30 km (19 miles) long, is Peru's second-largest lake after Titicaca. Most visitors arrive via day tours from Tarma, but anyone traveling overland from Huánuco via Cerro de Pasco will pass through the reserve.

Flat, rolling fields cut by clear, shallow streams characterize this cold, wet region between the highest Andes peaks and the eastern rain forest. Only heavy grasses, hearty alpine flowers, and tough, tangled berry bushes survive in this harsh climate, although farmers have cultivated the warmer, lower valleys into an agricultural stretch of orchards and plantations. The mountains are threaded with cave networks long used as natural shelters by humans, who hunted the llamas, alpacas, and vicuñas that graze on the plains. The dry season is June through September, with the rains pouring in between December and March.

The reserve is also the site of the **Santuario Histórico Chacamarca** (Chacamarca Historical Sanctuary), an important battle site where local residents triumphed over the Spanish conquistadors in August 1824.

Quechua of the Andes

The Quechua are the original mountain highlands dwellers. Their traditions and beliefs have survived Inca domination, Spanish conquests, and the beginning influences of modern technology. Throughout the region, locals speak Quechua before Spanish and wear traditional costumes woven on backstrap looms. Many Quechua make their living by farming maize and coca in the valleys or potatoes and quinoa in the higher altitudes, while other families herd llamas and alpacas on the cold, windy *puna*.

Walk through the narrow, cobbled streets of any village and you'll spot Quechua men by the large, patterned, fringed ponchos draped over their shoulders, their heads topped by matching tasseled cloths beneath big, cone-shape, felt hats. Knee-length pants are held up with a wide, woven belt that often has a local motif—such as the famous mountain train. Despite the cold, men usually wear rubber sandals, often fashioned from old tires.

Quechua women's attire is equally bright, with modern knit sweaters and a flouncing, patterned skirt over several petticoats (added for both warmth and puff). Instead of a poncho, women wear an *aguayo*, a length of saronglike fabric that can be tied into a sling for carrying a baby or market goods, or wrapped around their shoulders for warmth. Hats for the women differ from village to village; some wear black-felt caps with neon fringe and elaborate patterns of sequins and beads, whereas others wear a plain brown-felt derby. Women also wear rubber sandals for walking and working in the fields, but often go barefoot at home.

The Morochuco are a unique group of formerly nomadic Quechua who live near Ayacucho on the Pampas de Cangallo. They have light skin and blue eyes, and, unlike other Quechua, many Morochuco men wear beards. Cattle breeding and horse training are the main occupations. Renowned for their fearlessness and strength, the Morochuco fought for Peru's independence on horseback with Simón Bolívar, and local lore has it that they are the descendants of the army of Diego de Almagro, a Spanish hero killed by Pizarro.

The Morochuco are first-rate horseback riders—women and children included—who use their swiftness and agility to round up bulls on the highland *pampas*. Women ride in long skirts and petticoats, whereas men don thick wool tights and dark ponchos. Both men and women wear *chullos,* a wool hat with earflaps, beneath a felt hat tied under the chin with a red sash.

Look for gatherings of stone or adobe-brick homes with thatched roofs as you travel through the mountains. These typical Quechua homes are basic inside and out. Food is cooked either in an adobe oven next to the dwelling or over an open fire inside. Mud platforms with llama wool or sheepskin blankets make do for beds; occasionally a family will have the luxury of a wooden bed frame and grass mattress. All members of the family work in the fields as soon as they are able. Members of the *ayllu* (extended family) are expected to contribute to major projects like harvesting the fields or building a new home.

—By Holly S. Smith

8

A monument marks the victory spot. The sanctuary is within walking distance of Junín, and several trails lead around the lake and across the pampas. ■ TIP→ Bird fans stop here to spot Andean geese, flamingos, and other wildlife on day trips from Tarma. ⊠ *Carretera between Cerro de Pasco and Tarma.*

TARMA

350 km (217 miles) east of Lima; 25 km (16 miles) southeast of Junín.

The hidden mountain town known as "The Pearl of the Andes" has grown into a city of 55,000 whose traditions and sights illuminate its Peruvian roots. Long before the Spanish arrived, indigenous peoples built homes and temples in the hills that framed the town, the ruins of which local farmers continue to turn up as they turn the rich soil into flower and potato fields, coffee plantations, and orchards. The town's look is Spanish though, with a small Plaza de Armas and several colonial-style churches and mansions.

At an elevation of 3,050 meters (10,004 feet), Tarma has a cool and breezy climate, with crisp nights all year. ■ TIP→ Get out in these nights, too, as candlelight processions are a major part of the town's many festivals—notably the Fiesta San Sebastián in January, Semana Santa in March or April, Semana de Tarma in July, and Fiesta El Señor de Los Milagros in October. Tarma is definitely not a tourist town, but a place to visit for true Peruvian traditions and easy access to the jungle to the east.

Tarma's **Oficina de Turismo,** on the Plaza de Armas, can help you find qualified local guides for sights in the region.

GETTING HERE AND AROUND

Transportes Chanchamayo, Transportes DASA, and Transportes Junín all offer daily bus service, each two or three times a day, between Tarma and Lima. Transportes Chanchamayo also offers continuing service to Huancayo. *Colectivos* to all central highland cities can be found at corners throughout the city, just ask.

ESSENTIALS

Bus Transportes Chanchamayo ⊠ *Callao 1002* ☎ *064/321–882.* **Transportes DASA** ⊠ *Terminal Terrestre, Vienrich 664.* **Transportes Junin** ⊠ *Amazonas 669* ☎ *064/321–324* ⊕ *www.transjunin.com.pe.*

Internet B&B Locutorio Internet ⊠ *Chanchamayo 650, Tarma.*

Mail SERPOST ⊠ *Callao 356* ☎ *064/321–241.*

Visitor Information Oficina de Turismo ⊠ *2 de Mayo 775* ☎ *064/321–010* ⊕ *www.visitatarma.com.*

EXPLORING

Chanchamayo. Tarma sits at more than 3,000 meters (10,000 feet) but is a stone's throw from the ceja de selva (high jungle), where many of Peru's citrus plantations lie. For around S/50 ($20), you can organize a day trip from Tarma to visit Chanchamayo's magnificent waterfalls, butterfly-filled forests, and local tribal groups. These tours take guests to the major waterfalls in the area, including a refreshing dip in the

Laguna de Paca lakeside resort, near Jauja

30-meter Tirol Falls, a jungle lunch of *cecina* (cured pork) or *doncella* (river fish), a visit to the local Ashaninka tribe at Pampa Michi, and a tasting of local coffees and other artisanal products. For those who won't get to the Amazon during their time in Peru, this is an inexpensive way to experience the pleasures of jungle living. It is also a warm escape from the cool highland air. Peru Latino Tarma offers daily tours. ✉ *50 km (20 miles) from Tarma, La Merced.*

Gruta de Guagapo. Head northwest of Tarma 28 km (17 miles) to Palcamayo, then continue 4 km (2½ miles) west to explore the Gruta de Guagapo limestone cave system, a National Speleological Area. Guides live in the village near the entrance and can give you a basic short tour, but you'll need full spelunking equipment for deep cavern trips. Numerous tour operators in Tarma offer day trips of the caves and the surrounding villages. It is also possible to arrive at the caves independently by taking a *collectivo* at the corner of Jr. 2 de Mayo and Jr. Puno. ✉ *Palcamayo.*

San Pedro de Cajas. About 15 km (9 miles) northwest of Tarma is the town of San Pedro de Cajas, well known for its exquisite weaving and as an excellent place to buy good-quality, locally made wall hangings and rugs. The Cachi saline wells are about 2 km (1.25 miles) west of the town.

Señor de Muruhuay Sanctuary. The village of Acobamba is a 10-km (6-mile) drive from town in the direction of Chanchamayo, and is home to the El Señor de Muruhuay sanctuary. An image of the crucified Christ was said to have appeared here. ✉ *10 km (6 miles) from Tarma.*

WHERE TO EAT AND STAY

$ × **Restaurant Chavín de Grima.** This popular travelers' hangout is on
PERUVIAN   the plaza. There's kitschy Andean decor—pictures of snow-covered
mountains, patterned wall hangings—and lively lunchtime crowds.
They serve tamales and sweet coffee for breakfast, and *comida típica*,
including hearty stews, rice dishes, grilled meat, and fish for lunch and
dinner. $ *Average main: S/17* ⊠ *Lima 262* ☎ *064/321–341* ⌂ *Reservations not accepted.*

$ × **Restaurant Señorial.** Tarma's most upscale restaurant is still casual,
PERUVIAN   and locals don't bother with pomp and circumstance before digging
into hearty home cooking. The chefs show off their Andean flavors in
sancochado (meat and potato soup) and *picante de cuy* (guinea pig in
hot pepper sauce). You can also order pastas and sauces, grilled meats,
and fresh fish from the varied menu. $ *Average main: S/17* ⊠ *Huánuco
138* ☎ *064/323–130* ⌂ *Reservations not accepted* ▬ *No credit cards*
⊙ *No dinner Sun.*

$ ⊡ **Hacienda La Florida.** Experience life at a Spanish hacienda at this
B&B/INN   charming bed-and-breakfast that's a 10-minute drive from Tarma.
Fodor'sChoice   **Pros:** breakfast included; hiking trails lead from property. **Cons:** simple
★   accommodations; car ride from town. $ *Rooms from: S/120* ⊠ *6 km (4
miles) north of Tarma* ☎ *064/341–041 in Tarma, 01/344–1358 in Lima*
⊕ *www.haciendalaflorida.com* ↝ *5 rooms, 6 campsites* ⦿| *Breakfast.*

$ ⊡ **Hospedaje Residencial El Dorado.** This 19th-century *casona* a few blocks
HOTEL   from the plaza is the best budget find in Tarma—the sun bathes the terrace in warm light and the room's high ceilings give the hotel an airy
feel. **Pros:** good value; pleasant architecture. **Cons:** basic; some rooms
are noisy. $ *Rooms from: S/50* ⊠ *Huánuco 488, Tarma* ☎ *064/321–914*
⊕ *www.hospedajeeldoradotarma.com* ↝ *22 rooms.*

$$ ⊡ **Los Portales.** By far the most luxurious hotel in town, this recently
HOTEL   renovated colonial-style mansion surrounded by gardens offers more
warmth than grandeur. **Pros:** historic charm; friendly staff; loads of ame-
nities. **Cons:** filled during the week with business travelers. $ *Rooms
from: S/320* ⊠ *Castilla 512* ☎ *064/321–411* ⊕ *tarma.losportaleshoteles.
com* ↝ *45 rooms* ⦿| *Breakfast.*

SAN PEDRO DE CASTA

120 km (74 miles) northeast of Lima.

This compact Andean village is a collection of mud-brick and clapboard
homes and shops where you can watch craftspeople and farmers at
work on the highland plains. For many visitors, the town is a starting
point for the three-hour, uphill hike to the unusual rock formations at
Marcahuasi, 3 km (2 miles) from San Pedro, where winds have worn
the earth into a menagerie of animal shapes. Other hiking trails weave
through the grasslands around San Pedro, but you'll need to spend at
least one night to get used to the high altitude. Carry a water filtration
kit to drink from the lakes. San Pedro is about 40 km (25 miles) north
of Chosica, on the main highway between Lima and La Oroya. Most
visit from Lima, but the trip can be made as a day trip from Tarma.

QUECHUA LESSON

Here's a small sampling of Quechua words. It won't make you fluent, but people appreciate the effort when you learn a few of words of their language.

My name is . . . —Nuqap . . . sutiymi
Good-bye—rikunakusun
Good morning—windía
How are you?—Ima hinalla?
Thank you—añay

Words:
House—wasi
Mother—mama
Father—papa, tayta
Son—wawa
Daughter—wawa
Yes—arí
No—mana
Please—allichu
Hello—rimaykullayki, napaykullayki

Phrases:
What is your name?—Imataq sutiyki?

Numbers:
Zero—ch'usaq
One—huq, huk
Two—iskay
Three—kinsa, kimsa
Four—tawa
Five—pishqa, pisqa, pichqa
Six—soqta, suqta
Seven—qanchis
Eight—pusaq, pusac
Nine—isqun
Ten—thunka

TARMA SOUTH TO HUANCAYO

Traveling onward from Tarma's orchards, you leave the warm cradle of this Andean valley and head back into the crisp air above 3,500 meters. The road south to Huancayo runs along a high plain buffeted by wind and pocked by herds of highland cattle, and the Rio Mantaro leaves a crystalline gash in the otherwise uninterrupted landscape. Draining the massive Lago de Junín, the river has long sustained civilization in the Central Sierra, irrigating corn, artichoke, and potato fields throughout the region.

The road is a trip through Peru's complicated history and politics, with Huanca and Inca ruins surrounding Jauja, the former capital of the Peruvian viceroyalty, and Concepción, home to one of highland Peru's most stunning convents. The trip back in time ends as you approach Huancayo, a modern town enjoying the results of a decade-long mineral boom. Don't be thrown off by its hustle and bustle; Huancayo still pays respects to the traditions of its past, serving up some of the region's best cuisine and finest artisanship, all in the shadows of its colonial churches.

JAUJA

280 km (174 miles) southeast of San Pedro de Casta; 60 km (37 miles) south of Tarma.

Jauja has the distinction of having been Peru's original capital, as declared by Francisco Pizarro when he swept through the region; he changed his mind in 1535 and transferred the title to Lima. ■ **TIP→** Jauja still has many of the ornate 16th-century homes and churches that mark its place in the country's history. The Wednesday and Sunday markets display Andean traditions at their most colorful, showing the other side of life in this mountain town. Although there are several moderately priced hotels, many travelers come here on a day trip from Huancayo. Those who stay usually head to the lakeside **Laguna de Paca** resort area 4 km (2½ miles) from town.

CONCEPCIÓN

Fodor's Choice
★

15 km (9 miles) southeast of Jauja; 25 km (16 miles) northwest of Huancayo.

Convento de Santa Rosa de Ocopa. Originally a Franciscan foundation whose role was to bring Christianity to the Amazon peoples, the 1725 building now has a reconstructed 1905 church and a massive library with more than 25,000 books—some from the 15th century. The natural-history museum displays a selection of regional archaeological finds, including traditional costumes and local crafts picked up by the priests during their travels. A restaurant serves excellent, if simple, Andean food, and several spare but comfortable accommodations are in the former monks' quarters. Take a S/20 taxi ride for a round trip to the convent from Concepción's Plaza de Armas. Admission includes a guided tour. ⊠ *6 km (4 miles) outside Concepcón* ⊕ *www.municoncepcion.gob. pe* ⌦ *S/5* ⊗ *Wed.–Mon. 9–1 and 3–6.*

HUANCAYO

25 km (16 miles) southeast of Concepción; 40 km (25 miles) southeast of Jauja.

It's not hard to see how the modern city of Huancayo, which has close to 260,000 residents, was once the capital of pre-Inca Huanca (Wanka) culture. In the midst of the Andes and straddling the verdant Río Mantaro valley, the city has been a source of artistic inspiration from the days of the earliest settlers, and has thrived as the region's center for culture and wheat farming. A major agricultural hub, Huancayo was linked by rail with the capital in 1908, making it an endpoint to what was once the world's highest train line (but is now in second place). Although it's a large town, its little shops, small restaurants, blossoming plazas, and broad colonial buildings give it a comfortable, compact feel.

Huancayo was also a stronghold for the toughest Peruvian indigenous peoples, including the Huanca, who out-fought both the Inca and the Spanish. Little wonder that Peru finally gained independence in this region, near Quinua, in 1824. ■**TIP**➔ Still, the Spanish left their mark with the town's collection of hacienda-style homes and businesses, most with arching windows and fronted by brick courtyards with carefully groomed gardens. For an overview of the city, head northeast 4 km (2½ miles) on Giráldez, 2 km (1 mile) past Cerro de la Libertad Park, to the eroded sandstone towers in the hillsides at Torre-Torre.

The drive from Lima to Huancayo is breathtaking, with the road rising to more than 4,700 meters (15,416 feet) before sliding down to the valley's 3,272-meter (10,731-foot) elevation. As you enter the city, four-lane Calle Real is jammed with traffic and crammed with storefronts—but look more closely and you'll see the elegant churches and colorful markets tucked into its side streets, hallmarks of local life that make the city so charming. Women with long black braids beneath black-felt hats still dress in multitiered skirts and blouses with *mantas* (bright, square, striped cloths) draped over their shoulders. Note the intricate weavings—particularly the belts with the famous train worked into the pattern.

> **CURRENCY TIP**
>
> It's best to bring nuevo soles in bills smaller than 50 to the smaller towns of this region, as traveler's checks, credit cards, and U.S. dollars usually aren't accepted. Travel agencies or larger hotels might change money if you're in a pinch.

GETTING HERE AND AROUND

Huancayo's tiny Francisco Carle Airport (JAU) is 45 km (27 miles) north of Huancayo near Jauja. Although Huancayo is big, most of the areas of interest to travelers are within walking distance of the plaza. The exceptions are the craft villages in the Mantaro Valley. Combi vans circle the city streets looking for passengers for the 20–40-minute rides to each town, or you can take a comprehensive valley tour from any of the travel agencies in Huancayo for S/50. Taxis are another option, as they're quite economical.

ESSENTIALS

Bus Cruz del Sur ⊠ *Ferrocarril 151* ☎ *064/235–650* ⊕ *www.cruzdelsur. pe.* **ETUCSA** ⊠ *Puno 220* ☎ *064/232–638.* **Expreso Molina** ⊠ *Angaraes 334* ☎ *064/224–501.* **Ormeño** ⊠ *Mariscal Castilla 1379, Tambo* ☎ *064/251– 199* ⊕ *www.grupo-ormeno.com.pe.* **Turismo Central** ⊠ *Ayacucho 274* ☎ *066/223–128.*

Currency Banco de Crédito ⊠ *Real 1013* ⊕ *www.viabcp.com.*

Internet Inter Mail CyberCafe ⊠ *Loreto 337, in front of SUNAT, Huancayo.*

Mail SERPOST ⊠ *Huamanmarca 350* ☎ *064/231–271.*

Visitor Information Dirección de Comercio Exterior y Turismo de Huancayo ⊠ *Pachitea 201, inside train station* ☎ *064/222–575.*

EXPLORING

★ **Ferrocarril Central Andino.** The Central Highlands' Ferrocarril Central Andino once laid claim to being the world's highest rail route. With the 2006 opening of China's Qinghai-Tibet Railway, the Peru route was knocked down to second place. No matter, though: this is one of the country's most scenic areas, and tracks cut through the mountains and plains all the way from Lima to Huancayo.

The line these days is a shadow of what it once was, and trains ply the route only once or twice a month between May and November, requiring some careful planning if you want the journey to be a centerpiece of your visit to Peru. The railway's website lists departure dates, with Lima-Huancayo service operating mostly every other Friday. Trains depart the capital's Desamparados train station at 7 am for the 12-hour journey to Huancayo. Return trips to Lima usually take place the following Sunday.

8

The 335-km (207-mile) route twists through the Andes at an elevation of 4,782 meters (15,685 feet). The engine chugs its way up a slim thread of rails that hugs the slopes, speeding over 59 bridges, around endless hairpin curves, and through 66 tunnels—including the 1,175-meter- (3,854-foot-) long Galera Tunnel, which, at an altitude of 4,758 meters (15,606 feet) is its highest point.

Snacks, lunch, and soft drinks are included in the price (S/19578–S/35024 round-trip). You can request oxygen if you get short of breath over the high passes, and the mate de coca is poured freely. The decades-old *Clásico* cars are okay in a pinch, but the newer *Turístico* cars are much more comfortable with reclining seats and access to the observation and bar car. ✉ *Ticket Office, Av. José Gálvez Barrenechea 566, San Isidro, Lima* ☎ *01/226–6363* ⊕ *www.ferrocarrilcentral.com.pe* 💰 *S/19578–S/35024 round-trip.*

Museo Salesiano. Look for the well-preserved rain-forest creatures and butterflies from the northern jungles among the museum's more than 10,000 objects. Local fossils and archaeological relics are also on display. ✉ *2 blocks west of Real, across Río Shulcas, in Colegio Salesiano* ☎ *064/247–763* 💰 *S/5* ⊗ *Mon.–Sat. 9–noon and 2–6, Sun. 9–noon.*

🔥 **Parque del Cerro de la Libertad.** The Parque del Cerro de la Libertad is an all-in-one amusement site 1 km (½ mile) northeast of the city. You can picnic in the grass, watch the kids at the playground, swim in the public pool, dine at the restaurant, or stroll through the zoo. ■TIP➔ Folkloric dancers and musicians perform at the Liberty Hill Park amphitheater on weekends. A 15-minute walk from the park brings you to the site of Torre Torre, a cluster of 10–30-meter rock towers formed by wind and rain erosion. ⊠ *Giráldez* ⊗ *Daily dawn–dusk.*

Parque de la Identidad Huanca (*Huanka Identity Park*). The focus of the beautiful Parque de la Identidad Huanca is on the pre-Inca Huanca culture, which occupied the area but left few clues to its lifestyle. A 5-km (3-mile) drive from Huancao, the park has pebbled paths and small bridges that meander through blossoming gardens and past a rock castle just right for children to tackle. An enormous sculpture at the park's center honors the local artists who produce the city's *mates burilados* (carved gourds). ⊠ *San Antonio* ⊗ *Daily dawn–dusk.*

**OFF THE
BEATEN
PATH**

Warvilca. This ruined temple was built by the pre-Inca Huanca culture between 800 and 1200 AD. The closest village is Huari, which has a little museum on the main square with ceramic figures, pottery, and a few bones and skulls. ⊠ *6 km (3.5 miles) from Huancayo, near Huari* 🖼 *S/2* ⊗ *Daily 8–5.*

WHERE TO EAT

The local specialty is *papa a la huancaína* (potatoes covered in a spicy cheese sauce), served cold with an olive. Budget restaurants with set lunch menus are on Arequipa south of Antojitos, as well as along Giráldez. You can pick up a quick morning meal at the Mercado Modelo after 7 am, and juice stands, with fresh fruit brought in daily from the high jungle, are on every street.

$

PERUVIAN

✕ Detrás de la Catedral. With the cathedral only steps away, this restaurant has both delicious food and a romantic atmosphere. Wood tables and soft candlelight set the mood for a meal of roasted lamb, grilled trout, or pasta. Service can be slow, so be prepared to linger or take advantage of the free Wi-Fi. $ *Average main: S/20* ⊠ *Ancash 335* 🕾 *064/212–969.*

$

PERUVIAN

✕ Antojitos. The grilled meats, wood-smoked pizzas, and hearty sandwiches draw a diverse crowd of travelers and locals alike to this dimly lighted, wood-panel restaurant. The daily lunch special is filling and varied, and the locale is an excellent venue for lazy midday people watching. At night, try the *anticuchos* (grilled skewers of thin-sliced beef heart) and a glass of local wine while enjoying the live band, and stay for the nightclub atmosphere that prevails after midnight. $ *Average main: S/25* ⊠ *Puno 599* 🕾 *064/237–950.*

$

PERUVIAN

Fodor's Choice

★

✕ La Cabaña. Over-the-top decorations and labyrinthine rooms give this restaurant charm, but the food has made it a favorite. The wood-fired pizza is some of the best in the entire *sierra,* and the *parillada* (grilled meats) is a Peruvian classic executed to perfection. Wash it down with a pitcher of *calientitos* (hot spiced rum punch). The service can be slow, but it will all be worth is, as you sit in the garden on balmy days or by the fire on cooler ones, and enjoy superb cuisine, fine company, and live music. ■TIP➔ The owner is connected to the Casa de la Abuela hostel, and can arrange cooking classes, Spanish lessons, music instruction, and long-term local homestays. A book exchange, tourist information, and numerous maps are available. [$] *Average main: S/25* ✉ *Giráldez 652* ☎ *064/223–303.*

$ CAFÉ 🍴 **Panadería Coqui.** This pleasant café off the Plaza de la Constitución, with petite tables and high ceilings, has sandwiches, pastries, and decadent cakes available all day. Try the *café pasado con leche* (coffee extract with warm milk) to warm your bones after a day of highland sightseeing. A multicourse special is available at lunch. [$] *Average main: S/10* ✉ *Puno 296* ☎ *064/234–707* 🌐 *www.coquicafe.com.*

$ PERUVIAN ★ 🍴 **Restaurant Olímpico.** This upmarket restaurant, open for more than 60 years, still serves a downtown lunch crowd with cheap, hearty Andean specials. It's the kind of place you come to with your grandparents for a lingering Sunday lunch; it's popular and always crowded, but good food is guaranteed. Try the *lomo saltado* (stir-fried beef) or *papa a la huancaína* (potatoes covered in a spicy cheese sauce) for a taste of the Andes. [$] *Average main: S/30* ✉ *Giráldez 199* ☎ *064/219–515* 🌐 *www.olimpicorestaurante.com.*

WHERE TO STAY

$ HOTEL 🏨 **Hostal El Márquez.** Rooms at the fairly new El Márquez have been recently renovated but remain bland; some have flat-screen TVs, heaters, and cathedral views, while others don't, so choose carefully and negotiate hard. **Pros:** centrally located; recently renovated; modern comforts. **Cons:** bland; the hot water isn't always hot. [$] *Rooms from: S/190* ✉ *Jr. Puno 294* ☎ *064/219–026* 🌐 *www.elmarquezhuancayo.com* 🛏 *27 rooms, 2 suites* 🍽 *Breakfast.*

$ HOTEL 🏨 **Hotel Presidente.** The most popular lodging among visiting Limeños has the comforts of a modern hotel—rooms have contemporary furnishings and Andean fabrics and accents, TVs, phones, and private baths with hot water. **Pros:** good amenities; train packages. **Cons:** mostly business-oriented; service can be surly. [$] *Rooms from: S/215* ✉ *Real 1138* ☎ *064/231–275* 🌐 *www.huancavelicaes.hotelpresidente.com.pe* 🛏 *80 rooms, 15 suites* 🍽 *Breakfast.*

$ HOTEL 🏨 **Hotel Turismo Huancayo.** The hacienda-style exterior of this elegant hotel gives it a worldly charm that sets it above the younger options. **Pros:** excellent service. **Cons:** street and plaza in front often see protests; quality of rooms vary. [$] *Rooms from: S/150* ✉ *Ancash 729* ☎ *064/235–611* 🌐 *turistases.hotelpresidente.com.pe* 🛏 *80 rooms, 15 suites* 🍽 *Breakfast.*

NIGHTLIFE

Huancayo's nightlife is surprisingly spunky. Many restaurants turn into *peñas* with dancing, live music, and folkloric performances from Friday to Sunday between 7 pm and midnight (though some may start and end earlier). If you arrive around or after the time the show begins, expect to pay a cover of about S/7. Dance clubs are usually open from about 10 pm to 2 am and have a cover charge of S/10–S/14.

Café Bizarro. A trendy crowd of young locals and the occasional backpacker head to Café Bizarro, where the music swings from top-40 hits to live rock bands playing bad '80s covers. ✉ *Puno 656* ⏰ *Closed Sun.–Wed.*

La Cabaña. Listen to rollicking live *folklórico* and pop bands Thursday through Saturday here. ⊠ *Giráldez 652* ☎ *064/223–303.*

Taj Mahal. Video karaoke is the main attraction at the Taj Mahal when you're not dancing. ⊠ *Huancavelica 1052.*

SHOPPING

Huancayo and the towns of the surrounding Valle del Mantaro are major craft centers. The region is famous for its *mate burilado* (large, intricately carved and painted gourds depicting scenes of local life and historic events), many of which are made 11 km (7 miles) outside of town in the villages of Cochas Grande and Cochas Chico. Silver filigree and utensils are the specialties of San Jerónimo de Tunán, and exquisite knitwear, woolen sweaters, scarves, wall hangings, and hats are produced in San Agustín de Cajas and Hualhaus.

FOOD

Mercado Mayorista. Stretching around the blocks near the train station is the daily produce market. You'll need several hours to wander through the stalls of local crafts and foodstuffs, where you'll find traditional medicines and spices among such local delicacies as gourds, guinea pigs, fish, and frogs. ⊠ *Ferrocarril.*

HANDICRAFTS

Casa del Artesano. You'll find top-quality, locally made goods near the Plaza Constitución at Casa del Artesano, where artists sit shop-by-shop working on their various crafts. ⊠ *Real 495* ⊕ *www.casadelartesano.org.*

Sunday Market. The city's main shopping venue is the Sunday mercado, which is spread down one of the city's main thoroughfares and its side streets. In particular, look for mate burilado, mantas, straw baskets, and *retablos* (miniature scenes framed in painted wooden boxes). ⊠ *Av. Huancavelica* ⊙ *Sun. 8–6.*

8

EN
ROUTE

Valle de Mantaro. The wide Mantaro Valley stretches northwest of Huancayo, embracing not only the Río Mantaro but also a vast area of highlands lakes and plains. Trails run along the jagged mountainsides to archaeological sites and crafts villages. By road, you'll reach Cochas Chicas and Cochas Grandes, gourd-carving centers 11 km (7 miles) north of Huancayo, with some of the most talented *mate burilado* artists in the country. The road west leads 10 km (6 miles) to Hualhaus, a weaving village where you can watch blankets and sweaters being crafted from alpaca and lamb's wool dyed with local plants. About 5 km (3 miles) north is San Jerónimo de Tunan, where the Wednesday market specializes in gold and silver filigree. Cross the Río Mantaro and head 10 km (6 miles) west to Aco, a village of potters and ceramics artists. Group tours from Huancayo cover the valley, but the roads are good enough that you can drive on your own—although you won't have a guide or a translator. Minibuses from the Avenida Giraldez also reach these villages.

HUANCAYO TO AYACUCHO

The road from Huancayo to Huancavelica and on to Ayacucho shoots over high green plains before spilling into the folds of the Andes and tracing the cascading Mantaro River along a winding two-lane highway. In the rainy season, landslides or *huaycos* often block the road, making this trip a difficult one. Breathtaking scenery and vertigo-inducing climbs reward travelers who push onward.

Despite its seeming proximity on a map, Ayacucho lies at least 10 hours from Huancayo, as the road swerves south toward Lima, alternately cutting through high-altitude plains and winding in coils alongside steep crevasses. The thin air can be biting in the shade and scorching in the mid-afternoon sun, which beats down on the dry, barren landscape between the peaks. ■ TIP→ Look for spots of black, brown, and white— wild llamas, vicuñas, and alpacas that roam this cold, rocky range. Near Pucapampa the road rises to 4,500 meters (14,760 feet), often causing soroche in travelers while the resident (and rare) gray alpaca remains quite comfortable.

The road continues to rise higher, passing tiny Santa Inés and Abra de Apacheta, the latter at 4,750 meters (15,580 feet). The ever-changing scenery continues to be even more spectacular, with oxides painting the rocks and creeks a wash of vibrant colors. One of the highest roads in the world is 14 km (9 miles) farther, the 5,059-meter (16,594-foot) pass 3 km (2 miles) north of Huachocolpa. From here the journey is downhill into the wide, windy Valle Huanta, a landscape of lakes and hot springs, caverns, and ruins.

HUANCAVELICA

147 km (91 miles) south of Huancayo.

Spread out high in the Andes, colonial Huancavelica was founded by Spanish conquistadors in the 16th century, and they promptly discovered rich veins of silver and mercury threaded through the rocky hillsides. The abundant mercury was vital in the extraction of silver from mines in Peru and Bolivia, including Potosí. Although mining was difficult at 3,680 meters (12,979 feet), the Spanish succeeded in making the city an important profit center that today has grown to a population of around 40,000.

The Río Huancavelica slices through the city, dividing the commercial district on the south from the residential area in the north. The road between Huancayo and Huancavelica has been completely revamped in recent years, though it still winds through highland villages and vast pastures, and can be closed during the rainy season due to landslides. ■ TIP→ If you have a good map (or a good grasp of Spanish) and your own equipment, excellent hiking opportunities are in the surrounding mountains.

With improved transportation links, Huancavelica's traditional culture and relaxed atmosphere are more accessible to the adventurous traveler. You'll still see traditional costumes worn by women in the markets and shops and the narrow, cobbled streets are still lined with elegant, colonial-style mansions and 16th-century churches. Residents from all over the region crowd the sprawling Sunday market, as well as the daily food market at the corner of Muñoz and Barranca.

Most crafts and clothing are made in the villages on the outskirts of Huancavelica, and you're welcome to visit the artisans' shops. Other neighboring explorations include the viewpoints from Potaqchiz, a short stroll up the hill from San Cristóbal. Thermal baths are on the hillside across from town.

GETTING HERE AND AROUND

The town is quite compact, and a few short streets in the center contain nearly everything of interest. Few roads lead to Huancavelica; many mountain villages can only be reached on foot. A good, albeit steep, path starts from behind the rail station and has pleasant views of the city and surrounding mountains. The altitude is a common problem for visitors here, so take it slow and drink plenty of bottled water.

Instituto Nacional de Cultura. The best place for contacts on local culture in Huancavelica is the Instituto Nacional de Cultura, which offers language, music, and dance lessons, cultural talks, a library, and details on historic sights and regional history. ⊠ *Antonio Raimondi 193* ☎ *067/453–420* ⊙ *Mon.–Sat. 10–1 and 3–6.*

ESSENTIALS

Currency Banco de Crédito ⊠ *Toledo 383* ⊕ *www.viabcp.com.*

Mail Serpost ⊠ *Celestino Manchego Muñoz 757* ☎ *067/452-750.*

Visitor Information Oficina de Información Turistíca Municipal ⊠ *Plaza de Armas.*

EXPLORING

Iglesia de San Francisco. Begun in 1673, the Iglesia de San Francisco took nearly a century to complete. The dual white towers and red stone doorway—carved with regional motifs—make the church one of the most attractive buildings in town. ⊠ *Godos y Tagle* ☐ *Free* ⊙ *Mon.–Sat. 4–6.*

Feria Dominical. The Sunday Feria Dominical market attracts artists and shoppers from all the mountain towns. It's a good place to browse for local crafts—although you'll get better quality (and sometimes better prices) in the villages. ⊠ *Garma y Barranca* ⊙ *Sun. 8–3.*

Plaza de Armas. Huancavelica's Plaza de Armas is the main gathering place and a wonderful example of colonial architecture. Across from the plaza is the restored 17th-century cathedral, which contains a silver-plated altar. ⊠ *Plaza de Armas* ☐ *Free* ⊙ *Daily 24 hrs.*

OFF THE
BEATEN
PATH

Baños Termales de San Cristóbal. Locals believe that these hot-spring mineral baths, found in the tree-covered slopes north of town, have healing powers. Hundreds of pilgrims come from the surrounding villages during holy days. ⊠ *5 de Agosto, San Cristobal* ☎ *067/753–222* ☐ *S/3 private room, S/1.5 public area* ⊙ *Daily 6–5.*

WHERE TO EAT AND STAY

Restaurants line Barranca, Toledo, and the streets around the Plaza de Armas. All are casual and have a mix of Andean and continental cuisine. Most restaurants have an à la carte menu useful for sampling several dishes. Hotels usually have restaurants, or at least a small café or dining room.

$ HOTEL **Gran Hostal la Portada.** This relatively new hotel fills a much needed gap in Huancavelica, providing travelers with a clean bed, hot shower, and friendly service at a bargain price. **Pros:** great location; piping hot water; friendly service. **Cons:** building lacks charm. [$] *Rooms from: S/50* ✉ *Toledo 252, Huancavelica* ☎ *067/451–050* ✉ *h_laportada_hvca@hotmail.com* 🛏 *31 rooms, 13 with private bath* 💳 *No credit cards.*

$ HOTEL **Hotel Presidente Huancavelica.** The town's top hotel is in an attractive, Spanish-colonial building on the plaza. **Pros:** historic building; prime plaza setting. **Cons:** mixed amenities; pretty basic for the best hotel in town. [$] *Rooms from: S/180* ✉ *Carabaya y Muñoz* ☎ *067/452–760* 🌐 *huancavelicaes.hotelpresidente.com.pe* 🛏 *45 rooms, 40 with bath* 🍴 *Breakfast.*

QUINUA

37 km (23 miles) northeast of Ayachuco.

The Battle of Ayacucho, the decisive battle against Spain in the Peruvian War of Independence, took place on the Pampas de Quinua grasslands 37 km (23 miles) northeast of the city, near the village of Quinua, on December 9, 1824. Today a white obelisk rises 44 meters (144 feet) above the pampas to commemorate Peru's independence from Spain and cement the role of locals in bringing it about.

TIP→ Quinua is one of the craft centers of Peru. It's best known for its ceramics, and you'll find various examples on the windowsills and rooftops of the adobe houses. Miniature churches, delicately painted with ears of corn or flowers, are frequently seen symbols of good luck. The ubiquitous ceramic bulls are figures once used in festivities associated with cattle-branding ceremonies. Tours from Ayacucho bring you into the workshops of the many artisans in the village. Among the better-quality workshops are: Cerámica Artística Sánchez, Rumi Wasi, and Galería Artesanal Límaco; all on Jr. Sucre off the main plaza. Tours of Huari, Vilcashuaman, and Vischongo often include Quinua, but you can also get here by bus from Ayacucho.

Quinua museum. You can follow the surrounding events through exhibits in the compact Quinua museum. Come the first week in December to celebrate the town's role in Peru's democracy, when you'll see extravagant local performances, parties, parades, and crafts fairs. There's a little local market on Sunday. ✉ *Plaza de Armas* 🎫 *S/2* ⏲ *Tues.–Sun. 9–1 and 3–5.*

AYACUCHO

114 km (71 miles) south of Huancavelica; 364 km (226 miles) northeast of Pisco.

Tucked into the folds of the Andes, 2,740 meters (8,987 feet) up on the slopes, Ayacucho is a colorful, colonial-style town. Though its looks are Spanish—all glowing white-alabaster mansions with elegant columns and arches—it's primarily an indigenous town inhabited by people who still speak Quechua as a first language and don traditional costume for their daily routine. Locals greet visitors with warmth and amazement, and the city's 140,000 people revere artists with an energy matched only during religious celebrations like Carnaval and Semana Santa. Religion is a serious pursuit, too, in this city of churches, where more than 50 sanctuaries beckon worshippers at all hours.

Civilization in Peru began in the valleys around Ayacucho about 20,000 years ago. Dating back this far are the oldest human remains in the country—and perhaps in the Americas—found in a cave network at Piquimachay, 24 km (15 miles) west of the city. Over the centuries, the region was home to many pre-Hispanic cultures, including the Huari (Wari), who set up their capital of Huari 22 km (14 miles) from Ayacucho some 1,300 years ago. When the Inca arrived in the 15th century, they ruled the lands from their provincial capital at Vilcashuamán.

The Spanish came and conquered the reigning Inca, and Francisco Pizarro founded Ayacucho in 1540. First named Huamanga for the local *huamanga* (alabaster) used in handicrafts, Ayacucho grew from a small village into a broad city known for its many colonial-style churches. Nearly 300 years later it was the center of Peru's rebellion for independence from the Spanish, when the Peruvian army led by Antonio José de Sucre defeated the last Spanish at nearby Quinua on December 9, 1824. Iglesia Santo Domingo in Ayacucho sounded the first bells of Peru's independence, punctuating the city's role in bringing it about.

It took a century more before the city built its first road links west to the coast, and the road to Lima went unpaved through the 1960s. Ayacucho might have opened to tourism then, but for the influence of Abimael Guzmán Reynoso, a philosophy teacher at the University of Huamanga. His charismatic preaching encouraged a Maoist-style revolution as a panacea to the age-old problems of rural poverty among the country's indigenous peoples. He founded Sendero Luminoso (Shining Path) in the 1970s, and spurred it to militant action in March of 1982, when bombs and gunfire first shook the cobbled streets. The fighting between the Shining Path and the government killed thousands of Ayacuchanos, and by the 1990s the city was cut off from the rest of Peru. Alberto Fujimori's government arrested Guzmán in a posh Lima suburb in 1992, and the Shining Path fell apart thereafter. Although the city is now peaceful, tourism has been slow to establish itself outside of Semana Santa, and the city receives only about a thousand visitors a month. Those that do come consequently enjoy the benefits of hassle-free strolls down the cities well-built pedestrian promenades.

Ayacucho's resulting isolation from the modern world means that to visit is to step back into colonial days. Elegant white *huamanga* buildings glow in the sunlight, bright flowers spilling out of boxes lining high, narrow, wooden balconies. Beyond the slim, straight roads and terracotta roofs, cultivated fields climb the Andes foothills up to the snow. Electricity, running water, and phones are occasionally unreliable, but infrastructure has improved significantly in the last five years. Banks and

8

businesses hide in 16th-century *casonas* (colonial mansions). Women in traditional Quechua shawls draped over white blouses, their black hair braided neatly, stroll through markets packed with small fruit, vegetable, and craft stalls.

GETTING HERE AND AROUND

Most of the city can be explored on foot, as most tourist amenities, hotels, restaurants, and the bulk of the churches and colonial buildings are within a few blocks of the Plaza de Armas Getting to out-of-the-way workshops in Santa Ana and La Libertad requires a quick cab ride. Basic city tours (S/20) offered at every agency depart daily and will save you much of the hassle.

Ayacucho's Alfredo Mendívil Duarte Airport (AYP) is 4 km (2½ miles) from the city. You can take a taxi (about S/4), or catch a bus or *colectivo* from the Plaza de Armas, which will deliver you about a half block from the airport.

ESSENTIALS

Airport Alfredo Mendívil Duarte Airport ⊠ *Ejército 950* ☎ *066/312–088.*

Bus Cruz del Sur ⊠ *Av. Mariscal Cáceres 1264* ☎ *066/312–813.*
Expreso Molina ⊠ *Terminal Wari* ☎ *064/319–989.* **Internacional Palomino** ⊠ *Terminal Wari* ☎ *066/316–906* ⊕ *www.expresowari.com.pe.*
Ormeño ⊠ *Terminal Wari* ☎ *066/812–495.*

Currency Banco de Crédito ⊠ *Plaza de Armas* ⊕ *www.viabcp.com.*

Internet Multiservicios Shaddai ⊠ *Portal Constitución 9, Plaza de Armas* ☎ *066/315–528.*

Mail Serpost ⊠ *Jr. Asamblea 295* ☎ *066/312–224.*

Visitor Information iPerú ⊠ *Portal Municipal 48, Plaza de Armas* ☎ *066/318–305* ⊠ *Alfredo Mendívil Duarte Airport.* **La Dirección General de Industria y Turismo** ⊠ *Jr. Asamblea 481* ☎ *066/312–548.*

EXPLORING

Catedral. The twin bell towers of Ayacucho's Catedral, built in 1612 by Bishop Don Cristóbal de Castilla y Zamora, crown the Plaza de Armas. Step inside to view the cathedral's carved altars with gold-leaf designs, a silver tabernacle, and an ornate wooden pulpit, all built in a style mixing baroque and Renaissance elements. Look for the plaque inside the entrance that quotes from Pope John Paul II's speech during his visit in 1985. ⊠ *Asemblea* ☎ *066/312–590* 🍽 *Free* ⊙ *Mass time 4:30 pm–7 pm.*

Casa Ruiz de Ochoa. Across from the Iglesia Merced on the Plaza de Armas, you'll see the colonial-style Casa Ruiz de Ochoa. The building houses an art gallery with paintings, sculptures, and local crafts by Peruvian artists. The intricate 18th-century doorway mixes both European and indigenous techniques in a style known as *mestizo.* ⊠ *Dos de Mayo 210, Plaza Mayor* ☎ *066/314–612* 🍽 *Free* ⊙ *Weekdays 9 am–1 pm and 3 pm–5 pm.*

CLOSE UP

Sendero Luminoso (Shining Path)

Fighting what it considered a Marxist revolutionary war, Sendero Luminoso (Shining Path) first formed in the 1960s under the guidance of philosophy professor Abimael Guzmán and his "Gonzalo Thought." Following Peru's military coup in 1968 and its ambitious land reform in 1969, Peru's political left grew and fractured, with Sendero eventually forsaking politics and launching its "revolutionary war" in 1980 after 12 years of military rule. By burning ballot boxes in a town outside of Ayacucho, Sendero launched the opening salvo of its revolution.

Sendero promoted an exotic and violent philosophy of extreme Maoism. Guzmán and his disciples envisioned Peru as an agrarian utopia, and saw in Ayacucho's deep poverty and discontent the preconditions needed to destroy the country's existing political structure and replace it with a peasant revolutionary regime. Sendero's charismatic leadership built a core group of operatives who assassinated political figures and bombed police posts. To spread fear throughout the country, they hung dead dogs from lampposts. Their techniques ever more macabre, Sendero began committing atrocities against the very communities they claimed to be helping. Throughout the highlands, they used "people's trials" to purge those connected with the capitalist economy, including trade unionists, civic leaders, and the managers of farming collectives. What was once a "shining" path quickly became a bloody road to war.

Sendero's emergence was violent, but the government's response turned the conflict into a civil war. Peru's leaders sent in the military to quell what they viewed as a localized uprising, and the military in turn exacerbated the unrest by violating human rights and committing indiscriminate massacres of peasant populations. The anger of centuries of discrimination and disenfranchisement welled up and unleashed a torrent of senseless violence. The Truth and Reconciliation Commission released a 2003 report estimating that nearly 70,000 people died or disappeared during the conflict. The commission attributes half of these victims to Sendero, and at least one-third to government security forces.

The Dancer Upstairs, a film directed by John Malkovich, is a fascinating look at the search for, and capture of, Sendero leader Guzmán in 1992. With his arrest, Sendero began a rapid decline, although it remains active to this day, driven more by narcotrafficking riches than radical ideology. In 2012 Sendero kidnapped 36 employees of a major gas company near the VRAE (Apruímac and Ene river valley), the country's main coca-growing region. The military freed the employees, but in the process lost three of their own. As with so many of the world's insurgencies, profits from the drug trade will likely sustain low-level Sendero activities into the near future.

Meanwhile, although Peru's economy has grown over the last decade, rural highland peasants still live in desperate poverty, a potent source of conflict in one of South America's most unequal countries.

Joining Guzmán in jail is former President Alberto Fujimori, who spearheaded the fight against Sendero. The former president is currently serving a 25-year prison sentence for human rights violations.

—By Michael Goodwin

Huari. The wide plains that make up the 300-hectare (740-acre) Santuario Histórico Pampas de Ayacucho are scattered with relics of the Huari culture, which evolved 500 years before that of the Inca. Huari was its capital, thought to have once been home to 60,000 or more residents, and its surrounding fields contain a maze of tumbled stone temples, homes, and 12-meter (39-foot) walls. This is believed to have been the first urban walled settlement in the Andes, created by a civilization whose livelihood was based on such metalworking feats as bronze weapons and gold and silver jewelry. A small museum displays skeleton bits and samples of ceramics and textiles; opening times are at the whim of the workers. You can get here cheaply from Barrio Magdalena in Ayacucho via irregular buses, which continue to Quinua and Huanta for S/4. Most travel agents in town offer guided tours to the site for around S/60. ⊠ *22 km (14 miles) northeast of Ayacucho, Quinua Hwy.* 🖼 *Site: free; museum: S/3* ⊙ *Daily 8:30–5.*

Iglesia Santo Domingo. The 1548 Iglesia Santo Domingo is now a national monument. The first bells ringing out Peru's independence from the Spanish after the Battle of Ayacucho were sounded from here. The church's facade features Churrigueresque architectural elements, a style of baroque Spanish architecture popular in the 16th century, while the interior is coated in *pan de oro* (gold leaf). ⊠ *9 de Diciembre y Bellido, 2nd block* 🖼 *Free* ⊙ *Mass time 6:30 pm–7:30 pm.*

La Compañía de Jesús. You can't miss the ocher-color, baroque-style exterior of this Jesuit 17th-century church. The towers were added a century after the main building, which has religious art and a gilt altar. ⊠ *28 de Julio y Lima, 1st block* 🖼 *Free* ⊙ *Mass time 6:30 pm–7:30 pm.*

Museo Cáceres. In Casona Vivanco on the Plaza de Armas, the 17th-century Museo Cáceres honors Andrés Cáceres, an Ayacucho resident and former Peruvian president best known for his successful guerrilla leadership during the 1879–83 War of the Pacific against Chile. His Cáceres Museum is one of the city's best-preserved historic mansions, which today protects a mix of military memorabilia and ancient local artifacts, including stone carvings and ceramics. Note the gallery of colonial-style paintings. The **Museo de Arte Religioso Colonial** can also be found within these storied walls, and exhibits antique objects from the city's early days. ⊠ *Casona Vivanco, 28 de Julio 508, Plaza de Armas* ☎ *066/836–166* 🖼 *S/2* ⊙ *Weekdays 9–1 and 3–5, Sat. 9–1. Closed Sun.*

Museo de Arqueología y Antropología Hipólito Unánue. Regional finds from the Moche, Nazca, Ica, Inca, Canka, Chavín, Chimu, and Huari cultures are on display at here, at the Centro Cultural Simón Bolívar. Highlights of the archaeology and anthropology museum include ceremonial costumes, textiles, everyday implements, and even artwork from some of the area's oldest inhabitants. The museum is locally referred to as Museo INC. ⊠ *Centro Cultural Simón Bolívar, Independencia 502* ☎ *066/312–056* 🖼 *S/2* ⊙ *Daily 9–1 and 3–5.*

Palacio de Marqués de Mozobamba. Built in 1550 and now the home of the Escuela de Bellas Artes (School of Fine Arts), the Palacio de Marqués de Mozobamba is one of the city's oldest structures. The colonial-era, baroque-style architecture includes *portales* (stone arches) in front and

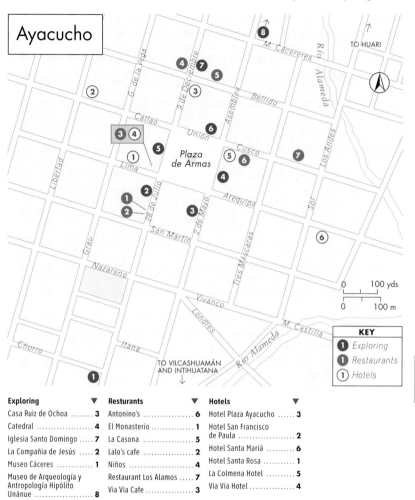

Ayacucho

TO HUARI

Plaza de Armas

TO VILCASHUAMÁN
AND INTIHUATANA

0 ____ 100 yds
0 ____ 100 m

KEY

- ① Exploring
- ① Restaurants
- ① Hotels

8

a monkey-shaped stone fountain in the courtyard. **TIP→ Notice the Andean carvings of snakes, cougars, and lizards etched into the stone.** Two Inca stone walls were discovered in 2003 during restorations. ✉ *Unión 47* ☎ *066/327-448* 🎟 *Free* ⏲ *Weekdays 8–1 and 3–6.*

Prefectura. Also known as the Boza and Solís House, the Prefectura, is tucked into a 1748, two-story *casona historica* (historic mansion). Local independence-era heroine María Prado de Bellido was held prisoner in the Prefecture's patio room until her execution by firing squad in 1822. ✉ *Portal Constitución 15* ⏲ *Weekdays 8–1 and 1:30–3:15.*

OFF THE BEATEN PATH

Vilcashuamán and Intihuatana. Four long hours south of Ayacucho on winding, unpaved roads is the former Inca provincial capital of Vilcashuamán, set where the north–south Inca highway crossed the east–west trade road from Cusco to the Pacific. You can still see the Templo del Sol y la Luna and a five-tiered platform, known as the Ushno, crowned by an Inca throne and surrounded by stepped fields once farmed by Inca. An hour's walk from Vilcashuamán (or a half-hour's walk south past the main road from Ayacucho) is Intihuatana, where Inca ruins include a palace and tower beside a lagoon. Former Inca baths, a sun temple, and a sacrificial altar are also on the grounds. Check out the unusual 13-angled boulder, one of the odd building rocks that are an Inca hallmark. Ayacucho travel agencies can organize tours of both sites (S/80), or you can catch a bus or *colectivo* for S/15. **TIP→ Ask around to confirm where these public transport options are leaving from, as pickup points change frequently.** ✉ *Vilcashuamán Hwy. Km 118* 🎟 *S/5* ⏲ *Daily 8:30–5.*

WHERE TO EAT

Outside of a few international restaurants catering to visiting tourists, Ayacucho stands by its Andean specialties. The city is famous for its filling, flavorful *puca picante* (a peanut-pork-and-potato stew), served with rice and topped with a parsley sprig. **TIP→ The city's favorite drink is the hot, creamy, pisco-spiked ponche (flavored with milk, cinnamon, cloves, sesame, peanuts, walnuts, and sugar).** The best time to sample this popular concoction is during Semana Santa. In the first week of November, Ayacuchanos are busy baking sweet breads shaped like horses (*caballos*) and babies (*guaguas*) to place in baskets for the spirits at the family gravesites. You'll find inexpensive restaurants where you can grab a cheap *almuerzo* (lunch) along Jirón San Martin. Many restaurants are closed Sunday morning.

$ PIZZA 🍴 **Antonino's.** The glow of the pizza oven on the rows of Chilean reds gives this small Italian restaurant a cozy, romantic feel. The menu offers only pizza, but each is a well-executed respite if you've been stuck eating regional dishes for a while. [$] *Average main: S/30* ✉ *Cusco 144* ☎ *066/319-505* 💳 *No credit cards.*

$ PERUVIAN 🍴 **El Monasterio.** The best restaurant in the pleasant colonial courtyard at the Centro Turístico San Cristóbal de Huamanga, home to several excellent restaurants and cafés, shops, and galleries, is El Monasterio. Located in the near corner, it cooks up regional specialties like *puca*

picante (pork-and-potato stew) and roasted cuy. $ *Average main: S/18* ✉ *Jr. 28 de Julio 178 int 116* ☎ *972/520–044* ▭ *No credit cards.*

$ ✕ **La Casona.** Dining in this Spanish-style home is like attending an

PERUVIAN intimate party in a fine hacienda. The sun bathes the leafy courtyard

★ during lunch, while the clientele tucks into the best of Ayacuchano cooking, including heaping plates of *puca picante* (pork and potatoes in red sauce) and fried trout. ■ TIP➜ The daily lunch special is a bargain, and includes an appetizer, entrée, dessert, and drink. $ *Average main: S/15* ✉ *Bellindo 463* ☎ *066/312–733.*

$ ✕ **Lalo's Café.** This modern, Parisian-style café attracts the city's well-

CAFÉ to-do and NGO workers in the mornings and evenings. It has coffees, teas, pastries, and light meals. The second location in Plaza More, also off Jirón 28 de Julio, offers decadent cakes that rival Peru's best. $ *Average main: S/15* ✉ *Jr. 28 de Julio 178* ☎ *066/311–331* ▭ *No credit cards* ☉ *Closed Sun.*

$ ✕ **Nino's.** The building is old Spanish style, but the food is modern,

CONTEMPORARY ranging in flavors from the meaty Andean parrillada to pizza, pasta, and sandwiches. Sit in the massive outdoor terrace and stay warm by the fire, a *calientito* in hand, while the well-lighted Iglesia Santo Domingo stands guard across the street. Come on weekends to catch bands that rock the crowd. $ *Average main: S/30* ✉ *9 de Diciembre 205* ☎ *066/314–537* ☉ *Daily 4 pm–1 am.*

$ ✕ **Restaurant Los Alamos.** This popular backpacker hangout begins the

PERUVIAN day with serious breakfasts: hearty egg and meat dishes, pancakes, pastries, and the like. This restaurant serves a little bit of everything, including Chinese food and Andean classics like fried guinea pig. After dark, huge dinners, such as pollo a la brasa and *tallarin verdes* (noodles with pesto) are often accompanied by local bands crooning crowd favorites under the awning of an ample covered terrace. $ *Average main: S/18* ✉ *Cusco 215* ☎ *066/312–782.*

$ ✕ **Via Via Cafe.** Perched above the Plaza de Armas, this wood-panel

INTERNATIONAL restaurant offers some of the best food in Ayacucho, from highland

Fodor's Choice specialties to backpacker favorites. Enjoy a relaxed breakfast of *pan*

★ *chapla* (local bread), eggs and fresh fruit while taking in the view of the Catedral from the expansive terrace. Daily specials feature organic produce, and a reasonably priced lunch special rounds out the varied Peruvian and International options. At night, the bar serves up classic cocktails as well as pricier Belgian trappist brews. The free Wi-Fi makes this a travelers hub without equal. $ *Average main: S/20* ✉ *Portal Constitución 4, Plaza de Armas* ☎ *066/312–834* ⊕ *www. viaviacafe.com/ayacucho.*

WHERE TO STAY

$ ⊡ **Hotel Plaza Ayacucho.** The city's most expensive hotel is in a gra-

HOTEL cious colonial building partly overlooking the Plaza de Armas. **Pros:** some rooms overlook Plaza de Armas; the place to stay for Semana Santa. **Cons:** room quality varies and rooms are in need of refreshing; stuffy atmosphere. $ *Rooms from: S/250* ✉ *Jr. 9 de Diciembre 184* ☎ *066/312–202* 🖴 *066/312–314* ↪ *69 rooms* ⏇*Breakfast.*

$ HOTEL **Hotel San Francisco de Paula.** At this rambling Spanish mansion, folk art, textiles, and local crafts lend charm to a building that dates back centuries. **Pros:** nice views of city and hills; regional art everywhere. **Cons:** plain rooms; poor lighting. [$] *Rooms from: S/216* ✉ *Callao 290* ☎ *066/312–353* 🌐 *www.hotelsanfranciscodepaula.com* 🛏 *42 rooms* 🍴 *Breakfast.*

$ HOTEL **Hotel Santa María.** Just three blocks away from the Plaza de Armas, Hotel Santa María is the most modern option in the city, with a sleek lobby, flat-screen TVs, and efficient service. **Pros:** cosmopolitan vibe; great price. **Cons:** doesn't feel quite like Ayacucho; farther from the plaza than other options. [$] *Rooms from: S/110* ✉ *Jr. Arequipa 320* ☎ *066/314–988* 🌐 *www.jianhoteles.com.pe* 🛏 *22 rooms* 💳 *No credit cards* 🍴 *Breakfast.*

$ HOTEL **Hotel Santa Rosa.** A block from the Plaza de Armas, the rooms in this pleasant little hotel have a mix of antiques, handmade fabrics, and contemporary furnishings, plus modern amenities like TV and Wi-Fi. **Pros:** beautiful courtyard; good restaurant; local charm with a modern feel. **Cons:** hot water isn't available all day; room sizes vary. [$] *Rooms from: S/125* ✉ *Jr. Lima 166* ☎ *066/315–830* 📠 *066/312–083* 🌐 *www.hotel-santarosa.com* 🛏 *40 rooms* 💳 *No credit cards* 🍴 *Breakfast.*

$ HOTEL **La Colmena Hotel.** Though the rooms are small, the quiet and pleasant courtyard makes this one of the city's most popular budget options. **Pros:** great regional restaurant; close to Plaza de Armas; lively atmosphere; all-day hot water. **Cons:** some rooms lack light; other rooms are noisy. [$] *Rooms from: S/60* ✉ *Cusco 140* ☎ *066/311–318* 🌐 *www.hotelcolmena.com* 🛏 *32 rooms* 🍴 *Breakfast.*

$ HOTEL **Via Via Hotel.** This new hotel and its eponymous café sit in a restored colonial building on the Plaza de Armas and offers some of the city's best, most eclectic lodging. **Pros:** excellent location; views of the plaza; great value. **Cons:** some rooms are noisy; service is inconsistent. [$] *Rooms from: S/100* ✉ *Portal Constitución 4, Plaza de Armas* ☎ *066/312–834* 🌐 *www.viaviacafe.com* 🛏 *14 rooms (8 singles)* 🍴 *Breakfast.*

8

NIGHTLIFE

Maxxo. The best disco in town, Maxxo gets going late and keeps going until the wee hours with a mix of local and international music, and a crowd to match it. ✉ *Mariscal Caceres 1035.*

Taberna El Buho. At Taberna El Buho, kick back with a pisco sour and listen to '80s rock before getting up the nerve to sing karaoke at Sol y Luna upstairs. ✉ *9 de Diciembre 288.*

Taberna Magía Negra. Admire the local art on the walls and dozens of upside-down black umbrellas on the ceiling while grabbing a drink or pizza at this "black magic" pub. ✉ *9 de Diciembre 293.*

SHOPPING

Ayacucho is the home of many of Peru's best artists, whom you can often visit at work in their neighborhood shops or galleries. Look for *retablos*, the multitiered, three-dimensional displays of plaster characters in scenes of the city's famed religious processions and historic battles. The busy Mercado Domingo (Sunday Market) in Huanta, an hour north, is fun to visit.

FOOD

Mercado Andrés Vivanco. Ayacucho's produce and meat market, this market is found behind the Arco del Triunfo in a one-story building; shops continue for several streets behind. ⊠ *Jr. 28 de Julio.*

HANDICRAFTS

Artesanías Huamanguina Pascualito. This store has an extensive collection of carvings. ⊠ *Cusco 101* ☏ *066/313–406.*

Mercado Artesanal Shosaku Nagase. The widest selection of handicrafts in Ayacucho, from retablos to sweaters, can be found at Mercado Artesanal Shosaku Nagase, about a kilometer north of the city center near the city jail. ⊠ *Plazoleta El Arco.*

Jose Gálvez. In Santa Ana, intricate Huamanga stone (alabaster) carvings are the specialty of Jose Gálvez. ⊠ *Plazoleta Santa Ana* ☏ *066/314–278.*

Urbano. Workshops owned by the artist family Urbano are among the best places to find finely crafted retablos. ⊠ *Peru 308 and 330.*

HOUSEHOLD ITEMS

Familia Sulca Alfombras. This shop is known for its beautiful carpets. ⊠ *Plazoleta Santa Ana 83* ☏ *066/317–119.*

TEXTILES

Galería de Arte Popular. This is the workshop of world-renowned weaver Alejandro Gallardo. ⊠ *Plazoleta Santa Ana 105* ☏ *066/311–215.*

Las Voces del Tapiz. Internationally famous weaver Edwin Sulca Lagos works out of Las Voces del Tapiz. ⊠ *Plazoleta Santa Ana 82* ☏ *066/314–243.*

Santa Ana neighborhood. The Santa Ana neighborhood is dotted with some of Peru's finest textile workshops. These local artists and their galleries are clustered around the Plazoleta Santa Ana, and most are happy to share their knowledge and even their life stories with visitors. In particular, look for complex *tejidos* (textiles), which have elaborate, and often pre-Hispanic, motifs that can take more than half a year to design and weave. Many artists painstakingly research their designs, pulling abstract elements from Huari ceremonial ponchos. These creations, made of natural fibers and dyes, can cost $400 USD or more for high-quality work. ⊠ *Plaza Santa Ana.*

The North Coast and Northern Highlands

WORD OF MOUTH

"The trip to Cajamarca was the most exciting bus trip of all! What views—often straight down!"

—Yokena

WELCOME TO THE NORTH COAST AND NORTHERN HIGHLANDS

TOP REASONS TO GO

★ **The Ancient World:**
Along the coast, Chavín, Moche, and Chimú ruins date as far back as 3,000 BC. In the highlands are Wari sites, and Kuélap, a stunning complex built by the Chachapoyans a thousand years before Machu Picchu.

★ **Superb Eating:** The north has undeniably one of Peru's most exciting regional cuisines. Abundant shellfish and extensive pre-Colombian influences make for some of Peru's favorite dishes, such as *arroz con pato* and *ceviche de conchas negras.*

★ **Outdoor Adventure:**
The highlands provide plenty of trekking, climbing, and rafting, especially around Huaraz, home of the highest mountains outside of the Himalayas.

★ **Colonial Architecture:**
Trujillo, on the coast, and Cajamarca in the highlands are two of the best places for colonial architecture.

★ **Beaches.** The far northern coast offers year-round sun, white-sand beaches, and a relaxed, tropical atmosphere.

The National Museum of the Royal Tombs of Sipan in Lambayeque.

1 **The North Coast.**
Explore almost unlimited archaeological sites, well-preserved colonial architecture, mangrove forests, and relaxed beach towns with year-round sun and surf. Fresh seafood is abundant, the climate is warmer, and life is more relaxed.

2 Huaraz and the Cordillera Blanca. Stunning snow-capped peaks, natural hot springs, and a lively bar and restaurant scene make this one of the north's most popular areas. With more than 40 peaks above 6,000 meters (19,500 feet) and the second-highest peak in all the Americas, this provides spectacular views and outdoor activities.

3 The Northern Highlands. See a landscape almost untouched by the modern world, with farm pastures, mountains, and herds of cows, goats, and sheep in Cajamarca. Head to Chachapoyas, where the Andes begin their descent to the Amazon, for extraordinary greenery and the astonishing ruins at Kuélap, often compared to Machu Picchu but built more than a thousand years before.

GETTING ORIENTED

Travel from one geographic region to another is quite challenging and only recommended for those without time constraints. Instead, choose a region and explore accordingly: for the north coast, travel from archaeological ruins to the beach in a south-north direction; for Huaraz and the Cordillera Blanca, use the town of Huaraz as your focal point—from there discover glaciers, snow-capped peaks, and natural hot springs; for the northern highlands, fly to Cajamarca to begin discovering the gateway to the Amazon.

Zona Reservada Santiago-Camainas

Bagua Grande

Pedro Ruíz Gallo

Chachapoyas

Kuélap

3

8

Cajamarca

3N

Sonchubamba

Cajabamba

10A **3**

Parque Nacional Río Abisea

Chuquícára

12 Huallanca

Caraz

Yungay

12A

Lagunas de Llanganuco

Chimbote

Carhuaz

Reserva de Biotera Huascaran

Bahía de Samanco

Playa Tortugas

Casma

Monterrey

Huaraz **2**

Punta El Huaro

Playa Grande

Chavín de Huántar

3N

Culebras

Cajacay

Huarmey

1 **1N**

Gramadal

Barranca

9

Cordillera Blanca.

Updated by
Nicholas Gill

Once passed up for the south, the north coast and northern highlands are increasingly becoming some of Peru's most sought after destinations for a variety of travelers. There are beaches, mountains, green fertile valleys, dry desert, and tremendous archaeological sites and museums. Aside from the coast, where getting up and down the Pan-American Highway is quick and buses are frequent, travel elsewhere in the region often requires time and patience.

Like the rest of Peru, there's incredible history behind the cities and towns you see today. First inhabited more than 13,000 years ago, the Chavín and Moche people later built colossal cities near the coast, to be replaced over time by civilizations like the Chimú and Chachapoyas. Eventually, all these were overtaken by the Inca, followed by the Spanish. Luckily, the extensive ruins and elaborate colonial-era mansions and churches are being preserved in many areas of the north.

A place of extraordinary natural beauty, the northernmost reaches of Peru have magnificent mountains, rare equatorial dry forests, and vast deserts. The steep, forested hills emerge from the highlands, and trekkers and climbers from around the world converge to hike the green valleys and ascend the rocky, snow-capped peaks towering more than 6,000 meters (19,500 feet) above the sea. The coast offers spectacular white-sand beaches, year-round sun, and an abundance of fresh seafood.

As Peru becomes a more popular international destination, tourism in the north is awakening, but is still light years behind Machu Picchu and Lake Titicaca. Come now and explore the relatively virgin territory that provides a rich peek into the cultural, historical, and physical landscape of Peru.

PLANNING

WHEN TO GO

The weather along the north coast is always pleasant, although it's sunnier from November to May. The northern highlands weather is more capricious—rainy season is November to early May, while it's drier from mid-May to mid-September. September and October have fairly good weather, but occasional storms frighten off most mountaineers.

PLANNING YOUR TIME

EXPLORING ANCIENT CIVILIZATIONS

If seeing the important archaeological sites, ruins, and museums is your main priority, start your journey in Trujillo with the important Moche pyramids of the Huaca de la Luna and Huaca del Sol, as well as Chán Chán, built by the Chimú people (but be sure to take at least a day to walk around and enjoy the spectacular colonial architecture). From here, head north to Chiclayo and peer into the Tomb of Sipán, the pyramids at Túcume, and explore world-class historical museums. If you can extend your trip past a week, probably for another four to five days, take the bus from Chiclayo to Chachapoyas and visit Kuélap, a precursor to Machu Picchu built over one thousand years before.

EXPLORING THE OUTDOORS

If you want to see the spectacular mountains of the highlands, head up (and up and up) to the mountain town of Huaraz. Drink lots of water and take a day or so to acclimatize to the altitude, taking in the local sights and hot springs. Take a three-day trek around the Cordillera Blanca. Discuss the numerous options with your guide. If you can extend your trip past a week, head to Trujillo to enjoy the architecture and ruins. Note: You can fly to Huaraz, but there's only one small flight per day, so it takes careful advance planning.

REST AND RELAXATION

If you want to take a week to relax, fly from Lima to Piura, walk around the city, eat in one of the excellent restaurants, and sleep in one of the first-rate hotels. After a relaxing breakfast at your hotel (almost always included in the price of your room), head to Máncora or Punta Sal for the next few days. Regardless of where you stay, you'll be able to relax on the beach or poolside, and—if you're inspired to get out of your beach chair—go on a fishing trip, learn to surf, or try the even more adventurous kite-surfing.

GETTING HERE AND AROUND

AIR TRAVEL

The easiest way to get around is by plane. You'll definitely want to fly to destinations like Piura, Tumbes, and Cajamarca. LAN (⊕ *www.lan. com*), Star Perú (⊕ *www.starperu.com*), and Taca (⊕ *www.taca.com*) fly to several cities in the region.

BUS TRAVEL

Bus service throughout the region is generally quite good. Oltursa (☏ *01/708–5000* ⊕ *www.oltursa.pe*) runs all the way up the coast. Other reputable companies for the coastal communities include Cruz del Sur (☏ *01/311–5050 in Lima* ⊕ *www.cruzdelsur.com.pe*) and

9

Expreso Chiclayo (☎ *074/233–071 in Chiclayo*). For the highlands, Móvil (⊕ *www.moviltours.com.pe*) is a good choice. Whenever possible, pay for a *bus-cama* or *semi-cama,* which gets you an enormous seat that fully reclines, and attendant service that includes at least one meal and a movie. Some buses have now even added Wi-Fi.

CAR TRAVEL

Driving can be a challenge—locals rarely obey road rules—but a car is one of the best ways to explore the region. The Pan-American Highway serves the coast. From there take Highway 109 to Huaraz and Highway 8 to Cajamarca. Small, reputable rental-car agencies are in Trujillo, Chiclayo, Piura, and Huaraz. Think twice before driving to archaeological sites; some are hard to find, and it's easy to get lost on the unmarked roads. Consider hiring a driver or taking a tour. Roads in the northern highlands are always in some disrepair.

TAXI TRAVEL

Taxi rides in town centers should cost around S/3 to S/6; rates go up at night. A longer ride to the suburbs or town environs costs from S/5 to S/20. Negotiate the price before you head off. Taxis hire out their services for specific places, ranging from S/15 and up depending on the distance, or around S/300 for the entire day.

HEALTH AND SAFETY

Use purified water for drinking and brushing your teeth. If you're out trekking, bring an extra bottle with you. Also, eat foods that have been thoroughly cooked or boiled. If vegetables or fruit are raw, be sure they're peeled. In the highlands, especially Huaraz, relax and take the time to acclimatize for a few days, drinking lots of water to avoid dehydration and altitude sickness.

In the big cities on the coast, be on your guard and take simple precautions, such as asking the concierge at the hotel to get you a taxi and carrying only the cash you need. In small coastal towns or in the highlands things are more secure, but be aware of your belongings at all times.

RESTAURANTS

The north coast has excellent seafood, while simpler, but equally delicious, meat-and-rice dishes are more common in the highlands. Some of Trujillo and Chiclayo's fancier restaurants expect you to dress up for dinner, but most spots along the coast are quite casual. Depending on the restaurant, the bill may include a 10% service charge; if not, a 10% tip is appropriate. Throughout the region, *almuerzo* (lunch) is the most important meal of the day. It's eaten around 2 pm. *Cena* (dinner) is normally a lighter meal. *Prices in the reviews are the average cost of a main course at dinner or, if dinner is not served, at lunch.*

HOTELS

Cities along the north coast, especially Trujillo and Chiclayo, have a wide range of lodgings, including large business hotels and converted colonial mansions. The latter, usually called *casonas,* offer personalized service not found in the larger hotels. In smaller towns, such as Yungay and Caraz, there are no luxury lodgings, but you'll have no problem finding a clean and comfortable room. The highlands have excellent lodges with horse stables and hot springs; you can also find family-run inns with basic rooms. Assume that hotels do not have air-conditioning unless otherwise indicated.

Finding a hotel room throughout the coastal and highlands areas ought to be painless throughout the year, although coastal resorts like Máncora and Punta Sal are often jammed in summer and holiday weeks. Sports enthusiasts head to Huaraz and Cajamarca in summer, so make reservations early. Plan at least two months in advance if you want to travel during Easter week or Christmas, when Peruvians take their holidays. *Prices in the reviews are the lowest cost of a standard double room in high season.*

TOURS

Condor Travel and Mayte Tours both organize tours to the ruins around Trujillo. Clara Bravo and Michael White are great guides for Trujillo, and also lead trips farther afield. Moche Toursis one of Chiclayo's best tour companies for trips to the Tomb of Señor Sipán.

There are many tour companies in Huaraz; Monttrek is among the best, arranging rafting, trekking, and mountain-climbing expeditions. Clarín Tours is said to be one of Cajamarca's best. In Piura, call Piura Tours.

In Chachapoyas, contact Vilaya Tours. The company arranges tours to Kuélap, as well as to the remote ruins of Gran Vilaya, which requires a 31-km (19-mile) hike, and to the Pueblo de Los Muertos, which requires a 23-km (14-mile) hike.

Contacts Clara Bravo and Michael White ⊠ *Cahuide 495, Trujillo* ☎ *044/243-347* ⊕ *trujilloperu.xanga.com.* **Clarín Tours** ⊠ *Del Batán 161, Cajamarca* ☎ *076/366-829* ⊕ *www.clarintours.com.* **Condor Travel** ⊠ *Jr. Independencia 553, Trujillo* ☎ *044/254-763, 877/236-7199 in U.S.* ⊕ *www.condortravel.com.* **Mayte Tours** ⊠ *Jr. San Martín 131, Tumbes* ☎ *07/278-2532* ⊕ *www.maytetours.com.* **Moche Tours** ⊠ *7 de Enero 638, Chiclayo* ☎ *074/232-184* ⊕ *www.mochetourschiclayo.com.pe.* **Monttrek** ⊠ *Av. Luzuriaga 646, Huaraz* ☎ *043/42-1121* ⊕ *www.monttrek.com.pe.* **Piura Tours** ⊠ *Jr. Ayacucho 585, Piura* ☎ *073/326-778.* **Vilaya Tours** ⊠ *Jr. Grau 624, Chachapoyas* ☎ *041/477-506* ⊕ *www.vilayatours.com.*

9

THE NORTH COAST

From pyramids to sun-drenched beaches, the north coast offers great diversity in landscape, weather, and activities. The north coast was, until recently, largely ignored by foreign tourists, but all the way up this sun-drenched stretch of coastal desert you'll find plenty of places to explore and relax, including well-preserved colonial architecture, numerous ancient ruins, excellent restaurants, reasonable beach resorts, and a friendly and relaxed people.

Rich in history and filled with an astonishing number of archaeological sites, especially from Trujillo to Piura, the northern coast redefines what is "old." Visit tombs, huge adobe cities, and unbelievable mummies. Explore museums filled with artifacts that date back to 3500 BC. In the far north, especially Máncora and Punta Sal, take off your watch and sink into the sand, soak up the sun, and eat up the luscious seafood.

NORTH COAST MENU

The coast serves mostly fresh seafood, often cold—a refreshing meal on a hot day. The highlander diet consists of root vegetables, like yucca and potato, and a variety of meats, where all parts of an animal are eaten. Both regions have spicy and nonspicy meals, so ask first.

Cabrito con tacu-tacu: This dish of kid goat with refried rice and beans tastes like Peruvian comfort food. It's rich in flavor, but has little spice.

Cangrejo reventado: This dish consists of boiled crab, eggs, and onions, and is usually served in the shell with a side of yucca. This is a fresh, spicy dish.

Cebiche de conchas negras: Cebiche made of black conch, believed to be an aphrodisiac, is one of the most symbolic dishes in the region, though it's not for everyone. The taste of the conch is quite strong.

Cuy: Guinea pig is one of the more popular dishes in Peru. It's a good but chewy meat usually served whole, so you need to decide whether this is something you want to see before eating.

Shámbar: Particular to Trujillo, this wheat and bean stew is a nice, semi-spicy meat alternative that is served only on Monday.

Parrilladas: At restaurants serving *parrilladas* (barbecues) you can choose from every imaginable cut of beef, including *anticucho* (beef heart) and *ubre* (cow udder).

GETTING HERE AND AROUND
Once in a city, it's extremely easy to get around via taxis or tours; however, getting from city to city requires more planning. There are flights to Tumbes, Piura, Chiclayo, or Trujillo from Lima, but not from city to city; the best option is to start by flying into a city and either renting a car or taking one of the many frequent, but long, bus rides to other towns.

BARRANCA

200 km (124 miles) northwest of Lima on Pan-American Hwy.

A nondescript town with little to visit except a large Chimú temple nearby, this is a stop for those who are either determined to see every archaeological site in Peru or do not have the time to go to Trujillo or Chiclayo but would like to see some northern ruins.

GETTING HERE AND AROUND
To get to Barranca, head north from Lima on the Pan-American Highway through the bleak, empty coastal desert, and pass several dusty villages.

EXPLORING
Paramonga. With its seven defensive walls, the gigantic fortress at Paramonga is worth a look. A small museum has interesting displays on Chimú culture. The archaeological site sits just off the Pan-American Highway, about 3 km (2 miles) north of the turnoff for Huaraz. For a few dollars you can take a taxi to the ruins from the nearby town of Barranca. ⊠ *Pan-American Hwy.* ☜ *S/5* ☉ *Daily 8–6.*

WHERE TO EAT AND STAY

$ ✕ **Don Goyo.** The best restaurant option in Barranca, Don Goyo offers
PIZZA a large selection of pizza, pasta, and grilled meat dishes. On the menu
is the requisite *pollo a la brasa* (rotisserie chicken), all pizzas are served
with garlic bread, and regardless of what you order, it will come with
a friendly smile. Fresh, homemade yogurts and cheeses are sold on
the premises. $ *Average main: S/10* ✉ *Jr. Gálvez 506* ☎ *01/235–2378*
⊟ *No credit cards.*

$ 🏨 **Hotel Chavín.** A full-service hotel at bargain prices, this is the best deal
HOTEL in Barranca. **Pros:** extensive facilities for a low price. **Cons:** location is
🕲 on a highly trafficked main road. $ *Rooms from: S/75* ✉ *Jr. Gálvez 222*
☎ *01/235–5025* ⊕ *www.hotelchavin.com.pe* ⤳ *72 rooms.*

CASMA

170 km (105 miles) north of Paramonga.

Once known as the "City of Eternal Sun," Casma, like Lima, is now
subject to cloudy winters and sunny summers. However, with its leafy
Plaza de Armas and a number of pleasant parks, it makes the best base
for visiting the nearby ruins. If you're not into the archaeology thing,
you might not want to include Casma in your itinerary.

GETTING HERE AND AROUND

Casma lies about six hours north of Lima. Cruz del Sur buses stop here
on their Lima–Trujillo routes. Once in town, mototaxis are the best
way to get around.

EXPLORING

Sechín. The origins of Sechín, one of the country's oldest archaeological sites dating from around 1600 BC, remain a mystery. It's not clear
what culture built this coastal temple, but the bas-relief carvings ringing
the main temple, some up to 4 meters (13 feet) high, graphically depict
triumphant warriors and their conquered, often beheaded enemies. The
site was first excavated in 1937 by the archaeologist J.C. Tello. It has
since suffered from looters and natural disasters. Archaeologists are still
excavating here, so access to the central plaza is not permitted. ∎ TIP➔ A
trail leading up a neighboring hill provides good views of the temple complex, and the surrounding valley. A small museum has a good collection
of Chavín ceramics and a mummy that was found near Trujillo. To get
to the ruins, head southeast from Casma along the Pan-American Highway for about 3 km (2 miles), turning east onto a paved road leading
to Huaraz. The ruins sit about 2 km (1¼ miles) past the turnoff. ▨ *S/6,
includes admission to Pañamarca* 🕘 *Daily 8–6.*

Pañamarca. Several other ruins are near the town of Casma, but the
heavily weathered Mochica city of Pañamarca is what to see after
Sechín. Located 10 km (6 miles) from the Pan-American Highway on
the road leading to Nepeña, Pañamarca has some interesting murals.
If they're not visible right away, ask a guard to show you as they are
often closed off. ∎ TIP➔ A taxi will take you to the ruins for about S/20
an hour; negotiate the price before you leave. ▨ *S/6, includes admission
to Sechín* 🕘 *Daily 8–6.*

9

WHERE TO EAT AND STAY

$ ✕ **El Tío Sam.** The best restaurant in Casma, this local favorite serves just

SEAFOOD about every type of seafood imaginable. The *arroz chaufa con mariscos* (shellfish with Chinese-style fried rice) is especially good, but if you're not in the mood for seafood, try the *cebiche de pato.* This isn't traditional cebiche, but cooked duck, served with rice, yucca, and beans. Don't be put off by the cement floor—the restaurant lacks polish, but it serves good food. $ *Average main: S/15* ⊠ *Av. Huarmei 138* ☎ *043/411–447.*

$ ⌂ **El Farol.** A respite from the dusty streets, gardens surround this pleas-

HOTEL ant hotel. **Pros:** calm and natural beauty transports you away from the city. **Cons:** service is a little too calm and requires patience. $ *Rooms from: S/120* ⊠ *Av. Túpac Amarú 450* ☎☎ *043/411–064* ⊕ *www.elfarolinn.com* ⇆ *23 rooms, 4 suites, 1 bungalow.*

PLAYA TORTUGAS

20 km (12 miles) north of Casma.

Playa Tortugas. An easy drive from the Sechín area and 20 km (12 miles) north of Casma, this small beach is a low-key base for exploring the nearby ruins. A ghost town in winter, it is much more pleasant, in terms of both weather and people, in summertime. The stony beach, in a perfectly round cove surrounded by brown hills, looks drab and offers limited hotel and restaurant options, but with its fleet of fishing boats and pleasant lapping waves, it's a relaxing destination. **Amenities:** restaurants; bathrooms. **Best for:** swimming.

GETTING HERE AND AROUND

Playa Tortugas is most easily reached by taxi from Casma. Expect to pay S/20 for the 15-minute drive.

WHERE TO STAY

$ ⌂ **Hospedaje Las Terrazas.** A pleasant stone walkway leads from the

B&B/INN lobby to the bamboo-ceilinged rooms, which are basic and clean, with a terrace and view of the bay. **Pros:** excellent views and relaxed atmo-sphere. **Cons:** bland furnishing and service. $ *Rooms from: S/50* ⊠ *Ca-leta Norte, Playa Tortugas* ☎ *043/94361–9042* ⊕ *www.lasterrazas.com* ⇆ *8 rooms* ⦿ *Breakfast.*

TRUJILLO

561 km (350 miles) northwest of Lima on Pan-American Hwy.

The well-preserved colonial architecture, pleasant climate, and archaeo-logical sites have made Trujillo a popular tourist destination. The Plaza de Armas and beautifully maintained colonial buildings make central Trujillo a delightful place to while away an afternoon. Occupied for centuries before the arrival of the Spaniards, ruins from the Moche and Chimú people are nearby, as is a decent museum. Combine this with a selection of excellent hotels, restaurants, and cafés, and you'll see why the City of Eternal Spring, officially founded in 1534, competes with Arequipa for the title of Peru's "Second City." The only serious problem for tourists is trying to fit in the time to visit all the sights—literally, since many places close from 1 to 4 for lunch.

GETTING HERE AND AROUND

Both LAN Perú and Star Perú fly from Lima to Trujillo's Aeropuerto Carlos Martínez de Pinillos (TRU), 5 km (3 miles) north of the city on the road to Huanchaco.

Almost everything is within walking distance in the center of the city, and for everything else there are reasonably priced taxis. If you don't have a car, ask your hotel to arrange for a taxi for the day or to tour a specific place. For the archaeological sights, another option is to join a day tour from a travel agency.

ESSENTIALS

Currency Scotiabank ✉ Pizarro 314 ☎ 044/256–600 ⊕ www.scotiabank.com.pe.

Mail DHL ✉ Av. Pizarro 318 ☎ 044/233–630 ⊕ www.dhl.com.pe.
Post Office ✉ Av. Independencia 286 ☎ 044/245–941.

Medical Hospital Belén ✉ Bolívar 350 ☎ 044/245–281.

Pharmacy Boticas Fasa ✉ Jr. Pizarro 512 ☎ 044/899–028.

Visitor Information iPerú ✉ Jr. Pizarro 402 ☎ 044/294–561 ⊕ www.peru.info.

Which Culture Was That Again?

The massive walls of Chan Chan, near Trujillo, once home to 10,000 dwellings.

It's a common question after a few days of exploring the extensive archaeological sites in the north. So many different civilizations were emerging, overlapping, and converging, that it can be difficult to keep track of them all.

Chavín: One of the earliest major cultures in northern Peru was the cat-worshipping Chavín. The Chavín empire stretched through much of Peru's northern highlands and along the northern and central coasts. Artifacts dating back to 850 BC tell us that the Chavín people were excellent artisans, and their pottery, with its florid, compact style, can be seen in the museums of Trujillo and Lima.

Moche: About 500 years later, a highly advanced civilization called the Moche emerged. It was their carefully planned irrigation systems, still in use today, that turned the desert into productive agricultural land. Their fine ceramics and large Moche pyramids, still standing near present-day Trujillo and Chiclayo,

give us insight about their architectural advances and daily lives. Such oddities as dragon motifs are perhaps a testament to commerce and intercultural exchange between South America and Asia. Despite voracious *huaqueros,* or looters, the tomb of the Lord of Sipán, discovered in 1987, was intact and untouched, revealing more about their complex culture.

Chimú to Inca: The Chimú came on the scene about AD 850. That civilization continued to conquer and expand until around 1470, when it, like most others in the area, was assimilated by the huge Inca empire. The awe-inspiring city of Chán Chán, built by the Chimú, sits near present-day Trujillo. Although the Inca center of power lay farther south in the Cusco–Machu Picchu area, its cultural influence stretched far beyond the northern borders of Peru and it was near present-day Tumbes that Pizarro, the Spanish pig farmer–turned-conquistador, first caught site of the glory of the Inca empire.

ARCHAEOLOGICAL SITES

Museo del Sitio. Begin your archaeological exploration at Chan Chan's Museo del Sitio. The entrance fee includes admission to the museum, plus Chán Chán, Huaca Arco Iris, and Huaca Esmeralda, so hold onto your ticket (you may also go directly to the ruins and purchase the same ticket there, for the same price). ■ TIP➡ This small but thorough museum has displays of ceramics and textiles from the Chimú empire. From Trujillo, take a taxi or join a tour from an agency. Each location is a significant distance from the next. Guides are available at the entrance of each site for S/10 or more (S/20 Chán Chán) and are strongly recommended, both for the information they can provide and also for safety reasons (a few robberies of visitors have occurred in the more remote sectors of the archaeological sites). At the museum, and all sites, there are clean restrooms and a cluster of souvenir stalls and snack shops, but no place to buy a full meal. ⊠ *Carretera Huanchaco, 5 km (3 miles) northwest of Trujillo* ☎ *044/206–304* ✎ *S/20, includes admission to Chán Chán, Huaca Arco Iris, and Huaca Esmeralda; ticket valid for 48 hrs* ⊘ *Daily 9–4.*

Fodor's Choice ★ **Chán Chán.** The sprawling adobe-brick capital city, whose ruins lie 5 km (3 miles) west of Trujillo, has been called the largest mud city in the world. It once held boulevards, aqueducts, gardens, palaces, and some 10,000 dwellings. Within the city were nine royal compounds, one of which, the royal palace of Tschudi, has been partially restored and opened to the public. Although the city began with the Moche civilization, 300 years later, the Chimú people took control of the region and expanded the city to its current size. Although less known than the Incas, who conquered them in 1470, the Chimú were the second-largest pre-Columbian society in South America. Their empire stretched along 1,000 km (620 miles) of the Pacific, from Lima to Tumbes.

Before entering this UNESCO World Heritage Site, see the extensive photographic display of the ruins at the time of discovery and postrestoration. Then, begin at the Tschudi complex, the Plaza Principal, a monstrous square where ceremonies and festivals were held. The throne of the king is thought to have been in front where the ramp is found. The reconstructed walls have depictions of sea otters at their base. From here, head deep into the ruins toward the royal palace and tomb of Señor Chimú. The main corridor is marked by fishnet representations, marking the importance of the sea to these ancient people. ■ TIP➡ You will also find renderings of pelicans, which served as ancient road signs, their beaks pointing to important sections of the city. Just before you arrive at the Recinto Funerario, the funeral chamber of Señor Chimú, you pass a small natural reservoir called a *huachaque*. Forty-four secondary chambers surround the funeral chamber where the king Señor Chimú was buried. In his day it was understood that when you pass to the netherworld you can bring all your worldly necessities with you, and the king was buried with several live concubines and officials and a slew of personal effects, most of which have been looted. Although wind and rain have damaged the city, its size—20 square km (8 square miles)—still impresses. ⊠ *Carretera Huanchaco, 5 km (3 miles) northwest of Trujillo* ☎ *044/206–304* ⊕ *www.chanchan. gob.pe* ✎ *S/20, includes admission to Huaca Arco Iris, Huaca Esmeralda, and Museo del Sitio; ticket valid for 48 hrs* ⊘ *Daily 9–4.*

9

Huaca Arco Iris. Filled with intriguing and unusual symbolic carvings, and with an urban backdrop, is the restored Huaca Arco Iris or Rainbow Pyramid. Named for the unusual rainbow carving (the area rarely sees rain), it's also known as the Huaca El Dragón, or Pyramid of the Dragon, because of the central role dragons play in the friezes. ■TIP→ This structure, built by the early Chimú, also has a repeating figure of a mythical creature that looks like a giant serpent. On the walls, mostly reconstructions, you will see what many archaeologists believe are priests wielding the knives used in human sacrifices. Half-moon shapes at the bottom of most of the friezes indicate that the Chimú probably worshipped the moon at this temple. ⊠ *La Esperanza* ⬛ *S/20, includes admission to Chán Chán, Huaca Esmeralda, and Museo del Sitio; ticket valid for 48 hrs* ⊙ *Daily 9–4.*

Huaca Esmeralda. Much like the other Chimú pyramids, the ruins' most interesting aspects are the carved friezes, unrestored and in their original state. The images include fish, seabirds, waves, and fishing nets, all central to the life of the Chimú. Like other Chimú pyramids on the northern coast, the ancient temple mound of Huaca Esmeralda, or the Emerald Pyramid, is believed to have served as a religious ceremonial center. The pyramid is in an area that's dangerous for unaccompanied tourists, so go with a guide. ⊠ *Huanchaco Hwy., 2 km (1 mile) west of Trujillo* ⬛ *S/20, includes admission to Chán Chán, Huaca Arco Iris, and Museo del Sitio; ticket valid for 48 hrs* ⊙ *Daily 9–4.*

Fodor's Choice **Huaca de la Luna and Huaca del Sol.** When you consider that these temples
★ were built more than 3,000 years ago, the mud and adobe pyramids near the Pan-American Highway and Río Moche are quite impressive. The Moche people were the first to spread their influence over much of the north coast, and all subsequent civilizations, including the Chimú and Incas, built upon what this group began.

The smaller of the two pyramids—the only one you can actually tour— is the Huaca de la Luna, the Pyramid of the Moon. The adobe structure is painted with anthropomorphic and zoomorphic reliefs. ■TIP→ Many of the figures picture the Moche god Ai-Apaec, whereas others depict fanciful creatures, notably dragons; the use of dragon images may point to cultural and commercial exchange between the cultures of South America and Asia. The Moche expanded the pyramid several times during their reign, covering up the exterior's original reliefs. Since 1990 archaeologists have slowly uncovered the ancient layers of the pyramid. Walk through to its very heart to glimpse some of its first facades. ■TIP→ On most days you're able to watch archaeologists as they uncover multicolor murals. Facilities include a flashy new museum not far from the entrance, a small craft market, cafeteria, restrooms, and parking area (free).

Although the nearby Huaca del Sol, or the Pyramid of the Sun, sits along the same entry road, it's not yet ready for the public. Standing more than 40 meters (130 feet) high—slightly shorter than it originally stood—with more than 140 million bricks, this is the largest adobe-brick structure in the New World. Scattered around its base are what some archaeologists believe are "signature bricks," with distinctive hand, finger, and foot marks that identify the community whose labor

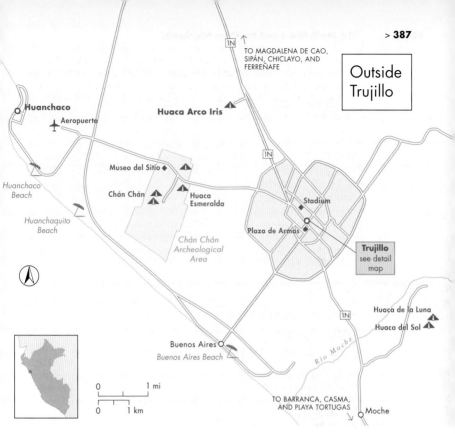

TO MAGDALENA DE CAO,
SIPÁN, CHICLAYO, AND
FERREÑAFE

Outside Trujillo

Huanchaco

Aeropuerto

Huaca Arco Iris

Huanchaco Beach

Museo del Sitio

Chán Chán

Huanchaquito Beach

Huaca Esmeralda

Chán Chán Archeological Area

Stadium

Plaza de Armas

Trujillo see detail map

Huaca de la Luna

Huaca del Sol

Buenos Aires

Buenos Aires Beach

Río Moche

0   1 mi

0   1 km

TO BARRANCA, CASMA,
AND PLAYA TORTUGAS

Moche

produced the bricks for their lords. ■ **TIP→** Researchers believe that the pyramid served as an imperial palace for the Moche people. Once a storehouse of untold treasures, it has been stripped clean over the centuries by huaqueros. So great were its riches that in 1610 the Spanish diverted the Río Moche to wash away the pyramid's base and lay bare the bounty within. Although many tourists wander around the base, this is not recommended as the structure may not be solid and it's possible to destory part of this important temple with a single step. ⊠ *10 km (6 miles) southeast of Trujillo* ☎ *044/221–269* ⊕ *huacasdemoche. pe* ⌲ *S/10; S/3 for museum* ⊗ *Daily 9–4.*

EXPLORING

More than any other city in Peru, Trujillo maintains much of its colonial charm, especially inside Avenida España, which encircles the heart of the city. This thoroughfare replaced a wall 9 meters (30 feet) high erected in 1687 to deter pirates. Two pieces of the wall stand at the corner of Estete and España.

TOP ATTRACTIONS

Casa Urquiaga. The enormous, elaborately carved wooden door is a stunning entrance to this beautifully restored neoclassical mansion from the early 19th century. ■ **TIP→** The house is owned by Peru's Central Bank; simply inform the guard that you'd like to go inside and look around. Don't miss the lovely rococo furniture and the fine collection of pre-Columbian ceramics. ✉ *Pizarro 446* ☎ *044/245–382* 🎫 *Free* ⊙ *Weekdays 9:30–3, weekends 10–1:30.*

Palacio Iturregui. One look at the elaborate courtyard with its two levels of white columns, enormous tiles, and three-tiered chandeliers and you'll know why this is called a palace rather than a house. From the intricate white-painted metalwork to the gorgeous Italian marble furnishings, every detail has been carefully restored and maintained. Originally built in 1842, it's now the home of the private Club Central de Trujillo. Unfortunately, the club only allows visitors limited access. You may only enter, for a small fee, weekdays 8–10:30 am and visit only the front courtyard 11–6. If you find these colonial-era mansions as fascinating as we do, get there early to visit the inside. The grand salon alone is worth it. ✉ *Pizarro 688* ☎ *044/234–212* 🎫 *S/6, or free to visit courtyard only* ⊙ *Inside club: weekdays 8–10:30; courtyard only: daily 11–6.*

NEED A BREAK?

De Marco. Try the homemade gelato at De Marco, a small bistro that also serves excellent-value criollo food at lunch and sponsors occasional peñas (folklore shows) at night. ✉ *Pizarro 725* ☎ *044/234–251.*

WORTH NOTING

Casa de la Emancipación. This branch of Banco Continental is unlike any bank you've ever been in. Go through the central courtyard and up to the small art gallery on the right. Enjoy the current exhibition, anything from modern to traditional artwork, and see a scale model of Trujillo when it was a walled city. ■ **TIP→** Continue to the back, taking in the chandeliers, the large gold mirrors and the small fountain, and imagine the day that, in this house, the city declared its independence from Spain on December 29, 1820. It later became the country's first capitol building and meeting place for its first legislature. ✉ *Pizarro 610* ☎ *044/246–061* 🎫 *Free* ⊙ *Mon.–Sat. 9:15–12:30 and 4–6:30 (frequent special events may affect these hrs).*

Casa del Mayorazgo de Facala. The open courtyard, from 1709, is surrounded by beautiful cedar columns, greenery, and bankers—as with many colonial mansions, this one is now owned by a bank. However, Scotiabank welcomes tourists and clients into the house to see its wonderfully preserved beauty. Notice the classic brown stucco-covered thick adobe walls and Moorish-style carved-wood ceiling. The security guards are happy to answer questions about the house. ✉ *Pizarro 314, entrance on corner of Bolognesí and Pizarro* ☎ *044/249–994* 🎫 *Free* ⊙ *Weekdays 9:15–12:30.*

Monasterio El Carmen. Still used as a nunnery, this handsome monastery, built in 1725, is regarded as the city's finest example of colonial art. It has five elaborate altars and some fine floral frescos. Next door is a museum, the Pinacoteca Carmelita, with religious works from the 17th and 18th centuries and an interesting exhibition on restoration techniques. ✉ *Av. Colón at Av. Bolívar* ☎ *044/233–091* 🎫 *S/3* ⊙ *Mon.–Sat. 9–1.*

Museo Cassinelli. This private museum in the basement of a gas station has a 2,800-piece collection, mostly concerning indigenous cultures. Of note are some spectacular portrait vases from the Moche civilization and whistling pots, which produce distinct notes that mimic the calls of various birds. ✉ *Av. Nicolás de Piérola 607* ☎ *044/246–110* 🖃 *S/6* ⊘ *Daily 9:30–1 and 3–7.*

Museo de Arqueología. Originally built in the 17th century, this museum displays pottery and other artifacts recovered from the archaeological sites surrounding Trujillo. There are excellent reproductions of the colorful murals found at the Huaca de la Luna, the pyramids southeast of the city. ✉ *Jr. Junín 682, at Jr. Ayacucho* 🖃 *S/6* ⊘ *Mon. 9–2:45, Tues.–Fri. 9–1 and 3–7, weekends 9–4.*

> ### FESTIVALS
>
> Considered the cultural capital of Peru, Trujillo is known for its festivities, including an international ballet festival, a contemporary art biennial, and a horse show. Consider coming to town for the Festival Internacional de la Primavera (International Spring Festival), held every year in late September or early October (check local listings for the exact dates). Trujillo is also busy during the last week of January, when it holds a dance competition called the National Fiesta de La Marinera. These events provide glimpses of traditional *criollo* culture.

🐣 **Museo del Juguete.** Puppets, puzzles, toys, games. What could be more fun than a toy museum? This private museum houses a large collection of toys from all over the world and shows the transformation of toys through the centuries. ▪TIP→ The toys from pre-Colombian Peru are especially interesting, giving a seldom-seen view into the daily lives of ancient people. You can't play with the toys so it may not be appropriate for very young children. ✉ *Jr. Independencia 705* ☎ *044/208–181* 🖃 *S/3* ⊘ *Mon.–Sat. 10–6.*

NEED A BREAK?

Museo Café Bar. Feel like you're part of the colonial history while enjoying delicious coffee at the Museo Café Bar. With a black-and-white-checkered marble floor, a dark-wood bar, floor-to-ceiling glass cabinets, and cushioned leather seats, it's a relaxed café in the afternoon and a hopping bar in the early evening. ▪TIP→ Come to soak up the atmosphere, not to satiate your appetite. ✉ *Corner of Junín and Jr. Independencia* ☎ *044/297–200.*

Plaza de Armas. Brightly colored, well-maintained buildings and green grass with walkways and benches make this one of the most charming central plazas. Fronted by the 17th-century cathedral and surrounded by the colonial-era mansions that are Trujillo's architectural glory, this is not, despite claims by locals, Peru's largest main plaza, but it's one of the nicest. ✉ *Plaza de Armas.*

WHERE TO EAT

Trujillo serves up delicious fresh seafood and a variety of excellent meat dishes. Try the cebiche made with fish or shellfish, *causa*, a northern cold casserole made of mashed potatoes and layers of fillings, tasty *cabrito al horno* (roast kid) or *seco de cabrito* (stewed kid), or *shámbar*, a bean stew tinged with mint.

9

$ PERUVIAN 🍴 **El Mochica.** It's crowded and busy, but a fun place to eat that specializes in regional cuisine. Start with an industrial-size portion of spicy cebiche *de lenguado* (sole marinated in citrus), followed by rice smothered with *camarones* (shrimp) or *mariscos* (shellfish). Join the many other enthusiastic diners at this local spot. There's a second location near the Huacas del Sol y de la Luna in the village of Moche. [$] *Average main: S/18* ✉ *Bolívar 462* ☎ *044/224–401* 🌐 *www.elmochica.com.pe.*

$ PERUVIAN Fodor's Choice ★ 🍴 **Fiesta Gourmet.** Born in Chiclayo decades ago, the Fiesta chain is widely considered the preeminent dining choice for those looking for modern interpretations of Peru's northern coastal cuisine such as *arroz con pato* (duck with rice) or suckling goat. This location, a sleek multilevel modern bistro open since 2008 in Vista Alegre, has become the city's top choice for fine dining. Try the creative dishes like grouper cebiche served hot and innovative cocktails, nearly all of which utilize pisco. [$] *Average main: S/30* ✉ *Av. Larco 954* ☎ *044/421–572* 🌐 *www.restaurantfiestagourmet.com.*

$ PERUVIAN ★ 🍴 **Las Bóvedas.** This elegant restaurant in the Hotel Libertador offers diners a beautiful space and delicious food. An impressive *bóveda,* or vaulted brick ceiling, arches over the dining room and plants fill the niches. The house specialty is the local delicacy, shámbar stew, garnished with *canchita* (fried bits of corn). It's served only on Monday. [$] *Average main: S/30* ✉ *Independencia 485* ☎ *044/232–741* 🌐 *www.libertador.com.pe/en/libertador/trujillo/gastronomy/.*

$ ECLECTIC 🍴 **Romano.** Although this Trujillo establishment looks like it's seen better days in its five-plus decades, Romano still offers diners good food and friendly service. For dinner, enjoy seafood and pasta dishes, followed by excellent homemade desserts. Skip the dimly lighted front room and, via a long, fluorescent-lighted hallway, enter the small, cozy back room with natural light and a more congenial feeling. [$] *Average main: S/15* ✉ *Pizarro 747* ☎ *044/252–251.*

$ PIZZA 🍴 **San Remo.** People come here for the best pizza in town. Select from a large list of pizzas, with every topping imaginable, or choose one of the many other dishes, mostly pasta, but also meat and poultry options. The deer head in the entryway, the stained-glass windows, and the small wooden bar add to an old-school atmosphere. There's an excellent selection of South American and European wines. [$] *Average main: S/15* ✉ *Av. Húsares de Junín 450* ☎ *044/293–333* 🕓 *No lunch.*

WHERE TO STAY

$ RESORT 👶 🏨 **Costa del Sol Trujillo.** If you want to stay outside the city, this modern hotel, recently bought by the Costa del Sol chain, who updated the bedspreads and general decor, is the best place to stay. **Pros:** quiet, attractive setting. **Cons:** can be isolating without a car. [$] *Rooms from: S/210* ✉ *Los Cocoteros 500, El Golf* ☎ *044/484–150* 🌐 *www.costadelsolperu.com* 🛏 *115 rooms, 5 suites* 🍽 *Breakfast.*

$$ HOTEL 🏨 **El Gran Marqués.** This upscale, full-service business hotel and spa is minutes from the city center. **Pros:** very efficient service. **Cons:** caters to business travelers and can be impersonal. [$] *Rooms from: S/325* ✉ *Díaz de Cienfuegos 145, Urb. La Merced* ☎ *044/481–710* 🌐 *www.elgranmarques.com* 🛏 *45 rooms, 5 suites* 🍽 *Breakfast.*

$ **Gran Bolívar.** A modern hotel
HOTEL hides behind the historic facade of
this centrally located lodging. **Pros:**
colonial architecture; beautiful central courtyard; central location;
good staff. **Cons:** some rooms have
lots of light, others have very little.
$ *Rooms from: S/224* ☒ *Jr. Bolívar
957* 📞 *044/262–200* ⊕ *www.
granbolivarhotel.com* 🛏 *28 rooms,
7 suites* ⦿ *Breakfast.*

$$ **Hotel Libertador.** On the Plaza de
HOTEL Armas, this elegant, upscale hotel
Fodor'sChoice is the best choice in Trujillo. **Pros:**
★ central location; beautiful architec-
ture. **Cons:** some rooms are better
than others. $ *Rooms from: S/340* ☒ *Independencia 485* 📞 *511/518–
6500* ⊕ *www.libertador.com.pe* 🛏 *74 rooms, 5 suites* ⦿ *Breakfast.*

$ **Los Conquistadores.** Near the Plaza de Armas, this uninteresting busi-
HOTEL ness hotel has large rooms with separate sitting areas. **Pros:** excellent
location; large rooms. **Cons:** bland furnishings; little natural light.
$ *Rooms from: S/230* ☒ *Diego de Almagro 586* 📞 *044/244–505* ⊕ *www.
losconquistadoreshotel.com* 🛏 *38 rooms, 12 suites* ⦿ *Breakfast.*

NIGHTLIFE

Luna Rota Pub. Luna Rota has live local music most evenings when it's
open; if not, a DJ fills in. The dance club downstairs mainly attracts a
40-and-over crowd, but upstairs the disco music blasts away. The party
doesn't get started until about midnight and lasts until the wee hours of the
morning. ☒ *Av. América Sur 2119* 📞 *044/242–182* ⊘ *Closed Sun.–Thurs.*

Runa's Martini Lounge. Conveniently set in a lovely colonial building just
off the plaza, this sleek bar and lounge attracts an upscale, 20- to 40-year-
old clientele who are content with skipping the club scene. Happy hours
and frequent drink promotions keep the cocktail prices down. ☒ *Jr.
Independencia 610* 📞 *044/203–295* ⊘ *Closed Mon. and Sun.*

Tributo. In a converted mansion with a friendly vibe, Tributo has live
music, mainly cover or "tribute" (hence, the name) bands on weekends.
☒ *Almagro and Pizarro* ⊘ *Closed Sun.–Wed.*

SHOPPING

Along Avenida España, especially where it intersects with Junín, stalls
display locally made leather goods, particularly shoes, bags, and coats. Be
wary of pickpockets during the day, and avoid it altogether after sunset.

Creaciones Cerna. For made-to-order boots or belts, check out this shop.
☒ *Bolognesi 567* 📞 *044/205–679.*

Los Tallanes. There's a wide selection of handicrafts here, mostly knick-
knacks made from seashells and totora reeds. ☒ *Jr. San Martín 455*
📞 *044/220–274.*

Luján. Pick up pieces of stylized Peruvian jewelry here. ☒ *Obregoso 242*
📞 *044/205–092.*

9

HUANCHACO

12 km (7½ miles) northwest of Trujillo.

Less than half an hour away from the city, Huanchaco is a little beach community where surfers, tourists, affluent *Trujillianos*, families, and couples easily mix. With excellent restaurants, comfortable hotels, and never-ending sunshine, this is a nice place to unwind for a couple of days or to live it up at one of the many annual fiestas. The Festival del Mar is held every other year during May, the Fiesta de San Pedro every June 29, and multiple surfing and dance competitions happen throughout the year.

▓ **TIP→** Head to the beach in the late afternoon to watch fishermen return for the day, gliding along in their caballitos de totora, traditional fishing boats that have been used for more than 1,000 years. These small, unstable boats, made from totora reeds, can be seen in Moche ceramics and other pre-Columbian handiwork. The boat's name, *caballitos,* means "little horse"; fishermen appear to be on horseback as they straddle on the boats.

GETTING HERE AND AROUND

Huanchaco sits well enough within the Trujillo orbit that taxiing it is the best way to get out here. The drive takes about 15 minutes and the fare runs about S/20.

ESSENTIALS

There is a GlobalNet ATM beside the Municipalidad, otherwise replenish your supply of cash at any bank back in Trujillo.

EXPLORING

El Santuario de Huanchaco. Although people come to Huanchaco for the beach, one of Peru's oldest churches, El Santuario de Huanchaco, on a hill overlooking the village, is a nice side trip. The Sanctuary of Huanchaco was built on a Chimú ruin around 1540. In the second half of the 16th century a small box containing the image of *Nuestra Señora del Socorro* (Our Lady of Mercy) floated in on the tide and was discovered by locals. The image, which is kept in the sanctuary, has been an object of local veneration ever since. ⊠ *At Andrés Rázuri and Unión* 🖅 *Free* ☉ *Daily 8–6.*

Puerto Pizarro. This small fishing port 14 km (9 miles) north of Tumbes on the way to the Ecuadorean border sits near the point where the Rio Tumbes and the Pacific Ocean meet. The mix of fresh and salt water is ideal for mangroves, not to mention the aquatic creatures that thrive among their roots. While tour operators in Tumbes and Mancora sell half-day or full-day tours starting from the port, it is just as easy to come here and arrange a trip directly. Prices are based on the time and the number of stops, which include bird and wildlife watching in the mangroves, a small reptile zoo, and tiny islands with pleasant beaches and informal beach shack restaurants. ⊠ *Puerto Pizarro, Tumbes.*

WHERE TO EAT AND STAY

$

SEAFOOD

✕ **Big Ben.** Skip the first floor and head upstairs to the terrace for great views of the beach at Huanchaco's largest and most popular restaurant. Enjoy Huanchaquero specialties, including *cangrejo reventado* (baked crab stuffed with egg) and *cebiche de mococho* (algae cebiche). Only open 11–6, this open-air restaurant serves lunch and sunset drinks from a special wine list or cocktail menu. $ *Average main: S/20* ⊠ *Av. Victor Larco 836* ☎ *044/461–378* ⊕ *www.bigbenhuanchaco. com* ⊘ *No dinner.*

$ **✕ Chocolate Café.** This cute coffeehouse serves as a nice break from sea-
CAFÉ   food if you find yourself spending too much time indulging in Huancha-co's cebicherias. The Dutch-and-Peruvian-owned café sources their coffee and other organic ingredients from local and regional producers. You can grab wraps, sandwiches, pastries, pies, and other light bites here as well. $ *Average main: S/10* ⊠ *La Rivera 752* ☎ *044/462–420.*

$ **✕ Club Colonial.** Formerly on the Plaza de Armas, this classic Huanchaco
SEAFOOD   eatery moved to the beachfront, to a sidewalk-facing patio in the hotel
Fodor's Choice   of the same name. Club Colonial combines recipes from the Old World
★   with ingredients from the New World, coming up with wonderful com-binations of fresh seafood, pasta, greens, meats, and more. There's everything from Basque-style sea bass to crepes covered with tropical fruit. The food hasn't changed much over the years, but the new loca-tion and sea view are a definite bonus. It's on a newly created street, so asking for directions can be tricky. It's closer to the surfers' section of the beach than the fishermen's area. $ *Average main: S/22* ⊠ *Av. La Rivera 514* ☎ *044/461–015.*

$ **Hotel Bracamonte.** This pleasant hotel, across the boulevard from
HOTEL   Playa Huanchaco, is popular with Peruvian families, especially in sum-
☺   mer, and has a pool set in beautifully landscaped grounds, a small res-taurant, a small playground, lots of grassy areas to play in, and a good "neighborhood" feel. **Pros:** if you have kids, this is the place to be. **Cons:** if you don't have kids, this is not the place for you. $ *Rooms from: S/150* ⊠ *Jr. Los Olivos 503* ☎ *044/461–162* ⊕ *www.hotelbracamonte. com.pe* ⇱ *31 rooms, 2 suites* ⦿ *No meals.*

$ **Las Palmeras.** Across from the tranquil Playa Los Tumbos, a beach
HOTEL   on the northern end of the waterfront, Las Palmeras is a welcom-
★   ing hotel once you get past the gated entrance. **Pros:** pristine and comfortable rooms with terraces and views; very quiet and relax-ing. **Cons:** difficult to find behind a closed gate; prices vary based on location of the room. $ *Rooms from: S/150* ⊠ *Av. Victor Larco 1150* ☎☎ *044/461–199* ⊕ *www.laspalmerasdehuanchaco.com* ⇱ *20 rooms, 1 suite* ⦿ *Breakfast.*

NIGHTLIFE

Huanchakero. A hotspot mainly filled with foreign travelers, this trendy restaurant and pub has an extensive menu with a range of Peruvian and Nikkei food, from sushi to ceviche. Their cocktails, many utilizing pisco that has been macerated in local fruits or herbs, are the most innovative on the strip and there's loud music for the after-dinner crowd. ⊠ *Av. La Rivera 115* ☎ *044/461–184.*

Sabes?. Worth checking out, especially on the weekend, this laid-back spot at the northern end of the main drag has good music and drinks. ⊠ *Larco 920* ☎ *044/461–555.*

SPORTS AND THE OUTDOORS

The beaches around Huanchaco are popular, though the water can be rather cold.

Playa Huankarote. This wide, rocky beach south of the pier, is less popular for swimming, but there's good surfing. **Amenities:** none. **Best for:** surfing; solitude. ⊠ *South of municipal pier.*

Playa Malecón. North of the pier, this is the town's most popular beach, and it is filled with restaurant after restaurant. Local craftspeople sell their goods along the waterfront walk and fishermen line their *caballitos de totora*, the reed fishing rafts that are used more as a photo op here or to rent to tourists than for actual fishing. There is more sand and fewer rocks the farther you move away from the pier. **Amenities:** food and drink. **Best for:** surfing; swimming; walking; sunset. ⊠ *North of municipal pier.*

MAGDALENA DE CAO

57 km (35 miles) northwest of Trujillo.

Chances are if you are coming to this small remote village in the Chicama Valley, it's to see the El Brujo archaeological complex, which is quickly growing in popularity.

GETTING HERE AND AROUND

As the site is about 1.5 hours from Trujillo by road and public transportation is sporadic, you'll either want to rent a car or join a tour from Trujillo.

EXPLORING

El Brujo. Just across the Rio Chicama lie the three huacas of El Brujo: La Huaca Prieta, Huaca Vieja, and Huaca Rajada. The Huaca Vieja in particular has drawn considerable interest due to the 2006 discovery of the well-preserved 1,600-year-old mummy, the Lady of Cao. The discovery of the tattooed Mochica ruler has been compared to the discovery of King Tut's tomb in Egypt, as it completely turned notions of power in pre-Colombian Peru upside down. Her tattoos even suggest that she had the ability to predict supernatural events. You can see her remains, as well as other artifacts found during the ongoing excavations, in the small site museum. The other two huacas are still not fully excavated, but the entrance fee covers all three, and they are a short walk from each other. ⊠ *Magdalena de Cao* 🖃 *S/11.*

SIPÁN

35 km (21 miles) east of Chiclayo.

This tiny village of about 1,700 doesn't offer much, but nearby is one of the country's major archaeological sites. Arrange for a taxi or tour to take you to the tomb of the Lord of Sipán.

EXPLORING

Tumba del Señor de Sipán (*Tomb of the Lord of Sipán*). The Tumba del Señor de Sipán was discovered by renowned archaeologist Walter Alva in 1987. The road to the archaeological site, not far from the town of

Sipán, winds past sugar plantations and through a fertile valley. You'll soon reach a fissured hill—all that remains of a temple called the Huaca Rajada. ■ TIP→ The three major tombs found here date from about AD 290 and earlier, and together they form one of the most complete archaeological finds in the Western Hemisphere. The tombs have been attributed to the Moche culture, known for its ornamental pottery and fine metalwork. The most extravagant funerary objects were found in the tomb, now filled with replicas placed exactly where the original objects were discovered. The originals are now on permanent display in the Museo Tumbas Reales de Sipán in Lambayeque. The Lord of Sipán did not make the journey to the next world alone—he was buried with at least eight people: a warrior (whose feet were amputated to ensure that he didn't run away), three young women, two assistants, a servant, and a child. The tomb also contained a dog and two llamas. Hundreds of ceramic pots contained snacks for the long trip. Archaeological work here is ongoing, as other tombs are still being excavated. 🖂 *S/10, S/20 for a guide (strongly recommended)* 🕙 *Daily 8–5:30.*

CHICLAYO

219 km (131 miles) north of Trujillo.

A lively commercial center, Chiclayo is prosperous and easygoing. Although it doesn't have much colonial architecture or special outward beauty, it's surrounded by numerous pre-Columbian sites. ■ TIP→ The Moche and Chimú people had major cities in the area, as did the Lambayeque, who flourished here from about 700 to 1370. Archaeology buffs flocked to the area after the 1987 discovery of the nearby unlooted tomb of the Lord of Sipán. Chiclayo is a comfortable base from which to visit that tomb as well as other archaeological sites.

GETTING HERE AND AROUND

LAN Perú, Taca, and Star Perú connect Lima with Chiclayo's Aeropuerto José Quiñones González (CIX) just outside the city. Star Perú also flies between Chiclayo and Trujillo.

For the most part, you'll need to take a taxi around Chiclayo. Within the city limits, each ride should cost about S/3; ask for help at your hotel to negotiate anything beyond the city. Look at the map before hailing a taxi, though, because some things are within walking distance.

ESSENTIALS

Currency Banco de Crédito 🖂 *Av. Balta 630* ⊕ *www.viabcp.com.*

Internet Africa Café Web 🖂 *San José 473* ☎ *074/229–431.*

Mail Post Office 🖂 *Elías Aguirre 140* ☎ *074/237–031.*

Medical Clínica del Pacífico 🖂 *Av. José Leonardo Ortiz 420* ☎ *074/232–141.*

Pharmacy Max Salud 🖂 *Av. 7 de Enero 185* ☎ *076/226–201.*

Visitor Information iPerú 🖂 *Siete de Enero 579* ☎ *074/205–703* ⊕ *www.peru.info.*

9

EXPLORING

Cathedral. The enormous Chiclayo cathedral, dating back to 1869, is worth a look for its neoclassical facade on the Plaza de Armas, and its well-maintained central altar. ✉ *Plaza de Armas* 🎫 *Free* ⏲ *Daily 6:30 am–1 pm and 3 pm–6 pm.*

Paseo Las Musas. For some fresh air and great people-watching, head to this pedestrian walking path. The path borders a stream and has classical statues depicting scenes from mythology. Try to ignore the excessive litter along this beautiful promenade. ✉ *La Florida and Falques.*

OFF THE BEATEN PATH

Fodor's Choice ★ Túcume. In Túcume, 35 km (21 miles) north of Chiclayo, you can see an immense pyramid complex, including Huaca Larga, one of the largest adobe pyramids in South America, as well as dozens of smaller ones spread across a dry desert. Go first to the small museum, **Museo de Sitio,** and take a tour with an English-speaking guide to learn about the history of the nearby ruins. Then follow your guide and climb 10 minutes to see the 26 giant pyramids, surrounded by the smaller ones, and the areas in between, which have yet to be excavated.

The rugged desert landscape, sprinkled with hardy little *algarrobo* (mesquite) trees, is probably very similar to what it looked like when—so the legend goes—a lord called Naymlap arrived in the Lambayeque Valley, and with his dozen sons founded the Lambayeque dynasty and built the pyramids we see today. **TIP→ Keep an eye out for burrowing owls as you make your way from the entrance toward the pyramids.**

Adjacent to the archaeological site there is a lovely hotel designed from adobe and algarobbo wood, **Los Horcones de Tucume** (*951/831–705, www.loshorconesdetucume.com*), whose architect/owner seemlessly incorporated pre-Colombian designs into the walled complex. There are 12 airy guest rooms with private terraces and a small pool at the hotel. They can arrange various horse-riding trips through algarobbo forests and meetings with local *curanderos*, or shamans. ☎ *076/422–027* 🎫 *S/10* ⏲ *Daily 8–5.*

WHERE TO EAT

Much like Trujillo, Chiclayo and Lambayeque offer *cabrito, causa,* and *tortilla de raya* (skate omelet). The area is more famous for King Kong, a large, crispy pastry that was invented around the time that the original movie premiered. It's filled with *manjar blanco,* a sweet filling made of sugar, condensed milk, and cinnamon boiled down until it's thick and chewy.

$ PERUVIAN Fodor's Choice ★

🍴 **Fiesta Gourmet.** In 1983 the Solis family began serving modern interpretations of *comida norteña* (typical food of northern Peru) out of their home. It quickly caught on and the restaurant outgrew the simple dining room expanding into an entire building as well as branches in Lima and Trujillo. Today Fiesta Gourmets are widely considered the go-to destinations for the cuisine of this region. Try the sumptuous *cabrito* (kid goat) and *arroz con pato* (duck with rice), as well as dozens of other local specialties and a long list of trendy pisco-based cocktails. [$] *Average main: S/30* ✉ *Salaverry 1820* ☎ *074/201–970* 🌐 *www.restaurantfiestagourmet.com* ⏲ *No dinner Sun.*

$ PERUVIAN 🍴 **Hebrón.** A friendly staff serves a wide range of national and international specialties from 7 am to midnight daily at this centrally located eatery. There's an excellent breakfast menu, free Wi-Fi, big corner windows for good people-watching, and a playground, Hebrónlandia, in the back. Families could easily spend half a day here. There are children's options on the menu, but the whole menu is kid-friendly and the size and price of these dishes is no different. [$] *Average main: S/10* ✉ *Av. Balta 605* ☎ *074/222–709.*

$ PERUVIAN 🍴 **La Parra.** Despite the bland decorations, this restaurant serves delicious grilled meats. La Parra specializes in parrilladas, with an extensive menu including every imaginable part of the cow. The *anticuchos* (beef heart) and *ubre* (cow udder) are well-prepared house specials. If this sounds unappetizing, you can always get grilled steak or head to the *chifa* (Chinese) restaurant next door, run by the same people. [$] *Average main: S/16* ✉ *Manuel María Izaga 752* ☎ *074/227–471.*

$ STEAKHOUSE ★ 🍴 **Marakos Grill.** Come here for the best barbecue in Chiclayo. The grilled-to-perfection *parrillas* (barbecue) combinations are the best options, serving groups ranging from two to seven, and including steak, ribs, chorizo sausages and more—plus your choice of side dishes. For the more adventurous eaters, try the tender *anticucho* (beef heart) or *avestruz* (ostrich). [$] *Average main: S/16* ✉ *Av. Elvira Garcia y Garcia 696* ☎ *074/232–840* 🌐 *www.marakosgrill.com.*

$ PIZZA 🍴 **Nueva Venecia.** This hugely popular Italian restaurant serves fantastic pizza on a wooden block fresh from the oven. The list of toppings is extensive and there are some pasta choices as well. You might have to wait on the street to get in, and once inside you'll feel the almost-stifling heat from the pizza ovens, but you're guaranteed good food and old-country charm. [$] *Average main: S/12* ✉ *Av. Balta 365* ☎ *074/233–384* ⏲ *Closed Sun.*

WHERE TO STAY

$ HOTEL 🏨 **Costa del Sol Chiclayo.** This modern tower just a few blocks from Chiclayo's main plaza is part of the growing Costa del Sol chain, which is aligned with Ramada. **Pros:** central location; great service; pool and gym. **Cons:** can be noisy outside. [$] *Rooms from: S/204* ✉ *Av. Balta 399* ☎ *074/227–272* 🌐 *www.costadelsolperu.com* 🛏 *74 rooms, 8 suites* 🍽 *Breakfast.*

$$ HOTEL 🏨 **Garza Hotel.** Don't be fooled by the bland exterior; inside there's a poolside bar and outdoor fireplace for cool nights, an admirable restaurant serving regional cuisine, a casino, efficient staff, and excellent accommodation. **Pros:** first-rate service and accommodation; central location. **Cons:** run of the mill decor. [$] *Rooms from: S/295* ✉ *Bolognesi 756* ☎ *074/228–172* 🌐 *www.garzahotel.com* 🛏 *91 rooms, 3 suites* 🍽 *Breakfast.*

$ HOTEL ★ 🏨 **Gran Hotel Chiclayo.** One of Chiclayo's best-known hotels which, at this writing was nearing the end of a year-long renovation, is now managed by the Casa Andina chain. **Pros:** central location; first-rate accommodation and amenities. **Cons:** occasionally large business groups overtake the hotel. [$] *Rooms from: S/240* ✉ *Av. Federico Villareal 115* ☎ *074/234–911* 🌐 *www.casa-andina.com* 🛏 *129 rooms, 16 suites* 🍽 *Breakfast.*

$ ⓣ **Inti Hotel.** With refurbished rooms and noise-proof glass for street-
HOTEL   side rooms, this hotel is one of the best deals in Chiclayo. **Pros:** quality
rooms at a low price. **Cons:** dimly lighted hallways; mediocre hotel
restaurant. ⓢ *Rooms from: S/125* ⊠ *Av. Luis Gonzales 622* ☎ *074/235–*
931 ⊕ *www.intiotel.com* ↴ *62 rooms, 2 suites* ⦿| *Breakfast.*

NIGHTLIFE AND THE ARTS

Bali Lounge. This lounge has an extensive menu of high-level, expensive Peruvian and Japanese-Peruvian fusion options, top shelf liquors,
imported beers, and an exuberant crowd listening to DJs pumping out
Latin Rock and 1980s pop. ⊠ *Av. José L. Ortiz 490* ☎ *074/235–932.*

Cafe 900. This bi-level restaurant and bar opens at 8 am for breakfast
and doesn't close until late. Decorated with old guitars and various
knickknacks and furnished with leather couches, it's one of the few
options in Chiclayo with charm. Tapas and sandwiches dominate the
long menu and there are 20 or so different desserts. There is also a
superb cocktail list with new looks at Peruvian favorites, like the *chil-
cano de hierba luisa* (made with lemongrass, pisco, lime, bitters, and
ginger ale). There's occasionally live jazz and folk music. ⊠ *Calle Izaga*
900 ☎ *074/209–268* ⊕ *www.cafe900.com* ⊙ *Closed Sun.*

Solid Gold. A favorite pastime of Chiclayans is karaoke. One of
the hottest places to show your vocal skills is the Gran Hotel Chiclayo's discotheque and bar Solid Gold. ⊠ *Av. Federico Villarreal 115*
☎ *074/234–911.*

SPORTS AND THE OUTDOORS

Pimentel. The closest beach to Chiclayo is this small port town, 14 km
(8½ miles) west of the city. Access via taxi should cost about S/20 each
way. Although the beach is not so attractive and the century-old curved
pier is now closed to the public, there are many other enjoyable sights
along the beach, including a small fleet of *caballitos de totora* and a
lively boardwalk lined with restaurants. Walk along and observe the old
colonial beach houses, the naval officers in white outside the maritime
station, and an excessive number of young Peruvian couples walking
hand in hand. **Amenities:** food and drink. **Best for:** swimming; surfing;
sunset. ⊠ *14 km west of Chiclayo, Pimentel.*

SHOPPING

Mercado Artesanal de Monsefú. For the best handicrafts in the area, go to
Mercado Artesanal de Monsefú, about 14 km (9 miles) south of Chiclayo. You can buy straw hats, baskets, cotton weavings, embroidery,
clay pots, wall hangings, all kinds of delicious snacks, and more. It's
well worth the trip (round-trip taxi from Chiclayo, including waiting
for you to shop, costs about S/35). ⊠ *Av. Venezuela.*

Mercado Central. Chiclayo's indoor Mercado Central on Avenida Balta
is no longer the city's main market. Once famed for its ceramics, weavings, and charms made by local *curanderos* (folk healers), now there's
mainly fresh food for sale, and a nice little "food court" in the back.
⊠ *Av. Balta and Vicente de la Vega.*

Mercado Modelo. Head over to the large, popular Mercado Modelo
beginning at the intersection of Avenida Balta and Avenida Arica. This

vast market has fresh meat, vegetables, and fruit from local farms, as well as clothing, pirated DVDs and CDs, handbags, and more. You can also ask at any of the stalls to point you to the southwest corner, where there is an extensive *mercado de brujos* (witch doctor's market), where dozens of herbalists, *curanderos*, and shamans offer their folk remedies, many of them made of dried animals like armadillos and llama fetuses. Wander around and enjoy, but don't lose your companions in the crowd. ✉ *Av. Balta and Av. Arica.*

LAMBAYEQUE

12 km (7 miles) north of Chiclayo.

This small town has some well-preserved colonial-era buildings, but the reason to come is for the outstanding museums. The museums' exhibits provide details about the Moche civilization, and original artifacts from the tomb in Sipán.

GETTING HERE AND AROUND

The town is small enough to walk around from place to place, or you can take an inexpensive taxi (S/3 within town) to the different museums. To get here from Chiclayo, you can easily hire a taxi or rent a car.

EXPLORING

Museo Arqueológico Nacional Brüning. Go to the archaeological museum to see how the different pre-Incan civilizations lived on a daily basis. Covering the Moche, Lambayeque, and other pre-Inca cultures such as the Cupisnique, Chavín, Chimú, and Sicán, there are excellent interpretive displays, showing how people fished, harvested, and kept their homes. There's also a wonderful photography exhibit of the archaeologist Hans Heinrich Brüning and his experiences in Peru beginning in the late 1800s. Descriptions are in Spanish, so an English-speaking guide is recommended. ✉ *Huamachuco and Atahualpa* ☎ *074/282–110* 🌐 *www.museobruning.com* 🎫 *S/10, S/20 for a guide* 🕘 *Daily 9–5.*

9

Fodor's Choice ★ **Museo Nacional Tumbas Reales de Sipán.** The impressive Museo Nacional Tumbas Reales de Sipán, which ranks among the country's best museums, displays the real artifacts from the tomb of the Lord of Sipán, one of the greatest archaeological finds of recent years. The stunning exhibits detail where every piece of jewelry, item of clothing, or ceramic vase was found. **TIP→ English-speaking guides are available to help with the Spanish-only descriptions and confusing order of exhibits.** All bags, cameras, and cell phones must be checked before you can enter the museum. ✉ *Av. Juan Pablo Vizcardo and Guzmán* ☎ *074/283–977* 🌐 *www.museotumbasrealessipan.pe* 🎫 *S/7, S/20 for a guide* 🕘 *Tues.–Sun. 9–5.*

WHERE TO STAY

$ HOTEL Fodor's Choice ★ 🏨 **Hosteria San Roque.** The most atmospheric place to base yourself while exploring the Chiclayo area's archaeological attractions is not in Chiclayo, but rather in this 18th century *casona* in Lambayeque. **Pros:** authentic, romantic. **Cons:** nothing nearby to do in the evenings. [$] *Rooms from: S/190* ✉ *2 de Mayo 437* ☎📠 *074/282–860* 🌐 *www.hosteriasanroque.com* 🛏 *20 rooms* 🍴 *Breakfast.*

FERREÑAFE

18 km (11 miles) northeast of Chiclayo.

Although it's produced more winners of the Miss Peru contest than any other town, Ferreñafe has other charms. The Iglesia Santa Lucia, begun in 1552, is a good example of baroque architecture. However, most visitors come to visit its excellent new museum.

EXPLORING

Museo Nacional Sicán. Although the Museo Nacional Sicán offers insight into the culture of the Sicán people, there are also unique exhibits on such topics as the *El Niño* effect and where the pre-Incan civilizations fit into world history. Visual timelines hammer home just how far back Peruvian history goes. See the exhibits introducing the Sicán (also known as the Lambayeque), including everything from common eating utensils to ceremonial burial urns, models of what their homes might have looked like, and a central room full of treasures from this coastal culture renowned for its amazing headdresses and masks. ⊠ *Av. Batán Grande* ☎ *074/286–469* 🔖 *S/8* 🕐 *Tues.–Sun. 9–5.*

OFF THE BEATEN PATH

Chaparrí Reserve. Although getting to the Chaparri Reserve on your own can be difficult, if you can get a group together or join a tour to this community-owned dry forest nature preserve a little more than an hour from Chiclayo it might just be one of your most memorable experiences in Peru. The 34,000 hectare reserve was created to help preserve rare native species such as the white winged guan, the Andean Condor, and guanaco (a type of camelid similar in appearance to a llama). Perhaps their most important work is protecting the spectacled bear, for which they have a rescue center that works to reintroduce rehabilitated animals into this last refuge for populations of the species.

Although you can visit the reserve anytime from 7 am to 5 pm, you'll up your chances at seeing wildlife if you stay overnight in the 12-room **Chaparri Ecolodge** (*084/255–718, www.chaparrilodge.com*) in the heart of the reserve. Stays include three daily meals and a guide to the reserve. ▪**TIP➜** Advance booking for day visits and overnight stays is highly recommended as space is limited and all visitors must be accompanied by a guide. ⊠ *75 km northeast of Chiclayo, Chaparrí* ☎ *072/221–4092* ⊕ *www.chaparri.org* 🔖 *S/30* 🕐 *Daily 7–5.*

PIURA

269 km (167 miles) north of Chiclayo.

The sunny climate, friendly people, and good food make Piura a delightful stop on your way north. Since most of the major flight and bus routes to the north-coast beaches travel through Piura, stopping here is not just easy, it's often required.

As Piura is a central commercial hub and the country's fifth-largest city (population 380,000), it's hard to believe how relaxed and friendly the city is to tourists. Historically, however, it's a community used to transitions. Founded in 1532 by Francisco Pizarro before he headed inland to conquer the Incas, the community changed locations three times before settling on the modern-day location along the banks of the Río Piura.

GETTING HERE AND AROUND

LAN Perú, Peruvian Airlines, and Taca fly between Lima and the Aeropuerto de Piura (PIU), 2 km (1 mile) east of the city.

The best way to get around Piura is to walk. However, inexpensive and safe taxis are available from the street if you have heavy bags or are ready for a siesta.

ESSENTIALS

Currency Banco de Crédito ✉ *Av. Grau 133* ☎ *073/336–822* 🌐 *www.viabcp.com.*

Medical Hospital Cayetano Heredia ✉ *Av. Independencia s/n, Urb. Miraflores* ☎ *073/303–208.*

Visitor Information iPerú ✉ *Av. Ayacucho 377* ☎ *073/320–249* 🌐 *www.peru.info.*

EXPLORING

Catedral de Piura. On the city's main square, the Catedral de Piura is worth a visit. Built in 1588, it's one of the country's oldest churches. Inside you'll find an altarpiece dedicated to the Virgen de Fátima dating back more than 350 years. ✉ *Plaza de Armas* 🎟 *Free.*

Museo Vicus. This archaeological museum, sometimes called the Museo Municipal, reopened in 2009 after an extensive renovation. The museum houses the city's collection of pre-Columbian ceramics and gold artifacts, primarily from the Vicus culture, as well as changing art exhibits. ✉ *Avs. Sullana and Huánuco* ☎ *073/30–2803* 🎟 *S/5* 🕒 *Tues.–Sun. 9–1 and 4–7.*

WHERE TO EAT AND STAY

$ PERUVIAN

🍴 **Capuccino.** This modern Peruvian restaurant has an extensive menu. Traditional rice and meat dishes, as well European-inspired salads, sandwiches, and entrées mix local and imported ingredients. Whether you choose the Thai salad or lomo saltado, expect to savor your meal. Relax in the serene dining room and don't forget to order dessert along with the delicious cappuccino. [$] *Average main: S/22* ✉ *La Libertad 1014* ☎ *074/301–111* 🌐 *www.capuccino-piura.com* 🕒 *Closed Sun.*

$$ PERUVIAN Fodor's Choice ★

🍴 **La Sirena D'Juan.** Although most of the restaurants in town offer backpacker grub, this narrow restaurant serves coastal Peruvian cuisine that rivals that of many of the top restaurants in the capital. Chef Juan Seminario, who attended culinary school in Lima, sources local ingredients, riding his motorcycle to the local market to pick up produce and working directly with artisanal fisherman. Mediterranean and Asian elements find their way into dishes such as a Nikkei style *tiradito* (sashimi-style fish with a spicy sauce) and house-made pastas. Despite being the best offering in town, prices are lower here than at most hotel restaurants. **TIP→ Check out the offfshoot tapas bar and café, Sirena Cafe Lounge, opened by Seminario and a partner at Avenida Piura 326.** [$] *Average main: S/36* ✉ *Av. Piura 316* ☎ *073/258–173* 🕒 *Closed Wed. and Sun.*

$
PERUVIAN
Fodor'sChoice
★

✕ **Picanteria La Santitos.** If you ask anyone in Piura the best place to go for typical dishes they'll tell you to go to the nearby town of Catacaos. If you want to stay in town, they'll tell you to come here. Two dining rooms with cracked white walls—one air-conditioned, one not—and waitresses in flowing peasant dresses make the setting for Piuran and regional dishes like *tamales verdes* (green tamales) and *seco de chavelo* (fried green bananas and pork) memorable. Wash everything down with an *algarobbina*, a pisco-based cocktail flavored with the syrup from the area's algarobbo trees. $ *Average main: S/16* ⊠ *La Libertad 1001* 🕿 *074/309–475* ⊗ *No dinner.*

$$
HOTEL

🛏 **Costa Del Sol Piura.** This business hotel, part of the Costa del Sol chain, offers modern rooms and facilities, along with excellent service. **Pros:** catering to business travelers means better all-around service. **Cons:** the modern architecture lacks charm; some rooms have little natural light. $ *Rooms from: S/319* ⊠ *Av. Loreto 649* 🕿 *074/302–864* ⊕ *www.costadelsolperu.com* ↳ *58 rooms, 10 suites* ⏐○⏐ *Breakfast.*

$
HOTEL
★

🛏 **Los Portales.** A venerable hotel on the tree-shaded Plaza de Armas, Los Portales has charming colonial architecture. **Pros:** beautiful colonial architecture; all the modern amenities one could want. **Cons:** some rooms are better than others. $ *Rooms from: S/194* ⊠ *Libertad 875* 🕿 *074/321–161* ⊕ *www.hotelportalespiura.com* ↳ *33 rooms, 2 suites* ⏐○⏐ *Breakfast.*

SHOPPING

Artesanías Lucas. This store has a respectable assortment of artisanal goods in Piura. ⊠ *Jr. Comercio 629.*

Catacaos. The tiny pueblo of Catacaos, 12 km (7 miles) southwest of Piura, is famous for its textiles, gold and silver figurines and jewelry, and excellent pottery. The small market, filled with street stalls and shops, is open daily until 6 pm. Look around as much as you like, but to get the best price, only closely examine what you really want to buy. The town also has excellent *picanterías* to sample northern cuisine. To get to Catacaos, take the Pan-American Highway. A taxi should cost around S/30 round-trip.

MÁNCORA

229 km (142 miles) north of Piura.

This laid-back beach destination, famous for its sunshine and white-sand beaches, has excellent waves for surfing, fishing, and diving. Although the relaxed but dusty town has tourist offices, restaurants, and small shops, the real draws are the hotels about 2 km (1¼ miles) south along **Las Pocitas,** a lovely string of beaches with rocky outcrops that hold tiny pools of seawater at low tide.

GETTING HERE AND AROUND

Comfortable Excluciva and Cruz del Sur buses ply the long 14-hour route between Lima and Máncora. If you wish to fly, LAN Perú connects Lima with the Aeropuerto de Tumbes (TCP), about an hour and a half away, while Star Peru flies seasonally to Talara, about an hour away. Taxis at the airport charge about S/100 for the trip to Máncora or Punta Sal. Once you arrive at Máncora, mototaxis are the best way to get around.

WHERE TO STAY

$$$$ DCO Suites, Lounge & Spa. When
HOTEL   it opened at the far end of Las Pocitas beach in 2008, Máncora and the entire northern coast of Peru had yet to see a hotel so hip. **Pros:** hip; clean; attracts a beautiful crowd. **Cons:** expensive; a long walk from town. $ *Rooms from: S/584 ⊠ Las Pocitas, 3 km south of Máncora ☏ 994/033–780 ⊕ www.hoteldco. com ⇨ 7 suites ◎ Breakfast.*

$ Hotelier Arte y Cocina. Sandwiched
HOTEL   between the fishing pier and the start
☕   of Las Pocitas beach, this small hotel is owned by the son of famed Peruvian TV chef Teresea Ocampo, whose recipes are used in the excellent beach-front restaurant, Donde Teresa. **Pros:** quiet and remote yet close to town; great restaurant. **Cons:** the restaurant has sporadic hours. $ *Rooms from: S/180 ⊠ 1 km south of Máncora ☏ 073/258–702 ⊕ www.hotelier.pe ⇨ 8 suites ◎ Breakfast.*

$ Las Pocitas. This full-service, family-friendly hotel has a large pool,
HOTEL   restaurant, bar, game area, and a beautiful beach. **Pros:** larger spaces
☕   than most hotels; all rooms are on the first floor and face the ocean. **Cons:** if all you want is the beach, you can stay somewhere else for less. $ *Rooms from: S/190 ⊠ Km 1162, Pan-American Hwy. ☏ 073/258–432 ⊕ www.laspocitasmancora.com ⇨ 21 rooms ◎ Breakfast.*

$ Los Corales. Directly on the beach with very reasonable rates, this
HOTEL   little lodging is one of the best deals in Máncora. **Pros:** offers the same
★   beachside location and service as other hotels at a lesser cost. **Cons:** open since 1992, it's one of the oldest properties in Mancora. $ *Rooms from: S/140 ⊠ Km 1215, Old Pan-American Hwy. N ☏ 073/258–309 ⊕ www.loscoralesmancora.com ⇨ 15 rooms ◎ Breakfast.*

$$$$ Mancora Marina Hotel. Better known as MMH, this dramatic white
HOTEL   hotel just south of town was designed by Jordi Puig, who designed the MV Aqua luxury riverboats in the Amazon. **Pros:** close to town; beautiful pool; decent restaurant and bar. **Cons:** pricey; the beach in front can get dirty. $ *Rooms from: S/536 ⊠ Mancora Chico ☏ 073/258–614 ⊕ www.mancoramarina.com ⇨ 12 rooms ◎ Breakfast.*

> **HOLD ON!**
>
> As a general rule, taxis are abundant, cheap, and safe throughout Peru. Enter the mototaxi, a three-wheeled motorcycle, attached to a double-seat, covered by an awning. No metal, no glass, nothing between you, the road and the other cars. The good news? Mototaxis often are slower and go only short distances. Whenever possible, take a regular taxi in a car. However, for those places—especially Máncora and Punta Sal—in which mototaxis are the main source of travel, hold on and enjoy the ride!

9

PUNTA SAL

25 km (15 miles) north of Máncora; 70 km (43 miles) south of Tumbes.

Sit on the beach, go for a swim, and relax in the afternoon sun—just what you want from a beach resort. That's probably why Punta Sal has become a popular vacation spot in recent years. A few kilometers north of the Pan-American Highway, hotels and resorts abound in this area, tourists and vacationing Limeños flock here for the blond-sand beach, comfortable ocean breezes, and sunny climate.

Surfers take to the waves at Máncora, the north's hot spot beach destination.

WHERE TO STAY

$
RESORT
Fodor's Choice
★

⛨ **Hotel Caballito de Mar.** This top-notch beach resort has tropical bungalows with private terraces, an excellent fresh seafood restaurant and beach access. **Pros:** first-rate service; larger family bungalows available; reasonable rates. **Cons:** only the suites have air-conditioning and minibar; prices nearly double during peak holidays. ⓢ *Rooms from: S/186* ✉ *Punta Sal, Km 1187, Pan-American Hwy. N* ☎ *072/540–058* ⊕ *www.hotelcaballitodemar.com* ⌖ *25 rooms* ⓄⒾ *Multiple meal plans.*

$
RESORT
ALL-INCLUSIVE

⛨ **Punta Sal Club Hotel.** Offering a variety of bungalows, rooms, and beach areas, this upscale, all-inclusive resort is the place to go for luxury and relaxation. **Pros:** top-quality hotel. **Cons:** regular rooms are nothing special; rates vary by season. ⓢ *Rooms from: S/195* ✉ *Punta Sal, Km 173, Sullana-Tumbes Hwy.* ☎ *072/540–088* ⊕ *www.puntasal.com.pe* ⌖ *12 rooms, 15 bungalows* ⓄⒾ *All-inclusive.*

TUMBES

183 km (114 miles) north of Piura; 70 km (43 miles) north of Punta Sal.

About an hour's drive north of the beach resorts of Máncora and Punta Sal is Tumbes, the last city on the Peruvian side of the Peru-Ecuador border. Tumbes played a major role in Peruvian history: it was here that Pizarro first saw the riches of the vast Inca Empire in 1528, which he would return to conquer in 1532. In the past, tensions were high—it wasn't until 1941 that Tumbes became part of Peru following a military skirmish. Tensions are now minimal. Hot, muggy Tumbes, is unlike anywhere else in the country. The coastal desert that has defined the Pan-American highway all the way to Chile is no more, and in its place is a landscape that is decidedly more tropical. There are mangrove forests and banana plantations. For most visitors Tumbes is just a transit point to or from Ecuador or a quick stop before an early flight. The city has few attractions or attractive places to spend the night. Though for those with the urge to explore, there are several excellent national parks, loads of inexpensive shellfish, and an atmosphere you will not find anywhere else in Peru.

If you find yourself crossing the border at Aguas Verdes, be extra aware of your personal belongings. Like many border towns, it has its fair share of counterfeit money, illegal goods, and scams to get money from foreigners.

GETTING HERE AND AROUND

Tumbes is the stopping point for most bus lines that travel the Pan-American Highway for the 18- to 19-hour trip to Lima, including Cruz del Sur. To get to Ecuador there are direct buses with CIFA to Guayaquil and Machala, where you can transfer to Cuenca. For most, flying will be their point of entry. Both LAN and Peruvian Airlines offer several flights per week from Lima to the Aeropuerto de Tumbes (TCP), which is just a few kilometers north of the city.

WHERE TO STAY

$ HOTEL **Costa del Sol Tumbes.** A member of the Costa del Sol chain, this hotel is in the heart of downtown and makes for a comfortable option in Tumbes, which has a dearth of nice places to stay. **Pros:** large, inviting pool area; the best hotel in town. **Cons:** Wi-Fi can be hit or miss. [$] *Rooms from: S/210* ✉ *Jr. San Martin 275, Tumbes* ☎ *072/523–991* 🌐 *www.costadelsolperu.com* *51 rooms, 3 suites* 🍴 *Breakfast.*

HUARAZ AND THE CORDILLERA BLANCA

The Cordillera Blanca is one of the world's greatest mountain ranges. The soaring, glaciated peaks strut more than 6,000 meters (19,500 feet) above sea level—only Asia's mountain ranges are higher. Glaciers carve their lonely way into the green of the Río Santa valley, forming streams, giant gorges, and glorious gray-green alpine lagoons. On the western side of the valley is the Cordillera Negra. Less impressive than the Cordillera Blanca, its steep mountains have no permanent glaciers and are verdant and brooding. A drive along the paved stretch of road through the valley offers spectacular views of both mountain ranges. You'll find an abundance of flora and fauna in the valley and in the narrow gorges that come snaking their way down from the high mountains. Deer, *vizcacha* (rodents resembling rabbits without the long ears), vicuñas, pumas, bears, and condors are among the area's inhabitants. You'll also find the 10-meter-tall (32-foot-tall) *puya raimondii* (the world's largest bromeliad), whose giant spiked flower recalls that of a century plant.

The valley between the Cordillera Blanca and the Cordillera Negra is often called the Callejón de Huaylas. It's named after the town of Huaylas in the northern part of the valley. **TIP→ The town is possibly the most important climbing and trekking destination in South America.** From here, arrange to go white-water rafting; head out on a 10-day trek through the vast wilderness; or stay closer to home, taking one-day excursions to the 3,000-year-old ruins at Chavín de Huántar, local hot

Discover Nature

Some of the most incredible flora and fauna live in protected areas near Máncora and Tumbes. Luckily, we can visit these important ecological areas, but only through a reputable tour operator and experienced guide. Do not believe it if someone tells you they can bring you there and back in an hour—if so they are probably referring to Puerto Pizarro. Most trips involve extensive driving, as well as hiking and camping. Including these areas in your itinerary isn't always possible, but the experience will leave you inspired and amazed.

Santuario Nacional Los Manglares de Tumbes: Crocodiles and a diverse collection of birds live in this mangrove reserve. Accessible only by unmotorized boat, this swamp forest is where the ocean water and river water meet, providing some of the most productive ecosystems on the planet.

Parque Nacional Cerros de Amotape: This area was created to protect the equatorial dry forest and its inhabitants. Living in this area are the condor, puma, boa constrictor, and approximately 100 other species of mammals, reptiles, and birds.

Zona Reservada de Tumbes: The dry forest and humid forest exist together in this protected zone, making it one of the more interesting areas to explore. As much of the flora and fauna in this area is in danger of extinction, this is also an extremely important area.

springs, a nearby glacier, and an alpine lagoon. Climbers come during the dry season to test their iron on the more than 40 peaks in the area exceeding 6,000 meters (19,500 feet). The 6,768-meter (21,996-foot) summit of Huascarán is the highest in Peru and is clearly visible from Huaraz on sunny days. To the south of Huaraz, the remote and beautiful Cordillera Huayhuash offers numerous trekking and climbing excursions as well. The outdoor options are limitless.

The area has been inhabited since pre-Inca times, and Quechua-speaking farmers still toil on the land, planting and harvesting crops much as they did thousands of years ago. The land in the valley is fertile, and corn and oranges are abundant. Up above, potatoes and other hearty crops grow on the steep terrain. The goddess Pachamama has always provided, but she can be iron-willed and even angry at times; every now and then she will shake her mighty tendrils and a section of one of the glaciers will crumble. The resulting rock and ice fall, called an *aluvión*, destroys everything in its path. In 1970 one such aluvión resulted from a giant earthquake, destroying the town of Yungay and almost all of its 18,000 inhabitants. Most of the towns throughout the area have suffered some damage from the numerous earthquakes, so not much colonial architecture survives. What remains are friendly, somewhat rugged-looking towns that serve as excellent jumping-off points for exploration of the area's vast wilderness and mountain ranges, hot springs, and 3,000-year-old ruins.

Continued on page 413

BIG MOUNTAINS
of the Cordillera Blanca

by Oliver Wigmore

The lofty ice-clad peaks of Cordillera Blanca soar above 6,000 meters (20,000 feet) and stretch for over 100 kilometers (62 miles) north to south across the Andes. These mountains, worshipped by Andean peoples for thousands of years, are now the idols of global adventure tourism.

Explore ancient ruins, ascend icy summits at the crack of dawn, hike isolated alpine valleys, be absorbed by the endless azure blue of glacial lakes, or put your feet up at a mountain lodge.

The formation of the present Andean mountain chain began as the Nazca plate collided with and was forced beneath the South American plate, driving the ocean floor up to produce the world's longest exposed mountain range. This resulted in the formation of the Pacific coastal desert, the highland puna, and the verdant Amazon basin. Since then the Andes have been the bridging point between these diverse environmental and ecological zones. The Cordilleras Blanca, Negra and Huayhuash, and the Callejón de Huaylas Valley were formed 4 to 8 million years ago, producing spectacular peaks and many distinct ecological niches.

The May to September dry season brings the most stable weather—and the big crowds. Increasingly people are battling the rain and snow for the isolation that comes with the off-season.

Peruvians cross a log bridge in the Jancapampa Valley, as the Cordillera Blanca looms before them.

CORDILLERA BLANCA

Taulliraju Mount, Cordillera Blanca, Huascaran National Park, Peru.

The Cordillera Blanca encompasses the mighty Huascarán, Peru's highest peak at 6,767 m (22,204 ft), and Alpamayo 5,947 m (19,511 ft), once proclaimed the most beautiful mountain in the world by UNESCO. Most of the Cordillera Blanca is within the Huascarán National Park, for which an entry ticket is required. Valid for one day or one month, these can be purchased at the entry gates or from the park headquarters in Huaraz.

Thanks to the newly paved road, the glacial lakes are now a popular day trip from Huaraz. Their beauty is still worth the trip.

HIGH POINTS

1. **The Santa Cruz Trek:** You ascend the Santa Cruz valley, crossing the Punta Union pass at 4,760 m (15,617 ft) beneath the breathtaking peaks, then descend to the spectacular azure blue of the Llanganuco Lakes. One of Peru's most popular alpine treks, it's often overcrowded, with litter and waste becoming a serious problem. For pristine isolation, look elsewhere.

2. **Pastoruri Glacier:** You can walk on a tropical glacier, ice-climb, ski, and witness the impacts of climate change. Popular day tours from Huaraz often combine the trip here with a visit to see the impressive Puya raimondii trees.

3. **Chavín de Huántar:** On the eastern side of the cordillera is Chavin de Huantar, where in around 900 BC the first pan-Andean culture developed. The Chavin culture eventually held sway over much of central Peru. The site can be visited on a long day trip from Huaraz.

4. **Olleros to Chavín Trek:** A short three-day trek across the Cordillera terminates at Chavin de Huantar. Guiding companies in Huaraz offer this trek with llama hauling your gear.

5. **Quilcayhuanca and Cojup Valley Loop:** This trek is becoming popular due to its relative isolation and pristine condition. It explores two spectacular high alpine valleys, crosses the 5,000 m (16,404 ft) Pico Choco Pass, passing beautiful glacial lakes, one of which caused the 1941 destruction of Huaraz city in a flood of mud, rocks, and ice.

6. **Laguna 69:** Spectacular glaciers encircle the lake and give it deep turquoise color. It can be seen on a long day hike from Huaraz. However, spending the night allows you to explore, and you will likely have the lake to yourself once the day trippers leave. This is an ideal acclimation trek.

7. **Alpamayo Basecamp:** An arduous week-long trek takes you on a northern route through the Cordillera, passing the spectacular north face of Nevado Alpamayo (5947 m/19,511 ft).

8. **Huascarán:** Peru's highest peak is one of the Cordillera's more challenging summits.

Climbing: Relatively easy three to five day guided summit climbs of Ishinka (5,550 m/18,208 ft), Pisco (5,752 m/18,871 ft) and Vallunaraju (5,684 m/18,648 ft) are arranged at any of the guiding outfitters in Huaraz. Prices and equipment vary—get a list of what's included. Many smaller companies operate purely as booking agencies for the larger companies.

1 The Santa Cruz Trek

Huaicayan

Cashapampa

Huaripampa

Artesonraju ▲

7 Alpamayo
5,947m
(19,511ft)

Pirámide ▲

▲ Caraz

Pisco
5,752m
(18,871ft)

0   3 mi
0   3 km

Caraz

Laguna 69 **6**

Huandoy ▲

Yanama

C O R D I L L E R A

(H U A S C A R A N)

▲ Chacraraju

Chopicalqui

▲ Contrahierbas

Pueblo
Libre

Yungay

Huascarán
6,768m
(22,204ft)

Utla

Chacas

C
O
R
D
I
L
L
E
R
A

Río Santa

Musho

Huaypan

Pompey

N
A
T
I
O
N
A
L

B
L
A
N
C
A

Hualcan ▲

Mancos

Shilla

Huaicán

▲ Copa

Utlo

▲ Copa

Copa Chico

Vicos ▲

Bayoraju ▲

▲ Paqcharaju

Carhuaz

Ranrahirca

Marcará

Vicos

Kekepatipa

Pashpa

Akilpo

▲ Toellaraju

Anta

Joncopampa

P
A
R
K

▲ Palcaraju

Taricá

Coltón

Ishinka
5,550m
(18,208ft) ◆

Pucaranra ▲

Jangas

Ranrapaica ▲

Pico Choco

Vallunaraju
5,684m
(18,648ft) ◆

COJUP
VALLEY

▲ Churup

Monterrey

Wilkawain

5 Quilcayhuanca and
Cojup Valley Loop

C
O
R
D
I
L
L
E
R
A

N
E
G
R
A

Pitec

QUILCAYHUANCA
VALLEY

Huaraz

Huahulac

Macashca

Río Santa

Chavín de
Huántar **3**

Pastoruri
Glacier **2**

4 Olleros

Agocancha

A llama—member of the camelid
family and provider of wool for
Andean weavers—Chavín, Cordillera Blanca.

GOOD TO KNOW

CLIMBING HISTORY

The first climbers in the region were probably pre-Colombian priests, attempting difficult summits to perform sacred rituals atop icy peaks. This climbing tradition was continued by the Spanish conquistadors who wanted to exploit the rich sulphur deposits atop many of Peru's volcanic cones, and to show their dominance over Mother Nature. Modern climbing in the region took off in 1932 when a German-Austrian expedition completed many of the highest summits, including Huascarán Sur. Since then the peaks of the Cordillera Blanca and Peru have attracted climbers from around the world for rapid-summit sport climbs and solo summits. Extended duration expeditions and large support crews are less common here than in the Himalayas.

SAFETY TIPS

This area is a high alpine environment and weather patterns are unpredictable. Be prepared for all weather possibilities. It's not uncommon to experience snow storms and baking sun over the course of a single day, and at night temperatures plummet. Sunburn, dehydration, exhaustion, and frostbite are all potential problems, but by far the major issue is *soroche* (altitude sickness). It's extremely important to pace yourself and allow enough time for acclimatisation before attempting any long-distance high-altitude treks or climbs.

(above) Cullicocha; (below) Sheperds hut, Huaraz.

ENVIRONMENTAL CHANGE

The warming climate is producing alarming rates of retreat in glacial water reserves of the Cordillera Blanca. The heavily populated Pacific coast relies almost exclusively on seasonal run-off from the eastern Andes for water supplies and hydroelectricity. The feasibility of transporting water across the Andes from the saturated Amazon basin is now being debated.

MAPS

For serious navigation, get the Alpenvereins-karte (German Alpine Club) topographic map sheets, which cover the Cordillera Blanca over two maps (north and south). They are sold by Casa de Guías and the gift store below Café Andino. Many local expedition outfitters sell an "officially illegal" copy with a little persuasion.

HUARAZ

400 km (248 miles) north of Lima.

Peru's number-one trekking and adventure-sports destination, Huaraz is an easy starting point for those wishing to explore the vast wilderness of the Cordillera Blanca. Unfortunately, the town has been repeatedly leveled by natural disasters. In the later part of the 20th century three large earthquakes destroyed much of Huaraz, claiming more than 20,000 lives.

Despite the setbacks and death toll, Huaraz rallied, and today it's a pleasant town filled with good-natured people. Being one of the most popular tourist destinations in northern Peru, Huaraz also has a great international scene; while the town has few sights, the lively restaurants and hotels are some of the best in the region. ■ TIP➔ Many businesses close between September and May, when the town practically shuts down without its hoards of climbers and trekkers. It can be hard to find an outfitter at this time; call ahead if you plan a rainy-season visit.

GETTING HERE AND AROUND

Most travelers come to Huaraz on an eight-hour bus ride from Lima, though the small airline LC Peru has several flights per week to the area's small airport in Anta, 32 km north of town. Getting around the city is quite easy, as it is small enough to walk almost anywhere. Or, if you've just arrived and are feeling a little breathless from the altitude, take a taxi for S/5. To enjoy any of the nearby treks and sights, hire a guide, as it's not safe to go alone.

ESSENTIALS

Currency Banco de Crédito ⊠ *Av. Luzuriaga 691* ☎ *043/421–170* ⊕ *www.viabcp.com.* **Scotiabank** ⊠ *José de Sucre 760* ☎ *043/721–500* ⊕ *www.scotiabank.com.pe.*

Mail Post Office ⊠ *Av. Luzuriaga 702* ☎ *043/421–030.*

Medical Hospital Victor Ramos Guardia ⊠ *Av. Luzuriaga, Cuadra 8* ☎ *043/421–861.*

Rental Car Monte Rosa ⊠ *Jr. José de la Mar 691* ☎ *043/421–447.*

Visitor Information iPerú ⊠ *Pasaje Atusparia* ☎ *043/428–812* ⊕ *www.peru.info.*

EXPLORING

Jirón José Olaya. To see Huaraz's colonial remnants, head to Jirón José Olaya, a pedestrian-only street where several houses with handsome facades still stand. It's best to visit on Sunday when there's a weekly *Feria de Comida Típica,* a regional street festival with local food and craft stalls. ⊠ *East of town center, on right-hand side of Raimondi and a block behind Confraternidad Inter Este.*

Mercado Central. For a pungent look at Andean culture, head to the Mercado Central. At this market you'll see fruits and vegetables grown only in the highlands as well as cuy, chickens, ducks, and rabbits, which you can purchase alive or freshly slaughtered. ⊠ *Entrance at Jr. de la Cruz Romero and Av. Cayetano Requena.*

9

Mirador de Retaquenua. The lookout point has an excellent view of Huaraz, the Río Santa, and the surrounding mountains. It's a 45-minute walk up, but the directions are complicated so it's best to hire a guide or, better yet, take a taxi. ⊠ *Av. Confraternidad Inter Sur and Av. Confraternidad Inter Este.*

Museo Arqueológico de Ancash. The small Museo Arqueológico de Ancash displays some very unique items, including a mummified baby and teenager, created by covering the dead with salt, *muña* (wild mint), *quinua* (a cornlike plant), and *izura* (pink earth). ■**TIP➔** Upstairs numerous skulls bear the scars (or rather holes) from trepanation, the removal of bone from the skull. Additionally, the museum has Chavín textiles and ceramics, and a delightful little park accessible through the bottom floor. Here you'll find original carved stones, benches, and a little café. ⊠ *Av. Luzuriaga 762* ☎ *043/421–551* ⊕ *www.huaraz.com/museo* ⊠ *S/5, includes a guide* ⊙ *Mon.–Sat. 9–5, Sun. 9–1.*

Plaza de Armas. Every few years, as a new mayor is elected, the town gets an updated Plaza de Armas, which is on the corner of Luzuriaga, the town's main drag, and José Sucre. Thanks to the current mayor, who removed a gigantic, towering statue of Christ, the plaza provides nice views of the surrounding mountains. There are several *ferias artesenales* (artisanal kiosks) bordering the plaza. ⊠ *Corner of Luzuriaga and José Sucre.*

Wilcahuaín. North of the city is a small archaeological site called Wilcahuaín. The Wari temple, dating back to AD 1100, resembles the larger temple at Chavín de Huántar. Each story of the crumbling three-tiered temple has seven rooms. There's a small museum and recently built basic bathroom facilities and a limited restaurant. Trained and knowledgeable local students will be your guide for a small tip (suggested minimum tip: S/15). ⊠ *8 km (5 miles) north of Huaraz* ⊠ *S/5* ⊙ *Daily 6–6.*

OFF THE BEATEN PATH

Glaciar Pastoruri. A popular day trip from Huaraz is a visit to the Pastoruri Glacier, where you can hike around the glacier and visit a glowing blue-ice cave. The rapidly shrinking ice field, which could disappear within the next few years, has become a symbol of global climate change. ■**TIP➔** On this trip you'll ascend to well above 4,000 meters (13,000 feet), so make sure you're used to the high altitude. Wear warm clothing, sunscreen, and sunglasses, as the sun is intense. Drink lots of water to avoid altitude sickness. The easiest and safest way to get here is with a tour company from Huaraz. The tour costs about S/20 to S/30 and takes eight hours. Admission to the glacier is S/5. You can also hire diminutive horses to take you up to the glacier from the parking lot for about S/15. It's not the most spectacular glacier in the world, but if you've never seen one up close, it's worth the trip. The glacier is about three hours south of Huaraz, off the main highway at the town of Recuay. ⊠ *70 km (43 miles) south of Huaraz.*

WHERE TO EAT AND STAY

$ ✕ **Creperie Patrick.** With a breezy terrace upstairs and a cozy bistro downstairs, this French eatery is an excellent choice. There's couscous and
FRENCH   fondue, as well as hard-to-find local dishes such as grilled alpaca. Don't

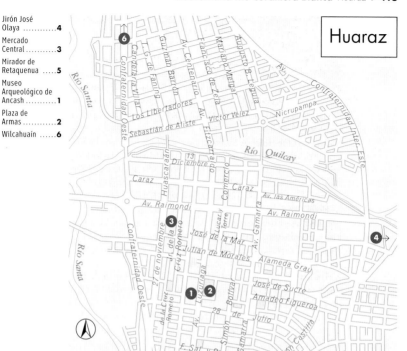

Huaraz

miss the sumptuous dessert crepes and good wine selection. After two decades in Peru, chef and owner Patrick Bertrand now makes homemade delicacies including his own liquors, jams, mustards, granola, and more. $ *Average main: S/18* ⊠ *Av. Luzuriaga 422* ☎ *043/426–037* ⊕ *creperiepatrick.com* ⊟ *No credit cards.*

$ ✗**El Horno.** With a terrace area for sunny afternoons and a recently

ITALIAN expanded dining room for the evenings, El Horno is a good stop any

★ time. ■**TIP➔** Here you'll find some of the finest pizzas in Huaraz—baked by a Frenchman, no less. The doughy crusts are superb and the service faultless. Excellent salads, sandwiches, pastas, and barbecued meats are also on the menu. If you are, by some chance, looking for French books, there is a French-only book exchange here as well. $ *Average main: S/15* ⊠ *Parque del Periodista 37* ☎ *043/424–617* ⊕ *www.elhornopizzeria.com* ⊟ *No credit cards* ⊘ *Closed Sun. No lunch Oct.–Apr.*

$ ✗**Piccolo Ristorante.** Walk straight to the outdoor patio in the back to

ITALIAN enjoy your meal in the peaceful Parque del Periodista. The Italian eatery specializes in pastas and pizza, but the international specialties like *filete de trucha a la piamontesa* (trout in herb sauce) and filet mignon round out the menu nicely. The breakfasts are especially good, as is the freshly brewed coffee. $ *Average main: S/18* ⊠ *Jr. Julián de Morales 632* ☎ *043/509–210.*

9

$ THAI ★ 🍴 **Siam de Los Andes.** Thai food high in the Peruvian Andes—who would have thought? It's probably the best Thai restaurant in Peru. Siam de Los Andes is a true anomaly in the land of tacu-tacu and pollo a la brasa. The light, delicate, and at times extremely spicy food is the real deal; from the chicken satay to the shredded pork, it's very good. The Thailand-born owner's secret? He takes regular trips to the homeland, importing those hard-to-find ingredients. [$] *Average main: S/25* ✉ *Augustin Gamarra 560* ☎ *043/428–006* 💳 *No credit cards* 🕒 *Closed Oct.–Apr. No lunch.*

$$ HOTEL 🏨 **Andino Club Hotel.** A Swiss-style chalet set high on the hill above Huaraz, Andino Club Hotel is one of the town's best lodgings. **Pros:** the best views in Huaraz. **Cons:** it's just outside the heart of central Huaraz. [$] *Rooms from: S/365* ✉ *Pedro Cochachín 357* ☎ *043/421–662* 🌐 *www.hotelandino.com* 🛏 *50 rooms, 4 suites* 🍽 *Breakfast.*

$ HOTEL 🏨 **Hotel San Sebastián.** Perched on the side of a mountain, this hotel has great views of the Cordillera Blanca. **Pros:** reasonable rates with first-rate accommodation. **Cons:** the decor could use a facelift. [$] *Rooms from: S/146* ✉ *Jr. Italia 1124* ☎ *043/426–960* 🌐 *www.sansebastianhuaraz.com* 🛏 *30 rooms, 1 junior suite.*

$ B&B/INN 🏨 **The Lazy Dog Inn.** The Canadian owners who built this ecofriendly adobe lodge and two private cabins are heavily involved with community and environmental activities in Huaraz and the Cordillera Blanca. **Pros:** cabins can sleep four to five people; secluded; close to nature; some rooms have fireplaces. **Cons:** far from town. [$] *Rooms from: S/210* ✉ *12 km east of Huaraz* ☎ *043/978–9330* 🌐 *www.thelazydoginn.com* 🛏 *5 rooms.*

NIGHTLIFE

To warm yourself up at night, enjoy one of the many cool bars and dance clubs.

Café Andino. This funky café offers light snacks, hot and cold beverages, free Wi-Fi, and a seemingly endless supply of newspapers and books in English. ✉ *Jr. Lucar y Torre 530, 3rd fl.* ☎ *043/421–203* 🌐 *www.cafeandino.com.*

el Tambo. The ever-popular el Tambo has low ceilings and curvy walls. There's a large dance floor where you can get down to salsa music until the wee hours of the morning. ✉ *José de la Mar 776* ☎ *043/423–417.*

Los 13 Buhos. This cool little lounge above Makondo's offers its own homebrew and inexpensive pub grub. ✉ *José de la Mar 812.*

Makondo's. The music at this dance club nearby el Tambo (another club on the strip) tends to be pop. ✉ *José de la Mar and Simón Bolívar* ☎ *043/423–629.*

X-treme Bar. For strong cocktails and loud rock music head to X-treme Bar. ✉ *Gabino Uribe and Luzurriaga* ☎ *043/423–150.*

SPORTS AND THE OUTDOORS

BIKING

If you're an experienced mountain biker, you'll be thrilled at what the area offers along horse trails or gravel roads, passing through the Cordilleras Blanca and Negra.

Mountain Bike Adventures. This shop rents Specialized bikes and has experienced guides to take you to the good single-track spots. ⊠ *Jr. Lucar and Torre 530* ☎ *043/424–259* ⊕ *www.chakinaniperu.com.*

CLIMBING AND TREKKING

If dreams of bagging a 6,000-meter (19,500-foot) peak or trekking through the wilderness haunt your nights, Huaraz is the place for you. Huaraz sits at a lofty 3,090 meters (10,042 feet), and the surrounding mountains are even higher. Allowing time to acclimatize is a life-saving necessity. Drinking lots of water and pacing yourself help avoid high-altitude pulmonary edema (commonly known as altitude sickness, or *soroche* in Peru). ■ TIP➔ The climbing and trekking season runs from May through September—the driest months. You can trek during the off-season, but drudging every day through thick rain isn't fun. Climbing during the off-season can be downright dangerous, as crevasses get covered up by the new snow. Even if you're an experienced hiker, you shouldn't venture into the backcountry without a guide.

The guided treks in the region vary by the number of days and the service. You can opt for smaller one-, two-, and three-day hikes, or an expedition of 10 to 20 days. Most guided treks provide donkeys to carry your equipment, plus an emergency horse. So many outfitters are in the area that looking for a qualified company can become overwhelming. Visit a few places, talk with the guides, and make sure you're getting what you really want.

Casa de Guías. An association of certified freelance guides, Casa de Guías offers excellent advice and personalized trips, including mountaineering and trekking as well as rock- and ice-climbing courses. ⊠ *Parque Ginebra 28/G* ☎ *043/427–545* ⊕ *www.casadeguias.com.pe* ☉ *Closed Sun.*

WHITE-WATER RAFTING

There's good rafting on the Río Santa with Class 3 and 4 rapids. The freezing cold glacial river water brings heart-pumping rapids. The most-often-run stretch of river is between Jangas and Caraz. The river can be run year-round, but is at its best during the wettest months of the rainy season, between December and April. Be prepared with the right equipment; the river is cold enough to cause serious hyperthermia.

Monttrek. One of the best rafting outfitters in Huaraz, the company also has friendly and experienced guides for trekking and mountaineering. ⊠ *Av. Luzuriaga 646, upstairs* ☎ *043/421–124* ⊕ *www. monttrek.com.pe.*

SHOPPING

Craft booths on either side of the Plaza de Armas have tables piled high with locally woven textiles.

Tatoo Adventure Gear. There is a large selection of quality gear here, mainly imported. ⊠ *Jr. Simón Bolívar 26* ☎ *043/422–966* ⊕ *www. tatoo.ws.*

CHAVÍN DE HUÁNTAR

110 km (68 miles) southeast of Huaraz.

GETTING HERE AND AROUND

If you have a car—and an excellent map and good sense of direction—you can head out and explore the windy, confusing roads. For all others, simply hiring an inexpensive taxi when needed will ensure that you arrive where you need to safely. Major trips and treks should be arranged with experienced, certified guides.

Fodor'sChoice
★

Chavín de Huántar. Although the ruins, which date as far back as 1500 BC, appear unimpressive at first—most of the area was covered by a huge landslide in 1945—underground you'll discover a labyrinth of well-ventilated corridors and chambers. ▓TIP➜ They're illumined by electric lights that sometimes flicker or fail altogether—it's wise to bring your own flashlight. Deep inside the corridors you'll come upon the **Lanzón de Chavín.** This 4-meter-high (13-foot-high) daggerlike rock carving represents a human-animal hybrid deity (complete with fangs, claws, and serpentine hair); it sits elegantly at the intersection of four corridors. Built by the Chavín, one of the first civilizations in Peru, little is known about this ancient culture, although archaeologists believe they had a complex religious system. The main deity is always characterized as a puma or jaguar. Lesser deities, represented by condors, snakes, and other animals, were also revered.

This is a fascinating archaeological site that you can day-trip to from Huaraz. Chavín de Huántar sits on the southern edge of Chavín, a tiny village southeast of Huaraz. On the drive from Huaraz you get good views of two Andean peaks, Pucaraju (5,322 meters/17,296 feet) and Yanamarey (5,237 meters/17,020 feet). Construction on the road may delay your journey—check on conditions before setting out. Tours from Huaraz visit the ruins, a small on-site museum, and the alpine Laguna de Querococha during the eight-hour tour. The tour costs about S/30 per person, not including the entrance fee to the ruins. If you'd prefer to get here on your own, regular buses run between Huaraz and Chavín, and you can hire a guide at the entrance to the ruins. ✉ *Chavín* 🎫 *S/11* 🕙 *Daily 8–4.*

MONTERREY

5 km (3 miles) north of Huaraz.

This area provides a quiet and attractive alternative to Huaraz. For some, it can feel isolating: there isn't a town center, just hotels and restaurants spread about. There are local hot springs and a nice hiking trail just behind Hotel Monterrey that leads across a stream and up into the hills, eventually taking you to the Wilcahuaín Ruins. And you're just a 15-minute drive from Huaraz.

GETTING HERE AND AROUND

To get to the Monterrey area, head north from Huaraz on what is popularly called the Callejón de Huaylas, passing attractive little villages and taking in spectacular scenery from the comfort of your car.

CLOSE UP

Life in the Andes

This region of the Andes has sustained some 12,000 years of cultural development. From Guitarrero Cave through the Chavín, Huari, and Inca cultures to the present day.

The highland puna has been the breadbasket for countless generations of Andean communities. Fertile glacial plains and mineral-rich rivers provide the nutrients for the rigorous growing cycles of traditional highland crops such as potatoes, while lower elevations allow the production of grains including quinoa, oats, barley, wheat, and corn. The region also provides pasture for wild and domestic herds of llamas, alpacas, and vicuñas. Various species of birds and waterfowl also inhabit the area, and sightings of the enormous condor are possible.

To this day traditional life remains a struggle. Indigenous populations continue to eke a meager existence from the land, while attempting to keep up with the rapidly changing face of a modernizing Peru. Increasingly young people are moving away from traditional life to find employment in the cities, mines, or Peru's booming tourism industry.

—Oliver Wigmore

EXPLORING

Los Baños Termales de Monterrey. Popular with locals, Los Baños Termales de Monterrey is a large public bathing area where you can soak your troubles away. Although the facilities could use some refreshing, a dip in the sulfur-rich waters is quite relaxing. For a more tranquil bath, as it can get very crowded on the weekends, you can rent a private tub. Didn't bring your bathing suit on your hiking trip? Don't worry, you can buy (or rent!) one here. ✉ *Av. Monterrey s/n, at Hotel Monterrey* ☎ *043/427–690* 🎫 *S/3.50* ⏲ *Daily 7–5.*

9

WHERE TO EAT AND STAY

$ PERUVIAN ★ ✕ **El Cortijo.** This outdoor restaurant has the absolute best barbecue around, from steaks to ribs. The plastic patio furniture, placed around the grass and centered on the large barbecue pit, add to the "downhome" feeling. Or maybe it's the swing set in the front. Either way, El Cortijo is a great place to spend part of a sunny afternoon—or perhaps the entire afternoon, as there are large portions and the service can be slow. It is open from 8 am to 7 pm. 💲 *Average main: S/12* ✉ *Carretera Huaraz–Caraz* ☎ *043/423–813* ⏲ *No lunch Oct.–Apr.*

$ B&B/INN Fodor's Choice ★ **El Patio de Monterrey.** A lovely hacienda built in the colonial style, El Patio is a great lodging option for those wishing to stay in the country, yet it's only 6 km (4 miles) from Huaraz. **Pros:** close to the city; luxurious country-estate. **Cons:** you may not see much else while you're here. 💲 *Rooms from: S/222* ✉ *Carretera Huaraz–Caraz, Km 206* ☎ *043/424–965* 🌐 *www.elpatio.com.pe* *25 rooms, 4 cabañas* 🍽 *Breakfast.*

CARHUAZ

35 km (22 miles) north of Huaraz.

A small, laid-back village, less touched by recent earthquakes, Carhuaz is a popular stop along the Callejón de Huaylas. A bright spot is the ice-cream shop, which scoops up excellent homemade *helado*. The town comes alive with bullfights, fireworks, dancing, and plenty of drinking during its festival honoring the Virgen de la Merced, held every year September 14–24. This is one of the best festivals in the region.

WHERE TO EAT

$ ✕ **Heladería El Abuelo.** You won't want to miss this ice-cream shop,
CAFÉ mostly for the fantastic flavors such as pisco sour and beer. The owner is a good source for information about the region; he also rents nice rooms in a lodge near town, **Hostal El Abuelo** (*043/394456, www.elabuelo-hostal.com*). Ⓢ *Average main: S/7* ✉ *La Merced 727* ☎ *043/394–149* 🚫 *No credit cards.*

YUNGAY

59 km (37 miles) north of Huaraz.

On May 31, 1970, an earthquake measuring 7.7 on the Richter scale shook loose some 15 million cubic meters of rock and ice that cascaded down the west wall of Huascarán Norte. In the quiet village of Yungay, some 14 km (8½ miles) away, people were going about their normal activities. Some were waiting for a soccer game to be broadcast on the radio, others were watching the Verolina Circus set up in the stadium. Then the debris slammed into town at a speed of more than 200 miles per hour. Almost all of Yungay's 18,000 inhabitants were buried alive. The quake ultimately claimed nearly 70,000 lives throughout Peru.

The government never rebuilt in Yungay, but left it as a memorial to those who had died. They now call the area **Campo Santo,** and people visit the site daily. ■ **TIP→** Walking through the ruined town, you'll see upturned buses, the few remaining walls of the cathedral, and, oddly, a couple of palm trees that managed to survive the disaster. There's a large white cross at the old cemetery on the hill south of town. It was here that 92 people who were tending the graves of friends and relatives were on high-enough ground to survive. You pay a nominal S/2 to enter the site.

New Yungay was built just beyond the aluvión path—behind a protective knoll. It serves as a starting point for those visiting the spectacular Lagunas de Llanganuco.

LAGUNAS DE LLANGANUCO

Fodor'sChoice **Lagunas de Llanganuco.** Make sure your camera memory card is empty
★   when you go to see these spectacular glaciers, gorges, lakes, and mountains. Driving through a giant gorge formed millions of years ago by a retreating glacier, you arrive at Lagunas de Llanganuco. The crystalline waters shine a luminescent turquoise in the sunlight; in the shade they're a forbidding inky black. ■ **TIP→** Waterfalls of glacial melt snake

Cordillera Huayhuash Treks

While much smaller than the Cordillera Blanca, the main chain of the Cordillera Huayhuash is known for its isolation and pristine environment. For years the area remained essentially off limits to foreign tourism as it was a major stronghold for the Shining Path movement that wracked much of Peru's central highlands with terrorism throughout the 1980s. Today this isolation is what makes the region so special. Treks in this region are measured in weeks not days, with road access and tourist infrastructure almost nonexistent. The opportunities to spot rare Andean wildlife are much greater here and the chances of meeting tour groups next to zero.

Cordillera Huayhuash Circuit: The major draw here is the Cordillera Huayhuash circuit. This taxing trek can take up to two weeks, passing some of the region's most spectacular mountain scenery. Access to this trail was traditionally via Chiquián, but the road has now been extended to Llamac. Tours and supplies are best organized in Huaraz, although Chiquián does provide some limited facilities, and porters and mules can be arranged here.

Siula Grande (6,344 meters, 20,813 feet): See the mountain made famous by Joe Simpson in his gripping tale of survival in *Touching the Void.*

Yerupaja (6,617 meters, 21,709 feet): The second-highest mountain in Peru.

—Oliver Wigmore

their way down the gorge's flanks, falling lightly into the lake. There are many *quenual* trees (also known as the paper-bark tree) surrounding the lakes. Up above, you'll see treeless alpine meadows and the hanging glaciers of the surrounding mountains. At the lower lake, called Lago Chinancocha, you can hire a rowboat (S/3 per person) to take you to the center of the lake. A few trailside signs teach you about local flora and fauna. The easiest way to get here is with an arranged tour from Huaraz (about S/30 plus entrance fee), though if you are going on the Santa Cruz trek you will probably start here. The tours stop here and at many other spots on the Callejón de Huaylas, finishing in Caraz. ☎ S/5.

EXPLORING

Fodor'sChoice ★ **Parque Nacional Huascarán.** Laguna Llanganuco is one of the gateways to the Parque Nacional Huascarán, a 340,000-hectare park created in 1975 to protect and preserve flora and fauna in the Cordillera Blanca. ■ TIP→ This incredible mountain range has a total of 663 glaciers and includes some of the highest peaks in the Peruvian Andes. Huascarán, which soars to 6,768 meters (21,996 feet), is the highest in Peru. The smaller Alpamayo, 5,947 meters (19,327 feet), is said by many to be the most beautiful mountain in the world. Its majestic flanks inspire awe and wonder in those lucky enough to get a glimpse. The monstrous Chopicalqui and Chacraraju rise above 6,000 meters (19,500 feet).

Within the park's boundaries you'll find more than 750 plant types. There's a tragic scarcity of wildlife in the park—most have been decimated by hunting and the loss of natural habitats. Among the 12 species of birds and 10 species of mammals in the park, you're most likely to see wild ducks and condors. With a great deal of time and an equal amount of luck you may also see foxes, deer, pumas, and viscachas.

The giant national park attracts campers, hikers, and mountain climbers. Myriad treks weave through the region, varying from fairly easy 1-day hikes to 20-day marathons. Within the park, you can head out on the popular **Llanganuco–Santa Cruz Loop,** a three- to five-day trek through mountain valleys, past crystalline lakes, and over a 4,750-meter-high (15,437-foot-high) pass. Other popular hikes include the one-day Lake Churup Trek, the two-day Quilcayhuanca–Cayesh trek, and the two-day Ishinca Trek. Check with guide agencies in Huaraz for maps, trail information, and insider advice before heading out.

Although experienced hikers who know how to survive in harsh mountain conditions may want to head out on their own, it's much safer to arrange for a guide in Huaraz. You can opt to have donkeys or llamas carry the heavy stuff, leaving you with just a daypack. The most common ailments on these treks are sore feet and altitude sickness. Wear comfortable hiking shoes that have already been broken in, and take the proper precautions to avoid altitude sickness (drink lots of water, avoid prolonged exposure to the sun, and allow yourself time to acclimatize before you head out). The best time to go trekking is during the dry season, which runs May through September. July and August are the driest months, though dry season doesn't mean a lack of rain or even snow, so dress appropriately.

Some hikers decide to enter the park at night to avoid paying the hefty S/65 for a multiday pass (from 2 to 30 days). The money from these fees goes to protect the wonders of the Andes; consider this before you slip in during the dead of night. (Nighttime safety is a concern, too.) You can purchase a pass at the Huaraz office of Parque Nacional Huascarán, at the corner of Rosas and Federico Sal, as well as at Llanganuco. ■TIP→ Be sure to carry a copy of your passport with you. ⊠ *Huaraz office of Parque Nacional Huascarán, Federico Sal y Rosas 555* ☎ *043/422–086* ⌦ *S/5 day pass, S/65 multiday pass* ⊗ *Daily 6–6.*

CARAZ

67 km (42 miles) north of Huaraz.

One of the few towns in the area with a cluster of colonial-era architecture, Caraz is at the northern tip of the valley—only a partly paved road continues north. North of Caraz on the dramatic road to Chimbote is the Cañon del Pato, the true northern terminus of the Callejón de Huaylas. Caraz is an increasingly popular alternative base for trekkers and climbers. While in town be sure to try the ultrasweet *manjar blanco, Peru's version of dulce de leche.*

WHERE STAY

$ B&B/INN Fodor's Choice ★ **Chamanna.** This cluster of cabañas among beautifully landscaped gardens is the town's best lodging. **Pros:** location provides peace and quiet; beautiful vistas; good restaurant. **Cons:** hiring taxis and traveling means less time to enjoy the great outdoors. [$] *Rooms from: S/90* ✉ *Av. Nueva Victoria 185* ☎ *044/689–257* 🌐 *www.chamanna.com* *10 cabañas, 5 with bath* 🍴 *No meals.*

THE NORTHERN HIGHLANDS

The green valleys and high mountaintops that comprise the northern highlands are certainly one of the area's biggest draws, as is the area's rich history. But few travelers venture here; it's hard to reach and far from the more popular destinations of Cusco, Puno, and Machu Picchu.

Several major archaeological sites are in the northern highlands. **TIP→** The pre-Inca fortress of Kuélap, near Chachapoyas, is one of the region's best-preserved ruins. The region's largest town, Cajamarca, is the center for exploration and was the site of one of history's quickest and wiliest military victories. It was here in 1532 that Pizarro and his meager force of 160 Spaniards were able to defeat more than 6,000 Inca warriors and capture Atahualpa, the new king of the Inca empire. Without a king, the vast empire quickly crumbled. In and around Cajamarca you'll find a handful of Inca and pre-Inca sites. There are also chances for horseback riding and hiking in the green valleys and hills.

CAJAMARCA

865 km (536 miles) northeast of Lima; 304 km (188 miles) northeast of Trujillo.

Cajamarca is the best place to stay if you want to explore the lovely landscape and rich history of the northern highlands; from here there are a number of daylong excursions to nearby ruins and hot springs.

The largest city in the northern highlands, it's a tranquil town of more than 150,000 people. Sitting in a large green valley surrounded by low hills, it feels a bit like Cusco minus all the tourists. The name Cajamarca means "village of lightning" in the Aymara language. It's fitting, for the ancient Cajamarcans worshipped the god Catequil, whose power was symbolized by a bolt of lightning. **TIP→** The area around town was first populated by the Cajamarcan people, whose major cultural influence came from the cat-worshipping Chavín, 3,000 years ago. The Inca conquered the region in about 1460, assimilating the Chavín culture. Cajamarca soon became an important town along the *Capac Ñan* or Royal Inca Road.

The arrival of the Spanish conquistador Pizarro and his quick-witted defeat of the Incas soon brought the city and much of the region into Spanish hands. Few Inca ruins remain in modern-day Cajamarca; the settlers dismantled many of the existing structures to build the churches that can be seen today. The town's colonial center is so well preserved that it was declared a Historic and Cultural Patrimony Site by the Organization of American States in 1986.

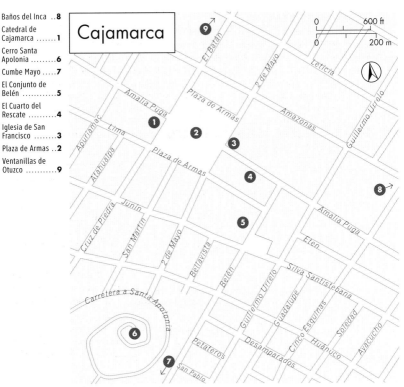

GETTING HERE AND AROUND

LAN Perú and LC Peru fly several times per week between Lima and the Aeropuerto de Cajamarca (CJA), 3 km (2 miles) east of town.

Most places are within walking distance, but taxis are abundant if you feel a little breathless from the altitude or want to go somewhere a little outside of the city center. If you like your taxi driver, arrange a pickup another day. For major exploration outside of the city, the best option is to join a tour for the day. Cajamarca is 2,650 meters (8,612 feet) above sea level. Although not very high by Andes standards, it's still quite high. Take your time, wear sunscreen, and drink plenty of water to avoid altitude sickness.

ESSENTIALS

Currency Banco de Crédito ⊠ *Jr. Apurimac 717* ☎ *076/362-742*
⊕ *www.viabcp.com.* **Scotiabank** ⊠ *Jr. Amazonas 750* ☎ *076/827-101*
⊕ *www.scotiabank.com.pe.*

Mail Post Office ⊠ *Jr. Amazonas 443* ☎ *076/364-065.*

Medical Hospital de Cajamarca ⊠ *Av. Mario Urtega 500* ☎ *076/822-557.*

Visitor Information iPerú ⊠ *Av. 13 de Julio s/n* ☎ *076/823-042*
⊕ *www.peru.info.*

EXPLORING

Baños del Inca. About 6 km (4 miles) east of Cajamarca are these pleasant hot springs offering several public pools and private baths with varying levels of quality, as well as some spa facilities such as a sauna and massage tables. Each service has a separate price, though everything is quite inexpensive. The central bath, Poza del Inca, is an intact Incan pool with a system of aqueducts built by the Incas and still in use today. Despite the large size of the complex, it's quite relaxing and popular with the locals. ■ TIP→ Don't forget to bring your swimsuit and a towel! ⊠ *Av. Manco Cápac* ☎ *076/348–563* ⊕ *www.ctbinca.com.pe* ✉ *S/6* ☉ *Daily 5–8.*

Catedral de Cajamarca. Originally known as the Iglesia de Españoles (because only Spanish colonialists were allowed to attend services), this cathedral on the Plaza de Armas was built in the 17th and 18th centuries. It has an ornate baroque facade that was sculpted from volcanic rock. Like many of the town's churches, the cathedral has no belfry; the Spanish crown levied taxes on completed churches, so the settlers left the churches unfinished, freeing them from the tight grip of the tax collector. ⊠ *Jr. Del Batán and Amalia Puga* ✉ *Free* ☉ *Daily 3–6.*

Cerro Santa Apolonia. At the end of Calle 2 de Mayo are steps leading to this hilltop *mirador*, or scenic lookout, to see a bird's-eye view of the city. At the top are many carved bricks dating to pre-Columbian times. ■ TIP→ One of the rocks has the shape of a throne and has been dubbed the Seat of the Inca. According to local legend, it was here that Inca rulers would sit to review their troops. You'll find pretty gardens and great views of the town. You can either walk or go by taxi (round-trip S/5). ⊠ *End of 2 de Mayo* ✉ *S/2* ☉ *Daily 8–6.*

OFF THE BEATEN PATH

Ventanillas de Otuzco (*Otuzco Windows*). One of the oldest cemeteries in Peru, the Ventanillas de Otuzco dates back more than 3,500 years. The ancient necropolis, 8 km (5 miles) northeast of Cajamarca, is comprised of several large burial niches carved into a cliff. From afar the niches look like windows, hence the area's name. On closer inspection you see that many of the burial niches have carved decorations. Sadly, the site is slowly being eroded by wind and rain. If you're inspired by this cemetery, you can go about 30 km (18 miles) from Combayo, in the same direction, and visit the better-preserved Ventanillas de Combayo. A three-hour guided tour to Ventanillas de Otuzco costs around S/25.

★ **El Conjunto de Belén.** Built in the 17th century, this large complex, originally a hospital, now houses the city's most interesting museums and a colonial church. At the **Museo Arqueológico de Cajamarca,** the town's archaeological museum, are exhibits of Cajamarcan ceramics and weavings. The pre-Inca Cajamarcans were especially famous for their excellent patterned textiles that were often dyed vivid shades of blue. The **Museo Etnográfico** has a few displays of everyday bric-a-brac—there's even an old saddle and a dilapidated coffee grinder—dating back to precolonial times. The **Iglesia de Belén** is a charming church with a polychrome pulpit and cupola. ⊠ *Jr. Belén and Jr. Junín* ☎ *076/362–903* ✉ *S/5, includes admission to entire Conjunto de Belén and El Cuarto del Rescate* ☉ *Mon., Wed.–Fri. 9–1 and 3–6, weekends 9–1.*

9

El Cuarto del Rescate. The Ransom Chamber is the only Inca building still standing in Cajamarca and, although the big stone room itself isn't much to look at, the history is enough to make this worth a visit. Legend has it that after Pizarro and his men captured Atahualpa, the Inca king offered to fill the chamber once with gold and twice with silver. The ransom was met, up to a marking on the stone wall, but the war-hardened Spaniards killed Atahualpa anyway. ✉ *Jr. Amalia Puga 750* ☎ *044/922–601* 🎟 *S/5, includes admission to Conjunto de Belén* ⏲ *Mon., Wed–Fri. 9–1 and 3–6, weekends 9–1.*

Iglesia de San Francisco. Built in the 17th and 18th centuries, the Church of San Francisco sits proudly on the Plaza de Armas in front of the main cathedral. The church's two bell towers were begun in Republican times and finished in 1951. The church was called the Iglesia de Indios (Church of the Indians) as indigenous peoples were not allowed to attend services at the main cathedral. ■ **TIP→ Inside you'll find catacombs and a small religious-art museum.** To the right of the church, the Capilla de la Virgen de Dolores is one of Cajamarca's most beautiful chapels. A large statue of Cajamarca's patron saint, La Virgen de Dolores, makes this a popular pilgrimage destination for local penitents. ✉ *Northeast corner of Plaza de Armas* 🎟 *S/3 for museum* ⏲ *Daily 3–6.*

Plaza de Armas. Like most colonial cities, this is the main square and includes a fountain, benches, and street vendors, making it a nice place to hang out. Built on roughly the same spot as the great plaza where the Atahualpa was captured and later killed, Cajamarca's Plaza de Armas no longer shows any sign of Inca influence. ✉ *Av. Lima and Arequipa.*

OFF THE BEATEN PATH

Cumbe Mayo. This pre-Inca site, 23 km (14 miles) southwest of Cajamarca, is surrounded by a large rock outcropping, where you'll find various petroglyphs left by the ancient Cajamarcans. There are also petroglyph-adorned caves so a guided tour is highly recommended. This site, discovered in 1937 by the famous Peruvian archaeologist J.C. Tello, also includes some of the most notable aqueducts in the Andes. Constructed around 1000 BC, the aqueduct was designed to direct the ample water from the Andes into the drier area of Cajamarca, where there was a large reservoir. Amazingly, more than 8 km (5 miles) of the ancient aqueduct are intact today. Guided tours cost around S/25 and take about four hours.

WHERE TO EAT

$ BAKERY

🍴 **Cascanuez.** This is the place in Cajamarca for decadent desserts and delicious coffee. Casanuez translates to "The Nutcracker," and Sugar Plum Fairies would approve of the extensive homemade pastries, tortes, and other tempting treats. There's also a small lunch and dinner menu with highland staples such as *caldo verde* (a culantro spiced potato soup) and grilled meats, but the desserts are their mainstay. [$] *Average main: S/12* ✉ *Av. Puga 554* ☎ *076/366–089.*

$ PERUVIAN ★

🍴 **El Batán.** Although the food is quite good, the real feast is the visual one: the restaurant building is a beautiful 18th-century mansion. The patio dining area, including a stained-glass roof, has iron chairs and a stone floor. The indoor dining room is just so-so though. In addition to picturesque surroundings, this criollo restaurant has specialty meat dishes, a menu in Spanish and English, a small art gallery upstairs, and live music on weekends. [$] *Average main: S/20* ✉ *Jr. Del Batán 369* ☎ *076/366–025* 🕒 *No dinner Sun.*

$ PERUVIAN ★ 🍴 **El Querubino.** Ask for the chef's daily specials or choose from a large selection of dishes, such as *causa de langostinos* (mashed potatoes with shrimp), roasted duck, fettucini with pesto sauce, or gnocchi with herbed sauce. El Querubino has the most extensive wine list in Cajamarca and nice details, such as monogrammed plates in pastel hues and walls painted a soft Tuscan yellow, but service is slow. [$] *Average main: S/24* ✉ *Av. Puga 589* ☎ *076/340–900.*

$ PERUVIAN 🍴 **La Chanita.** Step into the Mercado Central and walk past the buckets of varying regional potatoes, past the stalls selling *cuy* (guinea pig), *charqui* (dehydrated meat), and rainbow-color displays of quinoa and other Andean grains. In one corner of the market, during lunch only, you'll find a crowd of people lining up for *cebiche frito*, a locally famous fried version of cebiche where the fish is battered and topped in a spicy mayo and plated with leche de tigre and all the other usual cebiche fixings. You'll have to elbow your way to a counter seat; otherwise just take your plate and go. [$] *Average main: S/6* ✉ *Mercado Central, Jiron Apurimac* 🌐 *www.lachanita.com* 🕒 *No dinner.*

$ PERUVIAN 🍴 **Salas.** Across from the Plaza de Armas, this is where to get no frills, typical food from the region. Open 7–10 daily, the menu includes authentic regional specialties such as cuy, *perico* (a lake fish), and Spanish-style tortillas. There's also an extensive selection of piscos, top-shelf liquors, and wines. Although the furnishings and staff look like they have been there since the restaurant opened in 1947, the food is fresh and delicious. [$] *Average main: S/12* ✉ *Av. Puga 637* ☎ *076/362–867.*

WHERE TO STAY

$$ HOTEL 🏨 **Costa del Sol Cajamarca.** While it lacks the colonial antiques of many nearby B&Bs, the Cajamarca branch of Peruvian chain Costa del Sol, though seemingly quite modern, is actually designed from a historic mansion of a notable local family. **Pros:** clean; comfortable; superb location. **Cons:** the plaza can be quite noisy in the evenings. [$] *Rooms from: S/286* ✉ *Jr. Cruz de Piedra 707* ☎ *076/362–472* 🌐 *www.costadelsolperu.com* 🛏 *71 rooms* 🍽 *Breakfast.*

$ B&B/INN 🏨 **El Portal del Marqués.** Within Cajamarca's historic district, the rooms in this lovely casona surround two sunny courtyards. **Pros:** in the heart of Cajamarca city. **Cons:** the city can be noisy. [$] *Rooms from: S/160* ✉ *Jr. de Comercio 644* ☎ *076/368–464* 🌐 *www.portaldelmarques.com* 🛏 *31 rooms, 2 suites* 🍽 *Breakfast.*

$ B&B/INN 🏨 **Hotel El Ingenio.** Like many other hotels in the area, this is in a renovated hacienda with extensive grounds, but it is the best bargain in Cajamarca and only a 10-minute walk from the plaza. **Pros:** quality service at a very reasonable price. **Cons:** some rooms are better than others. [$] *Rooms from: S/220* ✉ *Av. Via de Evitamiento 1611–1709* ☎ *076/368–733* 🌐 *www.elingenio.com* 🛏 *33 rooms, 6 suites* 🍽 *Breakfast.*

9

$$$ HOTEL Fodor's Choice ★ 🏨 **Hotel Laguna Seca.** Come here to pamper yourself—this refurbished hacienda, which has well-manicured garden areas throughout its extensive grounds, offers private and public baths from the nearby thermal hot springs. **Pros:** relaxing; in-room hot-spring water; spa. **Cons:** outside the city limits. [$] *Rooms from: S/382* ✉ *Av. Manco Cápac 1098, Baños del Inca* ☎ *076/584–300* 🌐 *www.lagunaseca.com.pe* 🛏 *37 rooms, 5 suites* 🍴 *Breakfast.*

$ B&B/INN ★ 🏨 **La Posada del Puruay.** In the countryside, this hacienda is far from the noise of Cajamarca and has extensive gardens, a trout hatchery, and green hills for horseback riding and hiking. **Pros:** transported to another time and place; reasonable price. **Cons:** small number of rooms can be a drawback if you don't enjoy socializing with the other guests. [$] *Rooms from: S/235* ✉ *Carretera Porcón, Km 4.5* ☎ *076/367–028* 🌐 *www.posadapuruay.com.pe* 🛏 *7 rooms, 6 suites* 🍴 *Breakfast.*

DRINKING THE AGUARDIENTES

Aguardientes (homemade liqueurs) are common throughout the region. They're made in sundry flavors, including *mora* (blackberry), *maracuyá* (passion fruit), *café* (coffee), and *leche* (milk). Some jungle towns such as Chachapoyas and Pucallpa sell bottles of the stuff and are more than willing to offer tourists a sample of these strong, home-brewed liqueurs.

NIGHTLIFE

Entre Copas. For a trendy bar-restaurant with sushi and tapas on the menu, check out this spot, which is slightly more upscale than the other nightlife in Cajamarca. ✉ *Jr. Silva Santisteban 172* ☎ *076/341–535* 🌐 *www.entrecopas.pe.*

Cowboy Pub. This Western-theme local watering hole is popular with the town's miners. ✉ *Amalia Puga 212* ☎ *076/365–529.*

Los Frailones. This beautifully renovated casona has antiques throughout and offers an air of sophistication not often found in these parts. The waiters dress in monks' robes. The house has several levels, where you'll find a grill, a dance floor, and a cozy pub. There are peñas on weekends and sometimes during the week. ✉ *Av. Perú 701* ☎ *076/364–113* 🌐 *www.losfrailones.com.*

Up & Down. There is a dance floor in the basement here with overwhelmingly loud salsa and pop music. ✉ *Tarapacá 782.*

SPORTS AND THE OUTDOORS

A number of hikes are in the area around Cajamarca, from the rivers of the region, to past Inca and pre-Inca ruins. Most follow the *Capac Ñan,* or Royal Inca Road, that ran from Cusco all the way north to Quito. One of the most popular walks is to the pre-Inca necropolis of **Combayo.** To get to the trailhead, drive 20 km (12 miles) north of the Baños del Inca. The hike takes around four or five hours. The **Ruta del Tambo Inca** takes you to an old Inca *tambo,* or resting point. It's difficult to find this trailhead, and roads sometimes get washed out during the rainy season, so ask in town to confirm the following: drive 46 km (28 miles) from Cajamarca on the road to Hualgayoc. Near Las Lagunas turn onto a dirt road and follow the road to the milk depository at

Ingatambo. The trail begins here. The 16-km (10-mile) trip takes about eight hours. The best time to go trekking is during the dry season, May through September.

Clarín Tours. This tour company offers trips, with English-speaking guides, to many of the ruins in and around Cajamarca. ✉ *Jr. Del Batán 165* ☎ *076/366–829* ⊕ *www.clarintours.com.*

SHOPPING
The town of **Llacanora,** 13 km (8 miles) from the city on the road to the Baños del Inca, is a typical Andean farming community, now a cooperative farm, famous for agriculture and making reed bugles. People come to see the traditional village, but there are also several shops around town selling locally produced goods.

CHACHAPOYAS

460 km (285 miles) east of Chiclayo.

At the *ceja de la selva* (jungle's eyebrow), Chachapoyas is the capital of Peru's Amazonas department. ■ TIP➔ The town is a good jumping-off point for exploring some of Peru's most fascinating and least-visited pre-Inca ruins. The giant fortress at Kuélap, the Gocta waterfall, the Karajia sarcophagi, and the ruins of Purunllacta and Gran Vilaya are nearby. Despite the Amazonas moniker, there's nothing junglelike about the area around Chachapoyas. The surrounding green highlands constitute what most people would call a highland cloud forest. Farther east, in the region of Loreto (won by Peru in the 1942 border dispute with Ecuador), you'll find true jungle.

Chachapoyas is a sleepy little town of 20,000. It has a well-preserved colonial center and one small archaeological museum. Chachapoyas—difficult to reach because of the poor roads through the mountains—is most easily accessed from Chiclayo. Infrequent flights arrive here from Lima as well.

GETTING HERE AND AROUND
In town everything is close and within walking distance. There are plenty of taxis, but you'll have little chance of needing one. To get to the archaeological sites, you must go with a guide. The most enjoyable and cost-effective way of doing this is with a tour. There's no public transportation, and you cannot hire a guide once at the sites.

ESSENTIALS
Currency Banco de Crédito ✉ *Jr. Ortiz Arrieta 576* ☎ *041/477–430* ⊕ *www.viabcp.com.*

Medical Hospital Chachapoyas ✉ *Jr. Triunfo, Cuadra 3* ☎ *044/477–354.*

Visitor Information iPerú ✉ *Jr. Ortiz Arrieta 590* ☎ *041/477–292* ⊕ *www.peru.info.*

EXPLORING
Gocta Waterfall. Surprisingly, Gocta, a 771 meter (2,529 feet) waterfall, believed to be the third tallest in the world, wasn't brought to the attention of the Peruvian government until 2006. The falls, about 50

The circular structures at the pre-Inca city of Kuélep

km (31 miles) are strongest during the rainy season, from November to April, though during the dry season the sun will likely be out and you will be able to swim at the base of the falls. Occasionally, on the 2.5 hour hike from Cocachimba (you can hire guides there if you are not coming on a tour from Chachapoyas) you may be able to spot toucans or the endemic yellow tailed wooly monkey. ■ TIP→ The best way to appreciate the falls is by staying at the charming, 10-room **Gocta Lodge** (*042/526–694, www.goctalodge.com*), especially if you prefer the light of the morning or afternoon. ⊠ *hike from Cocachimba.*

Iglesia Santa Ana. The Iglesia Santa Ana is the town's oldest church. It was one of Peru's first "Indian churches," where indigenous people were forced to attend services. The church was built in the 17th century and is on a small square of the same name. ⊠ *Av. Santa Ana.*

Museo Arqueologíco. Showing artifacts from the area's ancient civilizations, a small display of Chachapoyan ceramics is at the Museo Arqueologíco. You'll also find a ghoulish display of mummies lying in the fetal position. ⊠ *Jr. Ayacucho 504* ☎ *041/477–045* 🎫 *Free* ⊙ *Weekdays 8–1 and 2–4:45.*

Pozo de Yanayacu. This small, rocky natural hot spring a few blocks west of the Plaza de Armas at the Pozo de Yanayacu isn't much, but is nice to look at. It's said the spring magically appeared during a visit from Saint Toribio de Mogrovejo. ⊠ *Jr. Salamanca, 2 blocks west of Jr. Puno.*

OFF THE BEATEN PATH

Museo Leymebamba. One of the most fantastic museums in all of Peru, the Museo Leymebamba, opened in 2000, can be found in this small village 60 km (40 miles) south of Chachapoyas. Inside are more than 200 mummies, some dating back over 500 years, that were discovered high on a limestone cliff above the Laguna de los Condores in 1997, as well as other artifacts from the Chachapoyas culture. If you get a group together a taxi from Chachapoyas will cost about S/150 round-trip, otherwise you can take a Cajamarca bound bus (via Celendin) and asked to be let off at Leymebamba. ✉ *60 km south of Chachapoyas, Leymebamba* ☎ *041/816–803* ⊕ *www.museoleymebamba.org* 💲 *S/12* ◷ *Tues.–Sun. 9:30–4:30. Closed Mon.*

Purunllacta. About 35 km (22 miles) southeast of Chachapoyas are the ruins of Purunllacta, a good place for hiking. With pre-Inca agricultural terraces, dwellings, ceremonial platforms, and roads extending for more than 420 hectares, but few tourists, this can be peaceful and also boring as you have no explanation of what you're seeing. To get here, drive to the town of Cheto. From the town it's a one-hour walk uphill to the site. Few people know about this or go, so ask in Cheto for directions to the trailhead, and don't be alarmed if you have to ask more than one person. There's no entrance fee. ✉ *35 km (22 miles) southeast of Chachapoyas.*

WHERE TO EAT AND STAY

$

PERUVIAN

✕ **El Tejado.** With windows overlooking the town's Plaza de Armas, this is one of the most elegant eateries in Chachapoyas. The criollo food is serviceable, and the staff is most attentive when the *dueña* (owner) is around. 💲 *Average main: S/15* ✉ *Jr. Santo Domingo 424* ☎ *041/477–592* 🚫 *No credit cards* ◷ *No dinner Sun.*

$

EUROPEAN

✕ **La Tushpa.** Probably the best eatery in town, La Tushpa has good grilled steaks served with homemade *chimichuri* (a green sauce made with herbs, garlic, and tomatoes). There are also pizzas and other items from the on-site bakery. Though the place feels institutional, the restaurant is more welcoming than most in the region, thanks to an extremely friendly wait-staff. Make sure to look at the Andean textiles hanging on the walls. Ask to see the owner's orchard garden, which he keeps above the restaurant. 💲 *Average main: S/18* ✉ *Jr. Ortiz Arrieta 769* ☎ *041/477–478.*

$

HOTEL

🏠 **Casa Andina Chachapoyas.** Under construction at this writing with a late 2012 estimated completion date, this new hotel from reliable mid-range Casa Andina chain shows just how far along the Chachapoyas area has come in the past few years. **Pros:** attractive setting; pool; newly built. **Cons:** far from town. 💲 *Rooms from: S/216* ✉ *Km 39 de la Carretera Pedro Ruiz* ☎ *01/213-9739* ⊕ *www.casa-andina.com* 🛏 *21* ◍ *Breakfast.*

$

B&B/INN

★

🏠 **Hostal Casa Vieja.** This colorful old house, which dates back to the 1800's, with its bougainvillea-filled courtyard and pleasant terraces, is the finest in Chachapoyas. **Pros:** amazing old house with modern touches. **Cons:** some rooms are better than others. 💲 *Rooms from: S/170* ✉ *Jr. Chincha Alta 569* ☎ *041/477–353, 512/466–7211 in U.S.* ⊕ *www.casaviejaperu.com* 🛏 *11 rooms, 3 suites.*

$

HOTEL

🏠 **Hotel Vilaya.** A pleasant, if slightly antiseptic, hotel in the center of Chachapoyas, the Hotel Vilaya has rooms with simple wooden furnishings. **Pros:** good service. **Cons:** unattractive building. 💲 *Rooms from: S/130* ✉ *Jr. Ayacucho 734* ☎ *041/477–664* ⊕ *www.hotelvilayachachapoyas.com* 🛏 *22 rooms* 🚫 *No credit cards* ◍ *Breakfast.*

9

$ **Puma Urco.** Simple, clean rooms
HOTEL and friendly staff make this a good
budget alternative. **Pros:** good
location. **Cons:** very basic rooms.
$ *Rooms from: S/142* ✉ *Jr. Amazonas 833* ☎ *041/477–871* ⊕ *www.hotelpumaurco.com* ⤴ *22 rooms*
†Ⓞ *Breakfast.*

CERAMIC STOP

About 10 km (6 miles) north of
Chachapoyas is the tiny pueblo of
Huancas, whose citizens are well
known for their pottery; this is a
good place to buy artisanal goods
and locally made ceramics.

NIGHTLIFE

La Estancia. The owner of this
friendly pub loves to chat with the customers about the region's history and natural beauty. ✉ *Jr. Amazonas 861* ☎ *041/478–432.*

La Reina. There is a large selection of *aguardientes* (locally distilled liquors) in flavors that range from *leche* (milk) to *mora* (blackberry) here. ✉ *Jr. Ayacucho 723* ☎ *041/477–618.*

KUÉLAP

72 km (45 miles) south of Chachapoyas.

GETTING HERE AND AROUND

A visit to Kuélap is an all-day affair. It's best to visit Kuélap with a tour group from Chachapoyas. The trip costs around S/60 per person. Vilaya Tours, in the Hotel Vilaya, is highly recommended. Remember to bring a hat for protection from the sun. Take frequent rests and drink lots of water to avoid altitude sickness.

★ **Kuélap.** The most impressive archaeological site in the area is this immense pre-Inca city, 72 km (45 miles) south of Chachapoyas. Most visitors to this region come solely to see the grand city. Little is known about the people who built it; archaeologists have named them the Chachapoyans or Sachupoyans. They were most likely a warlike people, as the city of Kuélap is surrounded by a massive defensive wall ranging from 6 to 12 meters (20 to 40 feet) high. The Chachapoyans left many cities and fortresses around the area. In 1472 they were conquered by the Inca Huayna Capac. If you've been to Machu Picchu, or just seen photographs, you'll recognize many similarities in this complex, built almost a thousand years before.

The city sits at a dizzying 3,100 meters (10,075 feet) above sea level, high above the Rio Utcubamba. The oval-shape city has more than 400 small, rounded buildings. The city's stonework, though rougher than that of the Inca, has geometric patterns and designs, adding a flight of fancy to a town seemingly designed for the art of war. The most interesting of the rounded buildings has been dubbed El Tintero (the Inkpot). Here you'll find a large underground chamber with a huge pit. Archaeologists hypothesize that the Chachapoyans kept pumas in this pit, dumping human sacrifices into its depths. ✉ *72 km (45 miles) south of Chachapoyas* 🎟 *S/12* ⊙ *Daily 6–6.*

UNDERSTANDING PERU

English–Spanish
Vocabulary

SPANISH VOCABULARY

ENGLISH	SPANISH	PRONUNCIATION

BASICS

ENGLISH	SPANISH	PRONUNCIATION
Yes/no	Sí/no	see/no
Please	Por favor	pore fah-**vore**
May I?	¿Me permite?	may pair-**mee**-tay
Thank you (very much)	(Muchas) gracias	(**moo**-chas) **grah**-see-as
You're welcome	De nada	day **nah**-dah
Excuse me	Con permiso	con pair-**mee**-so
Pardon me	¿Perdón?	pair-**dohn**
Could you tell me?	¿Podría decirme?	po-dree-ah deh-**seer**-meh
I'm sorry	Lo siento	lo see-**en**-toh
Good morning!	¡Buenos días!	**bway**-nohs **dee**-ahs
Good afternoon!	¡Buenas tardes!	**bway**-nahs **tar**-dess
Good evening!	¡Buenas noches!	**bway**-nahs **no**-chess
Good-bye!	¡Adiós!/¡Hasta luego!	ah-dee-**ohss**/**ah**-stah **lwe**-go
Mr./Mrs.	Señor/Señora	sen-**yor**/sen-**yohr**-ah
Miss	Señorita	sen-yo-**ree**-tah
Pleased to meet you	Mucho gusto	**moo**-cho **goose**-toh
How are you?	¿Cómo está usted?	**ko**-mo es-**tah** oo-**sted**
Very well, thank you	Muy bien, gracias	**moo**-ee bee-**en**, **grah**-see-as
And you?	¿Y usted?	ee oos-**ted**
Hello (on the telephone)	Diga/Aló	**dee**-gah/ah-**loh**

NUMBERS

1	un, uno	oon, **oo**-no
2	dos	dos
3	tres	tress
4	cuatro	**kwah**-tro
5	cinco	**sink**-oh
6	seis	saice

7	siete	see-**et**-eh
8	ocho	**o**-cho
9	nueve	new-**eh**-vey
10	diez	dee-**es**
11	once	**ohn**-seh
12	doce	**doh**-seh
13	trece	**treh**-seh
14	catorce	ka-**tohr**-seh
15	quince	**keen**-seh
16	dieciséis	dee-es-ee-**saice**
17	diecisiete	dee-es-ee-see-**et**-eh
18	dieciocho	dee-es-ee-**o**-cho
19	diecinueve	**dee**-es-ee-new-ev-eh
20	veinte	**vain**-teh
21	veinte y uno/veintiuno	**vain**-te-**oo**-noh
30	treinta	**train**-tah
32	treinta y dos	train-tay-**dohs**
40	cuarenta	kwah-**ren**-tah
43	cuarenta y tres	kwah-**ren**-tay-**tress**
50	cincuenta	seen-**kwen**-tah
54	cincuenta y cuatro	seen-**kwen**-tay **kwah**-tro
60	sesenta	sess-**en**-tah
65	sesenta y cinco	sess-**en**-tay **seen**-ko
70	setenta	set-**en**-tah
76	setenta y seis	set-**en**-tay **saice**
80	ochenta	oh-**chen**-tah
87	ochenta y siete	oh-**chen**-tay see-**yet**-eh
90	noventa	no-**ven**-tah
98	noventa y ocho	no-**ven**-tah-o-choh
100	cien	see-**en**
101	ciento uno	see-en-toh **oo**-noh

200	doscientos	doh-see-**en**-tohss
500	quinientos	keen-**yen**-tohss
700	setecientos	set-eh-see-**en**-tohss
900	novecientos	no-veh-see-**en**-tohss
1,000	mil	meel
2,000	dos mil	dohs meel
1,000,000	un millón	oon meel-**yohn**

COLORS

black	negro	**neh**-groh
blue	azul	ah-**sool**
brown	café	kah-**feh**
green	verde	**ver**-deh
pink	rosa	**ro**-sah
purple	morado	mo-**rah**-doh
orange	naranja	na-**rahn**-hah
red	rojo	**roh**-hoh
white	blanco	**blahn**-koh
yellow	amarillo	ah-mah-**ree**-yoh

DAYS OF THE WEEK

Sunday	domingo	doe-**meen**-goh
Monday	lunes	**loo**-ness
Tuesday	martes	**mahr**-tess
Wednesday	miércoles	me-**air**-koh-less
Thursday	jueves	hoo-**ev**-ess
Friday	viernes	vee-**air**-ness
Saturday	sábado	**sah**-bah-doh

MONTHS

January	enero	eh-**neh**-roh
February	febrero	feh-**breh**-roh
March	marzo	**mahr**-soh
April	abril	ah-**breel**

May	mayo	**my**-oh
June	junio	**hoo**-nee-oh
July	julio	**hoo**-lee-yoh
August	agosto	ah-**ghost**-toh
September	septiembre	sep-tee-**em**-breh
October	octubre	oak-**too**-breh
November	noviembre	no-vee-**em**-breh
December	diciembre	dee-see-**em**-breh

USEFUL PHRASES

Do you speak English?	¿Habla usted inglés?	**ah**-blah oos-**ted** in-**glehs**
I don't speak Spanish	No hablo español	no **ah**-bloh es-pahn-**yol**
I don't understand (you)	No entiendo	no en-tee-**en**-doh
I understand (you)	Entiendo	en-tee-**en**-doh
I don't know	No sé	no seh
I am American/British	Soy americano (americana)/inglés(a)	soy ah-meh-ree-**kah**-no (ah-meh-ree-**kah**-nah)/in-**glehs**(ah)
What's your name?	¿Cómo se llama usted?	**koh**-mo seh **yah**-mah oos-**ted**
My name is...	Me llamo...	may **yah**-moh
What time is it?	¿Qué hora es?	keh **o**-rah es
It is one, two, three...o'clock.	Es la una/Son las dos, tres...	es la **oo**-nah/sohn lahs dohs, tress
Yes, please/No, thank you	Sí, por favor/No, gracias	**see** pohr fah-**vor**/no **grah**-see-us
How?	¿Cómo?	**koh**-mo
When?	¿Cuándo?	**kwahn**-doh
This/Next week	Esta semana/la semana que entra	**es**-teh seh-**mah**-nah/lah seh-**mah**-nah keh **en**-trah
This/Next month	Este mes/el próximo mes	**es**-teh mehs/el **proke**-see-mo mehs
This/Next year	Este año/el año que viene	**es**-teh **ahn**-yo/el **ahn**-yo keh vee-**yen**-ay

Yesterday/today/ tomorrow	Ayer/hoy/mañana	ah-**yehr**/oy/mahn-**yah**-nah
This morning/ afternoon	Esta mañana/ tarde	es-tah mahn-**yah**-nah/ **tar**-deh
Tonight	Esta noche	es-tah **no**-cheh
What?	¿Qué?	keh
What is it?	¿Qué es esto?	keh es **es**-toh
Why?	¿Por qué?	pore **keh**
Who?	¿Quién?	kee-**yen**
Where is . . .? the train station?	¿Dónde está . . .? la estación del tren?	**dohn**-deh es-**tah** la es-tah-see-on del trehn
the bus stop?	la parada del autobus?	la pah-**rah**-dah del ow-toh-**boos**
the post office?	la oficina de correos?	la oh-fee-**see**-nah deh koh-**rreh**-os
the bank?	el banco?	el **bahn**-koh
the hotel?	el hotel?	el oh-**tel**
the store?	la tienda?	la tee-en-dah
the cashier?	la caja?	la **kah**-hah
the museum?	el museo?	el moo-**seh**-oh
the hospital?	el hospital?	el ohss-pee-**tal**
the elevator?	el ascensor?	el ah-**sen**-sohr
the bathroom?	el baño?	el **bahn**-yoh
Here/there	Aquí/allá	ah-**key**/ah-**yah**
Open/closed	Abierto/cerrado	ah-bee-er-toh/ ser-**ah**-doh
Left/right	Izquierda/derecha	iss-key-er-dah/ dare-**eh**-chah
Straight ahead	Derecho	dare-**eh**-choh
Is it near/far?	¿Está cerca/lejos?	es-**tah** sehr-kah/ **leh**-hoss
I'd like . . .	Quisiera . . .	kee-see-ehr-ah
a room	una habitación	**oo**-nah ah-bee-tah-see-**on**
the key	la llave	lah **yah**-veh
a newspaper	un periódico	oon pehr-ee-oh-dee-koh
a stamp	un sello de correo	oon **seh**-yo deh koh-**reh**-oh

I'd like to buy . . .	Quisiera comprar . . .	kee-see-**ehr**-ah kohm-**prahr**
cigarettes	cigarrillos	ce-ga-**ree**-yohs
matches	cerillos	ser-**ee**-ohs
a dictionary	un diccionario	oon deek-see-oh-**nah**-ree-oh
soap	jabón	hah-**bohn**
sunglasses	gafas de sol	**ga**-fahs deh sohl
suntan lotion	loción bronceadora	loh-see-**ohn** brohn-seh-ah-**do**-rah
a map	un mapa	oon **mah**-pah
a magazine	una revista	oon-ah reh-**vees**-tah
paper	papel	pah-**pel**
envelopes	sobres	**so**-brehs
a postcard	una tarjeta postal	oon-ah tar-**het**-ah post-**ahl**
How much is it?	¿Cuánto cuesta?	**kwahn**-toh **kwes**-tah
It's expensive/ cheap	Está caro/barato	es-**tah kah**-roh/ bah-**rah**-toh
A little/a lot	Un poquito/ mucho	oon poh-**kee**-toh/ **moo**-choh
More/less	Más/menos	mahss/**men**-ohss
Enough/too much/too little	Suficiente/ demasiado/ muy poco	soo-fee-see-**en**-teh/ deh-mah-see-**ah**-doh/ **moo**-ee **poh**-koh
Telephone	Teléfono	tel-**ef**-oh-no
Telegram	Telegrama	teh-leh-**grah**-mah
I am ill	Estoy enfermo(a)	es-**toy** en-**fehr**-moh(mah)
Please call a doctor	Por favor llame a un medico	pohr fah-**vor ya**-meh ah oon **med**-ee-koh

ON THE ROAD

Avenue	Avenida	ah-ven-**ee**-dah
Broad, tree-lined boulevard	Bulevar	boo-leh-**var**
Fertile plain	Vega	**veh**-gah
Highway	Carretera	car-reh-**ter**-ah
Mountain pass	Puerto	poo-**ehr**-toh
Street	Calle	**cah**-yeh

Waterfront promenade	Rambla	**rahm**-blah
Wharf	Embarcadero	em-bar-cah-**deh**-ro

IN TOWN

Cathedral	Catedral	cah-teh-**dral**
Church	Templo/Iglesia	**tem**-plo/ee-**glehs**-see-ah
City hall	Casa de gobierno	kah-sah deh go-bee-**ehr**-no
Door/gate	Puerta/portón	poo-**ehr**-tah/por-**ton**
Entrance/exit	Entrada/salida	en-**trah**-dah/sah-**lee**-dah
Inn, rustic bar, or restaurant	Taberna	tah-**behr**-nah
Main square	Plaza principal	**plah**-thah prin-see-**pahl**
Market	Mercado	mer-**kah**-doh
Neighborhood	Barrio	**bahr**-ree-o
Traffic circle	Glorieta	glor-ee-**eh**-tah
Wine cellar, wine bar, or wine shop	Bodega	boh-**deh**-gah

DINING OUT

Can you recommend a good restaurant?	¿Puede recomendarme un buen restaurante?	**pweh**-deh rreh-koh-mehn-**dahr**-me oon bwehn rrehs-tow-**rahn**-teh?
Where is it located?	¿Dónde está situado?	**dohn**-deh ehs-**tah** see-**twah**-doh?
Do I need reservations?	¿Se necesita una reservación?	seh neh-seh-**see**-tah oo-nah rreh-sehr-bah-**syohn**?
I'd like to reserve a table . . .	Quisiera reservar una mesa . . .	kee-**syeh**-rah rreh-sehr-**bahr** oo-nah meh-sah . . .
for two people	para dos personas	**pah**-rah dohs pehr-**soh**-nahs
for this evening	para esta noche	**pah**-rah **ehs**-tah **noh**-cheh

for 8:00 pm	para las ocho de la noche	**pah**-rah lahs **oh**-choh deh lah **noh**-cheh
A bottle of...	Una botella de...	**oo**-nah bo-**teh**-yah deh
A cup of...	Una taza de...	**oo**-nah **tah**-thah deh
A glass of...	Un vaso de...	oon **vah**-so deh
Ashtray	Un cenicero	oon sen-ee-**seh**-roh
Bill/check	La cuenta	lah **kwen**-tah
Bread	El pan	el pahn
Breakfast	El desayuno	el deh-sah-**yoon**-oh
Butter	La mantequilla	lah man-teh-**key**-yah
Cheers!	¡Salud!	sah-**lood**
Cocktail	Un aperitivo	oon ah-pehr-ee-**tee**-voh
Dinner	La cena	lah **seh**-nah
Dish	Un plato	oon **plah**-toh
Menu of the day	Menú del día	meh-**noo** del **dee**-ah
Enjoy!	¡Buen provecho!	bwehn pro-**veh**-cho
Fixed-price menu	Menú fijo o turistico	meh-**noo** **fee**-hoh oh too-ree-stee-coh
Fork	El tenedor	el ten-eh-**dor**
Is the tip included?	¿Está incluida la propina?	es-**tah** in-cloo-ee-dah lah pro-**pee**-nah
Knife	El cuchillo	el koo-**chee**-yo
Large portion of savory snacks	Raciónes	rah-see-**oh**-nehs
Lunch	La comida	lah koh-**mee**-dah
Menu	La carta, el menú	lah **cart**-ah, el meh-**noo**
Napkin	La servilleta	lah sehr-vee-**yet**-ah
Pepper	La pimienta	lah pee-me-**en**-tah
Please give me	Por favor déme	pore fah-**vor** **deh**-meh
Salt	La sal	lah sahl
Savory snacks	Tapas	**tah**-pahs
Spoon	Una cuchara	**oo**-nah koo-**chah**-rah
Sugar	El azúcar	el ah-**thu**-kar

Waiter!/Waitress!	¡Por favor Señor/Señorita!	pohr fah-**vor** sen-**yor**/sen-yor-ee-tah

EMERGENCIES

Look!	¡Mire!	**mee**-reh!
Listen!	¡Escuche!	ehs-**koo**-cheh!
Help!	¡Auxilio! ¡Ayuda! ¡Socorro!	owk-**see**-lee-oh/ ah-**yoo**-dah/ soh-**kohr**-roh
Fire!	¡Incendio!	en-**sen**-dee-oo
Caution!/Look out!	¡Cuidado!	kwee-**dah**-doh
Hurry!	¡Dése prisa!	**deh**-seh **pree**-sah!
Stop!	¡Alto!	**ahl**-toh!
I need help quick!	¡Necesito ayuda, pronto!	neh-seh-**see**-toh ah-**yoo**-dah, **prohn**-toh!
Can you help me?	¿Puede ayudarme?	**pweh**-deh ah-yoo-**dahr**-meh?
Police!	¡Policía!	poh-lee-**see**-ah!
I need a policeman!	¡Necesito un policía!	neh-seh-**see**-toh oon poh-lee-**see**-ah!
It's an emergency!	¡Es una emergencia!	ehs **oo**-nah eh-mehr-**hehn**-syah!
Leave me alone!	¡Déjeme en paz!	**deh**-heh-meh ehn pahs!
That man's a thief!	¡Ese hombre es un ladrón!	**eh**-seh **ohm**-breh ehs oon-lah-**drohn**!
Stop him!	¡Deténganlo!	deh-**tehn**-gahn-loh!
He's stolen my...	Me ha robado...	meh ah rroh-**bah**-doh...
pocketbook	la cartera	lah kahr-**teh**-rah
wallet	la billetera	lah bee-yeh-**teh**-rah
passport	el pasaporte	ehl pah-sah-**pohr**-teh
watch	el reloj	ehl rreh-**loh**
I've lost my...	He perdido	eh pehr-**dee**-doh
suitcase	mi maleta	mee mah-**leh**-tah
money	mi dinero	mee dee-**neh**-roh
glasses	los anteojos	lohs ahn-teh-**oh**-hohs
car keys	las llaves de mi automóvil	lahs **yah**-behs deh mee ow-toh-**moh**-beel

TELLING TIME AND EXPRESSIONS OF TIME

What time is it?	¿Qué hora es?	keh **oh**-rah ehs?
At what time?	¿A qué hora?	ah keh **oh**-rah?
It's...	Es...	ehs...
one o'clock	la una	lah **oo**-nah
1:15	la una y cuarto	lah **oo**-nah ee **kwahr**-toh
1:30	la una y media	lah **oo**-nah ee **meh**-dyah
It's...	Son las...	sohn lahs...
1:45	dos menos cuarto	dohs **meh**-nos **kwahr**-toh
two o'clock	dos	dohs
morning	la mañana	Lah mah-**nyah**-nah
afternoon	la tarde	lah **tahr**-deh
It's midnight	Es medianoche	ehs **meh**-dyah **noh**-cheh
It's noon	Es mediodía	ehs meh-dyoh-**dee** ah
In a half hour	En media hora	ehn **meh**-dyah **oh**-rah
When does it begin?	¿Cuándo empieza?	**kwahn**-doh ehm-**pyeh**-sah?

PAYING THE BILL

How much does it cost?	¿Cuánto cuesta?	**kwahn**-toh **kwehs**-tah?
The bill, please	La cuenta, por favor	lah-**kwen**-tah pohr fah-**bohr**
How much do I owe you?	¿Cuánto le debo?	**kwan**-toh leh **deh**-boh?
Is service included?	¿La propina está incluida?	lah proh-**pee**-nah ehs-**tah** een-kloo-ee-**dah**?
This is for you	Esto es para usted	**ehs**-toh ehs pah-rah oos-**tehd**

GETTING AROUND

Do you have a map of the city?	¿Tiene usted un mapa de la ciudad?	**tyeh**-neh oos-**tehd** oon **mah**-pah deh lah syoo-**dahd**?
Could you show me on the map?	¿Puede usted indicármelo en el mapa?	**pweh**-deh oo-**stehd** een-dee-**kahr**-meh-loh ehn ehl **mah**-pah?
Can I get there on foot?	¿Puedo llegar allí a pie?	**pweh**-doh yeh-**gahr** ah-**yee** ah pyeh?
How far is it?	¿A qué distancia es?	ah keh dees-**tahn**-syah ehs?
I'm lost	Estoy perdido(-a)	ehs-**toy** pehr-**dee**-doh(-dah)
Where is...	¿Dónde está...	**dohn**-deh ehs-**tah**...
the Hotel Rex?	el hotel Rex?	ehl oh-**tehl** rreks?
... Street?	la calle...?	lah **kah**-yeh...?
... Avenue?	la avenida...?	lah ah-beh-**nee**-dah...?
How can I get to...	¿Cómo puedo ir a...	**koh**-moh **pweh**-doh eer ah...
the train station?	la estación de ferrocarril?	lah ehs-tah-**syon** deh feh-rroh-cah-**rreel**?
the bus stop?	la parada de autobuses?	lah pah-**rah**-dah deh ow-toh-**boo**-ses?
the ticket office?	la taquilla?	lah tah-**kee**-yah?
the airport?	el aeropuerto?	ehl ah-eh-roh-**pwehr**-toh?
straight ahead	derecho	deh-**reh**-choh
to the right	a la derecha	ah lah deh-**reh**-chah
to the left	a la izquierda	ah lah ees-**kyehr**-dah
a block away	a una cuadra	ah **oo**-nah **kwah**-drah
on the corner	en la esquina	ehn lah ehs-**kee**-nah
on the square	en la plaza	ehn lah **plah**-sah
facing, opposite	enfrente	ehn-**frehn**-teh
across	al frente	ahl **frehn**-teh
next to	al lado	ahl **lah**-doh

near	cerca	sehr-kah
far	lejos	leh-hohs

ON THE BUS

I'm looking for the bus stop	Estoy buscando la parada de autobuses	ehs-**toy** boos-kahn-doh lah pah-rah-dah deh ow-toh-**boo**-sehs
What bus line goes...	¿Qué línea va...	keh **lee**-neh-ah bah...
north?	al norte?	ahl **nohr**-teh?
south?	al sur?	ahl soor?
east?	al este?	ahl **ehs**-teh?
west?	al oeste?	ahl oh-**ehs**-teh?
What bus do I take to go to...	¿Qué autobús tomo para ir a...	keh ow-toh-**boos** toh-moh pah-rah eer ah...
Can you tell me when to get off?	¿Podría decirme cuándo debo bajarme?	poh-**dree**-ah deh-seer-meh kwan-doh **deh**-boh bah-**hahr**-meh?
How much is the fare?	¿Cuánto es el billete?	**kwahn**-toh ehs ehl bee-**yeh**-teh?
Should I pay when I get on?	¿Debo pagar al subir?	**deh**-boh pah-**gahr** ahl soo-**beer**?
Where do I take the bus to return?	¿Dónde se toma el autobús para regresar?	**dohn**-deh seh **toh**-mah ehl ow-toh-**boos** pah-rah rreh-greh-**sahr**?
How often do the return buses run?	¿Cada cuánto hay autobuses de regreso?	**kah**-dah **kwahn**-toh ahy ow-toh-**boo**-sehs deh rreh-**greh**-soh?
I would like...	Quisiera...	kee-**syeh**-rah...
a ticket	un billete	oon bee-**yeh**-teh
a receipt	un recibo	oon reh-**see**-boh
a reserved seat	un asiento numerado	oon ah-**syehn**-toh noo-meh-**rah**-doh
first class	primera clase	pree-**meh**-rah **klah**-seh
second class	segunda clase	seh-**goon**-dah **klah**-seh
a direct bus	un autobús directo	oon ow-toh-**boos** dee-**rehk**-toh

| an express bus | un autobús expreso | oon ow-toh-**boos** ehks-**preh**-soh |
| ticketed luggage | equipaje facturado | eh-kee-**pah**-heh fahk-too-**rah**-doh |

ACCOMMODATIONS

I have a reservation	Tengo una reservación/ una reserva	**tehn**-goh **oo**-nah rreh-sehr-vah-**syohn**/ . . . **oo**-nah rre-**sehr**-vah
I would like a room for . . .	Quisiera una habitación por . . .	kee-**syeh**-rah **oo**-nah ah-bee-tah-**syohn** pohr . . .
one night	una noche	**oo**-nah **noh**-cheh
two nights	dos noches	dohs **noh**-chehs
a week	una semana	**oo**-nah seh-**mah**-nah
two weeks	dos semanas	dohs seh-**mah**-nahs
How much is it . . . for a day?	¿Cuánto es . . . por día?	**kwahn**-toh ehs . . . pohr **dee**-ah?
for a week?	por una semana?	pohr **oo**-nah seh-**mah**-nah?
Does that include tax?	¿Incluye impuestos?	een-**kloo**-yeh eem-**pwehs**-tohs?
Do you have a room with . . .	¿Tiene una habitación con . . .	**tyeh**-neh **oo**-nah ah-bee-tah-**syohn** kohn . . .
a private bath?	baño privado?	**bah**-nyoh pree-**bah**-doh?
a shower?	una ducha?	**oo**-nah **doo**-chah?
air-conditioning?	aire acondicionado?	**ay**-reh ah-kohn-dee-syoh-**nah**-doh?
heat?	calefacción?	kah-leh-fak-**syohn**?
television?	televisor?	teh-leh-bee-**sohr**?
hot water?	agua caliente?	**ah**-gwah kah-**lyehn**-teh?
a balcony?	balcón?	bahl-**kohn**?
a view facing the street?	vista a la calle?	**bees**-tah ah lah **kah**-yeh?
a view facing the ocean?	vista al mar?	**bees**-tah ahl mahr?
Does the hotel have . . .	¿Tiene el hotel . . . ?	**tyeh**-neh ehl oh-**tehl** . . . ?
a restaurant?	un restaurante?	oon rrehs-tow-**rahn**-teh?
a bar?	un bar?	oon bahr?

a swimming pool?	una piscina?	oo-nah pee-**see**-nah
room service?	servicio de habitación?	sehr-**bee**-syoh deh ah-bee-tah-**syohn**?
a safe-deposit box?	una caja de valores/ seguridad?	oo-nah kah-hah deh bah-**loh**-rehs/ seh-goo-ree-**dahd**?
laundry service?	servicio de lavandería?	sehr-**bee**-syoh deh lah-vahn-deh-**ree**-ah?

I would like . . .	Quisiera...	kee-**sye**-rah . . .
meals included	con las comidas incluidas	kohn lvahs koh-**mee**-dahs een-**kluee**-dahs
breakfast only	solamente con desayuno	soh-lah-**men**-teh kohn deh-sah-**yoo**-noh
no meals included	sin comidas	seen koh-**mee**-dahs
an extra bed	una cama más	oo-nah **kah**-mah mahs
a baby crib	una cuna	oo-nah **koo**-nah
another towel	otra toalla	oh-trah **twah**-yah
soap	jabón	hah-**bohn**
clothes hangers	ganchos de ropa	**gahn**-chohs deh **rroh**-pah
another blanket	otra manta	oh-trah **mahn**-tah
drinking water	agua para beber	**ah**-gwah **pah**-rah beh-**behr**
toilet paper	papel higiénico	pah-**pehl** ee-**hye**-nee-koh

This room is very . . .	Esta habitación es muy . . .	**ehs**-tah ah-bee-tah-**syohn** ehs muee . . .
small	pequeña	peh-**keh**-nyah
cold	fría	**free**-ah
hot	caliente	kah-**lyehn**-teh
dark	oscura	ohs-**koo**-rah
noisy	ruidosa	rruee-**doh**-sah

The . . . does not work	No funciona . . .	noh foon-**syoh**-nah . . .
light	la luz	lah loos
heat	la calefacción	lah kah-leh-fahk-**syohn**
toilet	el baño	ehl **bah**-nyoh
the air conditioner	el aire acondicionado	ehl **ay**-reh ah-kohn-dee-syo-**nah**-doh
key	la llave	lah **yah**-beh
lock	la cerradura	lah seh-rah-**doo**-rah
fan	el ventilador	ehl **behn**-tee-lah-

		dohr
outlet	el enchufe	ehl ehn-**choo**-feh
television	el televisor	ehl teh-leh-bee-**sohr**

May I change to another room?	¿Podría cambiar de habitación?	poh-**dree**-ah kahm-**byar** deh ah-bee-tah-**syohn**?

Is there...	¿Hay...	ahy...
room service?	servicio de habitación?	sehr-**bee**-syoh deh ah-bee-tah-**syohn**?
laundry service?	servicio de lavandería?	sehr-**bee**-syoh deh lah-vahn-deh-**ree**-ah?

EMAIL AND THE INTERNET

Where is the computer?	¿Dónde está la computadora?	**dohn**-deh eh-**stah** lah kohm-poo-tah-**doh**-rah

I need to send an email	Necesito enviar un correo electrónico	neh-seh-**see**-toh ehn-**byahr** oon koh-**reh**-yoh eh-lehk-**troh**-nee-koh

Can I get on the Internet?	¿Puedo conectarme con el internet?	**pweh**-doh koh-nehk-**tahr**-meh ahl **een**-tehr-net?

Do you have a Web site?	¿Tiene página web?	**tyeh**-neh **pah**-hee-nah web?

BARGAINING

Excuse me	Perdón	pehr-**dohn**

I'm interested in this	Me interesa esto	meh een-teh-**reh**-sah **ehs**-toh

How much is it?	¿Cuánto cuesta?	**kwahn**-toh **kwehs**-tah?

It's very expensive!	¡Es muy caro!	ehs muee **kah**-roh!

It's overpriced (It's not worth so much)	No vale tanto	noh **vah**-leh **tahn**-toh

Do you have a cheaper one?	¿Tiene uno más barato?	**tyeh**-neh **oo**-noh mahs bah-**rah**-toh?

This is damaged—do you have another one?	Está dañado, ¿hay otro?	ehs-**tah** dah-**nyah**-doh, ahy **oh**-troh?

What is the lowest price?	¿Cuál es el precio mínimo?	**kwahl** ehs ehl **preh**-syoh **mee-nee-moh?**
Is that the final price?	¿Es el último precio?	ehs ehl **ool**-tee-moh **preh**-syoh?
Can't you give me a discount?	¿No me da una rebaja?	noh meh dah **oo**-nah rreh-**bah**-hah?
I'll give you...	Le doy...	leh doy...
I won't pay more than...	No pago más de...	noh **pah**-goh mahs deh...
I'll look somewhere else	Voy a ver en otro sitio	voy ah behr ehn **oh**-troh **see**-tyoh
No, thank you	No, gracias	noh, **grah**-syahs

TOILETRIES

toiletries	objetos de baño	ohb-**jeh**-tohs deh **bah**-nyoh
a brush	un cepillo	oon seh-**pee**-yoh
cologne	colonia	koh-**loh**-nyah
a comb	un peine	oon **pay**-neh
deodorant	desodorante	deh-soh-doh-**rahn**-teh
disposable	pañales	pah-**nyah**-lehs
diapers	desechables	deh-seh-**chah**-blehs
hairspray	laca	**lah**-kah
a mirror	un espejo	oon ehs-**peh**-hoh
moisturizing lotion	loción humectante	loh-**syohn** oo-mehk-**tahn**-teh
mouthwash	enjuague bucal	ehn-**hwah**-geh boo-**kahl**
nail clippers	cortaúñas	kohr-ta-oo-**nyahs**
nail polish	esmalte de uñas	ehs-**mahl**-teh deh **oo**-nyahs
nail polish remover	quitaesmalte	kee-tah-ehs-**mahl**-teh
perfume	perfume	pehr-**foo**-meh
sanitary napkins	toallas sanitarias	toh-**ah**-yahs sah-nee-**tah**-ryahs

shampoo	champú	chahm-**poo**
shaving cream	crema de afeitar	**kreh**-mah deh ah-fay-**tahr**
soap	jabón	hah-**bohn**
a sponge	una esponja	**oo**-nah ehs-**pohn**-hah
tampons	tampones	tahm-**poh**-nehs
tissues	pañuelos de papel	pah-**nyweh**-lohs deh pah-**pehl**
toilet paper	papel higiénico	pah-**pehl** ee-**hyeh**-ee-koh
a toothbrush	un cepillo de dientes	oon seh-**pee**-yoh deh **dyehn**-tehs
toothpaste	pasta de dientes	**pahs**-tah deh **dyehn**-tehs
tweezers	pinzas	**peen**-sahs

Travel Smart Peru

GETTING HERE AND AROUND

Because of the massive Andes mountains that ripple through the country, most travelers choose to fly between the major cities of Peru. The good news is that domestic flights can be reasonable, sometimes less than $100 USD per segment.

TRAVEL TIMES FROM LIMA		
To	By Air	By Car/Bus
Cusco	1 hour	24 hours
Puno	2 hours	22 hours
Arequipa	1¼ hours	15 hours
Trujillo	1 hour	9 hours

■TIP→ Ask the local tourist board about hotel and local transportation packages that include tickets to major museum exhibits or other special events.

▮ AIR TRAVEL

Almost all international flights into Peru touch down at Aeropuerto Internacional Jorge Chávez, on the northwestern fringe of Lima. Flying times are for nonstop flights to Lima: from Miami 5 hours 45 minutes; Houston 6 hours 45 minutes; Los Angeles 8 hours 35 minutes; and New York 7 hours.

Airlines now include departure taxes on international and domestic flights in the cost of tickets.

The least expensive airfares to Peru are priced for round-trip travel. Airlines generally allow you to change your return date for a fee; most low-fare tickets, however, are nonrefundable.

Airline Security Issues Transportation Security Administration ⊕ www.tsa.gov.

AIRPORTS

Peru's main international point of entry is Aeropuerto Internacional Jorge Chávez (LIM), on the northwestern fringe of Lima. It's a completely modern facility with plenty of dining and shopping options, and flights that arrive and depart 24 hours a day. There are ATMs and currency exchange offices in the main terminal and the arrivals terminals. These are nowhere to be found in the departures terminal, so do your banking before heading through security.

Airport Information Aeropuerto Internacional Jorge Chávez ⊠ Av. Faucett s/n, Lima, Peru ☎ 01/517–3100 ⊕ www.lap.com.pe.

GROUND TRANSPORTATION

If your hotel doesn't offer to pick you up at the airport, you'll have to take a taxi. Arrange a ride with one of the official airport taxis whose companies have counters inside the arrivals area of the terminal. A taxi to most places in the city should cost no more than $20–$25 USD. It's a 20-minute drive to El Centro, and a 30-minute drive to Miraflores and San Isidro. During rush hour (8–10 am and 5–9 pm), driving times in Lima can double, so plan accordingly.

FLIGHTS

Dozens of international flights touch down daily at Lima's Aeropuerto Internacional Jorge Chávez, mostly from other Latin American cities. There are also plenty from the U.S. American flies from Miami, United flies from Houston and Newark. Delta has daily flights from Atlanta, and Spirit flies from Fort Lauderdale. The South American–based airline LAN flies from Los Angeles, Miami, and New York's JFK. Air Canada flies from Toronto.

If you're flying from other Latin American cities, you have a wide range of regional carriers at your disposal. LAN has flights from most major airports in the region, as does Taca. Brazil's TAM flies from Sao Paulo. Copa, affiliated with United, flies from its hub in Panama City. Aeroméxico flies from Mexico City, Aerolineas Argentinas flies from Buenos Aires, Avianca from Bogota, and Taca from San José, Costa Rica.

DOMESTIC

With four mountain ranges and a large swath of the Amazon jungle running through Peru, flying is the best way to travel from Lima to most cities and towns. LAN, the carrier with the most national flights, departs several times each day for Arequipa, Cajamarca, Chiclayo, Cusco, Iquitos, Piura, Puerto Maldonado, Tacna, Tarapoto, and Trujillo. LC Peru flies to Andahuaylas, Ayacucho, Cajamarca, Cusco, Huánuco, Huaraz, and Tingo Maria. Peruvian Airlines flies to Arequipa, Cusco, Iquitos, Piura, and Tacna. Star Perú flies to Andahuaylas, Ayacucho, Cusco, Huánuco, Iquitos, Juliaca, Pucallpa, Puerto Maldonado, Talara, Tarapoto, and Trujillo. Taca flies to Cusco.

LAN operates the majority of domestic flights within the country, frequently with service several times a day between major destinations, but its fares skew higher than the competition. LAN does offer lower fares—and you can see them on its website—but only residents of Peru are eligible to use them. Likewise for Taca's low-cost fares on the popular Lima-Cusco route. ⚠ If you buy a restricted-fare ticket, you will have to pay a $178.50 fee at check-in.

Airline Contacts Aerolineas Argentinas ✉ *Dean Valdivia 243, Of. 301, San Isidro, Lima, Peru* ☎ *800/333-0276 in North America, 01/513-6565 in Lima* ⊕ *www.aerolineas.com. ar.* **Aeroméxico** ✉ *Pardo y Aliaga 699, Of. 501-C, San Isidro, Lima, Peru* ☎ *800/237-6639 in North America, 01/705-1111 in Lima* ⊕ *www.aeromexico.com.* **Air Canada** ✉ *Italia 389, Of. 101, Miraflores, Lima, Peru* ☎ *888/247-2262 in North America, 01/626-0900 in Lima* ⊕ *www.aircanada. com.* **American Airlines** ✉ *José Pardo 392, Miraflores, Lima, Peru* ☎ *800/433-7300 in U.S., 01/211-7000 in Lima* ⊕ *www.aa.com.* **Avianca** ✉ *Edificio Torre Roja, Los Sauces 364, 1st fl., San Isidro, Lima, Peru* ☎ *800/284-2622 in North America, 01/440-4104 in Lima* ⊕ *www.avianca.com.* **Copa** ✉ *Centro Empresarial Torre Choca, Esquina Canaval y Moreyra con Halcones, Of. 105, San Isidro, Lima, Peru* ☎ *800/359-2672 in North America, 01/610-0808 in Lima* ⊕ *www.copaair.com.* **Delta Airlines** ✉ *Víctor Andrés Belaúnde 147, Of. 701 Edificio Real 3, San Isidro, Lima, Peru* ☎ *800/750-3284, 01/211-9211 in Lima* ⊕ *www.delta.com.* **LAN** ✉ *José Pardo 513, 1st fl., Miraflores, Lima, Peru* ☎ *866/435-9526 in North America, 01/213-8200 in Lima* ⊕ *www. lan.com.* **Spirit Air** ✉ *Aeropuerto Internacional Jorge Chávez, Callao, Peru* ☎ *800/772-7117, 01/517-2536 in Lima* ⊕ *www.spiritair.com.* **Taca** ✉ *José Pardo 811, 4th fl., Miraflores, Lima, Peru* ☎ *800/400-8222 in North America, 01/511-8222 in Lima* ⊕ *www.taca.com.* **TAM** ✉ *Alcanfores 495, Of. 507, Miraflores, Lima, Peru* ☎ *888/235-9826 in North America, 01/202-6900 in Lima* ⊕ *www.tam.com.br.*

Domestic Airlines LC Perú ✉ *Pablo Carriquiry 857, San Isidro, Lima, Peru* ☎ *01/204-1300* ⊕ *www.lcperu.pe.* **Peruvian Airlines** ✉ *José Pardo 495, Miraflores, Lima, Peru* ☎ *01/716-6000* ⊕ *www.peruvianairlines.pe.* **Star Perú** ✉ *José Pardo 485, Miraflores, Lima, Peru* ☎ *01/242-7720* ⊕ *www.starperu.com.*

▌ BUS TRAVEL

The intercity bus system in Peru is extensive, and fares are quite reasonable. Remember, however, that mountain ranges often sit between cities, and trips can be daunting. It's best to use buses for shorter trips, such as between Lima and Ica or between Cusco and Puno. That way you can begin and end your trip during daylight hours. If you stick with one of the recommended companies, like Cruz del Sur, you can usually expect a comfortable journey.

Second-class buses (*servicio normal*) tend to be overcrowded and uncomfortable, whereas the more expensive first-class service (*primera clase*) is more comfortable and much more likely to arrive on schedule.

Bus fares are substantially cheaper in Peru than they are in North America or Europe. Competing bus companies serve all major and many minor routes, so it can pay to shop around if you're on an extremely tight budget. Always speak to the counter clerk, as competition may mean fares are cheaper than the official price posted on the fare board.

For the 15-hour journey between Lima and Arequipa, Cruz del Sur's fares for its top service, called *Cruzero*, are $55 USD. Its less expensive service, called *Imperial*, is $22–$39 USD. Inka Express, which promotes itself to tourists rather than the local market, uses large, comfortable coaches for the popular eight-hour journey between Cusco and Puno. Tickets are $55 USD and the trip includes snacks and brief rest stops at points of interest along the way.

Tickets are sold at bus-company offices and at travel agencies. Be prepared to pay with cash, as credit cards aren't always accepted. Reservations aren't necessary except for trips to popular destinations during high season. Summer weekends and major holidays are the busiest times. You should arrive at bus stations early for travel during peak seasons.

Bus Information Cruz del Sur
✉ Javier Prado 1109, La Victoria, Lima, Peru
☎ 01/311–5050 ⊕ www.cruzdelsur.com.pe.
Inka Express ✉ La Paz 623, Urbanización El Ovalo, Wanchaq, Cusco, Peru ☎ 084/247–887
⊕ www.inkaexpress.com. Ormeño ✉ Javier Prado Oeste 1057, La Victoria, Lima, Peru
☎ 01/472–1710 ⊕ www.grupo-ormeno.com.pe.

▌ CAR TRAVEL

In general, it's not a great idea to have a car in Peru. Driving is a heart-stopping experience, as most Peruvians see traffic laws as suggestions rather than rules. That said, there are a few places in Peru where having a car is a benefit, such as between Lima and points south on the Pan-American Highway. The highway follows the Pacific Ocean coastline before it cuts in through the desert, and stops can be made along the way for a picnic and a swim at the popular beaches around Asia at kilometer 100. The highway is good, and although there isn't too much to see along

the way, it's nice to have the freedom a car affords once you get to your destination.

If you rent a car, keep these tips in mind: outside cities, drive only during daylight hours, fill your gas tank whenever possible, and make sure your spare tire is in good repair. In some areas, drivers caught using a cell phone while driving receive a hefty fine, especially on the coastal highway following the cliff along the Pacific Ocean between Lima and Miraflores, and San Isidro.

Massive road-building programs have improved highways. Nevertheless, even in some parts of Lima roads are littered with potholes. Outside of the cities, street signs are rare, lighting is nonexistent, and lanes are unmarked. Roads are straight along the coast, but in the mountains they snake around enough to make even the steadiest driver a little queasy. Fuel is pricey in Peru, with a gallon costing upwards of $6.

And then there are the drivers. When they get behind the wheel, Peruvians are very assertive. Expect lots of honking and last-minute lane switching when you're in a city. On highways you'll encounter constant tailgating and passing on blind curves. And remember the ancient car you sold five years ago? Chances are it is now plying Peru's roads. Take our word for it and leave the driving to someone else if you can. Consider hiring a car and driver through your hotel, or making a deal with a taxi driver for some extended sightseeing. Drivers often charge an hourly rate regardless of the distance traveled. You'll have to pay cash, but you'll often spend less than you would for a rental car.

The major highways in Peru are the Pan-American Highway, which runs down the entire coast, the Carretera Central, which runs from Lima to Huancayo, and the Interoceánica, which runs from Lima to Cerro de Pasco and on to Pucallpa before crossing through Brazil to the Atlantic Ocean. Most highways have no names or numbers; they're referred to by destination.

CAR RENTAL

If you plan to rent a car it's best to make arrangements before you leave home, and book through a travel agent who will shop around for a good deal. If you plan to rent during a holiday period, reserve early.

The minimum age for renting a car in Peru is 25, although some agencies offer rentals to under-25-year-olds for an additional fee. All major car-rental agencies have branches in downtown Lima as well as at Jorge Chávez International Airport that are open 24 hours. You can also rent vehicles in Arequipa, Chiclayo, Cusco, Tacna, and Trujillo.

The cost of rental cars varies widely, but is generally between $50 and $60 USD for a compact, $8 to $100 USD for a full-size car or small SUV. A daily $10–$20 USD collision damage waiver is usually added to your bill. Always make sure to check the fine print, as some companies give you unlimited mileage whereas others give you between 200 and 240 km (124 and 150 miles) free, then charge you a hefty 25 to 60 cents for every kilometer you drive above that. Many rental firms include in your contract a statement saying you may not take the vehicle on unpaved roads, of which there are many in Peru. Many also forbid mountain driving for certain types of vehicles in their fleets.

Always give the rental car a once-over to make sure that the headlights, jack, and tires (including the spare) are in working condition. Note any existing damage to the car and get a signature acknowledging the damage, no matter how slight.

GASOLINE

Gas stations are less plentiful in Peru than in the US or Europe, but can be found with some advance planning. In Lima gas stations should be easy to locate, but in Cusco, Arequipa, or smaller cities they may be on the outskirts and are often difficult to find. Make sure to ask your rental company where they're located. Stations along the highways are rare, so don't pass up on the chance to gas up. Many stations are now open 24 hours.

PARKING

If you have a rental car, make sure your hotel has its own parking lot. If not, ask about nearby lots. In the cities guarded parking lots that charge about $1 USD an hour are common. Don't park cars on the street, as theft is common.

ROADSIDE EMERGENCIES

The Touring y Automóvil Club del Perú will provide 24-hour emergency road service for members of the American Automobile Association (AAA) and affiliates upon presentation of their membership cards. (Towing is free within 30 km [18 miles] of several urban areas.) Members of AAA can purchase good maps there at low prices.

Emergency Services Touring y Automóvil Club del Perú ✉ *Trinidad Morán 698, Lince, Lima, Peru* ☎ *01/611-9999 emergencies, 01/615-9315 other calls* ⊕ *www.touringperu.com.pe.*

RULES OF THE ROAD

In Peru your own driver's license is acceptable identification, but an international driving permit is good to have. They're available from the American and Canadian automobile associations and, in the United Kingdom, from the Automobile Association and Royal Automobile Club. These international permits, valid only in conjunction with your regular driver's license, are universally recognized; having one may save you headaches with local authorities.

Speed limits are 25 kph–35 kph (15 mph–20 mph) in residential areas, 85 kph–100 kph (50 mph–60 mph) on highways. Traffic tickets range from a minimum of $4 USD to a maximum of $100 USD. The police and military routinely check drivers at roadblocks, so make sure your papers are easily accessible. Peruvian law makes it a crime to drive while intoxicated, although many Peruvians ignore that prohibition.

▌ TRAIN TRAVEL

Trains run along four different routes: between Cusco and Machu Picchu, between Cusco and Lake Titicaca, between Huancayo and Lima, and between Huancayo and Huancavelica. In addition there's a line between Puno and Arequipa that's operated for groups only. Tickets can be purchased at train stations, through travel agencies, or on the Internet. During holidays or high season it's best to get your tickets in advance.

Three companies offer train service to Machu Picchu. PeruRail, which has run the route since 1999, is operated by Orient-Express, the same company that runs one of the most luxurious and famous trains in the world, the Venice Simplon Orient Express between London and Venice. It operates service to Machu Picchu from Cusco (technically from the nearby town of Poroy, about 20 minutes outside the city) and the Sacred Valley towns of Ollantaytambo and Urubamba. Inca Rail and Andean Railways, which began service in 2010 and 2011, respectively, run service between Urubamba, Ollantaytambo, and Machu Picchu. Foreigners are prohibited from riding the very inexpensive local trains that travel the route. The Machu Picchu station is not at the ruins themselves, but in the nearby town of Aguas Calientes. ⇨ *See Chapter 6: Machu Picchu and the Inca Trail for more information about these trains.*

Three or four PeruRail trains a week, depending on season, take passengers on the 10-hour trip between Cusco and Lake Titicaca. The plush Andean Explorer is $210 USD one-way.

Note that there are two different train stations in Cusco. Estación Poroy serves the Machu Picchu route, and Estación Wanchaq serves the Lake Titicaca route.

Reserve and purchase your ticket as far ahead as possible, especially during holidays or high season. Reservations can be made directly with PeruRail through its website, or through a travel agency or tour operator.

Reservations Andean Railways
✉ *El Sol 576, Cusco, Peru* ☎ *084/221–199 in Cusco, 01/613–5288 in Lima*
⊕ *www.machupicchutrain.com.* **Inca Rail**
✉ *Plaza de Armas, Cusco, Peru* ☎ *084/233–030 in Cusco, 01/613–5288 in Lima*
⊕ *www.incarail.com.* **PeruRail** ✉ *Plaza de Armas, Cusco, Peru* ☎ *084/581–414, 01/517–1884 in Lima* ⊕ *www.perurail.com.*

Train Stations Estación Wanchaq (Cusco–Lake Titicaca route) ✉ *Pachacutec 503, Cusco, Peru* ☎ *084/581–400.*
Estación Poroy (Cusco - Machu Picchu Route) ✉ *Poroy, Cusco, Peru* ☎ *084/581–414.*

ESSENTIALS

▌ ACCOMMODATIONS

It's always good to take a look at your room before accepting it, especially if you're staying in a budget hotel. If it isn't what you expected, there might be several other rooms from which to choose. Expense is no guarantee of charm or cleanliness, and accommodations can vary dramatically within a single hotel. Many older hotels in some of the small towns in Peru have rooms with charming balconies or spacious terraces; ask if there's a room *con balcón* or *con terraza* when checking in.

If you ask for a double room, you'll get a room for two people, but you're not guaranteed a double mattress. If you'd like to avoid twin beds, you'll have to ask for a *cama matrimonial* (no wedding ring required).

Our local writers vet every hotel to recommend the best overnights in each price category, from budget to expensive. Unless otherwise specified, you can expect private bath, phone, and TV in your room. For expanded reviews, facilities, and current deals, visit Fodors.com.

APARTMENT AND HOUSE RENTALS

Apartment rentals are not a viable option in most parts of Peru. However, they're becoming more popular in Lima. One company that has proven reliable is Inn Peru, which rents apartments in the neighborhood of Miraflores. You can get a roomy two- or three-bedroom apartment for less than you'd pay for a shoebox-size hotel room.

Contacts Home Away ☎ 877/228–3145 ⊕ *www.homeaway.com*. **Inn Peru** ☎ 945/607–2173 in U.S., 01/998–578–350 in Peru ⊕ *www.innperu.com*. **Villas International** ☎ 415/499–9490 or 800/221–2260 ⊕ *www.villasintl.com*.

BED-AND-BREAKFASTS

Bed-and-breakfasts are a popular option all over Peru, but especially in tourist areas like Cusco, Arequipa, and Puno. Many are in charming older buildings, including colonial-era homes built around flower-filled courtyards. Breakfast ranges from a roll with butter and jam to a massive buffet.

Reservation Services Bed and Breakfast. com ☎ 512/322–2710 or 800/462–2632 ⊕ *www.bedandbreakfast.com*.

HOME EXCHANGES

With a direct home exchange you stay in someone else's home while they stay in yours. Some outfits also deal with vacation homes, so you're not actually staying in someone's full-time residence, just their vacant weekend place. Homeexchange.com costs $119.40 for a year membership.

Exchange Clubs Home Exchange.com ☎ 800/877–8723 or 310/798–3864 ⊕ *www.homeexchange.com*.

HOTELS

Peru's hotels range from $1 beds in municipal hostels to luxurious retreats tucked away in forgotten Andean valleys. In general, the highest quality hotels can be found in major cities (Lima, Arequipa, Cusco), but four- and five-star properties can still be found in smaller cities that cater to high-end tourism or business.

These hotels will generally feature hot water, modern fixtures, and 24-hour concierge service. Mid-level hotels may lack some of these features, and will generally feel dated in comparison. At the low-end, dormitories and bunk beds cater to backpackers and budget travelers. Prices tend to reflect the properties age and amenities, but specialty lodges in the jungle or highlands may offer few comforts at a given price point. The name of a hotel does not necessarily have anything to do with its luxuriousness. A *posada*, for example, can be at the high, middle, or low end. *Prices in the reviews are the lowest cost of a standard double room in high season. Our local writers vet every hotel to recommend the best overnights in each price category, from budget to expensive. Unless otherwise specified, you can expect private bath, phone, and TV in your room. For expanded reviews, facilities, and current deals, visit Fodors.com.*

■ COMMUNICATIONS

INTERNET

Email has become a favorite way to communicate in Peru. Lima, Cusco, and other larger cities have dozens of Internet cafés. (Look for a sign with an @ symbol out front.) Even on the shores of Lake Titicaca you can stop in a small shop and send an email message back home for about $1 USD. And many of the country's airports, including Lima's Jorge Chávez International Airport and Cusco's Teniente Alejandro Velasco Astete International Airport, offer wireless connections if you're traveling with your own laptop or wireless device. Even hotels that don't have wireless in their rooms will probably have a strong signal in the public areas.

Computer keyboards in South America are not quite the same as those in English-speaking countries. Your biggest frustration will probably be finding the "@" symbol to type an email address. On a PC you have to type "Alt+164" with the "Numbers Lock" on or some other combination. If you need to ask, it's called *arroba* in Spanish.

If you're traveling with a laptop, carry a converter if your computer isn't dual voltage (most are these days), otherwise your existing power cord will work just fine. Carrying a laptop could make you a target for thieves. Conceal your laptop in a generic bag, and keep it close to you at all times. Cybercafes lists more than 4,000 Internet cafés worldwide.

Contacts Cybercafes ⊕ *www.cybercafes.com.*

PHONES

The good news is that you can now make a direct-dial telephone call from virtually any point on earth. The bad news? You can't always do so cheaply. Calling from a hotel is almost always the most expensive option; hotels usually add huge surcharges to all calls, particularly international ones. In some countries you can phone from call centers or even the post office. Calling cards usually keep costs to a minimum, but only if you purchase them locally. And as expensive as international mobile phone calls can be, they are still usually a much cheaper option than calling from your hotel.

To call Peru direct, dial 011 followed by the country code of 51, then the city code, then the number of the party you're calling. (When dialing a number from abroad, drop the initial 0 from the local area code.)

CALLING WITHIN PERU

To get phone numbers for anywhere in Peru, dial 103. For an operator, dial 100, and for an international operator, dial 108. To place a direct call, dial 00 followed by the country and city codes. To call another region within the country, first dial 0 and then the area code.

To reach an AT&T operator, dial 0–800–50288. For MCI, dial 0–800–50010. For Sprint, dial 0–800–50020.

LOCAL DO'S AND TABOOS

CUSTOMS OF THE COUNTRY

Peru is one of South America's most hospitable nations. Even in the overburdened metropolis of Lima people are happy to give directions, chat, and ask a question you'll hear a lot in Peru, *¿De dónde viene usted?* (Where are you from?). Peruvians are quite knowledgeable and proud of the history of their country. Don't be surprised if your best source of information isn't your tour guide but your taxi driver or hotel desk clerk. That said, always consider what the person offering information might have to gain from directing you to a given hotel or tour agency, and try to ask a few people for information before settling on any one option.

GREETINGS

In the cities women who know each other often greet each other with a single kiss on the cheek, whereas men shake hands. Men and women often kiss on the cheek, even when being introduced for the first time. Kissing, however, is not a custom among the conservative indigenous population.

SIGHTSEEING

To feel more comfortable, take a cue from what the locals are wearing. Except in beach towns, men typically don't wear shorts and women don't wear short skirts. Bathing suits are fine on beaches, but cover up before you head back into town. Everyone dresses nicely to enter churches. Peruvian women wearing sleeveless tops often cover their shoulders before entering a place of worship.

OUT ON THE TOWN

Residents of Lima and other large cities dress up for a night on the town, but that doesn't necessarily mean a jacket and tie. Just as in Buenos Aires or Rio de Janiero, you should dress comfortably, but with a bit of style. In smaller towns, things are much more casual. You still shouldn't wear shorts, however. The posh clubs in Lima's Miraflores district may not let you enter without proper footwear, so leave the sandals at home.

LANGUAGE

Spanish is Peru's national language, but many indigenous languages also enjoy official status. Many Peruvians claim Quechua, the language of the Inca, as their first language, but most also speak Spanish. Other indigenous languages include the Tiahuanaco language of Aymará, which is spoken around Lake Titicaca, and several languages in the rain forest. English is now routinely taught in schools, and many older people have taken classes in English. In Lima and other places with many foreign visitors, it's rare to come across someone without a rudimentary knowledge of the language.

A word on spelling: Because the Inca had no writing system, Quechua developed as an oral language. With European colonization, words and place-names were transcribed to conform to Spanish pronunciations. Eventually, the whole language was transcribed, and in many cases words lost their correct pronunciations. During the past 30 years, however, national pride and a new sensitivity to the country's indigenous roots have led Peruvians to try to recover consistent, linguistically correct transcriptions of Quechua words. As you travel you may come across different spellings and pronunciations of the same name. An example is the city known as Cusco, Cuzco, and sometimes even Qosqo. Even the word Inca is frequently rendered as the less-Spanish-looking Inka.

A bit of terminology, too: The word *Indio* (Indian) is considered pejorative in Peru and Latin America. (We use the word only to describe an Indian restaurant.) To avoid offense, stick with *indígena* (indigenous) to describe Peru's Inca-descended peoples. Likewise, the words *nativo* (native) and *tribú* (tribe) rub people here the wrong way and are best left to old Tarzan movies.

CALLING OUTSIDE PERU

For international calls, you should dial 00, then the country code. (For example, the country code for the U.S. and Canada is 1.) To make an operator-assisted international call, dial 108.

Access Codes AT&T Direct ☎ *800/225-5288* ⊕ *www.att.com/esupport/traveler.jsp.* **MCI WorldPhone** ☎ *800/444-4444.* **Sprint International Access** ☎ *800/298-3266.*

CALLING CARDS

Public phones use phone cards that can be purchased at newsstands, pharmacies, and other shops. These come in denominations ranging from S/3 to S/40. Your charges will appear on a small monitor on the phone, so you always know how much time you have left. Instructions are usually in Spanish and English.

MOBILE PHONES

If you have a multiband phone (some countries use different frequencies than what's used in the United States) and your service provider uses the world-standard GSM network (as do T-Mobile and AT&T), you can probably use your phone abroad. Roaming fees can be steep: 99¢ a minute is considered reasonable. And overseas you normally pay the toll charges for incoming calls. It's almost always cheaper to text message than to make a call, since text messages have a very low set fee.

If you just want to make local calls, consider buying a new SIM card for a few soles (note that your provider may have to unlock your phone for you to use a different SIM card) and a prepaid service plan in the destination. You'll then have a local number and can make local calls at local rates. If your trip is extensive, you could also simply buy a new cell phone in your destination, as the initial cost will be offset over time.

■TIP→ If you travel internationally frequently, save one of your old mobile phones or buy a cheap one on the Internet; ask your cell-phone company to unlock it for you, and take it with you as a travel phone, buying a new SIM card with pay-as-you-go service in each destination.

Contacts Cellular Abroad. Cellular Abroad rents and sells GMS phones and sells SIM cards that work in many countries. ☎ *800/287-5072* ⊕ *www.cellularabroad.com.* **Mobal.** Mobal rents mobiles and sells GSM phones (starting at $29 USD) that will operate in 190 countries. Per-call rates vary throughout the world. ☎ *888/888-9162* ⊕ *www.mobal.com.* **Planet Fone.** Planet Fone rents cell phones for $21 per week, but per minute rates are expensive. ☎ *888/988-4777* ⊕ *www.planetfone.com.*

❚ CUSTOMS AND DUTIES

You're always allowed to bring goods of a certain value back home without having to pay any duty or import tax. But there's a limit on the amount of tobacco and liquor you can bring back duty-free, and some countries have separate limits for perfumes; for exact figures, check with your customs department. The values of so-called "duty-free" goods are included in these amounts. When you shop abroad, save all your receipts, as customs inspectors may ask to see them as well as the items you purchased. If the total value of your goods is more than the duty-free limit, you'll have to pay a tax (most often a flat percentage) on the value of everything beyond that limit.

When you check through immigration in Peru put the white International Embarkation/Disembarkation form you filled out in a safe place when it's returned to you. You will need it when you leave the country. If you lose it, in addition to being delayed, you may have to pay a small fine. You may bring personal and work items; a total of 3 liters of liquor; jewelry or perfume worth less than $300 USD; and 400 cigarettes or 50 cigars into Peru without paying import taxes. Likewise, travelers can bring one of each type of electronic device (for example, one laptop or one tablet). After that, goods and gifts will be taxed at 20% their value up to $1,000 USD; everything thereafter is taxed at a flat rate of 25%.

U.S. Information U.S. Customs and Border Protection ⊕ *www.cbp.gov.*

▌ EATING OUT

Most smaller restaurants offer a lunch-time *menú*, a prix-fixe meal ($3–$5 USD) that consists of an appetizer, a main dish, dessert, and a beverage. Peru is also full of cafés, many with a selection of delicious pastries. Food at bars is usually limited to snacks and sandwiches. *Prices in the reviews are the average cost of a main course at dinner or, if dinner is not served, at lunch.*

⇨ *For information on food-related health issues, see Health, below.*

MEALS AND MEALTIMES

Food in Peru is hearty and wholesome. Thick soups made of vegetables and meat are excellent. Try *chupes*, soups made of shrimp and fish with potatoes, corn, peas, onions, garlic, tomato sauce, eggs, cream cheese, milk, and whatever else happens to be in the kitchen. Corvina, a sea bass caught in the Pacific Ocean, is superb, as is a fish with a very large mouth, called *paiche*, that is found in jungle lakes and caught with spears. Or try piranha—delicious, but full of bones. *Anticuchos* (marinated beef hearts grilled over charcoal) are a staple, as is *pollo a la brasa* (rotisserie chicken), which is so popular that the government includes it in its inflation figures. Peru's *choclo* (large-kernel corn) is very good, and it's claimed there are more than 100 varieties of potatoes, served in about as many ways. And there is always *cebiche*, raw fish marinated in lemon juice then mixed with onions and *aji* (chili peppers) and served with sweet potatoes and choclo.

Top-notch restaurants serve lunch and dinner, but most Peruvians think of lunch as the day's main meal, and many restaurants open only at midday. Served between 1 and 4 pm, lunch was once followed by a siesta, though the custom has largely died out. Dinner can be anything from a light snack to another full meal. Peruvians tend to dine late, between 8 and 11 pm.

Unless otherwise noted, the restaurants listed in this guide are open daily for lunch and dinner.

RESERVATIONS AND DRESS

Peruvians dress informally when they dine out. At the most expensive restaurants, a jacket without a tie is sufficient for men. Shorts are frowned upon everywhere except at the beach, and T-shirts are appropriate only in very modest restaurants.

In this book we only mention reservations specifically when they are essential or when they are not accepted. For popular restaurants, book as far ahead as you can (often 30 days), and reconfirm as soon as you arrive. We mention dress only when men are required to wear a jacket and tie.

WINES, BEER, AND SPIRITS

Peru's national drink is the pisco sour, made with a pale grape brandy—close to 100 proof—derived from grapes grown in vineyards around Ica, south of Lima. Added to the brandy are lemon juice, sugar, bitters, and egg white, before sometimes being topped with a dash of cinnamon. It's a refreshing drink and one that nearly every bar in Peru claims to make best. Tacama's Blanco de Blancos from Ica is considered the country's best wine. Ica's National Vintage Festival is in March.

Peruvian beer (*cerveza*) is also very good. In Lima try Cristal and the slightly more upscale Pilsen Callao, both produced by the same brewery. In the south it's Arequipeña from Arequipa, Cusqueña from Cusco, and big bottles of San Juan from Iquitos, where the warm climate makes it taste twice as good. In Iquitos locals make Chuchuhuasi from the reddish-brown bark of the canopy tree that grows to 100 feet high in the Amazon rain forest. The bark is soaked for days in *aguardiente* (a very strong homemade liquor) and is claimed to be a cure-all. However, in Iquitos, it has been bottled and turned into a tasty drink for tourists. *Chicha*, a low-alcohol corn beer, is still made by hand throughout the highlands. An acquired taste, chicha can be found by walking through any doorway where a red flag is flying.

▍ELECTRICITY

The electrical current in Peru is 220 volts, 50 cycles alternating current (AC). A converter is needed for appliances requiring 110 voltage. U.S.-style flat prongs fit most outlets.

Consider buying a universal adapter, which has several types of plugs in one lightweight, compact unit. Most laptops and mobile phone chargers are dual voltage (i.e., they operate equally well on 110 and 220 volts), so require only an adapter. These days the same is true of small appliances such as hair dryers. Always check labels and manufacturer instructions to be sure. Don't use 110-volt outlets marked "for shavers only" for high-wattage appliances such as hair dryers.

Contacts Global Electric & Phone Directory. Global Electric & Phone Directory has information on electrical and telephone plugs around the world. ⊕ *www.kropla.com.*

▍EMERGENCIES

The fastest way to connect with the police is to dial 105. For fire, dial 116. The Tourism Police, part of the National Police of Perú, exists for the security and protection of travelers. Officers are usually found around hotels, archaeological centers, museums, and any place that is frequently visited by tourists. They almost always speak English.

Foreign Embassies Australia ⊠ *La Paz 1049, Miraflores, Lima, Peru* ☎ *01/630–0500.* **Canada** ⊠ *Bolognesi 228, Miraflores, Lima, Peru* ☎ *01/319–3200* ⊕ *www.peru.gc.ca.* **United Kingdom** ⊠ *Torre Parque Mar, José Larco 1301, 22nd fl., Miraflores, Lima, Peru* ☎ *01/617–3000* ⊕ *ukinperu.fco.gov.uk.* **United States** ⊠ *Av. La Encalada, Cuadra 17, Surco, Lima, Peru* ☎ *01/618–2000* ⊕ *lima.usembassy.gov.*

▍HEALTH

The most common illnesses are caused by contaminated food and water. In Lima, water supplies are chlorinated, and should be safe to use for brushing teeth and washing fruits and vegetables. Although many Limeños drink the tap water, travelers should drink bottled, boiled, or purified water and drinks to avoid any issues. Many higher quality hotels do purify their water, so inquire with the concierge. In the provinces, water may not be treated. Wash fruits and vegetables before eating, and avoid ice unless it is made with purified water. If you have problems, mild cases of traveler's diarrhea may respond to Imodium (known generically as loperamide) or Pepto-Bismol. Drink plenty of fluids; if you can't keep fluids down, seek medical help immediately. Infectious diseases can be airborne or passed via mosquitoes and ticks and through direct or indirect physical contact with animals or people. Some, including Norwalk-like viruses that affect your digestive tract, can be passed along through contaminated food. If you are traveling in an area where malaria is prevalent, use a repellent containing DEET and take malaria-prevention medication before, during, and after your trip as directed by your physician. Speak with your physician and/or check the CDC or World Health Organization websites for health alerts, particularly if you're pregnant, traveling with children, or have a chronic illness.

Medical Insurers International Medical Group ☎ *800/628–4664* ⊕ *www.imglobal.com.* **International SOS** ⊕ *www.internationalsos. com.* **Wallach & Company** ☎ *800/237–6615* *or 540/687–3166* ⊕ *www.wallach.com.*

SHOTS AND MEDICATIONS

No vaccinations are required to enter Peru, although yellow fever vaccinations are recommended if you're visiting the jungle areas in the east. It's a good idea to have up-to-date boosters for tetanus, diphtheria, and measles. A hepatitis A inoculation can prevent one of the most common intestinal infections. Those who might be around animals should consider a rabies vaccine. As rabies is a concern, most hospitals have anti-rabies injections. Children traveling to Peru should have their vaccinations for childhood diseases up-to-date.

According to the Centers for Disease Control and Prevention (CDC), there's a limited risk of cholera, typhoid, malaria, hepatitis B, dengue, and Chagas' disease. Although a few of these you could catch anywhere, most are restricted to jungle areas. If you plan to visit remote regions or stay for more than six weeks, check with the CDC's International Travelers Hot Line.

Health Warnings Centers for Disease Control & Prevention (*CDC*). ☎ 800/232–4636 *international travelers' health line* ⊕ www.cdc.gov/travel. **World Health Organization** (*WHO*). ⊕ www.who.int.

SPECIFIC ISSUES IN PERU

The major health risk in Peru is traveler's diarrhea, caused by viruses, bacteria, or parasites in contaminated food or water. So watch what you eat. If you eat something from a street vendor, make sure it's cooked in front of you. Avoid uncooked food, food that has been sitting around at room temperature, and unpasteurized milk and milk products. Drink only bottled water or water that has been boiled for several minutes, even when brushing your teeth. Order drinks *sin hielo,* or "without ice." Note that water boils at a lower temperature at high altitudes and may not be hot enough to rid the bacteria, so consider using purification tablets. Local brands include Micropur.

Mild cases of traveler's diarrhea may respond to Imodium, Pepto-Bismol, or Lomotil, all of which can be purchased in Peru without a prescription. Drink plenty of purified water or tea—*manzanilla* (chamomile) is a popular folk remedy.

The number of cases of cholera, an intestinal infection caused by ingestion of contaminated water or food, has dropped dramatically in recent years, but you should still take care. Anything raw, including cebiche, should only be eaten in the better restaurants.

Altitude sickness, known locally as *soroche,* affects the majority of visitors to Cusco, Puno, and other high-altitude locales in the Andes. Headache, dizziness, nausea, and shortness of breath are common. When you visit areas over 10,000 feet above sea level, take it easy for the first few days. Avoiding alcohol will keep you from getting even more dehydrated. To fight soroche, Peruvians swear by *mate de coca,* a tea made from the leaves of the coca plant. (If you are subject to any type of random drug testing through your workplace, know that coca tea can result in a positive test for cocaine afterward.) Some travelers swear by the prescription drug acetazolamide (brand name, Diamox), which should be taken 48 hours before arriving at altitude. Whether that's an appropriate course is for you and your health-care professional to decide.

Spend a few nights at lower elevations before you head higher. If you must fly directly to higher altitudes, plan on doing next to nothing for the first day or two. Drinking plenty of water or coca tea or taking frequent naps may also help. If symptoms persist, return to lower elevations. If you have high blood pressure or a history of heart trouble or are pregnant, check with your doctor before traveling to high elevations.

Mosquitoes and sand flies are a problem in tropical areas, especially at dusk. Take along plenty of repellent containing DEET. You may not get through airport screening with an aerosol can, so take a spritz bottle or cream. Local brands of repellent are readily available in pharmacies. If you plan to spend time in the jungle, be sure to wear clothing that covers your arms and legs, sleep under a mosquito net, and spray bug repellent in living and sleeping areas. You should also ask your doctor about antimalarial medications. Do so early, as some medications must be started weeks before heading into a malaria zone.

Chiggers are sometimes a problem in the jungle or where there are animals. Red, itchy spots suddenly appear, most often *under* your clothes. The best advice when venturing out into chigger country is to use insect repellent and wear loose-fitting clothing. A hot, soapy bath after being outdoors also prevents them from attaching to your skin.

OVER-THE-COUNTER REMEDIES

Over-the-counter analgesics may curtail *soroche* symptoms, but consult your doctor before you take these, as well as any other medications you may take regularly. Always carry your own medications with you, including those you would ordinarily take for a simple headache, as you will usually not find the same brands in the local *farmacia* (pharmacy). However, if you forgot, ask for *aspirina* (aspirin). Try writing down the name of your local medication, because in many cases the pharmacist will have it or something similar.

▌ HOLIDAYS

New Year's Day; Easter holiday, which begins midday on Holy Thursday and continues through Easter Monday (March or April); Labor Day (May 1); St. Peter and St. Paul Day (June 29); Independence Day (July 28); St. Rosa of Lima Day (August 30); Battle of Angamos Day, which commemorates a battle with Chile in the War of the Pacific, 1879–81 (October 8); All Saints' Day (November 1); Immaculate Conception (December 8); Christmas.

▌ MAIL

Letters sent within the country cost S/3 for less than 20 grams; letters and cards up to 20 grams sent to the United States and Canada cost S/7.20. Bring packages to the post office unsealed, as you must show the contents to postal workers. Mail service has been improving, and a letter should reach just about anywhere in a week from any of the main cities. For timely delivery or valuable parcels, use FedEx, DHL, or UPS, although be aware that customs can be very complicated.

DHL, FedEx, and UPS all have offices in Peru. Because of the limited number of international flights, overnight service is usually not available.

▌ MONEY

Peru's national currency is the nuevo sol (S/). Bills are issued in denominations of 10, 20, 50, 100, and 200 soles. Coins are 1, 5, 10, 20, and 50 céntimos, and 1, 2, and 5 soles. (The 1- and 5-céntimo coins are rarely seen.) At this writing, the exchange rate was S/2.6 to the U.S. dollar. Peru is not one of those "everybody takes dollars" places—many businesses and most individuals are not equipped to handle U.S. currency—so you should try to deal in soles.

You'll want to break larger bills as soon as possible. Souvenir stands, craft markets, taxi drivers, and other businesses often do not have change. Be aware that U.S. dollars must be in pristine condition, as moneychangers and banks will not accept a bill with even the slightest tear. Likewise, counterfeiting is a big problem in Peru, and you should check all bills (both dollars and soles) immediately to confirm that they are real. The easiest method is to ensure that the color changing ink does indeed change colors, from purple to black. Do not feel uncomfortable scrutinizing bills; you can be sure that any cashier will scrutinize your bills twice as hard.

Currency Conversion
Google ⊕ *www.google.com.* **Oanda.com**
⊕ *www.oanda.com.* **XE.com** ⊕ *www.xe.com.*

▌**TIP**➔ If you're planning to exchange funds before leaving home, don't wait until the last minute. Banks never have every foreign currency on hand, and it may take as long as a week to order. For the best exchange rates, you're better off to wait until you get to Peru to change dollars into local currency.

ATMS AND BANKS

Your own bank will probably charge a fee for using ATMs abroad; the foreign bank you use may also charge a fee, which currently stands at $5 per transaction. Nevertheless, you'll usually get a better rate of exchange at an ATM than you will at a currency-exchange office or even when changing money in a bank. And extracting funds as you need them is a safer option than carrying around a large amount of cash.

■ TIP→ PIN numbers with more than four digits are not recognized at ATMs in many countries. If yours has five or more, remember to change it before you leave.

ATMs (*cajeros automáticos*) are widely available, especially in Lima, and you can get cash with a Cirrus- or Plus-linked debit card or with a major credit card. Most ATMs accept both Cirrus and Plus cards, but to be on the safe side, bring at least one of each.

ATM Locations MasterCard Cirrus
☎ *800/424–7787 in North America, 800/307–7309 in Peru* ⊕ *www.mastercard.com.*
Visa Plus ☎ *800/843–7587*
⊕ *www.visa.com/atm.*

CREDIT CARDS

It's a good idea to inform your credit-card company before you travel. Otherwise, the credit-card company might put a hold on your card owing to unusual activity—not a good thing halfway through your trip. Record all your credit-card numbers—as well as the phone numbers to call if your cards are lost or stolen—in a safe place, so you're prepared should something go wrong. Both MasterCard and Visa have general numbers you can call (collect if you're abroad) if your card is lost, but you're better off calling the number of your issuing bank, since MasterCard and Visa usually just transfer you to your bank; your bank's number is usually printed on your card.

Although it's usually cheaper (and safer) to use a credit card abroad for large purchases (so you can cancel payments or be reimbursed if there's a problem), note that some credit-card companies *and* the banks that issue them add substantial percentages to all foreign transactions, whether they're in a foreign currency or not. Check on these fees before leaving home, so there won't be any surprises when you get the bill.

■ TIP→ Before you charge something, ask the merchant whether he or she plans to do a dynamic currency conversion (DCC). In such a transaction the credit-card processor (shop, restaurant, or hotel, not Visa or MasterCard) converts the currency and charges you in dollars. In most cases you'll pay the merchant a 3% fee for this service in addition to any credit-card company and issuing-bank foreign-transaction surcharges.

Dynamic currency conversion programs are becoming increasingly widespread. Merchants who participate in them are supposed to ask whether you want to be charged in dollars or the local currency, but they don't always do so. And even if they do offer you a choice, they may well avoid mentioning the additional surcharges. The good news is that you *do* have a choice. And if this practice really gets your goat, you can avoid it entirely thanks to American Express; with its cards, DCC simply isn't an option.

For costly items, try to use your credit card whenever possible—you'll come out ahead, whether the exchange rate at which your purchase is calculated is the one in effect the day the vendor's bank abroad processes the charge or the one prevailing on the day the charge company's service center processes it at home.

Major credit cards, especially MasterCard and Visa, are accepted in most hotels, restaurants, and shops in tourist areas. If you're traveling outside major cities, always check to see whether your hotel accepts credit cards. You may have to bring enough cash to pay the bill.

Before leaving home, make copies of the back and front of your credit cards; keep one set of copies with your luggage, the other at home.

Reporting Lost Cards American Express ☎ 800/528–4800 in North America, 0800–50629 in Peru ⊕ www.americanexpress. com. **Diners Club** ☎ 800/234–6377 in North America, 514/877–1577 collect from abroad ⊕ www.dinersclub.com. **Discover** ☎ 800/347–2683 in North America, 801/902–3100 collect from abroad ⊕ www.discovercard.com. **MasterCard** ☎ 800/627–8372 in North America, 636/722–7111 collect from abroad ⊕ www.mastercard.com. **Visa** ☎ 800/847–2911 in North America, 410/581–9994 collect from abroad ⊕ www.visa.com.

CURRENCY AND EXCHANGE

You can safely exchange money or cash traveler's checks in a bank, at your hotel, or at *casas de cambio* (exchange houses). The rate for traveler's checks is usually the same as for cash, but many banks have a ceiling on how much they will exchange at one time.

▮ TIP➔ Even if a currency-exchange booth has a sign promising no commission, rest assured that there's some kind of huge, hidden fee. (Oh…that's right. The sign didn't say no fee). Rates are always better at an ATM or a bank.

▮ PACKING

For sightseeing, casual clothing and good walking shoes are desirable and appropriate, and most cities don't require formal clothes, even for evenings. If you're doing business in Peru, you'll need the same attire you would wear in U.S. and European cities: for men, suits and ties; for women, suits for day wear, and for evening, depending on the occasion—ask your host or hostess—a cocktail dress or just a nice suit with a dressy blouse.

Travel in rain-forest areas will require long-sleeve shirts, long pants, socks, sneakers, a hat, a light waterproof jacket, a bathing suit (if you want to swim), sunscreen, and insect repellent. You can never have too many large resealable plastic bags, which are ideal for protecting official documents from rain and damp and quarantining stinky socks.

If you're visiting the Andes, bring a jacket and sweater, or acquire one of the hand-knit sweaters or ponchos crowding the marketplaces. Evening temperatures in Cusco are rarely above 40°F. For beach vacations, you'll need lightweight sportswear, a bathing suit, a sun hat, and lots of sunscreen. Peruvians are fairly conservative, so don't wear bathing suits or other revealing clothing away from the beach.

Other useful items include a travel flashlight and extra batteries, a pocketknife with a bottle opener (put it in your checked luggage), a medical kit, binoculars, and a calculator to help with currency conversions. A sarong or light cotton blanket can have many uses: beach towel, picnic blanket, and cushion for hard seats and, most important, always travel with tissues or a roll of toilet paper, as restrooms are not always stocked with these necessities.

Weather Weather.com ⊕ www.weather.com.

▮ PASSPORTS AND VISAS

Visitors from the United States, Canada, the United Kingdom, Australia, and New Zealand require only a valid passport and return ticket to be issued a 90-day visa at their point of entry into Peru.

Make two photocopies of the data page of your passport, one for someone at home and another for you, carried separately from your passport. While sightseeing in Peru, it's best to carry the copy of your passport and leave the original hidden in your hotel room or in your hotel's safe. If you lose your passport, call the nearest embassy or consulate and the local police. Also, never, ever, leave one city in Peru to go to another city (even for just an overnight or two) without carrying your passport with you.

GENERAL REQUIREMENTS FOR PERU	
Passport	Valid passport required for U.S. residents
Visa	Not necessary for U.S. residents with a valid passport
Vaccinations	Yellow fever vaccination required for those visiting infected areas
Driving	Driver's license required
Departure Tax	$31 USD for international flights; $6.82 USD for domestic flights; included in all fares

▮ RESTROOMS

In Lima and other cities, your best bet for finding a restroom while on the go is to walk into a large hotel as if you're a guest and find the facilities. The next best thing is talking your way into a restaurant bathroom; buying a drink is a nice gesture if you do. Unless you're in a large chain hotel, don't throw toilet paper into the toilet—use the basket provided, as unsanitary as this may seem. Flushing paper can clog the antiquated plumbing. Always carry your own supply of tissues or toilet paper, just in case.

Public restrooms are usually designated as *servicios higiénicos*, with signs depicting the abbreviation "SS.HH."

Find a Loo The Bathroom Diaries.
The Bathroom Diaries is flush with unsanitized info on restrooms the world over—each one located, reviewed, and rated.
⊕ *www.thebathroomdiaries.com.*

▮ SAFETY

Be street-smart in Peru and trouble generally won't find you. Money belts peg you as a tourist, so if you must wear one, hide it under your clothing. If you carry a purse, choose one with a zipper and a thick strap that you can drape across your body; adjust the length so that the purse sits in front of you. Carry only enough money to cover casual spending. Keep

camera bags close to your body. Note that backpacks are especially easy to grab or open secretly. Finally, avoid wearing flashy jewelry and watches.

Many streets throughout Peru are not well lighted, so avoid walking at night, and certainly avoid deserted streets, day or night. Always walk as if you know where you're going, even if you don't.

Use only "official" taxis with the company's name emblazoned on the side. Don't get into a car just because there's a taxi sign in the window, as it's probably an unlicensed driver. At night you should call a taxi from your hotel or restaurant.

Do not let anyone distract you. Beware of someone "accidentally" spilling food or liquid on you and then offering to help clean it up; the spiller might have an accomplice who will walk off with your purse or your suitcase while you are distracted.

Women, especially blondes, can expect some admiring glances and perhaps a comment or two, but outright come-ons or grabbing are rare. Usually all that is needed is to ignore the perpetrator and keep walking down the street.

▮**TIP➔** Distribute your cash, credit cards, IDs, and other valuables between a deep front pocket, an inside jacket or vest pocket, and a hidden money pouch. Don't reach for the money pouch once you're in public.

Contact Transportation Security Administration (*TSA*). ⊕ *www.tsa.gov.*

▮ TAXES

A 19% *impuesto general a las ventas* (general sales tax) is levied on everything except goods bought at open-air markets and street vendors. It's usually included in the advertised price and should be included with food and drink. If a business offers you a discount for paying in cash, it probably means they aren't charging sales tax (and not reporting the transaction to the government).

By law restaurants must publish their prices—including taxes and sometimes a 10% service charge—but they do not always do so. They're also prone to levy a cover charge for anything from live entertainment to serving you a roll with your meal. Hotel bills may also add taxes and a 10% service charge.

Departure taxes at Lima's Aeropuerto Internacional Jorge Chávez are $31 USD for international flights—all airlines now include the tax in their ticket prices—and $6.82 USD for domestic flights.

▌TIME

Peru is on Eastern Standard Time (GMT-0500) year-round, with no daylight saving time observed. From November to March the time in Peru is the same as in New York and Miami. The rest of the year, when the United States does observe daylight saving time, Peru is one hour behind the U.S. East Coast.

▌TOURS

Many people visiting Peru do so as part of a tour package. There is nothing wrong with that, especially for those who don't speak Spanish or are unaccustomed to foreign travel. On the other hand, do you really want to see the same sights as everyone else? There's no reason that you can't book your own tour. It's easy to arrange a custom itinerary with any travel agent.

Several Lima-based companies can arrange trips around the city as well as around the country. Long-established Lima Tours offers tours of the city and surrounding area as well as of the rest of the country. Lima Vision has some excellent tours, some of which include lunch at a traditional restaurant or a dinner show.

Recommended Companies Lima Tours ✉ *Jr. de la Unión 1040, El Centro, Lima, Peru* ☎ *01/619–6900* ⊕ *www.limatours.com. pe.* **Lima Vision** ✉ *Jr. Chiclayo 444, Miraflores, Lima, Peru* ☎ *01/447–0482* ⊕ *www.limavision.com.*

▌VISITOR INFORMATION

ONLINE TRAVEL TOOLS

Andean Travel Web, an independent website, has great information about regional destinations. Assisting travelers is iPerú, which has English- and Spanish-language information about the city and beyond. The website, in English and Spanish, is extremely helpful in planning your trip.

The most thorough information about Peru is available at South American Explorers. This nonprofit organization dispenses a wealth of information. You can also call ahead with questions, or just show up at its clubhouses in Lima (Miraflores) or Cusco (as well as Quito and Buenos Aires) and browse through the lending library and read trip reports filed by members. It costs $60 USD to join, and you can make up for that with discounts offered to members by hotels and tour operators.

All About Peru Andean Travel Web ⊕ *www.andeantravelweb.com.* **iPerú** ☎ *01/574–8000 in Peru* ⊕ *www.peru.info.* **South American Explorers** ✉ *Piura 135, Miraflores, Lima, Peru* ☎ *01/444–2150 in Peru, 800/274–0568 in U.S.* ⊕ *www.saexplorers.org.*

INDEX

PHOTO CREDITS

1, Hemis/Alamy. 3, JTB Photo Communications, Inc./Alamy. Chapter 1: Experience Peru: 6-7, Angelo Cavalli/eStock Photo. 8 (left), John Warburton-Lee Photography/Alamy.8 (center), Paul Kingsley/ Alamy. 8 (top right), Melvyn Longhurst/Alamy. 8 (bottom right), Galen Rowell/Mountain Light/Alamy. 11, mediacolor's/Alamy. 13, Sirois/age fotostock. 14, Jim Wileman/Alamy. 15, Arguelles/Shutterstock. 16, Pixonnet.com/Alamy. 17, Icon Sports Media Inc. 18, Toño Labra/age fotostock. 19, Galen Rowell/Mountain Light/Alamy. 20 (left), Alvaro Leiva/age fotostock. 20 (top center), GARDEL Bertrand/ age fotostock. 20 (top right), Beren Patterson/Alamy. 20 (bottom right), Alex Maddox/Alamy. 21 (top left), (c) Melastmohican | Dreamstime.com. 21 (bottom left), Philip Scalia/Alamy. 21 (bottom center), Toño Labra/age fotostock. 21 (right), Alun Richardson/Alamy. 23, Pictorial Press Ltd/Alamy. 24, CuboImages srl/Alamy. 25, Nathan Benn/Alamy. 27, James Brunker/Alamy. 28, Gonzalo Azumendi/age fotostock. 31, SouthAmerica Photos/Alamy. 37, Stephen H. Taplin. 41, Tony Morrison/South American Pictures. 42 (left), INTERFOTO/age fotostock. 42 (top right), Tony Morrison/South American Pictures. 42 (bottom right), J Marshall/Tribaleye Images/Alamy. 43 (left), Kathy Jarvis/South American Pictures. 43 (top right), Beren Patterson/Alamy. 43 (bottom right), TB Photo Communications, Inc./ Alamy. 44 (left), Danita Delimont/Alamy. 44 (top right), José Fuste Raga/age fotostock. 44 (bottom right), Tony Morrison/South American Pictures. 45 (left), Mireille Vautier/Alamy. 45 (right), Tim Jarrell. 46 (left),Visual Arts Library (London)/Alamy. 47 (right), public domain 47 (left), Classic Vision/ age fotostock. 47 (right), North Wind Picture Archives/Alamy. 48 (left), ZUMA Wire Service / Alamy. 48 (right), Mike Yamashita/Woodfin Camp/Aurora Photos. Chapter 2: Lima: 49, Scott Warren/Aurora Photos. 50 and 51 (top), Toño Labra/age fotostock. 51 (bottom), Timothy Hursley/SuperStock. 52, Toño Labra/age fotostock. 60, Charles Graham/eStock Photo. 65, CuboImages srl/Alamy. 83, Alexander S. Heitkamp/Shutterstock. 84, (top), Luke Peters/Alamy. 84 (bottom), Tim Hill/Alamy. 85 (top), Mo Al-Nuaimy/Flickr. 85 (bottom), Emilio Ereza / age fotostock. 86 (top right), Toño Labra/ age fotostock. 86 (center), Corey Wise/Alamy. 86 (bottom left), Mary Evans Picture Library/Alamy. 86 (bottom right), Toño Labra/ age fotostock. 87 (top), Michele Molinari/Alamy. 87 (center), Emilio Ereza/age fotostock. 87 (bottom), Jeffrey Jackson/Alamy. 91, José Fuste Raga/age fotostock. 94, Toño Labra/age fotostock. Chapter 3: The South: 101, Danilo Donadoni/age fotostock. 102, Olivier Renck/Aurora Photos. 103 (top), Will Steeley/Alamy. 103 (bottom), Luke Peters/Alamy. 104, Emmanuel LATTES/Alamy. 108, Anthony Ibarra/Alamy. 118, Danilo Donadoni/age fotostock. 129, JTB Photo Communications, Inc./Alamy. 130-131, Philip Scalia/Alamy. 132, Bennett Photo/Alamy. 133 (top), Tony Morrison/South American Pictures.133 (bottom), Dan Bannister/Shutterstock. Chapter 4: The Southern Coast of Lake Titicaca: 139, WYSOCKI Pawel/age fotostock. 140, South America Photos/Alamy. 141 (top), Vespasian/Alamy.141 (bottom), Sean Sprague/age fotostock. 142, Tolo Balaguer/age fotostock. 151, Mireille Vautier/Alamy. 155, Michael Woodruff/Shutterstock. 160, Philip Scalia/Alamy. 162, Gallo Images/ Alamy. 170, Jon Arnold Images Ltd/Alamy. 185, David Ranson/Shutterstock. 186-187, Jarno Gonzalez Zarraonandia/Shutterstock. 188, JTB Photo Communications, Inc./Alamy. 189 (top), GARDEL Bertrand/age fotostock. 189 (bottom), Danita Delimont/Alamy. 190 (top), Harry Papas/Alamy. 190 (bottom), Ian Nellist/Alamy. 194, FOTOPANORAMA /age fotostock. 198-99, Christophe Boisvieux / age fotostock. Chapter 5: Cusco & The Sacred Valley: 203, Kevin Schafer/age fotostock. 204, Robert Fried/Alamy. 205 (top), Bjorn Svensson/age fotostock.205 (bottom), Jon Arnold Images Ltd/Alamy. 206, Stephen H. Taplin. 216-217, Digital Vision/Super-Stock. 219, Mark Titterton/Alamy. 237, Kevin Schafer/Alamy. 248, Stephen H. Taplin. 255, James Brunker/Alamy. 257, Klaus Lang/Alamy. 258-259, Gonzalo Azumendi/age fotostock. 260 (top), Guylain Doyle/age fotostock. 260 (center), Ozimages/ Alamy. 260 (bottom), Danita Delimont/Alamy. 261 (top), GARDEL Bertrand/age fotostock. 261 (bottom), Danita Delimont/Alamy. 262 (top, Gail Mooney-Kelly/Alamy. 262 (bottom), Bjorn Svensson/ age fotostock. 265, David Noton Photography/Alamy.Chapter 6: Machu Picchu & the Inca Trail: 269 and 271 (top), Tim Jarrell. 271 (center), Andrew Holt/Alamy. 271 (bottom), Bryan Busovicki/Shutterstock. 272, SuperStock/age fotostock. 280-281, Robert Fried/Alamy. 282, Melvyn Longhurst/Alamy. 283, The Granger Collection, New York. 284 (left and right), Tim Jarrell. 284 (bottom), Stephen H. Taplin. 285 (left), Tim Jarrell. 285 (right), Fabricio Guzmán. 286 (top left), Robert Harding Picture Library Ltd/Alamy. 286 (top right), Rachael Bowes/Alamy. 286 (bottom), Christine McNamara. 287 (top left), Jordan Klein. 287 (top right), Tim Jarrell.287 (bottom), Nick Jewell/Flickr. 288, SouthAmerica Photos/Alamy. 289, Christine McNamara. 290, Ozimages/Alamy. 291, Melvyn Longhurst/Alamy. 292-293, Pep Roig/Alamy. 292 (left), Jason Scott Duggan/Shutterstock. 292 (right), Christine McNamara. 293 (left), Stephen H. Taplin. 293 (right), Robert Fried/Alamy. 294-295, Stephen H. Taplin. 299, Orient-Express Hotels. Chapter 7: The Amazon Basin: 301, Hemis /Alamy. 302, infocusphotos.com/ Alamy. 303 (top), Michael Doolittle/Alamy. 303 (bottom), Papilio/Alamy. 304, Michele Falzone/Alamy. 313, Mark Jones/age fotostock. 314-315 (background), Steffen Foerster/iStockphoto. 314 (top), Mark

NOTES

NOTES

ABOUT OUR WRITERS

Freelance journalist and consultant David Dudenhoefer has lived in Lima since 2006, though his work frequently takes him to the Amazon Basin—his favorite part of the country. Before moving to Peru, he lived in San Jose, Costa Rica, from where he covered the rest of Central America. He has contributed to nine Fodor's guides over the years. For this guide, he updated the Experience Peru, Lima, and Amazon Basin chapters.

Lima, Peru, and NYC-based writer and photographer Nicholas Gill updated the Southern Coast, the Southern Andes and Lake Titicaca, and the North Coast and Northern Highlands chapters of this guide. His work appears in publications such as *Conde Nast Traveler*, the *New York Times*, and the *Wall Street Journal*. Visit his personal website (⊕ *www. nicholas-gill.com*) or blog about Latin American food and drink (⊕ *www.newworldreview.com*) for more information.

As a project manager for an international NGO, Michael Goodwin has found his way from Puno's high plains, down to Lima's coastal expanse and back up to the spectacular ruins nestled in Cusco's cloud forests. Along the way, he has feasted on Peru's maritime bounty, danced at local festivals, and ambled through Quechua-only *sierra* villages. He has worked extensively in the Puno, Cusco, and Huancavelica regions, carrying out research on microfinance, education, and small businesses. Though originally from New York, Mike now resides full time in Lima, within easy striking distance of breathtaking camping and some of the world's best urban surf. He updated the Central Highlands and Travel Smart chapters.

Freelance travel writer Maureen Santucci first visited Peru in January 2008 and, after two more visits the same year, moved there that November. She has spent those four plus years living in Cusco and the Sacred Valley, allowing her to indulge her love of trekking as well as positioning her perfectly to update that chapter as well as the one on Machu Picchu and the Inca Trail. In addition to working with Fodor's, she writes a number of articles for online publication on traveling in South America in general and Peru in particular.